Early Hominids of Africa

Early Hominids of Africa

Edited by
Clifford J. Jolly

ST. MARTIN'S PRESS
NEW YORK

St. Martin's Press, Inc., 175 Fifth Avenue, New York, N.Y. 10010
Printed in Great Britain
Library of Congress Catalog Card Number 78–54136
ISBN 0–312–22461–3
First published in the United States of America in 1978

CONTENTS

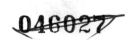

III. ANATOMICAL EVIDENCE

IV. THE INTERPRETATION OF HOMINID DIVERSITY

Preface

In 1924, a new chapter in the study of human ancestry was opened by Professor Dart's recognition of the hominid status of the Taung child – soon to become the type specimen of *Australopithecus africanus*. Just fifty years later a week-long conference took place in New York City, with the object of taking stock of the current state of knowledge and opinion concerning this specimen and the many others of its kind that had since come to light in Africa South of the Sahara. This book is the outcome of the conference.

The idea of such a meeting was first mooted in 1972 by a small group of palaeoanthropologists concerned about the state of communication in their field. On the one hand, new fossil hominid specimens, and new Plio-Pleistocene sites, were being discovered at an unprecedented rate, while on the other hand, more and more anthropologists were publishing interpretative schemes on the basis of general evolutionary theory. We were concerned at the gulf that seemed to be widening between those who discovered and had direct access to the material, and those who were developing general theories of hominid evolution, but who had no direct access to the newly discovered material. The primary aim of the conference was to help bridge this gap by bringing the palaeoanthropologists who had been most active in the recent phase of discovery and primary description of fossil hominids together with those who had been using the data to construct broad and sweeping models of the course of hominid evolution.

It was decided to focus our attention on a specific geographical region – Africa south of the Sahara – and upon a specific, if rather vaguely-defined, span of time, the Plio-Pleistocene. The beginning of the Pliocene, recently redefined to about 5 million years ago, is conveniently close to the time of the first appearance in the fossil record of specimens that are indisputably hominid in character. For the purposes of the conference, the close of the Plio-Pleistocene was defined as the time of disappearance of the australopithecines. Such a definition freed us from the constraints of formal time horizons that are the proper province of geology, but at the same time focussed our attention on particular issues. We were not primarily concerned with recognising the precursors of the Plio-Pleistocene hominids among the Miocene Hominoidea, or with tracing the evolution of humans in the Middle and Upper Pleistocene. The hominids of the period between – what we are calling the Plio-Pleistocene – present a set of problems that is unique to them, and reflects their transitional position in the course of human evolution. Did the early hominids undergo adaptive radiation, like most mammalian families, or are they to be regarded as members of a single variable lineage, like later humans? How dependent upon culture were the early hominids, and indeed, can one argue that all hominids are necessarily culture-bearing? What was the habitat of early hominids, and how far is it possible to reconstruct their position in the ecosystem of which they were a part? The conference was intended to bring together as wide as possible a spectrum of informed opinion to discuss such issues. We were fortunate in obtaining support from the National Science Foundation and from the Wenner-Gren Foundation for Anthropological Research, while the Wenner-Gren Foundation and New York University provided facilities and hospitality for the meetings. Almost all those invited to attend were able to do so. The conference convened in January 1974.

The joint sponsorship of the conference encouraged us to depart somewhat from the usual closed format of a study conference. We took advantage of the New York venue by holding the first few sessions of the conference in public. This enabled directors of some of the major research projects to lecture on their latest findings to an invited audience of anthropologists, both professional and student. Representatives of the news media also attended these sessions; in this way we recognized the newsworthy quality of human evolution, the notion of palaeoanthropology as entertainment. This is an aspect of our subject that the profession can ill afford to ignore, especially in the present economic climate. As the stream of popular books, magazine articles and television programmes attests, the general public entertains an enormous interest in the life-ways of early hominids, and in the more spectacular aspects of fossil-hunting. Whether this interest stems entirely from intellectual interest in human origins, or whether, as one suspects, it is also fed by the same fascination with the not-quite-human that sustains the horror-movie industry, it makes palaeoanthropology publicly saleable in a way that few other branches of biology can match. There are those who find the notion of the palaeoanthropologist as showman a distasteful one. Certainly, if the publicist becomes a sensationalist, distorting or concealing his discoveries in order to hit the headlines or to garner personal *kudos*, this is clearly antithetical to the aims and spirit of science. On the other hand, publicising and popularising the findings of palaeoanthropology, provided that this is done without distortion of the facts, can be regarded as partial repayment to the general public for the support it provides through public foundations and private donations to what is ultimately a non-utilitarian pursuit. It was in this spirit that the open sessions of the conference were planned.

The open sessions occupied the first two days of the conference. The remaining five days were devoted to round-table discussion at the Wenner-Gren Foundation's headquarters, each session being devoted to a particular aspect of early hominid biology. Each session opened with the presentation of a lead paper that had been prepared in advance and circulated to all participants. Discussion then followed. As will be apparent from the chapters that follow, the conference was far from achieving unanimity on the problems posed by the Plio-Pleistocene hominids of Africa. However, complete agreement was not the aim of the conference; after all, a science in which there is no more controversy is dead. We can claim that our objectives were accomplished in that issues were examined, positions stated and clarified, and opinions (sometimes) revised. In several sessions, points of view that had appeared widely disparate turned out to be closer than their respective proponents had believed. But, more importantly, even when a core of real disagreement was uncovered, such differences were delineated with a lack of acrimony that sometimes surprised veterans of previous 'Early Man' conferences. Hotel room discussions lasted well into the night, and links of collegiality were forged between specialists who hitherto had encountered each other only in the pages of journals.

Participants were asked to revise their contributions in the light of the discussion, and almost all were able to do so, thus obviating the need to reproduce the discussions themselves. Almost all the participants were able to submit a manuscript for publication, and in addition, Professor P.V. Tobias, who was unable to attend the conference, also sent a manuscript. Most took the opportunity to update their contributions in 1976.

The book is arranged to correspond, more or less, to the sessions of the conference. In the first section, the directors of major research projects introduce the sites at which they work, summarise the material that has been derived from them, and describe the current state of research. In the second part are grouped papers that discuss the information that can be derived from the *context* in which early hominid fossils are found – geological, taphonomic, faunal and archaeological. The third section includes papers that discuss the information about hominid adaptation that can be derived from the *anatomical characteristics* of the hominids themselves, especially their teeth, postcranial skeleton and the shape and volume of the endocranial cast. The papers in section four deal with the thorny problem of *diversity among Plio-Pleistocene hominids*; the ways in which this diversity can be interpreted in terms of phylogeny and expressed in terms of taxonomy. It is our hope that the work will stand, not just as a record of the state of the art 'fifty years on', but also a useful source-book for students of human evolution at all levels of specialisation.

It is a pleasure to record, on behalf of all participants in the conference, our appreciation of all the individuals and organisations who made possible the meetings themselves and the publication of their proceedings. To Mrs Lita Osmundsen of the Wenner-Gren Foundation for hosting the conference in the comfort and convenient surroundings of the Foundation's New York headquarters, and for unstintingly sharing with its organiser her experience and expertise in the care and handling of anthropologists; to Mrs Maria Brunet and the rest of the staff of the Foundation who so skilfully managed the logistics of travel and accommodation for our international group; to Dr Iwao Ishino, Dr Mary Green, and the National Science Foundation, for their support and personal interest in the conference; to President James Hester of New York University who delivered the opening address and provided an auditorium for the open sessions of the conference; to Professor John Buettner-Janusch for his hospitality and his help in organising the logistics of the open sessions; and to F.L. Brett, J. Klein and other students at N.Y.U. who ably operated projectors and tape recorders, we are most grateful. A special word of thanks is due to Mr Colin Haycraft who, in undertaking to publish this symposium volume, is pursuing the policy of service to anthropology for which Duckworth's is justly renowned.

Finally, a word of thanks from the editor to his fellow conferees; to all those who participated in the discussions or contributed to this volume, in the hope that each one found the experience as enjoyable and stimulating as I did.

1977 Clifford J. Jolly

PART I
THE SITES

M.D. Leakey

Olduvai fossil hominids: their stratigraphic positions and associations

Olduvai Gorge lies in the eastern part of the Serengeti plains in northern Tanzania. The gorge is 30 miles long, but only the eastern 13 miles are fossiliferous.

The study of the stratigraphic sequence at Olduvai is probably more detailed and more complete than that of any other lower or middle Pleistocene site. This is thanks to the work of Professor Richard L. Hay, of the Department of Geology and Geophysics, University of California, Berkeley. The basis on which he has established the stratigraphic sequence has been a long series of carefully measured sections throughout the length of the gorge. These have not only enabled various beds to be correlated but have also revealed the periods of faulting, which can be detected by the differential deposition on either side of a fault line, since there is a greater thickness on the downthrown side, where the sediments have filled the fault trough.

The original terminology for Olduvai formulated by H. Reck has been retained for the recent studies, so that the main sequence of deposits is still subdivided into Beds I to IV. The only part of the sequence that has had to be revised is what was formerly the upper part of Bed IV and Bed V. Lower Bed IV, which for a time was known as Bed IV A, is largely composed of fluvial and lacustrine deposits while the upper part consists of an entirely different set of deposits, largely of aeolian origin. Upper IV has, therefore, been re-named the Masek Beds (after a lake at the head of the gorge). The deposits formerly lumped together as Bed V have also required subdivision. The earlier part is known as the Ndutu Beds (named after a second lake at the head of the gorge) and the later part as the Naisiusiu Beds (a Masai word for the sound of wind rustling through dry grass). Major earth movements cut through the Ndutu Beds but the Naisiusiu Beds have nowhere been observed to be affected by faulting.

The Olduvai sequence, up to and including the Masek Beds, covers a time span from 1.9 to about 0.2 m.y. Within this period there is an

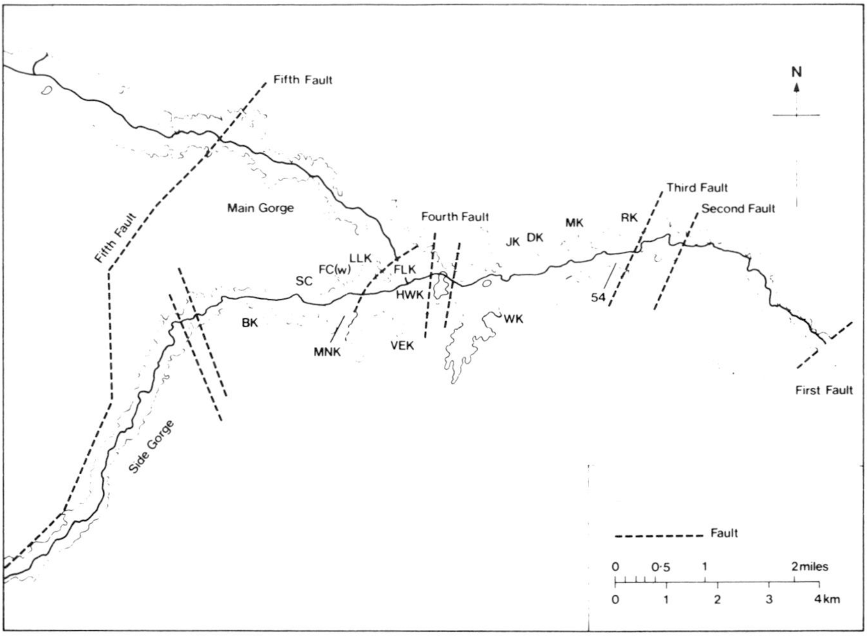

Figure 1. Map of Olduvai Gorge showing hominid sites.

unsurpassed record of hominid activities and of the hominids themselves.

Bed I

This is the earliest bed and it appears to represent a relatively short time span. The upper, fossiliferous part may be no more than 100,000 or 150,000 years in duration, while the entire bed including the basalt and underlying sediments spans about 300,000 years.

During Bed I times there was a permanent, saline lake in the Olduvai area. At its maximum extent, at the top of Bed I, it measured 14 miles across, where it is cut through by the present gorge. As far as it is possible to determine, the lake was bounded to the north by pre-Cambrian hills and to the south by the volcanic highlands. Living sites of the hominids are found principally along the southern shore where fresh water was available in the streams that flowed down into the lake from the highlands. Most of these sites appear to have been on the flats marginal to the lake and were probably at no great distance from the water's edge.

There are indications from the fauna – particularly from the microfauna – that the climate throughout Bed I times was wetter than it is today, and further, that it was wetter in lower Bed I than in upper Bed I. In lower Bed I there are urocyclid slugs, a group whose living representatives require a rainfall of 35 inches per year or else semipermanent mist (Verdcourt, 1963). These slugs are not found in upper Bed I. The varieties of rodents, too, indicate a climate wetter than today, but one that became drier during the course of Bed I. In lower Bed I there were swamp rats, whereas in upper Bed I gerbils are common, a group of rodents that favours warm, dry conditions (J-J. Jaeger, pers. comm.). Similarly, the species of elephant shrews also indicate more humid conditions than today (P.M. Butler, pers. comm.).

Even though the terminology used in describing Plio-Pleistocene hominids may be ripe for revision, I will employ the terms hitherto used in publications on Olduvai Gorge: *Australopithecus boisei, Homo habilis* and *Homo erectus*.

Unlike East Rudolf,[1] where remains of *Australopithecus* cf. *boisei* are extraordinarily common, Olduvai has only yielded one skull, a few teeth and a femoral fragment. Remains of *H. habilis* are far more numerous and in view of the robusticity of *A. boisei* remains compared to those of *H. habilis*, and consequent better chances of preservation, it is evident that *H. habilis* was the more common hominid at Olduvai.

Parts of 10 individuals of *H. habilis* have been found under well-documented conditions. Seven of these were directly associated with the Oldowan industry, while three were from the same levels as nearby Oldowan sites. In contrast, specimens of *A. boisei* with indisputable provenance have only been found on three occasions. These are the cranium from Bed I at site FLK, two deciduous teeth from BK and three teeth from SC, both the latter sites being in upper Bed II.

The repeated association of *H. habilis* remains with the Oldowan industry, the scarcity of *A. boisei* and the apparent absence of any other recognisable hominid taxon make it reasonable to assume the *H. habilis* was responsible for making the Oldowan tools. In fact, it is possible that the abundance of Oldowan artifacts at Olduvai compared to their relative scarcity at East Rudolf may be due to the greater numbers of *Homo habilis* in the Olduvai area.

Faunal remains from the living sites that were on the shores of the Bed I lake clearly indicate that successful hunting methods had been achieved. Scavenging from carnivore kills is likely also to have been a means of obtaining meat, but actual killing of the animals by the hominids is evidenced by three antelope skulls from upper Bed I that show depressed fractures over the right orbits; the positioning of these fractures is so accurate and so similar that one is led to conclude that the blows were delivered at close quarters, possibly with a club.

For a time it was believed that small game was hunted preferentially during the lower Pleistocene and that juvenile animals

1. East Rudolf is now known as East Turkana. Since this paper was written, new evidence has come to light and other changes in nomenclature have taken place; for instance, *Afrochoerus nicoli* is known as *Metridiochoerus compactus*.

were also more commonly represented than adults on the living sites. This has not proved to be the case at Olduvai where the most common bone debris on the Bed I sites belongs to medium-sized adult antelopes. Large animals such as hippos and rhinos are not so numerous as they are among the occupational debris of sites in Beds II, III and IV, but an elephant butchery or 'kill' site is known in upper Bed I at site FLK North (Leakey, M.D., 1971). Here, the partially disarticulated skeleton of a single animal was found embedded in clay and associated with a number of stone tools (Leakey, M.D., 1971, Figure 32). The animal may have been driven into the swamp by man or become trapped there accidentally, as sometimes happens today. In either case, man took advantage of the situation to obtain meat from the carcase.

The question of the size of the hominid bands that occupied the Bed I living sites probably will never be answered satisfactorily. Modern parallels, with Bushmen for example, cannot offer close analogies in view of the vastly different conditions concerning the game population and the hunting methods, as well as the unknown extent of scavenging on the living sites after they had been abandoned by the hominids, a factor that has surely appreciably altered the debris that we find today. Perhaps, at a guess, the bands may have numbered 20 or 30 individuals so that there was a sufficient number of males for hunting and defence without being too numerous to subsist as a group by hunting and gathering.

Bed I is the only period at Olduvai during which we have any

Figure 2. Photograph of modern stone circle; abandoned hut on the eastern side of Lake Baringo. Photo: W.W. Bishop.

evidence of cultural activity other than stone tools and debris on living sites, with the exception of a pits complex in Bed III of which the purpose remains obscure. At DK, in lower Bed I and at the same level as the cranium H.24 and mandible fragment H.4 attributed to *Homo habilis*, there is a circle of loosely piled lava blocks (Leakey, M.D., 1971, Figure 7). The circle is 12 to 14 feet in diameter and has the appearance of being an artificial structure. Many present-day parallels can be seen among nomadic peoples who live in a reasonably warm climate and require only temporary shelters. Among the Turkana in northern Kenya it is a common sight to see such stone circles marking abandoned villages. They are the result of building crude shelters or windbreakers from boughs stuck into the ground, with the tops bent inwards. In order to support them and avoid digging deep holes, stones are piled round the bases. I am indebted to W.W. Bishop for the photograph showing such an abandoned structure (Figure 2). In this case, however, the builder had departed from the traditional African round hut and built himself a square dwelling.

Another instance of a possible windbreak or thorn fence can be seen on the plan of the occupation floor at FLK where the cranium of *A. boisei* as well as remains of *H. habilis* were found. In this case no structure is preserved and the evidence is negative, consisting of a blank area, containing virtually no occupational debris, which encircles the central part of the living site on the windward side. Beyond the empty ring there were greater numbers of stone tools, bones and waterworn stones. This arrangement of the debris suggests the possibility of a barrier of some sort, sheltering the central area, over which discarded objects were thrown (Leakey, M.D. 1971, Figure 24).

The stone industry of Bed I is the Oldowan. It is homogeneous except for minor variations between sites and it is evident that no evolution in tool-making took place during Bed I times. The principal tools of the Oldowan are choppers, usually made on waterworn, fist-size stones in which the rounded natural surface forms a butt that can be held comfortably in the hand. The working edges were roughly flaked from both sides to form sharp, jagged cutting edges. Choppers are simple, primitive tools, but when newly-made are surprisingly effective for a number of purposes such as skinning and cutting meat off a carcass as well as rough wood working. For a time choppers were thought to be the only tools of the Oldowan and they were certainly the most common and the most obvious, but excavations at Olduvai have shown that the Oldowan industry also contains a number of other tools that were probably used for similar purposes, as well as small tools such as scrapers, burins or chisels. There are also many small, sharp flakes that show evidence of use along the edges. These must surely have served for disjointing bones, sharpening wooden tools and other purposes for which the rather thick-edged choppers were unsuitable.

Table 1 List of Olduvai Hominids as at 1.4.74*

Specimen number	*Date discovery*	*Site or locality*	*Stratigraphic position*	*Parts found*	*Taxonomic status*	*Associated stone industry*
H.1	1913	RK	Burial dated *c.* 17,000 BP	Complete skeleton	*Homo sapiens*	*Inferred* microlithic industry as at 2nd. Fault Naisiusiu Beds.
H.2	1935	MNK	Surface, base Bed IV	Two fragments, thick cranial vault	cf. *H. erectus*	*Inferred* Acheulean
H.3	1955	BK	*In situ*, upper Bed II	Deciduous molar and canine	cf. *A. boisei*	Developed Oldowan B
H.4	1959	MK	*In situ* lower Bed I	1 lower molar, 2 broken teeth	*H. habilis*	*Inferred* Oldowan
H.5	1959	FLK	*In situ*, Middle Bed I	Almost complete cranium	*Australopithecus boisei*	Oldowan
H.6	1959-60	FLK	Surface, *inferred* Middle Bed I	2 molars and skull fragments	cf. *H. habilis*	*Inferred* Oldowan
H.7	1960	FLK NN	*In situ* Middle Bed I	Mandible, parietals, hand bones etc.	*Homo habilis*	Oldowan
H.8	1960	FLK NN	*In situ* Middle Bed I	Foot bones	? *Homo habilis*	Oldowan
H.9	1960	LLK	Surface, Upper Bed II	Calvaria	*Homo erectus*	Nil
H.10	1960	FLK North	*In situ*, Upper Bed I	Terminal phalanx of big toe	*Homo* sp.	Oldowan
H.11	1962	DK	Surface, probably from Lower Ndutu Beds	Palate and maxillary arch, lacking crowns of teeth	*Homo* sp.	Nil
H.12	1962	VEK	Surface, from Upper Bed IV	Palate, occipital parts of parietals etc.	*Homo erectus*	Nil
H.13	1963	MNK Skull site	*In situ* and surface, Middle Bed II (lower part)	Mandible, maxilla and broken skull	*Homo habilis*	Oldowan
H.14	1963	MNK Skull site	Surface, *inferred* same level as H.13	Juvenile cranial vault fragments	*Homo* sp.	*Inferred* Oldowan
H.15	1963	MNK Skull site	*In situ* 1' above level of H.13	1 canine, 2 molars	*Homo* sp.	Nil

Table 1 (continued)

Specimen number	*Date discovery*	*Site or locality*	*Stratigraphic position*	*Parts found*	*Taxonomic status*	*Associated stone industry*
H.16	1963	FLK Maiko Gully	*In situ* lower Bed II	Crushed skull, upper and lower dentitions	? *Homo habilis*	*Inferred* Oldowan
H.17	1964	FLK Maiko Gully	Surface (stream bed)	Broken deciduous molar	*Homo* sp.	Nil
H.18	Not Valid					
H.19	1963	FC West	*In situ*, middle Bed II	Broken molar	*Homo* sp.	Status not determined
H.20	1959	HWK	Surface, *inferred* lower Bed II	Frag. prox. end L. femur	cf. *A. boisei*	Nil
H.21	1968	FLK North	Surface	Small, unworn upper L. M^1	*H. habilis*	Nil
H.22	1968	Side Gorge between MNK and VEK	Surface	R. side of mandible with P_3 – M_2	cf. *H. erectus*	Nil
H.23	1968	FLK	*In situ*, Masek Beds	L. side mandible with M_1, M_2, P_4	*Homo* sp.	Acheulean
H.24	1968	DK East	Surface, from lower Bed I	Crushed cranium	*H. habilis*	*Inferred* Oldowan
H.25	1968	Geologic locality 54	Surface, Bed IV	Frag. parietal in region of asterion	*Homo* sp.	Nil
H.26	1969	FLK West	Surface, probably from lower Bed II	Large, unworn R. lower M_3	cf. *A. boisei*	Nil
H.27	1969	HWK EE	Surface, upper Bed I	Unworn R. lower M_3	cf. *H. habilis*	Nil
H.28	1970	WK	Upper Bed IV	Shaft of L. femur and L. side pelvis	*H. erectus*	Acheulean
H.29	1969	JK	*In situ*, Bed III	Broken molar	*Homo* sp.	Indeterminate

Table 1 (continued)

Specimen number	*Date discovery*	*Site or locality*	*Stratigraphic position*	*Parts Found*	*Taxonomix status*	*Associated stone industry*
H.30	1969	Maiko Gully	Surface, lower Bed II	Parts deciduous and permanent dentitions	cf. ? *A. boisei*	Nil
H.31	1969	HWK East	Surface, upper Bed I	Broken molar	*Homo* sp.	Nil
H.32	1969	MNK	Surface, middle Bed II	Broken molar	*Homo* sp.	Nil
H.33	1969	FLK NN	Surface, Bed I	Vault frags. of v. thin skull	Indeterminate	Nil
H.34	1962	JK	*In situ*, Bed III	Slender femur and part tibia shaft	*Homo* sp.	Indeterminate
H.35	1960	FLK	*In situ*, middle Bed I	Tibia and fibula	cf. *Homo habilis*	Oldowan
H.36	1970-71	SC	*In situ*, upper Bed II	Nearly complete ulna	*H. erectus*	Indeterminate
H.37	1971	Camp Road, FLK South	Surface, probably from sandy conglomerate in middle Bed II	L. side of mandible with M_1, M_2	*H. Habilis*	Nil
H.38	1971	SC	*In situ*, upper Bed II	R. M_2 and 2 incisors	cf. *A. boisei*	Indeterminate
H.39	1972	HWK EE	In fallen block from upper Bed I	Upper dentitions: permanent teeth 12, deciduous teeth 5	cf. *H. habilis*	Nil
H.40	1972	FLK South	Surface, middle Bed II, probably from sandy conglomerate	Broken molar	*Homo* sp.	Nil
H.41	1972	HWK EE	*In situ*, lower Bed II	Upper molar	*H. habilis*	Developed Oldowan A.
H.42	1972	HWK EE	Surface, upper Bed I	Broken crown of upper premolar	cf. *H. habilis*	Nil
H.43	1960	FLK NN	*In situ*, middle Bed I	Two metatarsals	cf. *H. habilis*	Oldowan
H.44	1970	FLK	Surface, blow living floor	Crown of R. upper M^1	*H. habilis*	*Inferred* Oldowan
H.45	1960	FLK NN	Surface, below living floor	L. upper M^1 or M^2	*H. habilis*	*Inferred* Oldowan
H.46	1960	FLK NN	Surface, below living floor	Broken crown, worn premolar or molar	? *A. boisei*	*Inferred* Oldowan

*Several additional hominids have been found since this list was compiled.

Bed II

The conditions in Bed II are considerably more complex than in Bed I, in respect of the geology, the hominid population, the stone industries and even the fauna. A longer time span is involved, probably about 600,000 years.

Dr Hay has kindly contributed the following note for this paper on a particular aspect of the geological interpretation. He writes: 'Tuffs have proved of the greatest importance for correlating, and by studying their structure it is also possible to determine the environment at the time they were deposited. By studying a widespread tuff one can get information about the palaeogeography of a wide area for a particular period of time. The tuffs in Bed I are widespread, relatively thick and easy to recognize; those in Bed II are generally reworked, discontinuous and vary greatly in appearance over short distances. Only a few tuffs in Bed II are sufficiently widespread to allow correlation of the deposits in the eastern and western parts of the gorge. One of the two most important tuffs for correlation in Bed II is a thin band of fine-grained, laminated tuff, only 5 to 12 cm. thick, that is known as the 'bird print tuff' on account of the innumerable impressions of birds' feet that are perfectly preserved on its surface. These were clearly made by shore birds and are strikingly similar to prints made by small plovers round the shores of East African soda lakes today. The bird-print tuff can be recognized over an east-west distance of 10 km., both on its distinctive appearance and mineral composition. The impressions of birds' feet show that layers of ash formed the surface of a moist mud flat only slightly above the level of the lake or just below the surface of the water. The bird prints must have been quickly buried by succeeding ash showers or lacustrine muds.

'Because this tuff was deposited at very nearly the same level everywhere it can be used to show that the Olduvai lake basin was deformed as the underlying part of Bed II was deposited. This is determined from the fact that the uppermost tuff of Bed I, like the bird-print tuff, was nearly horizontal when it was deposited. If no deformation had taken place the two tuffs should, therefore, be separated by a nearly uniform thickness of beds. In actual fact, the bird print tuff ranges from about 10 to 35 feet above the tuff at the top of Bed I, over quite short distances. This reflects the beginning of faulting in the Olduvai area.

'The deposits of lower Bed II, below a marker tuff known as the Lemuta Member, closely resemble those of Bed I. They were laid down before the onset of faulting in the Olduvai region and under the same stable conditions. But the beginning of earth movements immediately after the deposition of the Lemuta Member brought about a great change in the palaeogeography. The perennial lake of

Bed I was drained and substantially reduced in size, while more river- and stream-channels came into being as a result of the altered drainage system. Although a lake did still exist, hominid occupation sites were more often in the channels than along the lake shore, a change of habitat that persisted throughout nearly all the subsequent living sites in the higher part of the Olduvai sequence. From the point of view of the archaeological record this was a disastrous change, since it is never possible to find occupational material in an undisturbed context at such sites. The reason for this change of habitat is difficult to understand, but it may have been for the advantage of conveniently close water supplies during the dry season, when water could probably be obtained by digging holes in the river beds. Trees growing along the watercourses would also give shade and add comfort to the camp-sites.'

Until now, the micro-vertebrate fauna obtained from Bed II above the Lemuta Member is very scarce and evidence concerning ecological conditions has to be based on the larger mammals. There was, in fact, a marked change in the fauna at the time of the Lemuta Member. Giant forms such as *Pelorovis oldowayensis, Afrochoerus nicoli* and *Theropithecus oswaldi* appear at Olduvai for the first time, while numbers of the animals present in Bed I no longer occur. This change in the fauna was considered in the past to mark the incoming of middle Pleistocene fauna, but if the boundary between the lower and middle Pleistocene is recognized to be at the Brunhes/Matuyama change of polarity (700,000 years), then the faunal change at the time of the Lemuta Member is still well within the lower Pleistocene.

It is now evident that the reduction of the lake and altered drainage pattern owing to the onset of faulting changed the topography of the Olduvai area at this time. Whether there was also a change in overall climatic conditions is not known at present.

Homo habilis continues into lower Bed II and also into the lower part of middle Bed II, but has not been found higher in the sequence. Where an identifiable stone industry occurs in association with remains of *Homo habilis* in Bed II, it has proved to be either Oldowan, or the first stage of the Developed Oldowan, in which there are no hand-axes.

Australopithecus boisei – or his descendants – lived on until the top of Bed II. Indeed, the first evidence of the existence of *Australopithecus* at Olduvai was the deciduous molar and canine found at site BK in upper Bed II during 1955, although, at the time, the teeth were not identified as australopithecine. The molar, however, was the subject of a prolonged correspondence in *Nature* between Louis Leakey and John Robinson who argued heatedly as to whether it was permanent or deciduous, upper or lower.

The third hominid taxon in Bed II is *Homo erectus*, which has been found only in the upper levels. Unfortunately, neither the massive cranium found by Louis Leakey in 1960 (H.9) nor the ulna found in

1970 (H.36) was associated with any identifiable stone industry.

The position regarding the stone industries of Bed II is complex and is still not fully understood. There is certainly a continuation of the Oldowan from Bed I that I have named the Developed Oldowan. It is characterized by choppers, spheroids, a variety of small tools and, from middle Bed II onwards, by a small number of poorly made, generally small bifacial tools. There is also an indisputable Acheulean industry first found a few feet above the Lemuta Member, where it probably dates to about 1.3 m.y. This early Acheulean is now known from two sites at the same stratigraphic level. It is in every respect typical of the Acheulean with a few cleavers as well as many hand-axes. These are generally made on large flakes struck from boulders with a minimum of simple retouch. Choppers, spheroids and small tools are rare and bifaces make up the greater part of the industry. This industry compares closely in general character with the Acheulean from west Natron and is of approximately the same age (Isaac 1965).

The Developed Oldowan and Acheulean can easily be distinguished from one another both in the nature of the bifaces and in the proportions of the tool types. Moreover, they continue as distinct industrial complexes through Bed III into upper Bed IV. However, the industries found at two sites, in middle and upper Bed II respectively, fit neither the Acheulean nor the Developed Oldowan. At both these sites (MNK and the lower floor at TK) choppers, spheroids and small tools are common, as they are in the Developed Oldowan, while bifaces are similarly rare. But, unlike the small, crude bifacial tools of the Developed Oldowan these tools are large, boldly flaked and appear to be typical of the Acheulean. On the basis of the bifaces – scarce though they are – the industries from these two sites would be termed Acheulean, whilst on the tool-kit as a whole they would fit best with the Developed Oldowan. Further field-work will certainly be necessary before the problem is solved.

Bed III

The red Bed III yielded very few fossils or artifacts over most of the area where it is exposed in the gorge. If Richard Hay's interpretation of how it was formed is correct, this is hardly surprising, since conditions must have been most unfavourable for human habitation. He considers that it represents a semi-arid alluvial plain lacking permanent streams, with alkaline soil and mudflats probably bearing only sparse vegetation. On the analogy of present-day red beds forming along the shore of Lake Natron, where the Peninj river flows into the soda lake, he has concluded that a chemical reaction that causes reddening takes place as a result of wetting and drying of the alkaline sediments along the shore. Certainly, there would be no inducement for man to live on the open, windswept flats at the edge of a soda lake (Bed I lake-shore living sites, judged on the presence of reed casts and fossil rhizomes, appear to have been in areas where there was vegetation along the shore).

There are, however, a number of sites in Bed III in one area on the north side of the gorge, where a wide river valley existed. Among these sites is JK, which has yielded an abundance of tools, but mostly very abraded and not in their original context. A hominid femur and part of a tibia shaft were also found at JK by M.R. Kleindienst in 1962. But these are so abraded and corroded by soil acids that their taxonomic position remains uncertain. The femur, however, appears to bear little resemblance to the femur from Bed IV attributed to *H. erectus*.

Bed IV

Bed IV was for a long time considered to be the top of the Olduvai sequence and of relatively recent date. But clearly this is not the case. Paleomagnetic samples from lower Bed IV have shown reversed polarity, indicating that the Matuyama Reversed Epoch had not yet come to a close. A date of not less than 700,000 years can therefore be assumed for this part of the deposit.

During Bed IV times there appear to have been a number of seasonal lakes with rivers draining into them. Man lived in or by the water courses, as he did during most of Bed II times. Micro-vertebrate fauna is almost unknown from Bed IV, but remains of hippopotamus are particularly common, together with crocodiles and catfish, as well as *Equus* and the three-toed equid *Stylohipparion*. This combination of riverine and savannah animals fully supports the geological interpretation of the conditions at this time.

The hominid remains from Bed IV can all be attributed to *Homo erectus*. They consist of the small, incomplete cranium H.12 that only just falls within the lowest limit of cranial capacity for the crania of *H. erectus* from the Far East, two fragments of cranial vault from MNK, the femur shaft and innominate bone from WK. These last are from upper Bed IV as is the cranium H.12, while the fragments from MNK are from the lower part of the Bed.

The sites excavated in lower Bed IV have yielded Acheulean industries. Each of these assemblages of tools differs to some extent from the others, but all can be classed unquestionably as Acheulean, both on the proportionate numbers of bifaces and their method of manufacture. In upper Bed IV, however, there is a series of sites which has yielded a different industry that closely resembles the Developed Oldowan from upper II and must represent a continuation of the same tradition.

Masek Beds

Only one site is known in the Masek Beds. This is probably due to the fact that desertic conditions largely prevailed at this time. The single site is at FLK, where a river channel cuts down into Bed IV from the overlying Masek Beds. Exceptionally large, well-made Acheulean handaxes were recovered from this site as well as a small fragment of human mandible (H.23) that is unfortunately too abraded for positive identification.

Ndutu Beds

One further group of deposits that almost certainly also belongs within the middle Pleistocene remains to be mentioned. These have been termed the lower Ndutu Beds by Richard Hay. Unlike bones from the upper Ndutu Beds, which are quite fresh in appearance, bones from these deposits are fully mineralized. The lower Ndutu Beds are only sparsely represented in the gorge, but one exposure has yielded a complete mandible of *Theropithecus* while a very damaged hominid palate (H.11) probably also comes from these deposits.

A site at the head of the gorge, on the shores of Lake Ndutu, has also been attributed to the lower Ndutu beds. This contains an Acheulean industry in which there is an abundance of spheroids.

Whatever the taxonomic positions of the Olduvai hominids and their relationship to other fossil hominids in East and South Africa may prove to be eventually, it is evident that at Olduvai itself there are still some outstanding questions.

Australopithecus boisei is present in characteristic form throughout Beds I and II; whether he was capable of formalized tool-making is a question still unresolved, although I consider it to be unlikely. The status of *Homo habilis* has been controversial ever since the specific name was set up (Leakey, Tobias and Napier, 1964) and continues to be so. But if we accept that this hominid was probably responsible for the Oldowan stone industry the term *Homo* rather than *Australopithecus* seems more suitable. The evidence for *H. habilis* being the tool-maker is not conclusive and probably never will be, but the cumulative data of repeated associations of his remains with Oldowan tools give reasonable grounds for this assumption. If we accept this and also consider certain morphological features of *Homo habilis* it is difficult to understand why no remains have been found later than H.13, in the lower part of middle Bed II (*c.* 1.5 m.y.). Subsequently, apart from *A. boisei* in upper Bed II, all the hominid fossils can be attributed to *Homo erectus* with the possible exception of the damaged femur and tibia fragment from Bed III.

Furthermore, it seems that we can no longer attribute without reservation all the lightly built post cranial remains from Olduvai to *H. habilis*. Some specimens appear to have australopithecine characters, for example, the astragalus of the FLK NN foot (Day and Wood, 1968). Does this imply that these remains should be attributed to the gracile *Australopithecus* (whose presence has hitherto been unsuspected) or to a female *A. boisei* or does it mean that *H. habilis* retained australopithecine affinities? These and other queries remain to be answered in the future.

REFERENCES

Day, M.H. and Wood, B.A. (1968) Functional affinities of the Olduvai Hominid 8 talus. *Man* 3, 440-55.

Isaac, G. Ll. (1965) The stratigraphy of the Peninj beds and the provenance of the Natron australopithecine mandible. *Quaternaria* 7, 101-30.

Leakey, M.D. (1971) *Olduvai Gorge* Vol. 3, *Excavations in Beds I and II*. London.

Leakey, L.S.B., Tobias, P.V. and Napier, J.R. (1964) A new species of the genus *Homo* from Olduvai Gorge. *Nature* (London) 202, 7-9.

Verdcourt, B. (1963) The Miocene non-marine mollusca of Rusinga Island, Lake Victoria and other localities in Kenya. *Sond. Palaeontographica* 121, Stuttgart.

R.E.F. Leakey

Koobi Fora: A Summary

The Koobi Fora area is today recognized as being one of the more important Plio-Pleistocene localities in Africa. The region (see Figure 1) covers close to 1000 sq.km. and large numbers of vertebrate fossils have been recorded from the sedimentary succession. The area was investigated for the first time during 1968 and subsequent years have seen a programme of systematic investigation. The research programme is coordinated by the National Museum of Kenya and is undertaken by a multi-national inter disciplinary team, the Koobi Fora Research Group. A variety of reports (see Appendix II) has appeared, covering interim results of the geological investigations, the archaeology, palaeontology and palaeo-anthropology, as well as various related studies.

The Koobi Fora region has been divided into a number of 'areas' with numerical references. These areas comprise naturally defined sedimentary outcrops and are of no significance except as geographical references within a vast area of sediment exposure. Localities of important discoveries, excavations and geological sections are recorded by area and are documented by aerial photographs at a scale of 1:24,000. The mapping of the region is yet to be completed at the microstratigraphic level although certain areas have been studied intensively. A broad picture of the geological history has been prepared in which the sedimentary units, faults and lithologies are documented. A correlation of key marker beds within the basin is possible and the various fossil discoveries are tied into a secure stratigraphic framework.

Attempts have been made to date the Koobi Fora sediments and fossils via a number of different approaches. The prolific faunas of the Koobi Fora formation correlate well with those from various parts of the Omo Shungura sequence. Conventional K-Ar methodology has provided dates for some of the major Koobi Fora tuffs which agree well with the vertebrate correlations. More refined radiometric methods and fission track analysis have, however, provided alternative

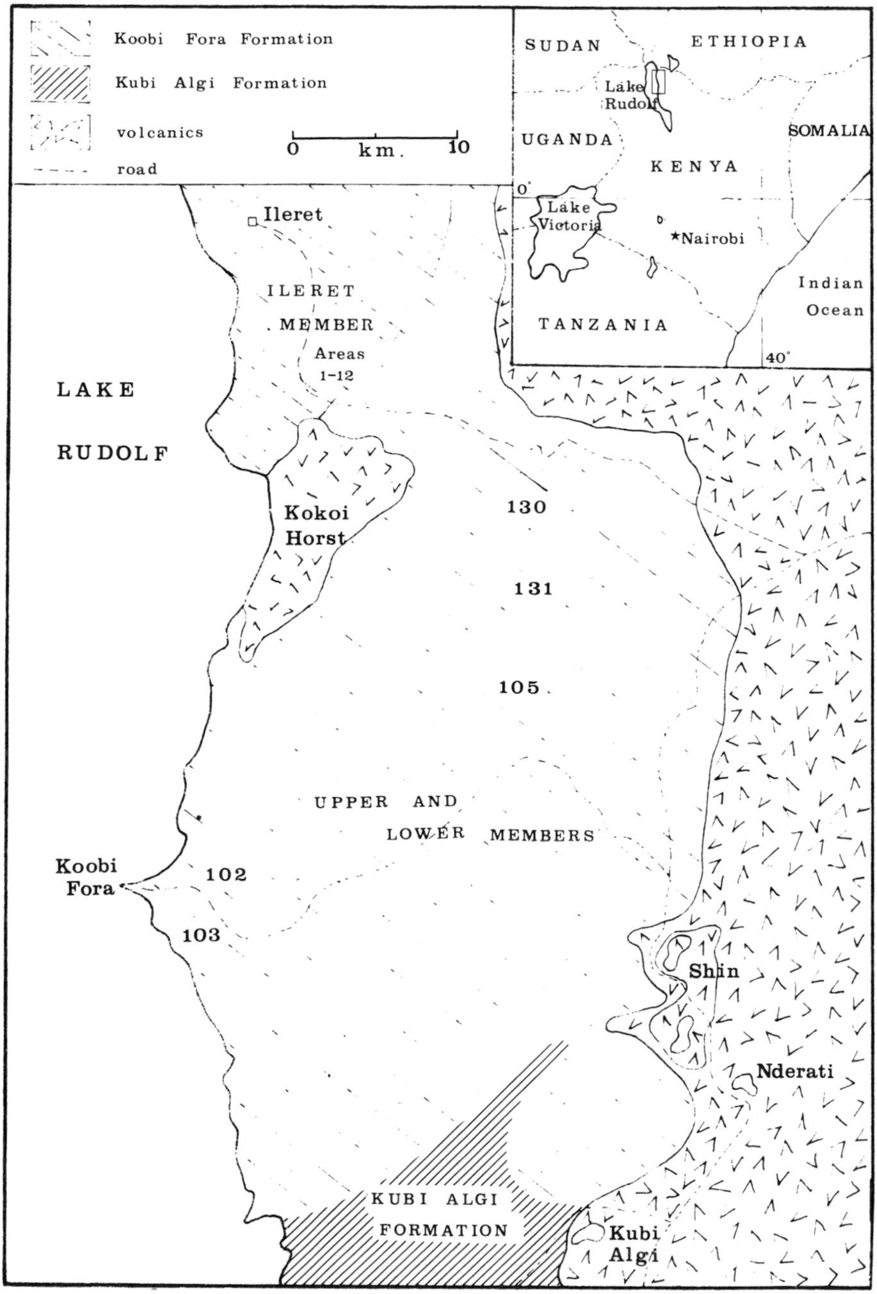

Figure 1. Map to show the fossiliferous exposures east of Lake Turkana and the geographical position of the areas indicated in Figure 2. The inset shows the position in Kenya of the enlarged map.

older dates for the same tuffs. Palaeomagnetic evidence is equivocal at this stage because too few areas have lengthy sedimentary sequences. The conventional radiometric results in combination with relative faunal dating permit the various local faunas to be correlated both within the basin and with the other important African Plio-Pleistocene localities. Which set of absolute ages is correct remains to be proven.

The large collection of fossil vertebrates includes more than 90 species. A full list of identified taxa is given in Appendix 1. The detailed comparison between faunas within the Lake Turkana basin is now in progress.

The fauna has been discussed by Maglio (1972), who proposed 4 faunal units: the *Notochoerus capensis* zone, the *Mesochoerus limnetes* zone, the *Metridiochoerus andrewsi* zone and the *Loxodonta africana* zone. There is some evidence of an extensive hiatus between the *Notochoerus capensis* and the *Mesochoerus limnetes* zones and that the *M. andrewsi* faunal zone is better documented here than elsewhere in Africa. The continuing programme of palaeontological research in the large area may yet provide further information on the transitional phases of vertebrate evolution during the Plio-Pleistocene. It would seem appropriate to re-stress the potential significance of palaeo-ecology and the need to understand better the reconstruction of palaeo-habitats in the Rudolf basin.

Invertebrate fossils are well represented in the sedimentary succession at Koobi Fora and are likely to prove important to the understanding of inter-basin correlations and palaeoenvironments. At the time of writing, a pioneer study by Peter Williams of Bristol University is not completed.

The archaeological programme has produced results of significance that are well covered elsewhere (Isaac, this volume). The artifact occurrences associated with the KBS tuff provide evidence for a well developed pattern of hominid tool making behaviour. Scanty indications exist for even earlier occurrences but these are yet to be fully investigated. The artifacts from the later Karari industry have been the subject of an extensive study by J.W.K. Harris. There are numerous sites with a high density of lithic material, often associated with fragmentary bone of prey animals. The apparent age for this series of sites is about 1.5 million years.

The hominid fossils from Koobi Fora are listed in Appendix 3 and have been the subject of various papers. The material has been provisionally assigned to either *Australopithecus* or *Homo* with an *indeterminate* category for specimens of uncertain affinities and fragmentary material that cannot be diagnosed. The hominid fossils are the subject of a major comparative study that will be published upon completion in monograph form. For the present, the evidence suggests the contemporary existence at East Rudolf of at least two broad forms of hominid; *Homo* and *Australopithecus*. The fossil hominids are recorded from the *Mesochoerus limnetes* zone through to the *Loxodonta africana* zone, a time span of at least a million years.

Discussion of the Koobi Fora hominids

The generic rank has been used as the most convenient taxonomic level. Until comprehensive studies are concluded, the fossil hominid remains have been sorted upon the basis of morphological traits and similarities. Considerable allowance has been made for variability within the sample and further sorting of the two 'generic' groups may lead to further divisions and a more complex systematic interpretation. Some workers approach the problem on the basis that sub-specific or at most specific distinctions have to be established before attempting attribution to a genus. Though the existence of such an approach is accepted, it has not been applied to the East Rudolf hominids and there does not seem to be any good reason to apply it.

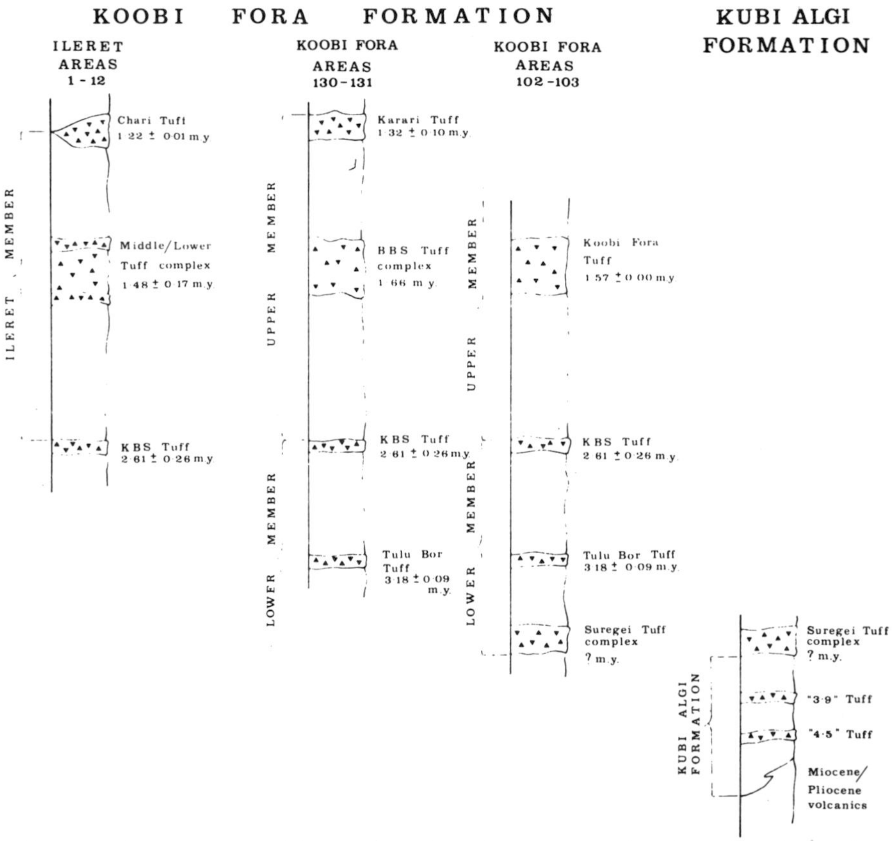

Figure 2. Composite simplified sections (not drawn to scale) to show the relationship of the major tuffs. The dates for these tuffs are from Fitch, F.J. and Miller, J.A., 'Conventional potassium-argon and argon 40/argon 39 dating of the volcanic rocks from East Rudolf', in *Earliest Man and Environments in the Lake Rudolf Basin*, ed. Coppens, Y. *et al.*, Chicago 1976, pp. 123-47.

The East Rudolf collection attributed to *Australopithecus* consists of cranial, mandibular and post-cranial elements. It would seem that within this group, there may be one form that is typically robust and which changes little through the time period represented at East Rudolf. Sexual dimorphism has been suggested to explain a large part of variability and this form bears striking resemblances to *Australopithecus boisei* from Bed I, Olduvai.

Until 1973, there did not seem to be any evidence for a 'gracile' form within the East Rudolf examples of the genus *Australopithecus*. The discovery of KNM-ER 1813, a well-preserved and almost complete cranium, has reopened this issue and requires that the previous attributions of more fragmentary fossils be re-examined. There does seem to be a clear suggestion that in addition to a sexually dimorphic robust species, there was in existence a 'gracile' species as well, both being distinct from *Homo*.

Fossils attributed to *Homo* are documented throughout the succession and as in the case of *Australopithecus*, various elements of the skeleton have been recovered. The earliest example, KNM-ER 1470, is dated at more than 2 million years. A number of other specimens are known from the *Mesochoerus limnetes* zone, while the greater proportion of the specimens are from the *Metridiochoerus andrewsi* and *Loxodonta africana* zones.

The material attributed to *Homo* shows variability, and specimens at the upper part of the sequence are different from material lower down. This may prove to be indication of a wide range of variation within a single chronospecies but it may instead be evidence for a more complex story involving more than one species.

A single specimen, KNM-ER 1482, is possibly of particular interest. The morphology of this mandible appears to differ markedly from other specimens from Koobi Fora. Certain mandibles from the Shungura Formation are quite similar but no detailed comparative studies have yet been concluded. It has been suggested that this might be evidence for a distinct hominid type, possibly an ancestral form for the typical Plio-Pleistocene examples. Systematic classifications can only be tentative until such time as the detailed comparative and functional studies have been concluded. The remarks above are made to encourage debate and to provide a summary of six rewarding years of research.

I should like to acknowledge and thank colleagues on the Koobi Fora Research Project for their contributions. I also thank the National Geographic Society, the National Science Foundation, the William H. Donner Foundation, private donors and the National Museum of Kenya for support over the period. In particular, I am indebted to Drs Walker, Wood and Day for their role in the careful description and study of the Koobi Fora hominids.

Appendix 1
Koobi Fora Faunal List

BOVIDAE (J. Harris)
Tragelaphus strepsiceros
Tragelaphus nakuae
Bovini gen. & sp. nov.
Pelorovis Oldowayensis
Pelorovis sp. nov.
Kobus ancystrocera
Kobus ellipsiprymnus
Kobus cf. *kob*
Kobus cf. *leche*
Kobus cf. *sigmoidalis*
Redunca sp.
Reduncini gen. & sp. nov.?
Hippotragus gigas
Oryx sp.
Parmularius angusticornis
Parmularius altidens
Parmularius sp. nov.
Connochaetes sp.
Megalotragus cf. *kattwinkeli*
?*Rabaticeras* sp.
Aepyceros sp.
Antidorcas recki
Gazella spp.

FELIDAE (M.G. Leakey)
Homotherium sp.
Megantereon eurynodon
cf. *Megantereon* sp.
Dinofelis barlowi
cf. *Dinofelis* sp.
Panthera cf *leo*
Panthera cf. *crassidens*

MUSTELIDAE (M.G. Leakey)
cf. *Aonyx* sp.

VIVERRIDAE (M.G. Leakey)
Genetta cf. *genetta*
Pseudociretta ingens

DEINOTHERIIDAE (J. Harris)
Deinotherium bozasi

ELEPHANTIDAE (Beden)
Elephas ekorensis
Elephas recki
Loxodonta adaurora
?*Loxodonta africana*

GOMPHOTHERIIDAE
Anancus sp.

EQUIDAE (Eisenmann)
Equus sp.
Hipparion sp.
Asinus sp.
Madoqua sp.

GIRAFFIDAE (J. Harris)
Sivatherium cf. *maurusium*
Giraffa jumae
Giraffa gracilis
Giraffa sp. nov.

SUIDAE (H.B.S. Cooke)
Nyanzochoerus pattersoni
Notochoerus capensis
Notochoerus euilus
Metridiochoerus andrewsi
Stylochoerus nicholi
Phacochoerus aethiopicus
Mesochoerus limnetes
Mesochoerus olduvaiensis

HIPPOPOTAMIDAE (S. Coryndon)
Hippopotamus gorgops
Hippopotamus sp. nov. (diprotodont)
Hippopotamus sp. nov. (pygmy tetraprotoc

HYAENIDAE (M.G. Leakey)
Crocuta crocuta
Hyaena hyaena

CANIDAE (M.G. Leakey)
Canis mesomalus
gen. cf. sp. indet.

RHINOCEROTIDAE (J. Harris)
Ceratotherium sinum germanoafricanum
Diceros bicornis subsp.

CERCOPITHECIDAE (M.G. Leakey)
cf. *Cercopithecoides* sp. nov.
Colobinae gen. et sp. nov.
Colobinae gen. et sp. indet.
Colobus sp.
Cercocebus sp.
Cercopithecus cf. *aethiops*
Cercopithecus sp.
Papio sp.
Theropithecus oswaldi
Theropithecus brumpti

HYSTRICIDAE
Hystrix sp.

THRYONOMYIDAE
Thryonomys sp.

ORYCTEROPODIDAE (M.G. Leakey)
Orycteropus sp.

CROCODYLIDAE (Tchernov)
Crocodylus cathafractus
Crocodylus sp. nov.
Euthecodon cf. *brumpti*

CHELONIA (R. Wood)
Geochelone sp.
Trionyx sp.

OSTEICHTHYES
Clarius sp.
Lates sp.
Polypterus sp.
Protopterus sp.

Appendix 2
Koobi Fora Research Project

Catalogue of Publications 1970 to January 1974

1. Leakey, R.E.F. (1970) New hominid remains and early artifacts from Northern Kenya. *Nature* 226, 223-4.
2. Behrensmeyer, A.K. (1970) Preliminary geological interpretation of a new hominid site in the Lake Rudolf basin. *Nature* 226, 225-6.
3. Fitch, F.J., and Miller, J.A. (1970) Radioisotopic age determinations of Lake Rudolf artifact site. *Nature* 226, 226-8.
4. Leakey, M.D. (1970) Early artefacts from Koobi Fora area. *Nature* 226, 228-30.
5. Leakey, R.E.F. (1970) In search of Man's past at Lake Rudolf. *National Geographic* 137, 712-32.
6. Leakey, R.E.F. (1971) Further evidence of Lower Pleistocene hominids from East Rudolf, North Kenya. *Nature* 231, 241-5.
7. Vondra, C.F., Johnson, G.D., Bowen, B.E., and Behrensmeyer, A.K. (1971) Preliminary stratigraphical studies of the East Rudolf Basin, Kenya. *Nature* 231, 245-8.
8. Maglio, Vincent J. (1971) Vertebrate faunas from the Kubi Algi, Koobi Fora and Ileret areas, East Rudolf, Kenya. *Nature* 231, 248-9.
9. Isaac, Glynn Ll., Leakey, R.E.F. and Behrensmeyer, A.K. (1971) Archaeological traces of early hominid activities, east of Lake Rudolf, Kenya. *Science* 173, 1129-34.

10. Leakey, R.E.F., Mungai, J.M. and Walker, A.C. (1971) New australopithecines from East Rudolf, Kenya. *Amer. J. phys. Anthrop.* 35, 175-86.
11. Leakey, R.E.F., Mungai, J.M. and Walker, A.C. (1972) New australopithecines from East Rudolf, Kenya (II). *Amer. J. phys. Anthrop.* 36, 235-51.
12. Leakey, R.E.F. (1972) Further evidence of Lower Pleistocene hominids from East Rudolf, North Kenya, 1971. *Nature* 237, 264-9.
13. Leakey, R.E.F. and Isaac, Glynn Ll. (1972) Hominid fossils from the area of Lake Rudolf, Kenya: photographs and a commentary on the context. In Washburn, S.L. and Dolhinow, P. (eds.), *Perspectives on Human Evolution 2*, San Francisco.
14. Maglio, V.J. (1972) Vertebrate faunas and chronology of hominid-bearing sediments east of Lake Rudolf, Kenya. *Nature* 239, 379-85.
15. Leakey, R.E.F. (1972) New evidence for the evolution of man. *Social Biology* 19, 99-114.
16. Leakey, R.E.F. (1973) Further evidence of lower Pleistocene hominids from East Rudolf, North Kenya, 1972. *Nature* 242, 170-3.
17. Bowen, B.E. and C.F. Vondra (1973) Stratigraphical relationships of the Plio-Pleistocene deposits, East Rudolf, Kenya. *Nature* 242, 391-3.
18. Leakey, R.E.F. (1973) Evidence for an advanced Plio-Pleistocene hominid from East Rudolf, Kenya. *Nature* 242, 447-50.
19. Leakey, R.E.F. (1973) Skull 1470. *National Geographic* 143, 818-29.
20. Leakey, R.E.F., and Wood, B.A. (1973) New evidence for the genus *Homo* from East Rudolf, Kenya, II. *Amer. J. phys. Anthrop.* 39, 355-68.
21. Johnson, G.D. (1974) Cainozoic lacustrine stromatolites from hominid-bearing sediments east of Lake Rudolf, Kenya. *Nature* 247, 520-3.
22. Day, M.H. and Leakey, R.E.F. (1973) New evidence for the genus *Homo* from East Rudolf, Kenya, I. *Amer. J. phys. Anthrop.* 39, 341-54.
23. Leakey, R.E.F., and Walker, A. (1973) New australopithecines from East Rudolf, Kenya. III. *Amer. J. phys. Anthrop.* 39, 205-22.
24. Leakey, R.E.F. (1972) Man and sub-men on Lake Rudolf. *New Scientist*, 385-7.
25. Leakey, M.G., and Leakey, R.E.F. (1973) New large Pleistocene colobinae (Mammalia, Primates) from East Africa. *Fossil Vertebrates of Africa* Vol. 3, 121-38.
26. Leakey, R.E.F. (1974) Further evidence of lower Pleistocene hominids from East Rudolf, North Kenya, 1973. *Nature* 248, 653-6.
27. Day, M.H. and Leakey, R.E.F. (1974) New evidence for the genus *Homo* from East Rudolf, Kenya. III. *Amer. J. phys. Anthrop.* 41, 367-80.
28. Leakey, R.E.F., and Wood, B.A. (1974) New evidence for the genus Homo from East Rudolf, Kenya. IV. *Amer. J. phys. Anthrop.* 41, 237-44.
29. Day, M.H., Leakey, R.E.F., Walker, A.C., and Wood, B.A. (1974) *Amer. J. phys. Anthrop.* 42, 461-76.
30. Leakey, R.E.F., and Wood, B.A. (1974) A hominid mandible from East Rudolf, Kenya. *Amer. J. phys. Anthrop.* 41, 245-50.
31. Wood, B.A. (1974) A *Homo* talus from East Rudolf, Kenya. *J. Anat.* 117, 652-3.
32. Wood, B.A. (1974) Morphology of a fossil hominid mandible from East Rudolf, Kenya. *J. Anat.* 117, 203-4.
33. Wood, B.A. (1974) Evidence on the locomotor pattern of *Homo* from

early Pleistocene of Kenya. *Nature* 251, 135-6.
34. Brock, A., and Isaac, G.Ll. (1974) Palaeomagnetic, stratigraphy and chronology of hominid-bearing sediments east of Lake Rudolf, Kenya. *Nature* (London) 247, 344-8.

Appendix 3
Koobi Fora hominids collected 1968-1973

KNM-ER No.	*Year*	*Area*	*Specimen detail*
164a	1969	104	parietal frag.
164b-c	1971	104	two phalanges, two vertebrae
403	1968	103	r. mandible
404	1968	7A	r. mandible M_2, M_3
405	1968	105	palate lacking teeth
406	1969	10	cranium lacking teeth
407	1969	10	cranium lacking face
417	1968	129	parietal frag.
725	1970	1	l. mandible
726	1970	11	l. mandible
727	1970	6A	r. mandible
728	1970	1	r. mandible
729	1970	8	mandible with dentition
730	1970	103	l. mandible with symphysis, l. M_1 –M_3
731	1970	6A	l. mandible
732	1970	10	demi-cranium, parietal P^4
733	1970	8	r. mandible, l. maxilla and cranial frags. M^1, M_3
734	1970	103	parietal frag.
736	1970	103	l. femur shaft
737	1970	103	l. femur shaft
738	1970	105	prox. l. femur
739	1970	1	r. humerus
740	1970	1	distal l. humerus frag.
741	1970	1	prox. l. tibia
801	1971	6A	r. mandible, M_3, M_2, and associated isolated teeth
802	1971	6A	isolated teeth
803	1971	8	associated skeletal element
805	1971	1	l. mandible
806	1971	8	isolated teeth
807A	1971	8A	r. maxilla frag. M^3, partial M^2
807B	1973	8A	r. maxilla frag. M^1
808	1971	8	isolated juvenile teeth
809	1971	8	isolated teeth
810	1971	104	l. mandible, M_3
811	1971	104	parietal frag.
812	1971	104	juvenile l. mandible frag.
813	1971	104	r. talus and tibia frag.
814	1971	104	cranial fragments

KNM-ER No.	*Year*	*Area*	*Specimen detail*
815	1971	10	prox. l. femur
816	1971	104	canine and molar frag.
817	1971	124	l. mandible frag.
818	1971	6A	l. mandible P_3–M_3
819	1971	1	l. mandible
820	1971	1	juvenile mandible with dentition
992	1971	1	mandible with dentition
993	1971	1	distal l. femur
997	1971	104	l. metatarsal III
998	1971	104	isolated incisor
999	1971	6A	cranial fragments
1170	1971	6A	cranial fragments
1171	1971	6A	isolated juvenile teeth
1462	1972	130	isolated M_3
1463	1972	1A	r. femur shaft
1464	1972	6A	r. talus
1465	1972	11	prox. l. femur frag.
1466	1972	6	parietal frag.
1467	1972	3	isolated M_3
1468	1972	11	r. mandible
1469	1972	131	l. mandible, M_3
1470	1972	131	cranium
1471	1972	131	prox. r. tibia
1472	1972	131	r. femur
1473	1972	131	prox. r. humerus
1474	1972	131	parietal frag.
1475	1972	131	prox. l. femur
1476	1972	105	l. talus and prox. l. tibia
1477	1972	105	juvenile mandible with dentition
1478	1972	105	cranial frags.
1479	1972	105	isolated molar frags.
1480	1972	105	isolated molar
1481	1972	131	l. femur, prox. and dist. l. tibia, dist. l. fibula.
1482	1972	131	mandible, r. P_4, l P_3–M_3
1483	1972	131	l. mandible, frag. M_2
1500	1972	130	associated skeletal elements
1501	1972	123	r. mandible
1502	1972	123	r. mandible frag. with M_1
1503	1972	123	prox. r. femur
1504	1972	123	dist. r. humerus
1505	1972	123	prox. l. femur
1506	1972	121	r. mandible, M_1, M_2, isolated P^3, P^4
1507	1972	127	juvenile l. mandible with dentition
1508	1972	127	isolated molar
1509	1972	119	isolated teeth C-M_3
1515	1972	103	isolated incisor
1590	1972	12	partial cranium with juvenile dentitio
1591	1972	12	r. humerus lacking head
1592	1972	12	dist. r. femur
1593	1972	12	cranial and mandibular frags.
1648	1972	105	parietal frag.
1800	1973	130	cranial frags.
1801	1973	131	l. mandible, P_4, M_1, M_3

KNM-ER No.	*Year*	*Area*	*Specimen detail*
1802	1973	131	mandible, l. P_4–M_2, r. P_3–M_2
1803	1973	131	frag. r. mandible
1804	1973	104	r. maxilla, P^3–M^2
1805	1973	130	cranium and mandible with dentition
1806	1973	130	mandible lacking teeth
1807	1973	103	shaft r. femur
1808	1973	103	associated skeletal and cranial elements
1809	1973	121	shaft r. femur
1810	1973	123	prox. l. tibia
1811	1973	123	l. mandible frag.
1812	1973	123	frag. r. mandible, isolated l. I_1, M_1
1813	1973	123	cranium
1814	1973	127	maxillary frags.
1816	1973	6A	immature mandible with dentition
1817	1973	1	r. mandible
1818	1973	6A	isolated I^1
1819	1973	3	isolated M_3
1820	1973	103	l. mandible, M_1
1821	1972	123	parietal frag.

D.C. Johanson and M. Taieb

Plio-Pleistocene hominid discoveries in Hadar, central Afar, Ethiopia

Introduction

While engaged in geological reconnaissance of the Awash River valley, one of the authors (M.T.) visited the central Afar in 1969 and located a series of fossiliferous lacustrine sediments of Plio-Pleistocene age near the Hadar River (Taieb, 1971). Other areas of fossil outcrops were subsequently located and late in 1971 Taieb collected a number of specimens of fossil vertebrates which were shown to the late L.S.B. Leakey and to M.D. Leakey at the Seventh Pan African Congress in Addis Ababa in December of that year. The Leakeys confirmed the Plio-Pleistocene age of the collection and encouraged the formation of an exploratory expedition to the Afar in order to ascertain the extent and nature of the fossiliferous sediments and to collect additional faunal remains.

In April and May of 1972 a small group composed of M. Taieb (geologist), D.C. Johanson (palaeoanthropologist), Y. Coppens (palaeontologist), and J. Kalb (geologist) participated in a geological and palaeontological survey in the central Afar. Numerous localities extremely rich in fossil vertebrates were found and selective palaeontological sampling was conducted. Geological observations suggested a varied set of depositional environments with extensive exposures of sediments and intercalated volcanics, offering the possibility of firm stratigraphic correlations and absolute dates.

The results (Taieb *et al.*, 1972) of this short exploratory expedition were so encouraging that it was decided to establish the International Afar Research Expedition (IARE) with the specific intention of launching a more extensive expedition as a combined French-American-Ethiopian effort. Funding became available from a number of sources, and it was possible to return to the central Afar during the fall of 1973.

This ten-week expedition (from October to December, 1973) was

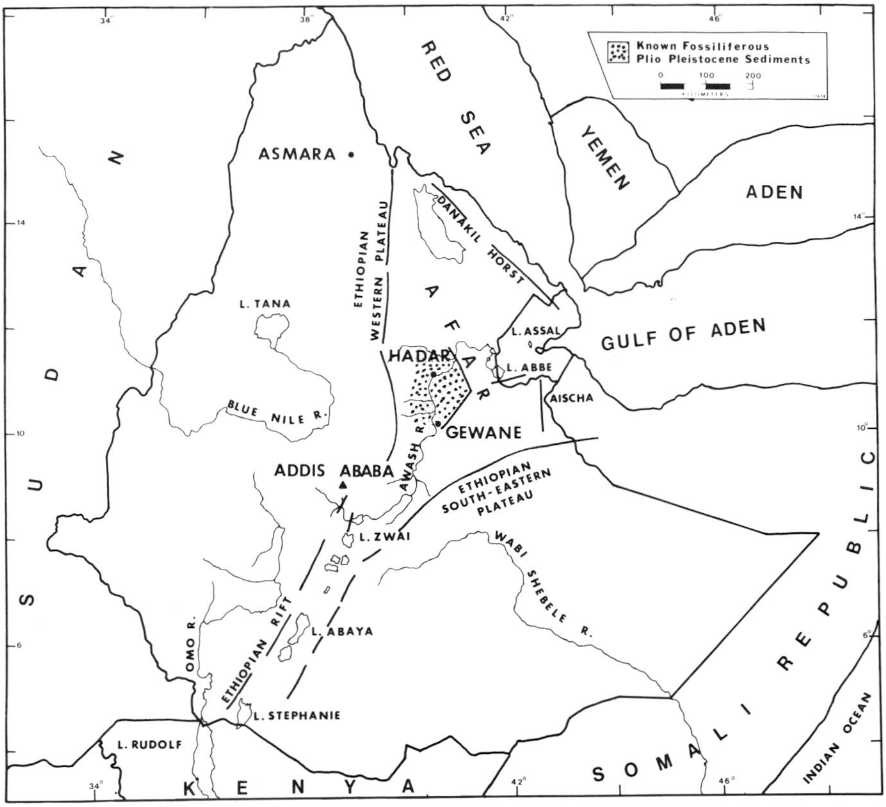

Figure 1. Map of Ethiopia.

joined by a number of additional scientists and students.[1] Our efforts were concentrated almost exclusively in the region of Hadar (Figure 1), although two weeks were also spent in the areas of Geraru and Amado. The decision to work in the Hadar area, rather than in one of the other areas located during the 1972 expedition, rested on a number of considerations. Firstly, localities had yielded a number of specimens of elephants and suids which suggested a considerable antiquity (about 3.0 m.y.) for the Hadar succession. Secondly, the localities in Hadar had proved to be exceedingly rich in splendidly preserved fossil specimens. Thirdly, the deposits are heavily dissected

1. These included: R. Bonnefille (palynologist, CNRS, Bellevue), C. Guerin (palaeontologist, University of Lyon), G. Corvinus (archaeologist, University of Tübingen), B.T. Gray (taphonomist, Case Western Reserve University), A.E. Dole (palaeontological survey, Case Western Reserve University), P. Planques (topographer, Institute Geographique National). Additional technical help was provided by N. Page (aerial photographs, CNRS, Bellevue), D. Peak (geographical mapping, Addis Ababa), and C. Guillemot (palaeontological survey, Paris). The National Museum in Addis Ababa provided us with an assistant, Ato Alemayehu Asfaw, who not only contributed valuable administrative help but also participated in palaeontological survey and collection.

exposing numerous fossiliferous horizons which can be traced laterally for great distances. Fourthly, the geological picture suggested a thick series of lacustrine and peri-lacustrine sediments. This setting has proven highly advantageous for faunal preservation at a number of other African Plio-Pleistocene sites such as Olduvai Gorge in Tanzania (L.S.B. Leakey, 1965) and East Rudolf in Kenya (Behrensmeyer, 1975).

In this contribution we provide some preliminary results of the 1973 expedition. The material is only just beginning to be studied in detail, but we feel that a number of results can be presented with the understanding that they are incomplete and will be substantially augmented in future publications.

The geological setting

The Afar triangle or Afar depression is a dominant geological feature in Ethiopia which is the result of the migration of the Nubian and Arabian plates (Tazieff *et al.*, 1972). It is especially important to geologists because it is the junction of three major rift systems: the Gulf of Aden, the Red Sea, and the East African rifts. This peculiar geological phenomenon of a triple junction has resulted in a large suite of geological events which have attracted the attention of geologists interested in continental drift, sea floor spreading, vulcanism, tectonics, oceanization, geothermal activity, geophysics, etc.[2]

The Afar triangle is approximately 130,000 sq.km. and is bounded by the western and south-eastern Ethiopian plateaus with the Danakil horst and the Red Sea to the north-east. Elevations in the Afar triangle range from about 600-700 m. in the south to 400-500 m. in the centre and less than 115 m. in the north. The unique geological history of the Afar depression has provided numerous and varied taphonomic settings advantageous to the accumulation; preservation, and exposure of fossil vertebrate remains (Taieb, 1974). Palaeoanthropological research in this area will substantially augment our knowledge of the Plio-Pleistocene time range for eastern Africa, revealing not only detailed information on geological, faunal, and ecological evolution but also faunal migrations into Africa from Eurasia.

The Hadar region (Figure 1) as thus far investigated is situated on the left bank of the Awash River at about 500 m. above sea level, only 14 km. east of the western Ethiopian plateau. The fossiliferous deposits are now estimated at approximately 20 sq.km., of which to date only about 2% has been intensively surveyed. It is known that the Hadar

2. 'Symposium on the Afar Region of Ethiopia and Related Rift Problems' was held in Clausthal-Zellerfeld, Germany on 1-6 April 1974.

sedimentary sequence is continuous with sediments to the west (Gona), south of the Awash River and to the east extending the exposures to several hundred sq.km.

The sediments in Hadar appear essentially horizontal, but in fact, dip 2.5° to the N-NE. The sequence does not appear to exhibit any substantial disconformities, but a number of minor faults are present trending SSW-NNE and SSE-NNW with displacements of from 5 to 20 m. Total thickness of the stratigraphic sequence (Figure 2) is estimated at nearly 110 m., but this estimate may well be increased when work is extended to the south and east.

At this stage of our research detailed geological interpretations of the Hadar section are impossible. However, the repetitive horizons of sands suggest fluctuating lake levels, and it is not impossible that these are related to ancient beaches. Appreciation of the

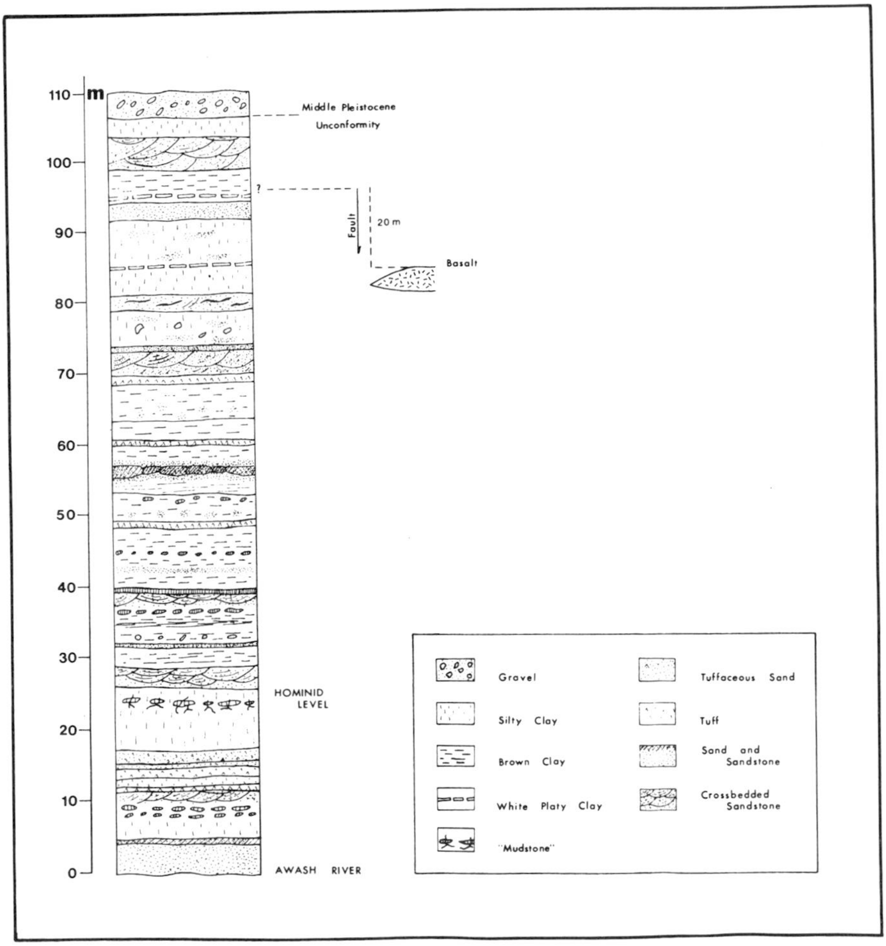

Figure 2. Generalized section of Hadar.

palaeogeomorphology, the palaeogeography, and the factors responsible for fluctuating water levels must await additional detailed stratigraphic studies. Variations in water level are probably related to volcano-tectonic activity in the axial zones of the Afar depression.

Fossiliferous occurrences are common throughout the succession. Sands appear to be most productive and while fossils do occur in other rocks, they are often less abundant and commonly fragmentary. However, a number of 'mudstone' horizons are locally rich in excellently preserved faunal remains which are frequently of small size and include, for instance, a half mandible of *Mastomys*.

Reliable radiometric estimates for the absolute age of the Hadar sequence are not presently available. However, a number of tuff horizons and a basalt are evident in the sequence (Figure 2). Field and laboratory research specifically directed at establishing an absolute geochronological framework for the sedimentary sequence is only just beginning.

Palaeontological considerations

In the Hadar region a total of 89 palaeontological localities have been collected and mapped. The fossil fauna is beautifully preserved, frequently nearly complete, heavily mineralized, and in a number of instances represented by associated and even articulated body parts. Most of our collection was from the surface, although small scale excavations of *in situ* fossils were occasionally undertaken.

Faunal remains were identified in the field by Johanson and Coppens, and a number of these identifications have been confirmed by various experts.[3] Table 1 presents a provisional list of the fossil vertebrates collected at Hadar in 1972 and 1973. The present faunal assemblage is sufficiently extensive to permit a preliminary biostratigraphic correlation with other sites in eastern Africa of Plio-Pleistocene age.

Suids and elephants have proved to be particularly useful in Plio-Pleistocene correlation as a result of their rapid evolution manifested in various trends, and due to their wide geographical distribution (Cooke and Maglio, 1972). *Notochoerus capensis* and *Nyanzachoerus pattersoni* are primitive suids known from the lower Shungura Formation and Kanapoi (Cooke and Ewer, 1972; Cooke and Maglio, 1972). Specimens of *N.* cf. *pattersoni* from the Hadar may be somewhat more evolved than those found at Kanapoi (Cooke, pers. comm.). In addition, *N. capensis* is known from Kubi Algi and *N.* cf. *pattersoni* from

3. Some specimens as well as a number of good illustrations have been shown to H.B.S. Cooke (Suidae), V. Maglio (Elephantidae), J. Harris (Giraffidae), J.J. Jaeger (Rodentia), C. Guerin (Rhinocerotidae), V. Eisenman (Equidae), and S. Coryndon (Hippopotamidae).

Table 1 Provisional list of the vertebrate species from Hadar, central Afar

Artiodactyla		
	Hippopotamidae	
		Hippopotamus sp., *H.* cf. *imagunculus*
	Suidae	
		Sus sp., *S.* cf. *waylandi* *Notochoerus* sp., *N.* cf. *capensis* *Notochoerus* sp., *N.* cf. *euilus* *Nyanzachoerus* sp., *N.* cf. *pattersoni*
	Giraffidae	
		Sivatherium maurusium *Giraffa* sp., *G.* cf. *jumae* *Giraffa* sp.
	Bovidae	
		Tragelaphus sp., *T.* cf. *nakuae* *Kobus* sp. *Aepyceros* sp. *Ugandax*
Perissodactyla		
	Equidae	
		Hipparion sp.
	Rhinoceratidae	
		Ceratotherium sp., *C.* cf. *simum*
Proboscidea		
	Elephantidae	
		Elephas recki *Loxodonta adaurora*
Deinotheroidea		
		Deinotherium sp.
Rodentia		
		Hystrix sp. *Mastomys* sp. *Xenohystrix* sp. *X.* cf. *crassidens*
Carnivora		
	Canidae	
		gen. et sp. indet.
	Hyaenidae	
		Crocuta sp.
	Mustelidae	
		gen. et sp. indet. ?*Enhydriodon* sp.

Table 1 continued.

	Felidae	
		?*Megantereon* sp.
		?*Dinofelis* sp.
Primates		
	Cercopithecidae	
		Papio sp.
		Theropithecus sp.
	Hominidae	
		Australopithecus sp.
		gen. et sp. indet.
Aves		
		gen. et sp. indet.
Reptilia		
		Crocodilus sp.
		Geochelone sp.
		Trionyx sp.
Osteichthyes		
	Siluridae	
		gen. et sp. indet.

Lothagam (Cooke and Ewer, 1972; Cooke and Maglio, 1972). The possible occurrence of *Sus waylandi* suggests a correlation with Kaiso (Cooke and Coryndon, 1970).

Elephas recki is the most abundant proboscidean, but *Loxodonta adaurora* is also represented by a fair number of specimens. In lamellar frequency, enamel thickness, number of plates, and the hypsodonty index, the *E. recki* material most closely resembles Stage 1 in Maglio's evolutionary scheme (Maglio, 1973). This suggests correlations with Kikagati in Uganda and again with the lower Shungura. *L. adaurora* spans a considerable length of time and changes slowly (Maglio, 1973). The Hadar specimens exhibit a number of features, such as low lamellar frequency and thick enamel, which may be representative of the earlier stages of *L. adaurora* evolution (before 3.0 m.y.).

The earliest representatives of the Hippopotamidae are characterized by having six incisors (hexaprotodont) and can be traced back to the Miocene (Coryndon, 1976). Coryndon (1976) believes that the specialized four-incisor (tetraprotodont) hippos did not arise until about four million years ago. It is interesting to note that among the Hadar collections only hexaprotodont hippos are present with no trace of the tetraprotodont form.

Other faunal elements have not been adequately studied to permit their use in biostratigraphic correlation. However, the giraffids, particularly *Giraffa*, may be similar to forms from the Baringo basin which are older than three million years (J. Harris, pers. comm.).

These presumed correlations with a portion of the fauna from Kanapoi, Lothagam, lower Shungura, Kikagati, Kubi Algi, and Baringo are consistent for the proboscideans, suids, hippopotamids, and giraffids. We feel (and see Taieb *et al.*, 1972) that on the basis of these biostratigraphic considerations the sedimentary sequence at Hadar is best interpreted as sampling a time period older than three million years. It is possible that the three million date may be somewhat adjusted, perhaps towards four million, when more extensive faunal analysis is performed.

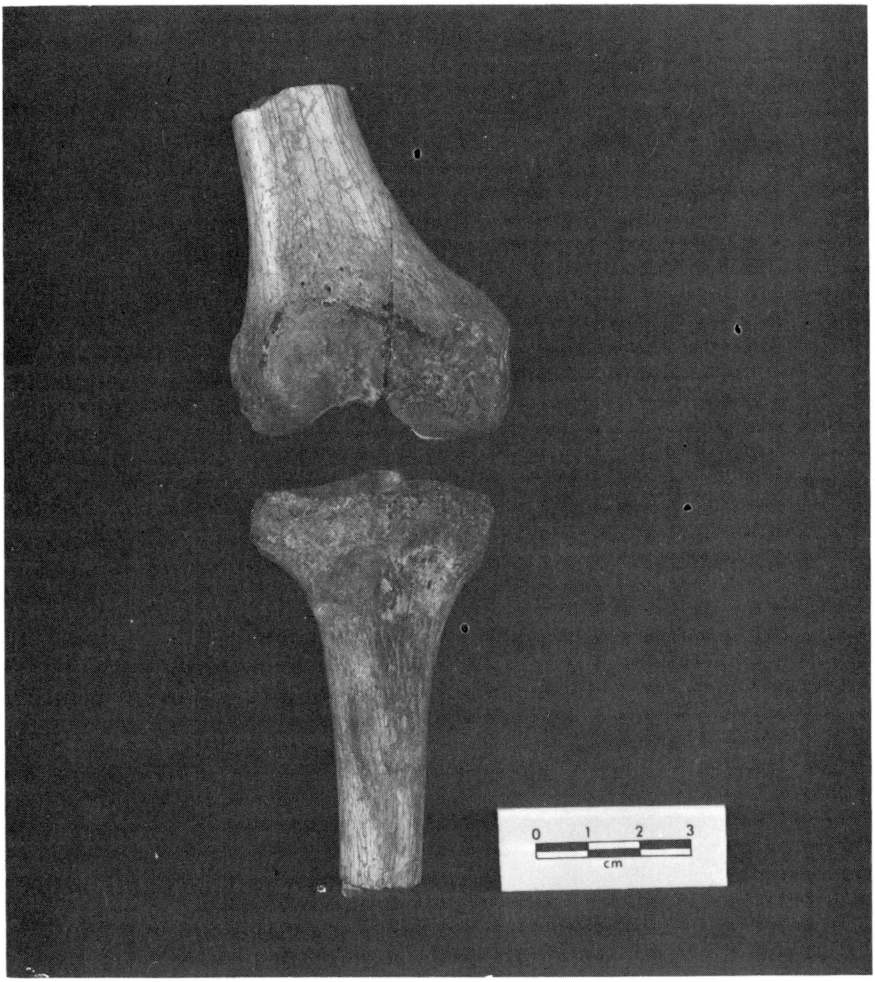

Figure 3. Anterior aspect of the right distal femur and proximal tibia from AL 129 (Hadar).

Hominid material

Presentation of the hominid specimens recovered from Hadar during the 1973 field season is intended to be merely introductory. Currently a more detailed anatomical description is being prepared (Johanson and Coppens) and will appear elsewhere.

Fossil hominid remains were first discovered on October 30, 1973, at a locality situated near the base of the stratigraphic sequence (Figure 2). Abundant vertebrate faunal remains of suids, proboscideans, hippopotamids, and rhinoceratids were collected from a very rich sand and sandstone horizon a few metres above the

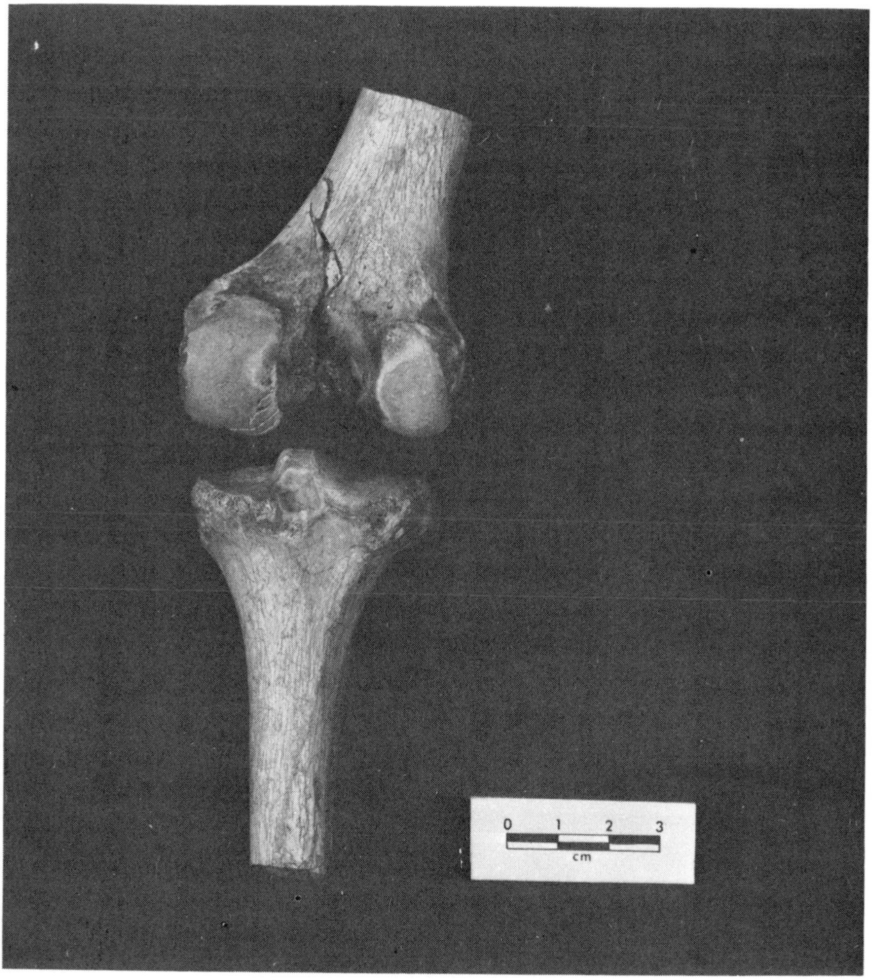

Figure 4. Posterior aspect of the right distal femur and proximal tibia from AL 129 (Hadar).

stratigraphic level presumed to have yielded the hominid material. Matrix adhering to the postcranial fragments matched a level of 'mudstone' (a fine grained calcareous sediment stained with hematite) underlying the sand and sandstone horizon (Figure 3 and 4).

The initial surface find of a right proximal tibia was followed by the discovery (within 10 m.) of a right distal femur (Figure 3 and 4). Subsequent survey resulted in the collection of an incomplete right proximal femur (Figure 5 and 6) 8.5 m. further up the slope, and a left proximal femur (Figures 5 and 6) some 80 m. to the north-east. The close association of the right proximal and distal femur and the proximal tibia strongly suggest that they represent a single individual.

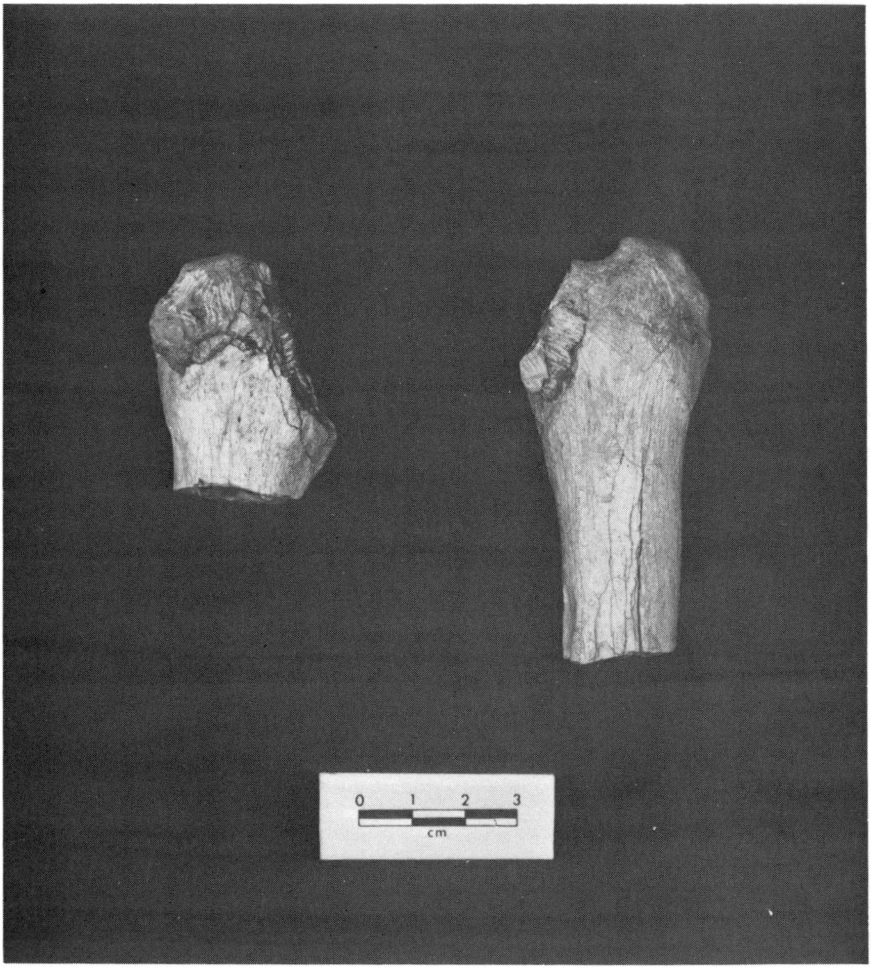

Figure 5. Anterior aspect of the right (AL 129) and the left (AL 128) proximal femora from Hadar.

The left and right proximal femora exhibit numerous resemblances in size and shape and are presumed to belong to the same individual. Intensive survey and careful sieving of the slope did not produce any additional hominid remains, but further examination of the locality is planned for the next field season.

Noteworthy is the rather small size of the postcranial specimens when compared to other Plio-Pleistocene hominids. For example, the distal femur is smaller than the two comparable Sterkfontein specimens (Sts 34 and Sts TM 1513). The morphology of the distal femur is characteristically hominid, with a marked bicondylar angle, a deep patellor groove with a high lateral ridge, and exhibiting a laterial condyle elongated antero-posteriorly with a flattened articular

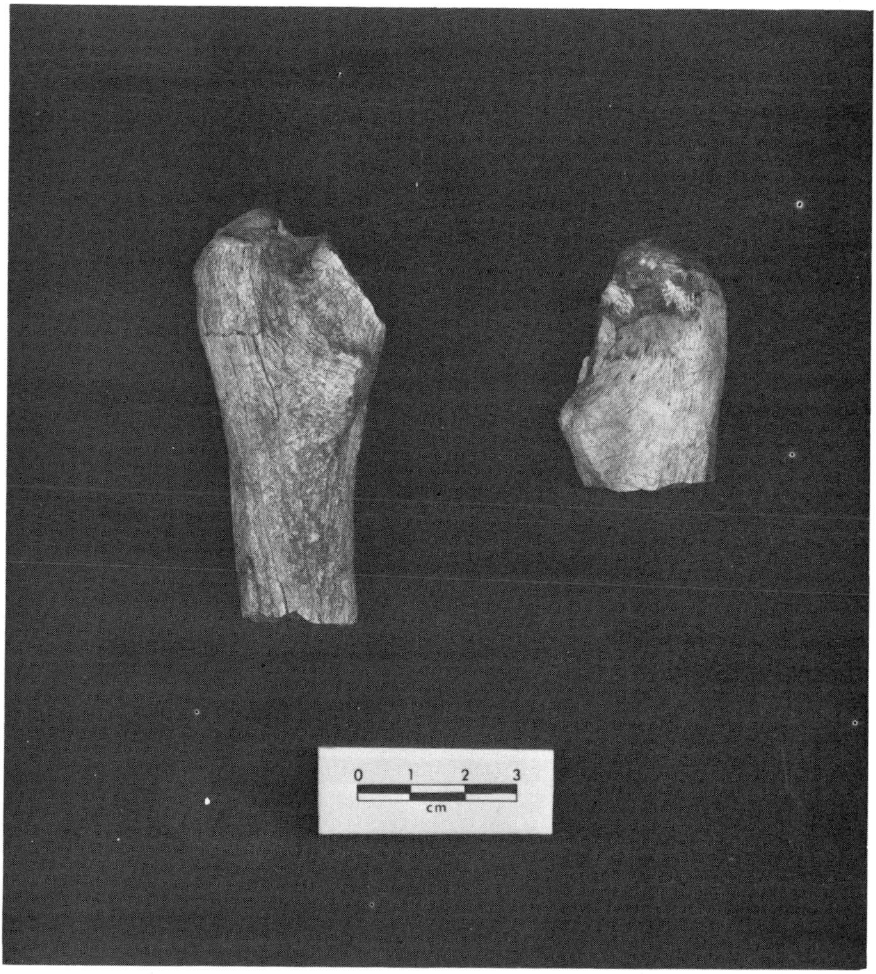

Figure 6. Posterior aspect of the right (AL 129) and the left (AL 128) proximal femora from Hadar.

surface (see Heiple and Lovejoy, 1971, for a discussion of these characteristics).

The two proximal femora are unfortunately incomplete and lack the femoral heads and most of the necks. However, muscle attachments are clearly marked and will provide valuable information regarding muscles important in bipedal locomotion. The cross-section of the femoral neck is flattened antero-posteriorly and is oval in outline.

The proximal tibia is mostly complete except for some abrasion around the periphery of the articular surface. It possesses rather high intercondylar tubercles with pronounced anterior and posterior intercondyloid fossae. The total articular surface is quite reduced with an estimated medial-lateral length of 51.0 mm. and an anterior-posterior length of about 33.0 mm. Detailed studies of the anatomy of this specimen will be particularly crucial since this portion of the postcranium is virtually unknown for Plio-Pleistocene hominids.

Early in December, just prior to closing the camp, a heavily eroded left temporal fragment of a hominid (Figures 7 and 8) was recovered at a locality situated approximately half a kilometre to the north-east of the postcranial material. Detailed stratigraphic work and extended survey here was impossible since the field session was near

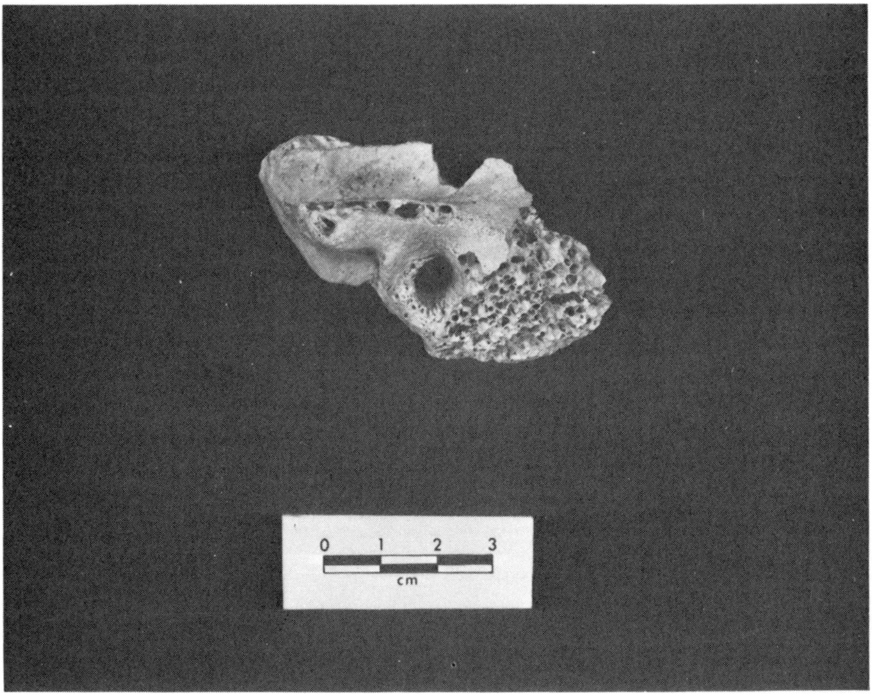

Figure 7. Lateral aspect of the hominid left temporal fragment from AL 166 (Hadar).

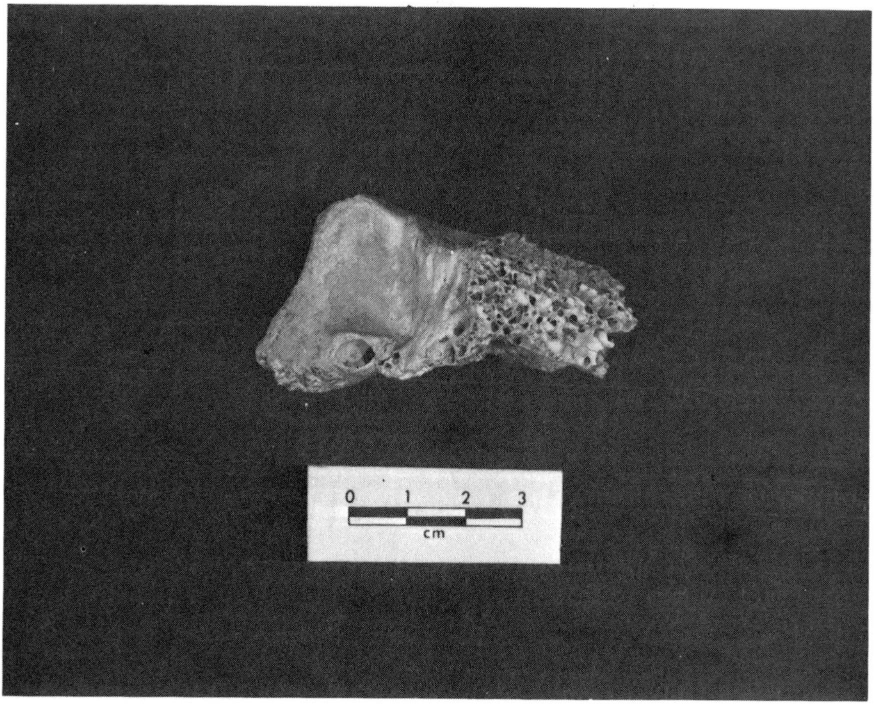

Figure 8. Basal aspect of the hominid left temporal fragment from AL 166 (Hadar).

completion. However, it appears that the cranial fragment is derived from a sandy horizon roughly equivalent to the stratigraphic position of the first hominid site.

The specimen has been extensively eroded with most of the petrous portion broken away. The mastoid and zygomatic processes are abraded exposing extensive pneumatization. The external auditory meatus is intact as is the entire glenoid fossa. The latter structure is rather broad with a quite reduced preauricular eminence.

Although in depth study of these specimens has not been completed, we would like to proffer some impressions concerning their taxonomic status. In the absence of comparable material of the same antiquity, it is, we believe, premature to assign the postcranial material more closely than to the family Hominidae. The cranial fragment presents a number of features, particularly in the mastoid and glenoid anatomy, that suggest to us that it is broadly comparable to some of the material from East Rudolf which has been referred to as *Australopithecus* (R.E.F. Leakey, 1970, 1971, 1972, 1973, 1974). It appears to be from a larger hominid than the postcranial material and may not belong to the same taxon. This is only a suggestion, but at all other localities in eastern Africa of this time range, at least two forms of hominids have been located.

Further study of the hominid remains promises to be exceedingly important, particularly in the case of the postcranial specimens. As most students of human evolution agree, bipedalism may have been the single most crucial event in the early stages of hominid evolution. If this was the case, then the Afar material represents the earliest direct evidence in eastern Africa of this unique locomotor adaptation that distinguishes man from the other primates.

Summary

Recent palaeonthropological research in Hadar, Ethiopia, has brought to light a number of exceedingly rich Plio-Pleistocene vertebrate localities which are provisionally dated in excess of three million years. The abundant vertebrate fossil remains in primary geological contexts greatly enlarge our understanding of this important time range in Africa.

The discovery of fossil hominid remains has now extended our knowledge of early man's geographical distribution some 800 km. north-east of previous discoveries. In addition, the recovery of associated postcranial remains provides concrete evidence of man's adaptation to bipedal locomotion at a very early date. The associated distal femur and proximal tibia make available a critical anatomical region for understanding various biomechanical aspects of early hominid bipedalism. Presence of a second form of hominid is suggested by the temporal fragment.

With additional field research in the central Afar we feel that a substantial contribution will be made to our understanding of not only the origins of man, but also the palaeoecological environment in which he interacted, and hopefully, various aspects of his palaeobehaviour.[4]

Acknowledgments

We would like to express our sincerest gratitude to the Ethiopian Government for their encouragement and permission to carry out this highly important research in Ethiopia.

Various forms of support such as petrol, food, some transportation and vehicle repair were provided by the Trapp Construction Company. We are grateful for their aid which was so kindly offered.

We appreciate Dr Jolly's invitation to contribute to this volume.

4. We would like to emphasize that this paper was presented shortly after completion of the first season of intensive fieldwork and more recent studies have required substantial revision. In particular, the stratigraphic position of the basalt is about 50 meters above the base of the section, and the faunal list has been considerably augmented.

Special gratitude is offered to the Wenner-Gren Foundation for their continued support of early man studies in Africa and especially to Mrs Lita Osmundsen for providing a congenial atmosphere in which to meet and discuss our findings.

Thanks to Bruce Frumker for photographic assistance.

Funding for this project was provided by the National Science Foundation (Grant Number GS-39624), the Wenner-Gren Foundation for Anthropological Research (Grant Number 2966-1834-R), and French CNRS and RCP. These contributions are greatly appreciated and without their support this work would not have been feasible.

References

Behrensmeyer, A.K. (1975) The taphonomy and palaeoecology of Plio-Pleistocene vertebrate assemblages east of Lake Rudolf, Kenya. *Bull. Mus. Comp. Zool.* 146 (10): 473-578.

Cooke, H.B.S., and Coryndon, S.C. (1970) Pleistocene mammals from the Kaiso Formation and other related deposits in Uganda. In Leakey, L.S.B., and Savage, R.J.G. (eds.), *Fossil Vertebrates of Africa*, Vol. 2, 107-224. London.

Cooke, H.B.S., and Ewer, R.F. (1972) Fossil Suidae from Kanapoi and Lothagam, north-western Kenya. *Bull. Mus. Comp. Zool.* 143 (3), 149-295.

Cooke, H.B.S., and Maglio, V.J. (1972) Plio-Pleistocene stratigraphy in East Africa in relation to proboscidean and suid evolution. In Bishop, W.W., and Miller, J.A. (eds.), *Calibration of Hominoid Evolution*, 1971 Wenner-Gren Symposium, 303-29. Edinburgh.

Coryndon, S.C. (1976) Fossil Hippopotamidae from Pliocene-Pleistocene successions of the Rudolf Basin. In Coppens, Y., *et al.* (eds.), *Earliest Man and Environments in the Lake Rudolf Basin: Stratigraphy, Paleoecology and Evolution*, 238-50. Chicago.

Heiple, K.C., and Lovejoy, C.O. (1971) The distal femoral anatomy of *Australopithecus*. *Amer. J. phys. Anthrop.* 35 (1), 75-84.

Leakey, L.S.B. (1965) *Olduvai Gorge 1951-1961*, Vol. 1. A preliminary report on the geology and fauna. London.

Leakey, R.E.F. (1970) New hominid remains and early artifacts from northern Kenya. *Nature* 226, 223-4.

Leakey, R.E. (1971) Further evidence of lower Pleistocene hominids from East Rudolf, north Kenya. *Nature* 231, 241-5.

Leakey, R.E.F. (1972) Further evidence of lower Pleistocene hominids from East Rudolf, north Kenya, 1971. *Nature* 237, 264-9.

Leakey, R.E.F. (1973) Further evidence of lower Pleistocene hominids from East Rudolf, north Kenya, 1972. *Nature* 242, 170-3.

Leakey, R.E.F. (1974) Further evidence of lower Pleistocene hominids from East Rudolf, north Kenya, 1973. *Nature* 248, 6536.

Maglio, V.J. (1973) Origin and evolution of the Elephantidae. *Trans. Amer. Phil. Soc.*, n.s., 63 (3), 1-149.

Taieb, M. (1971) Aperçus sur les formations quaternaires et la neotéctonique de la basse vallée de l'Awash (Afar méridional, Ethiopie). *C.R. somn. Soc. géol. Fr.*, 13 (2), 63-5.

Taieb, M. (1974) Evolution quaternaire du bassin de l'Awash (Rift éthiopien et Afar). Thèse d'Etat, l'Université de Paris VI.

Taieb, M. (1972) *et al.* Dépôts sédimentaires et faunes du Plio-Pléistocene de la basse vallée de l'Awash (Afar Central, Ethiopie). *C. R. Acad. Sci. Fr.* D. 275, 819-22.

Tazieff, H. (1972) *et al.* Tectonic significance of the Afar (or Danakil) depression. *Nature* 235, 144-7.

P.V. Tobias

The South African australopithecines in time and hominid phylogeny, with special reference to the dating and affinities of the Taung skull[1]

To anyone familiar with the now voluminous literature on the australopithecines, the recent claims that Taung is much younger than had earlier been believed should have come as no surprise. It is many years since doubts were first expressed on the correctness of the widely received view that Taung was among the oldest of the five South African australopithecine sites. Also, a number of years have passed since queries were first raised about the validity of assigning the fossils from Sterkfontein and Makapansgat to the same taxon as that represented by the Taung skull. It is the purpose of this chapter to present some of the evidence and to give a progress report on the study of the implications of the dates proposed for the South African australopithecine sites. The *prima facie* case for the likely taxonomic affinities of the Taung skull rests on the concept that two main hominid lineages (commonly known as gracile and robust) existed side by side in Africa for a fairly considerable length of time. The other consideration on which the *prima facie* case is based is the dating of the various East and South African representatives of these two lineages. It will therefore be necessary as well to review briefly the evidence supporting this concept and the present position of dating of the African early hominid sites.

African sites of early hominid discoveries

Several new sites of early hominid discoveries have come to light since the late 'sixties. These include the areas around Lake Rudolf, namely

[1] I warmly appreciate the kindness of the Editor, Dr Clifford Jolly, in desiring me to contribute a chapter to this work, even though circumstances had made it impossible for me to accept his invitation to participate in the Symposium held in New York City from 26th January to 2nd February, 1974.

Kanapoi (1965), Lothagam (1967), Omo (1967), Ileret and Koobi Fora (1968) and the sites around Lake Baringo, Chemeron (1965) and Chesowanja (1970). The last-mentioned site lies east of Lake Baringo in Central Kenya and yielded a partial hominid cranium with teeth in 1970 (Carney *et al.*, 1971). The newest site to have uncovered hominid remains is Afar-Awash in Central Ethiopia (Taieb *et al.*, 1972 and this volume), where, late in 1973, the International Afar Research Expedition recovered several hominid lower limb fragments and a cranial fragment. At 10-11° North, this site represents the most northerly of the East African early hominid sites: the other nine sites or areas related to the Eastern Rift Valley lie between 3° South (Olduvai and Garusi in northern Tanzania) and about 5° North (Omo in southern Ethiopia) (Tobias, 1972). On the other hand, the site of Yao near Koro Toro in northern Chad lies at a latitude of about 17-18° North. Furthermore, although the palaeontological wealth of East Rudolf had begun to be revealed by the late 'sixties (7 hominid specimens were discovered in 1968-9), the area has blossomed explosively since then. Its yield of hominid fossils is now about 107 specimens, while that of Omo is as high as 230 (Howell and Coppens, 1974), largely through the great number of isolated teeth and dental fragments. Table 1 lists all of the African early hominid sites, together with dates of the earliest and, as far as is known to me, the latest hominid discoveries at each. The dates given for each site are those for the first hominid discovery from that site and for the most recent hominid discovery known to the compiler.

Table 1 African sites of early hominid discoveries

South Africa:	Taung, Cape Province	1924
	Sterkfontein, Transvaal	1936-77
	Kromdraai, Transvaal	1938-54
	Makapansgat, Transvaal	1947-61
	Swartkrans, Transvaal	1948-76
Tanzania:	Garusi	1939
	Olduvai	1955-72
	Peninj	1964
Kenya:	*around Lake Baringo*	
	Chemeron (West Baringo)	1965
	Chesowanja (East Baringo)	1970
	around Lake Turkana (Rudolf)	
	Kanapoi (S.W. Rudolf)	1965
	Lothagam (S.W. Rudolf)	1967
	Ileret and Koobi Fora (E. Rudolf)	1968-76
Ethipia	Omo	1967-73
	Afar/Awash	1973-76
Chad:	Yayo (near Koro Toro)	1961

Latest discoveries of early hominids

As Table 1 makes clear, the latest finds of early hominids have come from Swartkrans and Sterkfontein in the Transvaal, Olduvai Gorge, East Rudolf, Omo and Afar/Awash. Not slowly, but with embarrassing rapidity, the total number of hominid specimens is climbing. Even the tally of individual hominid fossils compiled for Burg Wartenstein Symposium No. 48 in July 1970 and brought up to date in April 1971 is sadly behind the times. At that stage, the total number of teeth and other parts available was 1,427 specimens, comprising 405 from East Africa and 1,022 from South Africa (Tobias, 1972). An estimate would now add a further 55 from South Africa and 186 from East Africa, giving a total of about 1,669 specimens, with regional totals of about 1,077 from South Africa, 591 from East Africa and 1 from the Chad. These totals include all teeth, whether in jaws or isolated, as separate items. Totals have increased further since 1974.

Statistically, this may seem an excellent total. But it comprises hominid fossils spread over some 4.5 or more million years; at least three or four taxa; for each taxon, males and females; and different parts of the body, including 16 different kinds of permanent teeth and 10 of deciduous teeth, for each taxon. When the total is broken down into these numerous sub-sets, it will be appreciated that there are still many gaps: some taxa are poorly represented in males, females or both; some anatomical parts are in meagre supply. Nevertheless, the greatly amplified samples have made possible new studies on the morphology of the taxa represented. We are gaining new insights into the regional and functional complexes of early hominid anatomy and a clearer picture is beginning to emerge of the extent and role of sexual dimorphism and of the ranges of variation within populations, taxa and lineages.

The time-scale of East African hominids

The time-scale of hominid fossils and phylogeny in East Africa has in recent years been greatly clarified (Figure 1). As is well known, the new age determinations have been based upon the potassium-argon and ^{40}Argon/^{39}Argon radio-isotopic methods, palaeomagnetic reversal patterns, fission tracking and faunal correlations with radiometric dates. It is not necessary here to examine the claims and counter-claims for the hominid status of *Ramapithecus, Graecopithecus* or *Gigantopithecus*. These questions have recently been dealt with elsewhere, along with the related questions of whether hominid phylogeny has been long or short and whether the palaeontological and molecular evidences are really at variance with each other

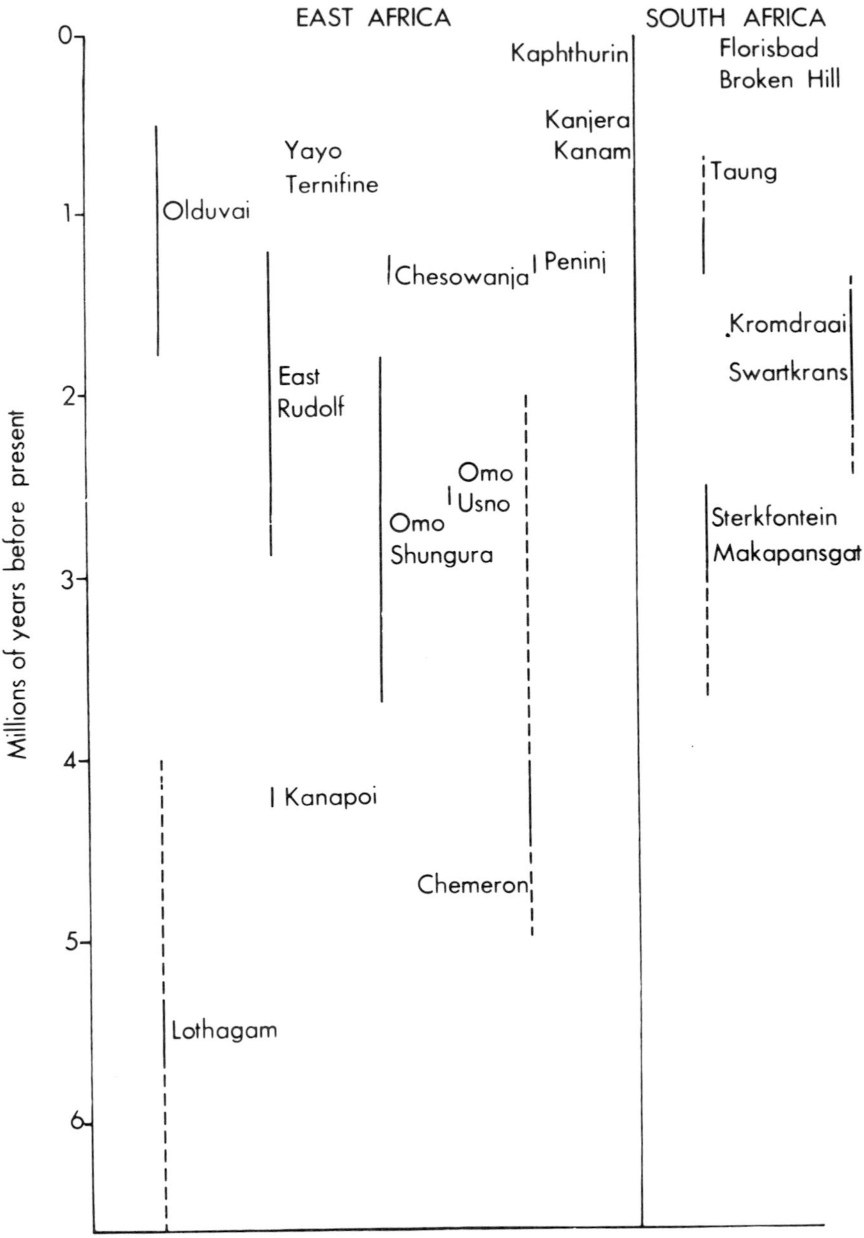

Figure 1. Chronological distribution of early hominids in the Plio-Pleistocene of Africa. For each East African hominid-bearing site, data for which are taken from Maglio (1973), the full duration in time of the deposit(s) at that site is indicated or suggested: a vertical solid line implies that hominid remains have been found throughout the sequence of deposits; an interrupted line with a solid segment indicates that only at the level of the solid segment have hominid fossils been found, though the deposits at that site, as a whole, cover a greater range of time. For the South African sites, the solid parts of the lines represent the tentative dates of the hominids based upon faunal comparisons by H.B.S. Cooke and V.J. Maglio; the interrupted lines indicate the dates estimated by T.C. Partridge for the opening of the caves.

(Tobias, 1975c). In any event, the challenging problems of the early Upper Tertiary are outside the scope of this volume. We shall therefore confine ourselves to the fossil hominids that followed the potentially exciting silent period in the hominid sequence of Africa, that hiatus between 14 and 5.5 million years (Phase E of Bishop, 1972).

There are apparently still some real problems of correlation, such as the seeming inconsistency or disagreement between the potassium-argon dates obtained for fossils in the Ileret and Koobi Fora areas of East Rudolf and those claimed for comparable fossils in the Omo basin, a relatively short distance away. However, this discrepancy does not seem to be in excess of several hundreds of thousands of years (Butzer, 1973) and perhaps a half million years at the outside. With this difficulty in mind, it is none the less clear that the well-attested East African early hominids span nearly 5.0 million years from about 5.5 m.y. BP to just over 1.0 m.y. BP.

It may be convenient to divide the East African sites into three groups on the basis of the age of the hominid-yielding strata:–

(a) *Early Pliocene hominids*: comprising a mandible from Lothagam (ca. 5.5 m.y.) and the distal part of a humerus from Kanapoi (ca. 4.4 m.y.). A temporal bone from the Chemeron Beds was previously thought to be ca. 4.5 m.y. but is now considered to be younger (Howell 1972), probably belonging in Group (b) or even (c).

(b) *Late Pliocene hominids*: Numerous teeth and a number of other bones from the lower and middle parts of the Omo/Shungura Formation (>4.0 – ca. 2.5 m.y.), the Omo/Usno Formation (ca. 2.5 m.y.) and the lowest part of the East Rudolf sequence (>3.0 – ca. 2.5 m.y.).

(c) *Lower and middle Pleistocene hominids*: Numerous remains from the upper part of the Omo/Shungura Formation (ca. 2.5->2.0 m.y.); the middle and uppermost parts of the East Rudolf exposures (ca. 2.5->1.0 m.y.); the Olduvai sequence from the Upper Member of Bed I to Bed IV (1.8-?>1.0 m.y.); the mandible of Peninj and the calvario-facial specimen from Chesowanja (>1.0 m.y.) (Bishop, 1971, 1972; Brock and Isaac, 1974; Brown, 1972; Butzer, 1971a, Butzer and Thurber, 1969; Carney *et al.*, 1971; Cooke, 1970, Cooke and Maglio, 1972; Coppens, 1970-71, 1973a, 1973b; Evernden and Curtis, 1965; Fleischer and Hart, 1972; Heinzelin, 1971, Heinzelin *et al.*, 1969; Howell, 1969, 1972; Hurford, 1974; Leakey, M.D., 1971; Leakey, R.E.F., 1970, 1971, 1972, 1973a; Leakey, R.E.F. *et al.*, 1971, 1972, 1973a, 1973b; Maglio, 1971, 1972, 1973; Patterson, 1966, Patterson *et al.*, 1970, Patterson and Howells, 1967).

The hominid taxa and lineages in East Africa

Various parts of this time range are occupied in East Africa by fossils identified as representing at least four hominid taxa, namely *Australopithecus cf. africanus, A. boisei, Homo habilis* and *H. erectus*. Three out of four of the names just mentioned have various synonyms attached to them; but it is not intended here to examine the diverse systems of nomenclature in use at present. The four names given above are those which the author has most generally employed and they will be used here. It is freely acknowledged that further studies and discoveries may eventually justify changes being made to one or more of these nomina.

(a) *The early Pliocene group of hominids*

In the earlier, poorly sampled early Pliocene group, the admittedly slender evidence suggests gracile australopithecine affinities. The most readily identifiable of the three earliest fossils, the mandible and lower first molar of Lothagam, closely resemble those of *A. africanus* (Patterson *et al.*, 1970). My own examination of the original specimen, kindly requested by Dr B. Patterson and Dr W.W. Howells during a visit to Harvard in 1968, confirmed for me that it is decidedly gracile, like the jaws of *A. africanus* and *H. habilis*, although the preserved parts – portion of the body of an isolated jaw and a worn first lower molar – are not necessarily the most diagnostic. Pilbeam (1972, p.150) goes further and states: 'In crown pattern, size, and proportions, and in other mandibular features, too, the specimen is very similar to *A. africanus* from Sterkfontein and Makapansgat. It possibly represents *A. africanus* and would extend the time range of that species further back in time.' Lasker (1973) unequivocally calls it the 'oldest *Australopithecus* specimen known' (p.422) and Simons (this volume) supports that view. It should be noted, however, that two colleagues have sounded caveats about Lothagam. R.E.F. Leakey (1973b, p.56) has stated that: 'In the absence of additional cranial and mandibular material from the Pliocene of Africa, there is every reason to be cautious as to its affinities.' He voices the possibility that the Lothagam mandible 'might represent a Pliocene survival of *Ramapithecus*'. Eckhardt (1975) has sounded more doubts. He states: 'We can safely conclude that the Lothagam specimen represents a middle to late Pliocene hominoid of medium to large size; anything beyond this is conjecture'.

Despite these queries and the fact that a detailed acount of the specimen has not yet been published, I believe it is more likely that the Lothagam mandible is of a gracile early hominid than of anything else and very probably of a species close to, or identical with, *A. africanus*. The fossil was derived from the lowest fossiliferous horizon at Lothagam (Patterson *et al.*, 1970), dated faunistically to between 5.0

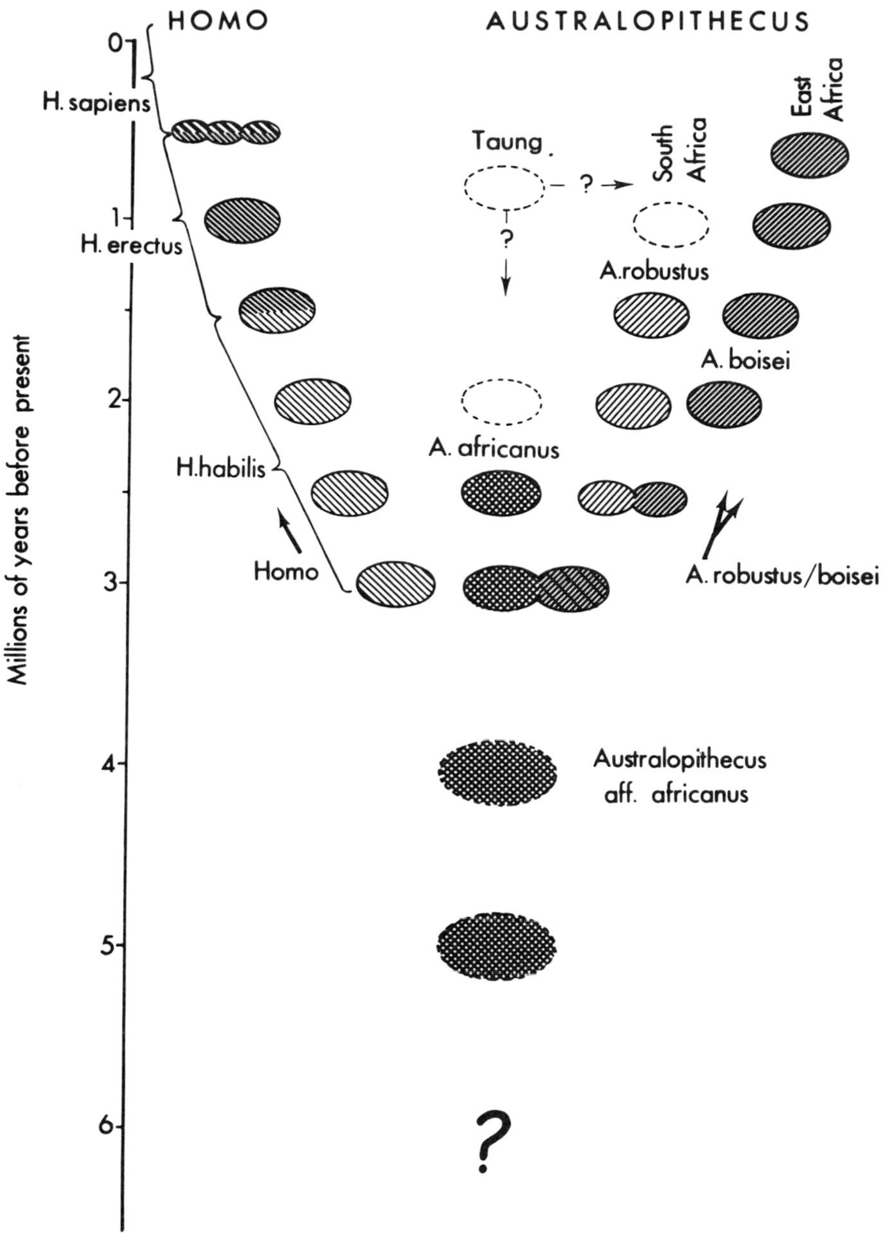

Figure 2. Hominid populations in Africa at various time levels in the Plio-Pleistocene. The oval figures at each time level represent the systematically identified, synchronic hominid populations represented in the fossil record of Africa at that time. At any one time level, the horizontal distance between a pair of ovals is roughly proportional to the morphological and taxonomic distance between the populations or taxa represented by the ovals. The anomalous position of the Taung skull is clearly indicated, its only near-contemporaries being *H. erectus* and the robust australopithecines. The queries (?) convey the uncertainty expressed in this chapter, as to whether the affinities of the Taung child lie with the gracile australopithecines, as traditionally believed and taught, or with the robust early hominids, as now seems to be *prima facie* likely.

and 5.5 m.y. (Maglio, 1970; Cooke and Maglio, 1972; Howell, 1972). This specimen appears therefore to be the oldest well-attested hominid in the Plio-Pleistocene time range of East Africa.

Kanapoi

A distal humeral portion was found at Kanapoi in the south-eastern part of Turkana District, northern Kenya. Howell (1972) has reviewed the evidence leading to a date for this specimen of between 4.0 and 4.5 m.y. On morphological grounds, it has been affined to the gracile *A. africanus* (Patterson and Howells, 1967). It should be noted, however, that, because the humeral fragment is said to be large, Pilbeam (1972, p.150) feels it is more reasonably assigned to the hyper-robust East African australopithecine, *A. boisei*.

Chemeron

This specimen is an isolated, well-preserved hominid temporal bone from the Chemeron Beds in the basin of Lake Baringo, Central Kenya (Martyn and Tobias, 1967). The Chemeron deposits have an inferred age of between about 2 and 5 m.y. and include an early fauna of about the same age as Kanapoi (4.0-4.5 m.y.). While it was previously thought that the hominid specimen was derived from this Pliocene horizon, it now seems likely that the part of the Chemeron sequence from which the hominid temporal bone was derived (the Upper Fish Beds) is of later age than 4.0 m.y., though how much younger is not at present known (Howell, 1972, p.356). On this revised view the Chemeron temporal might have to be removed from the Pliocene Group. The features of the bone reveal that it is of a hominid with many australopithecine but also a number of hominine characters; hence, in my original study of the isolated specimen, I was unable to decide between *Australopithecus* and early *Homo* (cf. *H. habilis*).

For economy of hypothesis, the Kanapoi humerus, the Lothagam mandible and the Chemeron temporal could all be accommodated within *A.* cf. *africanus*; but each of these three fossils has been regarded by one or other worker as possibly belonging to another taxon, in one instance not even necessarily a hominid taxon, while one of the three – Chemeron – may not belong in this Pliocene Group. It would be fair to conclude this section with the statement that the two earliest – Pliocene – hominids from East Africa are compatible with membership of *A. africanus*.

(b) *The late Pliocene group of hominids*

The late Pliocene group of East African hominids includes gracile hominids comparable with *A. africanus* and, from about 3.0 m.y. onwards, robust hominids, such as the East African semispecies, *A. boisei* (Tobias, 1973a). A third element appears somewhere between 3.0 and 2.5 m.y. BP, a population showing absolute enlargement of the endocranial capacity, and believed to represent an early species of *Homo*.

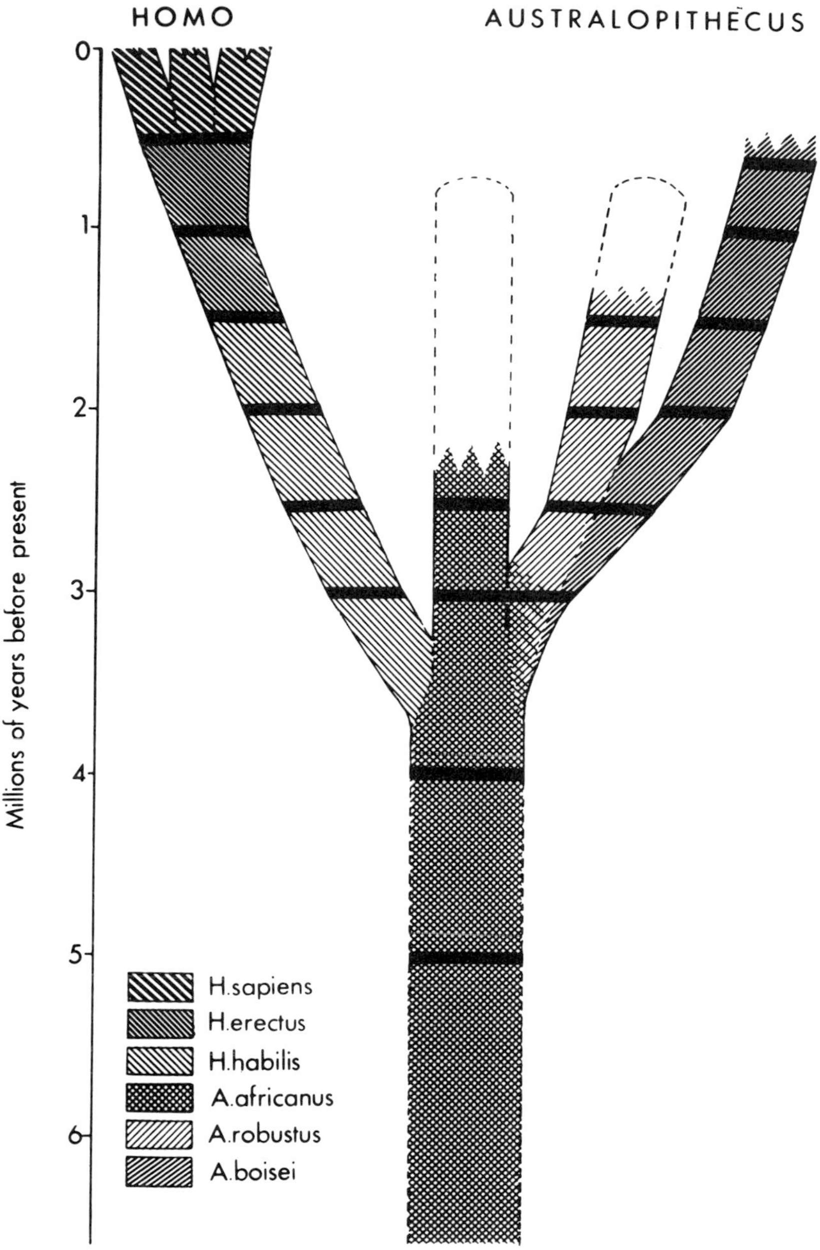

Figure 3. Provisional phylogenetic tree of the Hominidae during the Pliocene and the Pleistocene. The vertical, unbranched trunk of the tree is probably an over-simplified picture of hominid evolution during the Pliocene, owing to the paucity of hominid fossils dated to this period (6.0 to 3.5 m.y. BP). The branching of *Homo* from *Australopithecus* is shown as an early event (before 3.0 m.y. BP), in order to accommodate in *Homo* the East Rudolf specimen, KNM-ER-1470, which has been tentatively identified as possibly the earliest cranium attributable to *Homo*, at greater than 2.6 m.y. BP and perhaps as old as 2.9 m.y. BP (R.E.F. Leakey 1973b). The diagram suggests the possible extension of either *A. africanus* or *A. robustus* to a very recent period (<0.9 m.y. BP), as two alternative means of accommodating the Taung skull, in view of its proposed new young date of 0.7 to 0.8 m.y. BP.

(c) *The lower and middle Pleistocene group of hominids*

In the lower Pleistocene, we find East African hominids falling into two main morphological groups, the hyper-robust *A. boisei* and the ultra-gracile form to which has been given the name *Homo habilis* (Leakey, L.S.B. *et al.*, 1964). Later, in the middle Pleistocene, the surviving remnants of the robust australopithecine lineage are sympatric and synchronic with a more advanced hominid, *H. erectus*.

Thus, in East Africa, at each well-sampled time level from at least 3.0 m.y. BP up to about 1.0 m.y. BP, the hominid fossils may be sorted into, and classified as no fewer than two different populations, co-existing sympatrically. The differences among the synchronic and sympatric hominids are such as to justify their systematic ranking at least as separate species; at some time-levels, it would appear that even generic distinctness had been attained. These facts seemingly refute the so-called Principle of Competitive Exclusion according to which, on *a priori* grounds, it was supposed by some that only one hominid species had ever existed at any one time since the emergence of the Hominidae. It is logical to go one step further: since at each reasonably sampled time level in the 3 to 1 million year period the hominids sort themselves into gracile and robust taxa, the inference is justified that two (or more) different *lineages* of hominids co-existed in one relatively restricted geographical zone for some 2 million years at least (Tobias, 1973b, 1975a).

The time-scale of South African hominids: earlier faunal inferences

Ever since the first discovery of an australopithecine skull (1924), there have been surmises about the age of the South African fossil ape-men. Perhaps the earliest reference to the dating of any primate fossils from Taung actually precedes the discovery of *A. africanus* by M. de Bruyn in 1924. As early as 1920, some fossil baboons from Taung were sent to the South African Museum in Cape Town. On 19 May, 1920, a paper on these fossil baboons was read before the Royal Society of South Africa by S.H. Haughton, who was subsequently to become Director of the Geological Survey of the Union of South Africa and, still later, Honorary Director of the Bernard Price Institute for Palaeontological Research at the University of the Witwatersrand. Haughton's paper of 1920 was never published, though he did make his notes available to Dart (1926), Broom (1925), and J.H.S. Gear (1926). An abstract was published in 1925 and in it, Haughton stated, 'At present it seems impossible to correlate our inland Tertiary and Recent deposits with those of the Northern Hemisphere; but from the nature of the occurrence of the forms (a small species of baboon) it is probable that the form may extend back in point of time to a level contemporaneous with the early and possibly pre-Pleistocene of

Europe' (Haughton 1925). To accommodate the sample of 7 or 8 baboon skulls from Taung, Haughton proposed to create a new species, to be called *Papio antiquus*. However, as Haughton's paper was never published and as no type was designated, the name *P. antiquus* has to be regarded as a *nomen nudum* (Broom 1946). Instead, Gear (1926) recognized that the sample of cercopithecoids from Taung included two different species to which he gave the names *P. africanus* and *P. izodi*. The presence of the baboons reported on by Haughton led Wybergh (1920) to infer that 'the formation is relatively of great age and hardly to be classed as recent'. Haughton, in his unpublished notes made available to Dart (1940), also stated, 'We can justifiably look upon the limestone (of Taung) as a late Tertiary deposit'.

Thus, from a very early period in the half century of australopithecine studies, the view had been expressed that Taung was most ancient. A dissident view of the time was that of Broom who, in 1925 (p.570), asserted that, since he did not consider the difference between the Taung baboons and the living local baboons (*P. ursinus*) to be very striking, 'the Taungs skull is thus not likely to be geologically of great antiquity – probably not older than Pleistocene, and perhaps even as recent as the *Homo rhodesiensis* skull'. He added: 'When later or other associated mammalian bones are discovered, it may be possible to give the age with greater definiteness. At present all we can say is that the skull is not likely to be older than what we regard as the human period.'

So the view that the Taung skull is fairly recent has, too, been in the literature almost from the beginning of the discussion of *Australopithecus*.

It is of interest to note that, by 1930, Broom was attributing the Taung fauna to the lower Pliocene. At the same time, both A.L. du Toit and Broom (1930) 'independently suggested that the deposit is quite as likely to be Pliocene as Pleistocene'. This in essence had been the view of R.B. Young (1925), who had been responsible for the sending of the Taung hominid skull by the Limeworks Manager, Mr A.E. Spiers, to Dart in November, 1924; whilst A.W. Rogers, then Director of the Geological Survey of the Union of South Africa, is on record as declaring in June 1925 that 'there was no probability of the age of the deposit being determined' (quoted by Broom 1946, p.18).

In that state of uncertainty, we carry this review forward to the next phase – the discovery of australopithecine remains at Sterkfontein in 1936.

Very soon after the discovery of a hominid and other fauna at Sterkfontein in 1936, the idea became established in the literature that Taung was older than Sterkfontein. With the subsequent discovery in 1938 of the Kromdraai robust australopithecine and fauna, a faunal seriation of the three sites entered the picture. The fauna from Sterkfontein seemed to Broom (1936, 1937) at first to be 'of upper or possibly middle Pleistocene age' (1937, p.681). Broom (1938a) was initially inclined to regard Kromdraai as older than Sterkfontein and thus he recognized at that time the following sequence: Taung lower Pleistocene, Kromdraai middle Pleistocene, Sterkfontein upper Pleistocene. Later in the same year more faunal finds led him to push Sterkfontein back to the middle Pleistocene (1938b). By 1940, we find Dart speaking of the two Transvaal sites as belonging to 'two entirely different and more recent geological horizons (than Taung), as the concomitant fauna of divergent Pleistocene levels revealed' (Dart, 1940, p.175). He added: 'Dr Broom's discoveries thus widened the period of persistence of the terrestrialized man-ape fauna of South Africa from Taungs (Pliocene) to Kromdraai (middle Pleistocene) times.'

Broom listed the fauna from Taung in 1946. All but one of the 14 species enumerated had been described and named by Broom himself. However, it is important to note that he included in his list fauna from two other localities in the Taung area, namely those to which he gave the names Hrdlicka's Cave and Spiers' Cave (Broom, 1946, pp. 28-9). As these deposits were entirely separate from the Taung hominid locality, their contents do not necessarily throw any light on the age of the Taung hominid cave (that Broom called Dart's Cave). Nevertheless, Broom described all 14 species in his list as 'contemporaneous with *Australopithecus*'. It is to this entire assemblage from three different caves that Broom referred when he stated further on (p.30): 'Not one of the species found at Taungs occurs at Sterkfontein or Kromdraai; which seems definite proof that the ages of the deposits are very different. A number of the same genera occur, but the species are all quite different. Then a much larger number of the genera in the Taungs deposits are extinct than in the Sterkfontein and Kromdraai deposits; from which I think we may infer, as at least probable, that the Taungs deposit is very much older.'

The discovery of the hyaena, *Lycyaena*, at Sterkfontein, together with the presence of two sabre-tooth cats and the absence of horses, led Broom (1946, p.31) to propose that the Sterkfontein fossils were probably older even than his revised opinion of 1938, and he was now inclined to assign them to the Upper Pliocene. If this were so, and if the Taung deposit were much earlier, reasoned Broom, Taung 'may belong to an earlier part of the upper Pliocene – and possibly even to middle Pliocene'.

This view, that Taung was the oldest, Sterkfontein intermediate and Kromdraai the youngest, persisted unchallenged for close on 20 years after Broom's (1946) monograph appeared. The subsequent discovery of hominids at two further South African sites, Makapansgat (1947) and Swartkrans (1948), and the identification of comparable fauna from both, led Ewer in 1955 to incorporate these sites into the proposed sequence for South Africa. Basing her analysis on the Primates, Insectivora, Hyracoidea, Carnivora and Suidae, that is, those faunal groups of which at that time all the available material had been studied, she was able to conclude that 'the probable time sequence of the deposits is Sterkfontein and Makapan close together, with the former very probably the earlier; then Swartkrans and lastly Kromdraai, while the Taung deposit is most probably closest in time to Sterkfontein and Makapan' (Ewer, 1957, p.141). She admitted that the dating of Taung 'presents some difficulties', since 'the fauna is rather incompletely known, and the indications are that the environment was distinctly more desert-like than at the other deposits' (1957, p.139). 'However, the presence of *Procavia transvaalensis, Procavia antiqua* and *Parapapio jonesi* is sufficient to show that, in age, Taung does not differ widely from the other deposits. The presence of *Australopithecus africanus* and *Cercopithecoides williamsi* would seem to indicate that the relationship is closest with Sterkfontein and Makapan.'

The next development was the division of the faunas from these five australopithecine sites, as well as those from other non-hominid-bearing localities, of southern Africa into stages. Such a division had been attempted by Cooke in 1952. At that time, he recognized three groups of fauna associated respectively with the australopithecine breccias, deposits containing hand-axes and deposits with tools of the so-called middle Stone-Age Complex. Thus, initially, a single faunal stage was associated with the ape-man period. Subsequently, this australopithecine faunal stage was split into two sub-divisions, the Sterkfontein Stage and the Swartkrans Stage, while the ensuing two faunal stages were dubbed respectively the Vaal-Cornelia and the Florisbad-Vlakkraal Stages (Ewer and Cooke, 1964). Cooke had apparently set out the basis for this terminology in a short, unpublished paper prepared for the 1961 INQUA meeting in Warsaw (see Cooke, 1967, p.177). The same terms for the four faunal stages were used by Cooke in his paper to the 1961 Wenner-Gren Symposium on 'African Ecology and Human Evolution' (Cooke, 1963). Similar terms were published by Wells (1962). In their 1964 paper, Ewer and Cooke analysed the numbers of species common to 2 or more of the 5 South African sites: of the 150 species of mammals identified up to that time, only 21 were available for this inter-site comparison. This method suggested that, of the three sites in the Krugersdorp District, Sterkfontein was the oldest and Kromdraai the youngest, while Swartkrans was intermediate in age, 'but somewhat closer to Sterkfontein' (1964, p.40). Makapansgat was found to be not very different in age from Sterkfontein but perhaps 'just a little more recent than Sterkfontein and somewhat older than Swartkrans'. Although the fauna of Taung was very incompletely known, inter-site comparisons suggested that the Taung deposit was close in age to Sterkfontein and Makapansgat and rather older than Swartkrans and Kromdraai.

Later, the term 'Faunal Stage' was replaced by 'Faunal Span' to connote both a particular faunal assemblage and the temporal duration of its existence (Cooke, 1967). The faunas from Sterkfontein, Makapansgat and Taung were assigned to the Sterkfontein Faunal Span and those of Swartkrans and Kromdraai to the Swartkrans Faunal Span (Cooke, 1968).

Recent faunal dating of the Transvaal sites

More recent work has served largely to corroborate the sequence in respect of Sterkfontein, Makapansgat, Swartkrans and Kromdraai (Figure 1), though at the same time it has become clear that the division of the faunas from these sites into two Faunal Spans presents a much over-simplified picture. There are appreciable differences between the faunas of Swartkrans and of Kromdraai (Wells, 1969), and even between the Primates of Kromdraai A (the faunal site) and Kromdraai B (the australopithecine site) (Freedman and Brain, 1972). Similarly, Wells (1969) has pointed out that there are many differences between the faunas of Sterkfontein and Makapansgat Limeworks. He added (1969, p.94): '... it is difficult to determine whether these (differences) should be interpreted as ecological, regional or chronological; if the last view were taken, I suggest, contrary to the widely received opinion, that (Makapansgat) Limeworks could plausibly be regarded as earlier than Sterkfontein.'

Furthermore, even within two of the Sterkfontein cave breccias (called by Robinson, 1962, the Lower and Middle Breccias), evidence points to an undoubtedly lengthy lapse of time. The older breccia contains an australopithecine attributed to *A. africanus* and no stone implements; while the more recent breccia contains stone implements accompanying fragments of a hominid identified by Robinson as *A. africanus* (Robinson and Mason, 1957, Robinson, 1962), but possibly belonging instead to a more advanced hominid with small teeth (cf. *H. habilis*) (Tobias, 1965). Vrba (1974), in her comprehensive study of the Sterkfontein bovids, finds that they fall into three distinct groups, A, B, and C. Only the phase A bovids are associated with the Sterkfontein Faunal Span including the australopithecines. The phase B bovids are associated with the more advanced hominid, the stone tools and the upper or later breccia, and resemble most closely the bovids of the Swartkrans Faunal Span. Thus, the evidence of the hominids, the associated cultural remains (or absence of them) and the bovids all points to an appreciable time-lapse separating two levels within the Sterkfontein breccias.[2]

A logical step in this latest phase has been to attempt to correlate

[2] In the three years since this chapter was written, T.C. Partridge has proposed the division of the Sterkfontein Formation into 6 Members. It is Member 4 that contains fossils of *A. africanus* and of the Sterkfontein Faunal Span, while Member 5 contains fauna more closely allied to that of the Swartkrans Faunal Span, as well as stone implements and the hominid fragments I believed were of an early species of *Homo* (cf.

the fauna from southern Africa with the isotopically calibrated faunas of East Africa. The application of radiometric dating techniques to the East African faunal deposits, supported by palaeomagnetic and fission-tracking evidence, had provided an excellent series of calibrated faunal sequences from that area (Bishop *et al.*, 1971, Bishop and Miller, 1972; Cooke and Ewer, 1972; Cooke and Maglio, 1972; Maglio, 1970, 1971, 1972, 1973). Comparisons between South and East African species had often been made before (e.g. by Lavocat, 1957; L.S.B. Leakey, 1965; Ewer, 1967), while Gentry (1970) had likened the Makapansgat bovid, *Makapania broomi*, to an Omo specimen found below tuff G. On the then available evidence of dating, this East African horn core would be aged between 1.8 and 2.6 m.y.; newer evidence (Brown, 1972) has dated tuff G as 1.93 m.y. so the specimen from Omo would be older than 1.93 m.y. As Gentry (1970) pointed out, this comparison provided only slender indications of the age of Makapansgat Limeworks. Cooke (1970) has been the first to attempt a comparison with radiometrically dated East African faunal sequences. He has compared the fossil suids and *Elephas recki* from Makapansgat and Sterkfontein with calibrated lineages of Suidae and Proboscidea from East Rudolf and Omo (Shungura Formation). He finds their closest affinity to lie with corresponding forms in the middle Shungura and the lowest Koobi Fora (East Rudolf) formations. On this basis, he provisionally suggests that the Sterkfontein and Makapansgat breccias may be about twice as old as had hitherto been thought, possibly 'in the vicinity of 2.5 to 3.0 million years old'. V. Maglio supports Cooke's view, although he stresses that the faunal evidence is as yet far from adequate (1973, pers. comm.). A recent paper by Maier (1973) cites a later personal communication by Cooke: according to this, Cooke accepts an age approaching 3.0 m.y. BP for the oldest Makapansgat fauna and about 2.5 m.y. BP for Sterkfontein and 'upper Makapansgat'.[3]

For Swartkrans, an age of about 1.8-2.0 m.y. BP seems to be indicated (Cooke, 1970; Cooke, pers. comm. in Maier, 1973; Maglio, 1973).

Thus, faunal comparisons support the inference that Makapansgat and Sterkfontein contain the oldest hominid-bearing faunas in the Transvaal, though they would tend to reverse the order which Ewer

---

H. habilis). In August 1976, Member 5 yielded a skull that seems to confirm the belief that a hominid like *H. habilis* lived in Member 5 times and was probably the long-sought Sterkfontein tool-maker (A.R. Hughes and P.V. Tobias, *Nature*, January 1977).

[3] Further faunal comparisons by E. Vrba and palaeomagnetic results by A. Brock and P. McFadden confirm the late Tertiary age of the *Australopithecus*-bearing layers at Makapansgat and Sterkfontein. On the newer evidence the lowest Beds in the Makapansgat Formation would seem to be over 3.0 million years old (P.V.T., February 1977).

and Cooke (1964) had earlier suggested: that is, it now seems that Makapansgat is faunistically older than the Sterkfontein hominid-bearing breccia by half a million years or thereabouts. Further, the new faunal comparisons suggest a greater age for those sites than most workers have hitherto suspected – except for that early surmise of Broom (1946)!

Faunal questions about the Taung site

It has already been mentioned above that Broom (1930, 1946) based his inference on the early age of Taung on a composite list of species derived from three different cave deposits, Dart's, Hrdlicka's and Spiers' Caves. It was mentioned, too, that Ewer and Cooke (1964) had stressed the 'very incompletely known' fauna of the Taung deposit. Indeed, Ewer (1956, 1957) had stressed the difficulty of dating the Taung deposit. On the other hand, in his various faunal correlations and tabulations, Cooke included Taung, without qualification, in the earliest or Sterkfontein Faunal Span (Cooke, 1963, 1967, 1968).

Despite these difficulties, the notion that Taung was the oldest of the five South African sites, or at least was of an age with Makapansgat and Sterkfontein as the oldest group of southern sites, remained virtually unchallenged in the literature for very nearly 20 years from 1946. The author's former teacher, L.H. Wells, has long cherished doubts on this score. In 1962, one finds him stating, '... the *Australopithecus* type site at Taung probably also belongs to this (Sterkfontein Faunal) stage, though its fauna displays local peculiarities' (Wells, 1962, p.37). This gently expressed doubt had intensified by the time of the Wenner-Gren Foundation Symposium on 'Background to Evolution in Africa' in July-August 1965. In his paper at that meeting, Wells gave a provisional correlation of the main South African faunal localities. In his Table 1, it is noteworthy that Taung is shown with a question mark and it is placed in a non-committal position between the Sterkfontein and Swartkrans faunal assemblages (Wells, 1967, p.101). By this Wells meant to imply not that it was intermediate in age, but that he could not decide whether its affinities were with the Sterkfontein or the Swartkrans Faunal Span. This interpretation is apparent from the context and, more particularly, from the discussion recorded at the end of Wells's paper (pp. 105-6). It is worth citing the brief discussion in full:

WELLS: What, if any, is the justification for considering the Taung fauna as belonging to the Sterkfontein rather than the Swartkrans stage?

EWER: This is slight and is based on the smaller forms which *seem* to indicate closer resemblances to Makapansgat and Sterkfontein than to Swartkrans. However, the designation was very tentative and statistically the numbers present are not significant.

WELLS: The new short-faced baboon, *Papio wellsi* from Taung, seems to be very close to one from Swartkrans; most of the other Taung primates, including perhaps *Australopithecus*, have a long time range.

The cercopithecoids referred to, it should be noted, were derived from the lower, *non*-hominid-bearing breccia, that is, a part of the Taung deposit that is appreciably older than the australopithecine-bearing breccia (Peabody, 1954; Butzer, 1974). Indeed, Butzer places the lower cercopithecoid breccia and the upper australopithecine breccia in two successive phases of one geomorphological cycle, namely Norlim 2 and 3. Wells's point about the affinities of the cercopithecoids of Taung was underlined when, in 1970, Freedman published an up-to-date checklist of cercopithecoids from all of the early hominid sites in South Africa: this showed the significant absence from Taung of *Parapapio broomi* – which is the commonest cercopithecoid at Sterkfontein and Makapansgat (Freedman and Stenhouse, 1972, Table 6). Moreover, his list showed that there are two species of *Papio* at Taung, another two at Kromdraai and one at Swartkrans, but none at Makapansgat or Sterkfontein. It would certainly seem that the primates in the Taung cercopithecoid breccia are more recent than those of the Sterkfontein Faunal Span: *a fortiori*, *Australopithecus* at Taung is younger, by a still more substantial margin, than the Sterkfontein Faunal Span.

These considerations led Wells (1969, p.94) to his most forthright statement on the younger dating of Taung:

> Those faunal elements most closely connected with the type specimen of *Australopithecus africanus* do not clearly favour equating this part of the deposit with Sterkfontein and Makapansgat Limeworks rather than with Swartkrans or even Kromdraai, and certainly do not warrant the view that the Taung child is the earliest South African Australopithecine. Some of the animals recorded from Taung may however belong to parts of the deposit appreciably older than the Australopithecine breccia.

Thus, before the end of the sixties, the relative faunal dating had tended to re-sort the sites, so as possibly to place Taung on an equivalent time-level with Swartkrans or even Kromdraai. That is, Taung could be equal in age to the most recent of the four other South African sites. Although practically a decade has elapsed since these doubts were expressed and Wells's alternative faunal dating was suggested, little note seems to have been taken of his claims and they were overlooked by most writers, until recently stressed by the author (Tobias, 1973c, 1974a, 1974b). A wider acquaintance with this history would clearly have paved the way and prepared the minds of one's colleagues for a readier acceptance of the recent claims made by Partridge (1973) and by Butzer (1974) that Taung is relatively young in geological age.

Other approaches to the dating of the South African sites

Our excavation at Sterkfontein was begun in 1966 on the 100th anniversary of the birth of the late Dr Robert Broom, F.R.S. and has continued without interruption ever since. Prime objectives were the elucidation of the stratigraphy of the deposit and the uncovering of materials which might prove suitable for one or other method of dating (Tobias and Hughes, 1969). Thus far, in this fourth phase of systematic excavations at Sterkfontein, from 1966-1974 (Tobias, 1973d), we have a few positive results to report on the geochronometric attack on the site. A number of different approaches are being pursued in conjunction with our collaborators in laboratories in various parts of the world. Macdougall and Price (1974) have studied calcite crystals from the marrow cavities of fossil bones from Makapansgat and Swartkrans for fission tracks; but the absence of the expected numbers of tracks indicates that track annealing at ambient temperatures has occurred, thus apparently vitiating the use of this technique for dating the australopithecine deposits. Amino acid analyses of collagen in the fossil bones are beginning to yield some results (Carmichael, Tobias and Dodd, 1974), but it will be some time before the method can be used for age determination. J. Wilkinson (1973) has thrown considerable light on the stratigraphic sequence of the Sterkfontein breccias and cave system, as have the largely unpublished researches of T.C. Partridge and A.B.A. Brink. A first search for palaeomagnetism reversals was fruitless (Tobias and Hughes, 1969), but new attempts are to be made by A. Brock. The quest for materials amenable to radio-isotopic dating has so far drawn a blank.

By 1972, the only geochronometric front on which there had been appreciable progress was that of faunal dating, as reviewed above. It was against this background that T.C. Partridge, despairing of the outcome of our search for suitable radio-isotopes or other dateable materials, late in 1972 developed a geomorphological approach to the dating of these caves.

Geomorphological dating of the South African sites

Dr T.C. Partridge is a geomorphologist and a member of the team investigating Sterkfontein. Late in 1972, he developed a revolutionary new approach to determine the approximate date when the

Australopithecus-bearing caves were actually opened to the exterior.* Partridge (1973, 1974) has attempted to gauge the dates of 'holing through' of Sterkfontein, Makapansgat, Swartkrans and Taung. The underlying premise was that the original opening of the caves was effected through incision and widening of river valleys in a single erosion cycle, the Post-African I. He estimated the rate of migration of cyclic nickpoints, assuming that nickpoint migration was subject to linear decline (as a mean representation) to a culminating point of zero at the stream sources. In addition he estimated the rate of recession of the flanks of valleys related to the caves. By reading off the migration rates on the graph of linear decline, he was able to make time-place transpositions. On this basis, he estimated the approximate date of opening of four of the caves as follows:–

Makapansgat 3.7 million years BP
Sterkfontein 3.3 million years BP
Swartkrans 2.6 million years BP
Taung <0.9 million years BP

Partridge presented these results to the South African Archaeological Society in Johannesburg on 28 February, 1973. Later that year, he published them in *Nature* (1973).

Partridge's challenging claims have elicited severe criticism from some of his colleagues (e.g. de Swardt, 1974, and an anonymous correspondent in *Nature*, March 8, 1974, 248, pp. 100-1), who cavil at his use of geomorphological data, assumptions and inferences for geochronometric purposes. Indeed, it is likely that geomorphologists will argue for a long time on the validity of utilizing geomorphological data for dating purposes; obviously a mere palaeoanthropologist such as myself is not qualified to comment on this aspect.

The critical comments offered by de Swardt (1974) and by the *Nature* correspondent (8th March, 1974) reporting on the New York Conference on African Hominidae of the Plio-Pleistocene, refer to a number of supposed uncertainties, such as the identification of the Post-African I surface, the dates of inception of planation cycles, the allegedly conflicting eyidence of deep-sea cores, the influence of various lithologies on the migration rates of nickpoints and the very recognition of erosional nickpoints. Partridge (1974 and 1975, in preparation) has given unhesitating replies to all of the criticisms raised. He admits – as his initial paper clearly did – that various

* The caves in the Transvaal dolomite have formed underground and initially under the surface of the water-table. By gradual extension of the underground cavities, hastened by roof collapses, and assisted by the weathering away of the outside land surface, sooner or later such subterranean caves acquired external openings. It was only after the land-surface had 'holed through' to the cave that surface-derived materials, including animal bones and soil, could gain access to the interior of the cavity, fall to the bottom and so begin the process of forming breccia (Brain 1958, this volume).

sources of error inhere in his method and the assumptions it relies upon, but he is led to conclude that the margin of error so introduced would be relatively small. He reiterates that the range of possible inaccuracies 'is considered to be sufficiently small to permit the technique to be used *to derive general orders of age* and *a relative sequence of dates for cave opening* – all that I originally claimed for my results' (Partridge, 1974, p.684, italics mine).

Although I am not competent to comment on these geomorphological issues nor on the validity of Partridge's replies to his critics, it is nevertheless of importance to note that Partridge's dates are in broad terms corroborated by the faunal datings adduced by Cooke and Maglio: they confirm the general order of high antiquity which faunal comparison had already attributed to three of the Transvaal sites. Furthermore, Partridge's young date for Taung is more or less in keeping with the faunal inferences of Wells and, moreover, with the results of a new study of Taung by Dr K. Butzer (1974).

Butzer (1974) has arrived at a dating for Taung by a study of the inferred and correlated sequences of geomorphological events. His study confirms that Taung is no older than Swartkrans and Kromdraai. Indeed, he relates the Taung hominid to a younger geomorphological cycle than that postulated by Peabody (1954) and this cycle appears immediately to predate the middle Pleistocene 'Younger Gravels' of the Vaal river. His late lower Pleistocene age estimate for Taung is virtually identical with the date of opening of the Taung cave arrived at by Partridge. Butzer's study may therefore be considered to validate, to a certain extent, the assumptions and methodology of Partridge, as well as their applicability to Taung, a point which has apparently been questioned.

The concurrence of three independent lines of research on the fauna, the dates of cave opening and the sequences of geomorphological events suggests strongly that Partridge's approach may be valid.

In a word, as Dr E.D. Gill of Australia pointed out to me in a letter recently, Partridge's contribution is useful as giving an independent estimate of time and in providing a challenge to other estimates.

Comparison of faunal and geomorphological dates

For each of three Transvaal sites, the date of cave opening determined by Partridge (1973) is somewhat older than the faunal date proposed by Cooke and Maglio. Table 2 makes this clear:–

Table 2 Tentative dates proposed for three Transvaal australopithecine sites

Site	*Date of Cave Opening* (Partridge)	*Faunal Date* (Cooke and Maglio)	*Discrepancy*
Makapansgat Limeworks	ca. 3.7 m.y. BP	ca. 3.0 m.y. BP	ca. 0.7 m.y.
Sterkfontein	ca. 3.3 m.y. BP	ca. 2.5–3.0 m.y. BP	ca. 0.3–0.8 m.y.
Swartkrans	ca. 2.6 m.y. BP	ca. 2.0 m.y. BP	ca. 0.6 m.y.

It is possible that errors, systematic or otherwise, may have entered into both sets of dates. On the other hand, recent developments in our understanding of the stratigraphy of some of these sites suggest another explanation for the discrepancies. At Sterkfontein, it is now known that there is a fairly considerable depth of breccia below or deep to the lowest level of the main quarry ('type site'). The emptying of the Middle Pit in the north-west part of the main quarry by A.R. Hughes made it possible for Brink and Partridge (1970) to descry a bone-bearing breccia below and clearly earlier than a thick band of travertine, that itself underlies the hominid-bearing breccia. The breccia excavated on the surface is nearly vertically above further breccias exposed in some of the underground caverns, and it seems highly probable that the surface breccias are continuous with those in the underground caves. Only the lowermost portion of that great depth of 30 m. or more of consolidated breccia would have accumulated on the first opening of the cave. It is that lowermost breccia that would be dated as slightly younger than Partridge's estimated 'date of cave opening'. On the other hand, the faunal remains that Cooke and Maglio compared with the East African calibrated faunas were derived from the breccia near the surface down to a depth of not more than 12 m. below datum: to this upper fraction of the deposit, or at least a part of it, the faunal date of ca. 2.5 m.y. BP would apply. Since Vrba (1974) has shown a succession of bovids *within* this upper 12 m., it is not inconceivable that the lower moiety of the breccia, too, may have accumulated over hundreds of thousands of years, as Butzer (1971b) inferred.

The deep, lower breccia of Sterkfontein, referred to above, is richly fossiliferous. Although no systematic listing of fauna from that part of the breccia has been given, it does seem likely that fossils have been identified from that part of the cave deposit. In 1931 or 1932, one of Dart's former research students, J.H.S. Gear, together with the Goedvolk brothers, identified antelope and baboon fossils from a deep deposit well below the surface workings (see Tobias, 1973d, for an account of this previously unrecorded fossil collecting endeavour at Sterkfontein). No trace of these specimens has been found in a recent search at the South African Institute for Medical Research, from which Professor J.H.S. Gear recently retired as Director. The other fossil occurrence that seems almost certainly to have come from these lowermost breccias is that of *Lycyaena silberbergi* Broom about 1946. The specimen which was the first-discovered Transvaal fossil belonging to the genus *Lycyaena* was found by Dr H.K. Silberberg of Johannesburg (Broom, 1948; Ewer, 1967). According to Broom (1946, p.83): 'The spot where it was found is about directly below the spot where the type skull of Plesianthropus was found, but at about 60 feet lower level.' This would almost certainly place the specimen in the lowest part of the Sterkfontein breccias, where T.C. Partridge and the author have recently located a number of good mammalian fossils in situ; but no systematic work has yet been carried out at this level. Broom added, however: 'Though this working is so much lower, the other specimens I found here did not seem to indicate any difference in age' (Broom, 1946, p.83). We have, however, no record of other faunal species identified from this low level and proposed to carry out systematic work there soon, as an extension of our ongoing Sterkfontein programme. I believe it is very likely that the fauna from the oldest breccia may well show differences from the identified species from higher in the deposit.

Hence the long stratigraphy of Sterkfontein presents a reasonable reconciliation between the faunal date and the proposed date of cave opening. It is perfectly possible that both dates may be correct!

Similarly, though the evidence from Makapansgat is at this stage less clear-cut, there, too, we have indications of a lengthy cycle of deposition after cave opening, but antedating the suid and elephantid remains which have been correlated with calibrated lineages in East Africa. There is an appreciable depth of breccias with intercalated travertines below the level from which were derived the pig and elephant fossils (Tobias, 1973c). Furthermore, the occurrence of differences in the faunal content of various strata within the Makapansgat deposit has been suggested by Dr J. Kitching (quoted by Maier, 1970). In other words, at Makapansgat, too, Partridge's date of cave opening is compatible with Cooke's and Maglio's faunal date.

Thus, at both Sterkfontein and Makapansgat, the considerable depth of the breccia body may account for the discrepancy of hundreds of thousands of years between the first opening of the caves and the deposition of those breccias dated faunistically. It remains to be seen whether Dr C.K. Brain's excavation at Swartkrans (1970) reveals there a similar lengthy sequence of early breccias to account for the discrepancy of some 600,000 years between the proposed date of cave opening and Cooke's tentative faunal date of the australopithecine deposit.

The dating of Taung

Three different and independent studies, as we have seen, concur in assigning a relatively recent date to Taung. On Wells's (1969) faunal analysis Taung is *at least as young* as the Swartkrans Faunal Span. On Butzer's (1974) proposed correlations between the sequences of geomorphological cycles, Taung immediately antedates the Middle Pleistocene 'Younger Gravels' of the Vaal River. Moreover, applying his geomorphological approach to the Orange-Vaal-Harts-Buxton river systems, Partridge (1973) has inferred that the Taung cave did not open until <0.9 m.y. BP.

Since both Butzer and Peabody agree that the cercopithecoid breccia was deposited appreciably before the hominid-bearing breccia at Taung, it follows from Partridge's proposed date of cave opening that the Taung hominid skull, coming from the upper part of the deposit, may in fact be as young as 0.8 or even 0.7 m.y. BP.

If the new faunal and geomorphological age estimates are even approximately correct, the australopithecines of Makapansgat and Sterkfontein are respectively about 2.2 and 1.7 m.y. earlier than that of Taung. It would follow, too, that the South African cave deposits may span as great a period of time as 3 million years, from 3.7 m.y. BP to 0.7 m.y. BP, while the hominids thus far discovered would seem to span some 2.3 millions of years, from 3.0 m.y. BP to 0.7 m.y. BP.

South African hominid taxa

Within a span of close on 3 million years, at least three different hominid taxa are represented in the five South African sites, namely *A. africanus, A. robustus* (called by some *Paranthropus robustus*) and *Homo* sp. (from Swartkrans and from the later breccia, possibly of the Swartkrans Faunal Span, exposed in the West Pit of Sterkfontein). We may divide these southern hominids into groups:–

(a) *late Pliocene hominids*: numerous cranial, dental and post-cranial remains from Makapansgat and Sterkfontein (2.5-3.0 m.y. BP)

(b) *lower and middle Pleistocene hominids*: these stem from the Sterkfontein Member 5 ('middle breccia' of Robinson) (? 2.0 or less m.y. BP), Swartkrans (ca. 1.8-2.0 m.y. BP), Kromdraai (perhaps between 1.0 and 1.8 m.y. BP) and Taung (<0.9 m.y. BP).

The earlier specimens, those in group (a), provide our best evidence of the more slenderly-built or gracile australopithecines. They are commonly assigned to *A. africanus* (though Broom, 1936, regarded the Sterkfontein hominid as a separate species from Taung, namely *A.*

transvaalensis and, subsequently, as a separate genus, *Plesianthropus transvaalensis* Broom 1938b, while Robinson, 1954, considered that they were distinct at the subspecific level, *A. africanus transvaalensis*, as compared with the Taung subspecies, *A. africanus africanus*).

The Makapansgat sample shows, too, a number of features reminiscent of *A. robustus*: these traits have been variously explained as indicative of hybridization between gracile and robust australopithecines (Tobias, 1967); or of a polymorphism present in *A. africanus* prior to, and close to, the point of speciation into gracile and robust taxa (Tobias, 1973b); or of the presence of both *A. robustus* and *A. africanus* at Makapansgat (Aguirre, 1970).

Most specimens in group (b) are commonly attributed to *A. robustus* from Swartkrans and Kromdraai; or to *Homo* sp. from Swartkrans (formerly called *Telanthropus capensis*). In addition, some or all of the jaw and tooth fragments from the uppermost breccias exposed in the West Pit of the Sterkfontein deposit, though originally assigned to *A. africanus* (Robinson, 1957, 1958, 1962), are thought to represent *Homo* sp., possibly *H. habilis* (Tobias, 1965, p.187), a view supported by the 1976 finding of StW 53 in Member 5 (Hughes and Tobias, 1977).

The position of Taung in group (b) is exceptional. It is the holotype of *A. africanus* and yet it is the only specimen of *A. africanus* in the very large sample comprising group (b). On the other hand, all of the gracile specimens in group (a), also a sizeable sample, are assigned to *A. africanus*. From what we have seen, there may well be a lapse of 2 million years between the gracile hominids (called *A. africanus*) in group (a) and the type specimen of *A. africanus* in group (b). At the same time, if we accept the new later dating for Taung, its only known near-contemporaries are the last of the robust australopithecines and *Homo erectus*. It may well be enquired whether the earlier fossils of the gracile lineage have been correctly assigned to *A. africanus* (Tobias, 1973c).

Provisional pattern of hominid evolution in Africa

Now that we have a fair idea of the taxonomic affinities and of the spread in time of the various South and East African hominids, it is possible to plot the early hominids against time. Although there are several competing classificatory systems, I have adhered to a widely-accepted system that recognizes only two genera, *Homo* and *Australopithecus*. Within *Australopithecus* are one polymorphic species, *A. africanus*, and a superspecies, *A. robustus*, comprising two semispecies, *A. robustus* and *A. boisei*. Within *Homo* are early *Homo* sp., *H. habilis, H. erectus* and *H. sapiens*. Early *Homo* sp. and *H. habilis* may be a single polymorphic taxon with early representatives at East Rudolf and late representatives at Olduvai, or they may be related to each other in some different manner.

A generally clear-cut pattern of hominid phylogeny seems to emerge when the various taxa are arranged on a time axis (Figures 2 and 3). We may read this provisional phylogenetic tree of the hominids as follows.

The ancestral Pliocene population of hominids was *A. africanus* or a species very similar to it. This relatively unspecialized hominid is best represented in the samples from Makapansgat and Sterkfontein. About 3.0 m.y. BP (or even earlier), a branch of *A. africanus* underwent strong selection for cerebral enlargement, out of proportion to overall bodily size. This branch represented the emergent *Homo* lineage. Perhaps its earliest known member is R.E.F. Leakey's (1973b) large-brained hominid cranium, KNM-ER 1470, found below the KBS tuff in the East Rudolf zone, which has been dated radiometrically to 2.6 m.y. BP.[4] The evidence seems to support the inference that this *Homo* lineage was characterized by strong dependence upon tool-making and tool-using; and by a variable degree of bipedalism. It differentiated further into the subsequent species of *Homo*, spreading gradually to become global in distribution. In its dysharmonic brain enlargement, tooth and jaw reduction, development of speech, prolongation of infancy and life stages, and ultimately complete dependence for survival on extra-corporeal aids such as implements, this line of higher hominoid development was quite atypical, as compared with other mammalian lineages.

More typical of the pattern of mammalian evolution was the subsequent fate of those australopithecine populations that were not involved in the transformation to *Homo*. Some populations of *A. africanus* continued with relatively little change after the emergence of *Homo*: they seem to have survived, for example at Sterkfontein, for another few hundreds of thousands of years. Others underwent dental specialization and developed an increasingly robust body, under dietary or behavioural influences, thus giving rise to the late, robuster lineages of *Australopithecus*. In South Africa, this trend produced the moderately large *A. robustus* and in East Africa the excessively robust *A. boisei*. As these two robust forms were nowhere sympatric, though synchronic, it has been suggested that they might be regarded as a superspecies comprising South and East African semispecies (Tobias 1973a). These lines of specialization diverged away from the *Homo* lineage and were, it seems, *not* characterized by strong dependence upon implemental activities. Having spawned two derivative lineages, *Homo* and *A. robustus*/*A. boisei*, *A. africanus* largely disappeared from the scene some hundreds of thousands of years later.

4. A much younger date has been subsequently proposed for it (Curtis, G.H., *et al.*, 1975, *Nature*, 395-8).

The anomalous position of the Taung child

If the Taung child is as young as the recent claims would make it, it would be the most recently-surviving australopithecine that Africa has so far furnished. The implications of this late survival for the taxonomy, ecology and phylogeny of the early African hominids require special comment, especially in view of the hiatus of 2 million years between the gracile hominids of Sterkfontein and Makapansgat and the hominid of Taung. From no other site than Taung do we have evidence of the survival of *A. africanus* (as we understand it from the Makapansgat and Sterkfontein fossils) to so late a period as <1.0 m.y. B.P. Indeed, it is true to claim that our concept, our mental picture of the gracile australopithecine, is based almost entirely on the large and excellent sample from Sterkfontein and to a lesser extent on the smaller though beautifully preserved sample from Makapansgat, rather than on the type specimen from Taung – for the simple reason that Taung is a juvenile specimen, representing an individual of 5 or 6 years of age at the time of death.

For many years I have pondered the relationship between Taung and the Sterkfontein hominids. As a research student one could not but be impressed at the many differences between the Taung and Sterkfontein hominids that Broom (1938b, 1946) was at pains to demonstrate. But my doubts became more serious when Wells (1967) first started expressing misgivings about the supposed high antiquity of Taung. In the very year following the publication of Wells's opinion, when I addressed a Wenner-Gren Supper Conference at the Foundation's New York City headquarters (April 1968), I queried whether the Sterkfontein and Makapansgat fossils, as well as the Garusi fragment from Tanzania, had been correctly assigned to the same species as the Taung skull. A year later, in the Yearbook of Physical Anthropology for 1967 (Tobias, 1969, p.27), I raised the specific query:

> Among many unresolved problems to which I should like to draw attention are the following:
>
> 6. The Taung skull is the type specimen of *A. africanus*. Are the Sterkfontein and Makapansgat fossils (as well as the fragment from Garusi in Tanzania) correctly assigned to this species (the only permanent teeth shown by the Taung skull are the upper and lower first molars)?

In July 1970, at the Wenner-Gren Symposium on Functional and Evolutionary Biology of Primates, I reiterated the same query (Tobias, 1972). The question of the permanent first molars being the only ones permitting comparison with reasonable samples of gracile and robust australopithecine teeth from the Transvaal was considered important, because so few deciduous teeth were available for comparison. For instance, when Robinson (1956, p.138) sought to establish the character of the lower first deciduous molar as 'a point of great importance and one of the clearest indicators of the dichotomy in the australopithecine group', while there was a reasonable sample of dm1 from robust australopithecines (9 or 10 teeth from 6 or 7 individuals), the gracile sample with which to compare the Taung pair comprised a single pair of dm1 from the opposite sides of one mandible from Sterkfontein. Obviously such a sample could give no concept of the variability of dm1 in the gracile hominids; and I remained doubtful of the claims that were made in respect of the dm1 as an indicator of gracile or robust status. Since none of the deciduous teeth was supposed to distinguish so effectively the gracile from the robust hominids as the dm1, one had to fall back on the permanent teeth. The first permanent molar is not the most useful tooth for distinguishing early hominids. So my doubts deepened. There remain the unerupted germs of some other permanent teeth in the Taung jaws, which the radiological study of G.H. Sperber (1973) has visualized in their crypts.

Even in the teeth that were available, one was plagued by those differences that Broom had pointed out in the thirties and forties. Was Taung the same sort of creature as Sterkfontein and Makapansgat? The new young dates proposed for Taung by Wells, Partridge, and Butzer gave added point to the uncertainties.

If Taung lived less than one million years ago, its only known contemporaries were *Homo erectus* and the last of the robust australopithecines. Was Taung a third contemporary hominid, the last of the gracile australopithecines? It is of course possible that while *A. africanus* was evolving into *Homo* in East Africa, a southerly branch of the species persisted in southern Africa for another couple of millions of years as a relict population of virtual 'living fossils'. In that event, the apparently chronologically isolated position of the Taung child may be the freakish consequence of unrepresentative sampling and discovery and of the imperfection of the fossil record. Further discoveries of hominids may reveal that a considerable body of gracile australopithecines survived as a third lineage, contemporary with the robust hominids and the evolving lineage of *Homo*. Yet if they did, it is more than a little surprising that our large stockpile of fossils from 16 different sites or areas, many of them in the time zone in question, does not appear to include many clear-cut examples of gracile australopithecines in the 2 million years period. Such a survival for 2 million years would itself pose contingent questions: if there really is such a gap between Taung and the early gracile hominids, and if they are in the same lineage, how are we to account for this lengthy survival of the species when all around, including southern Africa, other australopithecines were hominizing into *Homo* or specializing into

A. robustus? The query I raised (Tobias, 1973c) was: *is* the child of Taung in the same lineage as the gracile australopithecines of Makapansgat and Sterkfontein?

The hypothesis suggested was that Taung does not belong to the gracile lineage. If not, it could represent one or other of the two well-known groups of hominids which were its contemporaries. Clearly it is not *Homo erectus*: its brain size alone would rule out that possibility (Tobias, 1971). There remain the last of the robust hominids. The possibility must be seriously countenanced that the Taung child may represent a population which is a late survivor of the robust australopithecine lineages. We do not know the date of the Kromdraai hominid site but it may not be very much older than the new date proposed for Taung. Furthermore, in East Africa, there are at least two examples of late-surviving robust hominids – represented by the Peninj mandible from northern Tanzania and the Chesowanja calvario-facial specimen found east of Lake Baringo in central Kenya. Both of these East African fossils are dated to just *over* 1 million years; Taung is considered to be just *under* 1 million years. So there is evidence that the robust forms survived to a relatively recent period: the possibility that Taung represents a very late surviving robust australopithecine is therefore fully in keeping with this evidence.

Does the morphology of the Taung child allow it to be placed in the robust lineage?

Comments on the morphology of the Taung skull

As already mentioned, the adult morphology of the Taung australopithecine is not available. Furthermore, it remains true that, to this day, no detailed comprehensive assessment of the 'total morphological pattern' (Le Gros Clark, 1964) of the Taung skull has been made. Dart's 300-page monograph prepared in the years following the discovery was not published (Dart, 1940). In any event, at that stage, no other specimens of juvenile australopithecines were available for comparison – nor, for that matter, of any other African early hominids of whatever individual age group. The difficulties of comparing the child specimen from Taung with the fossils of older individuals subsequently discovered has already been alluded to, especially the fact that the Taung child presented only the permanent first molars in an erupted state. Nevertheless, from an early date, Broom was impressed by the differences between the Taung specimen and the Sterkfontein fossils.

When Broom described the first australopithecine specimen from Sterkfontein, he assigned it to a new species (*A. transvaalensis*) 'as though certainly allied to the Taungs ape it is evidently considerably later in time' (Broom, 1937). Broom (1938b) rightly pointed out that there were few points in which a comparison could be made between the Taung and Sterkfontein specimens. In 1938, he found part of a juvenile mandible at Sterkfontein: he commented on 'the interesting fact that the lateral incisors are considerably larger than the central ones' and added that the shape of the symphysis was so different from that of Taung 'that it seems advisable to place *A. transvaalensis* in a distinct genus, for which the name *Plesianthropus* is proposed' (Broom, 1938b, p.377).

Meantime, Wells (1931) in his study on 'growth changes in the Bushman mandible', had called attention to certain points in the structure of the Taung mandible. He stated: 'The body of the *Australopithecus* mandible is relatively short, while the ascending ramus is narrow and unusually high. These features imply a small degree of prognathism combined with marked "subgnathism"'. The accumulation of several australopithecine mandibles from Sterkfontein and Kromdraai enabled Broom by 1946 to develop Wells's comment and to add: 'It seems to show that the adult Australopithecus [i.e. of Taung] had a very high ascending ramus such as we find in the adult Paranthropus [i.e. of Kromdraai]' (Broom, 1946, p.36).

Broom (1946, p.64) drew attention as well to the fact that the Carabelli pit on the Sterkfontein upper molars was distinct and even much developed, whereas in the Taung upper permanent molars the pit is slight as it is in the Kromdraai upper molars. Again, Broom pointed out that the first lower deciduous molar of Sterkfontein (at that stage represented only by a mesial half of the crown) differed markedly from the corresponding teeth of Taung and Kromdraai (p.72). Elsewhere he stated (p.128): 'The imperfect lower first milk molar of the Sterkfontein ape is so different from the corresponding tooth of Australopithecus (Taung) that it further confirms the opinion that the two forms are generically distinct.' Similarly, he mentioned resemblances between the Taung first lower molar and that of Kromdraai, including reference to a sixth cusp (tuberculum sextum) (p.106), although of course he also cited differences, such as the fact that the cusps of the Kromdraai child's first lower molar are distinctly more pointed than in Taung.

Although Broom (1946) finally believed that all three groups of australopithecines – those of Sterkfontein, Kromdraai and Taung – should be regarded as distinct genera, it is at least of interest that he was able to find so many resemblances between Taung and Kromdraai and differences between Taung and Sterkfontein.

The discovery of further juvenile jaws and teeth at Sterkfontein enabled Broom and Robinson (1950) to give a completer description of the deciduous teeth of the Sterkfontein australopithecine. They drew attention to more differences between the Taung and Sterkfontein hominids. Speaking of the upper deciduous molars, they stated (p.49):

> If the teeth of Plesianthropus [i.e. Sterkfontein ape-man] be compared with those of Australopithecus [i.e. Taung hominid] it will be seen that while there is essential agreement there are a number of important differences. The Australopithecus teeth are a little more worn. They are slightly smaller. In the 1st tooth there is in Plesianthropus a little hollow corresponding to the Carabelli pit. There is hardly a trace of this in Australopithecus. In the 2nd tooth while there is a Carabelli cusp in Plesianthropus, there is not even a pit in Australopithecus. Further there is a very distinct posterior fovea in Plesianthropus, while there is no trace of it in Australopithecus.

Of the lower second deciduous molar, they drew attention to the fact that 'the tooth is smaller and considerably narrower than in Australopithecus' (p.54). The mesial buccal groove of this tooth in the Sterkfontein specimen has no distinct pit, whereas in the Taung dm_2 'there is a well developed pit, and a bar of enamel forming a sort of cingulum below it' (p.54). Such a pit is a feature of all 10 dm_2's from Swartkrans (Robinson, 1956, p.140), as it is of the robust M_1's of Swartkrans (p.102) and of Kromdraai (p.104). Again, referring to the Sterkfontein dm_2, they stated, 'The posterior cusp (mesoconid) is small and there is in Plesianthropus no 6th cusp, as there is in Australopithecus' (Broom and Robinson, 1950, p.54). Finally, they laid great stress on the difference in the lower milk canine: 'The remarkable fact that the milk lower canine (of Sterkfontein) has a small anterior cusp, which does not occur in Australopithecus, seems to justify the placing of the Sterkfontein ape-man in a distinct genus' (pp. 54-5).

Schepers (1946, 1950), in his studies on endocranial casts, drew attention to differences between the endocast of Taung and those of Sterkfontein. For example, while the earlier-found Sterkfontein endocasts have a distinct downward concavity of the temporal lobe axis, the Taung and Kromdraai endocasts were said to show a marked medial deflection at the tip (Schepers 1946, p.185). Again, while the endocast of Sterkfontein 5 shows a 'forward specialization', the endocast of an adult from Taung would have shown greater expansion upwards and backwards, according to Schepers (1950, p.103). On the other hand, Holloway's studies tend to align Taung with the gracile australopithecines. Thus, his new determination (1970) of the Taung capacity as 440 c.c. (estimated for the adult) would tend to relate it more closely to the Sterkfontein capacities than to those of robust australopithecines. Indeed, the value of 440 c.c. is smaller than the lower limit of the 95% confidence limits of the robust australopithecines (478-560 c.c.) based upon a sample of four values from South and East African robust specimens (Tobias, 1975b). Another feature tending to distinguish gracile from robust australopithecines is the 'advanced' form of the cerebellar hemisphere in which respect Holloway groups the Taung endocast with that of some gracile australopithecines from Sterkfontein and Makapansgat (Holloway, 1972, pp. 177-8, and see Tobias, 1967, pp. 88-92). He states that the gracile and robust forms differ, too, in the degree of folding of the cortex, expansion of the parietal cortex, overall size and shape of the brain, in which respects Taung resembles two Sterkfontein specimens: this gracile sample of three that show increased cortical folding are, however, all from young individuals (Holloway, 1972, p.185).

When the Swartkrans monograph appeared, Broom and Robinson (1952) stated unequivocally of the Taung M_1: 'This tooth resembles that of *P. crassidens* [i.e. the Swartkrans australopithecine] more closely than it does that of *Plesianthropus* [i.e. of Sterkfontein]' (p.67).

Bronowski and Long (1951, 1952) made what must be one of the earliest attempts to apply the statistics of discrimination in palaeoanthropology, when they compared the lower milk canines of Taung and of Kromdraai with those of modern man and apes. While showing the remoteness of the australopithecine teeth from those of apes and their proximity to those of modern human beings, they also showed that the Taung and Kromdraai teeth very closely resembled each other in size and shape. In a subsequent study (1953), they extended the multivariate statistical analysis to deciduous canines from Swartkrans and Sterkfontein. While the ape-man teeth formed a fairly compact group closely resembling the homologues of modern man, it is interesting to note that, in their size and shape distance from the human sample, the Taung teeth (with an *S* value of 5.9) were closer to those of Kromdraai and Swartkrans (with *S* values ranging from 1.0 to 6.7), while the Sterkfontein teeth with *S* values of 10.6 and 11.9 were farthest removed, in fact 'unacceptably remote', and the authors stated that 'a value of *S* as high as these would be expected to occur in modern European man only once in a thousand times'. Thus, in size and shape, the Taung lower milk canine is closest to those of Kromdraai and Swartkrans.

By the time Robinson (1956) made his important study of the teeth of the Australopithecinae, he had fairly large samples at his disposal. His study led him to align the teeth of Taung with the Sterkfontein and Makapansgat dentitions, despite the fact that, like Broom previously, he recognised and stressed a number of features in which the Taung teeth differed from those of Sterkfontein and Makapansgat and resembled those of Swartkrans or Kromdraai, or both. Thus, he drew attention again to the pit that terminates the mesial buccal groove on the Taung M_1, a feature that occurs regularly in the Swartkrans M_1's. He stressed the clear-cut distinction between Taung with its definite tuberculum sextum on dm_1 (op.cit., p.137), dm_2 (op.cit., p.143) and M_1 (op.cit., p.107) and the Sterkfontein and Makapansgat homologues which lack the tuberculum sextum. In this respect, too, the Taung teeth closely resemble the Swartkrans homologues, in which the presence of tuberculum sextum is a consistent finding (in respect of M_1 and dm_2 – op.cit., pp. 118 and 140) while it 'may be present' in the Swartkrans dm_1 (p.138).

Likewise, apart from the general resemblances in size and shape of the Taung lower milk canines to those of the robust australopithecines to which Bronowski and Long had drawn attention, the deciduous lower canines of Taung are clearly distinguishable in a number of morphological respects from those of Sterkfontein (Robinson 1956, p.133) 'in a fashion which suggests a real difference between them but more specimens are required to indicate the ranges of variation before this can definitely be established'. This difference in the lower milk canines was stated to be part of Robinson's reason for separating Taung and Sterkfontein at the subspecific level.

Although Robinson claimed that the Taung dm_1 and dm_2 were 'similar in type' to, or 'of the same sort' as, those of Sterkfontein and 'different from the type possessed by the Swartkrans and Kromdraai forms', this interpretation is not unequivocal, as a careful examination of his Figure 38 (p.135) and Figure 48 (p.156), as well as an examination of the original specimens, suggests.

More recently, Sperber (1973), in the latest detailed odontoscopic and odontometric study on the South African early hominid fossils, including a number of measurements never before taken on these teeth, has uncovered additional fine morphometric traits distinguishing the Taung teeth from those of Sterkfontein and Makapansgat and, in some instances, aligning them with those of the South African robust australopithecines. Professor Sperber, a colleague and former research student of mine, has generously allowed me to quote his unpublished thesis to this effect.

On morphological grounds, therefore, there seems to be sufficient evidence to call into question any facile assumption that 'it is obvious' or 'indisputable' that the Taung child skull belongs to the gracile lineage. The case briefly presented above would justify a detailed and comprehensive study of the entire Taung skull (including a re-study of the dentition and of the morphology of the endocast), in comparison with the now much larger sample of available juvenile and adult specimens of both gracile and robust australopithecines from East as well as South Africa. Only a new and meticulous study of the Taung skull will permit Dart's child of 1924 to show itself in its true colours. Just 50 years after the disclosure of the Taung skull (Dart, 1925), its discoverer and nominator, Emeritus Professor Raymond A. Dart, has recently generously invited me to undertake such a study.

Taxonomic implications if the Taung skull is transferred to the robust Australopithecine lineage

In the original comment in *Nature* on the taxonomic implications of a transfer of the Taung skull to the robust lineage, I was in error, as Dr T.R. Olson has kindly pointed out (1974). In the last three sentences of my paper (Tobias, 1973c), I misinterpreted the International Code of Zoological Nomenclature. Further, in raising the possibility of a change of name for Taung, I took for granted, though I did not expressly state, that this could come about only if an appeal to the Commission under Clause 79 of the Code were successful. The correct position is as follows (Tobias, 1974c).

We may assume that the original designation of *A. africanus* as the type-species of the new nominal genus *Australopithecus* was valid, in the light of Articles 67 to 70 of the Code. Moreover, we may accept the validity of Dart's procedure in basing the new nominal species on the Taung skull as its holotype, in accordance with Articles 72 and 73 of the Code.

If we accept that these procedures were valid and if we do find ourselves facing the necessity of transferring the Taung skull to the robust lineage, then it is clear that real problems would follow rigid adherence to the Code (with the exception of its Article 79).

Taung, it has been suggested, may not represent *A. africanus* in the sense in which this taxon is understood from the Makapansgat and Sterkfontein fossil hominids, though it does of course represent *A. africanus*, the original nominal species. If this hypothesis proves correct, it would follow that Taung on one hand, and Makapansgat and Sterkfontein on the other, may represent two different taxa. In this event, the possibility was tentatively raised (Tobias, 1973c) that the taxon represented by the Taung skull may belong to the robust lineage – and we have here cited morphological and geochronological evidence that provides some *prima facie* support for such transfer of Taung from the gracile to the robust lineages. If Taung proves to be robust, the confusing position set forth by Olson (1974) would follow, namely that the robust australopithecines would need to be added to the hypodigm of *A. africanus*, whilst the gracile australopithecines from Makapansgat and Sterkfontein would either remain as part of the hypodigm of a vastly more variable *A. africanus*, or need to be removed to form the hypodigm of another species (for which, as Dr Olson points out, the nomen *A. transvaalensis* is available). Since there is abundant evidence that the gracile and robust australopithecines are taxonomically distinct, the last-mentioned course would probably need to be adopted.

Such removal of the gracile australopithecines of Makapansgat and Sterkfontein from *A. africanus* would cause immense confusion, for our image of the species, *A. africanus*, is at present based largely on the hominids from these two sites, rather than on the skull of the Taung child, even although the latter is the holotype.

No less of a muddle would follow if palaeoanthropologists were now required to call the robust (but not the gracile) australopithecines *A. africanus*. It was to avert such appalling ambiguity that I raised the possibility of the holotype (the Taung skull) being removed from the hypodigm of *A. africanus*, though I assumed, and should have added, 'if an appeal to the Commission under Article 79 of the Code were successful'. It is to meet such unusual circumstances of extreme instability and confusion that Article 79 permits such an appeal to the Commission. In the present, as yet hypothetical case, it is reasonable to expect that such an appeal would be permissible under the Code; indeed it might well be justified. If such an appeal were successful, the gracile australopithecines of Sterkfontein and Makapansgat would then legitimately continue to be called *A. africanus*, but the Taung skull would no longer be a part of that species, let alone its holotype.

Meantime, the entire discussion has helped to establish the case for a comprehensive re-study of the Taung skull.

Acknowledgments

The many original studies that have gone into this survey and tentative synthesis have benefited greatly from my lengthy association with Professor R.A. Dart, the late Dr L.S.B. Leakey, Dr M.D. Leakey, R.E.F. Leakey, A.R. Hughes, Dr T.C. Partridge and Dr C.K. Brain. To all of them, I express my profound gratitude. Thanks are extended, too, to Mr J. Wilkinson, Dr C. Jolly, Dr K. Butzer, Dr T.R. Olson, Mrs K. Copley, Miss C.J. Orkin, Mr P. Faugust and Mrs S.M. Clarke, as well as to my research students who have stimulated me to attempt this review.

The detailed researches which have made possible my own part of the work reviewed in this chapter were generously subvented by the University of the Witwatersrand, Johannesburg, and especially its Bernard Price Institute for Palaeontological Research, the Council for Scientific and Industrial Research (Pretoria), the Wenner-Gren Foundation for Anthropological Research, the L.S.B. Leakey Foundation and the National Science Foundation.

References

Aguirre, E. (1970) Identificacion de 'Paranthropus' en Makapansgat. *Cronica del XI Congreso Nacional de Arqueologia, Merida 1969*, 98-124.

Bishop, W.E. (1971) The late Cenozoic history of East Africa in relation to hominoid evolution. In Turekian, K.K. (ed.), *The Late Cenozoic Glacial Ages*, 493-527. New Haven/London.

Bishop, W.W. (1972) Stratigraphic succession 'versus' calibration in East Africa. In Bishop, W.W. and Miller, J.A. (eds.), 219-46.

Bishop, W.W. *et al.* (1971) Succession of Cainozoic vertebrate assemblages from the Northern Kenya Rift Valley. *Nature* 233 (41), 389-94.

Bishop, W.W. and Miller, J.A. (eds.) (1972) *Calibration of Hominoid Evolution.* Edinburgh.

Brain, C.K. (1958) *The Transvaal Ape-man Bearing Cave Deposits. Transvaal Mus. Memoir* 11, 1-131.

Brain, C.K. (1970) New finds at the Swartkrans australopithecine site. *Nature* 225, 1112-19.

Brink, A.B.A. and Partridge, T.C. (1970) *Notes on Sterkfontein Deposit Stratigraphy* (unpublished).

Brock, A. and Isaac, G. Ll. (1974) Palaeomagnetic stratigraphy and chronology of hominid-bearing sediments east of Lake Rudolf, Kenya. *Nature* 247, 344-8.

Bronowski, J. and Long, W.M. (1951) Statistical methods in anthropology. *Nature* 168, 794-5.

Bronowski, J. and Long, W.M. (1952) Statistics of discrimination in anthropology. *Amer.J. phys. Anthrop.* 10, 385-94.

Bronowski, J. and Long, W.M. (1953) The australopithecine milk canines. *Nature* 172, 251.

Broom. R. (1925) Some notes on the Taungs skull. *Nature* 115, 569-71.

Broom, R. (1930) The age of *Australopithecus*. *Nature* 125, 814.

Broom, R. (1936) A new fossil anthropoid skull from South Africa. *Nature* 138, 486-8.

Broom, R. (1937) Discovery of a lower molar of *Australopithecus*. *Nature* 140, 681-2.

Broom, R. (1938a) More discoveries of *Australopithecus*. *Nature* 141, 828-9.

Broom, R. (1938b) The Pleistocene anthropoid apes of South Africa. *Nature* 142, 377-9.

Broom, R. (1946) The occurrence and general structure of the South African Ape-Men. Part 1 of *The South African Fossil Ape-Men, the Australopithecinae. Transvaal Mus. Memoir* 2, 11-153.

Broom, R. (1948) Some South African Pliocene and Pleistocene mammals. *Ann. Transvaal Mus.* 21, 1-38.

Broom, R. and Robinson, J.T. (1950) Further evidence of the structure of the Sterkfontein Ape-Man, *Plesianthropus*. Part I of *Sterkfontein Ape-Man, Plesianthropus. Transvaal Mus. Memoir* 4, 11-83.

Broom, R. and Robinson, J.T. (1952) *Swartkrans Ape-Man,* Paranthropus crassidens. *Transvaal Mus. Memoir* 6, 1-123.

Brown, F.H. (1972) Radiometric dating of sedimentary formations in the lower Omo valley, southern Ethiopia. In Bishop, W.W. and Miller, J.A. (eds.), 273-87.

Butzer, K.W. (1971a) The Lower Omo Basin: geology, fauna and hominids of Plio-Pleistocene formations. *Naturwissenschaften* 58, 7-16.

Butzer, K.W. (1971b) Another look at the australopithecine cave breccias of the Transvaal. *Amer. Anthrop.* 73 (5), 1197-201.

Butzer, K.W. (1973) Dawn in the Rudolf Basin. *S.Afr.J.Sci.* 69, 292-3.

Butzer, K.W. (1974) Palaeoecology of South African australopithecines: Taung revisited. *Curr. Anthrop.* 15 (4), 367-82.

Butzer, K.W. and Thurber, D.L. (1969) Some late Cenozoic sedimentary formations of the Lower Omo Basin. *Nature* 222, 1132-7.

Carmichael, D.J., Tobias, P.V. and Dodd, C.M. (1975) A partial biochemical characterization of fossilized bone from Makapansgat, Swartkrans and Queen Charlotte Islands. *Comp. Biochem. Physiol.* 51B, 257-262.

Carney, J., Hill, A., Miller, J.A. and Walker, A. (1971) Late australopithecine from Baringo district, Kenya. *Nature* 230, 509-14.

Clark, Le Gros, W.E. (1964) *The Fossil Evidence for Human Evolution* (2nd ed.). Chicago.

Cooke, H.B.S. (1952) Quaternary events in South Africa. In Leakey, L.S.B. and Cole, S. (eds.), *Prehistory: First Pan-Afr. Cong., Nairobi 1947*, 26-36.

Cooke, H.B.S. (1963) Pleistocene mammal faunas of Africa with particular reference to Southern Africa. In Howell, F.C. and Bourlière, F. (eds.), *African Ecology and Human Evolution*, 65-116. Chicago.

Cooke, H.B.S. (1967) The Pleistocene sequence in South Africa and problems of correlation. In Bishop, W.W. and Clark, J.D. (eds.), *Background to Evolution in Africa*, 175-184. Chicago.

Cooke, H.B.S. (1968) Evolution of mammals on the southern continents. II. The fossil mammal faunas of Africa. *Quart. Rev. Biol.* 43 (3), 234-64.

Cooke, H.B.S. and Ewer, R.F. (1972) Fossil Suidae from Kanapoi and Lothagam, Northwestern Kenya. *Bull. Mus. Comp. Zool.* 143 (3), 149-296.

Cooke, H.B.S. and Maglio, V.J. (1972) Plio-Pleistocene stratigraphy in East Africa in relation to proboscidean and suid evolution. In Bishop, W.W. and Miller, J.A. (eds.), 303-29.

Coppens, Y. (1970-1) Localisation dans le temps et dans l'éspace des restes d'hominidés des formations plio-pleistocénes de l'Omo (Ethiopie). *C. R. Acad. Sci.* 271, 1968-71, 2286-9; 272, 36-9.

Coppens, Y. (1973a) Les restes d'hominidés des séries inférieures et moyennes des formations plio-villafranchiennes de l'Omo en Ethiopie (récoltes 1970, 1971 et 1972). *C. R. Acad. Sci.* 276, 1823-6.

Coppens, Y. (1973b) Les restes d'hominidés des séries supérieures des formations plio-villafranchiennes de l'Omo en Ethiopie. *C. R. Acad. Sci.* 276, 1981-4.

Dart, R.A. (1925) *Australopithecus africanus*: the man-ape of South Africa. *Nature* 115, 195-9.

Dart, R.A. (1926) Taungs and its significance. *Natural Hist.* 26 (3), 315-27.

Dart, R.A. (1929) A note on the Taungs skull. *S. Afr. J. Sci.* 26, 648-58.

Dart, R.A. (1940) The Status of *Australopithecus*. *Amer. J. phys. Anthrop.* 26, 167-86.

De Graaff, G. (1961) A preliminary investigation of the mammalian microfauna in Pleistocene deposits of caves in the Transvaal system. *Palaeontologia Africana* 7 (1960), 59-118.

Eckhardt, R.B. (1975) *Gigantopithecus* as a hominid. In Tuttle, R.H. (ed.), *Paleoanthropology, Morphology and Paleoecology*, 105-129. The Hague.

Evernden, J.F. and Curtis, G.H. (1965) The potassium argon dating of Late Cenozoic rocks in East Africa and Italy. *Curr. Anthropol.* 6 (4), 343-85.

Ewer, R.F. (1957) Faunal evidence on the dating of the Australopithecinae. In Clark, J.D. and Cole, S. (eds.), *Proc. IIIrd Pan-Afr. Cong. on Prehist., 1955*, 135-142.

Ewer, R.F. (1967) The fossil hyaenids of Africa – a reappraisal. In Bishop, W.W. and Clark, J.D. (eds.), *Background to Evolution in Africa*, 109-23. Chicago.

Ewer, R.F. and Cooke, H.B.S. (1964) The Pleistocene mammals of Southern Africa. In Davies, D.H.S. (eds.), *Ecological Studies in Southern Africa*, 35-48. The Hague.

Fleischer, R.L. and Hart, H.R. (1972) Fission track dating: techniques and problems. In Bishop, W.W. and Miller, J.A. (eds.).

Freedman, L. (1970) A new check-list of fossil Cercopithecoidea of South Africa. *Palaeont. Afr.* 13, 109-10.

Freedman, L. and Brain, C.K. (1972) Fossil Cercopithecoid remains from the Kromdraai australopithecine site (Mammalia: Primates). *Ann. Transvaal Mus.* 28 (1): 1-16.

Freedman, L. and Stenhouse, N.S. (1972) The *Parapapio* species of Sterkfontein, Transvaal, South Africa. *Palaeont. Afr.* 14: 93-111.

Gear, J.H.S. (1926) Preliminary account of the baboon remains from Taungs. *S.Afr.J.Sci.*, 23: 731-747.

Gentry, A.W. (1970) Revised classification for *Makapania broomi* Wells and Cooke (Bovidae, Mammalia). *Palaeont. Afr.* 13, 63-7.

Haughton, S.H. (1925) Note on the occurrence of a species of baboon in limestone deposits near Taungs. *Trans. Roy. Soc. S. Afr.* 12, 68.

Heinzelin, J. de (1971) Observations sur la formation de Shungura (Vallée de l'Omo, Ethiopie). *C. R. Acad. Sci.* 272, 2409-11.

Heinzelin, J. de and Brown, F.H. (1969) Some early Pleistocene deposits of the lower Omo valley: the Usno formation. *Quaternaria* 11, 29-46.

Howell, F.C. (1969) Remains of Hominidae from Pliocene/Pleistocene formations in the Lower Omo Basin, Ethiopia. *Nature* 223, 1234-9.

Howell, F.C. (1972) Pliocene/Pleistocene Hominidae in eastern Africa: absolute and relative ages. In Bishop, W.W. and Miller, J.A. (eds.), 331-68.

Howell, F.C. and Coppens, Y. (1974) Inventory of remains of Hominidae from Pliocene/Pleistocene formations of the Lower Omo Basin, Ethiopia (1967-1972). *Amer. J. phys. Anthrop.* 40, 1-16.

Holloway, R.L. (1970) Australopithecine endocast (Taung specimen, 1924): a new volume determination. *Science* 168, 956-8.

Holloway, R.L. (1972) New australopithecine endocast, SK 1585, from Swartkrans, South Africa. *Amer. J. phys. Anthrop.* 37, 173-86.

Holloway, R.L. (1973) Endocranial volumes of early African hominids and the role of the brain in human mosaic evolution. *J. hum. Evol.* 2 (6), 449-59.

Hurford, A.J. (1974) Fission track dating of a vitric tuff from East Rudolf, North Kenya. *Nature* 249, 236-7.

Lasker, G.W (1973) *Physical Anthropology*. New York.

Lavocat, R. (1957) La faune de rongeurs des grottes à Australopithèques. *Palaeont. Afr.* 4 (1956), 69-75.

Leakey, L.S.B. (1965) *Olduvai Gorge 1951-1961*, Vol. I. *A preliminary report on the geology and fauna*. Cambridge.

Leakey, L.S.B., Tobias, P.V. and Napier, J.R. (1964) A new species of the genus *Homo* from the Olduvai Gorge. *Nature* 202, 7-9.

Leakey, M.D. (1971) *Olduvai Gorge*, Vol. 3. *Excavations in Beds I and II, 1960-1963*. Cambridge.

Leakey, R.E.F. (1970) Fauna and artifacts from a new Plio-Pleistocene locality near Lake Rudolf in Kenya. *Nature* 226, 223-4.

Leakey, R.E.F. (1971) Further evidence of Lower Pleistocene hominids from East Rudolf, North Kenya. *Nature* 231, 241-5.

Leakey, R.E.F. (1972) Further evidence of lower Pleistocene hominids from East Rudolf, North Kenya, 1971. *Nature* 237, 264-9.

Leakey, R.E.F. (1973a) Further evidence of lower Pleistocene hominids from East Rudolf, North Kenya, 1972. *Nature* 242, 170-3.

Leakey, R.E.F. (1973b) Australopithecines and Hominines: a summary on the evidence from the Early Pleistocene of East Africa. In Zuckerman, S. (ed.), *The Concepts of Human Evolution*, *Symp. Zool. Soc. London* No. 33, 53-69.

Leakey, R.E.F., Mungai, J.M. and Walker, A.C. (1971) New australopithecines from East Rudolf, Kenya. *Amer. J. phys. Anthrop.* 35, 175-86.

Leakey, R.E.F., Mungai, J.M. and Walker, A.C. (1972) New australopithecines from East Rudolf, Kenya (II). *Amer. J. phys. Anthrop.* 36, 235-51.

Leakey, R.E.F. and Walker, A.C. (1973a) New Australopithecines from East Rudolf, Kenya (III). *Amer. J. phys. Anthrop.* 39, 205-22.

Leakey, R.E.F. and Wood, B.A. (1973b) New evidence of the genus *Homo* from East Rudolf, Kenya (II). *Amer. J. phys. Anthrop.* 39, 355-68.

MacDougall, D. and Price, P.B. (1974) Attempt to date early South African hominids using fission tracks in calcite. *Science* 185, 943-44.

Maglio, V.J. (1970) Early Elephantidae of Africa and a tentative correlation of African Plio-Pleistocene deposits. *Nature* 225, 328-32.

Maglio, V.J. (1971) Vertebrate faunas from the Kubi Algi, Koobi Fora and Ileret Areas, East Rudolf, Kenya. *Nature* 231, 248-9.

Maglio, V.J. (1972) Vertebrate faunas and chronology of hominid-bearing sediments east of Lake Rudolf, Kenya. *Nature* 239, 379-85.

Maglio, V.J. (1973) Origin and evolution of the Elephantidae. *Trans. Amer. Phil. Soc.* n.s. 63 (3), 1-149.

Maier, W. (1970) New fossil Cercopithecoidea from the lower Pleistocene cave deposits of the Makapansgat Limeworks, South Africa. *Palaeont. Afr.* 13, 69-107.

Maier, W. (1973) Paläoökologie und zeitliche einordnung der südafrikanischen Australopithecinen. *Z. Morph. Anthrop.* 65 (1), 70-105.

Martyn, J.E. and Tobias, P.V. (1967) Pleistocene deposits and new fossil localities in Kenya. *Nature* 215, 476-480.

Olson, T.R. (1974) Taxonomy of the Taung skull. *Nature* 252, 85.

Partridge, T.C. (1973) Geomorphological dating of cave opening at Makapansgat, Sterkfontein, Swartkrans and Taung. *Nature* 246, 75-9.

Partridge, T.C. (1974) Geomorphological dating of cave openings in South Africa; reply to A.M.J. De Swardt. *Nature* 250, 683-4.

Patterson, B. (1966) A new locality for early Pleistocene fossils in northwestern Kenya. *Nature* 212, 577-8.

Patterson, B., Behrensmeyer, A.K. and Sill, W.D. (1970) Geology and fauna of a new Pliocene locality in northwestern Kenya. *Nature* 226, 918-21.

Patterson, B. and Howells, W.W. (1967) Hominid humeral fragment from early Pleistocene of northwestern Kenya. *Science* 156, 64-6.

Peabody, F.E. (1965) Travertines and cave deposits of the Kaap escarpment of South Africa, and the type locality of *Australopithecus africanus* Dart. *Bull. Geol. Soc. Amer.* 65, 671-706.

Pilbeam, D. (1972) *The Ascent of Man: an Introduction to Human Evolution*. New York.

Robinson, J.T. (1954) The genera and species of the Australopithecinae. *Amer. J. phys. Anthrop.* 12 (2), 181-200.

Robinson, J.T. (1956) *The dentition of the Australopithecinae. Transvaal Mus. Memoir* 9, 1-179.

Robinson, J.T. (1957) Occurrence of stone artifacts with *Australopithecus* at Sterkfontein. *Nature* 180, 521-4.
Robinson, J.T. (1958) The Sterkfontein tool-maker. *The Leech* 28, 94-100.
Robinson, J.T. (1962) Australopithecines and artifacts at Sterkfontein. *S.Afr. archaeol. Bull.* 17, 87-107.
Robinson, J.T. and Mason, R.J. (1957) Occurrence of stone artifacts with *Australopithecus* at Sterkfontein. *Nature* 180, 521-4.
Schepers, G.W.H. (1946) The endocranial casts of the South African ape-men. Part II of *The South African Fossil Ape-men, the Australopithecinae. Transvaal Mus. Memoir* 2, 167-272.
Schepers, G.W.H. (1950) The brain casts of the recently discovered *Plesianthropus* skulls. Part II of *Sterkfontein Ape-man,* Plesianthropus. *Transvaal Mus. Memoir* 4, 89-117.
Sperber, G.H. (1973) The morphology of the cheek teeth of early South African hominids. PhD dissertation, Faculty of Science, Univ. of the Witwatersrand, Johannesburg.
Swardt, A.M.J. De (1974) Geomorphological dating of cave openings in South Africa. *Nature* 250, 683.
Taieb, M., Coppens, Y., Johanson, D.C. and Kalb, J. (1972) Dépôts sédimentaires et faunes du Plio-Pleistocene de la basse vallée de l'Awash (Afar central, Ethiopie). *C. R. Acad. Sci.* 275 (sér. D), 819-22.
Tobias, P.V. (1965) *Australopithecus, Homo habilis*, tool-using and tool-making. *S. Afr. archaeol. Bull.* 20, 167-92.
Tobias, P.V. (1967) *Olduvai Gorge*, Vol. 2. *The cranium and maxillary dentition of* Australopithecus (Zinjanthropus) boisei. London.
Tobias, P.V. (1968) New African evidence on human evolution. Wenner-Gren Found. Supper Conf., New York City, April 1968.
Tobias, P.V. (1969) Commentary on new discoveries and interpretations of early African fossil hominids. In Genoves, S. (ed.), *Yearbook of Physical Anthropology 1967*, 24-30.
Tobias, P.V. (1971) *The Brain in Hominid Evolution.* New York/London.
Tobias, P.V. (1972) Progress and problems in the study of early man in sub-Saharan Africa. In Tuttle, R. (ed.), *The Functional and Evolutionary Biology of Primates*, 63-93. Chicago/New York.
Tobias, P.V. (1973a) Darwin's prediction and the African emergence of the genus *Homo.* In *L'Origine dell'Uomo. Atti del Colloquio Internazionale, Roma, Ott. 1971* 182, 63-85.
Tobias, P.V. (1973b) New developments in hominid palaeontology in South and East Africa. *Ann. Rev. Anthrop.* 2, 311-34.
Tobias, P.V. (1973c) Implications of the new age estimates of the early South African hominids. *Nature* 246, 79-83.
Tobias, P.V. (1973d) A new chapter in the history of the Sterkfontein early hominid site. *J. S. Afr. Biol. Soc.* 14, 30-44.
Tobias, P.V. (1974a) The Taung skull revisited. *Nat. Hist.* (New York), 83 (10), 38-43.
Tobias, P.V. (1974b) Recent studies on Sterkfontein and Makapansgat and their bearing on hominid phylogeny in Africa. *S. Afr. Archaeol. Soc.*, Goodwin Ser. No. 2, 5-11.
Tobias, P.V. (1974c) Taxonomy of the Taung skull (Reply to Dr T.R. Olson). *Nature* 252, 85-6.

Tobias, P.V. (1975a) New African evidence on the dating and the phylogeny of the Plio-Pleistocene Hominidae. *Trans. Roy. Soc. New Zealand*, Bull. 13, 289-96.

Tobias, P.V. (1975b) Brain evolution in the Hominoidea. In Tuttle, R.H. (ed.), *Primate Functional Morphology and Evolution*, 353-392. The Hague.

Tobias, P.V. (1975c) Long or short hominid phylogenies? Palaeontological and molecular evidences. In Salzano, F.M. (ed.), *The Role of Natural Selection in Human Evolution*, 89-118. Amsterdam.

Tobias, P.V. and Hughes, A.R. (1969) The new Witwatersrand University excavation at Sterkfontein. *S. Afr. Archaeol. Bull.* 24, 158-69.

Vrba, E.S. (1974) Chronological and ecological implications of the fossil Bovidae at the Sterkfontein australopithecine site. *Nature* 250, 19-23.

Wells, L.H. (1931) Growth changes in the Bushman mandible. *J. Anat.* (Lond.) 66, 50-63.

Wells, L.H. (1962) Pleistocene faunas and the distribution of mammals in Southern Africa. *Ann. Cape Prov. Mus.* II, 37-40.

Wells, L.H. (1967) Antelopes in the Pleistocene of Southern Africa. In Bishop, W.W. and Clark, J.D. (eds.), *Background to Evolution in Africa*, 99-107. Chicago.

Wells, L.H. (1969) Faunal subdivision of the Quaternary in Southern Africa. *S. Afr. archaeol. Bull.* 24, 93-5.

Wilkinson, M.J. (1973) Sterkfontein Cave System: evolution of a Karst form. M.A. dissertation, Dept. of Geography, Univ. of the Witwatersrand, Johannesburg.

Wybergh, W. (1920) The limestone resources of the Union. In *Limestones of Natal, Cape and Orange Free State provinces. Memoir S. Afr. geol. Survey* No. 11.

Young, R.B. (1925) Calcareous tufa deposits of Campbell Rand, from Boetsap to Taungs native reserve. *Trans. Geol. Soc. S. Afr.* 28, 55-67.

F. Clark Howell

Overview of the Pliocene and earlier Pleistocene of the lower Omo basin, southern Ethiopia

For Louis Leakey – colleague, inspiration, and closest friend. This is a measure of what we have sought to do.

Introduction

Since the fortuitous discovery and insightful recognition of *Australopithecus africanus* a half century ago, the African continent has proved to be of primary importance for investigations into hominid origins and the earlier evolution of the Hominidae. The initial twenty-five years thereafter witnessed devoted, episodic, and highly fruitful efforts to obtain further remains of such early Hominidae in the fossil-rich cavern infillings of South Africa. As a consequence of that research, the reality and the apparent complexity of hominid origins was forcefully demonstrated.

In the past fifteen years, after the remarkable discovery in 1959 of *Australopithecus* at Olduvai Gorge, Tanzania, sustained field programmes have been mounted in eastern Africa to seek early Hominidae and to investigate their world in situations in and adjacent to the Rift Valley System. The persistent field researches at Olduvai Gorge have been the catalyst for such interests. Subsequently, small scale explorations were mounted in the Kenya section of the Rift Valley, in the Baringo area and in the Kerio drainage area south of the Rudolf basin. Slightly later, extensive and intensive field programmes were developed in the more northern portions of the Rudolf basin itself.

A major interdisciplinary effort was initiated in 1966 in the northern reaches of the greater Rudolf basin, in the valley of the lower Omo river, in southern Ethiopia. The research has been highly rewarding and has afforded an unexpected and diverse array of data bearing on early Hominidae, their age, and the world of their time. The scope of these researches is briefly set out here.

The lower Omo basin was first visited by European explorers (Count Samuel Teleki von Szék and Ludwig Ritter von Höhnel) in 1888, after their discovery of Lake Rudolf (von Höhnel *et al.*, 1891; von Höhnel, 1938). In 1896 Maurizio Sacchi, geographer with the ill-starred (second) Bottego Expedition (Vannutelli and Citerni, 1897, 1899; cf. Sclater, 1899), was the first to note the existence there of flat-lying, undeformed sediments with freshwater mollusca exposed to the north of the Omo delta. He lost his life in southern Ethiopia the next year, but his collections were subsequently studied and published by de Angelis d'Ossat and Millosevich (1900). These deposits have recently been investigated by the Omo Research Expedition (Butzer, Brown and Thurber, 1969; Butzer and Thurber, 1969) and defined as the Kibish Formation (Butzer, 1975), considered now to be of largely later Pleistocene to Holocene age.

Emil Brumpt, naturalist with the Bourg de Bozas expedition (Bourg de Bozas, 1903, 1906), was the first (in 1902) to recover vertebrate fossils from older, tectonically disturbed deposits underlying these largely horizontal sediments. Their importance for the study of the Cenozoic of sub-Saharan Africa, then practically unknown, was first noted by Haug (1912, p.1727), who recorded the occurrence of silurid fish, crocodilians (two species), chelonians, a hipparionine, rhinoceros, hippopotamus, a suid, various bovids, and deinothere and elephant. Subsequently the remains of the aquatic reptile *Euthecodon* (=*Tomistoma*) *brumpti* (Joleaud, 1920b, 1930; Boulenger, 1920), a deinothere and *Elephas* (Joleaud, 1928), hippopotamus (Joleaud, 1920a), and a hipparionine and *Equus* (Joleaud, 1933) were described from Brumpt's collections, deposited at the Muséum national d'histoire naturelle, Paris.

The first geological reconnaissance and extensive palaeontological prospection of these older fossiliferous deposits was effected by the late Camille Arambourg, between January 30 and March 13, 1933 as part of the activities of the Mission Scientifique de l'Omo (Arambourg and Jeannel, 1933; Jeannel, 1934). Arambourg (1943) subsequently reported on the geological results of this work and on the substantial collection of fossil vertebrates, including fish (9 species), reptiles (6 species), and mammals (29 species) (Arambourg, 1947). These deposits, which Arambourg (1943) considered to extend some 90 kms. up the lower Omo valley, were informally termed 'depôts anciens du Lac Rodolphe' or 'depôts fluviolacustres de la vallée de l'Omo' or simply 'Omo Beds'.

During World War II this area was occupied by Allied military forces from Kenya. Some fossils were collected and sent to the Coryndon Museum in Nairobi, of which the late L.S.B. Leakey was then Honorary Curator. In early 1942 he dispatched his assistant, Heselon Mukiri, to the lower Omo valley where he spent three weeks collecting a substantial number of mammalian fossils (now housed in the National Museums of Kenya, Nairobi). These collections, the precise geological provenance of which are of course unknown, represent a diversity of taxa. Except for some suids, which Leakey (1943) designated a new genus (*Pronotochoerus jacksoni*) and two new species (*Gerontochoerus scotti, Mesochoerus heseloni*), they remain undescribed.

A further reconnaissance of these fossiliferous sediments was made by the author in July-August, 1959, resulting in the recognition of the geological complexity of the deposits and of their vertebrate fauna (Howell, 1968). Subsequently in 1966 the formation of an international Omo Research Expedition was authorized by the Imperial Ethiopian Government. An extensive geological reconnaissance of the area was made by F.H. Brown (1969) in 1966, after which various participants of the expedition have worked annually in the lower Omo basin, during the summer months, since 1967.

Geological setting

The lower Omo basin, like the Rudolf basin to the south, is related to the Turkana depression of the Eastern Rift Valley (Baker, Mohr and Williams, 1972). It appears to represent a northward continuation of the depression into the southwestern margin of the Ethiopian plateau. The Omo basin is considered a tectonic depression (Merla, 1963), down-warped and down-faulted after episodes of planation of the adjacent highlands during the late Mesozoic and Palaeogene. Although the structure of the highly folded and faulted area to the south-west is known (Walsh and Dodson, 1969), that of the lower Omo basin and the highlands to the north-west and to the east remain to be investigated (Butzer, 1970). Projected gravity surveys in the lower Omo valley will help in part to resolve this problem. The Korath volcanics (Nakua), a low range of hills to the north-east of Sanderson's Gulf, are a series of basalt flows and coalescent tuff cones (Brown and Carmichael, 1969). They were extruded in late Pleistocene times along a line of tensional faulting, several fractures of which are recognized to transect the Plio-Pleistocene deposits farther east.

Stratigraphy

The lower Omo basin preserves and exposes the thickest, most continuous fossiliferous record of Pliocene and earlier Pleistocene sedimentation ever discovered in relation to the East African Rift System. The Plio-Pleistocene succession exposed in the lower Omo

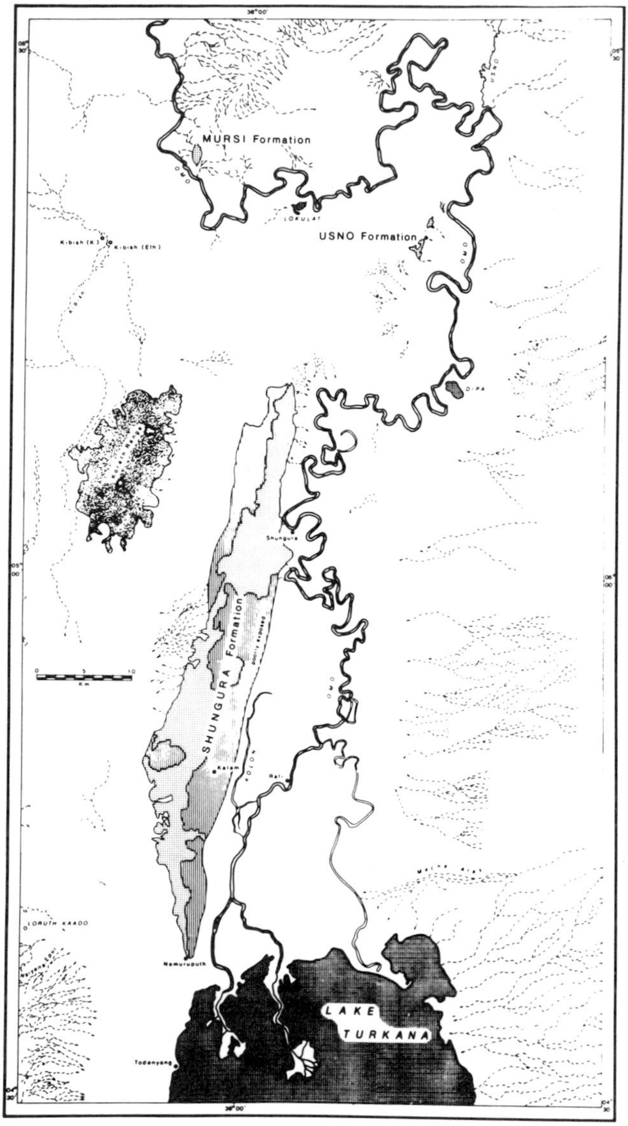

Figure 1. The lower Omo basin, southern Ethiopia, and situation of formations comprising the Omo Group.

basin is now known to have an aggregate measured thickness in excess of one kilometre (actually 1093 metres). The sediments outcrop discontinuously over an area of some 200 km.[2] in four sectors of the basin (Figure 1). These respective exposures have been given formational status, on a geographical basis, and together comprise the Omo Group (de Heinzelin, Brown, and Howell, 1970). All the formations have been surveyed and mapped on aerial photographs (taken for the expedition by Robert Campbell in 1967 and 1970) at a scale of 1:10,000, or smaller. These Omo Group formations can be defined as a set of somewhat consolidated sediments (clays, silts, sands) and pyroclastics (tuffs and, rarely, extrusive lavas), usually tectonically deformed by tilting and subsequent faulting, which discordantly underlie horizontal sediments comprising the Kibish Formation. Their radiometric age (Brown and Lajoie, 1970; Brown, 1972; Brown and Nash, 1976), palaeomagnetic record (Shuey, Brown and Croes, 1974; Brown and Shuey, 1976) and vertebrate fauna (Howell and Coppens, and Coppens and Howell, 1974), indicate a Pliocene and earlier Pleistocene age for their accumulation.

Minerals contained in the Mursi and Usno basalts, and in pumices and tuffs of the Usno and Shungura Formations afford a means of radiometric age determination by potassium argon. Thirty determinations have been made thus far. All are stratigraphically and biostratigraphically consistent and, with two exceptions, all are also consistent with the palaeomagnetostratigraphy established for the Shungura and the Usno Formations (see below). The results indicate that: (a) the Mursi Formation sediments have an age of 4.1 m.y.; (b) that the Nkalabong Formation has an age of 3.95 m.y.; (c) that the Usno Formation has an age of 3.3 m.y. (basalt) to 2.97 m.y. (main tuffs), the principal fossiliferous horizon closely approximating the latter figure; and (d) that the Shungura Formation encompasses a time span of about 2 m.y. (from approximately 3.3 to 1.34 m.y.).

Mursi Formation

This formation crops out south-west of the Nkalabong highlands at the Yellow Sands locality (5°24′N, 35°57′E). The locality was first recognized by C. Arambourg, F.C. Howell and R.E. Leakey in the course of aerial reconnaissance flown by Keith Mousley in late May, 1967. The locality was surveyed by R.E. Leakey in July-August 1967, mapped by John van Couvering in August 1967, and its stratigraphy studied by K.W. Butzer in 1967, 1968, and in July 1969. The latter effort was abruptly terminated by a destructive, but not deadly, helicopter crash (Butzer and Thurber, 1969; Butzer, 1971). The Mursi Formation has a thickness of some 140 metres, comprising four semi-conformable members (Butzer, 1976), the uppermost of which is an extrusive basalt with radiometric age determinations of 4.05 m.y. (Brown and Lajoie, 1970; Brown, 1972) and 4.4-4.1 m.y. (Fitch and Miller, 1976).* Below the basalt occurs a massive palaeosoil, the upper part of which has been altered thermically during the lava's emplacement. A detailed microstratigraphy of the Mursi Formation was made by J. de Heinzelin and P. Haesaerts in August 1973,

* Brown, in 1967, observed poor exposures of tuffs and sediments north of the Nkalabong highland seemingly lacking in vertebrate fossils which underlay or were intercalated with a substantial succession of thin basalt flows. These basalts unconformably overlay an older group of volcanics (F.H. Brown, pers. comm.).

coupled with palaeontological survey conducted by Clark Howell and palaeo-magnetic studies by F.H. Brown and R.W. Shuey. The three principal sedimentary members of the formation recognized by Butzer (1975) have now been further subdivided to produce a total of eight units (J. de Heinzelin and P. Haesaerts, pers. comm.). A vertebrate megafauna of very limited diversity occurs in the sixth sedimentary unit (Member II of K.W. Butzer) below the capping basalt. The third unit from the top has yielded a molluscan assemblage of 10 species which is broadly similar to that (smaller) assemblage from the base of the Usno Formation (Gautier, 1976).

Loruth Kaado Formation

This formation, which at this stage of research hardly merits formal status, outcrops at the northern end of the Laburr massif. The deposits include tuffs, fine sediments and piedmont-derived clastics, and related fine sediments and tuffites. A small molluscan assemblage is taxonomically comparable with that obtained from the Basal Member, Shungura Formation (van Damme and Gautier, 1972; Gautier, 1976) and is suggestive of a quiet water, perhaps small embayment habitat. The occurrence has still to be surveyed and investigated in detail.

Nkalabong Formation

This formation crops out south-west of the Nkalabong highlands a little to the north of the Yellow Sands locality (Mursi Formation). It overlies unconformably the uppermost faulted (basalt) member of that formation. The Nkalabong Formation represents some 90 metres of fluviolacustrine sediments and intercalated tuffaceous deposits comprising three members (Butzer and Thurber, 1969; Butzer, 1976). A lapilli tuff overlying fluviatile sands of Member II afforded a radiometric age of ~ 3.95 m.y. (Fitch and Miller, 1969).

Usno Formation

This formation crops out toward the north-eastern margin of the basin west of the confluence of the (seasonal) Usno stream and the Omo river (5°18′N; 36°12′E). The sediments occur on the upthrust side of a fault with the Omo river meandering a short distance along the downthrown side. Active gullying has taken place along the scarp, and these deposits are visible in a series of shallow exposures or along steep bluffs above the river. There are eight major areas of exposures (Figure 2). The deposits are tilted WNW, with a general strike of N25°E, and a general dip of 10° to 14°WNW.

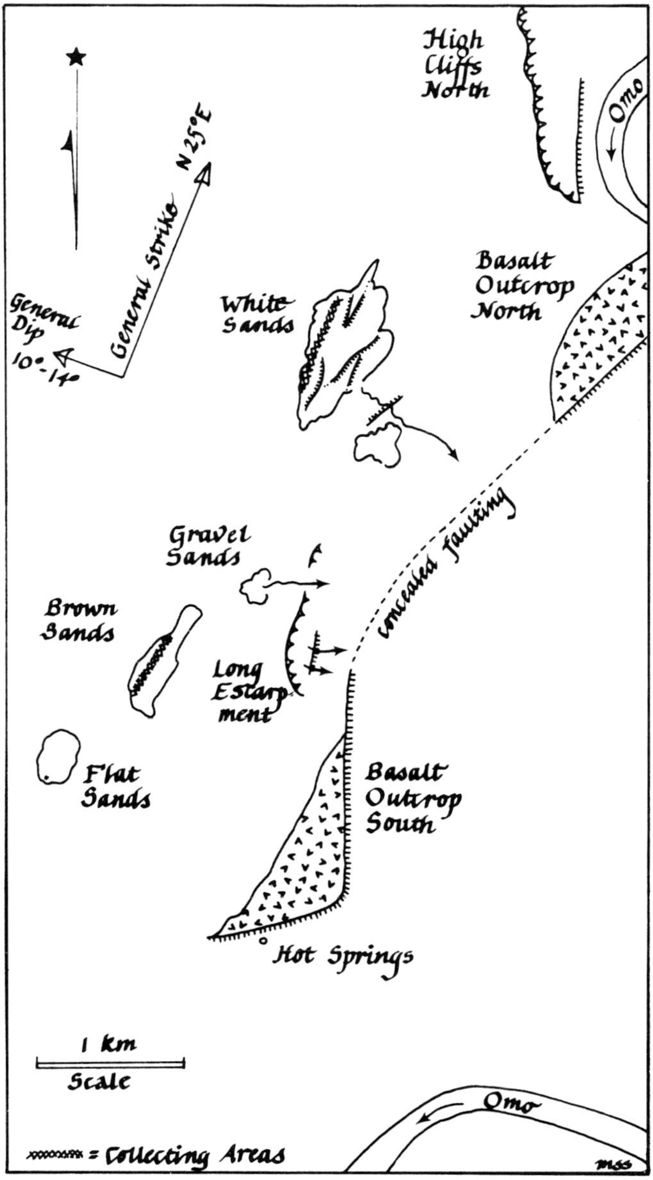

Figure 2. Principal exposures of the Usno Formation.

De Heinzelin and Brown (1969), after the discovery and initial investigation of these localities in 1967, provisionally subdivided the Usno Formation into an informal 9-fold succession. Further study by J. de Heinzelin and P. Haesaerts in 1973 has afforded a detailed micro-stratigraphy and led to a revision of the previous informal subdivision. Over 10 metres of sediments are exposed beneath the basalt which varies in thickness up to 2.5 metres and has afforded a whole rock age of ~3.31 m.y. (Brown and Nash, 1975). The main

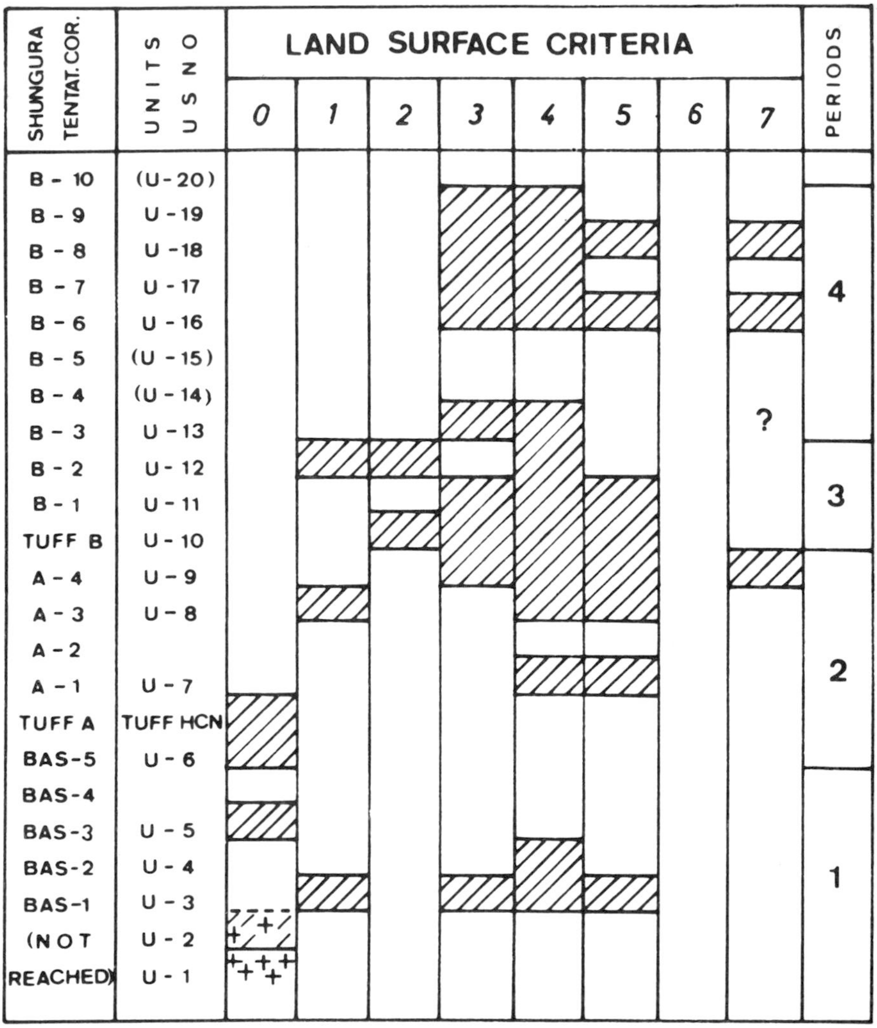

Figure 3. Land surface development for units of the Usno Formation and proposed correlation with the lower members of the Shungura Formation.

sedimentary sequence overlying the basalt has a measured thickness of 172 metres. The basalt and these sediments have been subdivided into 20 units (U-1 to U-20 upwards). Units U-2 to U-6 are exposed at the High Cliffs North locality, units U-6 to U-8 at the Gravel Sands and White Sands localities, units U-9 to U-13 at the Brown Sands and White Sands localities, units 14 and 15 between the Brown Sands and Flat Sands localities, and units U-16 to U-20 at the Flat Sands locality. A tuff in unit U-10 which underlies the main fossiliferous horizon (in unit U-12) at the White Sands and Brown Sands localities has afforded ages of ~2.64 and 2.97 m.y.; the latter is regarded (Brown and Nash, 1976) as the most reliable age. Older fossiliferous horizons occur at the Gravel Sands locality in units U-6 and U-7, and also at the eastern margin of the White Sands locality. The youngest occurrence of vertebrate fossils is in units U-19 and U-20 at the Flat Sands locality.

The age relation of the Usno Formation sediments to the protracted succession represented by the Shungura Formation has been a matter of concern since their discovery. On the basis of the initial radiometric measurements of Usno pyroclastics it was suggested (de Heinzelin, Brown, and Howell, 1970) that the most probable correlation was with lower Member C (the Usno basalt with tuff C and the three part Usno tuff with a subsidiary tuff higher in the sequence in Member C). The recent detailed stratigraphic studies of the Usno Formation have shown this correlation to be unlikely, as has also a more complete understanding of the respective assemblages of fossil vertebrates and the results of palaeomagnetic investigations. The correlation now proposed (Figure 3) is based on detailed comparisons of the sequences of deposits and their characteristics in the Shungura and Usno Formations. The Usno Formation is now regarded as correlative with Shungura Formation Basal Member through unit B-10 of Member B. This interpretation rests primarily on: the position and nature of the molluscan fauna (Gautier, 1976; Van Damme and Gautier, 1972) of the Usno U-3 and Shungura Basal Member-1 shellbeds, indicative of a similar lacustrine environment; the close depositional similarities found between Shungura tuff A and unit A-1, and an Usno tuff (designated High Cliffs North tuff) and unit U-7; the similarity in position of a major and complex pedogenesis in Shungura unit A-4 and Usno unit U-9; the close depositional similarity found between Shungura tuff B and the Usno unit U-10 tuffs; and the comparable relative situation of palaeosoils in Usno units U-16 to U-19 and Shungura units B-6 to B-9. This correlation would thus equate the principal fossiliferous horizons (with Hominidae) of the White Sands and Brown Sands localities of the Usno exposures with the base (unit B-2) of Shungura Formation, Member B. The younger fossil vertebrate assemblage from the Flat Sands locality would equate with that of units B-9 to B-10 of Member B. This interpretation is consistent with vertebrate palaeontological evidence, with available radiometric age determinations, and is now confirmed by palaeomagnetics of Usno Formation sediments.

Shungura Formation

This formation was first suggested as a stratigraphic entity by de Heinzelin and Brown (1969; cf. Butzer and Thurber, 1969) and was formally defined by de Heinzelin, Brown, and Howell (1970). It includes the ancient fluviolacustrine beds from which E. Brumpt, and subsequently C. Arambourg, collected some classic (and type) Omo fossil vertebrates. Its complexity, substantial thickness, and the significance of its tuffs for radiometric dating and for extensive mapping were first demonstrated by Brown (1969). The formation outcrops only on the west side of the Omo river between 5° and 5°10′N and comprises a series of fluvial, deltaic and lacustrine sands, silts, and clays and a set of 12 principal widespread tuffs (labelled A to L) as well as numerous subsidiary intercalated tuffs (de Heinzelin, Haesaerts and Howell, 1976). These deposits are faulted and tilted to the west and are of late Neogene to earlier Pleistocene age. The measured aggregate thickness of the formation (base unknown and top unconformably overlain by Kibish Formation) is nearly 770 metres. The thickness of the principal exposures east of Korath (Nakua) Hills is 670 metres (extending from the Basal Mb. through middle Mb. J-4). The thickness of the exposures south of Korath Hills and west of Kalam police post (from upper Mb. C to an uppermost shellbed of Mb. L) is 387 metres. The differences in thickness are presumably related to differential subsidence (see below).

This sequence of deposits has been subdivided into a number of members through the (convenient) occurrence of a series of widespread, usually readily distinguishable volcanic ash horizons (designated A to L upwards) (de Heinzelin, 1971). Each member (except the Basal Mb.) is represented by a major or principal tuff and its *overlying* sediments (de Heinzelin, 1971; de Heinzelin *et al.*, 1970).* These marker horizons at the base of the principal volcanic tuffs are true chronohorizons and are essentially isochronous over the whole lower Omo basin. (Essentially the same interpretation and procedure was followed by R.L. Hay at Olduvai Gorge and has been utilized by Ian Findlater in East Rudolf).

There is no single, simple east-to-west type section, due to tectonic disturbance. However, exposures of ca. half a kilometre in width, and extending west from the vicinity of Shungura village (on the river) toward the Korath hills, include all members through Mb. J. Members C upwards, including extensive outcrops of Mbs. G through L, crop out south of the Korath hills, and west of Kalam police post, where the type sections of Members K and L have been drawn. Mapping in 1972 and 1973 clearly demonstrated the interrelationships of these sets of sediments in the two major areas of exposure of the Shungura Fm. and permitted their correlation.

A particular lithologic sequence occurs repeatedly through much of the Shungura Formation. The sequence consists of silt and clay overlain successively by coarse sand, medium sand, fine sand, silt and clay. In general the sands are yellowish grey to light brown, poorly

* This procedure (cf. Bonnefille *et al.*, 1973), adopted for ease of mapping since tuffs could be readily mapped from the prominent morphology of the tuff cuestas, replaced an initial informal terminology, that of a 'series' of sedimentary units *below* a capping tuff (Arambourg, Chavaillon, Coppens, 1967, 1969). Any initial designation of 'series' is thus placed into this formal terminology by a lower letter designation (thus Mb. G = 'series' H; Mb. F = 'series' G, etc.).

cemented, cross-bedded, and composed of fragments of quartz, feldspar, lithic fragments and bits of chalcedony. The clayey silts are brown to reddish brown and may contain gypsum or halite. There are also many minor tuffs in the succession, aside from the major tuffs which define the members. These minor tuffs occur only discontinuously along strike, but their position within a member is constant. All tuffs are composed predominately of volcanic glass and have only a small admixture of foreign fragments. In general the major tuffs are less contaminated than the minor tuffs. Pebbles and cobbles of pumice occur in many of the tuffs, but most of the material is of sand and silt size.

These repetitive sequences of coarser to finer sediments are basically similar, but may vary in thickness and competeness. They are termed cyclic units and evidently represent sheets of meandering stream deposits (Allen, 1965a, 1970). They are defined as formal units in the type sections of members and are numbered successively upward (B-1, B-2, etc.) above the relevant tuff (tuff B, etc.); the exception is the Basal Member which comprises these sediments *below* tuff A. They may be traced over kilometres, although surficial cover or faulting may effect disjunction between outcrops. Correlation between more distant outcrops have been effected through the enumeration of cycles between known marker horizons (customarily the major tuffs A-L), and through the recognition of similar or identical sequences of deposits. The principle is of course well established and in numerous instances has led to the recognition of reliable chronosequences. These have led to the definition of local chronozones (see Hedberg, 1971, pp. 21-2), as the greater the complexity of events the more diagnostic is the resultant fit. The units of the Shungura Formation can be considered chronozones, although they are somewhat diachronous, given their formation by the lateral displacement of a meander belt. Thus in a strict sense they represent para-chronostratigraphic units.

The general outlines of the lower Omo basin were apparently delineated prior to the accumulation of Omo Group sediments (Butzer, 1970; Butzer and Thurber, 1969). The Mursi Formation sediments are similar to those of the Shungura Formation and represent deposits of an ancestral Omo river and Lake Rudolf. The river bed and the lake shore (as is seen in the Ileret and Koobi Fora areas of East Rudolf) probably shifted substantially through time. The basic geographical features of the lower Omo basin are thought to have been essentially as they are now, except that the Korath Range was probably absent, and there is the possibility that the adjacent highlands had a different elevation. Certainly there was a large river flowing over a broad plain from north to south, though its ancient course is not certainly known, and emptying into a lake. There is the possibility that the river's course was more direct and lacked the extensive easterly deviation past the Nkalabong highlands

(F.H. Brown, pers. comm.). At any rate this was the general palaeogeographic setting.

The principal characteristics of the members of the Shungura Formation are summarized in Table 1 (after de Heinzelin, Haesaerts and Howell, 1976). These include their thicknesses, number of units and subunits, number of major and minor tuffs, number of structured palaeosoils, number of vertebrate fossiliferous horizons, and invertebrate fossil occurrences.

Table 1. Principal characteristics of members of the Shungura Formation

Shungura Formation Members	Thickness in Meters	Number of Units	Number of Sub-units	Major and Minor Tuffs	Structured Paleosoils	Vertebrate Fossil Horizons	Molluscan Associations	*Etheria* Beds	Ostracod Beds
Mb. L	>48,60	9	15	6	5	4	4	1	4
Tuff L	0,40	1	1	1	—	—	—	—	—
Mb. K	26,40	4	>5	6	2	1	—	—	—
Tuff K	3,60	1	2	2	—	—	—	—	—
Mb. J	43,00	7	12	10	2	5	2	—	—
Tuff J	6,60	1	1	1	—	—	—	—	—
Mb. H	48,00	7	7	5	—	7	3	1	—
Tuff H	10,00	1	1	1	—	—	—	—	—
Upp. Mb. G	97,60	16	20	4	—	27	2	—	3
Low. Mb. G	112,60	13	28	11	2	16	—	3	—
Tuff G	6,00	1	2	1	—	—	—	—	—
Mb. F	35,50	5	9	2	—	5	—	—	—
Tuff F	7,20	1	4	1	—	3	—	—	—
Mb. E	35,00	5	13	5	1	6	—	2	—
Tuff E	2,00	1	2	1	—	1	—	—	—
Mb. D	37,00	5	11	5	1	5	—	—	—
Tuff D	4,00	1	2	2	—	1	—	—	—
Mb. C	78,00	9	32	12	3	12	1	4	—
Tuff C	1,80	1	3	2	—	1	—	—	—
Mb. B	84,40	12	44	13	8	16	1	2	—
Tuff B	13,00	1	4	4	—	2	—	—	—
Mb. A	31,60	4	10	5	2	2	—	—	—
Tuff A	3,20	1	1	1	—	—	—	—	—
Basal Mb.	>32,00	5	10	3	—	5	1	—	—
Total	>767,50	112	>239	104	26	119	14	13	7

The Shungura Formation represents three episodes of lacustrine incursions into the basin during an otherwise protracted period of largely fluviatile (floodplain and delta plain) environments. Brief lacustrine depositional situations are recorded at the very base (lowest Basal Member) and the top (uppermost Member L) of the sequence. Lagoonal estuarine prodeltaic followed by shallow, fully lacustrine

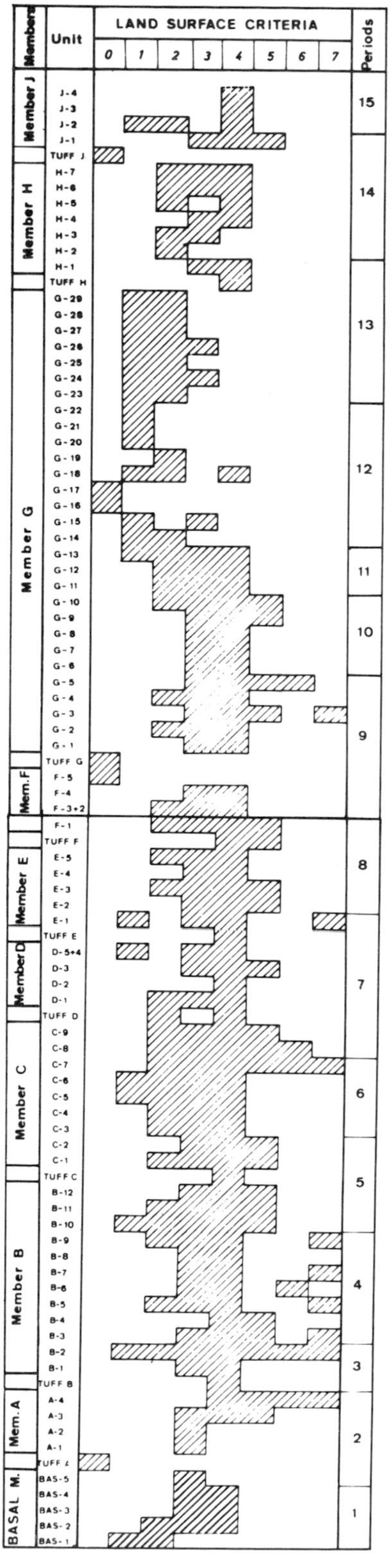

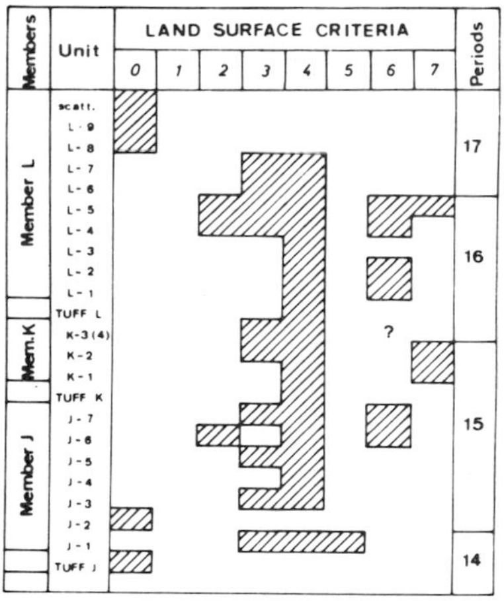

Figure 4. Land surface development and depositional periods of the Shungura Formation. 0 = sedimentary features only; 1 = sesquioxide sheets, siderite concretions and septaria indicative of shallow water and ground water registering Ph changes; 2 = desiccation cracks; 3 = mulching in silts, or slickensides in clays and silty-clays; 4 = rootcasts, indicating substantial traces of rootlets or rhizomes; 5 = incipient reduced soil, with or without calcic concretions and mottling; 6 = incipient oxidized soil, with colour or a brittle horizon, and polyhedral fracture; 9 = developed soil with structure, peds, and with or without coatings.

depositional situations predominated during the accumulation of the middle third of Member G.

The detailed nature of palaeoenvironmental situations associated with these principal depositional regimes has been elucidated through the recognition, mapping, and analysis of the components of fluvial sedimentary cycles in type sections and along strike, and through study of the varied expressions of land surfaces and attendant weathering horizons.

The members and units of the formation and their respective land surface criteria are summarized in Figure 4. From this diagram the sequence can be divided into successive sedimentary periods, of which 17 have been distinguished (de Heinzelin, Haesaerts and Howell, 1976). In this respect the main tuffs, which form the basis for the stratigraphic subdivision of the sequence are extraneous and incidental, as are too the numerous minor tuffs which are incorporated in almost every unit.

Geomagnetic polarity measurements

Continental sediments and lavas, as well as marine sediments, are now well-known to register the orientation of the earth's magnetic field at the time of their deposition. The unusually thick, essentially continuous record of deposition represented in the Omo formations affords a unique opportunity to examine the sequence of polarity changes over a period of several million years. This record can then be compared with the well-defined epochs and events of the known Magnetic Polarity Time Scale.

The Shungura Formation affords a long, very complete, and also complex magnetostratigraphy for the Matuyama Epoch and the preceding Gauss Normal Epoch (Shuey, Brown and Croes, 1974; Brown and Shuey, 1976). At present this is the most complete continental record of polarity changes known (Figure 5) and is comparable to that recorded in sediments from deep sea cores. The results are in large part concordant with the results of K/Ar age measurements (except those on tuff B toward the base of the sequence). Of particular interest is the complexity of normal events in the earlier part of the Matuyama Reversed Epoch (Brown and Shuey, 1974) which has been suspected from analysis of remnant magnetism of lavas and deep sea cores, but has been difficult to document fully due to range of error in K/Ar dating, the incompleteness of lava successions, and the usually slow sedimentation rate in marine basins. The sequence records essentially all of the Matuyama Reversed Epoch, including the Jaramillo, Gilsa/Olduvai, and three earlier normal events, and essentially all of the preceding Gauss Normal Epoch, with the Kaena and Mammoth Reversed Events, and the later portion of the earlier Gilbert Reversed Epoch.

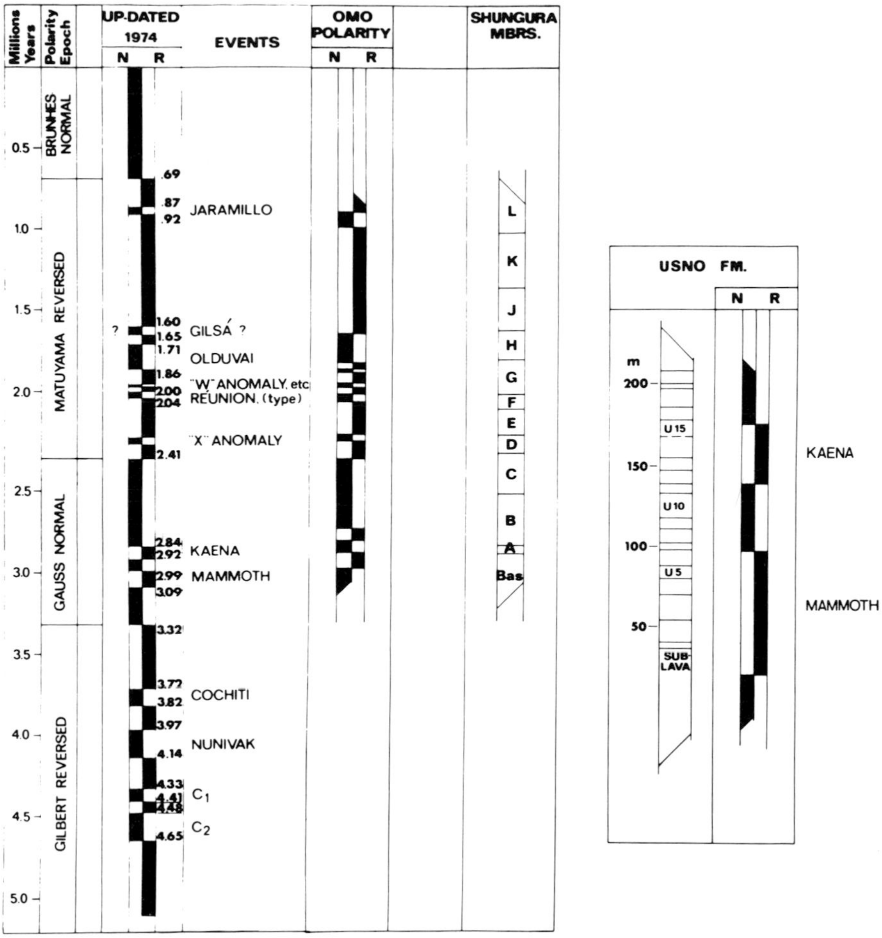

Figure 5. Magnetostratigraphy of the Shungura and Usno Formations.

The Usno Formation documents three normal intervals and two intervening reversed intervals. On the basis of comparative stratigraphy, biostratigraphy (vertebrate and invertebrate), and radiometric age determinations the sequence can be demonstrated to equate closely with the earliest of the Shungura Formation and to encompass the Gauss Normal Epoch with the Kaena and Mammoth Reversed Events (Brown and Shuey, 1975).

Depositional environments and taphocoenoses

The sediments of Omo Group formations largely reflect lacustrine and fluviatile depositional environments. Lacustrine environments are less commonly represented. They occur essentially at the beginning of the Omo succession, prior to and subsequent to ~4 m.y. ago, and toward and at the end of the succession, ~1.85 m.y. ago and ~1.6 to 1.4 m.y. ago.

The Mursi Formation reflects deltaic and fluvio-littoral deposition prior to 4.1 m.y. ago (Butzer, 1976). The depositional environment was initially lacustrine prodeltaic and offshore with shellbeds and mudflats; subsequently there was deposition in a delta distributary channel (with rolled macrovertebrate fossils), ultimately abandoned and filled with vitric tuff; delta fringe conditions and desiccation of closed basins ensued, followed by a return to lacustrine prodeltaic and offshore environments with shellbeds and mudcracks, and evidence of drowned trees persisting until the return of distributary channel conditions. The end of the sedimentary sequence is truncated by the development of a massive structured palaeosoil after which there were basalt extrusions.

The Mursi Formation affords not only the oldest, but one of the few major vertebrate fossil assemblages from a marginal lacustrine distributary channel situation. This assemblage is distinctive in that only a relatively few larger species are represented, often by postcranial parts. Three proboscideans are present, a gomphothere (*Anancus*) being very rare; hippo is not uncommon; rhino is infrequent; two bovid genera (*Aepyceros* and *Tragelaphus*) are quite frequent; a single suid (*Nyanzachoerus*) is common.

The upper member (III) of the Nkalabong Formation again reflects the recurrence of shallow littoral lacustrine conditions about 3.9 m.y. ago in association with ash falls from explosive volcanism. Butzer (1976) considers the Liwan beds, exposed at the eastern edge of Lokomarinyang along the western margin of the basin, to represent a pene-contemporaneous occurrence indicative of lacustrine conditions over most of the lower Omo basin. Vertebrate fossils are unknown in the Nkalabong Formation and, so far as hasty reconnaissance revealed, in the Liwan beds as well.

Lacustrine conditions are subsequently evidenced in the lower-most unit of the Basal Member of the Shungura Formation. Fragmentary vertebrate fossils, representing but a few identifiable taxa, and mollusca are recorded from the very restricted exposures of this sedimentary unit. These sediments show normal remnant magnetization and are considered to represent the base of the Gauss Normal Epoch, about 3.3 m.y. ago (Shuey, Brown, and Croes, 1974). It is possible that the decalcified and cemented shellbed overlying the Usno Formation basalt also reflects shallow lacustrine conditions, perhaps of short duration, at a comparable time.

Lacustrine sedimentation under delta fringe and prodeltaic conditions is again reflected in the middle third (units G-14 to G-22, or period 12 in Figure 5) of Member G of the Shungura Formation. These shallow lacustrine deposits encompass a short pre-Olduvai Normal Event (still unnamed) and the initial part of the Olduvai Normal Event (Shuey, Brown and Croes, 1974). The sediments are largely silts and clays, finely laminated and often gypsiferous. Abundant limonitic and calcareous septaria and ostracod-bearing sands are present. Some coarser sediments intercalated with these clays and silts could have been deposited as river mouth bars and in delta distributary channels. Silicified wood is often abundant in these deposits, and fish remains and Crocodilia are commonly found, the former often in a well-preserved state. Remains of higher vertebrates, particularly mammals, are uncommon to rare, and then almost always in fragmentary condition (as in units G-16, G-20 and G-21). However, in the transitional fluvio-lacustrine sands, interbedded with silts, at the base (unit G-13) of this sequence a number of localities afford substantial concentrations of a diversity of vertebrate taxa. These occurrences may sometimes include associated and partially complete individual skeletons in circumstances considered to be transitional deltaic sediments. One hominid occurrence (Omo 75) is known.

In upper Member H (H-2 to J-1) transitional lacustrine to prodeltaic conditions are recorded, usually with poor vertebrate fossil associations. In upper Member L at the end of the Shungura succession near shore lacustrine situations (with shellbeds) are evidenced, again with very sparse occurrences of vertebrates.

With these exceptions most of the Plio-Pleistocene sedimentation and related fossil occurrences in the lower Omo basin reflect alluvial landscapes. Fluviatile settings predominate in the lower portions (Members I, II) of the Nkalabong Formation (Butzer, 1976), in the Usno Formation, and essentially all of the Shungura Formation (through lower Member G). There are, however, important differences and variations within this general setting.

The Usno Formation comprises 19 sedimentary units above the extrusive basalt (unit U-1). After the brief episode of shallow lacustrine conditions (unit U-3-1) the succession reveals a prolonged period of fluviatile and fluvio-deltaic sedimentation, including marsh and swamp situations comparable in many respects to that recorded in the lower three members of the Shungura Formation (Figure 4). Significant vitric tuff accumulations occur at three horizons in the succession (units U-6; U-10 and U-11); they are the counterparts of Shungura Formation tuffs A and B. Subsidiary tuffs associated with other fine sediments occur higher in the succession (units U-12, U-17 and U-20) and these, at least in part (like U-20), have their equivalents also in the Shungura Formation (eg., the B-10-1 tuff). The successive accumulations of coarse clastic products, which generally incorporate vertebrate fossils at four localities, all reflect to a greater or a lesser extent the proximity of piedmont alluvial fans, drained by the Usno and related streams, along the eastern margin of the basin and affording quantities of basement complex detritus.

The Gravel Sands, Brown Sands/White Sands, and Flat Sands deposits represent three successively younger concentrations of vertebrate fossils in the Usno Formation. Gravel Sands (in U-6 and U-7), which equates with the upper part of the Basal Member, Shungura Formation, is not particularly fossiliferous and only a dozen identifiable specimens have been collected there (mostly bovid, a few hippo, *Giraffa*, cercopithecoids, and *Protopterus*). Flat Sands, the youngest occurence (in U-19 and U-20) which equates with the upper part (probably about unit B-9) of Member B, Shungura Formation, is substantially more productive of vertebrates from fluviatile sands interbedded with floodplain silts and with clays. Over 50 identifiable specimens have been collected, about half bovid and hippo, some cercopithecoids and suids, and a few proboscideans, including deinothere and an hipparionine.

By comparison the Brown Sands and White Sands occurrences are extremely productive of vertebrates, yielding in excess of 1500 identifiable specimens (Howell, Fichter and Eck, 1969). White Sands has yielded the largest assemblage. At these sites two subunits of unit U-12, a light gravel and medium sands, and an underlying gravelly sand, are interbedded with clay silts, a laminated tuff, and stratified sands with silt and clay lenses. In some instances the finer sands and silts yield more complete specimens and even associated skeletal elements of individuals may occur (eg. bovids, suids, elephant, cercopithecoids). In the coarser sediments at both localities specimens are usually disarticulated, incomplete or fragmentary. Both localities have yielded a substantial diversity of vertebrate taxa including fish, aquatic and other reptiles and nearly fifty species of mammals, including Hominidae.

Most members of the Shungura Formation represent deposits of a large meandering river system. Its sinuosity was undoubtedly substantial, perhaps even on the order of some meander belts of the present lower Omo river. However, the details of the ancient hydrographic system have still to be elucidated. In many respects the present lower Omo river can serve as an appropriate model for much of the Plio-Pleistocene situation in the lower Omo basin.

The fining-upwards sedimentary cycles (Allen, 1965b, 1970) characteristic of the Shungura Formation merit consideration. The basal coarse sands are moderately sorted, frequently cross-bedded, composed predominantly of quartz, feldspar and fragments of chalcedony and chert. The measured attitudes of cross-beds generally indicates north-to-south-flowing currents. Reefs of the river oyster *Etheria* suggest a stable bed with a persistent supply of fresh, flowing water, as these molluscs require such a habitat. Such conditions only obtain in a fluvial situation along the river channel below the usual water mark. The coarse sands at the base of these units are thus thought to represent fairly well sorted, coarse sediments accumulated at or near the bottom of the channel and on the point bars of meander bends.

The overlying medium and fine sands are similar mineralogically, have similar bedding features, and are moderately sorted. They may contain silt interbeds. They could represent the higher levels of point bar deposits formed by hydraulic sorting. They might also be the consequence of rises in lake level leading to coarse sand and pebble gravel deposition upstream and finer sands in their former place.

The finer silts and clays presumably represent levee and over-bank deposits on the river floodplain. The clays are in places reduced and show rootcasts and calcareous concretions suggestive of situations with standing water in river edge flood basins.

Palaeosoils are recognizable at the tops of many clayey silt beds. Soil development is generally weak and the grade of oxidation moderate. Reduced clays, with rootcasts and calcareous concretions, have been interpreted as swamp soils. The porous tops of tuffs sometimes contain concretions and abundant rootcasts, even mammalian remains, and weak soil profiles are developed.

Most sediments are shallow-water deposits, and as they comprise over 700 metres of section, the area of deposition must have been subsiding. In this situation the river could migrate back and forth across its flood-plain and fail to remove completely deposits accumulated previously. Truncated cyclic units are known in many instances, and well-preserved channels are evident (tuff F shows several such instances, with channels infilled with fine pebble gravel and coarse sands overlain by medium to fine sand, the distinctive tuff lithology making the channel relations particularly apparent).

Extensive channelling occurred during two main intervals in this fluviatile succession. Three major episodes of cut-and-fill in upper Member B attended the accumulation of unit B-10 which attains a cumulative thickness nearly double (about 40 metres) that of its actual thickness (20 metres). Subsequently, the sediments of Member D were largely accumulated in a series of substantial channels with dissections of several metres.

The meandering river situation was in part replaced by braided stream situations on at least two occasions. This occurred during the deposition of Member F (unit F-1) and early in Member G times (units G-3 to G-5). During these intervals channels were diverted and rejoined around intervening channel islands or braid bars. The riverine flood-plain was less continuous and permanent than previously and channel banks were shallower and broader. There were doubtless attendant transformations in distribution and structure of the fringing riverine forest, in the vegetation of the floodplain(s), and in the nature and diversification of microhabitats and ecotones in those portions of the basin. Such transformations may be reflected in the palynological record, and in the micromammal record as well.

A substantial diversity of depositional environments is represented within such a riverine system (Leopold, Wolman, and Miller, 1964; Allen, 1965a) – channels with point bars enclosed between meander loops; flood-plains and their abandoned and weathered terraces; levees with crevasses and crevasse splays; alluvial ridges with abandoned channels and meander loops, and associated ox-bow lakes, backswamps, marshes and mudflats; and floodbasins with variably expressed dry, poorly vegetated, or more permanently watered situations with denser, more established vegetation patterns. Microstratigraphic studies at the unit and intraunit level in members of the Shungura Formation reveal the varied microsedimentary situations with which the abundant Omo vertebrate assemblages are associated. They afford the requisite data for taphonomical studies, both for surface occurrences and for a series of excavated situations (Johanson, Boaz and Splingaer, 1976).

Some of these varied fossil occurrences include (de Heinzelin, Haesaerts and Howell, 1976) –

(a) those on or in palaeosoils, incorporated in calcic concretions which have afforded protection from cracking and dissolution (with various land mammals, including cercopithecoids and hominids);
(b) those in porous tops of major tuffs (particularly D, E, F and G) (with land mammals, including cercopithecoids and hominids);
(c) those on reduced horizons constituting ancient swamp soils (with land mammals, including cercopithecoids, hominids and artifact occurrences, as well as hippopotamus, aquatic reptiles and fish);
(d) those in transitional sand/silt situations attendant upon flood-plain construction and evidently constituting accumulations in small ponds or other ephemeral water bodies (usually rich and varied land mammal assemblages, often exceptionally well-preserved *in situ*, but extremely friable and quickly dispersed and destroyed upon surface exposure);
(e) those derived by reworking from palaeosoils and gentle washouts, including erosion of shallow embankments and levees (abundant concentrations of smaller skeletal parts, and including micromammals – particularly lowermost and upper Member B and in upper Member C); in other situations incipient floodplains have been alluviated and buried under sheets of fluviatile sands from divergent channels resulting in extensive overall dispersal of coarse elements (fossils) and small derived clastics (particularly the case for a number of artifactual occurrences in lower Member F);
(f) those in small pebble gravels where sorting has produced extensive vertebrate tooth and fragmentary bone concentrations (rich examples, with a great diversity of vertebrates, including some hominids, are known in upper Member B and lower Member G);

(g) those in erosional channels, in cross-bedded sands, and sometimes even in coarse gravels (with concentrated, mixed faunal assemblages, including some autochthonous aquatic reptiles and allochthonous skeletal parts of both small and large land vertebrates);

(h) those in tuff-choked erosional channels, as in the tuff facies D′, E′, F′, and G′ (extraordinarily dense, rich and diverse vertebrate assemblages, including usually teeth of Hominidae, associated usually with baked clay pebbles and pumices – two large excavations in lower F′ expose such situations).

The repeated inflow into the lower Omo basin of vast quantities of volcanic ashes was surely of significance for the sedimentary regime of this ancient river system. Over a hundred intercalations of volcanic ashes have been identified in the Shungura Formation, suggesting an accumulation rate of 20,000 years per tuff (according to the radiometric and magnetostratigraphic scales) or 1 tuff per 7.5 metres of sediment. These tuffs represent episodic, but repetitive and immediate, introductions of foreign pyroclastic products into the sedimentary regime throughout the lithologic sequence. Except for their lateral continuity there are no significant differences between the major tuffs (A to L) and the minor tuffs. The tuffs are composed almost exclusively of volcanic glass shards; the shards are fresh and angular, often with small glass bubbles or elongate vesicles. In some instances (e.g. upper Member B and middle Member D) fresh, angular sanidines may occur. The petrography and composition of the tuffs (as indicated by heavy minerals, trace elements, and refractive indices) demonstrate that they are peralkaline rhyolites of pantelleritic type. They have a high silica content – nearly 70% quartz and anorthoclase phenocrysts, and aenigmatite, sodic hedenbergite, and artvedsonitic sodic amphibole heavy minerals (in pumices). Some tuffs contain cinders or pumices, sometimes in remarkable quantity and of large size (up to 60-70 cms. diameter in the case of tuff D), and they also show vesiculation (Brown, 1972; Brown and Nash, 1976).

The source of these volcanic products is still uncertain. No appropriate nearby source is known, and all the known sources within the Rudolf basin have a different chemical composition. Brown (1972) concluded that: 'The source of the pyroclastic material is unknown, but probably lies on the eastern side of the Omo basin along the divide between it and the Ethiopian Rift Valley, or along the western edge of the rift valley itself.' A source in the middle reaches of the Omo drainage basin, and possibly Mt. Damota (near Soddu, Sidamo province), some 275 kilometres distant, and the rocks of which are silica rich and peralkaline, now appears likely (Brown and Nash, 1976). Pantelleritic ignimbrites do occur extensively, covering an area of some 150 thousand square kilometres, over much of western and southern Ethiopia, including the upper Omo basin (Mohr, 1968).

These ignimbrites have an (inferred) late Tertiary age and hence would fall, at least in part, within the time span of the Omo Group formations.

The difficulty of identifying the precise source could well be the consequence of the type of eruption. It could indicate either that there was no cone formation, that there was subsequent caldera collapse consequent upon emptying of the magma reservoir, or that the sources were fissures. The former would suggest Plinian eruptions which were repetitive, paroxysmal and productive of glowing avalanches (nuées ardentes) and great volumes of pumice and ash, lifted high in the air through violent explosions, blown and drifted substantial distances, subsequently to blanket large areas. However, remnants should be preserved of collapse craters and calderas from such a source. Conceivably a series of fissures, situated along lines of fracture(s) related to rift tectonics, could have provided sources. In such a situation the attendant cinder and ash cones could have been largely destroyed because of their substantial age and their setting in an erosive, highland situation. However, ring structures, and traces of associated, once more extensive lava flows should be preserved.

The agencies responsible for the deposition of the tuffs within the lower Omo basin are still inadequately understood. It is more than likely that several different depositional processes are responsible for their accumulation.

It has been suggested that several occurrences most reasonably represent primary ashfalls over littoral-foreshore or shallow lacustrine situations. Butzer (1976; also Butzer and Thurber, 1969) suggests this is the case for a laminated tuff (his IIf) for the (middle) Mursi Formation and those tuffs of the upper Member (III) of the Nkalabong Formation. In the Shungura Formation tuff A, as well as several minor tuffs, are laminated and diatomitic, while major tuffs H, J and K-*a* and minor tuffs present in (upper) Member G, and in Members K and L, are more massively stratified. All are regarded as primary ashfalls (de Heinzelin, Haesaerts and Howell, 1976).

Many tuffs are medium-to coarse-grained, and have large current cross-beds or climbing ripple marks indicative of rapid deposition by fluviatile agencies. Moreover, the large pebbles, cobbles and even boulders of pumice (present in tuffs D, E, F, G, G-3, J, 14, and L), and large lumps of baked red argillite (in tuffs B-*a*, D-3, E, E-3, F, and G-3) are generally too large to have been wind-transported, and are derived from a quite distant volcanic source. The purity of the tuffs may simply be a consequence of the dilution of the normal sediment load by vast quantities of ash, or partly as a consequence of the hydraulic characteristics of glass fragments, since glass is less dense than the sediments normally carried by the river and this would lead to hydraulic sorting.

If these tuffs originated as glowing cloud (nuée ardente) eruptions they could represent ash flows or ignimbrites (Smith, 1960; Ross and

Smith, 1961) or ground surge pyroclastic deposits (Sparks and Walker, 1973). The flowage of such a fluidized mass varies according to its relative density, and the ratio of gas to pyroclastic fragments. It is well-known that several cubic miles of pumice and ash may be erupted over a period of only a few days (as in the Valley of Ten Thousand Smokes in Alaska, as described by Curtis, 1968), so that catchment areas and their drainage systems would be glutted with these eruptive products.

Fluviatile transport of such eruptive products is a likely depositional agency in many instances. However, in others there is certain evidence to suggest the possible activity of pyroclastic flows or of ground surges, as the features are unfamiliar in fluviatile situations. These features include: the simultaneous deposition of tuff in a variety of situations, including abandoned meanders, backswamp clays, landsurfaces, as well as inactive channels; – the extensive lateral continuity of tuffs, traceable over several tens of kilometres in some instances, although lateral changes from pure ash to pisolitic tuff to stratified tuffite in channels is demonstrable; – the sharp, generally non-erosional nature (except in active channel situations) of the basal contact of many tuffs, and in the case of directly underlying fine sediments, their distinctive physical modification (evidenced in induration, texture, and breakage); – the occurrence of dense rootcast networks, calcareous rhizome mats, and even of biogenic features; – and some indications, in the case of Member C, of seemingly unrolled lava cobbles and scoriae. This would seem to suggest that in the case of certain major tuffs, and particularly D, E, F, G, K(*a*) and L, that emplacement occurred through agencies that were not merely fluviatile in nature.

Investigation of these volcanic products, and their source area, is obviously of importance not only because of their usefulness as stratigraphic marker horizons, their suitability for radiometric age determination, and their rapid emplacement and significance as isochronous surfaces. The catastrophic intensity and protracted activity of the volcanic source(s) produced a series of temporally delimited palaeoenvironmental disturbances. These doubtless had their effects on the nature and distribution of habitats in and about the basin. The attendant effects on natural communities may well have been substantial and of considerable palaeoecological importance, with attendant implication for hominid adjustments over this protracted interval of time.

Palynology and vegetational history

The Omo succession is almost unique* in sub-Saharan Africa in

* Samples of early Pleistocene age at Olduvai Gorge and East Rudolf now demonstrate that, with appropriate palynological techniques, microfloral assemblages will be recovered there as well (R. Bonnefille, pers. comm.).

preserving both macrofloral and microfloral fossils essential to the reconstruction of Pliocene plant communities. There is every expectation that the vegetational history of the basin, and relationships with the adjacent highlands, can ultimately be determined for a time span of some 3 m.y. from silicified wood, seeds and pollen. Such a vegetational history would be the first such sequence ever established in Africa, or the whole of the Old World tropics for that matter, and is unique as well in its association with extensive fossil vertebrate assemblages and early Hominidae.

Pollen samples processed from four members of the Shungura Formation provide indications of the nature and diversity of plant associations and of their transformations over a period of about a million years (3-2 m.y. ago) (Bonnefille, 1972; also 1970). They have been compared with the current local atmospheric pollen rain and the pollen content of riverine sediments, as well as with the composition and diversity of plant communities in the basin and the adjacent highlands. The principal associations are those of bush, wooded grassland, riverine and montane forests. The montane forest elements, currently restricted to higher elevations (above 2300-2500 metres), are evidently allochthonous.

The available evidence indicates that montane forest was present in the adjacent highlands and that the lower Omo basin supported substantial wooded savannah as well as riverine forest communities during this million year interval. All spectra contain relatively higher percentages of montane (allochthonous) elements than do present Omo sediments.

There is evidence for changes in the nature, composition and extent of plant communities between the lower (2.4 to 3 m.y.) and the middle (2 m.y.) portions of the Shungura succession (Bonnefille, 1976). A more humid montane forest was replaced by associations of more drought-resistant trees. Overall, the representation of arboreal species show increased percentages of taxa with reduced water requirements. There is also a marked overall decrease (by some 50%) of arboreal taxa. There is an accompanying increase in non-arboreal pollen, although the consistent representation of nearly 50% grasses indicates well-developed savannah conditions throughout the sequence. A change in the composition of grasses, especially those of Andropogonaeae, demonstrates, however, that the savannah came to assume a different structure and aspect. This is also confirmed by the presence of certain herbaceous species. A marked decrease in *Typha* and Cyperaceae also denotes reduction in the amount and distribution of local water sources and bodies in the course of this interval. These changes apparently reflect decreased rainfall.

Over 40 species of woody plants have been identified (R. Dechamps, 1976, pers. comm.), taxa scarcely represented in the Omo now, and often unknown in pollen spectra. Dechamps' findings document the mosaic nature of the vegetation, the presence of open forests, wooded savanna and gallery forest between 4 and 2.5 m.y., and progressively more open associations between 2 and 1 m.y.

These transformations in plant communities, their composition and distribution, are being investigated further, particularly with regard to earlier and later portions of the Omo succession. The results to date are in accord with the sedimentary and microfaunal evidence. They are profoundly important for the full-scale interpretation of palaeo-environments.

Palaeontology and faunal history

The Omo succession affords rich and diverse assemblages of invertebrate and vertebrate fossils which document the history of life in this portion of the Rift Valley System between ~4.5 and 1.0 m.y. ago. This essentially continuous record of deposition, fossiliferous throughout, for Pliocene and early Pleistocene times, is exceptional for eastern Africa. As a consequence of many radiometric age determinations and an extended palaeomagnetic stratigraphy it now constitutes the basis of comparison for this time range for other known fossiliferous situations in eastern Africa.

Invertebrates

Freshwater molluscan assemblages are now known from all Omo Group formations. As this time range has been and is still largely unknown or ill-documented in tropical Africa, this sequence is not only of interest for understanding the development of invertebrate faunas in African inland basins, but also because it affords a faunal zonation for this portion of the Rift Valley System. It is of considerable importance for temporal correlation and palaeoenvironmental interpretation within the Rudolf basin (Van Damme and Gautier, 1972).

Three major invertebrate assemblages are known from the Pliocene and earlier Pleistocene time range of the lower Omo basin (Gautier, 1976). They show distinct differences in composition, in extinction of species, in the appearance of new species, in adaptations to particular biotopes, and in biogeographic affinities. The assemblage from the later Shungura Formation (upper Mb. G and Mb. H) is distinctive in the number of endemic forms, the new immigrants, the replacement of older species, and its overall endemic character. An assemblage from the latest Pleistocene is also known and affords important evidence for the origin and evolution of invertebrate life in recent East African lakes, and particularly the Rudolf basin.

Vertebrates

The record of vertebrate life during the time span of the Omo Group formations is extremely abundant and varied. It provides an unusually complete representation of vertebrate life, its transformation through 3 m.y. of geological time in a Rift Valley setting, as well as interesting and important insights into problems of biogeography, species diversity, and extinctions.

Nine species of fish have been identified and published from these formations (Arambourg, 1947). A large number of new and largely compete specimens have been recovered, particularly from the lacustrine episode in Shungura Formation Member G. There are a number of new taxa still to be described. They are particularly important for appreciation of past hydrographic systems, in part disturbed by crustal movements and/or by climatic changes during the later Cenozoic, as well as for ascertaining biogeographic affinities, and for the study of evolutionary changes in 'closed' and 'open' drainage basins.

Terrestrial and aquatic chelonians are well-represented though not frequently wholly preserved. Three genera of pelomedusid, trionychid and testudinid Chelonia have been described (Arambourg, 1947), and F. de Broin has continued the study of this interesting group. They are of palaeoenvironmental as well as, particularly, biogeographic significance in respect to distributions and diversity during the African later Neogene.

Aquatic crocodilians are abundant and ubiquitous throughout the Omo Group Formations. They are of interest since they show affinities in part with other hydrographic systems within Africa, still broader temporal and biogeographic affinities outside Africa, as well as autochthonous distributions within this portion of the Rift System. At least four taxa are represented (Tchernov 1976). The narrow-snouted *Euthecodon brumpti*, a tomistomid derivative, occurs throughout the sequence, perhaps as more than one form; related species are known from older (Lothagam) as well as contemporaneous (East Rudolf; Kanapoi) fossiliferous localities around the Rudolf basin. The Nile crocodile (*Crocodilus niloticus*) is represented also throughout the sequence, and is of course present at most late Neogene and Pleistocene localities in eastern Africa. The slender-snouted crocodile, *C. cataphractus*, restricted to the Congo basin now, is recorded from the Omo (cf. Arambourg, 1947), from an unconfirmed provenance (probably later rather than earlier in the succession), and is also recorded at East Rudolf; it is unknown elsewhere. A new species of broad, short-snouted crocodile is also represented, both early (Mbs. B and C) and late (Mb. K) in the Omo succession; it is also recorded at East Rudolf and in lower Olduvai.

P. Brodkorb has recognized some 6 families of birds in the Usno Formation and 6 members of the Shungura Formation.

Mammals are extremely abundant, often well preserved, and represented by an extraordinary diversity of taxa in Omo Group formations. Over 40,000 identifiable fossil specimens have been collected, from surface survey and from controlled excavations, and catalogued by the recent expedition. They afford a unique biostratigraphy in a radiometrically dated and magnetostratigraphically controlled succession of extended duration. It is an unparalleled sample for the study of mammalian biostratigraphy and biogeography and evolutionary change (phyletic evolution), extinctions, species diversity, and palaeoecology for the Pliocene and earlier Pleistocene time range in equatorial Africa.

Eleven orders and 33 families (of 50 living families), including 4 extinct families, are documented in the mammalian fossil record of the Omo succession. Ninety-nine genera and over 140 species, exclusive of Hominidae, have been identified thus far (cf. Coppens and Howell, and Howell and Coppens, 1974). The representation of species in the Mursi and Usno Formation, and in the successive members of the Shungura Formation, is set out in Table 2.

Micromammals are known from various members of the Shungura Formation. Two species of Muridae are known in Members C and G, Hystricidae are known in the Usno Formation and Mbs. C, E, and H, J, and L, and Hyracoidea (*Gigantohyrax*, a Makapan Limeworks taxon) are known in Mb. C. However, two large assemblages have been recovered from washing and sorting operations at two hominid-bearing localities, and include Chiroptera, Insectivora, Rodentia, Prosimii, and small Carnivora (Viverridae). These assemblages (Figure 6), from upper Member B and lower Member F, show interesting and significant differences in composition (Jaeger and Wesselman, 1976). That from Member B is the most substantial and overall most diverse, having 6 species of Muridae (3 in C, 3 in F, and 4 in G), 1 species of Cricetidae (3 in F), 2 species of Sciuridae (2 in F), 1 species of Thryonomyidae (1 in F), 1 species of Hystricidae (2 in F), 3 species of Chiroptera (3 in F), 3 species of Insectivora (1 in F), 2-3 species of Lorisidae (0 in F), 1 species of Hyracoidea (also in B and C), and 1 species of Viverridae (1 in F). Noteworthy are differences in the frequency and differing species representation of Muridae (particularly those characteristic of 'closed' habitats), the markedly increased frequency of Gerbillinae, and the appearance of Dipodidae and of Bathyergidae, all indicative of substantially more 'open' habitat situations in Member F times. The older assemblage is indicative of wooded savannah as well as riverine forest and moist lowland forest. This is confirmed by sedimentary and palynological evidence. Ultimately the Omo succession will afford a microvertebrate biostratigraphy of primary importance for biogeographic and biostratigraphic comparisons with other African hominid-bearing localities as well as with sequences in northern Africa and in Eurasia. The rodents already recognized show resemblances both to species known from early Olduvai (Bed I) as well as to some from australopithecine sites in southern Africa.

Some aspects of species diversity, extinctions, phyletic evolution,

Table 2 Mammalian species represented in formations of the Omo group

Taxa	*Mursi Fm.*	*Usno Fm.*	*Basal Mb.*	*A*	*B*	*C*	*D*	*Shungura Formation E*	*F*	*G*	*H*	*J–K–L*
Proboscidea	3	4	?	3	4	3	3	2	2	2	2	3
Rhinocerotidae	2	2	?	?	2	2	2	1	2	2		
Equidae	1	1	?	1	1	1	1	1	2	4	3	2
Chalicotheriidae			?			1	1					
Hippopotamidae	1	2	?	1	1	3	2	1	2	3	3	3–4
Suidae	2	4–5	?	4	6	6	3+	3	5	6	4	4+
Giraffidae		4	?	1	4	4	3		3	4	1	3
Camelidae			?		1		1		1	1		
Bovidae			?									
Tragelaphini	1	1			2	3	3	3	2+	3+	1	1
Reduncini	1				4	6	3+	5	3	5+		3+
Hippotragini						1+		1		?		
Neotragini								1	1	1		
Alcelaphini		1+			1+	1+	1	1	1	1+		2
Aepycerotini	1	1			1	1	1	1	1	1	1	1
Bovini		1+			1+	2+	1	1+	1+	3+	1	1
Antilopini		1+			1+	1	2		2+	2+	1	1+
Carnivora			?									
Hyaenidae		4			1	2		1	2	2		1
Felidae	?	5–6		1	5	6	2	2	6+	6	1	1
Mustelidae		2			1	1		2	2			
Viverridae		1			2	5	1	3	1	3		
Primates			?									
Lorisidae					2–3							
Colobinae		1		1	2	3	2	2	2	2	1	2
Cercopithecinae		5		2	5	4	2	2	4	5	3	4
Total	12	45–47	?	14	47–48	56	35	33	48	56	22	32–33

and immigration among other mammalian groups are worthy of brief mention.

Proboscidea

Five proboscideans are represented early in the succession (Beden 1976). The gomphothere *Anancus* persists only into the Mursi Formation. *Stegodon* persists into upper Mb. B. The early loxodont, *L. adaurora*, persists into Mb. C (but is apparently absent from the Usno Formation, perhaps for ecological reasons). *Loxodonta*, represented by another species, is present in Mb. D. The extant species of *Loxodonta, L. africana*, apparently appears about Mb. J times. *Deinotherium* occurs throughout the Omo succession and seemingly becomes extinct by Mb. L times (as is the case in Olduvai, upper Bed II). The extinct *Elephas recki* appears at the base of the sequence, persists throughout, and has a complex phyletic evolution through four stages. It is a species of particular significance in biozonation of the African Pliocene and Pleistocene (Maglio, 1973; 1970).

Rhinocerotidae

An extinct, primitive species of white rhino, *Ceratotherium praecox*, is present only in the Mursi Fm. The extant white rhino (*C. simum*) and black rhino (*Diceros bicornis*) occur throughout the sequence, from the Usno Fm. through Mb. G at least, their presence subsequently being uncertain (either due to sampling and/or ecological factors). (Hooijer, 1976; Guerin, 1976).

Chalicotheriidae

This extinct perissodactyl is everywhere rare, but is documented in Mbs. D and G of the Shungura Fm. (Hooijer, *op. cit.*; Guerin, *op. cit.*).

Equidae

Two genera are represented, *Hipparion* and *Equus* (Eisenmann, 1976; Hooijer, 1976). The diversity and evolution of *Hipparion* is complex, with four species probably represented. The primitive *H. turkanense*, first known at Lothagam, is known only from the Mursi Fm. In the Usno Fm. and the lowermost members (A and B, perhaps C), another large and perhaps descendant species, *H.* cf. *albertense*, is represented. The characteristic gracile, hypsodont species *H. ethiopicum* is present thereafter, from Mb. F through Mb. L. Another, dwarf form, referred to *H.* cf. *sitifense*, seems to be present in Mbs. F and G, and is the characteristic species in this time range in northern Africa.

Equus appears suddenly in Mb. G as a new immigrant. Three species are represented. A large species, referred to *E. oldowayensis*, is most common, and occurs from Mbs. G through L. Another very large, new species is also present, but ill-known in lower Mb. G; it is also recorded in lower and upper Koobi Fora, East Rudolf. Another small species, the size of extant *E. burchelli granti*, apparently is also present.

Hippopotamidae

This family reveals an unexpected diversity in this time range. Five, perhaps six, species are represented in Omo Group formations (Coryndon and Coppens, 1973; Coryndon, 1976). A large hexaprotodont species, *H.* sp. nov. 'D', occurs in the earliest part of the succession (through Mb. B), the same species first well-documented at Lothagam and Kanapoi. This species ultimately becomes the tetraprotodont, slender-limbed species, *H. protamphibius*, which is so characteristic and unique to the Omo succession and which persists into Mb. H. A small hexaprotodont species, *H.* sp. nov. 'A', perhaps related to the former, appears sporadically from Mbs. C through G. The remaining species are tetraprotodont. A pygmy tetraprotodont (*H.* sp. nov. 'B'), which also occurs in upper East Rudolf and in lower Olduvai, occurs sporadically in Mbs. C, G, H, and finally in K and L. The large tetraprotodont, *H. gorgops*, so characteristic of Olduvai (and now also known at East Rudolf), appears first in Mb. G and is present thereafter.

The extant species, *H. amphibius*, the African evolutionary history of which is extremely poorly known, may also be present in the uppermost several members of the Shungura Fm. The distinctive diprotodont hippo of East Rudolf, *H.* sp. nov. 'C', if represented at all in the Omo succession, appears only at the end of the Shungura Fm. (perhaps Mb. K). It is difficult to conceive of this unusual diversity as other than a series of complex, still ill-appreciated ecological adjustments.

Suidae

This family epitomizes diversity, extinctions, and phyletic evolution through this 3 m.y. time range. Six genera and some 12 species are documented (Cooke, 1976). Two species of *Nyanzachoerus, N. pattersoni* and *N. jaegeri* (ex-*N. plicatus*) are variably represented in the Mursi and Usno Formations and the lower members of the Shungura Fm.; both were first documented at Kanapoi. Three or four species of the phacochoerine genus *Notochoerus* are known. The most primitive species *N. capensis* is restricted to the Usno Fm. (and is also known at Kanapoi and Kubi Algi, E. Rudolf). *N. euilus* is present in the Usno Fm. and the lower members (A through C) of the Shungura Fm.; a related, presumably derivative species, *N. 'scotti'*, occurs from Mbs. B through H and demonstrates an interesting phyletic evolution of the molar dentition. The suine genus *Mesochoerus* is represented by *M. limnetes* in the Usno Fm. and Mbs. A through G of the Shungura Fm., after which it evolves into *M. olduvaiensis*, the characteristic species at Olduvai.

The aberrant phacochoerine genus *Metridiochoerus* is represented by the small species *M. jacksoni* which occurs regularly and essentially unchanged through the Shungura Fm. from Mbs. B through K (and has a long evolutionary history at Olduvai as well). The related genus, *Stylochoerus*, is represented by *S. nicoli* (ex-*Afrochoerus*), a species with peculiar elephantine-like canines, is represented in the two uppermost members of the Shungura Fm. The extant genus *Phacochoerus* is represented by two species, *P. antiquus*, present in Mbs. G and H, and probably the extant species *P. aethiopicus*, which seemingly appears from Mb. G upwards.

Giraffidae

Sivatherium and three species of *Giraffa* have a continuous documentation from the Usno Fm. and the lower members (B and C) of the Shungura Fm. through Mb. G and, apparently, also into the uppermost members of that formation. All species are documented at the same horizon in several instances. The giraffine species include the distinctive slender-limbed *G. gracilis*, the large species *G. jumae*, and a new diminutive, okapi-sized species (also now known at a number of localities in eastern Africa), *G. pygmaeus* (Harris, 1976).

Camelidae

An extinct species of *Camelus*, perhaps with affinities to the extinct *C. thomasi* of North Africa, is documented in five members (B, D, F, G, J) of the Shungura Fm., first in Mb. G (Grattard, Howell and Coppens, 1976). It is another and unexpectedly early immigrant into eastern Africa, and has a subsequent documentation at Olduvai Gorge (upper Bed II) as well as at Marsabit (Gentry and Gentry, 1970).

Bovidae

Eight tribes are represented in the Omo formations (Gentry, 1976, 1977). Of the smallest species only Neotragini are known, and only by fragmentary remains in the middle members of the Shungura Formation. Hippotragini are unknown except for a miniscule record in Mbs. C, E, G. Antilopini are always rare and their diversity is surely poorly recorded. The extinct springbuck, *Antidorcas recki*, occurs repeatedly from early (Mb. B) to late (Mb. K). The Usno Fm. and Mbs. D and F thru K all yield few indeterminate antilopines, with *Gazella* sp. definitely recorded in D, F and H. The extinct *G. praethomsoni* is certainly known only in the Usno Fm. and Mb. G. The

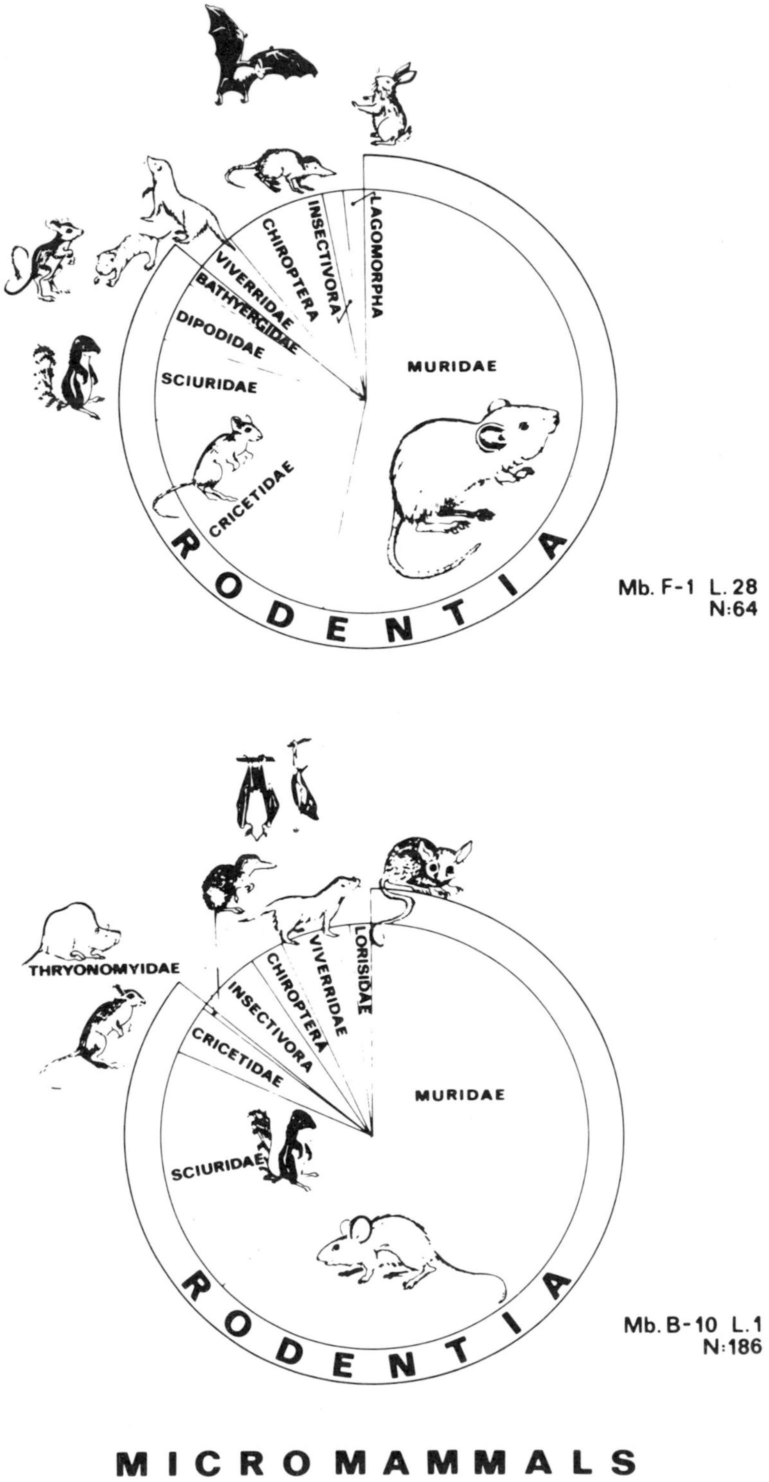

Figure 6. Micro-mammalian assemblages from upper Member B and lower Member F, Shungura Formation.

occurrence of an extinct blackbuck species, *Antilope subtorta*, affords an interesting link with southern Asia (Pinjor zone, Upper Siwaliks).

The remaining five tribes are the most common bovids, although quite unequally represented. Alcelaphini are always infrequent and usually have the poorest representation, although they occur in the Usno Fm. and throughout the Shungura Fm. (increasing in frequency in Mbs. D, E, and F). The extinct hartebeest, *Megalotragus*, occurs from Mb. G onwards (but may also have an earlier history in the Omo). Another wildebeest, whether *Connochaetes* or the extinct *Oreonagor* is uncertain, is documented in Mb. B. The extinct *Parmularius altidens* occurs late in the Shungura Fm., and a related form may occur as early as Mb. C. An extinct species of herola, *Beatragus antiquus*, is definitely documented in Mb. H. Except in Mbs. B and C bovines are always in very low frequency in the Shungura as well as the Usno Fms. An ancient, short-horned species of the buffalo *Syncerus* is in Mbs. B, C, and G. The extinct genus *Pelorovis* is documented as early as Mb. C and again in Mb. F, but is better known in Mb. G, as a species ancestral to, or identical with *P. oldowayensis* (of Bed II Olduvai). An extinct genus of Asiatic water-buffalo, *Hemibos*, first known from the Upper Siwaliks (Pinjor zone), is present in Mb. G, and perhaps E, and affords another indication of extra-African faunal affinities.

Tragelaphini and Reduncini are most abundant and varied and with *Aepyceros* form the bulk of the bovid fauna. *Aepyceros* is ubiquitous and represents from 30 to nearly 50% of the Usno and Shungura Fm. bovid fauna. An early form is also known from the Mursi Fm. Four or five species of Tragelaphini are represented. The extant greater kudu (*Tragelaphus strepsiceros*) appears first in Mb. G. The common kudu in the middle members (C through G) is the extinct *T. gaudryi*. Another, indeterminate species is also present in Mbs. C, D, and E. A primitive bushbuck, *T. pricei*, is present in Mb. C. The most common and persistant species is *T. nakuae*, first recognized in the Omo by Arambourg (1947), which occurs in the Usno Fm. and in the Shungura Fm. through Mb. K, in strongly decreasing frequency after Mb. E. This species preserves markedly boselaphine features and is strongly reminiscent of *Selenoportax vexillarius* from the Middle Siwaliks.

Reduncines are more diverse than tragelaphines, and customarily show reversed frequencies with the former group. Reduncines are essentially unknown from the Mursi Fm. and are undocumented in the Usno Fm. At least seven taxa are recorded in the Shungura Fm., with particularly high frequencies in Mbs. B and G. Three taxa are particularly characteristic of the Omo succession – *Menelikia lyrocera* (recorded as late as Mb. K), *Kobus sigmoidalis* (recorded as late as Mb. J), and *Kobus ancystrocera* (recorded as late as Mb. G). The former two species in particular show an interesting phyletic evolution through the Shungura Fm. in respect to cranial and horn core morphology. *K.*

sigmoidalis is considered to be ancestral to both the waterbuck, *K. ellipsiprymnus* (which appears in Mb. G) and the lechwe, *K. leche*. *Kobus kob* may be present in Mb. G, and is known subsequently from the uppermost members of the Shungura Fm. In Mb. B the upper Siwaliks form *K.* cf. *patulicornis* appears to be represented, and in Mbs. B and C another, previously unknown *Kobus* sp. is known. A species of *Redunca* is also present in several members of the Shungura Fm.

Carnivora

Carnivores are never common fossils and are usually, and not unexpectedly, fragmentary and incomplete. Larger taxa are more adequately represented than smaller taxa, particularly viverrids and the lesser felids. Over 25 carnivores are known thus far from the Usno and Shungura Formations, and include 9 viverrids, at least 3 mustelids, 5 hyaenids, 2 machairodontines, and more than 6 felines (Howell and Petter, 1976). There is still no record of Canidae from Omo Group formations, surely a sampling and ecological bias. The stratigraphic distribution of these carnivores, and their presence or absence, must in part reflect this latter bias, but in some instances repetitive occurrences and first appearances must have significances which supersede these biases.

Noteworthy among Viverridae is the documentation of *Viverra leakeyi* (Usno Fm. and Mbs. B to G) a Laetolil and Langebaanweg species; *Pseudocivetta ingens*, an Olduvai Bed I, and now Lower Koobi Fora species; *Civettictis civetta* (Mbs. C to F), and a large *Viverra* sp. (Mb. F).

Noteworthy among Mustelidae is the occurrence of an extraordinarily large lutrine, tentatively referred to *Enhydriodon* sp. nov. (Usno Fm., Mbs. B, C, E, and F), and including elements of the dentition and postcranial parts, hitherto unknown. A species of *Lutra* also occurs in the Usno Fm.

Hyaenids are next to felids the most common carnivores in the Omo succession. Four genera and five species appear to be represented. *Percrocuta* appears to be represented in the Usno Fm., and *Euryboas* (Mb. F) in the Shungura Fm. A small hyaena comparable to *H. hyaena makapani* is apparently represented in the Usno Fm. and Mbs. B and C, Shungura Fm. A larger *Hyaena* sp. occurs in the Usno Fm. and throughout (Mbs. B through K) the Shungura Fm. *Crocuta* appears first in Mb. G, Shungura Fm., in accordance with its belated appearance in stratigraphically and/or radiometrically well-documented presence elsewhere throughout Africa.

Felidae are the most common carnivores. The machairodontines *Megantereon* and *Homotherium* are associated in the Usno Fm. and in the Shungura Fm. from Mbs. B through G. The specific attributions of their remains is still uncertain, the remains being fragmentary. The 'false sabretooth' feline *Dinofelis* is persistently present in the Usno

Fm. and through Shungura Fm. Mbs. A through G. Four species have been recognized elsewhere. *D. barlowi* is known from a cranium in Mb. B, but the specific identity of other, fragmentary specimens has still to be determined. The extinct leopard-sized feline *Acinonyx* (ex-*Panthera*) *crassidens*, first documented at Kromdraai and then in Olduvai (Bed I) (Petter 1973) and now at East Rudolf (M.G. Leakey 1976), is known in the middle members (C, F, G) of the Shungura Fm. This species is also known in the earlier Quaternary of China and in the Siwaliks of India. A leopard, *P. pardus*, is represented in the Usno Fm. and early (Mb. B) and later (Mb. G) in the Shungura Fm. Lion, *P. leo*, is first documented in Mbs. H and L. The Omo clearly demonstrates the earlier appearance of *P. pardus* by comparison with *P. leo*, and both species appear later in Europe (in the Cromerian) than in Africa. Cheetah, *Acinonyx*, is seemingly only represented in Mb. G. Smaller felines are still poorly known, with indeterminate representatives in the Usno Fm. and several members of the Shungura Fm., including *Felis (Lynx) caracal* in Mbs. B and F.

Primates exclusive of Hominidae

Prosimians, at least two species of galagines, are recorded only in the Mb. B microfaunal assemblages.

Cercopithecoidea are common and very diversified in both the Usno and the Shungura Formations (Eck, 1976). Three and probably four taxa of Colobinae are represented, but they represent less than 10% of the total cercopithecoid fauna. A small *Colobus* sp. is known from Mb. K, and presumably another, about the size of *C. polykomos*, is known from Mb. L. Colobinae sp. indet. A, rather larger than *C. polykomos*, is known from Mbs. B and C, but its affinities are unclear; they may be with *Cercopithecoides williamsi*, a South African taxon. The most abundant species is Colobinae gen. et. sp. nov. which occurs in the Usno Fm. and throughout the Shungura Fm. It is a large form, comparable in size to *Paracolobus* and *Cercopithecoides molletti*, but is distinctive in its cranial and dental morphology. Finally Colobinae sp. indet. C is present in Mbs. C through G and is an exceptionally large form, comparable in size to an anubis baboon. Both sp. indet. A and C may ultimately prove to be unique to the Omo.

Representatives of the Cercopithecinae are much more common and at least four taxa can be distinguished. A small *Cercopithecus* sp. is represented in the Usno Fm. and in the lower (Mbs. B, C) and the upper (Mbs. G and J) members of the Shungura Fm. (Eck and Howell 1972). Two small Papionini are known, but their affinities are unclear – gen. et sp. indet A is restricted to the Usno and the lower (Mbs. B, C) Shungura Fm., is smaller than *Parapapio jonesi* and shows resemblances to *Cercocebus*; gen. et sp. indet. B, which occurs in Mbs. B through L of the Shungura Fm., is similar in both size and morphology to *P. jonesi* or *P. broomi*. *Papio* occurs in the Usno Fm. and throughout the Shungura Fm. (to Mb. L) and although broadly similar to modern representatives of the genus may prove to be distinctive in facial morphology.

Theropithecus is by far the most abundant cercopithecine, about 90% of all specimens recovered (and over 80% of all the Cercopithecoidea). It is represented in the Usno Fm. and throughout the Shungura Fm. (to Mb. L). The characteristic and dominant form (through Mb. G) is *T. brumpti*, restricted to the Omo except for one other occurrence from Kubi Algi, East Rudolf. This species is theropithecine in overall dental, mandibular and cranial morphology, but has a most distinctive facial morphology unknown in any other cercopithecoid primate. The more widespread species *T. oswaldi* was also present, however, and seems to have made its appearance by (at least) Mb. F times and subsequently to have become the dominant species.

The extraordinary fossil record preserved in the Omo Group formations affords a basis for assessing overall resemblances between successive faunal assemblages. Various methods of comparison may be employed, and various approaches which utilize the aggregate body of stratigraphic, radiometric and palaeomagnetic evidence will ultimately be appropriate. A useful and expedient measure is

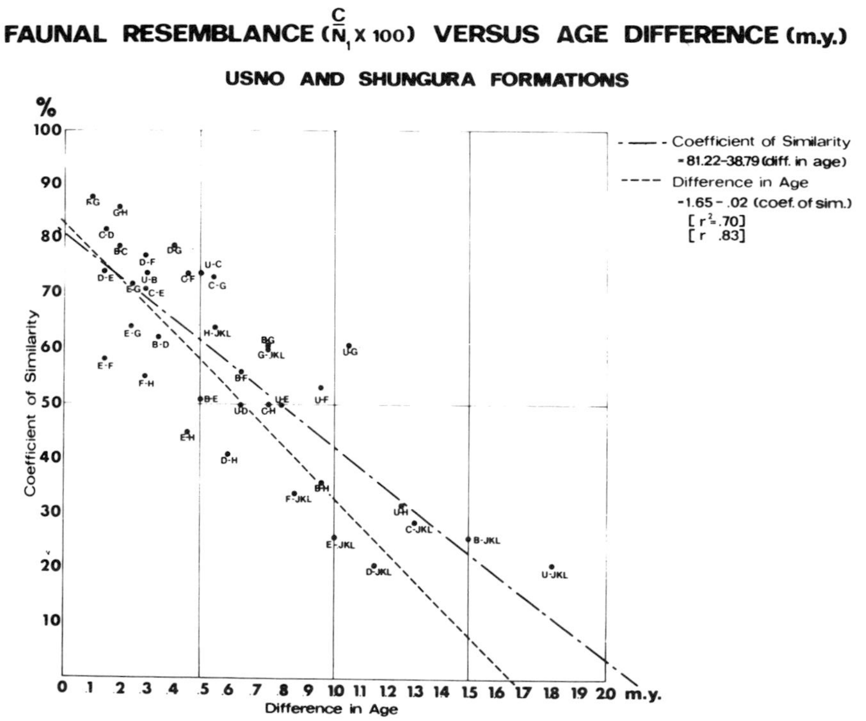

Figure 7. Indices of faunal resemblance between mammal assemblages from the Usno Formation and members of the Shungura Formation.

Simpson's (1960) index of faunal resemblance which measures the number of taxa in common as a function of the smaller of any two assemblages. Figure 7 shows the values obtained in such comparisons for the larger elements in the mammalian fauna plotted against differences in age between the samples compared. The relationship between the similarity index and age difference is clearly demonstrated, regardless of whatever other factors might be operative in effecting faunal resemblance. The Omo succession thus affords a useful comparative baseline for evaluating other faunal assemblages for which stratigraphic and age control may be less clearly defined.

Hominidae

Cultural evidence

Occurrences of hominid artifactual materials have been surely demonstrated in two members of the Shungura Formation. They are suspected, from survey, to occur in other members, but occurrences suitable for excavation have still to be found and tested so they remain unconfirmed.

The youngest occurrences are in fossiliferous gravels of channels in lower Member G (units G4/5). They are situated above tuff G dated 1.93 m.y. in sediments with normal remanent magnetism which must represent a Reunion Normal Event. Several out-crops were tested and yielded fresh and abraded small quartz artifacts. Concentrations in association with fine sediments suitable for excavation have still to be discovered.

Numerous artifact occurrences are now known in a number of areas of exposures of Member F (Merrick *et al.*, 1973; Merrick, 1976; Merrick and Merrick, 1977; Chavaillon, 1976, also 1970, 1971; Coppens, Chavaillon and Beden, 1973). These situations are above tuff F dated at 2.04 m.y. in sediments with reversed followed by normal remanent magnetism. This would seem to represent the initial Reunion Normal Event and the end of the preceding reversed interval (after the 'X' Normal Event).

Four occurrences have been tested and excavated in the first sedimentary unit (F-1) of Member F and maps prepared of the areal extent of the artifactual horizon(s). They occur either in relation to stream channels or to temporary land surfaces associated with marginal flood basins or backswamps. Pollen is preserved in some of these situations, and others may preserve associated mammalian fossils. Sites containing artifacts that are secondarily derived as well as others with artifacts in primary context are represented. All these occurrences are distinguished by their relative low artifact density (2 to $10/m^2$), very small size of artifacts, absence of large core-like tools, infrequency of retouched flakes, edge-damaged flakes and flake tools, and the predominant use of vein quartz as raw material (lava, chalcedony or chert is extremely rare). For the most part the collection represents waste products from artifact manufacture from pebbles and lumps of quartz.

Other artifact concentrations are now known to occur in slightly younger, fine sediments (unit F-3) of Member F in several areas of exposure (Chavaillon 1976). The density is very much greater (120 to 191/m^2) than any of the earlier occurrences, the artifacts may be much larger, cores are present (including the flakes struck from them), retouched pieces are more common, and a substantial diversity of raw materials were employed.

The occurrences are certainly relevant to an understanding of the cultural capabilities and technological practices of early Hominidae, their dietary habits, and the nature and variety of palaeoenvironments which they exploited. The seemingly 'sudden' appearance of lithic artifacts in the Omo succession, long after the first documentation of the presence of Hominidae, is unexpected and puzzling. It still requires explanation in respect to palaeoenvironmental factors as well as the palaeobiology and adaptive adjustments of the hominids of that time.

Skeletal remains

Ninety-one localities, two in the Usno Formation and the remainder in the Shungura Formation, have afforded skeletal parts of Hominidae (Howell, Coppens and de Heinzelin, 1974; Howell and Coppens, 1976). In the Shungura Formation nine of twelve members have yielded Hominidae. In all, hominids derive from 35 stratigraphic units. On the basis of conventional potassium-argon age

Table 3 Inventory by geological formation (and member) of skeletal parts of Hominidae, Omo succession. (i=incomplete; f=fragment)

	Localities	*Crania*	*Mandibles*	*Teeth*	*Postcrania*
Shungura Formation:					
Mb. L	2	—	—	2	—
Mb. K	2	1i	—	1	—
Mb. H	2	—	—	1	1
Mb. G	24	2i;f	5	42	3
Mb. F	14	—	1	57	—
Mb. E	10	1i	2	24	2
Mb. D	10	—	—	13	1
Mb. C	19	2f	1	36	2
Mb. B	6	—	—	11	1
Usno Formation:	2	—	—	21	—
Totals:	91	4i;ff	9	208	10

Total specimens 234

determinations and palaeomagnetic measurements these fall within a time span of 2.9 to 1 m.y. ago. The provenience and nature of the specimens are set out in Table 3. These remains are frequently fragmentary, and most often represent the dentition. However, they are informative in regard to hominid diversity and taxonomy in this important time range.

An overview of Omo Hominidae is given elsewhere by Howell and Coppens (1976). Some of the material has been discussed, and illustrated, by Arambourg and Coppens (1967, 1968), Coppens (1970a,b, 1971, 1973a,b), Howell (1969a,b), Howell and Coppens (1973), and Howell and Wood (1974). Four hominid taxa appear to be represented in this time range in the lower Omo basin.

(a) Remains from the Usno Formation and from Members B, C, D, E, and F and the lower units of G of the Shungura Formation are attributed to *Australopithecus* aff. *africanus*. The oldest specimens are generally small, with simple dental morphology, and might ultimately prove, with additional, more complete material, to represent a distinctive, though related lower taxonomic category.

(b) Some specimens from units of Members E, F, and G, and perhaps from L, of the Shungura Formation are attributed to a robust australopithecine, *Australopithecus boisei*.

(c) A very few teeth and partial cranium from localities in Members G (lower and uppermost), H, and perhaps L, are remarkably similar to those attributed to *Homo habilis* (Hominids 7 and 13) from Olduvai Gorge and East Rudolf.

(d) From (uppermost) Member K are cranial fragments with features diagnostic of *Homo erectus*.

Thus, the Omo succession appears to reveal the presence of *A. africanus*, or an allied diminutive species between ~3.0 and 2.5 m.y. ago; the persistence of this, or a derivative species until ~1.9 m.y. ago; the presence of a robust australopithecine, *A. boisei* between ~2.1 and nearly 1.0 m.y. ago; the appearance, by ~1.85 m.y. ago, of a hominid dentally like specimens assigned to *Homo habilis*; and, by ~1.1 m.y. ago (at least) *Homo erectus* is present.

Conclusions

In recent years very substantial progress has been made toward understanding various aspects of the Pliocene and the Pleistocene of the lower Omo basin in southern Ethiopia. The study of the late Pleistocene and recent sedimentation and depositional environments, as well as the natural communities in the basin, afford important data for the evaluation and interpretation of Pliocene and early Pleistocene conditions. The principal late Cenozoic geologic formations are now mapped, their stratigraphy measured in detail, and their depositional environments ascertained. Conventional potassium-argon dating has afforded an internally consistent and sound chronological framework. This framework has been confirmed and extended through rigorous and intensive palaeomagnetic sampling, resulting in one of the most complete magnetostratigraphic records ever obtained in continental sediments. A major gap in current knowledge is the absence of geophysical data for this area as neither gravity nor seismic surveys has been undertaken.

The history of life preserved in the Pliocene/Pleistocene sediments is rich and varied. Molluscan assemblages have afforded an important biostratigraphy as well as useful indications of palaeoenvironments. The prolonged and diverse vertebrate fossil record, in stratigraphic contexts the ages of which are well established radiometrically and magnetostratigraphically, affords not only an exceptional biostratigraphy, but an unusual opportunity to investigate important, unresolved questions of phyletic evolution, species diversity, extinctions, and faunal exchange. These and other matters of palaeobiological interest can also be related, through microstratigraphic, pedological, palynological and microvertebrate evidence, to other aspects of palaeoecology in the basin. And the occurrences of Hominidae now affords another opportunity for intensive and comparative investigations into the earlier biological evolution and diversification of Hominidae and the development of capabilities for culturally patterned behaviour.

Acknowledgments

The work of the many participants of the Omo Research Expedition has only been realized through the authorization and encouragement of the Imperial Ethiopian Government and, in particular, its Antiquities Administration. The cooperation of the Kenya government has enabled the expedition to function effectively across national frontiers. To both, and to the many colleagues participating in the expedition, the author is deeply grateful.

References

Allen, J.R.L. (1965a) A review of the origin and characteristics of alluvial sediments. *Sedimentology* 5, 89-191.

Allen, J.R.L. (1965b) Fining-upwards cycles in alluvial succession. *Liverpool Manchester geol. J.* 4, 229-46.

Allen, J.R.L. (1970) Studies in fluvial sedimentation: a comparison of fining-upwards cyclothems, with special reference to coarse-member composition and interpretation. *J. Sed. Petrol.* 40, 298-323.

Angelis d'Ossat, G. and Millosevich, F. (1900) Studio geologico sul materiale raccolto da M. Sacchi. Secondo spedizione Bòttego (Afrique orientale). Rome, Società Geografica Italiana.

Arambourg, C. (1943) Mission scientifique de l'Omo (1932-1933). Géologie-Anthropologie, Tome 1, fasc. 2, pp. 60-230. Mémoire, Muséum national d'histoire naturelle, Paris.

Arambourg, C. (1947) Mission scientifique de l'Omo (1932-1933). Paléontologie, Tome 1, fasc. 3, pp. 231-562. Mémoire, Muséum national d'histoire naturelle, Paris.

Arambourg, C., Chavaillon, J. and Coppens, Y. (1967) Premiers résultats de la nouvelle mission de l'Omo (1967). *C. R. Acad. Sci.*, Paris, 265-D, 1891-6.

Arambourg, C., Chavaillon, J. and Coppens, Y. (1969) Résultats de la nouvelle mission de l'Omo (2e campagne 1968). *C. R. Acad. Sci.*, Paris, 268-D, 759-62.

Arambourg, C. and Coppens, Y. (1967) Sur la découverte dans le Pléistocène inférieur de la vallée de l'Omo (Ethiopia) d'une mandibule d'australopithécien. *C. R. Acad. Sci.*, Paris, 265-D, 589-90.

Arambourg, C. and Coppens, Y. (1968) Découverte d'un australopithécien nouveau dans les gisements de l'Omo (Ethiopie). *S. Afr. J. Science* 64, 58-9.

Arambourg, C. and Jeannel, R. (1933) La mission scientifique de l'Omo. *C. R. Acad. Sci.*, Paris, 196, 1902-4.

Baker, B.H., Mohr, P.A. and Williams, L.A.J. (1972) Geology of the Eastern Rift system of Africa. *Geological Society of America*, Special Paper 136, 67 pages.

Beden, M. (1976) Proboscideans from Omo Group formations. In Coppens, Y. *et al.* (eds.), *Earliest Man and Environments in the Lake Rudolf basin: Stratigraphy, Paleoecology and Evolution*. Chicago.

Bonnefille, R. (1970) Prémiers résultats concernant l'analyse pollinique d'échantillons du Pléistocène inférieur de l'Omo (Ethiopie). *C. R. Acad. Sci.*, Paris, 270-D, 2430-3.

Bonnefille, R. (1972) Considérations sur la composition d'une microflore pollinique des formations plio-pléistocènes de la basse vallée de l'Omo (Ethiopie). In Van Zinderen Bakker, E.M. (ed.), *Palaeoecology of Africa* 7, 22-7.

Bonnefille, R. (1976) Palynological evidence for an important change in the vegetation of the Omo Basin between 2.5 and 2 million years. In Coppens, Y. *et al.* (eds.), *Earliest Man and Environments in the Lake Rudolf basin: Stratigraphy, Paleoecology and Evolution*. Chicago.

Bonnefille, R., *et al.* (1973) Situation stratigraphique des localités à hominidés des gisements Plio-Pléistocènes de l'Omo en Ethiopie. *C. R. Acad. Sci.*, Paris, 276, 2781-4, 2879-82.

Boulenger, G.-A. (1920) Sur le gavial fossile de l'Omo. *C. R. Acad. Sci.*, Paris, 170, 913-4.

Bourg de Bozas, R. (1903) D'Addis-Ababá au Nil par le lac Rodolphe. *La Géographie* 7, 91-112.

Bourg de Bozas, R. (1906) *Mission scientifique du Bourg de Bozas de la Mer Rouge à l'Atlantique à travers l'Afrique tropicale, Octobre 1900, Mars 1903*. Paris.

Brown, F.H. (1969) Observations on the stratigraphy and radiometric age of the 'Omo Beds', lower Omo basin, southern Ethiopia. *Quaternaria* 11, 7-14.

Brown, F.H. (1972) Radiometric dating of sedimentary formations in the lower Omo valley, southern Ethiopia. In Bishop, W.W. and Miller, J.A. (eds.), *Calibration of Hominoid Evolution*, 273-87. Edinburgh.

Brown, F.H. and Carmichael, I.S.E. (1969) Quaternary volcanoes of the Lake Rudolf region: 1. The basanite-tephrite series of the Korath range. *Lithos* 2, 239-260.

Brown, F.H. and Lajoie, K.R. (1971) Radiometric age determinations on Pliocene-Pleistocene formations in the lower Omo basin, southern Ethiopia. *Nature* 229, 483-5.

Brown, F.H. and Nash, W.P. (1976) Radiometric dating and tuff mineralogy of Omo Group deposits. In Coppens, Y. *et al.* (eds.), *Earliest Man and Environments in the Lake Rudolf basin: Stratigraphy, Paleoecology and Evolution.* Chicago.

Brown, F.H. and Shuey, R.T. (1976) Magnetostratigraphy of the Shungura and Usno Formations, lower Omo Valley, Ethiopia. In Coppens, Y. *et al.* (eds.), *Earliest Man and Environments in the Lake Rudolf basin: Stratigraphy, Paleoecology and Evolution.* Chicago.

Butzer, K.W. (1970) Geomorphological observations in the lower Omo basin, southwestern Ethiopia. In Lauer, M. (ed.), *Argumenta Geographica,* Carl Troll Festschrift; *Colloquium Geographicum* 12, 177-92.

Butzer, K.W. (1971) The lower Omo basin: geology, fauna and hominids of Plio-Pleistocene age. *Naturwissenschaften* 55, 7-16.

Butzer, K.W. (1976) The Mursi, Nkalabong and Kibish Formations, lower Omo basin, Ethiopia. In Coppens, Y. *et al.* (eds.), *Earliest Man and Environments in the Lake Rudolf basin: Stratigraphy, Paleoecology and Evolution.* Chicago.

Butzer, K.W., Brown, F.H. and Thurber, D.L. (1969) Horizontal sediments of the lower Omo basin: the Kibish Formation. *Quaternaria* 11, 15-29.

Butzer, K.W. and Thurber, D.L. (1969) Some late Cenozoic sedimentary formations of the lower Omo basin. *Nature* 222, 1132-7.

Chavaillon, J. (1970) Découverte d'un niveau Olduwayen dans la basse vallée de l'Omo (Ethiopie). *C. R. seances Soc. préhist. franc.* 1, 7-11.

Chavaillon, J. (1971) Etat actuel de la préhistoire ancienne dans la vallée de l'Omo (Ethiopie). *Archéologia* 38, 33-43.

Chavaillon, J. (1976) Evidence for the technical practices of early Pleistocene hominids. Shungura Formation, lower valley of the Omo, Ethiopia. In Coppens, Y. *et al.* (eds.), *Earliest Man and Environments in the Lake Rudolf basin: Stratigraphy, Paleoecology and Evolution.* Chicago.

Cooke, H.B.S. (1976) Suidae from Pliocene-Pleistocene strata of the Rudolf basin. In Coppens, Y. *et al.* (eds.), *Earliest Man and Environments in the Lake Rudolf basin: Stratigraphy, Paleoecology and Evolution.* Chicago.

Cooke, H.B.S. (1977) The Pliocene-Pleistocene Suidae. In Cooke, H.B.S. and Maglio V.J. (eds.), *Mammalian Evolution in Africa.* Harvard.

Cooke, H.B.S. and Maglio, V.J. (1972) Plio-Pleistocene stratigraphy in East Africa in relation to proboscidean and suid evolution. In Bishop, W.W. and Miller, J.A. (eds.), *Calibration of Hominoid Evolution,* 303-29. Edinburgh.

Coppens, Y. (1970a) Localisations dans le temps et dans l'espace des restes d'Hominides des formations plio-pléistocène de l'Omo (Ethiopie). *C. R. Acad. Sci.*, Paris, 172-D, 1968-71.

Coppens, Y. (1970b) Les restes d'hominidés des séries inferieurs et moyennes des formations plio-villafranchiennes de l'Omo en Ethiopie. *C. R. Acad. Sci.*, 271-D, 2286-9.

Coppens, Y. (1971) Les restes d'hominidés des séries supérieurs des formations plio-villafranchiennes de l'Omo en Ethiopie. *C. R. Acad. Sci.*, Paris, 272-D, 36-9.

Coppens, Y. (1973a) Les restes d'hominidés des séries inférieures et moyennes des formations plio-villafranchiennes de l'Omo en Ethiopie (récoltes 1970, 1971 et 1972). *C. R. Acad. Sci.*, Paris, 276:1823-1826.

Coppens, Y. (1973b) Les restes d'hominidés des séries supérieures des formations plio-villafranchiennes de l'Omo en Ethiopie (récoltes 1970, 1971, et 1972). *C. R. Acad. Sci.*, Paris, 276, 1981-4.

Coppens, Y., Chavaillon, J. and Beden, M. (1973) Résultats de la nouvelle mission de l'Omo (campagne 1972): Découverte de restes des hominidés et d'une industrie sur éclats. *C. R. Acad. Sci.*, Paris, 276, 161-4.

Coppens, Y. and Howell, F.C. (1974) Les faunes de mammifères fossiles des formations plio-pléistocènes de l'Omo en Ethiopie (Proboscidea, Perissodactyla, Artiodactyla). *C. R. Acad. Sci.*, Paris, 278, 2275-8.

Coryndon, S.C. (1976) Fossil Hippopotamidae from Pliocene-Pleistocene successions of the Rudolf basin. In Coppens, Y. *et al.* (eds.), *Earliest Man and Environments in the Lake Rudolf basin: Stratigraphy, Paleoecology and Evolution.* Chicago.

Coryndon, S.C. and Coppens, Y. (1973) Preliminary report on Hippopotamidae (Mammalia, Artiodactyla) from the Plio-Pleistocene of the lower Omo basin, Ethiopia. *Fossil Vertebrates of Africa* 3, 139-57.

Curtis, G.H. (1968) The stratigraphy of the ejecta from the 1912 eruption of Mount Katmai and Novarupta, Alaska. *Geol. Soc. of Amer., Memoir* 116, 153-210.

Dechamps, R. (1976) Resultats préliminaires de l'étude de bois fossiles de la basse vallée de l'Omo (Ethiopie sud occidentale). *Mus. Roy. Afr. Centr., Tervuren (Belg.), Dept. Géol. Min. Rapp. Ann. 1975*, 59-65.

Eck, G.G. (1976) Cercopithecoidea from Omo Group deposits. In Coppens, Y. *et al.* (eds.), *Earliest Man and Environments in the Lake Rudolf basin: Stratigraphy, Palaeoecology and Evolution.* Chicago.

Eck, G.G., and Howell, F.C. (1972) New fossil *Cercopithecus* material from the lower Omo basin, Ethiopia. *Folia Primatologia* 8, 325-55.

Eisenmann, V. (1976) Equidae from the Shungura Formation. In Coppens, Y. *et al.* (eds.), *Earliest Man and Environments in the Lake Rudolf basin: Stratigraphy, Paleoecology and Evolution.* Chicago.

Fitch, F.J. and Miller, J.A. (1969) Age determinations on feldspar from the lower Omo basin. *Nature* 222, 1143.

Fitch, F.J. and Miller, J.A. (1976) Conventional Potassium-Argon and Argon-40/Argon-39 dating of volcanic rocks from East Rudolf. In Coppens, Y. *et al.* (eds.), *Earliest Man and Environments in the Lake Rudolf basin. Stratigraphy, Paleoecology and Evolution.* Chicago.

Gautier, A. (1976) Assemblages of fossil freshwater mollusks from the Omo Group and related deposits in the Lake Rudolf basin. In Coppens, Y. *et al.* (eds.), *Earliest Man and Environments in the Lake Rudolf basin: Stratigraphy, Paleoecology and Evolution.* Chicago.

Gentry, A.W. (1976) Bovidae of the Omo Group deposits. In Coppens, Y. *et al.* (eds.), *Earliest Man and Environments in the Lake Rudolf basin: Stratigraphy, Paleoecology and Evolution.* Chicago.

Gentry, A.W. (1977) Artiodactyla: Camelidae: Tragelidae: Bovidae. In Cooke, H.B.S. and Maglio, V.J. (eds.), *Mammalian Evolution in Africa.* Harvard.

Gentry, A.W. and Gentry, A. (1969) Fossil camels in Kenya and Tanzania. *Nature* 222, 898.

Grattard, J.-L., Howell, F.C. and Coppens, Y. (1976) Remains of *Camelus* from the Shungura Formation, lower Omo valley. In Coppens, Y. *et al.* (eds.), *Earliest Man and Environments in the Lake Rudolf basin: Stratigraphy, Paleoecology and Evolution*. Chicago.

Guerin, C. (1976) Rhinocerotidae and Chalicotheriidae (Mammalia, Perissodactyla) from the Shungura Formation, lower Omo basin. In Coppens, Y. *et al.* (eds.), *Earliest Man and Environments in the Lake Rudolf basin: Stratigraphy, Paleoecology and Evolution*. Chicago.

Harris, J.M. (1976) Pleistocene Giraffidae (Mammalia, Artiodactyla) from East Rudolf, Kenya. *Fossil Vertebrates of Africa* 4, 283-332.

Haug, E. (1912) *Traité de géologie*. II: *Les Périodes géologiques*. Paris.

Hedberg, H.D. (ed.) (1971) *Preliminary Report on Chronostratigraphic Units*. International Subcommission on Stratigraphic Classification, Report No. 6, 39 pages. International Geological Congress, 24th Session, Montreal, 1971.

de Heinzelin, J. (1971) Observations sur la formation de Shungura (vallée de l'Omo, Ethiopie). *C. R. Acad. Sci.*, Paris, 272-D, 2409-11.

de Heinzelin, J. and Brown, F.H. (1969) Some early Pleistocene deposits of the lower Omo valley: the Usno Formation. *Quaternaria* 11, 31-46.

de Heinzelin, J., Brown, F.H. and Howell, F.C. (1970) Pliocene-Pleistocene formations in the lower Omo basin, southern Ethiopia. *Quaternaria* 13, 247-68.

de Heinzelin, J., Haesaerts, P. and Howell, F.C. (1976) Plio-Pleistocene formations of the lower Omo basin, with particular reference to the Shungura Formation. In Coppens, Y. *et al.* (eds.), *Earliest Man and Environments in the Lake Rudolf basin: Stratigraphy, Paleoecology and Evolution*. Chicago.

von Höhnel, L. (1938) The Lake Rudolf region: Its discovery and subsequent exploration (1888-1909). *J. Roy. Afr. Soc.* 37, 21-45, 206-26.

von Höhnel, R.L. *et al.* (1891) Beiträge zur geologischen Kenntnis des östlichen Afrika. *Denkschr. d. Akad. d. Wiss. Wien, Math.-naturw. K1.* 58, 140 pages.

Hooijer, D.A. (1976) Evolution of the Perissodactyla of the Omo Group deposits. In Coppens, Y. *et al.* (eds.), *Earliest Man and Environments in the Lake Rudolf basin: Stratigraphy, Paleoecology and Evolution*. Chicago.

Howell, F.C. (1968) Omo research expedition. *Nature* 219, 567-72.

Howell, F.C. (1969a) Remains of Hominidae from Pliocene-Pleistocene formations in the lower Omo basin, Ethiopia. *Nature* 223, 1234-9.

Howell, F.C. (1969b) Hominid teeth from White Sands and Brown Sands localities, lower Omo basin (Ethiopia). *Quaternaria* 11, 47-64.

Howell, F.C. and Coppens, Y. (1973) Deciduous teeth of Hominidae from the Pliocene-Pleistocene of the lower Omo basin, Ethiopia. *J. human Evol.* (R. A. Dart Memorial Issue) 2, 461-72.

Howell, F.C. and Coppens, Y. (1974) Les faunes de mammifères fossiles des formations plio-pléistocènes de l'Omo en Ethiopie (Tubulidentata, Hyracoidea, Lagomorpha, Rodentia, Chiroptera, Insectivora, Carnivora, Primates). *C. R. Acad. Sci.*, Paris, 278, 2421-4.

Howell, F.C. and Coppens, Y. (1976) Hominidae from the Usno and Shungura Formations, lower Omo valley. In Coppens, Y. *et al.* (eds.),

Earliest Man and Environments in the Lake Rudolf basin: Stratigraphy, Paleoecology and Evolution. Chicago.

Howell, F.C., Coppens, Y. and de Heinzelin, J. (1974) Inventory of remains of Hominidae from Pliocene-Pleistocene formations of the lower Omo basin, Ethiopia (1967-1972). *Amer. J. phys. Anthrop.* 40(1), 1-16.

Howell, F.C., Fichter, L.S. and Eck, G. (1969) Vertebrate assemblages from the Usno Formation, White Sands and Brown Sands localities, lower Omo basin; Ethiopia. *Quaternaria* 11, 65-88.

Howell, F.C., Fichter, L.S. and Wolff, R. (1969) Fossil camels in the Omo Beds, southern Ethiopia. *Nature* 223, 150-2.

Howell, F.C. and Petter, G. (1976) Carnivora from Omo Group formations, southern Ethiopia. In Coppens, Y. *et al.* (eds.), *Earliest Man and Environments in the Lake Rudolf basin: Stratigraphy, Paleoecology and Evolution*. Chicago.

Howell, F.C. and Wood, B.A. (1974) An early hominid ulna from the Omo basin, Ethiopia. *Nature* 249, 174-6.

Jaeger, J.-J. and Wesselman, H.B. (1976) Fossil remains of micro-mammals from the Omo Group deposits. In Coppens, Y. *et al.* (eds.), *Earliest Man and Environments in the Lake Rudolf basin: Stratigraphy, Paleoecology and Evolution*. Chicago.

Jeannel, R. (1934) *Un cimetière d'éléphants*. Paris, Société des Amis du Muséum national d'histoire naturelle.

Johanson, D.C., Boaz, N. and Splingaer, M. (1976) Paleontological excavations in the Shungura Formation, lower Omo basin, 1969-1973. In Coppens, Y. *et al.* (eds.), *Earliest Man and Environments in the Lake Rudolf basin: Stratigraphy, Paleoecology and Evolution*. Chicago.

Joleaud, L. (1920a) Contribution a l'étude des hippopotames fossiles. *Bull. Soc. géol. de France*, sér. 4, 20, 13-26.

Joleaud, L. (1920b) Sur la présence d'un gavialidé du genre *Tomistoma* dans le Pliocène d'eau douce de l'Ethiopie. *C. R. Acad. Sci.*, Paris, 170, 816-18.

Joleaud, L. (1928) Eléphants et dinothériums pliocènes de l'Ethiopie: contribution à l'étude paléogéographique des proboscidiens africains. *Intern. Géol. Congress, Madrid, 14th session*, 3, 1001-7.

Joleaud, L. (1930) Les crocodiliens du pliocène d'eau douce de l'Omo (Ethiopie). Contribution a l'étude paléobiogéographique des *Tomistoma* et des crocodiles à museau de gavial. *Soc. géol. de France, Livre Jubilaire, 1830-1930*, 2, 411-23.

Joleaud, L. (1933) Un nouveau genre d'Equidé quaternaire de l'Omo (Abyssinie): *Libyhipparion ethiopicum*. *Bull. Soc. Géol. de France*, sér. 5, 3, 7-28.

Leakey, L.S.B. (1943) New fossil Suidae from Shungura, Omo. *J. E. Afr. Uganda Nat. Hist. Soc., Nairobi*, 17:45-61.

Leakey, M.G. (1976) Cercopithecoidea of the E. Rudolf succession. In Coppens, Y. *et al.* (eds.), *Earliest Man and Environments in the Lake Rudolf basin: Stratigraphy, Paleoecology and Evolution*. Chicago.

Leakey, M.G. and Leakey, R.E.F. (1973) New large Pleistocene Colobinae (Mammalia, Primates) from East Africa. *Fossil Vertebrates of Africa* 3, 121-38.

Leopold, L.B., Wolman, M.G. and Miller, J.P. (1964) *Fluvial Processes in Geomorphology*. San Francisco and London.

Maglio, V.J. (1970) Early Elephantidae of Africa and a tentative correlation of Plio-Pleistocene deposits. *Nature* 225, 328-32.

Maglio, V.J. (1973) Origin and evolution of the Elephantidae. *Trans. Amer. Phil. Soc.* n.s. 63(3), 1-149.

Merla, G. (1963) Missione geologica nell'Etiopia meridionale del Consiglio nazionale delle ricerche 1959-1960: Notizie geomorfologiche e geologiche. *Giornale di Geologia* ser. 2, 31, 1-56.

Merrick, H.V. (1976) Recent archaeological research in the Plio-Pleistocene deposits of the lower Omo, southwestern Ethiopia. In Isaac, G.L. and McCown, E.R. (eds.), *Human Origins, Louis Leakey and the East African Evidence*, 461-81. Menlo Park, Cal.

Merrick, H.V. *et al.* (1973) Archaeological occurrences of early Pleistocene age from the Shungura Formation, lower Omo valley, Ethiopia. *Nature* 242, 572-5.

Mohr, P.A. (1968) The Cainozoic volcanic succession in Ethiopia. *Bull. volcanologique* 32, 5-14.

Petter, G. (1973) Carnivores pléistocènes du ravin d'Olduvai (Tanzanie). *Fossil Vertebrates of Africa* 3, 43-100.

Reilly, T.A. *et al.* (1966) Age and polarity of the Turkana lavas, northwest Kenya. *Nature* 210, 1145-6.

Ross, C.S. and Smith, R.L. (1961) Ash-flow tuffs: their origin, geologic relations and identification. *U.S. Geol. Survey*, professional paper 366.

Sclater, P.L. (1899) Results of the second Bòttego expedition into eastern Africa. *Science* 10, 951-5.

Shuey, R.T. *et al.* (1974) Magnetostratigraphy of the Shungura Formation, southwestern Ethiopia: fine structure of the lower Matuyama polarity epoch. *Earth and Planetary Science Letters* 23, 249-60.

Simpson, G.G. (1960) Notes on the measurement of faunal resemblance. *Amer. J. Sci.* 258-A, 300-11.

Smith, R.L. (1960) Ash flows. *Bull. Geol. Soc. America.* 71, 795-842.

Sparks, R.S.J. and Walker, G.P.L. (1973) The ground surge deposit: a third type of pyroclastic rock. *Nature-Phys. Sci.* 241, 62-4.

Tchernov, E. (1976) Crocodilians from the late Cenozoic of the Rudolf basin. In Coppens, Y. *et al.* (eds.), *Earliest Man and Environments in the Lake Rudolf basin: Stratigraphy, Paleoecology and Evolution.* Chicago.

Van Damme, D. and Gautier, A. (1972) Molluscan assemblages from the later Cenozoic of the lower Omo basin, Ethiopia. *Quaternary Research* 2(1), 25-37.

Vannutelli, L. and Citerni, C. (1897) Relazione preliminare sui risultati geografici della seconda spedizione Bottego. *Bulletino Società Geografica Italiana*, ser. 3, 10, 320-30.

Vannutelli, L. and Citerni, C. (1899) *Seconda spedizione Bottego: L'Omo. Viaggio di esplorazione nell'Africa orientale.* Milano.

Walsh, J. and Dodson, R.G. (1969) Geology of North Turkana. *Kenya Geol. Survey Rept.* 82, 42 pages (1:500,000 map).

C.K. Brain

Some aspects of the South African australopithecine sites and their bone accumulations

This paper is in two parts: the first provides a brief survey of the current research position at each of the five South African australopithecine sites, while the second deals with some specific problems in the interpretation of the bone accumulations of which the australopithecine remains form a part.

1. Current work at the sites

The five South African sites are Taung, Sterkfontein, Makapansat, Kromdraai B and Swartkrans. As is well known, the fossils occur in calcified cave fillings, the caves having resulted from the solution of pre-Cambrian dolomite limestone, except in the case of Taung where the cavity developed in a secondary cliff travertine, deposited against the dolomite escarpment edge.

(a) Taung

Very little organized palaeontological or geological work was done at Taung in the twenty years following the investigations of Peabody and his associates (Peabody, 1954). More recently, studies have been undertaken by Butzer, results of which are currently in the press. In a recent paper, Partridge (1973) has presented geomorphological evidence indicating a maximum age for the deposit in which the fossils occur. He has attempted to assess the rate of nickpoint migration inland from the coast along the Orange-Vaal-Harts-Buxton river system and has argued that the hominid-bearing deposit must postdate the arrival of the Post-African I nickpoint. This event is placed at 0.87 million years BP.

(*b*) *Sterkfontein*

In his report on the 1957/8 excavations at the Sterkfontein Extension Site, Robinson (1962) described a sequence of three breccias: the lower, middle and upper units. The lower breccia is regarded as the oldest in the fossil cavern and is extensively exposed in the type site and elsewhere. The stratigraphically higher levels of this breccia have yielded almost all the remains of *Australopithecus* from the site as well as the faunal remains recovered during the pre-1948 excavations of Broom and Robinson. No stone artifacts have so far been found in the lower breccia unit.

The middle breccia was regarded by Robinson as resting unconformably on the upper surface of the lower breccia and as filling a gap created by the partial collapse of lower breccia material into an adjacent and lower cavern. The middle breccia was considered to be the sole source of the Sterkfontein artifacts and has also provided some fragmentary hominid remains. Subsequent minor adjustments in the lower and middle fillings again created a limited amount of space beneath the roof of the western end. This was filled by the material now known as the upper breccia, apparently a rather insignificant deposit.

An extensive and long-term research project at Sterkfontein was started in 1966, the objectives of which have been described by Tobias and Hughes (1969). The clearing of the rubble from the type site and adjacent hilltop areas has exposed many new sections and has shown the cave filling to be more extensive that previously thought, particularly in the western areas.

A detailed study of the underground cave system at Sterkfontein has recently been undertaken by Wilkinson (unpublished M.Sc. thesis, Department of Geography, Witwatersrand University) which clarifies some of the relationships of underground breccia exposures to those on the surface. Geological and geomorphological studies in the Sterkfontein valley have been undertaken by Partridge (1973) and Brink (unpublished), while sedimentological research on the Sterkfontein breccias is in progress by Butzer (pers. comm.).

The most significant remaining problem at Sterkfontein is, to my mind, clarification of the stratigraphic and temporal relationships of the lower and middle breccias as described by Robinson. Why is stone culture apparently restricted to the middle breccia and absent from the lower unit where remains of *Australopithecus* are abundant? What is the precise nature of the hominids associated with the abundant artifacts from the middle breccia of the 'Extension Site'? (See Wallace's contribution to this volume.) It is hoped that the current work of Tobias and Hughes will answer these and other questions.

An exhaustive study of the fossil Bovidae from the Type Site (Broom/Robinson excavations) and Extension Site (Robinson 1957-8 excavations) has just been undertaken by Dr E.S. Vrba (Department of

Palaeontology, Tranvaal Museum) (Vrba, 1974). The study included material from breccia dumps provided by Tobias and Hughes. On the basis of the bovid remains, clear faunal differences appear to exist between the lower and middle breccia units, while the composition of the faunas suggests habitat changes during the timespan covered by the two accumulations.

(*c*) *Makapansgat Limeworks*

Fieldwork is still being undertaken at this site intermittently by teams from the Bernard Price Institute and Anatomy Department of the Witwatersrand University, while geomorphological investigations have been made by Partridge (1973) and Brink. Sedimentological studies by Butzer are in progress (pers. comm.).

In a recent paper, Tobias (1973) reports that he has discovered 'a succession of breccias and travertines below the supposed basal travertine', and suggests that these may span the time gap between the date of cave opening inferred by Partridge (1973), i.e. 3.67 million years, and the proposed, though tentative faunal date of 2.5 to 3.0 million years of Cooke and Maglio (as quoted by Tobias, 1973).

The greatest concentration of fossil bones at Makapansgat Limeworks occurs in the Phase I grey breccia. The question of how this remarkable accumulation was built up in what was obviously a deep subterranean situation remains an important one. In a recent paper Maier (1973) has provided a reconstruction in which the bones of the grey breccia levels accumulated as heaps below narrow vertical shafts, linking the cavern with surface occupation sites.

(*d*) *Kromdraai B*

No serious work has been done at Kromdraai since the excavation of 1955 when an attempt was made to define the northern wall of the Kromdraai B deposit, and decalcified breccia was excavated to a depth of 14 ft. A ground survey done by the writer in 1973 (Brain, in press) confirmed that the three deposits of Kromdraai A, B and C represent calcified fillings of enlarged joint planes or lineaments in the dolomite, orientated E-W in the case of Kromdraai A (the Faunal Site) and B (the Australopithecine Site), but N-S in the case of Kromdraai C, a small deposit apparently associated with the original entrance to site B (see Figure 1).

Analysis of the fossil fauna from KB and comparison with that of KA suggests strongly that the deposits are not of the same age (Freedman and Brain, 1972; Hendey, 1973). It is not clear which of the two is definitely the older. No fauna has so far been isolated from KC.

The sample of fossil bones available for study from the solid and decalcified breccia of KB consists of 4,985 fragments. An

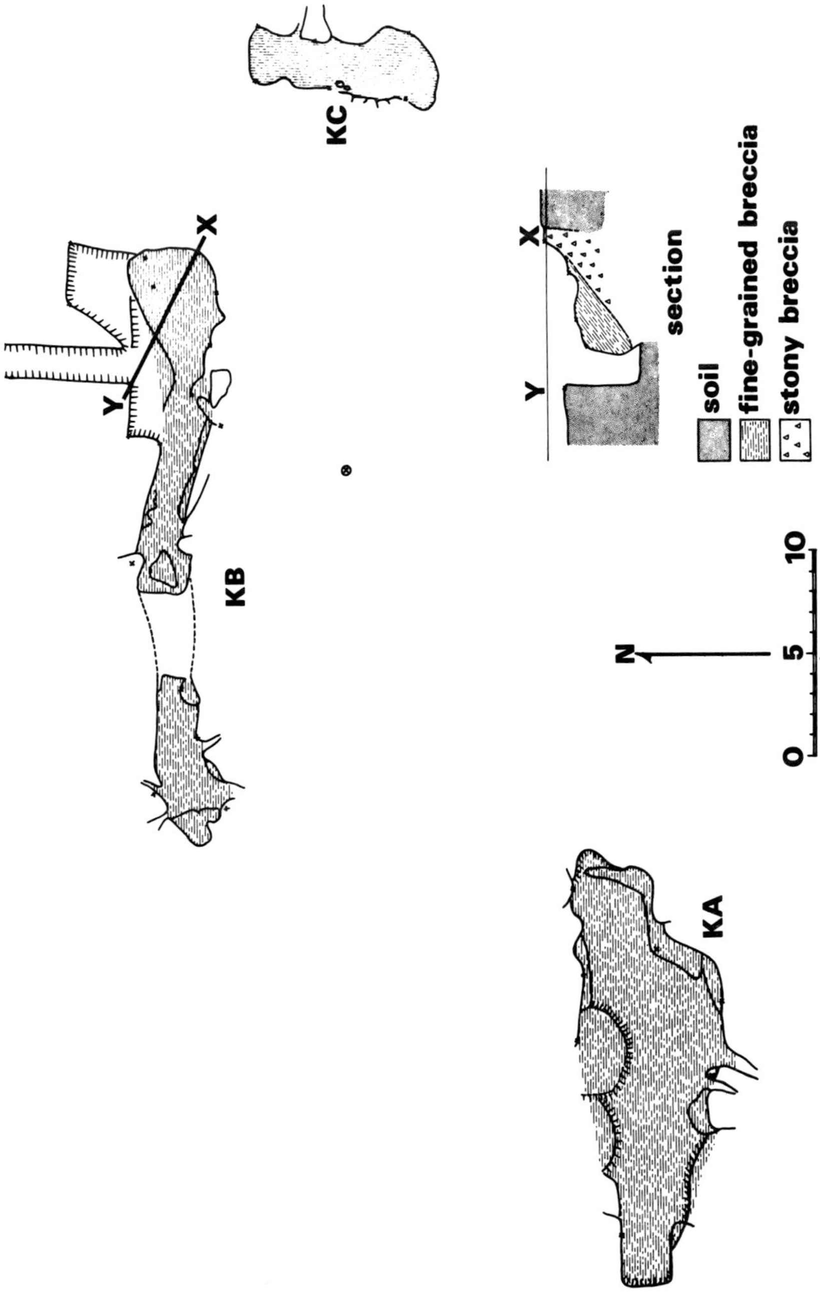

Figure 1. Plan of the Kromdraai A, B and C deposits. The type specimen of *Paranthropus robustus* was found near point X in the KB breccia.

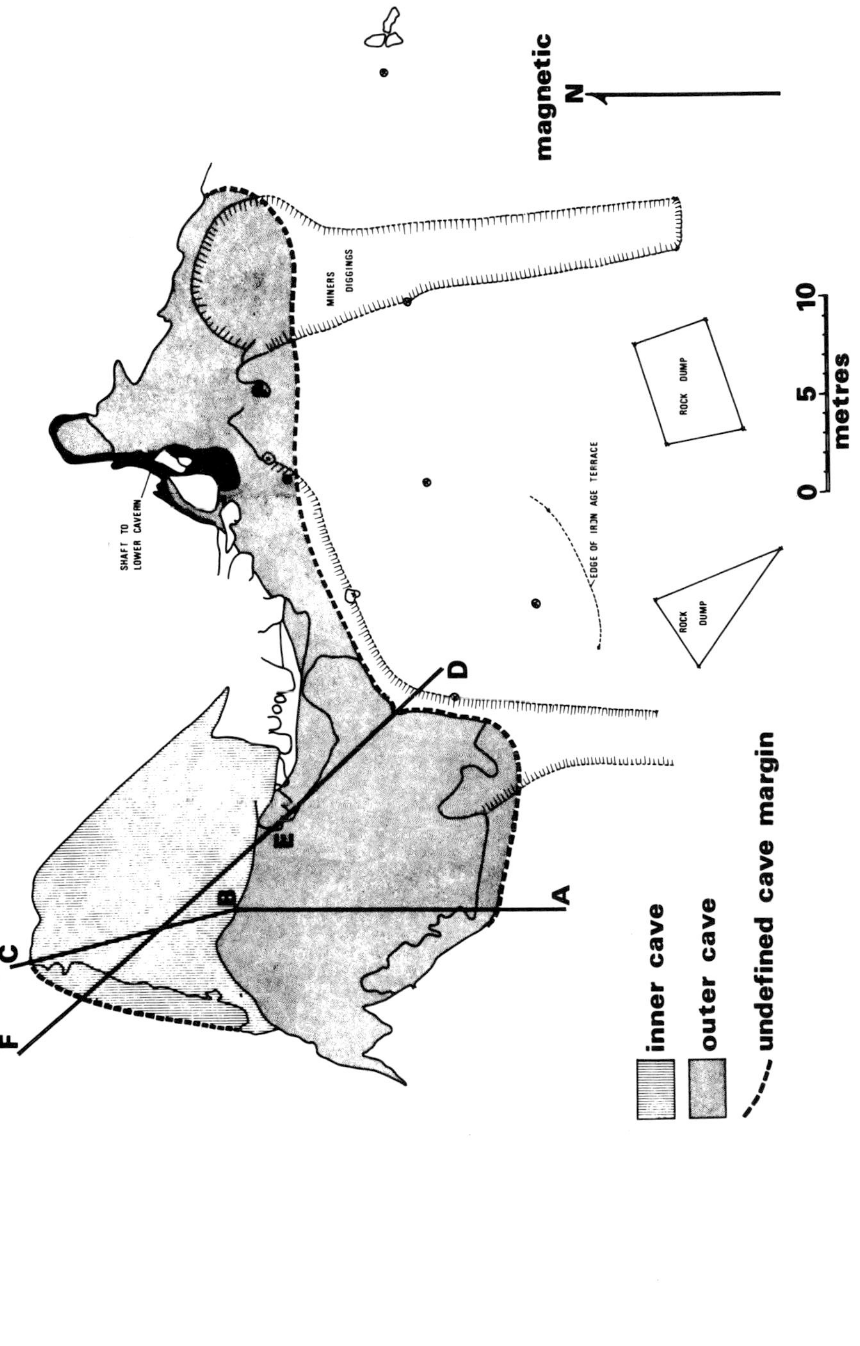
magnetic
N
0
5
10
metres
MINERS
DIGGINGS
ROCK DUMP
ROCK
DUMP
EDGE OF IRON AGE TERRACE
SHAFT TO
LOWER CAVERN
A
B
C
D
E
F
inner cave
outer cave
undefined cave margin

interpretation of this bone accumulation has been attempted (Brain, 1975) and will be discussed further shortly.

(*e*) *Swartkrans*

The objectives and progress of the current fieldwork at Swartkrans have been reviewed in several publications (e.g. Brain 1967, 1970, 1973a). The most time-consuming part of the present project has been the removal of miner's rubble from the entire cave area and the hand-sorting of fossil-bearing breccia from this. A list of the fossil hominids recovered to date as a result of this work has recently been compiled (Brain, 1973b).

With the completion of the clearing operation, all available profiles are now visible and detailed surveys of the surface and underground features are in progress. Professor K.W. Butzer is cooperating on the stratigraphic and sedimentological aspects. The Swartkrans cave system may still be divided conventiently into an outer and inner cave, separated by a floor block over which a substantial travertine boss had been laid down, while a lower cave underlies almost the entire length of the outer cave, beneath its north wall. As shown in Figure 2, the outer cave has a length in the E-W direction of 45 m., and a width on the west side of 13 m. Dimensions of the inner cave are approximately 16 m. (E-W) by 11 m. (N-S) and the cave descends to about 19 m. below the natural hillside surface.

The filling of the outer cave is generally referred to as the pink breccia[1] while that of the inner cave is designated the stratified brown breccia. A third breccia unit, the identity of which was pointed out to me by Professor Butzer, is sandwiched in time between the end of the accumulation period of the pink breccia and the beginning of that of the stratified brown. It is termed the orange breccia and is interbedded in the upper levels of the inner cave's floor travertine. The orange breccia has recently yielded a flattened hominid cranium (SKW 29) and was almost certainly the source of the beautiful *Paranthropus* mandible SK 23, recovered during the lime-mining operation of 1950 by Dr Robinson. This was previously thought to have come from the stratified brown breccia, which however has probably not yielded any fossil hominids to date.

Reconstructed vertical sections showing some suggested stages in the formation of the Swartkrans cave system are given in Figure 4. The sections are through the western end of the site and run SE-NW, approximately along the line of section D-E-F indicated in Figure 2.

Figure 4a shows a stage at which the outer cave has filled with soil,

1. Since this paper was written, a great deal of new information has become available on the relationships of the Swartkrans breccias. Two members have now been formally recognised and a new sequence of stages in the formation of the cave system proposed. The reader is referred to Brain, 1976b and Butzer, 1976.

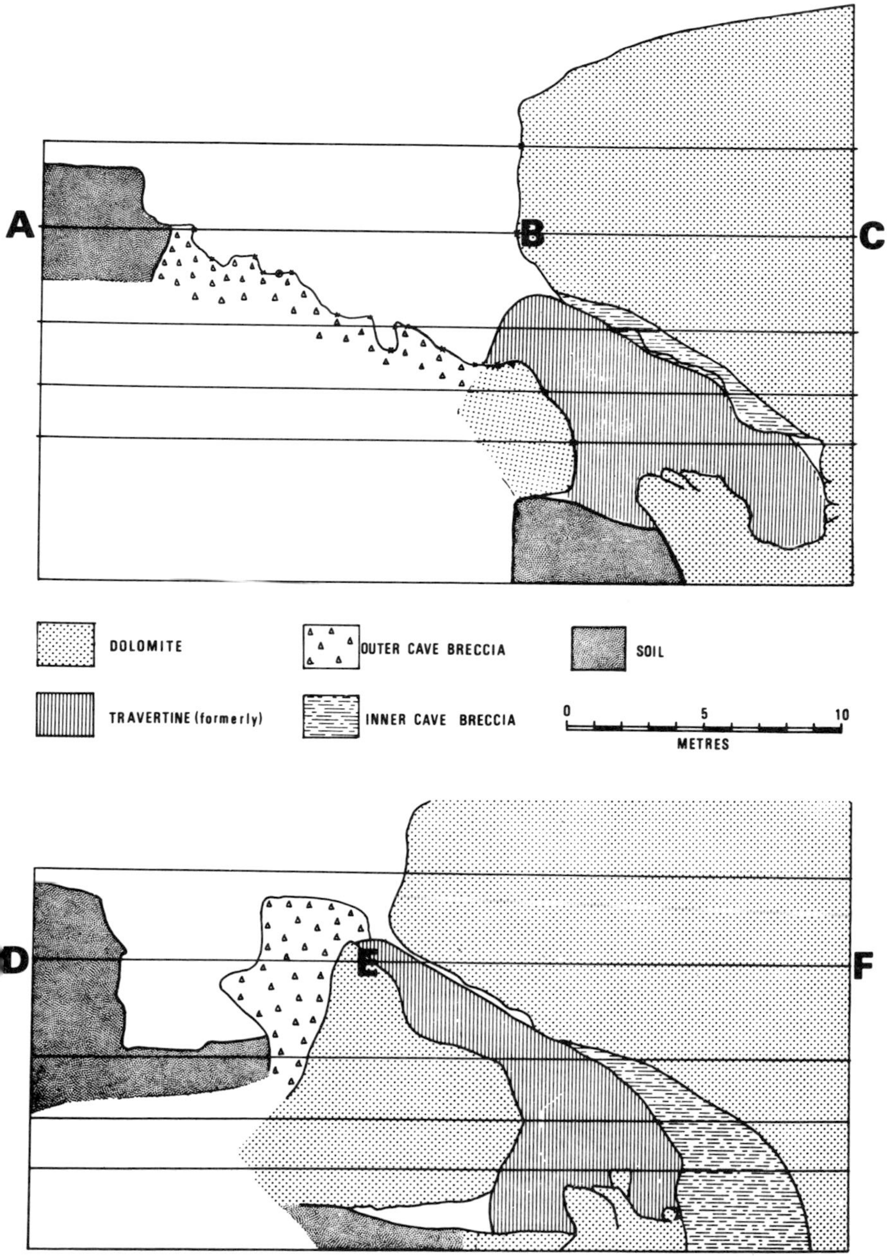
A
B
C
DOLOMITE
OUTER CAVE BRECCIA
SOIL
TRAVERTINE (formerly)
INNER CAVE BRECCIA
0
5
10
METRES
D
E
F

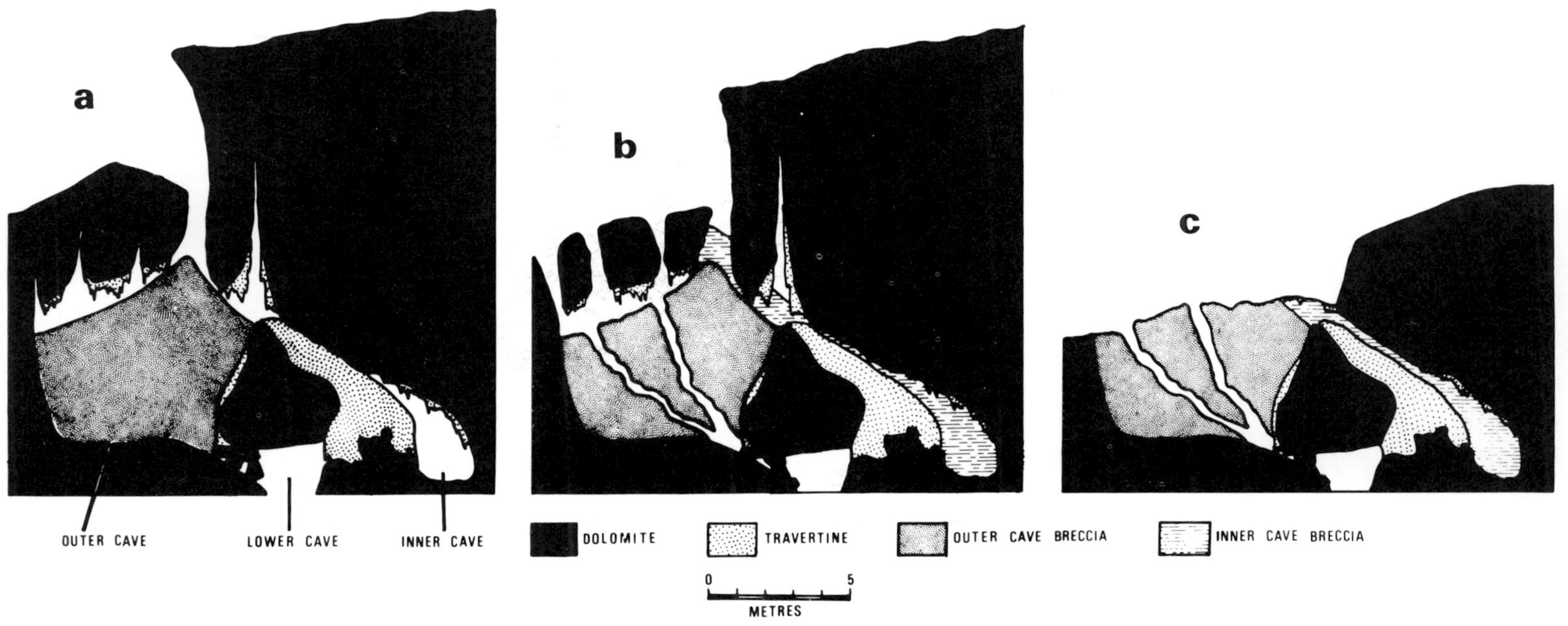

Figure 4. Reconstructed sections through the western end of the Swartkrans cave system. The sections are discussed in the text.

rock, bones and debris destined to form the pink breccia. This has entered through a presumed near-vertical shaft of unknown dimensions and depth. The inner cave is still sealed by the travertine boss deposited over the floor block which subsided originally from the cave roof.

Figure 4b reconstructs the cave system after a considerable but undefined lapse of time. Under the weight of the outer cave breccia (which deposit has now been calcified), the floor block has subsided further, by an estimated 1 m. Access has thus been provided to the inner cave which has filled up with the sediment now known as the stratified brown breccia. This material appears to have been laid down in standing water, and where it abuts against the outer cave breccia an unconformable contact exists. The dolomite roof over the outer cave has been eroded and broken up by aven formation. Rainwater percolating down through the outer cave breccia, en route to the lower cave, has carved a series of irregular and ramifying channels through the breccia mass. Some of these remained empty, as natural gutters for storm water, others have become choked with sediment in varying degrees of calcification.

Figure 4c shows the situation as it was this century, before mining or excavation occurred. Erosion has removed the roof over the entire outer cave. Channels through the breccia are still leading water down to the lower cave, which now has an appreciable deposit of soil in it, particularly at the western end.

Homo *at Swartkrans: the problem of channel formation in the outer cave breccia*

During the first year of palaeontological work at Swartkrans, abundant remains of robust australopithecines were discovered in the pink breccia of the outer cave by Dr Robert Broom and Dr J.T. Robinson. Then on April 29, 1949, a mandible was discovered by Dr Robinson that appeared strikingly different from those already found. It was described by Broom and Robinson (1949) as belonging to *Telanthropus capensis*, a form 'somewhat allied to Heidelberg man and intermediate between one of the ape-men and true man'. The mandible, that of a mature adult and now designated Sk 15, preserved the left M_1-M_3 and right M_2-M_3. Closely associated with the specimen was the buccal half of the crown of a RP_4 (SK 43), a LP_3 (SK 18a) and the proximal end of a radius (SK 18b). These are thought to come from one individual.

In September 1949, part of the right mandibular corpus of an old adult was found. Designated SK 45, it contained M_1 and M_2 and the alveolus for M_3. It was described by Broom and Robinson (1950) in a paper entitled 'Man contemporaneous with Swartkrans ape-man'. At about the same time a maxillary fragment (SK 80) was discovered. It came from an old adult with well-worn teeth. Both this specimen and the mandibular fragment were referred to *Telanthropus capensis* by Robinson (1953) in his paper on '*Telanthropus* and its phylogenetic significance'.

The genus *Telanthropus* was subsequently sunk by Robinson (1961) and the Swartkrans specimens transferred to *Homo erectus*.

In July 1969 Mr R.J. Clarke assembled hominid cranial fragments collectively designated SK 846b and 847, which had previously been referred to *Paranthropus robustus*. After assembly of SK 846b and 847, it was found that there was a perfect join across the left side between the posterior palatal fragment of SK 847 and the maxillary fragment SK 80, previously classified as *Homo*. The composite cranium SK 846b/847/80 was re-allocated to *Homo* sp. in a paper on 'More evidence for an advanced hominid from Swartkrans' by Clarke, Howell and Brain (1970).

The excavation of Broom and Robinson spanned a depth of about 15 ft. of the outer cave breccia immediately to the south and west of what is today called the 'Paranthropus face'. The dimensions of the outer cave involved were 12-16 ft. in a N-S direction and 24-30 ft. E-W. Fairly uniform pink breccia, typical of the outer cave, was encountered almost throughout, but in April 1949 a small volume of rather different matrix was broken into against the south margin of the excavation. From it came the mandible, SK 15, the two isolated teeth and proximal radius. Broom and Robinson wrote:

> Though this [the mandible, SK 15] was discovered in the same cave as the large ape-man, it is clearly of considerably later date. In the main bone breccia of the cave deposit there has been a pocket excavated and refilled by a darker type of matrix. The pocket was of very limited extent, being only about 4 ft. by 3 ft. and about 2 ft. in thickness. The deposit was remarkably barren, there being no other bones in it except the human jaw and a few remains of very small mammals. We are thus at present unable to give an age of the deposit except to say that it must be considerably younger than the main deposit. If the main deposit is upper Pliocene, not improbably the pocket may be lower Pleistocene.

When describing the second *Telanthropus* specimen, the mandibular fragment SK 45 (which came from typical outer cave pink breccia), Broom and Robinson (1950) again referred to the provenance of SK 15: 'It is unfortunate that we cannot give any more precise dating to the jaw. The pocket in the main deposit is somewhat different in material and must be of later date, but it may not be geologically much later.'

When Robinson wrote his paper in 1953 on '*Telanthropus* and its phylogenetic significance', he described the second specimen (maxillary fragment SK 80) from the main outer cave breccia and inclined to the view that all the *Telanthropus* specimens, including the controversial SK 15 mandible, were contemporaneous with the *Paranthropus* remains. Robinson (Broom and Robinson, 1952) had in fact expressed the opinion the year before that there was insufficient evidence at that stage to decide whether the material was coeval with or later than *Paranthropus* and its associated fauna.

In the meanwhile, a fluorine test was undertaken by Dr K.P. Oakley on bone from the SK 15 pocket and the results were compared with those on bones from the undoubted *Paranthropus* breccia. No significant difference in fluorine content was found between the two samples, suggesting that any large age difference was unlikely, provided the fluorine method could reliably be applied in calcified sediments, which has unfortunately not yet been established.

Another piece of evidence which contributed to Robinson's suggestion that the SK 15 pocket was contemporaneous with the man *Paranthropus* deposit came from sediment studies which I undertook at the time. Grading of the SK 15 pocket sediment was found to be broadly similar to that of main *Paranthropus*-bearing breccia sediment adjacent to the pocket. Figures obtained were as follows:

Grade	Particle sizes (mm)	Breccia in contact with *Telanthropus* mandible (SK 15)	Closest available *Paranthropus*-bearing breccia
Fine Gravel	4.7 – 2.0	3.8%	3.6%
Coarse sand	2.0 – 0.42	8.3%	3.7%
Sand	0.42 – 0.15	11.1%	13.0%
Fine sand	0.15 – 0.05	23.9%	26.0%
Silt	0.05 – 0.005	44.0%	44.5%
Clay	0.005	9.0%	9.3%
		100.1%	100.1%

The carbonate content of the matrix in contact with the *Telanthropus* mandible was found to be 46.0% (based on a sample weighing 301.5 gm.), while 72 samples of outer cave pink breccia (the undoubted *Paranthropus*-bearing deposit) gave a range of 59.6-90.0%, with a mean value of 76.8% (Brain, 1958). It appeared that the only distinct difference between the sediment of the SK 15 pocket and that of the surrounding pink breccia was a reduced carbonate content in the former.

It was on the basis of evidence such as this that Robinson assumed that the SK 15 matrix represented a decalcified pocket contemporaneous with the main breccia. The view was supported by Brain (1958).

Some more recent evidence on the SK 15 pocket will now be discussed. Clearing of the entire surface of the outer cave breccia has recently revealed a number of features not previously visible. It is now obvious that the breccia has been considerably affected by the presence of the lower cave beneath the northern margin of the outer cave. A complicated system of solution channels has developed through the outer cave breccia, serving as gutters leading storm water from the natural hillside surface (at present coinciding with the breccia surface) down to the lower cave and to the level of subterranean standing water. Two major solution shafts developed, descending through the breccia mass and then leading to the lower cave. One was in the SW corner of the outer cave filling, the other just to the east of the 'Paranthropus face'. Between them, a ramifying system of minor channels, each seldom more than a metre wide, make their way down at an overall angle of about 45 degrees, from the southern surface of the breccia mass to the lower cave beneath the northern wall. The channels are clearly long-term solution features; their surfaces are etched and weathered and secondary stalactites have been deposited on the breccia surfaces themselves. The channels are either empty, acting as active gutters today, or are choked partially or completely with sediment. The fillings may be completely calcified, with calcium carbonate contents in excess of 60% by weight, or may be incoherent. In grading, the channel fill sediments closely resemble that of the primary breccia, as it is to be expected since the source of both sediments is the hillside dolomite soil on the surface slopes.

At least three channels pass through the outer cave breccia at the base of the excavation section of Broom and Robinson. These, and the various other channels are now being surveyed and incorporated into the plans and sections. It is already apparent that one of the channels (the middle one of the three) almost certainly linked up with the brown breccia pocket in which Dr Robinson found SK 15. The pocket, as depicted in Robinson's paper (1952, p.10) now seems to represent a partially calcified channel-fill in section, which proceeds obliquely down to the lower cave beneath.

Following this particular channel upwards towards the south, one encounters a pocket of loose chocolate soil, containing abundant bone, before the filling is once again calcified into a solid brown breccia higher up. The upper calcified part of the fill contains a bifacial artifact, partially exposed and still in place, together with some visible bone. The interface between the calcified fill and the primary breccia on either side is sometimes difficult to detect.

About two cubic metres of chocolate brown, loose fill were removed from the channel immediately below the calcified portion referred to above. On sieving, this sediment was found to contain a total of 851 bone fragments, including one hominid fossil, a left maxillary piece with P^2-M^2 and part of M^3. This has not yet been described, but is designated SKW 12. Minimum numbers of animals represented by the bone fragments are listed in Table 1. Specific identifications are not given as the material is being studied at present. In addition to the remains listed, two pieces of shell indicate the presence of at least one ostrich egg shell.

Table 1 Individual animals based on remains from the Channel Pocket

	No. of individuals
Hominid	1
Antelope Class I	3
Antelope Class II	5
Antelope Class III	2
Antelope Class IV	1
Zebra	1
Jackal	2
Small felid	1
Hyrax (2 species)	5
Hare	1
Tortoise	1
Guineafowl	1
Francolin	1
Total	25

Table 2 Lengths of bones from the Channel Pocket

Length in cm.	*Bone flakes*	*Other bone pieces*	*Totals*
0–1	2 (0.5%)	2	4 (0.5%)
1–2	29 (7.5%)	52	81 (9.5%)
2–3	97 (25.1%)	115	212 (24.9%)
3–4	112 (29.0%)	95	207 (24.3%)
4–5	62 (16.1%)	73	135 (15.9%)
5–6	40 (10.0%)	49	89 (10.5%)
6–7	26 (6.7%)	34	60 (7.1%)
7–8	9 (2.3%)	15	24 (2.8%)
8–9	4 (1.0%)	8	12 (1.4%)
9–10	3 (0.8%)	8	11 (1.3%)
10–11	2 (0.5%)	8	10 (1.2%)
11–12	0 (–)	1	1 (0.1%)
12–13	0 (–)	1	1 (0.1%)
14–15	0 (–)	1	1 (0.1%)
16–17	0 (–)	1	1 (0.1%)
17–18	0 (–	1	1 (0.1%)
18–29	0 (–)	1	1 (0.1%)
Totals	386 (99.5%)	465	851 (100.0%)

The bones are extremely fragmented, 75% of them being less than 5 cm. in length (see Table 2). 45% of the total fragments consist of 'bone flakes' (as defined in Brain, 1974) from the long bones of the larger mammals, and in this respect the bone assemblage closely resembles those representing primitive human food remains. In an attempt to define criteria whereby Stone Age human food remains in southern African caves may be recognized, the writer has recently studied bone accumulations from four intensively occupied cave sites; Pomongwe, Rhodesia; Bushman Rock, Transvaal; Wilton, Cape and

Fackelträger, South West Africa. Although the proportions of prey animals varied greatly at each site, all the accumulations showed more than 50% of bone flakes, resulting from the smashing of long bones during extraction of marrow. Stone tools were presumably used and the abundant presence of bone flakes seems to be a reliable indicator of human activity (Brain, unpublished).

The hyrax remains come from two species, a large and a small, and on the basis of damage suffered, more closely resemble human food remains than those of leopard-size carnivores which appear to predominate in the main outer cave breccia. The 25 hyrax bones from the channel pocket are listed in Table 3.

Table 3 Procavia skeletal parts from the Channel Pocket

Minimum number of individuals = 5

Maxillary fragments	5
Mandibular fragments	3
Isolated teeth	3
Humerus shaft	1
Distal humerus pieces	9
Proximal radius piece	1
Femur shaft	1
Distal tibia piece	1
Calcaneus	1
Phalanx	1
Total	26

In view of recently acquired information on channel formation through the outer cave breccia, it now seems likely that the brown breccia pocket from which Dr Robinson obtained the *Homo* mandible, SK 15, was not, in fact, contemporaneous with the primary *Paranthropus*-bearing breccia after all. It appears to have formed part of a calcified filling to a channel leading down to the lower cave.

Channel cutting could have occurred at any time subsequent to the consolidation of the outer cave breccia and is still progressing today. First indications are that the fill in question dates to the Acheulean cultural period, vague though this term may be, and that the bone fragments represent food remains of human hunters rather than carnivores. The *Homo* fossils themselves may have resulted from natural deaths in the vicinity of the occupation site. The bones from the channel fill form a contrast to those from the primary breccia, both as to fragmentation and species present. Tortoise and ostrich eggshell have, for instance, not been recorded among the 14,000 bones examined from the primary breccia thus far. They are ubiquitous among Stone Age human food remains elsewhere.

While it seems that the *Homo* mandible SK 15 (and associated radial fragment) postdate the accumulation of the primary breccia by an undefined interval, there is no reason to believe that the other specimens (SK 846b/847/80 and SK 45), recovered from the primary breccia itself, should differ in age from the main *Paranthropus* sample.

It is hoped that careful excavation of primary breccia and defined channel fills, shortly to be undertaken, will clarify the age relationships of the deposits, their fauna and culture.

2. *Interpretation of australopithecine-bearing bone accumulations: evidence from skeletal disproportions*

The interpretation of a complete bone accumulation or representative sample thereof from a cave generally has several objectives:

1. To identify the animals whose bones are represented in the accumulation.
2. To estimate the minimum number of individuals involved.
3. To list the skeletal parts by which the animals are represented.
4. To decide what agencies were responsible for collecting the bones.
5. To reconstruct the behaviour of the hominids or other animals responsible for the accumulation.
6. To attempt environmental reconstructions.

In very few cases will a bone accumulation consist of complete and undamaged skeletons. This can only be expected where burial and preservation have been perfect. Generally, however, the natural processes of carnivore (including hominid) action, disintegration and decay will have selectively removed certain parts of the skeletons while leaving others. If we know what destructive influences have been at work, it should be possible to predict which parts of a given skeleton will survive and which will disappear. The study and interpretation of skeletal disproportions in bone accumulations can provide a good deal of information about the history of the accumulation in question.

Dart's interpretation of the Makapansgat bone accumulation

Professor R.A. Dart's pioneering interpretation (1957) of 7,159 bone fragments from the grey breccia of the Makapansgat Limeworks revealed some striking and unexpected disproportions in skeletal parts. The bones were found to come predominantly from antelope (293 individuals; 39 large, 126 medium, 100 small and 28 very small) but the other animals included 45 baboons, 20 pigs, 17 hyaenas, 7 porcupines and 5 australopiths. Dart concluded that the bones had been collected originally by the hominids, who used the adhering meat as food and the bones themselves for tools.

Returning to the disproportions, Dart found that parts of skull were exceptionally common, making up 34.5% of all the recognizable fragments. Vertebrae, on the other hand, were unaccountably rare, a total of only 163 being found; only 1.4% of what there should have been. Among the scarce vertebrae, the atlas and axis were abnormally abundant, while tail vertebrae were not represented at all.

Similar remarkable disproportions were found in the limb bones, parts of the fore-limbs being much more abundant than those of the hind-limbs. Turning to the individual bones of the limbs, Dart found that some ends of such bones were more common than others. In the humerus, 336 distal ends were found but only 33 proximal ones, a ratio of 10:1. Similarly in the tibia, the ratio of distal to proximal ends was 119:64.

In attempting to explain these disproportions, Dart suggested that the australopiths brought back only certain parts of the prey animals to the cave. They concentrated particularly on bones which made good tools: mandibles for saws and scrapers, distal humeri for clubs. Parts missing from the fossil collection were either not brought back at all or, as in the case of tails, were used for special purposes outside the cave. They may have served as 'whips or signals in hunting'.

An alternative explanation for Dart's disproportions: the evidence of the Hottentots' goats

It is obvious that a bovid skeleton consists of individual parts differing widely in shape and strength characteristics. If the parts of a complete skeleton are all subjected to the same destructive treatment, such as early hominid or hyaena feeding action, weathering or abrasion, certain skeletal elements will survive far better than others. Delicate parts such as scapula blades or ribs will disappear long before robust ones like astragali or distal humeri. Clearly what was needed was a test situation where complete skeletons could be subjected to known destructive influences, so that the composition of the surviving residue could be studied, while the reasons for survival could be evaluated. This situation was found among Topnaar Hottentot villages in the Central Namib of South West Africa.

The Hottentot goat study has been described in various publications (Brain, 1967, 1969 and 1976). The eight villages are scattered along the lower reaches of the Kuiseb River inland from Walvis Bay, and here about 150 Hottentots maintain 2,000 goats in the Kuiseb River bed. The goats provide the people with their only regular source of meat. The goats are butchered and cooked in a manner which has been described in detail; the marrow-containing bones are broken with a stone hammer and anvil and the remains simply discarded for the domestic dogs to gnaw. No other scavengers are normally involved. The residue, representing skeletal parts found unchewable by Hottentots and their dogs, is left to bleach on the desert surface.

A collection of 2,373 goat bone fragments was made around the Hottentot villages. These were found to have come from a minimum of

Table 4 Skeletal parts in the goat bone sample from South West Africa

	Skeletal part		*Totals*
Skull	Horns and cores	385	
	Cranial fragments	70	
	Maxillary fragments	57	512
Mandible	Complete half mandibles	38	
	Mandibular fragments	150	188
Loose teeth		15	15
Vertebrae	1st cervical (atlas)	12	
	2nd cervical (axis)	14	
	Other cervical	12	
	Thoracic	21	
	Lumbar	31	
	Sacral	1	
	Caudal	0	
	Fragments	24	115
Ribs		174	174
Scapula	Head portion	28	
	Other fragments	31	59
Pelvis	Acetabular portion	34	
	Other fragments	21	55
Humerus	Proximal ends	0	
	Distal ends	82	
	Shaft fragments	114	196
Radius and ulna	Complete bones	3	
	Proximal ends	62	
	Distal ends	19	
	Shaft fragments	123	207
Femur	Proximal ends	18	
	Distal ends	9	
	Shaft fragments	88	115
Tibia	Proximal ends	13	
	Distal ends	72	
	Shaft fragments	152	237
Metacarpal	Complete bones	8	
	Proximal ends	24	
	Distal ends	15	
	Shaft fragments	53	100
Metatarsal	Complete bones	9	
	Proximal ends	30	
	Distal ends	11	
	Shaft pieces	51	101
Astragalus	Complete	16	16
Calcaneum	Complete	14	14
Phalanges	Complete	21	21
Bone flakes		248	248
			2373

Table 5 Goat mandibles from South West Africa (age classes estimated on tooth eruption)

		Number of goats	
Age class		*Left side*	*Right side*
Under 6 months		1	0
6–12 months		17	23
12–20 months		7	6
Over 20 months		28	35
	Totals	53	64

Table 6 Goat bones from South West Africa, survival of parts

Part	*Number found*	*Original number*	*% Survival*
Half mandibles	117	1128	91.4
Humerus, distal	82	128	64.0
Tibia, distal	72	128	56.3
Radius and ulna, proximal	65	128	50.8
Metatarsal, proximal	39	128	30.4
Axis	14	64	21.9
Atlas	12	64	18.8
Metacarpal, distal	23	128	18.0
Radius and ulna, distal	22	128	17.2
Metatarsal, distal	20	128	15.6
Femur, proximal	18	128	14.1
Astragalus	16	128	12.5
Calcaneus	14	128	10.9
Ribs	170	1664	10.2
Tibia, proximal	13	128	10.1
Lumbar vertebrae	31	384	8.1
Femur, distal	9	128	7.0
Cervical 3 – 7 vertebrae	12	320	3.8
Phalanges	21	768	2.7
Thoracic vertebrae	21	832	2.5
Sacrum	1	64	1.6
Caudal vertebrae	0	1224	0
Humerus, proximal	0	128	0

64 individual goats, whose ages were estimated on tooth eruption and wear (Table 5). The bone fragments were analysed as to skeletal parts (Table 4) and, working with a minimum number of 64 individual goats, the percentage survival for each skeletal part was calculated. Half mandibles were found to be the most numerous parts, with a survival value of 91.4%. Distal humeri and caudal vertebrae were found to be completely absent (survival 0%). These results are given in Table 6. A similar survival table was drawn up for the

Makapansgat bovid remains (Table 7). Comparison of the two tables shows that, although the order of disappearance of parts among the Makapansgat and goat bone samples is not identical, it is strikingly similar.

The conclusion is reached that the survival of skeletal parts, under any particular destructive regime, is not random but may be correlated with physical characteristics of the bones (or particular portions of bones). Working with the proximal and distal ends of goat limb bones, it was found that those which survived best had high specific gravities, indicating the presence of compact bone, while fusion of epiphyses also occurred early. Those parts, such as proximal humeri, which had low specific gravities and epiphyses which fused late, survived extremely poorly, if at all. The correlation of survival value with these qualities is set out in Table 8.

It is concluded that the disproportions observed by Dart need not have resulted from deliberate hominid selection. The survival pattern could well have resulted from, for instance, hominid or carnivore hunting, upon which scavenging action has been superimposed.

Table 7 Bovid bones from Makapansgat, survival of parts

Part	*Number found*	*Original number*	*% Survival*
Half mandibles	369	586	62.9
Humerus, distal	336	586	57.3
Radius and ulna, proximal	279	586	47.6
Metacarpal, distal	161	586	27.4
Metacarpal, proximal	129	586	22.0
Scapula	126	586	21.5
Tibia, distal	119	586	20.3
Radius and ulna, distal	114	586	19.5
Metatarsal, distal	110	586	18.8
Metatarsal, proximal	107	586	18.3
Pelvis, half	107	586	18.3
Calcaneus	75	586	12.8
Tibia, proximal	64	586	10.9
Astragalus	61	586	10.4
Femur, distal	56	586	9.6
Axis	25	293	8.5
Atlas	20	293	6.8
Humerus, proximal	33	586	5.6
Sacrum	16	293	5.5
Femur, proximal	28	586	4.8
Cervical 3 – 7 vertebrae	47	1465	3.2
Lumbar vertebrae	30	1758	1.7
Phalanges	47	3516	1.3
Ribs	66	7618	0.9
Thoracic vertebrae	24	3809	0.6
Caudal vertebrae	1	4688	0

Table 8 Goat bones: correlation of percentage survival with specific gravity and epiphyseal fusion time

Part		*Survival %*	*S.G.*	*Fusion time (months)*
Humerus				
	Proximal	0	0.58	17
	Distal	64.0	0.97	4
Radius and ulna				
	Proximal	50.8	1.10	4
	Distal	17.2	0.97	21
Femur				
	Proximal	14.1	0.75	18
	Distal	7.0	0.72	20
Tibia				
	Proximal	10.1	0.82	25
	Distal	56.3	1.17	15

Disporoportions and their interpretation in the Swartkrans bone accumulation

A sample of 14,000 bone fragments from the outer cave breccia of Swartkrans has been examined. Of this, 3,600 specimens came from the Broom/Robinson excavations of 1949-53. The rest have come from blocks of breccia blasted out during the two mining episodes at the site (early 1930s and 1950-2). All the specifically identifiable specimens have been processed (with the exception of mammalian microfauna which is being studied separately) and a minimum of 522 individual animals has been listed to date. This figure is provisional as the collection is still being studied. As will be seen from Table 9, the assemblage is made up of at least 72 individual hominids, 69 cercopithecoids, 55 carnivores, 223 bovids and 103 other mammals. Although the bovids have been studied in detail (Vrba, unpublished)[2] the results have not yet been published and the animals are consequently simply grouped in size classes as follows (as discussed in Brain, 1974).

Antelope Class I : Live weight 0-50 lbs or 0-23 kg.
Antelope Class II : Live weight 50-185 lbs or 23-84 kg.
Antelope Class III : Live weight 185-650 lbs or 84-296 kg.
Antelope Class IV : Live weight more than 650 lbs or 296 kg.

For comparative purposes, the minimum numbers of individual animals from Kromdraai B are listed in Table 10, while a comparison of percentages of different animal groups represented at Kromdraai B and Swartkrans is provided in Table 11. It will be seen that cercopithecoids are proportionally the most numerous animals at

2. This work has been published in the interim. See Vrba (1976).

Table 9 Minimum numbers of individual animals from Swartkrans

Hominids		
Homo sp.	2	
Paranthropus robustus	70	
		Total 72
Cercopithecoids		
Papio robinsoni	23	
Dinopithecus ingens	16	
Simopithecus danieli	9	
Parapapio jonesi	4	
Cercopithecoides williamsi	4	
Cercopithecoid indet.	13	
		Total 69
Carnivores		
Panthera aff. *leo*	3	
Panthera pardus	12	
Dinofelis sp.	1	
Megantereon sp.	1	
Hyaena brunnea	3	
Crocuta crocuta	6	
Hyaenictis forfex	1	
Euryboas silberbergi	4	
Hyaenid indet.	4	
Canis mesomelas	10	
Vulpes pulcher	2	
Otocyon recki	1	
Lycaon sp.	1	
Proteles sp.	2	
Carnivores		
Mellivora sp.	1	
Herpestes sp.	2	
Cynictis sp.	1	
		Total 55
Bovids		
Antelope Class I	12	
Antelope Class II	116	
Antelope Class III	82	
Antelope Class IV	13	
		Total 223
Other mammals		
Equus capensis	13	
Equus quagga	12	
Hipparion steytleri	1	
Tapinochoerus meadowsi	7	
Phacochoerus antiquus	4	
Libytherium olduvaiensis	1	
Procavia antiqua	37	
Procavia transvaalensis	24	
Hystrix sp.	4	
		Total 103
	Total individual animals	522

Table 10 Minimum numbers of individual animals from Kromdraai B

Hominids		
Paranthropus robustus	6	Total 6
Cercopithecoids		
Papio robinsoni	18	
p. angusticeps	14	
Cercopithecoides williamsi	5	
		Total 37
Carnivores		
Panthera pardus	2	
? *Dinofelis* sp.	1	
? *Megantereon* sp.	1	
Hyaena cf. *brunnea*	3	
Canis sp.	4	
Proteles sp.	1	
Viverra sp.	1	
Herpestes sp.	2	
		Total 15
Bovids		
Antelope Class I	5	
Antelope Class II	11	
Antelope Class III	7	
Antelope Class IV	1	
		Total 24
Other mammals		
Phacochoerus antiquus	1	
Procavia sp.	1	
Lepus sp.	2	
		Total 4
Reptiles		
cf. *Testudo* sp.	3	
cf. *Cordylus giganteus*	1	
cf. *Crocodylus niloticus*	1	
		Total 4
	Total individual animals	91

Table 11 Numbers of individual mammals from Kromdraai B and Swartkrans, expressed as percentages of the totals

	KB		SK	
	Individuals	*% of total*	*Individuals*	*% of total*
Homo	0	0	2	0.4
Paranthropus	6	6.7	70	13.4
Cercopithecoids	37	43.3	69	13.2
Carnivores	15	17.4	55	10.4
Bovids	24	27.9	223	42.8
Other mammals	5	4.7	103	19.8
Totals	86	100.0	522	100.0

Kromdraai B (43.3%), while bovids dominate at Swartkrans (42.8%). Carnivores are exceptionally abundant at both sites (17.4% at KB and 10.4% at SK) while the fact that 13.8% of all animals recorded at Swartkrans are hominids is quite extraordinary. *Paranthropus* was clearly either a very common animal in Swartkrans times or was a favoured prey victim for the carnivores which used the site. The results listed in Table 11 are shown graphically in Figure 5.

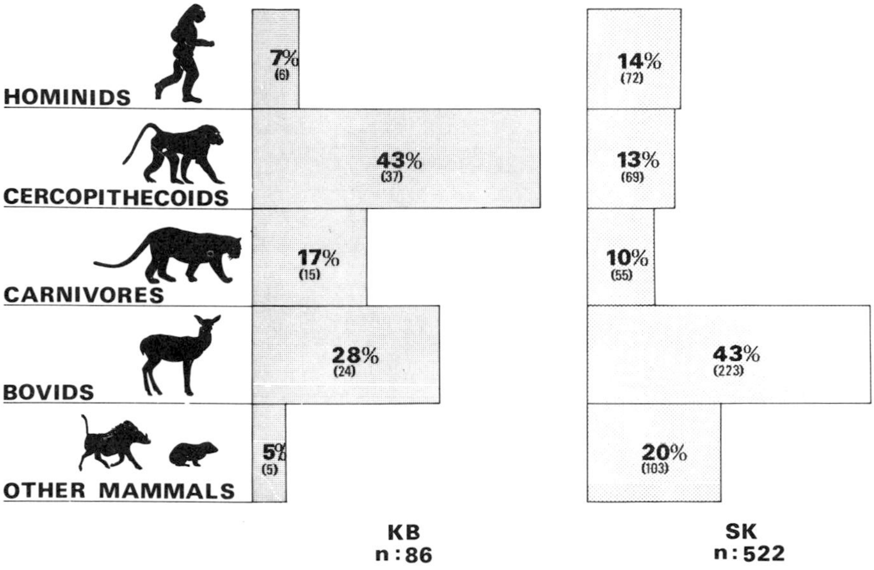

Figure 5. Histograms of percentage abundance of the various animal groups represented in the Swartkrans and Kromdraai B bone accumulations. The minimum number of individual animals so far identified from Kromdraai B is 86, and from Swartkrans, 522.

Thc *Paranthropus* remains from Swartkrans show a remarkable bias in favour of cranial parts. The minimum number count of 70 individuals is based on 192 separate specimens made up as follows:

Skulls and calvarial pieces	17
Mandibles and mandibular pieces	26
Maxillary pieces	19
Isolated teeth	120
Postcranial bones	10

When we examine the situation with the Swartkrans antelope of similar original live weight (Antelope Class II), we find a very different situation. Although the highest minimum individual count is still based on cranial specimens, other parts of the skeletons are well represented. A provisional estimate of Antelope Class II minimum individual numbers is 116 and, on this basis, percentage survival of limb-bones has been calculated. Results for the Swartkrans antelope

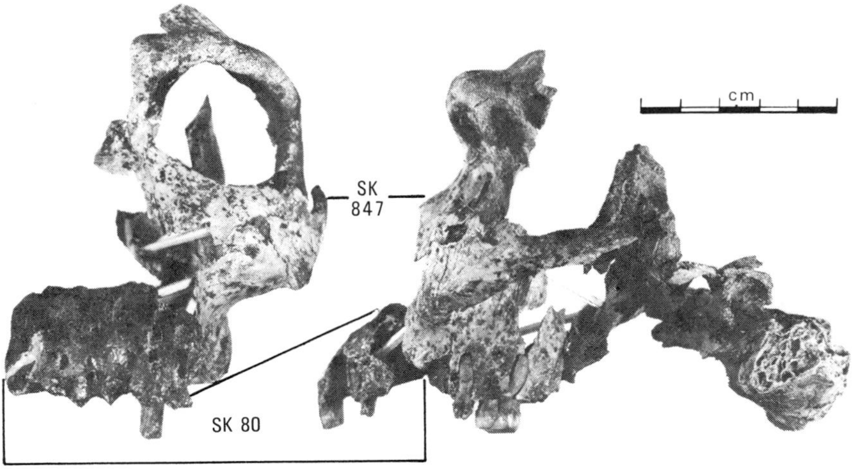

Figure 6. The composite cranium SK 847/80 which has been attributed to *Homo sp.* It comes from the australopithecine-bearing breccia at Swartkrans.

(Class II) and *Paranthropus* remains are given in Table 12. It will be seen that overall survival for the antelope limb-bones is 29.1% while that for *Paranthropus* is 0.25%.

What is the reason for the survival of antelope skeletal parts while those of hominids have largely disappeared?

A possible answer has come from some recent studies which I have undertaken on the feeding behaviour and food remains of cheetahs. Although cheetahs may have had nothing to do with the Swartkrans

Table 12a Antelope Class II live weight 50-200 lb.

Minimum number of individuals, based on cranial pieces: 116

	Left	*Right*	*Unsided*	*Totals*
Humerus				
Proximal end	2	0	21	23
Distal end	73	55	0	128
Radius and ulna				
Proximal end	36	56	2	94
Distal end	26	40	0	66
Femur				
Proximal end	22	15	8	45
Distal end	20	17	2	39
Tibia				
Proximal end	20	19	1	40
Distal end	47	57	1	105
			Total	540

$$\% \text{ Survival} = \frac{540}{1856} \times 100 = 29.1$$

Table 12b Paranthropus robustus

Minimum number of individuals, based on cranial pieces: 70

	Left	*Right*	*Unsided*	*Totals*
Humerus				
Proximal end	0	0	0	0
Distal end	0	1	0	1
Radius and ulna				
Proximal end	0	0	0	0
Distal end	0	0	0	0
Femur				
Proximal end	0	2	0	2
Distal end	0	0	0	0
Tibia				
Proximal end	0	0	0	0
Distal end	0	0	0	0
			Total	3

% Survial = $\frac{3}{1120}$ x 100 = 0.25

bone accumulation, they are amenable animals in the study of carnivore feeding action. Studies on cheetah food remains have been made in various parts of South and South-West Africa and it has been established that minimal damage is generally done to the skeletons of bovid prey in the 50-200 lb. live-weight range. Typical damage is restricted to delicate parts like the ends of the ribs, scapula blades and vertebral spines. In a series of controlled experiments, using five captive cheetahs, the pattern of damage to bovid skeletons was established. Experiments were repeated with baboon prey of similar live weight. In some cases the contrast was dramatic and the entire vertebral column, as well as parts of the limbs, disappeared.

The tentative conclusion has been reached that primate skeletons are more vulnerable to carnivore damage than are bovid skeletons of equivalent original live-weight. The full implications of this suggestion are not yet fully understood, but the apparent fact that primate skeletons suffer more severely than equivalent bovid ones might account for the striking *Paranthropus*/bovid discrepancies mentioned above.

Hyrax skeletal disproportions at Swartkrans

Hyraxes are well represented among the fossil fauna from Swartkrans. Two species, differing in size, have been identified: *Procavia transvaalensis* and *P. antiqua*. On the basis of cranial remains, at least 24 individuals of the former species are represented and 37 of the latter. As shown in Table 13, post-cranial bones are virtually absent in the outer cave sample so far studied.

Table 13 Procavia at Swartkrans: skeletal parts

Minimum number of individuals		*Procavia transvaalensis*	24
		p. antiqua	37
		Total	61

		P. transvaalensis	*P. antiqua*
Crania, complete or fragmentary		16	18
Maxillary pieces		8	35
Mandibular pieces		24	71
Isolated teeth		11	18
	Totals	59	142
Distal ends of humeri		4	88
Other post-cranial bones		10	0
	Totals	14	8

What is this strong cranial bias likely to mean?

A study of hyrax remains resulting from Stone Age human feeding activity has been made at Pomongwe Cave in Rhodesia. Here hyraxes have been eaten over a 70,000 year span and their remains are preserved in the hearths of the hunters. A very uniform pattern of bone damage has emerged and an analysis of the 1,192 hyrax bone pieces from Pomongwe is given in Table 14. The parts which remain are apparently those which could not be chewed by the hunters. It is interesting to notice that 186 distal humeri are present but only 21 proximal ends, indicating that the proximal ends could generally be chewed off with ease, but the distal end was usually discarded.

The hyrax skeletal pattern seen at Pomongwe is quite different from that encountered in the australopithecine breccia at Swartkrans, and the suggestion is that carnivore rather than hominid action is reflected in the Swartkrans hyrax disproportions.

In South-West Africa a study has been made of three caves habitually used by leopards as lairs. In each, cranial remains of hyraxes have been found, but there was an almost total absence of post-cranial bones.

The possibility that leopards habitually eat the whole bodies of hyrax prey, leaving only cranial pieces, has been investigated in experiments with a captive leopard. In six trials, the only bone fragments remaining were all skull parts with teeth. It seems highly likely that the hyrax remains in the Swartkrans outer cave breccia could have resulted from carnivore feeding action, probably that of leopards.

Leopards are the most individually numerous of the carnivores from Swartkrans and on the basis of various lines of evidence (Brain, 1970),

Table 14 Pomongwe Cave, Rhodesia: Procavia and Heterohyrax, skeletal parts

Minimum number of individuals			
Based in maxillary fragments		74	
Based on mandibular fragments		76	
Based on distal humeri		96	
Composite minimum number in all levels		114	
			Totals
Skull	Maxillary pieces	187	
	Mandibular pieces	199	
	Isolated teeth	16	
	Miscellaneous skull pieces	71	
			473
Vertebrae	Atlas	18	
	Axis	9	
	Other	79	
			106
Scapula	Pieces		38
Pelvis	Pieces		36
Ribs	Pieces		32
Humerus	Proximal ends	21	
	Distal ends	186	
			207
Ulna	Complete bones	5	
	Proximal ends	56	
	Distal ends	5	
			66
Radius	Complete bones	6	
	Proximal ends	6	
	Distal ends	9	
			21
Femur	Proximal ends	38	
	Distla ends	18	
	Shaft pieces	29	
			85
Tibia	Complete bones	2	
	Proximal ends	30	
	Distal ends	13	
			45
Fibula	Fragments		3
Phalanges	Complete		3
Pieces of limb bone shaft			77
		Overall total	1192

it seems likely that they may have been major predators of the robust australopithecines as well as some of the other fauna.

Figure 7. Characteristic remains of a hyrax, *Procavia capensis*, after a leopard feeding experiment. On the left is the head, with the skull sheared off posteriorally; above is the plucked hair; below, the stomach.

Figure 8. A feeding experiment with a group of captive cheetahs. The prey is springbuck, *Antidorcas marsupialis*.

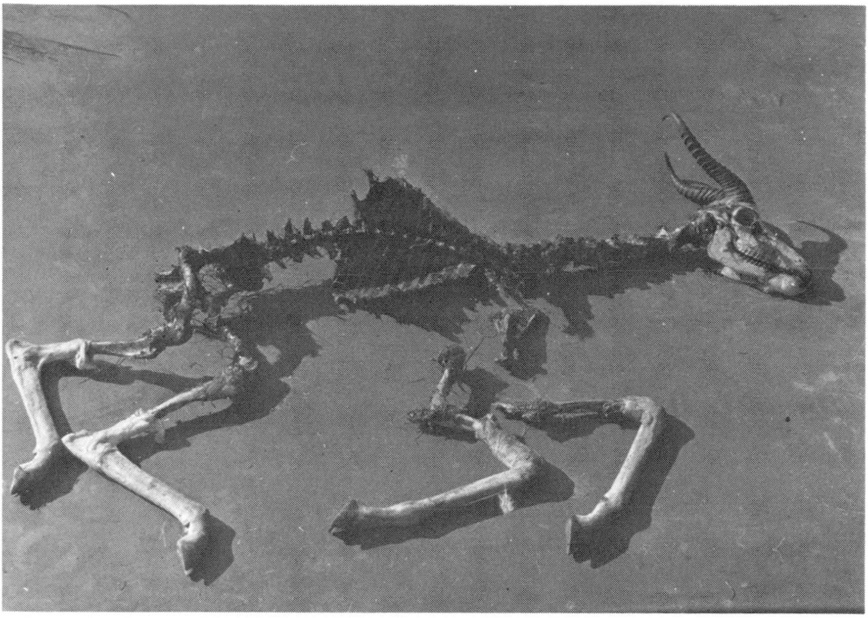

Figure 9. Remains of a springbuck after a feeding experiment in which five adult cheetahs participated. Damage to the skeleton is minimal except to the ribs, vertebral processes and tail. The missing right humerus was damaged by a rifle bullet.

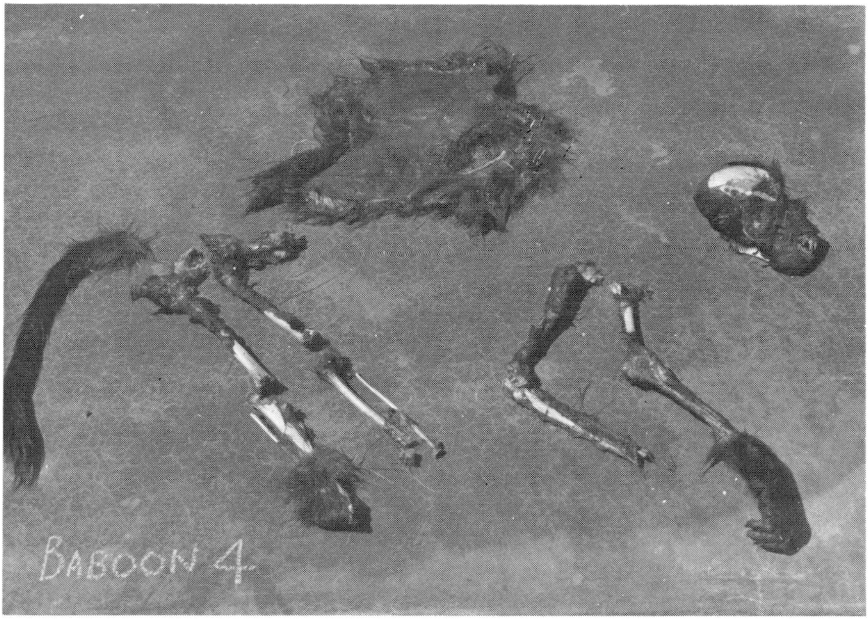

Figure 10. Remains of an adult baboon (*Papio ursinus*) after five cheetahs had fed on it in an experimental situation. Apart from the tail, the whole vertebral column had disappeared.

Acknowledgments

The research reported on here would not have been possible without the generous support of the Wenner-Gren Foundation for Anthropological Research in New York and the South African Council for Scientific and Industrial Research. This is gratefully acknowledged.

Thanks are due to the Board of Control of the Bernard Price Institute for Palaeontological Research, owners of the Swartkrans site, for kindly allowing the Transvaal Museum operations to continue there.

References

Brain, C.K. (1958) The Transvaal ape-man-bearing cave deposits. *Mem. Transv. Mus.* 11, 1-131.

Brain, C.K. (1967) The Transvaal Museum's fossil project at Swartkrans. *S. Afr. J. Sci.* 63, 378-84.

Brain, C.K. (1967) Hottentot food remains and their bearing on the interpretation of fossil bone assemblages. *Scientific Papers of the Namib Desert Research Station* 32, 1-11.

Brain, C.K. (1969) The contribution of Namib Desert Hottentots to an understanding of australopithecine bone accumulations. *Scientific Papers of the Namib Desert Research Station* 39, 13-22.

Brain, C.K. (1970) New finds at the Swartkrans australopithecine site. *Nature* 225, 1112-19.

Brain, C.K. (1973a). The significance of Swartkrans. *J. S. Afr. Biol. Soc.* 13, 7-23.

Brain, C.K. (1973b) Seven years' hard labour at Swartkrans. *Bull. Transv. Mus.* 14, 5-6.

Brain, C.K. (1974) Some suggested procedures in the analysis of bone accumulations from Southern African Quaternary Sites. *Ann. Transv. Mus.* 29, 1-8.

Brain, C.K. (1975) An interpretation of the bone assemblage from the Kromdraai australopithecine site, South Africa. In Tuttle, R. (ed.), *Palaeoanthropology, Morphology and Palaeoecology*, 225-43. The Hague.

Brain, C.K. (1976a) Some principles in the interpretation of bone accumulations associated with primitive man. In Isaac, G.H. and McLown, E.R. (eds.), *Human Origins, Louis Leakey and the East African Evidence*, 96-116. California.

Brain, C.K. (1976b) A reinterpretation of the Swartkrans Site and its remains. *S. Afr. J. Sci.* 72, 141-6.

Brain, C.K. (in press) Swartkrans and Kromdraai compared. Paper presented at IX INQUA congress, Christchurch, 1973.

Broom, R. and Robinson, J.T. (1949) A new type of fossil man. *Nature* (London), 322.

Broom, R. and Robinson, J.T. (1950) Man contemporaneous with the Swartkrans ape-man. *Amer. J. phys. Anthrop.* n.s. 8, 151-6.

Broom, R. and Robinson, J.T. (1952) Swartkrans Ape-man *Paranthropus crassidens*. *Mem. Transv. Mus.* 6.

Butzer, K.W. (1976) Lithostratigraphy of the Swartkrans formation. *S. Afr. J. Sci.* 72, 136-41.

Clarke, R.J., Howell, F.C. and Brain, C.K. (1970) More evidence of an advanced hominid at Swartkrans. *Nature* (London) 225, 1217-20.

Dart, R.A. (1957) The osteodontokeratic culture of *Australopithecus prometheus*. *Mem. Transv. Mus.* 10, 1-105.

Freedman, L. and Brain, C.K. (1972) Fossil cercopithecoid remains from the Kromdraai australopithecine site. *Ann. Transv. Mus.* 28, 1-16.

Hendey, Q.B. (1973) Carnivore remains from the Kromdraai australopithecine site. *Ann. Transv. Mus.* 28, 99-112.

Maier, W. (1973) Paläoökologie und zeitliche Einordnung der südafrikanischen Australopithecinen. *Z. Morph. Anthrop.* 65, 70-105.

Partridge, T.C. (1973) Geomorphological dating of cave openings at Makapansgat, Sterkfontein, Swartkrans and Taung. *Nature* 246, 5428, 75-9.

Peabody, F.E. (1954) Travertines and cave deposits of the Kaap Escarpment of South Africa and the type locality of *Australopithecus africanus* Dart. *Bull. Geol. Soc. Amer.* 65, 671-706.

Robinson, J.T. (1952) The australopithecine-bearing deposits of the Sterkfontein area. *Ann. Transv. Mus.* 22, 1-19.

Robinson, J.T. (1953) *Telanthropus* and its phylogenetic significance. *Amer. J. phys. Anthrop.* 11, 445-502.

Robinson, J.T. (1961) The australopithecines and their bearing on the origin of man and of stone tool making. *S. Afr. J. Sci.* 57, 3-13.

Robinson, J.T. (1962) Sterkfontein stratigraphy and the significance of the extension site. *S. Afr. archaeol. Bull.* 17, 66, 87-107.

Tobias, P.V. and Hughes, A.R. (1969) The new Witwatersrand University excavation at Sterkfontein. *S. Afr. archaeol. Bull.* 24, 158-69.

Tobias, P.V. (1973) Implications of the new age estimates of the early South African hominids. *Nature* 246, 5428, 79-83.

Vrba, E.S. (1974) Chronological and ecological implications of the fossil Bovidae at the Sterkfontein australopithecine site. *Nature* 250, 1923.

Vrba, E.S. (1976) The fossil Bovidae of Swartkrans, Kromdraai and Sterkfontein. *Mem. Transv. Mus.* 21, 1-166.

PART II

GEOLOGICAL, FAUNAL AND ARCHAEOLOGICAL EVIDENCE

Anna K. Behrensmeyer

The habitat of Plio-Pleistocene hominids in East Africa: taphonomic and micro-stratigraphic evidence

Introduction

This paper is primarily concerned with recent studies on the relationship of hominid fossils to sedimentary environments in the Koobi Fora Formation east of Lake Rudolf,[1] Kenya. The large sample of hominid fossils from a variety of sedimentary environments at East Rudolf provides the first opportunity for detailed taphonomic and palaeoecological investigation of the environmental context of early man. Preliminary studies were carried out during the 1973 season to determine the relationship of the hominid fossils to fluvial and lake margin deposits, representing two major vertebrate-preserving environments in the Koobi Fora Fm. Methods of investigation are still being refined, and the problems and results presented below represent the initial stages in what will, we hope, prove a valuable line of research in the story of hominid evolution.

Previous work has been done on the relationships of the vertebrate faunas in general to the sedimentary environments of East Rudolf (for example Behrensmeyer, 1976). Lake margin and fluvial depositional environments preserve faunas which differ in the proportions of various mammalian groups. These groups include suids, bovids and equids with modern counterparts that have varying preferences for grassland or bush habitats. In seven faunas sampled from specific sedimentary environments at East Rudolf, three delta (=lake) margin deposits preserved a higher proportion of bush-preferring mammals, while two fluvial channels and one open mudflats deposit preserved more grassland-preferring forms (assuming habitat preferences similar to those of the modern counterparts). Sampling was extensive

[1] In Kenya, Lake Rudolf has been renamed Lake Turkana. The area of fossiliferous exposures previously called East Rudolf is currently referred to as 'Koobi Fora' or 'East Turkana' by Kenyan workers. (Ed.)

enough to indicate that in general more grassland mammals are associated with fluvial deposits, while both bush and grasslands forms occur in lake margin deposits in the fossiliferous units of the Koobi Fora Fm. Taphonomic evidence indicates that this is not due to factors of differential preservation. Thus it appears that some palaeoecological record is preserved in the distribution of the East Rudolf faunas.

The object of this paper is to examine the patterns of distribution of the hominid fossils and their associated faunas and to compare these with the patterns previously established for the associations of faunas and depositional environments at East Rudolf.

General palaeoenvironmental setting

The overall palaeogeography of the north-eastern part of the Lake Rudolf Basin can be reconstructed as shown in Figure 1, with two major drainage components represented in deltaic deposits of the Ileret area and along the Karari-Fora Ridge. These systems apparently aggraded at different rates, with prodeltaic conditions lasting for some time after the deposition of the KBS tuff in the Ileret area while delta plain and fluvial conditions were present contemporaneously along the Fora Ridge. Details on regional geology and stratigraphy are available in Bowen and Vondra (1973), Vondra and Bowen (1976), and the sedimentologic history of the area has been recently studied by Findlater (1976). Differential uplift and erosion also affected the two areas, creating an unconformity in the north-eastern Fora Ridge and Karari Ridge deposits while deposition continued, apparently without break (?), in the Ileret area. Evidence indicates short-term tectonic and/or climatic instability over the East Rudolf area in general, with wide fluctuations in base level resulting in alternating periods of channel cutting, deltaic deposition and lacustrine transgression.

The setting for the inhabitants (floral and faunal) during the Plio-Pleistocene period represented by the Koobi Fora Fm. was thus characterized by occasional spatial shifts in ecological zones. As the drainage systems were probably not extensive, climatic change to drier conditions would have had pronounced effects on the productivity of the East Rudolf ecosystem. It seems likely that the river systems, if not ephemeral, suffered greater seasonal fluctuation than rivers with larger drainage basins such as the Omo River. Seasonal migrations of animals into and out of the East Rudolf area during the Plio-Pleistocene seems highly probable. The general environmental stability of the East Rudolf area through time was probably much more tenuous than in the Omo Basin to the north, with its large, high-altitude catchment area. Plio-Pleistocene stratigraphy in the Omo Basin indicates a relatively stable major river

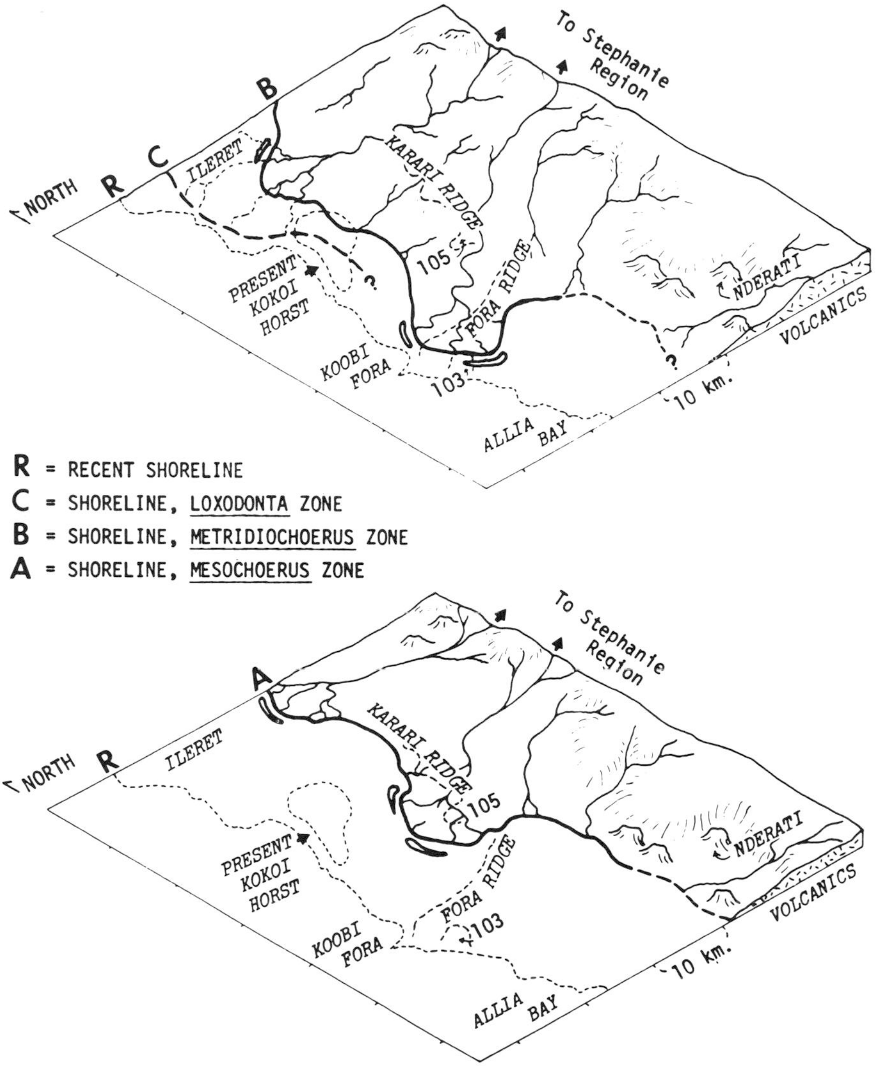

Figure 1. Hypothetical shorelines and drainage patterns for the Koobi Fora Fm. vertebrate-bearing deposits. Adapted from an unpublished figure by G.Ll. and B. Isaac and based in part on Vondra and Bowen (1975).

system with one lacustrine incursion during the time spanned by the Koobi Fora Fm. (Brown *et al.*, 1971; Butzer, 1971).

The palaeogeography of East Rudolf indicates that faunal interchange and gene flow with adjacent areas (including the Omo) was not geographically restricted, except possibly by extensions of Lake Rudolf. The Plio-Pleistocene fauna of the Koobi Fora Fm. consists of a diverse assemblage of vertebrates, with good fossil representation of the larger ungulates and primates but so far poor representation of the micro-fauna. The faunal diversity among large vertebrates is more comparable to that of the Serengeti, Nairobi or Kafue National Parks than to East Rudolf today, indicating generally wetter conditions in Plio-Pleistocene times.

Such evidence helps to characterize the general environment of the East Rudolf hominids. Additional information for palaeoecological reconstruction is derived from the geologic, palaeontologic and archaeologic evidence currently available and from analogies with comparable recent environments, particularly along the shores of Lake Rudolf. The hypothesized Plio-Pleistocene environment at East Rudolf included abundant vegetation, a large and diverse fauna of herbivores and carnivores, and seasonal climatic fluctuations with attendant faunal migrations. The terrain was generally flat, sloping upward toward the east, with probably some higher volcanic areas toward the east and north-east. Local relief may have been of the order of 10-100 m. during periods of incision. The lake margins were probably low-gradient and generally swampy, with extensive areas of mud flats which were seasonally covered with grass. It is likely that distributary systems supported coalescing gallery forests and interdistributary bush, with open areas of deltaic plain covered with grass and low bush. The fluvial channels were probably typically bordered by gallery forest which laterally gave way to grass-covered flood-plains. Interfluve areas may have been mixed savannah and open acacia woodland.

Hominids in relation to sedimentary environments in the Koobi Fora Formation

Method of study

Micro-stratigraphic sections and faunal collections were made for 88 out of the 110 hominid sites known at East Rudolf as of September, 1973. Polaroid and 35 mm. black-and-white photographs were also taken of each site. The original position of the hominid specimen and critical stratigraphic data were marked on the polaroid photos in the field. Due to limitations of time, sites of isolated teeth and specimens discovered in remote areas were not included in the initial study.

The stratigraphic data provide the basis for the crucial interpretation of the sedimentary context of each hominid fossil. Sections were made from 1 to 2 m. below the position of the hominid find to the top of the outcrop associated with the site. Examples of sections are shown in Figure 2. Since most of the hominids occurred on the surface (only 9% have been found *in situ*), an effort was made to determine which beds in each section were the most probable source. This was done on evidence from specimen matrix, local topography, and by careful tracing of obviously fossiliferous units in the vicinity of the find. In 64% of the sites, it was possible to assign specimens to a

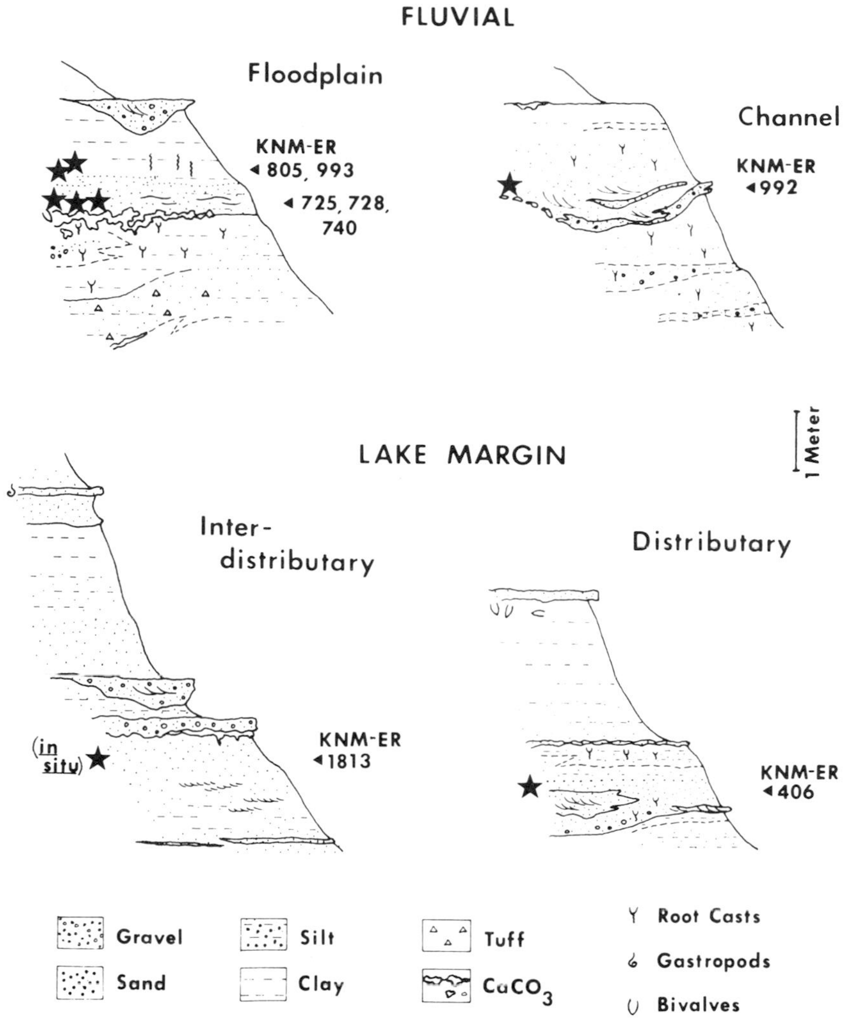

Figure 2. Examples of microstratigraphic sections showing the positions of selected hominid fossils in their depositional environments.

stratigraphic range of 1 to 3 m. with 90-95% confidence. About 21% of the hominids could be tied to a specific bed. In other cases, a range of 10 to 20 m. was the best possible stratigraphic resolution.

Microstratigraphic data plus studies of lateral relationships of the sedimentary units and the general context within the Koobi Fora Fm. enabled 84 out of the 110 sites to be assigned with confidence to fluvial or lake margin sedimentary environments. The two environments are defined as shown in Figure 3. It was more difficult to place specimens in finer categories such as 'channel', 'floodplain', 'distributary' and 'interdistributary'. A total of 48 specimens can be so assigned, with somewhat less confidence except for *in situ* examples.

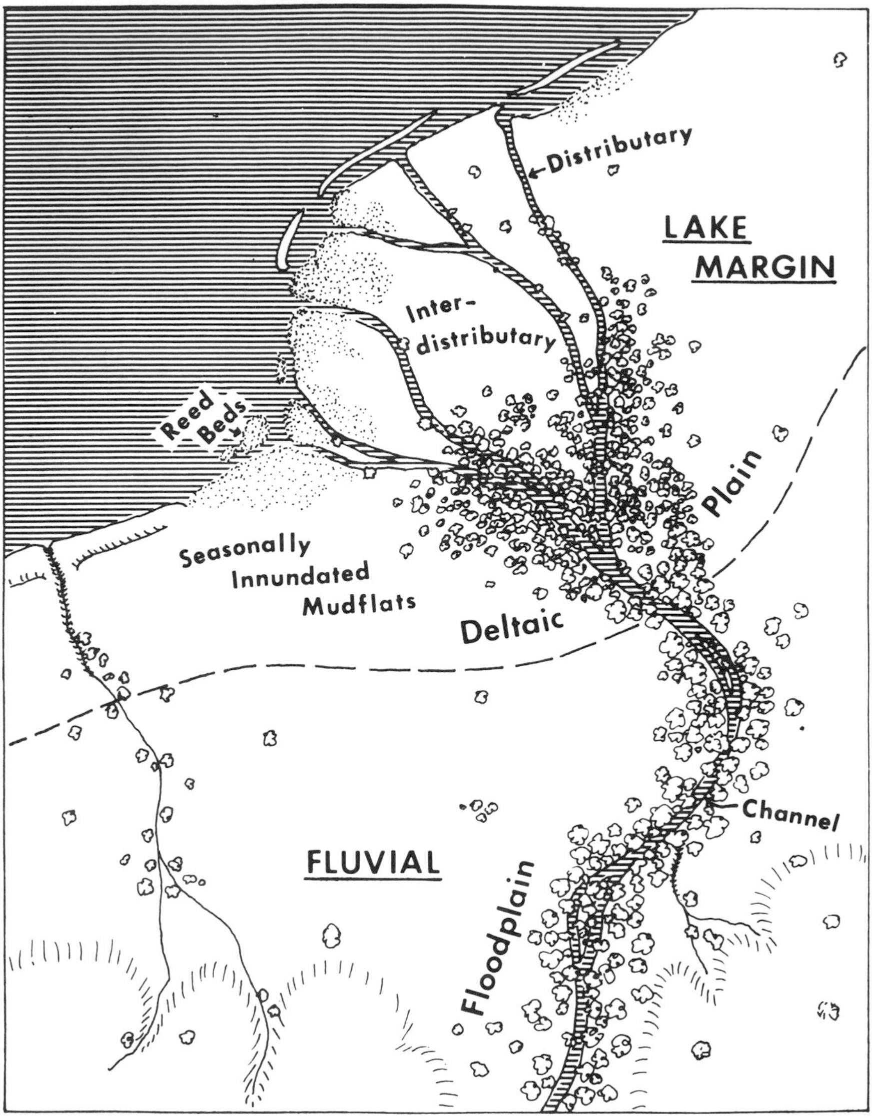

Figure 3. Generalized representation of the Koobi Fora Fm. environments of deposition.

Hominid distribution according to sedimentary environment

Of the 84 hominids that can be assigned to a major environment, 39 occur in fluvial deposits while 45 occur in lake margin deposits. This is not a significant difference from a 50/50 ratio, although a slightly greater hominid abundance in lake margin sediments is consistent with overall better preservation of fossils in this environment.

Many of the hominids can be separated into the two major taxa currently recognized by some workers at East Rudolf, *Homo* and

Table 1 Distribution of hominid taxa according to environment of burial

	Homo	*Australopithecus*	*Total*
By environment			
Fluvial	7	25	32
	KNM-ER 803, 807, 813, 820, 992, 1466, 1815	KNM-ER 405, 725, 726, 728, 729, 733, 738, 739, 741, 805, 810, 812, 814, 818, 819, 993, 1463, 1468, 1476, 1477, 1478, 1500, 1804, 1806, 1817	
Lake margin	18	15	33
	KNM-ER 730, 731, 736, 737, 1470, 1472, 1475, 1481, 1501, 1502, 1590, 1591, 1593, 1802, 1808, 1809, 1810, 1811	KNM-ER 403, 404, 406, 407, 732, 727, 801, 815, 1464, 1465, 1469, 1471, 1505, 1592, 1816	
Total	25	40	65
Excluding mandibles			
Fluvial	5	12	17
Lake margin	12	9	21
Total	17	21	38

Australopithecus (Leakey, 1973). Taxonomic problems are unavoidable, but a sample of 65 'less controversial'[2] specimens can be used to test the relative abundances of the two taxa in fluvial and lake margin deposits. Data are given in Table 1. *Australopithecus* is abundant in fluvial environments while *Homo* is rare, but both occur in comparable numbers in lake margin environments. Chi-Square tests show that the abundance figures in fluvial deposits differ significantly from the proportions in the lake margin deposits (Chi-Square = 7.33, $p \leq .025$). This pattern of hominid distribution may conceivably be due to sampling errors, taphonomic factors, or original variation in the ecological distribution of the hominids. I discuss these possibilities in a later section.

Fifty hominids which could be assigned to subenvironments were distributed in comparable numbers in channel, floodplain and distributary deposits, with slightly fewer in interdistributaries (Table 2). When 'less controversial' specimens are separated into taxa, distributions show that all subenvironments appear to reflect the pattern of occurrence demonstrated in Table 1, even though sample numbers are small.

2. The sample of 65 'less controversial' hominid specimens was designated with the help of taxonomic assignments by R.E.F. Leakey, F.C. Howell and B. Wood. There is little about that palaeoecologic interpretations will vary according to taxonomy of the hominid specimens. It would be interesting to test the environmental distribution using a variety of classifications.

Table 2 Distribution of hominid taxa according to subenvironments

By subenvironment	*Homo*	*Australopithecus*	*Total*
Channel	2	14	17
	KNM-ER 813, 992, 1466	KNM-ER 405, 726, 738, 739, 741, 810, 812, 814, 1476, 1477, 1478, 1500, 1804, 1806	
Floodplain	4	10	14
	KNM-ER 803, 807, 820, 1815	KNM-ER 725, 728, 729, 733, 805, 819, 993, 1463, 1468, 1817	
Distributary	5	6	11
	KNM-ER 1470, 1501, 1502, 1809, 1811	KNM-ER 403, 801, 406, 1464, 1465, 1469	
Interdistributary	4	4	8
	KNM-ER 1475, 1481, 1590, 1802	KNM-ER 404, 407, 727, 732	
Total	16	34	50

Hominid distribution according to faunal zone

All three faunal zones recognized by Maglio (1972) for the Koobi Fora Fm. have produced numerous hominid fossils, as shown in Table 3. Of the 'less controversial' taxonomic sample, *Australopithecus* is more common in the *Metridiochoerus andrewsi* and *Loxodonta africana* zones than *Homo*, while *Homo* is slightly more abundant in the *Mesochoerus limnetes* zone. This may be in part due to patterns of sedimentation, since fluvial deposits are more common in the Upper Member and partially equivalent Ileret Mb. of the Koobi Fora Fm., which include the upper two faunal zones, than in the Lower Mb. *Mesochoerus* zone.

Table 3 Distribution of hominid taxa in the Koobi Fora Formation

	By faunal zone	*Homo*	*Australopithecus*	*Total*
Ileret Mb.	*Loxodonta africana*	7	17	24
Upper Mb.	*Metridiochoerus andrewsi*	5	17	22
Lower Mb.	*Mesochoerus limnetes*	7	3	10

More fluvial deposits apparently mean more australopithecines in the hominid samples. The possibility that the population of australopithecines increased over the entire area during Upper Member time is countered by the fact that their numbers do not increase in the Upper Member lake margin deposits.

The distribution of hominid skeletal parts

A variety of associated and isolated skeletal parts form the hominid sample in all three faunal zones. These are distributed between fluvial and lake margin deposits as shown in Table 4. Most skeletal parts are present in comparable numbers in both sedimentary environments. Cranial remains and femora are somewhat more common in lake margin deposits, although the sample is too small for statistical significance. Of the 11 partial to relatively complete crania recovered from East Rudolf, 8 were found in lake margin deposits, indicating that this was the more favourable environment for cranial preservation.

Table 4 Distribution of hominid skeletal parts in fluvial and lake margin environments of burial. A = Australopithecus and H = Homo

		Fluvial		*Lake margin*		*Total*
Isolated parts only	Mandible	18	2 *H*	16	6 *H*	34
			13 *A*		6 *A*	
	Maxilla	4	1 *H*	0		4
			2 *A*			
	Crania (including parietals)	3	1 *H*	9	2 *H*	12
			1 *A*		3 *A*	
	Humerus	2	0 *H*	3	0 *H*	5
			1 *A*		0 *A*	
	Femur	4	0 *H*	11	4 *H*	15
			3 *A*		4 *A*	
	Tibia	1	0 *H*	2	0 *H*	3
			1 *A*		1 *A*	
	Talus	1	1 *H*	1	0 *H*	2
			0 *A*		1 *A*	
	Metapodial	1	0 *H*	0		1
			0 *A*			
	Associated parts (including skull and mandible)	5	1 *H*	3	3 *H*	8
			4 *A*		0 *A*	
	Total	39		45		84

The presence of a variety of skeletal parts, plus the presence of associated elements and relatively complete crania, indicate that in general the hominids were buried in the vicinity of their place of death. It seems improbable that remains were transported to the fluvial and lake margin depositional environments from more upland regions, particularly since few show evidence of transport abrasion.

Table 4 also provides information on the distribution according to environment of skeletal parts from the 'less controversial' sample assigned to *Homo* and *Australopithecus*. The two taxa have comparable representation in lake margin deposits, except for the associated material which consists of 3 *Homo*, but no *Australopithecus*. In the fluvial deposits, *Australopithecus* is represented by more different elements, and by more associated material, than *Homo*.

Summary

The associations of the hominid specimens with fluvial and lake margin environments indicate that:

1. Approximately equal numbers of hominids were buried in each environment.
2. *Homo* and *Australopithecus* were buried in comparable numbers in lake margin environments, but *Australopithecus* is significantly more abundant in fluvial environments.
3. The East Rudolf hominids were buried in the general vicinity of areas inhabited (at least temporarily) by the original populations.
4. Greater abundance of *Australopithecus* in the Upper Mb. of the Koobi Fora Fm. can be explained by the increase in fluvial deposits in the Upper Mb. compared with the Lower Mb.

Faunal and taphonomic analysis of hominid sites in the Koobi Fora Formation

Method of study

Collecting at each hominid site was directed toward obtaining a sample of the faunal groups and skeletal parts most clearly associated with the hominid-bearing bed or beds. An area of 200-400 sq.m. was chosen at each site according to outcrop and drainage patterns. All bones of mammals found on the surface were collected, and where possible identified and recorded. An effort was made to determine minimum numbers of individuals for comparisons between sites and groups of sites. This contrasts with the 'squares' method used for sampling the Koobi Fora Fm. for faunas associated with specific sedimentary environments (Behrensmeyer, 1976), in that it provides a larger faunal sample for statistical purposes. (In this method, surface bone concentrations were sampled using 10x10 m. squares spaced at least 20 m. apart over the outcrops being sampled.) The ultimate goal is to compare the *relative* numbers of abundant faunal groups from hominid site samples with the proportions of these groups associated with the fluvial and lake margin deposits in general, as determined by the 'squares' method.

Additional taphonomic information was derived by examining the surface of the hominid bones for evidence of weathering prior to burial, transport abrasion, and carnivore or scavenger activity. Comparisons were made with recent bones in various stages of weathering.

Skeletal proportions in the faunas associated with hominid sites

Analysis of the skeletal proportions was based on the five most common elements as determined in the environmental bone samples from East Rudolf (Behrensmeyer, 1975). These are: teeth, vertebrae, scapulae, radii, ulnae and phalanges, all of which are common in the hominid site samples. The comparative data on the relative proportions of these elements in the hominid site samples and in the environmental 'squares' samples are given in Table 5. The data for minimum numbers of skeletal parts are not comparable in an absolute sense because each hominid site was sampled over a larger area than the 10x10 m. squares used for the 'squares' sampling.

Table 5 Minimum numbers totals and comparative percentages of five common skeletal parts in hominid site and 'squares' faunal samples (from fauna other than hominids)

	Hominid Sites				*Squares*			
	Fluvial		*Lake margin*		*Fluvial*		*Lake margin*	
	Min. #s	%	Min. #s	%	Min. #s	%	Min. #s	%
Teeth	174	50	155	41	291	77	191	51
Vetebrae	77	22	104	28	28	7	79	21
Scapulae	22	6	30	8	14	4	24	6
Radii/ulnae	32	9	43	12	21	6	21	6
Phalanges	42	12	43	12	26	7	62	16
Total min. #s	380 (27 sites)		377 (38 sites)		347 (125 squares)		375 (88 squares)	

As indicated in Figure 4, skeletal proportions in both the fluvial and the lake margin hominid site sample are more comparable to the lake margin 'squares' samples than to the fluvial 'squares' samples. This shows relatively less removal of vertebrae and less concentration of teeth in fluvial deposits associated with hominids than is typical for fossiliferous fluvial deposits at East Rudolf. It is possible that hominids were only preserved in depositional situations where taphonomic alteration of the original death assemblages was minimal, and this would suggest burial close to the site of death. However, such hypotheses must be subjected to additional sampling and taphonomic investigations before they can be accepted.

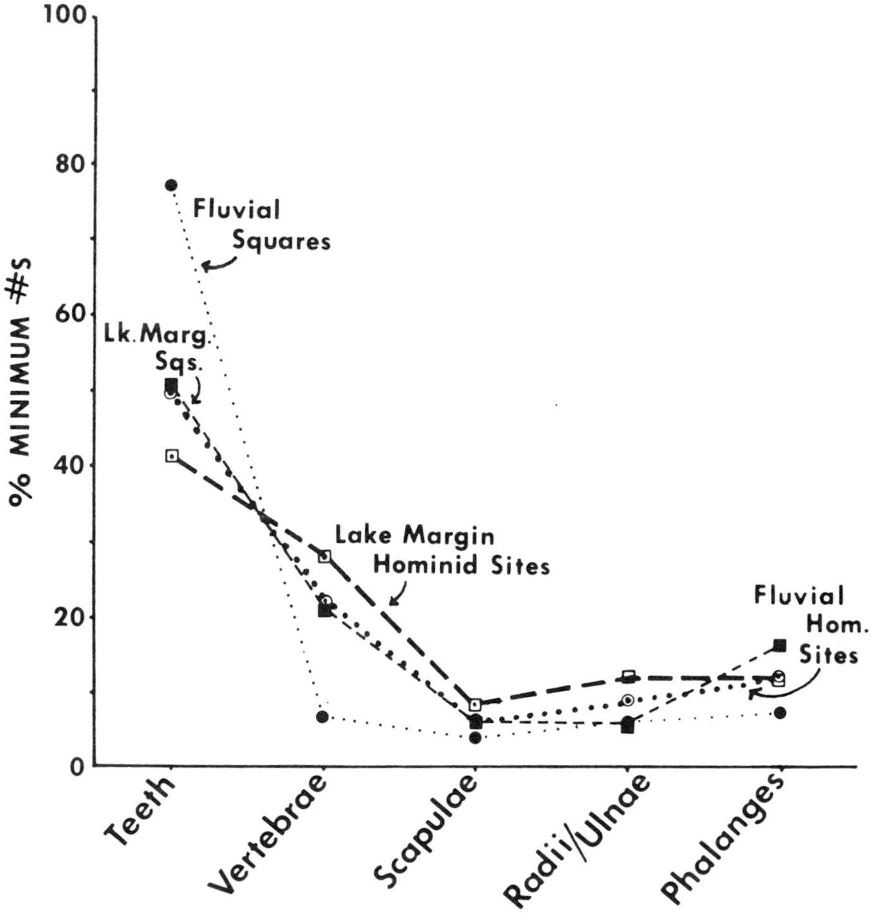

Figure 4. Comparison of the proportions of five skeletal parts in bone assemblages from hominid sites and from sedimentary environments sampled for more general patterns using 10x10 m. squares.

Additional taphonomic aspects of the hominid remains

Hominid specimens show the complete range of preservation from fresh, unweathered examples to weathered cores of bones consisting of little more than cancellous material. Some of the weathering characteristics can be related to pre-burial surface exposure. In particular, many of the mandibles show longitudinal cracks along the ramus about midway down from the tooth row. These are so consistent in character that similar structural responses to surface desiccation seem highly probable. Other cracking patterns, such as the radial cracking on crania (e.g. KNM-ER 1470, 732) probably also indicate predepositional surface weathering.

There is more evidence for breakage and gnawing of the bones by carnivores and scavengers. The KNM-ER 1470 cranium shows gnaw-marks on the outer rim of the right orbit (noted by Alan Walker). A tibia found in 1973 (KNM-ER 1810) has puncture marks with radial cracks, probably due to carnivore teeth. In the sample of 84 specimens, 8 show clear evidence of gnawing or biting, and others have suggestions of carnivore activity.

Both *Homo* and *Australopithecus* specimens from the 'less controversial' sample have a spectrum of weathered to fresh surface characteristics. There is no particular pattern of fresh or weathered specimens associated with either the fluvial or lake margin environments.

Faunal proportions associated with Hominid sites

In this paper, I consider only the particular groups which proved useful in the overall analysis of faunas from particular sedimentary environments (Behrensmeyer, 1975, 1976). These are given along with minimum numbers for both the hominid site and environmental ('squares') sample in Table 6. As in the case of skeletal parts, only *relative* proportions can be compared.

Table 6 Comparisons of the proportions of faunal groups in hominid sites and squares samples

	Hominid Sites		*Squares*	
	Fluvial	*Lake margin*	*Fluvial*	*Lake margin*
Bovids	*66 42%	72 40%	114 74%	82 43%
Suids	45 29%	39 22%	47 19%	30 16%
Equids	13 8%	21 12%	24 10%	15 8%
Hippos	32 21%	47 26%	59 24%	65 34%
Mesochoerus	18 55%	21 60%	6 23%	10 59%
Metridiochoerus				
Notochoerus	15 45%	14 40%	20 77%	7 41%
Alcelaphine (*Damaliscus*-size)	16 45%	10 40%	21 38%	18 53%
Alcelaphine (*Megalotragus*)	5 14%	6 24%	13 24%	2 6%
Reduncine	15 42%	9 36%	20 37%	14 41%

*Minimum numbers of individuals and percentage given for each grouping.

The proportions of bovids, suids, equids and hippos in fluvial and lake margin deposits are shown in Figure 5. In the 'squares' samples, the proportions of these four groups are very similar in both major environments (and are consistent within all seven of the different deposits sampled) except for hippos, which are more abundant in the lake margin environments. The hominid site samples from the two environments contrast in showing no such difference in the proportion

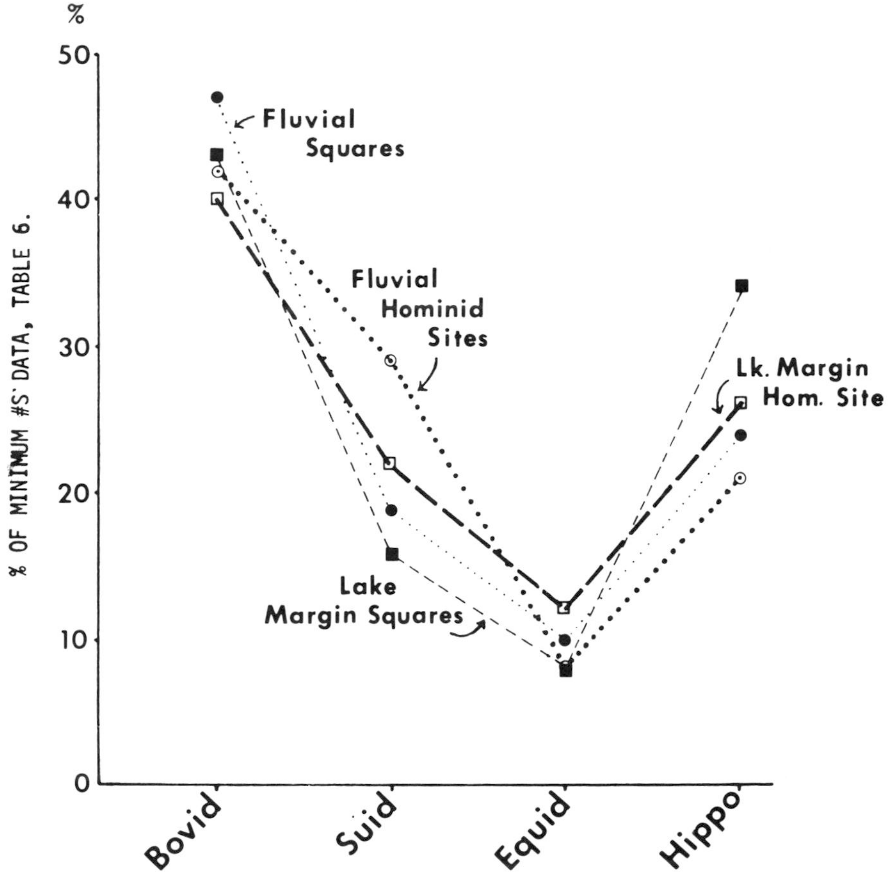

Figure 5. Proportions of four major mammal groups in faunal samples from hominid sites and 10x10 m. squares.

of hippos. Also, the fluvial hominid sites are disproportionately high in suids.

The suids can be separated in the low-crowned *Mesochoerus* (probably a bush form) and the high-crowned *Metridiochoerus* and *Notochoerus* (probably grazers) (Cooke, 1976). Table 6 shows that the fluvial hominid sites have more mesochoers than are found in the fluvial 'squares' samples.

The three bovid groups included in Table 6 also show similar proportions in the hominid site and 'squares' samples. *Megalotragus* is somewhat more abundant in the lake margin hominid site assemblages. Alcelaphines of today generally prefer open grassland while reduncines are bush to mixed habitat forms (Gentry, 1976).

Summary

Much of the data on taphonomic and faunal aspects of the hominid sites are yet to be analysed. However, preliminary results on selected components of the fossil assemblages indicate that:

1. The taphonomic history of burial assemblages associated with hominid sites in lake margin environments differs from that in lake margin environments sampled by the 'squares' method. More vertebrae and fewer teeth in the fluvial hominid site assemblages indicate less differential removal of these elements than appears to be 'normal' for fluvial thanatocoenoses in the Koobi Fora Fm., according to the 'squares' data.
2. Faunal peculiarities of the hominid site assemblages indicate a higher proportion of suids (chiefly *Mesochoerus*) in the fluvial environments, and fewer hippos in the lake margin samples than in the 'squares' samples for these environments.

Discussion, interpretation and speculation

Data given above on the distribution of *Homo* and *Australopithecus* in fluvial and lake margin deposits show that there are significant differences in the relative abundances of the two forms in different sedimentary environments. Why should there be more *Australopithecus* than *Homo* in the fluvial deposits, but equal representation in lake margin deposits? The pattern of occurrence may be due to sampling, taphonomy or ecology, and each possibility warrants more detailed consideration.

1. Sampling

(*a*) Collecting bias. Prospecting was done without taxonomic bias in either sedimentary environment, and large areas of deposits representing both environments have been thoroughly explored. This should not be a factor.

(*b*) Sample size. The sample of 65 'less controversial' specimens is large enough to represent statistically real trends in the population sampled (i.e. the population of buried hominids), and indirectly, the original population(s) of hominids.[3] A useful comparison can be made with the sample size necessary to show a 50/50 ratio between left and right paired body parts, where presumably taphonomic and collecting bias would be nil. Table 7 shows that a sample of 29 mandibles from both fluvial and lake margin deposits does not deviate significantly from a 50/50 left: right ratio, and the sample of all elements (61) is very close to a 50/50 ratio.

3. Considering the collecting as a technique of binomial sampling, the probability is $\leq .001$ that the proportions of hominid taxa in fluvial deposits do *not* represent a real trend in the population being sampled (Simpson *et al.*, 1960, p.199).

Table 7 Proportions of right and left hominid parts

	Right #	*Left* #	*Total*
Mandibles	12	17	29 (41% Right
All other paired parts	18	14	32 59% Left)
Total	30	31	61

2. *Taphonomy*

It has been suggested that the greater abundance of *Australopithecus* in fluvial environments may be due to relatively better preservation of their robust mandibles (Behrensmeyer, 1975). Mandibles form 42% of the 'less controversial' sample. Table 1 gives the environmental abundances of skeletal parts excluding mandibles. The pattern of unequal distribution of *Australopithecus* and *Homo* in fluvial deposits but equal distribution in lake margin deposits persists. The sample size is

Figure 6. Taphonomy, simply stated, is the study of the processes of fossilization. This photograph shows the effects of some taphonomic processes on the skeleton of a modern-day Oryx (a type of antelope) which was killed by lions on the delta of the Tulu Bor River at East Rudolf. Three of the oryx's limbs have been removed by the lions or later scavengers. A recent flood of the Tulu Bor has inundated the floodplain with several centimeters of water, causing the burial of the lower part of the skeleton in silt. However, unless a much larger flood covers the entire skeleton, it will be scattered and destroyed by surface processes, leaving only a few fragments as potential fossils. This illustrates the typical pattern of events leading to fossilization of skeletal parts in a floodplain situation that is comparable to one of the depositional environments which preserved fossil hominids at East Rudolf in the Plio-Pleistocene.

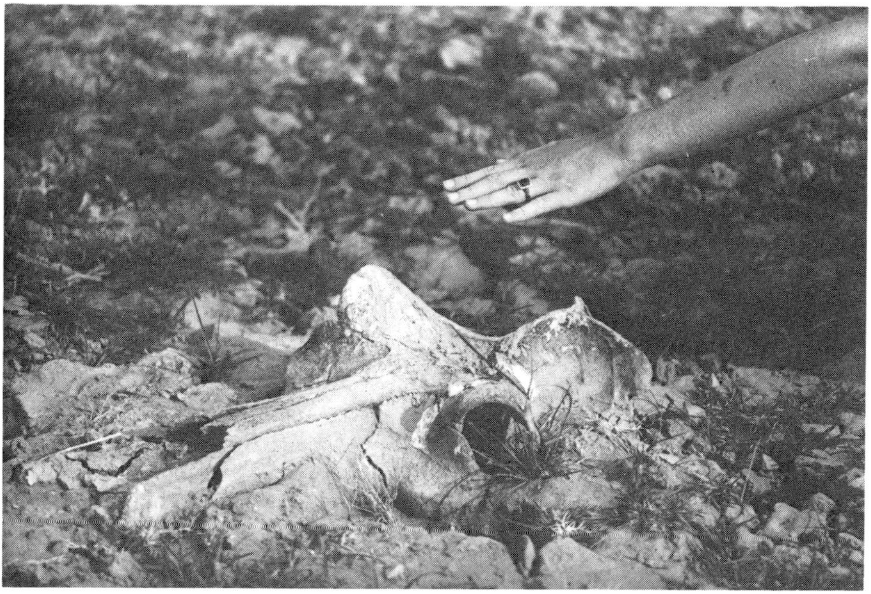

Figure 7. The partially buried skull of a modern hippopotamus lies in lake margin deposits only a few metres away from the shoreline of Lake Rudolf. The muds surrounding the skull were laid down during the yearly high stand of the lake, when water covered this area to a depth of perhaps half a meter. The retreat of the lake during the dry season has exposed the upper part of the skull to desiccation, cracking and trampling by shoreline animals. If it survives to be inundated and buried by the next rise in lake level, the teeth and palate are likely to be better preserved than the upper part of the skull. This illustrates taphonomic processes which also would have affected the preservation of lake margin hominid remains during the Plio-Pleistocene.

small, but the Chi-Square tests shows that the pattern is still close to the acceptable level of statistical significance (Chi-Square = 2.98, p. = 0.10-0.05). It is evident that a taphonomic bias towards preservation of the robust mandible in fluvial environments is not the sole cause of the disproportionate number of *Australopithecus*, although it may be a contributing factor.

Taphonomic factors which would result in the observed pattern of hominid distribution for skeletal parts other than mandibles are difficult to support with the available evidence. Post-cranial elements of the two taxa would have comparable hydraulic behaviour and differential transport of *Homo* remains out of the fluvial system seems unlikely. The effects of predation on the two forms should have resulted in comparable fragmentation and destruction of bones, excepting mandibles and crania. Other taphonomic processes may have been operating, but there is no available evidence which can satisfactorily account for the observed pattern of occurrence of the hominid taxa.

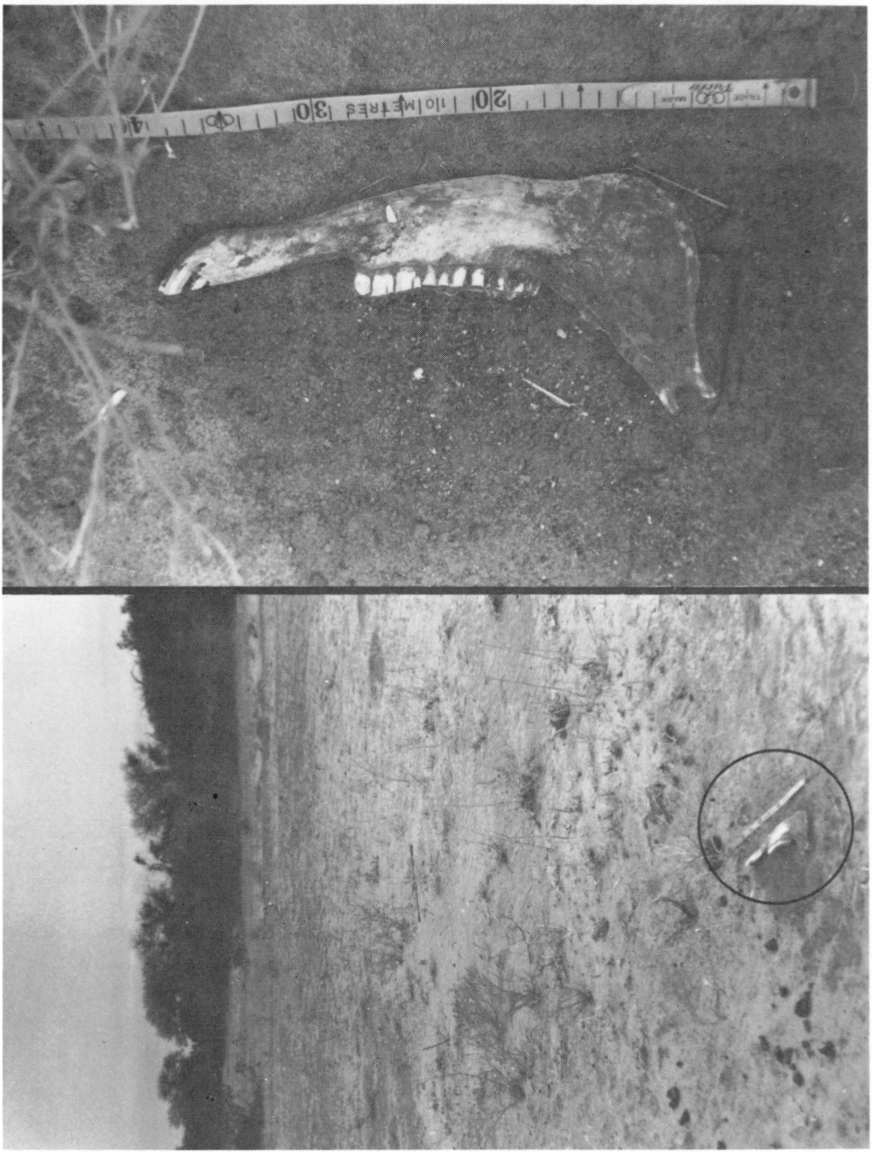

Figure 8. River processes tend to move and sort bones according to shape and weight, leaving the flattest and heaviest skeletal parts closest to the place where the animal died. This half-mandible of a recent cow has been partially buried by overbank levee deposits of the Tulu Bor River, East Rudolf. It has been isolated from other parts of the original skeleton, which are probably farther downstream. Half-mandibles and teeth are often the most common fossils in river deposits due to this process of sorting. Hominid remains in Plio-Pleistocene river deposits at East Rudolf often consist of mandible parts and teeth, showing that the hominid bones were subjected to similar taphonomic processes. (Note: in the photograph, the Tulu Bor River's main channel lies just behind the row of trees in the background. The mandible is oriented with its symphysis pointing downstream.) Scale in centimetres.

3. Ecology

The obvious hypothesis based on an ecological interpretation is that more *Australopithecus* remains were buried in the fluvial environments because more of this form were available to be buried, i.e. more lived and died there. According to an ecological hypothesis, both *Homo* and *Australopithecus* occupied the lake margin areas, in comparable numbers, while *Australopithecus* was much more abundant in the fluvial environments throughout the period sampled by the Koobi Fora Fm.

There is some evidence to support this hypothesis, although sample sizes are only large enough to indicate trends:

1. The number of associated skeletal parts is greater for *Australopithecus* than *Homo* in the fluvial deposits.
2. In general, skeletal representation (number of different parts) is better for *Australopithecus* than *Homo* in fluvial deposits, while it is comparable in lake margin deposits.

Additional samples and alternative taxonomic assignments of existing specimens should be used to test the validity of these points.

Various members of the Suidae and Bovidae have shown differential representation in the fluvial and lake margin deposits which can be best explained ecologically (Behrensmeyer, 1975). As previously stated, bush-preferring forms occur somewhat more frequently in the lake margin environments while grassland forms are more abundant in fluvial deposits. Accordingly, it seems that the ecological hypothesis indicates that *Australopithecus* may have been associated with the grasslands-habitat fauna.

The faunal association of the hominid taxa can be indirectly tested using the faunas collected from the hominid sites. From Table 6, it appears that the fluvial hominid sites (mostly *Australopithecus*) typically have more *Mesochoerus* and fewer *Megalotragus* than the 'squares' fluvial assemblages. In lake margin deposits, *Megalotragus* is more common and hippos are less so than in the 'squares' samples. There are no observable differences between *Homo* and *Australopithecus* site assemblages in the lake margin environment, but sample sizes are small.

This suggests that although *Australopithecus* was inhabiting the fluvial environments, it was not necessarily associated with the open grasslands fauna that is typically represented in the fluvial deposits. It may have been more a part of the gallery forest or bush associations found along streams and rivers. Much of the interpretation depends on the habitat of *Mesochoerus*. Both *Homo* and *Australopithecus* apparently inhabited the mixed open and closed habitats near the lake. Whether or not they were separated into different sub-habitats there cannot be determined from the data.

Table 8 Hominid 'clusters' found at the same stratigraphic level

Area	*KNM-ER#*	*Taxon*	*Environment*	*Faunal zone*
1	{ 725, 728	*Austr.*	Floodplain	*Loxodonta*
	{ 1815	*Homo*		
	{ 740	?		
	{ 993, 805	*Austr.*		
1	739	*Austr.*	Channel	*Loxodonta*
	741, 992	*Homo*		
6	1466	*Homo*		
11	726, 1468	*Austr.*		
6A	{ 801, 1464, 1816	*Austr.*	Distributary	*Metridiochoerus*
	{ 802, 1170, 1171	?		
8 + 8A	819, 1817	*Austr.*	Floodplain or deltaic plain	*Loxodonta*
	820	*Homo*		
103	736, 737, 730	*Homo*	Lake margin	*Metridiochoerus*
	734	?		
104	810, 814, 1804	*Austr.*	Floodplain and channel	*Metridiochoerus*
	816, 997, 998	?		
	813	*Homo*		
105	405	*Austr.*	Channel	*Metridiochoerus*
	{ 738, 1477, 1476,	*Austr.*		
	{ 1478	*Austr.*		
	1479, 1480	?		
130	{ 1805	?	Channel	*Loxodonta*
	{ 1806	*Austr.*		

{ = Found at same horizon.

The stratigraphic and environmental data provide ample evidence that the two hominid taxa were 'contemporaneous', i.e., living in the same time and place. Particularly in the lake margin habitats, it seems likely that ecological separation, if any, was not strongly spatial. The stratigraphic resolution is generally poor in terms of time, on the order of hundreds or even thousands of years even for fossils on essentially the same horizon. There may well have been seasonal fluctuations in the hominid populations along the lake margin, as there are among various animals today, which are obscured in the record.

Of interest in the problem of contemporaneity are the common occurrences of 'clusters' of hominid fossils in the East Rudolf deposits. At least 41 (37%) out of the 110 hominid specimens occur in groups which can be firmly attributed to only 8 different stratigraphic levels. In some cases there is good evidence for relating the finds to a single restricted horizon. Table 8 gives the specimens included in these 'clusters'. A microstratigraphic section of one example is given in Figure 2. Specimens assigned to *Homo* and *Australopithecus* occur at the same level ($< \pm 1.5$ m.) in at least three cases. Several of the 'clusters',

Figure 9. Occasionally whole carcasses are mummified before carnivores and scavengers have the opportunity to disarticulate and fragment the bones. This Oryx died of old age or disease, and the softer external parts were consumed by vultures. However, in the dry, hot climate of East Rudolf, the skin of the Oryx soon became too dessicated and tough for the vultures to penetrate, thereby preserving the skeleton essentially intact. The mummified carcass would probably float for some distance if picked up by a sudden flood and might be buried still intact. This illustrates one means of preserving whole skeletons in the fossil record. Articulated parts are extremely rare in the Plio-Pleistocene sediments of East Rudolf, and it seems that this mode of preservation was uncommon. However, it probably did occur from time to time, offering tantalizing possibilities for spectacular fossil discoveries. Scale in 10 cm. intervals.

however, are composed exclusively of one or the other taxon. *Australopithecus* clusters occur in fluvial deposits and the one *Homo* cluster is lake margin. The pattern of 'clusters' appears to contrast with the occurrences of the other more common members of the fauna, which are spread out through the sequence of sedimentary units. In part the clusters may be an artifact of intensive collecting around the site of the first hominid find in the area. However, the number of isolated finds plus the occurrence of widely separated sites which, on geological investigation, turn out to be at the same stratigraphic level, indicate that clusters are a genuine aspect of the hominid record at East Rudolf.

Conclusions

The study of hominids in relation to sedimentary environments is only in its infancy. Additional sampling at East Rudolf, comparative data from areas other than East Rudolf, and particularly a well-established taxonomy will be essential to confirm or revise the ideas and hypotheses presented in this paper. However, the approach shows promise as a means of placing hominids in a general palaeoecological setting in Plio-Pleistocene Africa.

It is important at this stage in the research to keep data and interpretation as separate as possible. The data on hominids in relation to East Rudolf sedimentary environments show that:

1. Both fluvial and lake margin sedimentary environments preserve comparable numbers of hominid fossils at East Rudolf.
2. There is a significantly greater number of *Australopithecus* remains from fluvial deposits than *Homo*, while the two taxa occur in similar numbers in lake margin deposits. The taxonomic designations are based on assignments by R.E. Leakey, F.C. Howell and B. Wood as of January, 1973.
3. Skeletal representation is better for *Australopithecus* in fluvial environments and is comparable for *Homo* and *Australopithecus* in lake margin environments.
4. *Australopithecus* is more abundant than *Homo* in the Upper Mb. of the Koobi Fora Fm. while the two taxa occur in comparable abundance in the lower Mb. (*Mesochoerus* zone).
5. There appears to be less sorting of fluvial thanatocoenoses associated with the hominid sites than is typical of bone assemblages from this environment, as determined by 'squares' sampling.
6. More suids (chiefly *Mesochoerus*) are preserved with the fluvial hominid site faunas than is typical of fluvial faunas as determined by 'squares' sampling. Fewer hippos are associated with the lake margin hominid sites.

7. Artifact concentrations and 'camp-sites' are found in deltaic situations in the *Mesochoerus* zone and in fluvial situations (both proximal and distal to the lake shore) in the *Loxodonta* zone (Isaac *et al.*, 1976). Therefore, artifact sites occur where both hominid forms are commonly preserved as fossils.

My inferences from these data, for the purposes of discussion, include the following:

1. The evidence indicates that the most reasonable explanation for the patterns of abundance of *Homo* and *Australopithecus* (as used in this paper) in fluvial and lake margin environments of deposition is ecological. More Australopithecines lived (or died) in fluvial habitats, probably gallery forest and bush near rivers, than *Homo*. Both inhabited lake margins.
2. Hominids in lake margin habitats (both taxa) inhabited drier areas of the shorelines and deltaic plains where fewer hippos were preserved.
3. Hominid carcases were subject to scavenging in the same manner as other animals in the fauna.
4. Interesting (although perhaps tenuous) similarities exist between East Rudolf hominid distribution patterns and those of Olduvai and the Omo Basin. Olduvai Beds I and II represent a lake margin situation similar in some respects to that of East Rudolf, and both hominid taxa appear to be present. In the Omo Shungura Fm., the hominid-bearing sediments are primarily fluvial, and many of the hominid remains appear to represent *Australopithecus*.

Postscript

Although not directly relevant to the palaeoecological setting of the East Rudolf hominids, the sedimentary context of the Lothagam mandible (Patterson *et al.*, 1970; Simons, this volume) should be placed on record. The specimen was found on the surface in clear association with Lothagam-1C (Patterson *et al.*, 1970). It was derived from fluvial deposits probably associated with the upper portions of a prograding deltaic system emptying northward into Lake Rudolf. Further stratigraphic investigations are being conducted by Mr Dennis Powers of Princeton University.

Acknowledgments

I would like to express my thanks to Richard Leakey and Glynn Isaac for their assistance and helpful comments during the course of research for this paper. Invaluable field assistance and helpful discussions were provided by John Barthelme, Bernard Wood, Glynn Isaac, Kamoya Kameu and Andrea Kilonzo. Maeve Leakey has assisted with timely correspondence and comments. I am also grateful to Clark Howell for suggestions on hominid taxonomy.

The research was made possible through the support of the Wenner-Gren Foundation for Anthropological Research (Grant 2957-1834-R). Much of the background information which made this study feasible is a result of the cooperative effort of the East Rudolf Research Project, which has been jointly sponsored by the National Science Foundation and the National Geographic Society.

References

Behrensmeyer, A.K. (1975) The taphonomy and paleoecology of Plio-Pleistocene vertebrate assemblages east of Lake Rudolf, Kenya. *Bull. Mus. Comp. Zool.* (Harvard), 146 (10), 475-574.

Behrensmeyer, A.K. (1976) Fossil assemblages in relation to sedimentary environments in the East Rudolf succession. In Coppens, Y. *et al.* (eds.), *Earliest Man and Environments in the Lake Rudolf Basin: Stratigraphy, Paleoecology and Evolution.* Chicago.

Bowen, B.E. and Vondra, C.F. (1973) Stratigraphical relationships of the Plio-Pleistocene deposits, East Rudolf, Kenya. *Nature* 242, 391-3.

Brown, F.H., de Heinzelin, J. and Howell, F.C. (1971) Pliocene-Pleistocene formations in the Lower Omo Basin, southern Ethiopia. *Quaternaria* 13, 247-68.

Butzer, K.W. (1971) The Lower Omo Basin: geology, fauna and hominids of Plio-Pleistocene formations. *Naturwissenschaften* 58, 7-16.

Cooke, H.B.S. (1976) Suidae from Pliocene-Pleistocene strata on the Rudolf Basin. In Coppens, Y. *et al.* (eds.), *Earliest Man and Environments in the Lake Rudolf Basin: Stratigraphy, Paleoecology and Evolution.* Chicago.

Findlater, I.C. (1976) *Stratigraphic analysis and palaeoenvironmental interpretation of a plio-pleistocene sedimentary basin east of Lake Turkana.* Unpublished Ph.D. Thesis, University of London, 252pp.

Gentry, A. (1976) Bovidae of the Omo Group deposits. In Coppens, Y. *et al.* (eds.), *Earliest Man and Environment in the Lake Rudolf Basin: Stratigraphy, Paleoecology and Evolution.* Chicago.

Isaac, G.L., Harris, J.W.K. and Crader, D. (1976) Notes on the archaeological evidence from the Koobi Fora Formation. In Coppens, Y. *et al.* (eds.), *Earliest Man and Environments in the Lake Rudolf Basin: Stratigraphy, Paleoecology and Evolution.* Chicago.

Leakey, R.E. (1973) Further evidence of lower Pleistocene hominids from East Rudolf, Kenya, 1972. *Nature* 242, 170-3.

Maglio, V.J. (1972) Vertebrate faunas and chronology of Hominid-bearing sediments east of Lake Rudolf, Kenya. *Nature* 239, 379-85.

Patterson, B., Behrensmeyer, A.K. and Sill, W.D. (1970) Geology and fauna of a new Pliocene locality in north-western Kenya. *Nature* 212, 918-21.

Simpson, G.G., Roe, A. and Lewontin, R.C. (1960) *Quantitative Zoology.* New York.

Vondra, D.F. and Bowen, B.E. (1976) Plio-Pleistocene deposits and environments, East Rudolf, Kenya. In Coppens, Y. *et al.* (eds.), *Earliest Man and Environment in the Lake Rudolf Basin: Stratigraphy, Paleoecology and Evolution.* Chicago.

Karl W. Butzer

Geoecological perspectives on early hominid evolution

Biological and geological approaches to palaeoecology

The past fifteen years have seen the crystallization of a new ecological orientation in the study of early hominids. This is not to say that ecological considerations had been lacking in previous work. Rather, I mean to emphasize that the scope and objectivity of ecological inference has attained a level of significance to warrant the concept of a 'palaeoanthropology'. Early landmarks, in my own view, are Brain's (1958) sedimentological studies of the australopithecine cave breccias, Bishop's (1963) palaeogeographical inferences on Miocene fossil sites in East Africa, and Robinson's (1963) hypothesis of dietary differentiation based on differential attribution and morphology of australopithecine dentitions. More recent milestones, that need no enumeration here, include continuing sedimentological work at a range of sites in Africa and Eurasia, the innovative taphonomic studies launched during the last few years, the biomechanical approach to locomotory adaptations of early hominids, and a number of thought-provoking models for hominid evolution. There can be no question that, despite the great debts owed to earlier workers, the state of the art is radically different now from what it was in 1958. In part this can be attributed to a greater awareness of the component contributions to the study of early hominids. But we also owe an equally great debt to those individuals willing to experiment with increasingly specialized analytical approaches.

Traditional palaeoecological interpretation was pre-eminently based on key faunal elements found within collections of large vertebrates. In order to overcome the intrinsic problems of dealing with extinct genera or species, work on the functional morphology of extinct megafauna was attempted, particularly since World War I. The persistence of uncertainties in this realm, and the appearance of derived or apparently aberrant forms in many collections, led to greater emphasis on total faunal assemblages, rather than on 'guide' fossils. At the same time, increasing attention was given to statistical analyses that emphasized habitat preferences of various forms. Studies of micro-vertebrates, primarily rodents, were added to the spectrum in the 1930s and, for a while, generated over-optimistic hopes for precise environmental and stratigraphical insights. No matter how essential such data were and remain, the facts are that despite such innovations, faunal studies by themselves were seldom conclusive and sometimes erroneous.

A fresh approach was necessary in faunal interpretation, taking into consideration the complex geological and, at times, cultural processes that operate in selection and preservation of bone. The resulting science of taphonomy, linking biology to geology, is developing rapidly at a crucial time, and promises to become of prime importance within the next few years. Pertinent examples are given by Behrensmeyer (this volume) and Brain (this volume), with an historical and methodological summary provided by Behrensmeyer (1975).

The potential geological contribution to early hominid palaeoecology has long been inhibited both by the inability of specialists from other subfields to utilize geological information properly, and by the lack of specialization or flexibility of most field geologists.

Traditionally, palaeontologists and archaeologists have sought geological assistance in the relative dating of sites. Their environmental inferences tended to be those suggested by their faunas or inferred from the suggested correlation of their site with a seemingly universal event such as a glacial or an interpluvial. Even if sound, site-specific geological data had been available, it is as probable as not that these would have been ignored in favour of more comprehensible, higher levels of generalization. Reversal of this tendency to ignore site-specific geological information has been slow and only partially successful, and some recent palaeontological and archaeological reports continue to include contradictions between unwarranted secondary generalization and the primary, site-specific data.

The blame for jumping from regional stratigraphic deductions directly to palaeoenvironmental inferences, based on primitive world models, lies mainly with the geologists themselves. The tools of the trade necessary even to identify broad genetic classes of sediments have been developed far too slowly in comparison to the rate of geological exploration during the last 150 years. Such basic categories as water, wind, ice, and wave-deposited materials have, until quite recently, been identified on the basis more of intuition than of scientific criteria. Although many sediments are unequivocal even in the field, others can only be identified after laboratory analysis. This applies particularly to the nuances of distinction necessary to isolate one of the many possible depositional environments involved in water action.

Partly as an offshoot of scientific exploration for petroleum since the 1930s, the new subfield of sedimentology has been able to cope increasingly well with marine and coastal sediments, but advances in interpreting the rapid facies changes of thin or discontinuous terrestrial sediments have been far less satisfactory. It is therefore not surprising that the early geologists applied simplistic stratigraphic frameworks – more suitable for subdivision of the Cretaceous or Tertiary – to an intricate Pliocene and Pleistocene record, bypassing empirical assessment of their supposedly diagnostic criteria. It is less excusable that Plio-Pleistocene field geologists, now commonly armed with sophisticated stratigraphic concepts, frequently continue to identify sediments, palaeosols, and erosional or depositional forms and structures with little or no analytical precision.

Against this background of geological mediocrity, the more meticulous course charted by the work of better, government geological surveys over the years has been dramatically accelerated in terms of palaeoanthropological interests through the exacting studies of C.K. Brain or Richard Hay, of W.W. Bishop and his students, of Carl Vondra and his associates. Although there is no simple, common denominator to describe the techniques applied by these geologists, their cumulative impact has been to place dozens of key Cenozoic sites into a reasonable scientific framework of interpretation.

On other, intermediate ground between biology and geology, we find increasing application of microscopic studies of diatoms, ostracods and, above all, pollen. These techniques, so eminently successful in deciphering late Pleistocene environments, promise much for the late Tertiary and early Pleistocene record. However, their cumulative impact for early hominid contexts is still relatively small. At this point, one can only hope for further, successful palynological as well as macrobotanical studies at critical sites in this time range.

Last but not least, as this conference has also served to demonstrate, the hominid fossils themselves have been increasingly subject to careful scrutiny in terms of functional morphology. They are finally proving capable of yielding detailed information on masticatory activities, locomotory mechanisms, and the like.

All these biological, geological, and anatomical innovations come at a time when palaeobiological and palaeobehavioural theorists have begun to formulate ecological hypotheses to help explain diverse aspects of early hominid differentiation or the specific evolution of the hominine line. Realistic ecological models will ultimately need to be the product of an interdisciplinary synthesis, employing the input of critically evaluated data processed by the diverse methods of the broad spectrum of scientists with palaeoanthropological focus or avocation. Thus far there has probably been a little too much assertion of apparent interrelationships, that are based on an incomplete appreciation of the complexity and conditional testimony of data from unfamiliar subdisciplines. Despite the continuing compartmentalization of institutions, individuals must strive to communicate to the degree that they can appreciate that no data of any category are wholly unequivocal. Thus a late Tertiary faunal assemblage cannot be simply equated with a specific vegetation and ecozone, nor can a sediment necessarily yield a reliable diagnosis on either macro or micro-depositional environments.

No palaeoecological generalizations – as opposed to limited site-specific inferences – relevant to Tertiary and Pleistocene hominids are established beyond reasonable doubt. No matter how quantitative a contributing subdiscipline may aspire to be, the compendium of palaeoanthropological sciences is necessarily an inexact one by virtue of the multivariate character of interacting organic and inorganic phenomena in nature. As scientists we remain obliged to continue to question the assumptions underlying our methods, and search for new ways to achieve fuller and more accurate resolution. The techniques of the behavioural, biological, or geological subdisciplines relevant to anthropology are never infallible and must therefore remain flexible. Similarly, the body of general information must never be elevated to the status of dogma, whether it be from our own or a cognate subdiscipline with data that we are less able to evaluate critically.

The potential contributions of the geological sciences to both data input and synthesis in palaeoanthropology are considerable, if for no other reason than that a palaeophysical geography is indispensable in both palaeoprimatology and prehistory. Admittedly, interpretations in geomorphology, sedimentology, or even basic stratigraphy are no less difficult than is the isolation of specific variables in any ecological system. But the overall information so derived does, at the very least, set potential structures on the assumptions on which palaeobiological or palaeobehavioural models are based.

Geo-ecological perspectives on Tertiary hominoid evolution

Three key ecological problems can be considered in regard to Tertiary hominid evolution in Africa: (1) What ecological contexts can be identified for the more advanced Oligocene and Miocene primates, and do these contexts change or diversify through time? (2) Does the evidence support the common assumption of Mio-Pliocene desiccation? (3) Is there adequate background information to allow for hypotheses of Tertiary geographic speciation in Africa? These points will be considered, in order, with general implications discussed in the concluding section of this paper. At issue are the various ecological adaptations inferred by palaeontologists and anatomists for the different Tertiary hominoids. Such views, as well as certain neontological inferences, are fundamental to the divergent theories that have been proposed for hominid origins among brachiating or knuckle-walking forms, or that envisage a sequence of arboreal, semi-arboreal and, ultimately, ground-dwelling adaptations through time. The geo-ecological evidence is, at this juncture, sufficiently specific to set certain strictures on unfettered speculation about early adaptations.

The earliest hominoids are associated with the Oligocene Jebel el-Qatrani Formation (*c.* 37-27 million years) of the Fayum. These primate localities come from the upper portions of point-bar deposits, laid down on the channel margins of sinuous to meandering, low-gradient, medium-velocity streams crossing a large, featureless deltaic plain (Bowen and Vondra, 1974). The occurrence of abundant, large branching logs in these point-bar deposits suggests the presence of a gallery forest with trees more than 33 m. tall. The locus of the fossil wood and vertebrates – of which all larger forms are disarticulated – indicates accumulation in the wake of periodic, bankfull floods. Throughout the vertical span of the Jebel el-Qatrani Formation there are numerous horizons of carbonate enrichment, with abundant root casts (2 mm.-2 cm. diameter); these are interpreted as pedo-genetic carbonate horizons formed by capillary action and evaporation, or by downward movement of carbonates during alternate wet and dry periods. Bowen and Vondra (1974) correctly infer periodic aridity and further suggest that savannah vegetation covered the interstream areas.

In other words, the Oligocene primates of the Fayum utilized flat-lying areas close to a perennial but flood-prone river, situated in a semi-arid environment (see also Frakes and Kemp, 1972: Figure 2). A belt of fringing, riverine forest is verified, but an ecological mosaic including open vegetation was almost certainly present well within the delta plain.

The second group of Tertiary hominoids comes from Miocene beds associated with the Eastern Rift of Kenya and Uganda. These sites are bracketed as younger than 23 and older than 12.3 million years by a large number of K/Ar dates (Bishop *et al.*, 1969; Bishop, 1971). Bishop (1963; see also Andrews and Van Couvering, 1974: Table 3) recognizes three repetitive lithofacies for fifteen fossiliferous localities (10 of which include primates): (a) lacustrine deposition of clays, silts, sands and tuffs, with fish bones; some non-sequences suggest episodic emergence; (b) subaerial accumulation of free-fall tuffs with occasional, coarser pyroclastic agglomerates, and fluvial interbeds that include land snails and fossil wood; (c) fluvial or fluvio-lacustrine aggradation of quartzose sands, grits and gravels, commonly with a proportion of fine volcanic ash in the matrix or, more rarely, coarse pyroclastic agglomerates. For eight such sites that can be localized with respect to a related, former volcanic centre, that source was 10 to 35 km. distant, and Bishop (1963) notes that most of the primate localities were situated 16-20 km. away. Even the fossiliferous beds at Napak, located a bare 10 km. from the former vents, form persistent, extensive, almost flat-lying strata, certainly deposited on or below the toeslope of the volcano (see Bishop, 1963: Figure 2).

The geological evidence therefore indicates that these East African fossil assemblages come from lake margins, sandy to gravelly stream channels, and other level surfaces prone to sheetfloods or overbank discharge; all come from the lower part of the topographic relief represented in these areas, and none can be linked with mountain slopes.

The coarse detrital nature of all the fluvial and many of the lacustrine sediments clearly implies seasonal periodicity of discharge. To some degree, the violent dissemination of pyroclastics must have contributed to this condition. However, the dominance of bed-load sediments among non-aeolian facies implies that traction and saltation were characteristic modes of transfer, i.e. fluvial transport was high-competence, turbulent, and somewhat torrential. At the same time, there are numbers of carbonate horizons, e.g. at Napak (see Bishop, 1968), that would be favoured by alkaline pyroclastics but that, nonetheless, demand marked seasonality of soil moisture and incomplete leaching. Finally, the clay-pellet dune deposits of Rusinga can only be interpreted as the result of seasonal or aperiodic desiccation of once lacustrine environments, regardless of the chemical environment (see Andrews and Van Couvering, 1974). Whitworth (1953) was correct in drawing attention to the clearcut seasonality and aperiodic variations of moisture to be deduced from the geological record.

Whether the climate was semiarid or subhumid cannot be more precisely deduced from such criteria. But, beyond question, the moist tropical conditions responsible for deep pedogenesis and 'savannah planation' in Uganda had terminated by the end of the Oligocene (see De Swardt, 1964; Bishop and Trendall, 1967), at about the same time that the Indian tectonic plate began to drift past East Africa, to cut off the monsoonal rains derived from the Indo-Pacific easterly belt (Frakes and Kemp, 1972). Although the rift valleys had not yet formed in early Miocene times, large volcanic centres were rising rapidly from the dissected plains. The geological evidence suggests a complex mosaic of depositional environments, and a regional setting no wetter than the modern Lake Victoria catchment. This would, implicitly, suggest the presence of extensive areas of open woodland or even 'savannah'.

This geological interpretation of the early, as opposed to mid-Miocene, sites of East Africa appears to be difficult to reconcile with some of the biological evidence. It was initially argued that the macrobotanical evidence from Rusinga, Napak, and Bukwa spoke for gallery forests amid open, thorny woodland or savannah (Chaney, 1933; Chesters, 1957). Similarly, the faunal assemblages (see lists in Bishop, 1967) have generally been interpreted in favour of a forest-savannah mosaic (see, for example, Whitworth, 1958), and include swamp/riverine, forest, and savannah forms. However, the mollusca from the 23 to 17 million-year-range sites are interpreted by Verdcourt (1963, 1972, and in Walker, 1969) as indicative of large tracts of unbroken, evergreen rainforest, with at least 1000 mm. precipitation. Andrews and Van Couvering (1974; also A.C. Hamilton, in Walker, 1969) arrive at a similar conclusion for the floras, suggesting extensive tracts of evergreen forest, at least in part of lowland character. Lastly, the early Miocene megafauna includes very few demonstrably open-country forms such as are indeed verified for mid-Miocene sites such as Ft. Ternan (see Andrews and Walker, 1974).

Closer evaluation of the actual data minimizes the apparent contradictions. For example, non-marine mollusca reflect specific micro-habitats rather than regional vegetation. In detail, the molluscan assemblages would also imply contradictory conclusions, with the poorly-represented freshwater mollusca including a prominent number of *Lanistes carinatus* – a form today restricted to aquatic situations in dry areas, while a number of the terrestrial species suggest dry forest, bush, or savannah. In fact, Verdcourt (1963, p.35) points out that there also were drier habitats, with 'riverine forest and woodland cutting through areas of savannah, with rainfall as low as 30 inches per year', and that 'a lowland evergreen flora and fauna coexisted with a savannah flora and fauna'. The floras are equally equivocal, with *Juncellus* cf. *laevigatus* at Bukwa being a herb today found around the margins of alkaline, i.e. non-outlet lakes, while the bulk of the forest trees and epiphytes are compatible with a riparian forest. It is significant that some grasses are present, a number of the forms are thorny, and overall leaf size is relatively small. Finally, the Miocene megafauna (although only occasionally determined beyond the generic level) changed considerably between 17 and 14 million years ago, in large part reflecting on the large-scale Afrasian faunal exchange made possible by the new landbridge opened at that time. In other words, the recent biological re-evaluations have primarily served to clarify the distinctiveness of early and mid-Miocene environments in East Africa:

(*a*) The early Miocene, pre-rift setting closely resembled the Lake Victoria catchment, including some central volcanoes, enjoying a comparable median rainfall of 1000 mm. The vegetation presumably was a mosaic of lowland and montane, evergreen forest, interspersed with riparian vegetation and stretches of open, deciduous woodland or parkland.

(*b*) The mid-Miocene, proto-rift setting was more diversified, since the accelerated rift-fracturing (Baker *et al.*, 1972) created volcanic mountains, horst blocks, and grabens with an increasingly complex mosaic of forest and open vegetation, wet mountain slopes and extensive rainshadows, lowland semi-

> deserts and lake plains. The median rainfall was probably only slightly lower, but the range of variation from place to place may have been twice as great. This trend to increasing areas of open vegetation continued through the later Miocene, as the topographic diversity of the rifts and their margins was accentuated.

The mid-Miocene *Ramapithecus* materials of Ft. Ternan are associated with subaerial volcanics, interbedded with current-bedded or ripple-marked fluvial strata and floodplain soils – the surfaces of which are fossiliferous, including oriented bones and aquatic forms (crocodile and freshwater crabs) (Bishop, 1963; Andrews and Walker, 1974). They date between *c.* 14 and 12.5 million years ago (Bishop *et al.*, 1969). The Ft. Ternan fauna (Simons, 1969; Andrews and Walker, 1974) encompasses galeria-riverine, forest, and open-country forms – the last including ostrich, and cursorial bovids as well as giraffids – just as does the Nagri fauna coeval with *Ramapithecus* in the Siwalik Series of north-west India (Tattersall, 1969a, 1969b; Prasad, 1971).[1] Although the Indian examples of *Ramapithecus* pertain to the upper, rather than middle Miocene, the geological environment is similar to that of the East African sites. The presumed Nagri-age beds of India consist predominantly of clayey sands deposited in meandering channels, with clayey overbank deposits important in some sectors, and common but localized lag gravels (Krynine, 1937; Johnson and Vondra, 1972). The Nagri biozone is situated midway in a sequence that becomes progressively coarser grained through time, with channel sands replacing flood silts, a decreasing role for post-depositional chemical weathering, but increasing carbonate content. The geological evidence favours a warm, moist climate with increasingly marked seasonality of rainfall, and moderate basin relief. Apart from common remains of palms, the macrobotanical remains suggest a forest and open woodland mosaic of Indo-Malayan type on the alluvial plains of the Himalayan foothills (see Prasad, 1971).

The newly published mandible *Graecopithecus*, from Pyrogos, near Athens (Koenigswald, 1972) is of interest here since it is attributed to *Ramapithecus* by Simons (this volume). The find comes from a sandy reddish clay, associated with an open country or even a grassland fauna that includes *Hipparion*, and may be a little younger than the Nagri (Freyberg, 1950; Simons, this volume). Thus, pending adequate study or publication of the Pyrgos site, *Ramapithecus* would seem to have a similar geo-ecological context on two, if not three continents.

1. The so-called Nagri biozone may be the first horizon of this sequence to contain *Hipparion* (Simons *et al.*, 1971; Hussain, 1973), although some specimens are from the Chinji, if the older field records are correct (D. Pilbeam, pers. comm.). It seems best therefore to equate the Chinji-Nagri transition with the approximate time of first appearance of *Hipparion*, ca. 11.5 million years ago (see Van Couvering, 1972; Delson, 1973).

In overview, the contextual data on the Miocene hominoids of East Africa allows several interim conclusions:

(*a*) *Terrain*. The Miocene hominoids of East Africa – and Eurasia – had theoretical access to several meso-habitats, much as in the case of the Oligocene Fayum. Unlike the Fayum case, where the primate fossils essentially come from a single depositional micro-environment, the East African hominoid remains come from several. In addition, some fossils of the East African 'lowland' thanatocoenoses may potentially have been derived from the higher mountain slopes of their watersheds. However, there is no sound palaeo-geographic evidence to differentiate the East African dryopithecines into high-lying (forest) and low-lying (savannah-woodland) biotopes (cf. Pilbeam, 1969).

(*b*) *Vegetation*. The early Miocene, like the Oligocene hominoid fossils, appear to derive from contexts that were predominantly wooded, but where open vegetation was present nearby or at moderate distance. The mid- and late Miocene specimens come from contexts that were partly wooded, and partly open. In each case a mosaic of vegetation must be assumed, and in every case geological processes could potentially have derived a particular fossil from either a closed or open habitat. The probabilities are that most of the Oligocene and early Miocene hominoids were arboreal, and that most of the available mid to late Miocene specimens were semi-arboreal or terrestrial. Such probabilities are inadequate to discuss ecological adaptations, however. They furthermore obscure the potential significance of mosaic environments in providing a wealth of ecologic opportunities for adaptive radiation. Yet the assumptions in the literature (e.g. Napier and Davis, 1959), including Simons's (this volume) characterization of early Miocene apes as 'tree-dwelling and feeding' in a 'wet, densely forested' environment, have about the same likelihood as our own unacceptable probability statement. The cautious conclusions of Andrews and Van Couvering (1974) – to the effect that *Barinipithecus*, and very possibly also *Limnopithecus legetet, Dryopithecus major*, and *Dryopithecus gordoni*, were forest forms – are based on limited but direct and specific faunal associations. But even here there is lingering uncertainty, and unequivocal generalizations are not yet warranted. It therefore remains to be demonstrated on purely anatomical grounds that the Miocene apes show ecological divergence.[2] Nonetheless, it may be significant that

2. The now-disputed presence of *Oreopithecus* at Fort Ternan would not alter this fact: although widely held to be an arboreal form (Hürzeler, 1958), the 1958 specimen of this problematic lineage at its Italian type site was buried in the sapropelic mud of a shallow swamp – rich in algae, water plants and sedges, but with no trees in proximity (Teichmüller, 1962; Weyland, 1962; Lorenz, 1968).

the first known dental adaptations to a grinding mastication among the hominoids (*Ramapithecus*) coincide with evidence for more open vegetation during the mid-Miocene and specifically with the mixed faunal spectrum from Ft. Ternan (Andrews and Walker, 1974).

(*c*) *Climatic change*. Despite the number of semi-arid or arid meso-habitats created in the Eastern Rift during the Mio-Pliocene, there is no evidence for a significant increase in overall aridity. Instead the wealth of ecological opportunities provided by the rift systems persisted in some form or other, despite any zonal or altitudinal shifts of climate. An objective evaluation of the admittedly meagre Tertiary record of other parts of Africa shows climatic alternations on a fairly large scale, but no demonstrable trend. The biggest stumbling block, much like the 'Great Arid' of Australia, is the Kalahari System and its apparent equivalents, the 'Continental Terminal' of West Africa and Mozambique. Accumulating stratigraphic evidence indicates a mid-Eocene to Miocene age for most of these sandstones, with various episodes of superficial aeolian and colluvial reworking through the Pliocene and Pleistocene (Haughton, 1963; Clark, 1963; Grove, 1969; Michel, 1973). In fact the original accumulation of the Kalahari Sands is best attributed to the relatively cool currents sweeping the western margins of a semi-enclosed South Atlantic Ocean during Eocene times (see Frakes and Kemp, 1972).

It remains to consider the recent hypothesis of geographic speciation of the Hominoidea in Africa and Asia as detailed by Kortlandt (1972). A variety of water barriers and arid zones are invoked to allow: (a) evolution of the australopithecines from part of an ancestral dryopithecine stock, *c.* 14 to 5 million years ago, east of a Nile-Zambezi barrier; (b) West of the Nile-Zambezi, speciation of gorilla and chimpanzee, made possible by a Niger-Benué barrier in Plio-Pleistocene times and subsequent wet-dry alternations of climate; (c) further isolation and independent evolution of 'humanoids' postulated in Arabia after *c.* 24 million (*Dryopithecus-Ramapithecus* lineage) and in Eurasia after *c.* 15 million years ago (*Dryopithecus-Gigantopithecus* lineage). Without commenting on the biological merits or fossil evidence for such a scheme, the environmental arguments must be faulted.

First and foremost the Miocene 'Nile-Zambezi barrier' is highly vulnerable. In the critical Western Rift, there is an extended erosional break between the (early?) Miocene lacustrine or fluvio-lacustrine beds (Mohari, Kabuga, Kisegi formations) and the Pliocene Kaiso Formation (*c.* 5.2 million years) (Gautier, 1970; Cooke and Maglio, 1972; Bishop and Trendall, 1967). Whether or not local basins of deposition (? Passage beds, Bishop, 1968) persisted is immaterial, since the bulk of the sediments reflect shallow lakes with strongly fluctuating margins, laid down long before the gradual sinking of the rift floor that only began in Kaiso times. This Miocene but pre-rift situation in Uganda and the eastern Congo applies more broadly to the southern Sudan and south-central Africa, and hardly constitutes a zoogeographic 'barrier'. Even after rifting had begun, the persistance of complex mosaic environments and a lack of through-drainage – much as in the Eastern Rift – minimizes the impediments of such zones to faunal movements.

A Plio-Pleistocene 'Niger-Benué barrier' is little more convincing. Buser (1966), Tricart (1965), Blanck (1968), and Michel (1973) have shown that the middle and upper Niger drainage was finally integrated quite late in the Pleistocene, with prolonged intervals of internal drainage that terminated on plains of coalescent alluvial fans. Similar conditions are suggested for the southern fringes of the Chad Basin (Pias, 1968), with only brief and incidental overflow from the Chad to the Atlantic drainage.

There is also a complication to Kortlandt's stepwise mid-Tertiary migration of African apes to and isolation in Arabia and Eurasia. The Sahara-Arabian desert axis is verified since Palaeozoic times, impeding migration via Suez, while downwarping and downfaulting of the Gulf of Aden and the Red Sea rifts began during the early Oligocene (Gass, 1970). Further, the limited occurrence of Miocene megafaunas from the Arabian Peninsula can probably be attributed to a geological situation unfavourable for potential fossil sites. On the west and south Arabian coasts, the Miocene is recorded only by narrow segments of marine beds, evaporites, reef limestones, and some coarse detrital beds that seem to lack mammalian fossils; in eastern Saudi Arabia, broad expanses of similar, but sand-veneered and poorly-exposed rocks form part of the Mesopotamian-Persian Gulf geosyncline (Powers *et al.*, 1966; Beydoun and Greenwood, 1968) – a structure that has also failed to yield significant localities with Miocene mammals in Syria and Iraq, where more intensive research has been under way for several generations. The localization of Miocene shoreline facies and the nature of the interdigited terrestial sediments leaves little doubt that most of the peninsula was exposed to semi-arid and arid denudational processes, just as was the eastern Sahara at this time (Butzer and Hansen, 1968, Ch. 9; Whiteman, 1971); the presence of large vertebrates in the early Miocene fluvial beds of northern Egypt is directly linked to the presence of a major, allochthonous river (see Said, 1962, p.200).

Geo-ecological contexts of East African Plio-Pleistocene hominids

Plio-Pleistocene hominids have been discovered and studied from several key East African areas, all situated within the Eastern Rift: the Rudolf Basin (Lower Omo, East Rudolf, Kerio Basin), the Baringo Basin, Olduvai Gorge and the Natron Basin. Intensive research has been under way at these localities for many years but, not surprisingly, publication is still incomplete for most. The level of geological research has also been uneven, with overemphasis on stratigraphy and limited attention to site-specific depositional environments in many cases. As a result, it is at present impossible to provide a comprehensive overview of meso-environments and depositional media associated with these fossils and contemporaneous archaeological sites.

The Rudolf Basin

The present status of geo-ecological research in the Lower Omo Basin and East Rudolf has been recently revealed by a workshop, *Stratigraphy, Paleontology and Evolution in the Lake Rudolf Basin*, held in Nairobi on 8-20 September, 1973, under the sponsorship of the Wenner-Gren Foundation and National Geographic Society. Since these materials have been published in revised form (Coppens *et al.*, 1976), the Rudolf Basin contexts will be reviewed briefly but critically here.

In effect, composite interpretation of the geology has proven to be controversial. The East Rudolf sequence, established primarily by Vondra and Bowen (1976), includes some 325 m. of sediment deposited along two stream systems on the north-eastern margins of Lake Rudolf. Radiometrically (Fitch and Miller, 1976) these beds range in age from 4.5 to 1.2 million years. In the field the East Rudolf sediments proved to be carefully interpreted by standard sedimentological criteria, with reference to contemporary depositional environments. The taphonomic studies by Behrensmeyer (1976; this volume) have also elucidated the nature of diverse fossil assemblages, although excavation of several of the key hominid sites was at first poorly coordinated with either sedimentological or taphonomic work.

The Omo Valley sequence is represented both by 230 m. of sediment (Mursi, Nkalabong Formations) along the north-western margins of the basin, dating from greater than 4.4 to less than 3.9 million years BP (Butzer, 1971a, 1976) and, more significantly, by a further 700 m. (Shungura Formation) of hominid-bearing deposits in the Omo type area, dating from greater than 3.7 to 1.2 million years BP on the basis of K/Ar dates, or 3.2 to 0.8 million on the basis of the magnetostratigraphy (de Heinzelin and Haesaerts, 1976; de Heinzelin, 1971; Brown *et al.*, 1970; Brown, 1976; Brown and Shuey, 1976; de Heinzelin and Brown, 1969). The Omo sequence is related to a distinctive sub-basin of Rudolf, namely an early Omo River or its key local tributaries. Interpretation of the Mursi and Nkalabong beds is based on comprehensive studies of particle size in relation to the modern Omo Delta. The methods used were comparable to those employed at East Rudolf. The Shungura Formation, although stratigraphically subdivided and mapped in meticulous detail, lacks sedimentological study and raised controversy in the field; in particular, a number of visiting geologists felt that the deposits were generally related to lower energy levels than envisaged by de Heinzelin, with the lower stratigraphic units possibly delta fringe, interdistributary or fluvio-lacustrine (rather than riverine fluvial) and the central units delta plain (rather than floodplain). Not all of the many palaeosols recognized within the Shungura were convincing in the field, and relevant laboratory analyses have only just begun. Relative stratigraphic correlations between the Omo and East Rudolf are impeded by these methodological problems, and mineralogy of the widespread volcanic tuffs has so far proved of limited help only.

The faunal successions of Omo and East Rudolf do not match directly with the dates presently assigned to the strata. The elephants, suines, and certain bovids (Maglio, 1972; Cooke, 1976; Gentry, 1976) of the Omo (and to some extent, of other East African sites) suggest that if the Omo dates are right, the East Rudolf radiometric dates are, relatively speaking, several hundred thousand years 'too old'. However, these East Rudolf Ar^{40}/Ar^{39} determinations are age spectra datings, liable to multiple interpretation and they find only equivocal support in the palaeomagnetic data of Brock (1976). Recent palaeomagnetic work in the Omo (Brown and Shuey, 1976) shows that many of the Omo K/Ar dates are probably too old rather than too young. However, this new magnetostratigraphy also suggests an alternative interpretation of that from East Rudolf, whereby the KBS tuff would be 0.55 million years younger. Clearly, the issue is not yet resolved.

'Gracile' australopith cranial materials at East Rudolf begin with specimen 1470 near 3.0 (alternatively 2.3) million years BP and the outstanding KBS archaeological site (Wood, 1976; Isaac *et al.*, 1976) at 2.6 (alternatively 2.05) million years BP; 'robust' forms span a range from greater than 2.6 (or 2.0) to 1.2 million years BP. 'Gracile' teeth in the Omo first appear between about 2.7 and 3.0 million years BP (just below horizon B-10 at Shungura; Usno Fm.), but verified archaeological materials (Bonnefille *et al.*, 1973; Chavaillon, 1976; Merrick *et al.*, 1973) are no older than 2.0 million years BP; robust forms here primarily date 2.4 to 2.0 million years BP.

The East Rudolf hominids and occupation sites come from deltaic and floodplain deposits, including the silty or sandy channels of ephemeral streams or distributaries, and extensive interdistributary marshes and mudflats that probably were seasonally dry (Behrensmeyer, 1976). There is as yet no clear pattern indicating occurrences of the 'non-robust' and robust hominids in different sedimentary environments. However, the frequency of robust australopithecine is significantly greater than that of 'non-robust' hominids in fluvial deposits, whereas the two taxa occur in similar numbers in lake-margin deposits. From these taphonomically-derived observations Behrensmeyer (this volume) suggests that rather greater numbers of robust hominids inhabited the galeria woodland of fluvial habitats than did 'non-robust' forms; both inhabited the more open vegetation of the shorelines and deltaic plains.

Again, in the lower Omo region, both the robust and gracile forms not only overlap temporally but may occasionally be found at the same sites. Other than that the bulk of the sites appear to be related to river or distributary channels of the Omo and its delta, no further generalizations can be offered at this time. Interestingly, Behrensmeyer (this volume) notes that the preponderance of robust hominids compares with that from fluvial depositional environments in East Rudolf. Fragmentary pollen records indicate that regional vegetation patterns were broadly similar to those of today (Bonnefille, 1976). Yet the earliest archaeological sites apparently coincide with palynological evidence for relatively dry conditions *c.* 2 million years ago, a trend verified by long-term change in the mammalian faunas (Howell, this volume).

Hominid fossils have been obtained from two areas of exposures in the Kerio Basin, at Kanapoi and Lothagam. On faunistic grounds the Kanapoi hominid elbow fragment probably dates *c.* 4 to 4.5 million years. It relates to a thick fluvio-lacustrine depositional sequence (Patterson, 1966; Patterson *et al.*, 1970), and probably derives from a sandy lakeshore facies (Behrensmeyer, pers. comm.). The partial mandible of the Lothagam-1(C) gracile hominid is possibly dated *c.* 6.0-5.5 million years, on faunal arguments, including correlation with the Baringo sequence, and comes from a thick and fairly rapid aggradational sequence, predominantly fluvial and probably deltaic (Patterson *et al.*, 1970). This fossil was closely linked with sandy channel units, characterized by perennial discharge, as indicated by the presence of *Etheria* (Behrensmeyer, pers. comm.).

The Baringo Basin

In recent years intensive field research in the Baringo Basin has yielded an increasing wealth of fossils and artifacts. Since the contexts as well as the materials themselves have at best been published in preliminary form, only a tentative summary is given here. The oldest hominoid fossil, a molar, possibly of a hominid, comes from the late Miocene Ngorora Formation, which is younger than 12 and older than 9 million years (Bishop and Chapman, 1970; Bishop, 1971). The tooth crown was recovered from a manganese palaeosol horizon, marking a land-surface on a low-energy alluvial plain. A hominid tooth was recovered from the Lukeino beds, *c.* 6.5 to 6.0 million years old on faunal grounds (Bishop *et al.*, 1971), in 1973 (Bishop, pers. comm.). This fossil comes from Lukeino unit B, which consists of diatomaceous silty tuffs, both massive and laminated, and essentially of lacustrine origin. The Chemeron hominid temporal fragment comes from gritty fluvial beds being built out across a fluvio-lacustrine interface, prior to extrusion of a lava dated 2.0 million years (Martyn and Tobias, 1967; Bishop *et al.*, 1971). Finally, there is the partial cranium of a robust australopithecine at Chesowanja (Carney *et al.*, 1971). Significant recent revision of the local stratigraphy indicates that this fossil and four artifactual horizons come from the low-energy delta-fringe deposits (clays, channel silts, grits or tuffs, and algal silts) of the Chemoigut Formation, which is considerably older than originally believed (1.2 million year date on capping basalt) (W.W. Bishop, pers. comm.).

Olduvai Gorge and the Natron Basin

The stratigraphy, general environmental setting, and archaeological data for Bed I and lower Bed II of Olduvai Gorge have been adequately published (Hay, 1971, 1976; M.D. Leakey, 1971). The key hominid and occupation sites of these units are found in a suite of interfingering lacustrine and alluvial deposits, laid down *c.* 1.8 to 1.7 million years ago. A soda lake of 10 to 14 km. diameter in the basin centre was at times chemically stratified, with a sheet of fresh or brackish water over hypersaline water at depth. This lake was relatively fresh at its south-eastern margin, where the sites were associated with the fluctuating shoreline or shallow, intermittent drainage lines debouching from alluvial-pyroclastic fans at the foot of high, volcanic mountains. A substantial aquatic flavour to most of the faunal assemblages also suggests that a lake was nearby. It seems that the ranges of both the gracile and robust hominids overlapped on the lake-shore and there appears to be no evidence that the various hominids were associated with different micro-environments.

The enigmatic early hominid remains from the Laetolil beds of Garussi Korongo, near Lake Eyasi, have taken on added dimensions since both the fauna and strata appear to be of considerable antiquity. There is a geological re-examination by R.L. Hay (1976, p.187), but the exact provenance of the hominid fossils remains to be assessed.

The Peninj mandible of the Natron Basin, pertaining to a robust australopith, completes the roster of key Rift Valley fossils. Dating a little earlier than 1.52 million years, the fossil comes from fluvial clayey sands that form part of a deltaic sequence (Isaac, 1967, 1972a).

The Afar

The cranial and lower limb bone fragments from the Afar Depression of Ethiopia (Johanson, this volume) are as yet not securely linked with a complex depositional sequence that appears to include at least a half dozen disconformities (Kalb, pers. comm.). Thus a faunal age cannot now be assigned with any confidence. In general, the various faunal horizons appear to be linked with fluvio-deltaic, rather than lacustrine facies; the lake basin in question was of tectonic origin and although time-transgressive, relatively restricted in size (Kalb, pers. comm.).

Geo-ecological contexts of South African australopithecines

The first australopithecine discovered, the Taung juvenile, was traditionally thought to have inhabited the treeless margins of the Kalahari Desert, with a way of life different from that of extant arboreal apes (Dart, 1925). This conception, apparently reinforced by Brain's (1958) cave sediment analyses from the Sterkfontein Valley and Makapansgat, led to Robinson's (1963) theory of dietary differentiation between gracile and robust australopithecines. A second traditional belief, in the great antiquity of the Taung fossil, is still widely held with most authors ranking Taung as the earliest South African hominid. In effect, a recent geomorphological study of the Gaap Escarpment (Butzer, 1975a) requires a revised stratigraphic age, as well as a different palaeo-climatic interpretation of the Taung australopithecine from that suggested by Peabody (1954).

At least four, repetitive, geomorphological cycles can be delineated for the Gaap Escarpment. Such cycles began with a phase (1) of accelerated aeolian activity under warm-dry conditions, with limited colluvial and fluvial processes that produced thin but extensive veneers of aeolian sediments and wash. Phase (2) was marked by accelerated fluvial and colluvial activity as surficial sediments accumulated in valleys and cave fissures, while cool-wet conditions in at least some instances led to active frost-weathering and talus accumulation. Phase (3) was also wet and probably cool, but ground cover and infiltration were optimal, leading to large-scale and protracted spring discharge and fluvial activity, with accumulation of tufa aprons and carapaces, and local filling of cave fissures with clayey sediment and flowstones. Finally, phase (4) saw declining spring and fluvial activity, erosion, karstic solution, and the formation of fissures and caves as ground cover deteriorated under the influence of an increasingly dry and warm climate.

The australopith cave complex at Taung was originally opened by karstic solution during phase (4) of the first, Thabaseek cycle. The earliest, 'dry phase' deposits of these caves accumulated during phase (2) of the second, Norlim cycle, and consist of well-sorted pink sand of aeolian origin but colluvial reworking. Judging by my own analyses of the matrix of the faunal specimens, Peabody (1954) was correct to infer that the 'dry phase' deposits included most or all of the Taung fauna, but not the hominid. The subsequent, 'wet phase' deposits accumulated during phase (3) of the Norlim cycle and consist of pink clayey silt and flowstones, the fine detritus of which was derived from montmorillonitic, residual dolomite soils by colluviation. Study of the matrix adhering to the skull leaves little doubt that *Australopithecus africanus* was embedded and fossilized in these 'wet phase' deposits, so that it is somewhat younger than the bulk of the Taung fauna.

Tentative correlation of the Gaap tufa cycles with the revised Vaal stratigraphy (Butzer *et al.*, 1973) places Norlim phase (2) no older than the youngest ('70 ft.') stage of the Vaal 'Older Gravels' – presumably of late lower Pleistocene age and possibly including Acheulean implements *in situ* (Helgren and Butzer, 1974). This and recent considerations of the Taung fauna (Wells, 1969; Freedman and Stenhouse, 1972) suggest that Taung is no older than Swartkrans and Kromdraai, rather than coeval with Sterkfontein and Makapansgat, as suggested by Cooke (this volume). The less than 870,000-year 'age' concurrently suggested by Partridge (1973) on independent, geomorphological argumentation is not contradictory with my interpretation, even though it would make Taung much younger than Swartkrans. However, even if Partridge's (1973) basic geomorphological assumptions were acceptable (and they are not – see Helgren and Butzer, 1974; Bishop, this volume), his calculations would not be applicable to Taung – where the Harts River has rapidly eroded soft Karroo sediments from a Palaeozoic valley, and where the 'Post-African' knickpoint at Buxton-Norlim is little else than an exhumed pre-Cambrian cuesta, fossilized by Karroo sediments and subject to limited retreat in Plio-Pleistocene times (Butzer, 1975a).

The environmental model offered for the Gaap tufa cycles argues strongly for a wetter and possibly cooler climate contemporary with the Taung hominid (Butzer, 1975a). A precipitation mean of 600-800 mm. (compared with 450 mm. today) is suggested, implying that this late representative of the gracile australopithecine lineage lived in a subhumid or humid setting, much like the Transvaal australopithecines, and not in a semi-desert environment as previously assumed.

The Transvaal australopithecine breccias have been studied by Brain (1958, 1967, and this volume). His basic evidence on cavern enlargement and sediment facies provides a background indispensible to evaluating the depositional environments of the South African hominid fossils. This schematic evolution for the Transvaal dolomite karst is as follows:

(*a*) Underground solution, which creates the dolomite cavern.
(*b*) Initial sedimentation of travertines and dripstones, interbedded with some residual sediment, resulting from further cavern enlargement – with no direct access to the exterior.
(*c*) Opening of a small and tenuous surface connection (karstic conduit) introduces limited quantities of soil wash and external rubble, admixed with slowly accumulating travertines and roof

fall. Bone and guano present, locally in concentration.

(*d*) Opening of a large vent (sink-hole?), leading to rapid sedimentation of soil wash and rubble, admixed with roof blocks and incidental travertines. Further bone and guano accumulation.

Brain (1958) attempted to assess the external climate by detailed study of the angularity of quartz sand grains, and of the ratio of chert to quartz sands. These results were subsequently generalized by Cooke (1963) and utilized by Robinson (1963, 1972) to help argue his dietary hypothesis, on the grounds that robust australopithecines were present in the Transvaal at times of wetter climate and lusher vegetation than their gracile counterparts. This apparent environmental dichotomy has been most explicitly stated by Kortlandt (1972), who believes that the robust South African australopiths inhabited 'sudanian and miombo woodlands' with 'very dense undergrowth', the gracile australopiths a 'sahelian, dry-sudanian, mopane' vegetation.

It has already been argued (Butzer, 1971b) that each of the fossiliferous, detrital cave fills of the Transvaal basically represents colluvial sediments compatible only with an incomplete mat of vegetation, and an environment roughly comparable to or drier than that of today. Since then, systematic sediment work on a large suite of samples, carried out in cooperation with C.K. Brain, has begun to show that each sedimentary unit of each cave is more or less unique at the micro-environmental level. Thus, the 'pink' or 'Paranthropine' breccia at Swartkrans begins with a rapid accumulation of blocks and residual soil below a newly opened sink-hole – bringing in an older residue from a former surface depression or external cave; subsequent beds, including the 'brown' breccia, record slow, episodic erosion of surface soils that were then washed into the cave interior and perhaps locally intermixed with travertines or channelled into pools of standing water. Preliminary X-ray studies of the clay minerals appear to confirm that long periods of slope stability and pedogenesis marked the depositional breaks within the cave. Combined with evidence for significant changes of the water-table, these alternations do point to major climatic changes, changes of the magnitude of those recorded on the Gaap Escarpment or at the 4-million-year Pliocene site of Virginia (Butzer, 1973). But both the patterns of slope stability and instability can theoretically be reconciled with an open regional vegetation, possibly punctuated by trees in sink-holes and valley bottoms (see Butzer, 1976a, for details).

Similar site-specific inferences can be made for Sterkfontein (see Butzer, 1971c:427ff.), where the 'type site' fossil matrix is distinct from that at the 'extension site'. At Makapansgat both the past micro-facies and the contemporary analogues are different from those of the Sterkfontein Valley. Interestingly, the 'basal red breccia' is a distinctly fluvial, crossbedded deposit derived from an allochthonous stream; the upper units, with detritus increasingly derived from local sources, are conformably interbedded with lenticles of 'grey breccia', which include the so-called osteodontokeratic collections. The younger units at Makapansgat can be interpreted much along the lines originally suggested by Brain (1958).

Perhaps the most significant ecological results of the past and recent work on the australopithecine cave breccias would seem to be that (a) the Transvaal sites and Taung both imply approximately comparable, open but not arid, regional environments, while (b) the deposits in each case include a substantial component of soil wash that introduced bone and hominid remains from outside. Brain (this volume) provides strong arguments that leopard lairs contributed much or most of this bone debris.

In terms of dating the elephants and suids appear to suggest faunal dates of 2.5 to 3.0 million years for Makapansgat and Sterkfontein, and of 1.8 million years for Swartkrans (Cooke, this volume, and discussion). Partridge (1973) computes 'opening' dates of 3.7, 3.3 and 2.6 million years respectively for these three sites. However, acceptance of such geomorphologic 'dates' also depends on many demanding assumptions, not the least of which is an acceptance of L.C. King's pan-African denudation chronology (see Butzer *et al.*, 1973; Bishop, this volume) and, granted that, a positive identification of certain isolated valley-head knickpoints with a cycle of pediplanation allegedly working its way upvalley over the past 20 million years (Helgren and Butzer, 1974). It is therefore apparent that the South African australopithecine sites remain undated, although some hope for geomagnetic applications does remain (Brock, pers. comm.).

Conclusions and outlook

Despite the general, rather than site-specific nature of much of the incomplete data available, several conclusions of interest can be drawn:

(*a*) All of the Tertiary hominoids and Plio-Pleistocene hominids examined died in proximity of water – stream, lakeshore, or karstic sink-hole. Each specimen was immediately, or within a reasonable span of time, either transported short distances by moving waters of low to moderate energy, or buried on the spot by standing water. This underscores the axiomatic yet intimate relationship of the available hominoid fossils to permanent or seasonal sources of water, whether in the valley bottoms of East Africa or on the High Veld of South Africa. Except for the Fayum Proto-Nile delta, all of the sites were situated at reasonable derivative or exploitative distances from moderate or high topographic relief – the Transvaal, the mountainous margins of the Rudolf and Baringo basins, the volcanic cones of western Kenya and the adjacent Eastern Rift, or, in India, the nascent Himalayas. This strongly cautions against the simple assumption that the Hominoidea were restricted to relatively low-lying alluvial or lacustrine plains. Indeed, the subtle yet significant variety of the geological environments represented suggests further that we may already be able to see well beyond the bias of those highly selective factors favouring subaqueous fossil preservation in relatively low-lying topography. Stated more specifically, the geo-ecological composite reviewed here does not support the notion that early hominid lowland sites were preferentially situated along sandy stream channels (cf. Isaac, 1972b).

(*b*) The sites discussed, despite the fragmentary nature of the record, all imply complex environmental mosaics that certainly included local or riparian thickets or forest, and in all probability also embraced a variety of more open vegetation types. Thus there is no sound geological – nor, as yet, faunal – evidence to argue for arboreal adaptations of the early Hominoidea; such must, instead, be argued independently from the functional morphology of the fossils or from relevant adaptations of certain modern forms. Equally, the spectrum of sites reviewed here allows for but does not demonstrate a temporal trend for the Hominoidea in general or the Hominidae in particular to occupy progressively more open environments. This does not contradict Jolly's (1970) model for an early adaptive shift to seasonal eating of cereals. If my views are correct, similar forest-grassland mosaics as were available to the australopithecines 2 million years ago were already accessible to an early hominid contender, such as *Ramapithecus*, over 10 million years earlier. Thus, although the preferred macroenvironment changed but little, new or broader ecological niches may well have been exploited by one or other lineage. Nonetheless the implications are that extensive open habitats were present but uncommon in close proximity to the Oligocene and early Miocene sites, whereas they were regionally prominent in the vicinity of the mid-Miocene and later sites of East Africa.

(*c*) The distribution of Tertiary Hominoidea through tropical Africa and mid-latitude Eurasia raises no questions in terms of temperature tolerances, since higher latitudes were substantially warmer at that time (see Hamilton, 1968; Schwarzbach, 1968). For the late Pliocene and early Pleistocene this distribution appears to have been restricted to somewhat lower latitudes, probably a consequence of declining planetary temperatures. Comparatively aberrant is the higher latitude (27°25′S) of Taung, possibly contemporary with a cool climatic anomaly. However, early hominids or their cultural traces continue to be elusively absent from suitable depositional media both in the Cape area (e.g., Langebaanweg, 33°S, Butzer, 1975b) or the Maghreb (e.g., Atlantic Morocco, Ain Hanech, etc., 33-36°N). Thus there is as yet no evidence for australopithecine dispersal beyond those macroecological limits circumscribing the range of the Miocene ancestral stock.

(*d*) Although the late Tertiary record of the Siwalik Series does indicate a conspicuous drying trend over 10 million years or more, nothing comparable can be cited for Africa. Mio-Pliocene desiccation is certainly not demonstrable in East Africa and the evidence for a systematic or pulsating trend to greater aridity in southern Africa is tenuous at best. It would therefore be advisable to abandon long-term desiccation or increased seasonality as a mechanical, *deus ex machina* factor stimulating new ecological adaptations (cf. Robinson, 1963; Jolly, 1970). In effect, the geological information shows that the dietary hypothesis (cf. Robinson, 1963) must stand or fall on the as yet wholly inadequate cultural record and on the fossil morphology *per se*. Instead, the available evidence shows indisputably that robust and gracile hominids in the Plio-Pleistocene time range shared overlapping geographical ranges. They may or may not have utilized the same ecological niche, and further, detailed taphonomic work such as that in East Rudolf may yet prove general preferences for different micro-environments. In the meanwhile we can only speculate that the sympatric continuation of two or more closely-related species or lineages for no less than 2 (and possibly more than 4) million years does suggest that they were not directly competitive.

(*e*) Altogether, the geo-ecological perspectives presented here disprove more than they prove. In general, they offer no support for deterministic models of hominization. Specifically, they show that many specious 'ecological' arguments are indeed spurious. In fact no case has yet been made to the effect that environmental changes promoted biological, social, or cultural adaptations in late Tertiary or early Pleistocene times (see Butzer, 1977). Any new adaptations that were implicitly made, either initially at the level of a *Ramapithecus*, or later, as hallmarks of possible ecological differentiation among australopithecine lineages, would seem to have been made to different or more diversified ecological niches within the same environmental mosaic shared by *Ramapithecus* and the australopithecines over a 12 million years span. If we are to develop more complex, causally-oriented, feedback models, then clearly we must have much more detailed and exacting scientific data from different relevant subfields. Much has already been gained over the traditional study of fossils in isolation, by working in multidisciplinary groups whose broad range of results is increasingly effective for integrated interpretations. Nonetheless, multidisciplinary teams do not by themselves ensure a successful interdisciplinary approach, and the impasse that remains after a decade of incredibly expensive research projects suggests that the vital contributing earth scientists and biologists must by all means be integrated into future research strategies.

Acknowledgment

This paper owes much to the consistent material support of the Lichstern endowment of the Department of Anthropology, University of Chicago.

References

Andrews, Peter and Van Couvering, J.A.H. (1975) Palaeoenvironments in the East African Miocene. In Szalay, F. (ed.), *Approaches to Primate Paleobiology. Contrib. Primatol.* 5, 62-103.

Andrews, Peter and Walker, A.C. (1974) The Primate and other fauna from Fort Ternan, Kenya. In Isaac, G.L. and McCown (eds.), *Human Origins: Louis Leakey and the East African Evidence.* Menlo Park, Cal., 279-304.

Baker, B.H., Mohr, P.A. and Williams, L.A.J. (1972) Geology of the eastern Rift system of Africa. Special Paper, Geological Society of America, 136, 1-67.

Behrensmeyer, A.K. (1975) The taphonomy and palaeoecology of Plio-Pleistocene vertebrate assemblages east of Lake Rudolf, Kenya. *Bull. Mus. Comp. Zool. Harvard.*) 146, 473-578.

Behrensmeyer, A.K. (1976) Fossil assemblages in relation to sedimentary environments in the East Rudolf succession. In Coppens, Y. *et al.*, 383-401.

Behrensmeyer, A.K., this volume.

Beydoun, Z.R. and Greenwood, J.E.G.W. (1968) Aden Protectorate and Dhufar. In *Lexique stratigraphique international* (Paris), 3, fasc. 1062, 1-128.

Bishop, W.W. (1963) The later Tertiary and Pleistocene in eastern Equatorial Africa. *Viking Fund Publications in Anthropology* 36, 246-75.

Bishop, W.W. (1967) The later Tertiary in East Africa: volcanics, sediments, and faunal inventory. In Bishop, W.W. and Clark, J.D. (eds.), *Background to Evolution in Africa*, 31-56, Chicago.

Bishop, W.W. (1968) The evolution of fossil environments in East Africa. *Trans. Leicester Lit. Phil. Soc.* 62, 22-44.

Bishop, W.W. (1971) The late Cenozoic history of East Africa in relation to hominoid evolution. In Turekian, K.K. (ed.), *The Late Cenozoic Glacial Ages*, 493-528. New Haven.

Bishop, W.W., this volume.

Bishop, W.W. and Chapman, G.R. (1970) Early Pliocene sediments and fossils from the northern Kenya Rift Valley. *Nature* 226, 914-18.

Bishop, W.W. *et al.* (1971) Succession of Cainozoic vertebrate assemblages from the northern Kenyan Rift Valley. *Nature* 233, 389-94.

Bishop, W.W., Miller, J.A. and Fitch, F.J. (1969) New potassium-argon age determinations relevant to the Miocene fossil mammal sequence in East Africa. *Am. J. Sci.* 267, 669-99.

Bishop, W.W. and Trendall, A.F. (1967) Erosion-surfaces, tectonics and volcanic activity in Uganda. *Quart. J. Geol. Soc. Lond.* 122 (1966), 385-420.

Blanck, J.P. (1968) Schema d'évolution géomorphologique de la Vallée du Niger entre Tombouctou et Labbezanga (République du Mali). *Bulletin de Liaison, Association Sénégalaise pour l'Etude du Quaternaire de l'Ouest Africain* 19-20, 17-26.

Bonnefille, R. (1976) Palynological evidence for an important change in the vegetation of the Omo Basin between 2.5 and 2 million years. In Coppens, Y. *et al.* (eds.), 421-32.

Bonnefille, R. *et al.* (1973) Situation stratigraphique des localités à hominidés des gisements plio-pléistocènes de l'Omo en Ethiopie. *C. R. Acad. Sci.*, D 276, 2781-4, 2879-82.

Bowen, B.E. and Vondra, C.F. (1974) Palaeoenvironmental interpretations of the Oligocene Jebal el-Qatrani Formation, Fayum Depression, Egypt, U.A.R. *Essays on African Paleontology* (2), Cairo, Geological Survey of Egypt, 115-38.

Brain, C.K. (1958) The Transvaal ape-man-bearing cave deposits. Pretoria, *Transvaal Mus. Mem.* 11, 1-131.

Brain, C.K. (1967) Procedures and some results in the study of Quaternary cave fillings. In Bishop, W.W. and Clark, J.D. (eds.), *Background to Evolution in Africa*, 285-301. Chicago.

Brain, C.K., this volume.

Brock, A. and Isaac, G.L. (1976) Reversal stratigraphy and its applications at East Rudolf. In Coppens, Y. *et al.* (eds.).

Brown, F.H. and Nash, W.P. (1976) Radiometric dating and tuff mineralogy of Omo Group deposits. In Coppens, Y. *et al.* (eds.), 50-63.

Brown, F.H., De Heinzelin, J. and Howell, F.C. (1970) Pliocene-Pleistocene formations in the Lower Omo Basin, southern Ethiopia. *Quaternaria* 13, 247-68.

Brown, F.H. and Shuey, R.T. (1976) Magnetostratigraphy of the Shungura and Usno Formations, Lower Omo Valley, Ethiopia. In Coppens, Y. *et al.* (eds.), 64-78.

Buser, H. (1966) Der Einfluss von Paläostrukturen auf die Entwicklung der Entwässerungssysteme Westafrikas. *Zeitschrift, Deutsche Geologische Gesellschaft* 166 (1964), 651-74.

Butzer, K.W. (1971a) The Lower Omo Basin: geology, fauna and hominids of the Plio-Pleistocene formations. *Die Naturwissenschaften* 58, 7-16.

Butzer, K.W. (1971b) Another look at the australopithecine cave breccias of the Transvaal. *Amer. Anthrop.* 73, 1197-201.

Butzer, K.W. (1971c) *Environment and Archeology: an Ecological Approach to Prehistory*. Chicago.

Butzer, K.W. (1973) On the geology of a late Pliocene *Mammuthus* site, Virginia, Orange Free State. *Researches, National Museum Bloemfontein* 2 (11), 386-93.

Butzer, K.W. (1975a) Paleoecology of South African australopithecines: Taung revisited. *Current Anthropology* 15, 367-82, 398-426.

Butzer, K.W. (1975b) Provisional comments on the sedimentary sequence of Langebaanweg 'E' Quarry, Cape Province, South Africa. *Quaternaria* 17 (1973), 237-43.

Butzer, K.W. (1976) The Mursi, Nkalabong, and Kibish formations, Lower Omo Basin (Ethiopia). In Coppens, Y. *et al.* (eds.), 12-23.

Butzer, K.W. and Hansen, C.L. (1968) *Desert and River in Nubia: geomorphology and prehistoric environments at the Aswan Reservoir.* Madison.

Butzer, K.W. *et al.* (1973) Alluvial terraces of the Lower Vaal Basin, South Africa: a re-appraisal and re-investigation. *J. Geol.* 81, 341-62.

Butzer, K.W. (1976a) Lithostratigraphy of the Swartkrans Formation. *S. Afr. J. Sci.*, 72, 136-41.

Butzer, K.W. (1977) Environment, culture and human evolution, *Amer. Scientist*, in press.

Carney, J. *et al.* (1971) Late australopithecine from Baringo District, Kenya. *Nature* 230, 509-14.

Chaney, R.W. (1933) A Tertiary flora from Uganda. *J. Geol.*, 41, 702-9.

Chavaillon, J. (1976) Evidence for the technical practices of Early Pleistocene hominids. In Coppens, Y. *et al.* (eds.), 565-73.

Chesters, K.I.M. (1957) The Miocene flora of Rusinga Island, Lake Victoria, Kenya. *Palaeontographica* B-101, 30-67.

Clark, J.D. (1963) *Prehistoric cultures of Northeast Angola and their significance for tropical Africa.* Museu do Dundo, Publicacoẽs Culturais, 62, 2 vols.

Cooke, H.B.S. (1963) Pleistocene mammal faunas of Africa, with particular reference to southern Africa. *Viking Fund Publications in Anthropology* 36, 65-116.

Cooke, H.B.S. (1976) Suidae from Pliocene-Pleistocene strata of the Rudolf Basin. In Coppens, Y. *et al.* (eds.), 251-63.

Cooke, H.B.S., this volume.

Cooke, H.B.S. and Maglio, V.J. (1972) Plio-Pleistocene stratigraphy in East Africa in relation to proboscidean and suid evolution. In Bishop, W.W. and Miller, J.A. (eds.), *Calibration of Hominoid Evolution*, 303-30. Toronto.

Coppens, Y. *et al.* (eds.) (1976) *Earliest Man and Environments in the Lake Rudolf Basin: Stratigraphy, Paleoecology and Evolution.* Chicago.

Dart, R.A. (1925) *Australopithecus africanus*, the man-ape of South Africa. *Nature* 115, 195-9.

De Heinzelin, J. (1971) Observations sur la formation de Shungura (Vallée de l'Omo, Ethiopie). *C. R. Acad. Sci.* (Paris), 272, 2409-11.

De Heinzelin, J. and Brown, F.H. (1969) Some early Pleistocene deposits of the lower Omo Valley: the Usno Formation. *Quaternaria* 11, 31-46.

De Heinzelin, J. and Haesaerts, P. (1976) Plio-Pleistocene formations of the Lower Omo Basin, with particular reference to the Shungura Formation. In Coppens, T. *et al.* (eds.) 24-49.

Delson, E. (1973) Fossil colobine monkeys of the circum-Mediterranean region and the evolutionary history of the Cercopithecidae. Unpublished dissertation, Columbia University.

De Swardt, A.M.J. (1964) Lateritisation and landscape development in parts of equatorial Africa. *Zeitschrift für Geomorphologie* 8, 313-33.

Fitch, F.J. and Miller, J.A. (1976) Conventional K/Ar and Argon-40/Argon-39 dating of volcanic rocks from East Rudolf. In Coppens, Y. *et al.* (eds.), 123-47.

Frakes, L.A. and Kemp, E.M. (1972) Influence of continental positions on early Tertiary climates. *Nature* 240, 97-100.

Freedman, L. and Stenhouse, N.S. (1972) The *Parapapio* species of Sterkfontein, Transvaal, South Africa. *Palaeontologia africana* 14, 93-112.

Freyberg, B. von (1950) Das Neogengebiet nordwestlich Athen. *Analecta geologica Helvetica* 3, 65-86.

Gass, I.G. (1970) The evolution of volcanism in the junction area of the Red Sea, Gulf of Aden and Ethiopian rifts. *Phil. Trans. Roy. Soc. London* A. 267, 369-81.

Gautier, A. (1970) Fossil fresh water mollusca of the Lake Albert-Lake Edward Rift (Uganda). *Ann. Mus. Roy. Afr. Cent.* (Tervuren), Sciences Géologiques, 67, 1-144.

Gentry, A.W. (1976) Bovidae of the Omo Group deposits. In Coppens, Y. *et al.* (eds.), 275-92.

Grove, A.T. (1969) Landforms and climatic change in the Kalahari and Ngamiland. *Geog. J.* 135, 191-212.

Hamilton, W. (1968) Cenozoic climatic change and its cause. In *Causes of Climatic Change: Meterological Monographs*, 8 (30), 128-33.

Haughton, S.H. (1963) *The Stratigraphic History of Africa South of the Sahara.* Edinburgh.

Hay, R.L. (1971) Geologic background of Beds I and II: stratigraphic summary. In Leakey, M.D., *Olduvai Gorge*, vol. 3, 9-18. London.

Hay, R.L. (1976) *Geology of the Olduvai Gorge*, Berkeley.

Helgren, D.M. and Butzer, K.W. (1974) Alluvial terraces of the lower Vaal Basin: reply. *J. Geol.* 82, 665-6.

Howell, F.C., this volume.

Hürzeler, J. (1958) *Oreopithecus bambolii* Gervais: a preliminary report. *Verhandlungen, Naturforschende Gesellschaft Basel* 69, 1-48.

Isaac, G.Ll. (1967) The stratigraphy of the Peninj group. In Bishop, W.W. and Clark, J.D. (eds.), *Background to Evolution in Africa*, 229-54. Chicago.

Isaac, G.Ll. (1972a) Chronology and the tempo of cultural change during the Pleistocene. In Bishop, W.W. and Miller, J.A. (eds.), *Calibration of Hominoid Evolution*, 381-430. Toronto.

Isaac, G.Ll. (1972b) Comparative studies of Pleistocene site locations in East Africa. In Ucko, P.J., Tringham, R. and Dimbleby, G.W. (eds.), *Man, Settlement and Urbanism*, 165-76. London.

Isaac, G.Ll., Harris, J.W.K. and Crader, D. (1976) Archaeological evidence from the Koobi Fora Formation. In Coppens, Y. *et al.* (eds.), 533-51.

Johnson, G.D. and Vondra, C.F. (1972) Siwalik sediments in a portion of the Punjab re-entrant: the sequence at Haritalyangar District, Bilaspur, H.P. *Himalayan Geology* 2, 119-42.

Jolly, C.J. (1970) The seed-eaters: a new model of hominid differentiation based on a baboon analogy. *Man* 5, 5-26.

Koenigswald, G.H.R. von (1972) Ein Unterkiefer eines fossilen Hominoiden aus dem Unterpliozän Griechenlands. *Koninklijke Nederlandse Akademie der Wetenschappen*, Series B, 75, 385-94.

Kortlandt, A. (1972) *New Perspectives on Ape and Human Evolution*. Amsterdam.

Krynine, P.D. (1937) Petrography and genesis of the Siwalik series. *Amer. J. Sci.* 34, 422-46.

Leakey, M.D. (1971) *Olduvai Gorge*, vol. 3: *Excavations in Beds I and II, 1960-63.* London.

Lorenz, H.G. (1968) Stratigraphische und micropaläontologische Untersuchungen des Braunkohlengebietes von Baccinello (Prov. Grosseto, Italien). *Rivista Italiana di Paleontologia e Stratigrafia* 74, 147-270.

Maglio, V.J. (1972) Vertebrate faunas and chronology of hominid-bearing sediments east of Lake Rudolf, Kenya. *Nature* 239, 379-85.

Martyn, J. and Tobias, P.V. (1966) Pleistocene deposits and new fossil localities in Kenya. *Nature* 215, 476-80.

Merrick, H.V. *et al.* (1973) Archaeological occurrences of early Pleistocene age from the Shungura Formation, Lower Omo Valley, Ethiopia. *Nature* 242, 572-75.

Michel, P. (1973) *Les bassins des fleuves Sénégal et Gambie: étude géomorphologique.* Paris, Office de la Récherche Scientifique et Technique Outre-Mer, *Mémoire* 63, 3 vols., 1-752.

Napier, J.R. and Davis, P.R. (1963) The forelimb skeleton and associated remains of *Proconsul africanus. Fossil Mammals of Africa* (British Museum, Natural History) 16, 1-69.

Partridge, T.C. (1973) Geomorphological dating of cave openings at Makapansgat, Sterkfontein, Swartkrans and Taung. *Nature* 246, 74-9.

Patterson, B. (1966) A new locality for early Pleistocene fossils in north-eastern Kenya. *Nature* 212, 577-8.

Patterson, B., Behrensmeyer, A.K. and Sill, W.D. (1970) Geology and fauna of a new Pliocene locality in north-western Kenya. *Nature* 226, 918-21.

Peabody, F.E. (1954) Travertines and cave deposits of the Kaap Escarpment of South Africa and the type locality of *Australopithecus africanus*. *Bull. Geol. Soc. Amer.* 65, 671-706.

Pias, J. (1968) Contribution a l'étude des formations sédimentaires tertiares et quaternaires de la cuvette tchadienne. *Cahiers*, Office de la Récherche Scientifique et Technique Outre-Mer (Pédologie), 6, (3-4), 367-77.

Pilbeam, D.R. (1969) Tertiary *Pongidae* of East Africa: evolutionary relationships and taxonomy. *Peabody Museum Bulletin* 31, 1-185.

Powers, R.W. *et al.* (1966) Geology of the Arabian Peninsula: sedimentary geology of Saudi Arabia, *Professional Paper*, U.S. Geological Survey, 560D, 1-146.

Prasad, K.N. (1971) Ecology of the fossil *Hominoidea* from the Siwaliks of India. *Nature* 232, 413-14.

Robinson, J.T. (1963) Adaptive radiation in the australopithecines and the origin of man. *Viking Fund Publications in Anthropology* 36, 385-416.

Robinson, J.T. (1972) *Early Hominid Posture and Locomotion*. Chicago.

Said, R. (1962) *The Geology of Egypt*. Amsterdam.

Schwarzbach, M. (1968) Das Klima das rheinischen Tertiars. *Zeitschrift der deutschen geologischen Gesellschaft* 118 (1966), 33-68.

Simons, E.L. (1969) The late Miocene hominid from Ft. Ternan, Kenya. *Nature* 221, 448-51.

Simons, E.L., this volume.

Simons, E.L., Pilbeam, D. and Boyer, S.J. (1971) Appearance of *Hipparion* in the Tertiary of the Siwalik Hills of North India, Kashmir and West Pakistan. *Nature* 229, 408-9.

Tattersall, I.M. (1969a) Ecology of North Indian *Ramapithecus*. *Nature* 221, 451-2.

Tattersall, I.M. (1969b) More on the ecology of North Indian *Ramapithecus*. *Nature* 224, 821-2.

Teichmüller, M. (1962) Die *Oreopithecus*-führende Kohle von Baccinello bei Grosseto (Toskana/Italien). *Geologisches Jahrbuch* 80, 69-110.

Tricart, J. (1965) Rapport de la mission de réconnaissance géomorphologique de la vallée moyenne du Niger. *Mémoire*, Institut Fondamentale de l'Afrique Noire (Dakar) 72, 1-196.

Van Couvering, J. (1972) Radiometric calibration of the European Neogene. In Bishop, W.W. and Miller, J.A. (eds.), *Calibration of Hominoid Evolution*, 247-72. Toronto.

Verdcourt, B. (1963) The Miocene non-marine mollusca of Rusinga Island, Lake Victoria and other localities in Kenya. *Palaeontographica* 121, 1-37.

Verdcourt, B. (1972) The zoogeography of the non-marine mollusca of East Africa. *Journal of Conchology* 27, 291-348.

Vondra, C.F. and Bowen, B.E. (1976) Plio-Pleistocene deposits and environments, East Rudolf, Kenya. In Coppens, Y. *et al.* (eds.), 79-83.

Walker, A. (1969) Fossil mammal locality on Mount Elgon, eastern Uganda. *Nature* 223, 591-3.

Wells, L.H. (1969) Faunal subdivision of the Quaternary in southern Africa. *S. Afr. Archaeol. Bull.* 24, 93-5.

Weyland, H. (1962) Floristische Beobachtungen bei der Mazeration von Braunkohlenproben von Baccinello in der Toskana (Italien). *Geol. Jb.* 80, 111-16.

Whiteman, A.J. (1971) *The Geology of the Sudan Republic*. Oxford.

Whitworth, T. (1953) A contribution to the geology of Rusinga Island, Kenya. *Quart. J. Geol. Soc. Lond.* 109, 75-92.

Whitworth, T. (1958) Miocene ruminants of East Africa. *Fossil Mammals of Africa* (British Museum, Natural History) 15, 1-50.

Wood, B.A. (1976) Remains attributable to *Homo* in the East Rudolf succession. In Coppens, Y. *et al.* (eds.), 490-506.

Glynn Ll. Isaac

The archaeological evidence for the activities of early African hominids[1]

Reconstruction

If an observer could be transported back through time and climb a tree in the area where the Koobi Fora Formation was accumulating – what would he see?

As the upper branches are reached, the climber would find himself in a ribbon of woodland winding out through open areas. A kilometre or so away to the west would be seen the swampy shores of the lake, teeming with birds, basking crocodiles and *Euthecodons*. Here and there are schools of hippos. Looking east, in the distance some ten or twelve kilometres away lie low, rolling hills covered with savannah vegetation. From the hills, fingers of trees and bush extend fanwise out into the deltaic plains. These would include groves of large *Acacia, Celtis* and *Ficus* trees along the water courses, fringed by shrubs and bushes. Troops of colobus move in the tree tops, while lower down are mangabeys. Scattered through the bush, the observer might see small groups of waterbuck, impala and kudu, while out in the open areas beyond would be herds of alcelaphine antelope and some gazelle (*Megalotragus* and *Antidorcas*). Amongst the undergrowth little groups of *Mesochoerus* pigs rootle, munching herbage.

Peering down through the branches of the tree, the climber would see below the clean sandy bed of a watercourse, dry here, but with a tidemark of grass and twigs caught in the fringing bushes and showing the passage of seasonal floods. Some distance away down the channel is a small residual pool.

Looking out beyond the bushes he can see large open flood plains,

1. This review was prepared for a volume commemorating the life's work of Louis Leakey, *Perspectives in Human Evolution#4*, edited by G.Ll. Isaac and E.R. McCown, 1976. The paper was circulated and discussed at the New York symposium and is reprinted in this volume at the editor's request. Only the concluding sections of the two versions differ. A brief postscript has been added, drawing attention to some advances and revisions since the paper was written, and citing some new references.

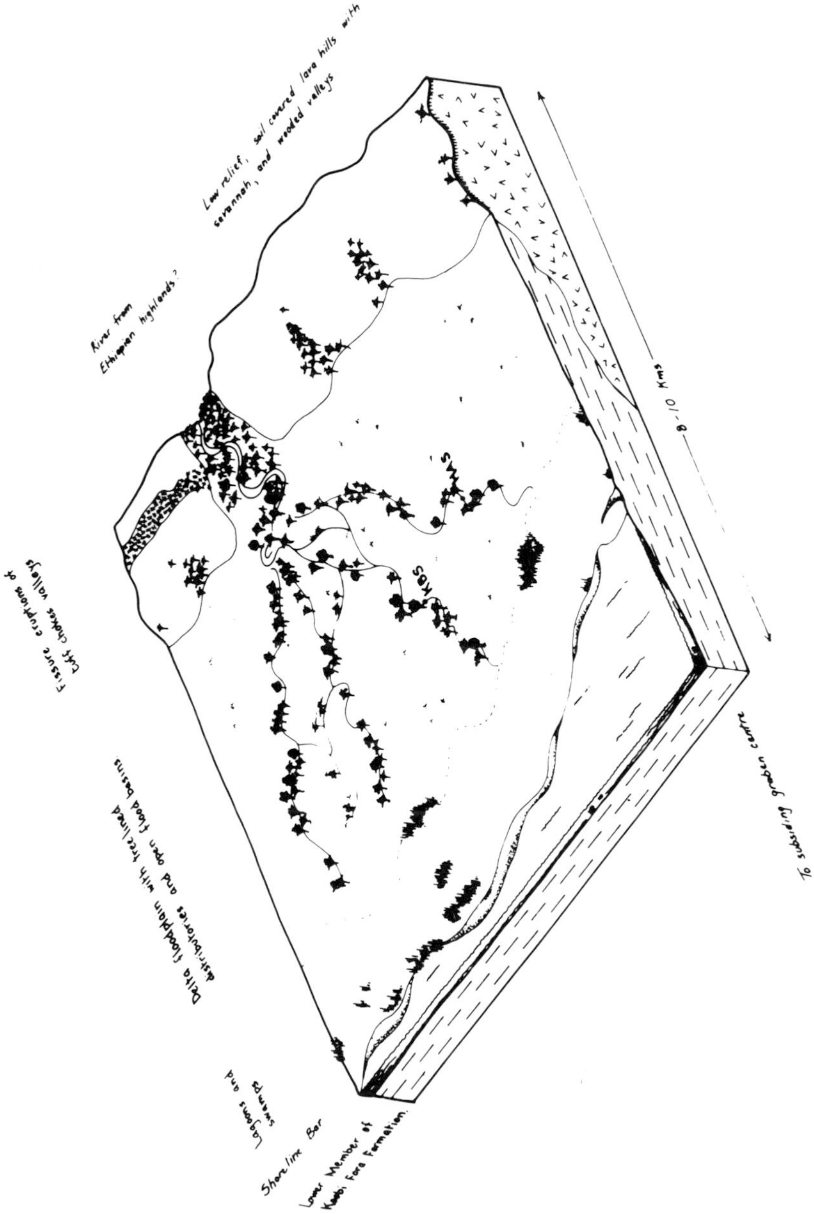

Figure 1. A reconstruction of the setting of the Plio-Pleistocene archaeological sites at East Rudolf. Details are conjectural but the main features are established from geological and palaeontological evidence.

covered with grasses and rushes, partly dry at those seasons of the year when the lake is low and when the river is not in spate. Far across the plains, a group of four or five men approach; although they are too far off for the perception of detail, the observer feels confident that they are men because they are striding along, fully upright, and in their hands they carry staves.

To continue the reconstruction in a more purely imaginative vein: as the men approach, the observer becomes aware of other primates below him. A group of creatures has been reclining on the sand in the shade of a tree while some youngsters play around them. As the men approach, these creatures rise and it becomes apparent that they too are bipedal. They seem to be female, and they whoop excitedly as some of the young run out to meet the arriving party, which can now be seen to consist mainly of males. The two groups come together in the shade of the tree, and there is excited calling, gesturing and greeting contacts. Now the observer can see them better, perhaps he begins to wonder about calling them men: they are upright and formed like men, but they are rather small, and when in groups they do not seem to engage in articulate speech. There are a wealth of vocal and gestural signals in their interaction, but no sustained sequential sound patterns.

The object being carried is the carcase of an impala and the group congregates around this in high excitement; there is some pushing and shoving and flashes of temper and threat. Then one of the largest males takes two objects from a heap at the foot of the tree. There are sharp clacking sounds as he squats down and bangs these together repeatedly. The other creatures scramble round picking up the small sharp chips that have been detached from the stones. When there is a small scatter of flakes on the ground at his feet, the stone worker drops the two chunks, sorts through the fragments and selects two or three pieces. Turning back to the carcase, this leading male starts to make incisions. First the belly is slit open and the entrails pulled out; the guts are set on one side, but there is excited squabbling over the liver, lights and kidneys: these are torn apart, some individuals grab pieces and run to the periphery of the group. Then the creatures return to the carcase; some of the males pull at limbs, while another severs skin, muscle and sinew so as to disengage them from the trunk. Each adult male finishes up with a segment of the carcase and withdraws to a corner of the clearing, with one or two females and juveniles congregating around him. They sit chewing and cutting at the meat, with morsels changing hands at intervals. Two adolescent males sit at the periphery with a part of the intestines. They squeeze out the dung and chew at the entrails. One of the males gets up, stretches his arms, scratches under his armpits and then sits down. He leans against the tree, gives a loud belch and pats his belly ... *End of scenario.*

Jane Lancaster (1967) pointed out that in dealing with early hominids we ought to make an imaginative leap and realize that we are dealing with an adaptive system that no longer exists. The system presumably had some structural features held in common with that of man, some in common with that of the apes, and very probably it also had unique components and configurations. In hindsight we can see that the system was continuously evolving in the sense that it never reached equilibrium – but in terms of those who lived it, it was presumably more or less constant over hundreds of generations, and it must have been not just promising, but downright effective, otherwise we could not be here to indulge our curiosity over its nature.

The scenario, fanciful though it is, does serve to bring into sharp focus how little we know about the aspects of early hominids that really matter. For instance, what if we included the encounter between two hominid bands, or between different hominid species in the glimpse? How would those have looked? We have direct evidence for tool making at a place on a tree-lined stream channel where bones also accumulated, but the rest of the behaviour pattern sketched is an extrapolation. Food sharing, division of labour, pair-bonding with economic involvements are envisaged in this reconstruction, but all we can in fact say is that at some stage these behaviours did become critical ingredients of human adaptation.

In contrast with our ignorance of hominid behaviour, we are steadily learning more about its context and concomitants. Thus as geological, palaeontological and palynological research progresses we can speak with more and more confidence about the setting of early hominid life and death, and the description of the scene for the scenario may not be too far from the truth. Similarly, as hominid fossil finds continue to mount in numbers, we are getting better and more complete information on the appearance and physical capabilities of early hominids. However, human evolution is characterized more by changes in behaviour and social organization than by changes in anatomy, and what one would really like to know is how these came about: what were the formative stages like? What influence if any do they have on the character of the end product?

Table 1 sets out in an oversimplified and elementary fashion some of the contrasts that I know between men and their closest living relatives. This crude list helps me to symbolize my stance, which is that the evolutionary transformation with which we are concerned was a complex one, involving intricately inter-related anatomical, physiological, economic, technological and cultural components.

As an archaeologist, I am primarily concerned with the physical traces of activities, but these will remain as rather dull stones and bones unless they are considered as parts of broader patterns of habit, behaviour and ecology.

Table 1 Changes which have occurred in the evolutionary development of mankind since divergence from the last common ancestor shared with any living ape

I *Anatomical and physiological changes*

A. *Visible in fossils*	B. *Not readily visible in fossils*
– Modification of hind limbs for full bipedal locomotion	– Changes in skin and skin glands
– Modification of hands and arms for more effective carrying and tool use	– Reduction in body hair
– Enlargement of the brain	– Continuous sexual receptivity of female
– Reduction and remodeling of the jaws	– Partial reorganization of the brain
	– Modification of the vocal tract

II *Behavioural changes*

A. *Directly detectable by archeology*	B. *Not directly detectable by archeology*
– Increasing dependance on manufactured EQUIPMENT and TOOLS	– LANGUAGE
– Great increase in MEAT-EATING (= hunting until recently).	– Subtle controls on displays of emotion
– Increasing interdependence through FOOD-SHARING	– Greatly increased CO-OPERATION and DIVISION OF LABOUR
– Re-organisation of behavior around a 'camp' or HOME-BASE	– Great increase in social bonding mechanisms: 'marriage', kinship, reciprocation
	– Great increase in symbolism

Relationships of sites and finds to local and regional ecology and geography

Although our knowledge of the archaeology of early man is currently expanding in a most encouraging way, it should be borne in mind that it still depends on a mere handful of significant excavated sites: Olduvai Gorge Beds I and II (M.D. Leakey, 1971); Peninj Formation (Isaac, 1967); Shungura Formation (Coppens, Chavaillon and Beden, 1973; Chavaillon, 1976; Merrick *et al.*, 1973); and Koobi Fora Formation (M.D. Leakey, 1970a; Isaac *et al.*, 1971; Isaac *et al.*, 1976). The review will focus on these East African sites with Olduvai occupying a pivotal position, both because of the qualities of the evidence available there and because Mary Leakey has compiled and published more complete data for Olduvai than are available for any

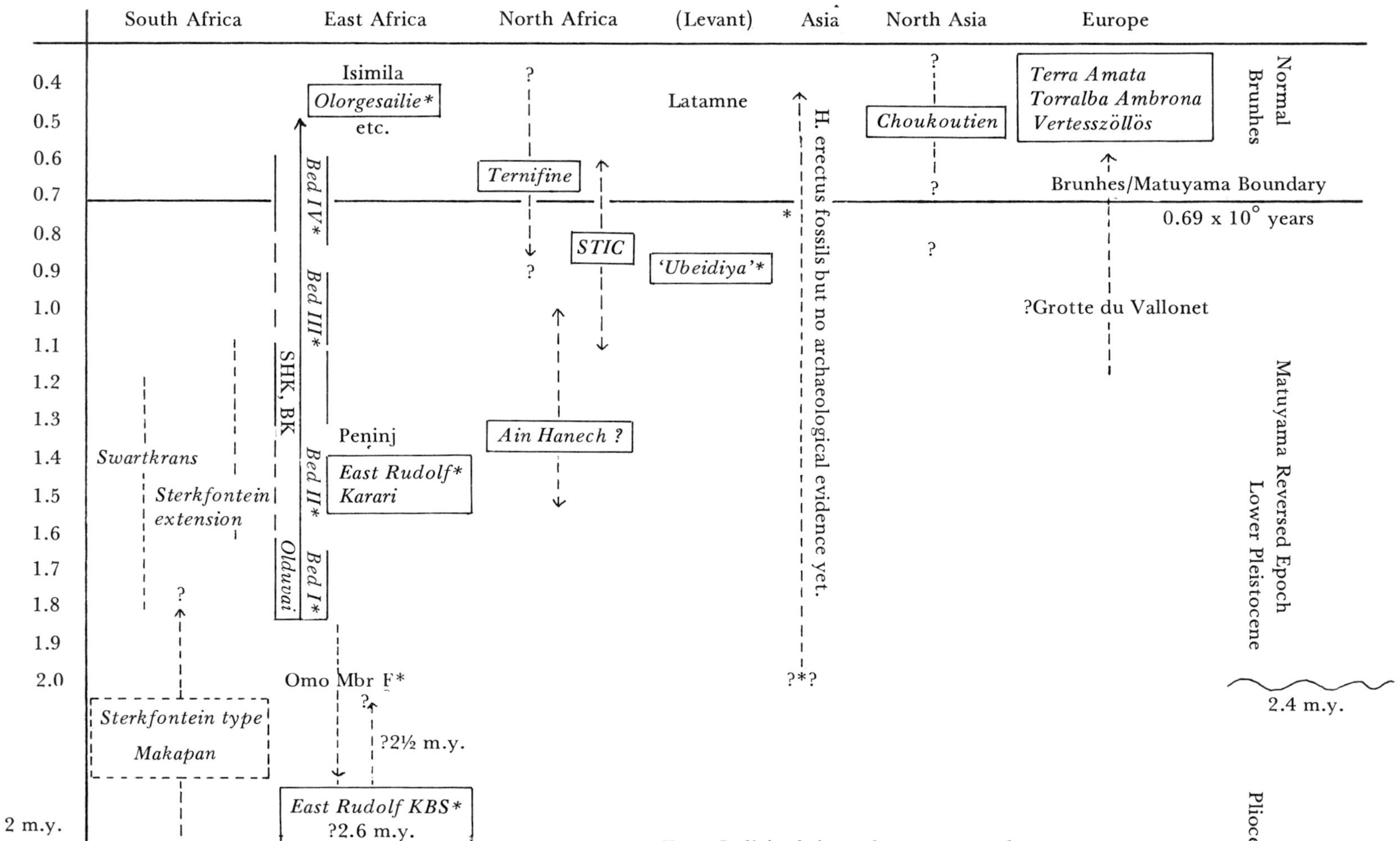

Key: Italicised sites = bone preserved.

other site. For East Rudolf I have drawn on our own largely unpublished field and laboratory data, of which a summary is currently in press. Comments on the Shungura evidence depend both on the published reports and on comprehension gained during field exchanges between the East Rudolf and the Omo teams.

The application of K-Ar dating and palaeomagnetic stratigraphy to these East African sedimentary formations has placed them for us on a chronometric time scale. We can be sure that all these documents relate to the time span between about $2\frac{1}{2}$ and $1\frac{1}{2}$ million years. Within this span, some time placements are debatable. Olduvai Bed I is securely dated to 1.83 ± .13 (Curtis and Hay, 1972) but there is current discussion about whether the KBS Industry at East Rudolf is really as sold as $2\frac{1}{2}$ million years, or whether it might be closer to 2 million years. However, the chronological uncertainties within East Africa are on a much smaller scale than those affecting estimates of the age relations of palaeoanthropological sites in most other regions. For instance estimated ages for Makapan and Sterkfontein range from more than 3 million years to perhaps less than 2 million years. These uncertainties notwithstanding, the following important sites outside East Africa are presumed to be at least in part coeval with the East African material under review:

North Africa:	Ain Hanech (Arambourg, 1950; Balout, 1955; Howell, 1960
	Sidi Abderahman and related sites (Biberson, 1961)
Ethiopia:	Melka Kontouré (Chavaillon, 1967, 1970)
South Africa:	Makapansgat (Dart, 1957; Tobias, 1967)
	Sterkfontein (Robinson and Mason, 1962; Tobias and Hughes, 1969; M.D. Leakey, 1970b)
	Swartkrans (Brain, 1970; M.D. Leakey, 1970b)

Some of the Javanese palaeoanthropological sequence may also overlap this time range, but because of chronological uncertainties and because archaeological investigation *senu stricto* has not been carried out, this sequence has not been considered further. All archaeological sites in the temperate zone of Eurasia now appear to be younger than 700,000 years (see Butzer and Isaac, 1975).

Three components of the evidence are now widely recognized, and form convenient headings for this review: artifacts and equipment, food refuse (usually bone), and spatial configuration within sites. What follows is a necessarily rather cursory survey of the information now available under these headings. By way of conclusion I offer some speculations on overall interpretation – one archaeologist's 'model' of the evolution of hominid behaviour.

Stone artifacts

Stones which show clear signs of having been fractured by hominids occur in Plio-Pleistocene deposits in several parts of Africa. These occur both as isolated stray pieces and in concentrated patches on old ground surfaces. For obvious reasons it is the material from the concentrations that is most often studied. At the best studied and most important localities we can be certain that an unusual agency, presumably hominids, was concentrating stone and causing its fracture in a systematic way. This process generates two distinctive classes of objects: lumps of stone from which flakes have been removed, and comparatively thin slivers of stone fractured from larger blocks. Clearly the two series are in part complementary, though assemblages are not always balanced with regard to numbers of each, or of raw material composition. The first series includes choppers, discoids, polyhedrons and some heavy-duty scrapers etc., which can perhaps be conveniently grouped under the collective term 'core tools'. The second class includes flakes, flake fragments, angular fragments etc. Where no further modification is evident, the term 'debitage' is often used. Items showing chipping and/or battering attributable to damage in use are termed 'utilized'; items showing modification by the removal of small trimming flakes are designated as tools and are termed 'scrapers', 'awls', 'burins' etc. as appropriate. The structure and definition of this terminology is clearly set out in Dr Mary Leakey's monograph (1971, pp. 3-8) and certainly does not require detailed repetition here. For the benefit of those not extensively initiated into the mysteries of stone artifact terminology, let me stress that in spite of the literal, non-technical meaning of the words used, the distinctions involved are *morphological*; they do not depend on recurrent judgments about *function*. Thus the distinction between a tool and a non-tool depends largely on whether the piece is judged to show purposive design for use, not on whether the piece was actually used as a tool. For this reason choppers, polyhedrons and scrapers etc., which are systematically shaped by flake removals, are classified as tools, while raw flakes are relegated to debitage, in spite of the fact that many of us believe that these were very important as implements. The term 'artifact' remains neutral and covers anything shaped by the hand of man, whether by design or as a by-product; it can be contrasted with the category of 'manuports' which are items believed to have been introduced but not shaped by man. Figure 2 summarizes the frequency distributions of percentage incidence of these major categories in Plio-Pleistocene assemblages. The questions may now be asked: what can these simple manufactures teach us about human evolution? What useful question can we pose, with some hope of getting valid answers?

It seems to me that artifact assemblages contain potential

information on the following broad topics:

1. The *levels of craft competence* of the makers, and the *intensity of involvement* with, or *dependence* on equipment (material culture).
2. *Function* and *adaptation*, the need for particular forms of artifacts in economic and social life.
3. *Tradition*: that is, culturally determined craft practices and design norms. This information can in turn be used to attempt assessments of culture-historic interrelations and distinctions.
4. The extent of *transportation of some materials*.

Until recently most of the endeavours of palaeolithic archaeology were concerned with topic number three, and to a lesser extent with topic number one. We know distressingly little about the function of

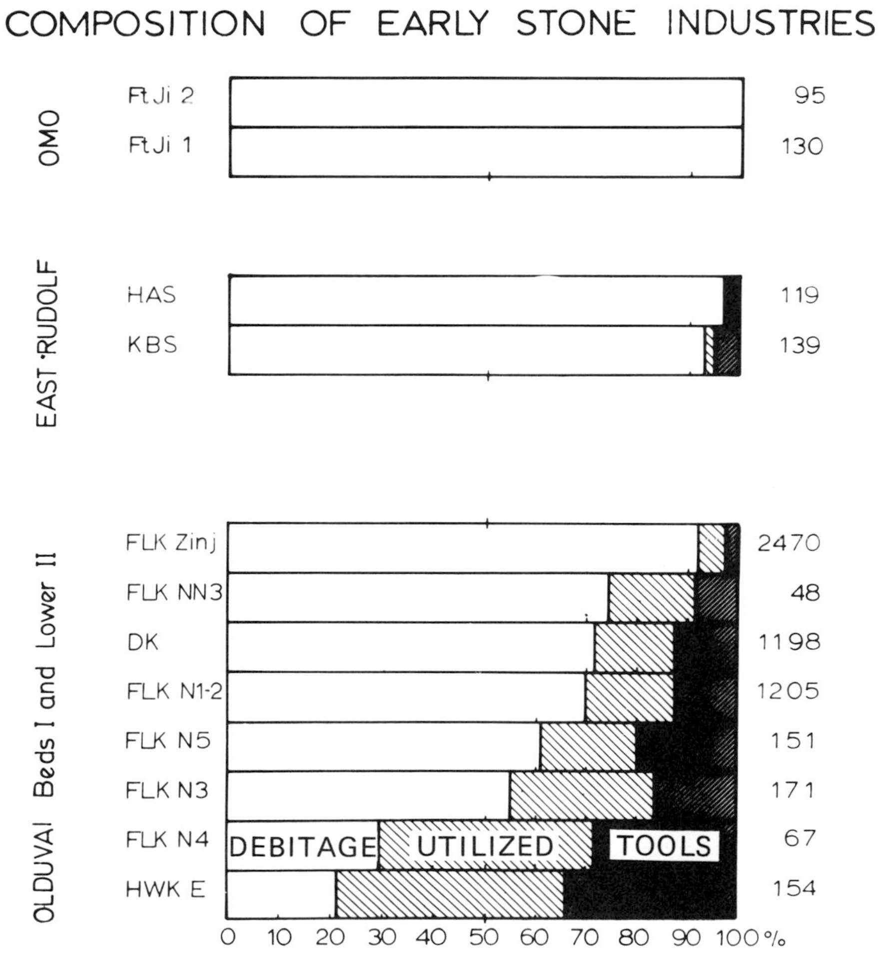

Figure 2. Bar diagram showing the percentages of the three main categories, 'Debitage', 'Utilized' and 'Tools', in various Plio-Pleistocene assemblage samples.

stone artifacts, partly because of lack of emphasis on this in enquiries and partly because clear evidence is difficult to obtain.

Before trying to unravel these strands of information from the tangle of an assemblage, it is necessary to ask what determines the form of a stone artifact? As a gross simplification one can enumerate four primary factors:

1. The physics of conchoidal fracture.
2. The size, form and detailed mechanical properties of available stone.
3. The needs of the makers for certain kinds of working edges.
4. Prevailing cultural norms with regard to artifact form (= 'fashion', 'style', 'tradition').

When comparatively simple artifact forms are compared, the possibility has to be borne in mind that some similarities and some differences may have been occasioned by purely mechanical contingencies; these should not be interpreted as being indicative of important cultural connections or distinctions. An example of this phenomenon may be the marked differences between the Shungura Formation assemblages made of small quartz pebbles and other Plio-Pleistocene assemblages made from lava cobbles and blocks. We simply cannot tell whether the Shungura craftsmen were more or less advanced, and also we cannot tell what cultural norms they held in common with Olduvai and Koobi Fora craftsmen.

Levels of competence and intensity of involvement with implements

The earliest known archaeological sites are marked as documents of hominid behaviour by the presence of clear-cut artifacts. These relics signal that a major behavioural shift in the direction of the human condition had already occurred. Without the artifacts it is very difficult to identify traces of hominid behaviour of any kind, as can be seen from the continuing uncertainty about the osteo-dontokeratic culture and the Makapan evidence for the predatory behaviour of *A. africanus*.

One question that arises is as follows: was the process of initial involvement in stone artifact production a long, slow, gradual development, or have thresholds been crossed, that is to say, innovations which rapidly brought about a certain technological situation which may then have persisted for long periods with little change?

We do not yet have enough evidence to answer this question, but it seems to me that the actual trajectory of development probably lay somewhere between even, steady progression and a stepwise pattern of change. These are simply opposite extremes in possible conceptualization of the origins of stone tool manufacture. It does seem likely to me that the empirical discovery of the effects of conchoidal fracture was a threshold. This discovery immediately creates two families of artifact form: sharpened lumps of stone (core tools) and sharp slivers and fragments (flakes etc.). As I have indicated, these are in fact the fundamental components of the earliest known assemblages.[2]

Clearly some hominids, by the time of Olduvai Bed I, had firmly established the basic techniques of achieving conchoidal fracture (M.D. Leakey, 1971). If, as seems likely, the Koobi Fora Formation, Lower Member sites are substantially earlier, then this position had been achieved by about two and a half million years ago (M.D. Leakey, 1970a; Isaac *et al.*, 1971; Isaac, postscript to this paper). There seems no way of judging how much further back the record of these practices will be traced. We have to get out into the field and search.

Louis Leakey found a stone, in the excavation at the 14 million year old Miocene site of Fort Ternan, which seemed to him to have been damaged by use (L.S.B. Leakey, 1968). He also concluded that the variety of lava of which the stone is composed is extraneous to the deposits. In default of detailed geological studies it is hard to evaluate the possibility that the stone is a manuport. Unfortunately, also, the signs of use, while suggestive, are not unambiguous. For the time being, tool-using activities by *Ramapithecus wickeri* seem to me to be possible, but unproven.

One possible view of the three earliest excavated artifact assemblages (Olduvai I, Shungura F and Koobi Fora Lower Member) is that they each represent the intersection of elementary control over stone fracture with the form in which stone was available in the particular area. Under this view, the specific design-tradition element in each of these would be small. This is a possibility that I think should be considered; I do not regard it as in any way established. Elimination or validation will require the development of fresh procedures of analysis since it cannot be ascertained from typological analysis.

Can we detect any progressive changes in the known Plio-Pleistocene record of technology, that is, in the period before one million BP? The crucial evidence in this connection comes from Olduvai Gorge where Dr Mary Leakey has shown very clearly that there were important changes: 'There was an overall increase in the tool kit ... the average number of tool types for seven Oldowan levels in Bed I and the base of Bed II amounts to only six; the figure has risen to over ten for nine Developed Oldowan levels in Bed II' (M.D. Leakey, 1971, p.269).

In the Koobi Fora Lower Member and the Shungura samples which are currently believed to be slightly older than the better known

2. A partial exception may be the Shungura Formation Industry (Merrick, *et al.*, 1973; Coppens *et al.*, 1973). In this instance it seems likely that the artifacts were generated by smashing small pebbles. Under these circumstances the core tool series is very poorly represented.

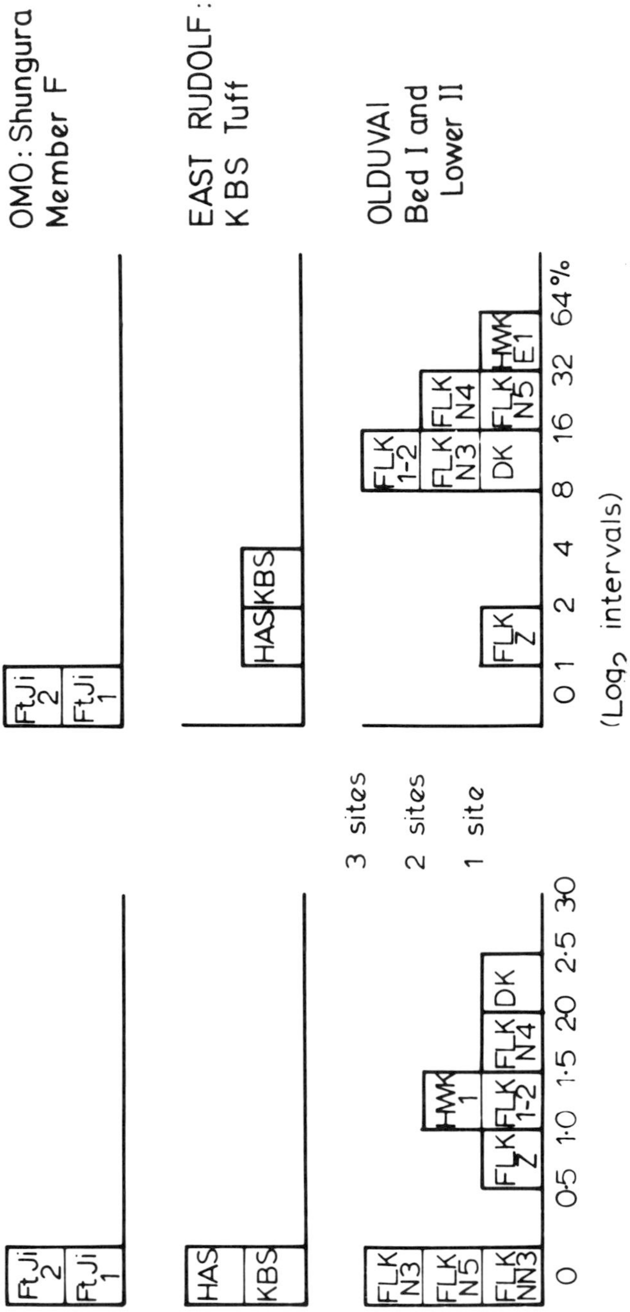

Figure 3. Histograms showing the frequency distributions of percentage representation of 'small tools' (scrapers etc.) and of core-tools (choppers etc.) in the Plio-Pleistocene samples from East Africa. Olduvai data from M.D. Leakey (1971, p.265) recalculated relative to the entire set including waste. Omo data from Merrick *et al.*, 1973.

Olduvai series, even fewer tool type categories *sensu stricto* are represented (see Figure 3). This could be an illusion created by inadequate sampling but it is suggestive.

Some time between one, and one and a half million years ago, hand-axes and cleavers began to be made. In some cases these were made by the application of bifacial retouch to large flakes, which were also a technical novelty. Where these forms preponderate the whole aspect of the assemblages appears suddenly quite different from all the previous assemblages and from some contemporary ones. Dr Mary Leakey summed up the situation, saying of Middle Bed II:

> Up to and including this level there is no suggestion whatever of duality in the known lithic assemblages which are remarkably constant in character ... In middle Bed II, however, the first unquestionable bifaces appear. ... At some sites they occur in sufficiently large numbers (over 50 per cent of the tools) for the term 'Acheulian' to be applied without hesitation to the industry ... At other sites bifaces occur in small numbers (an average of 6 per cent of the tools) in assemblages that are otherwise wholly Developed Oldowan in character. (M.D. Leakey, 1971, p.269)

At East Rudolf a similar situation is being observed: the contrast between the KBS industry (Lower Member ~ $2\frac{1}{2}$ m.y.) and the Karari industry (Upper Member ~ $1\frac{1}{2}$ m.y.) in the Koobi Fora Formation, varies in its specifics but it also involves a great increase in the number of types, and a rise in assemblage diversity. Bifaces also seem to appear in the later Karari industry, but so far have never been found dominating an assemblage. Mary Leakey's data also show a marked rise in the maximum density of artifacts (Figure 4, based on M.D. Leakey, 1971, p.260). Our data at East Rudolf show a similar contrast between the early and the late sites with a rise in density of at least an order of magnitude. It is hard to know what the behavioural significance of this rise may be. Factors to bear in mind include the following:

- (*a*) Stone tool making had become a more facile and habitual behaviour.
- (*b*) Sites were more intensively occupied (longer duration, or more recurrent visits, or both).
- (*c*) Better bags or baskets had developed for carrying raw material to site.

In summary, the East African evidence does document progressive developments. Two arbitrary divisions in a continuum can perhaps be recognized: first an early set of industries is known which has less typological diversity and perhaps lower occurrence densities. This includes the classic Oldowan of Bed I and Lower II, the KBS industry and presumably the Shungura industry, although this is different and

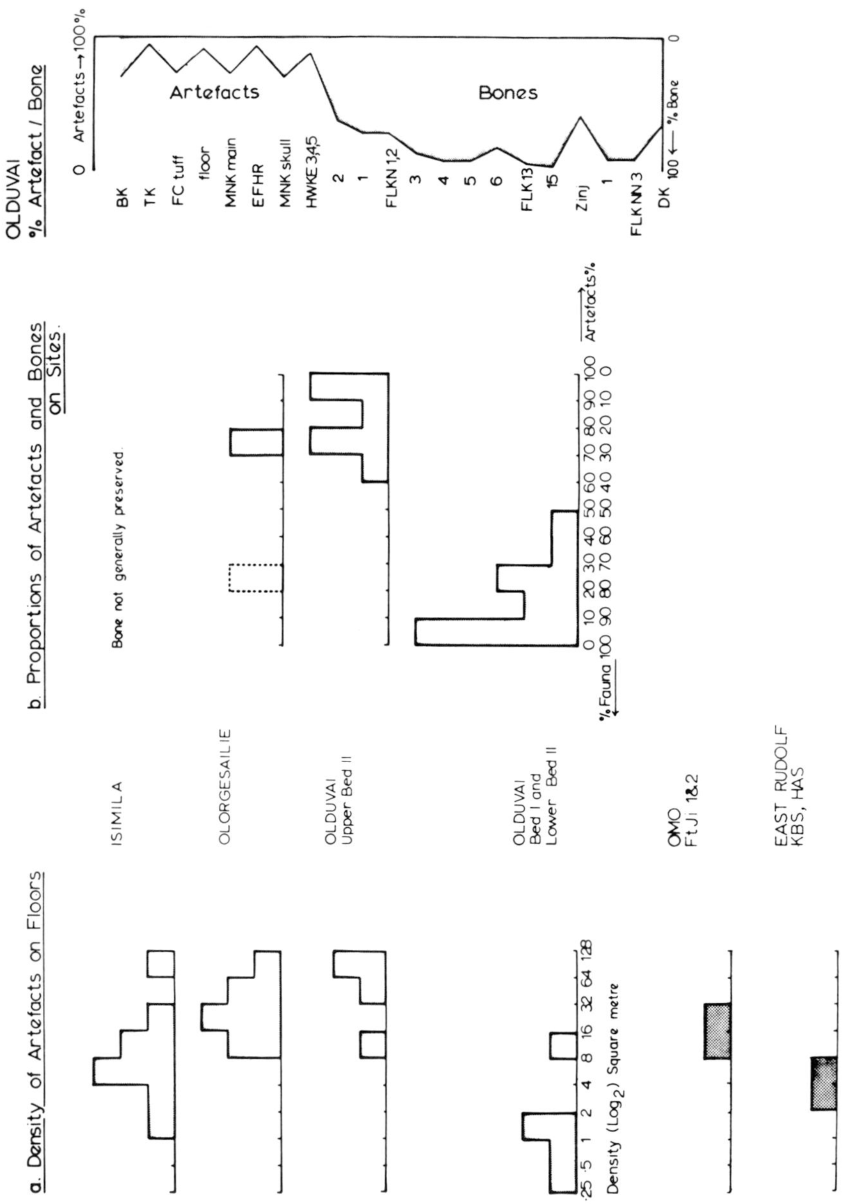

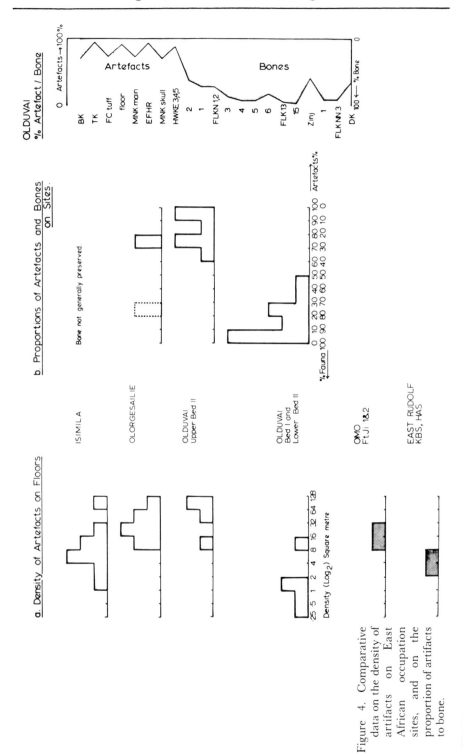

Figure 4. Comparative data on the density of artifacts on East African occupation sites, and on the proportion of artifacts to bone.

distinctive. This series is believed to span a time interval of ~ 2.6 to ~ 1.6 million years. We do not know whether the phase began with the rapid establishment of stone knapping following the 'discovery' of conchoidal fracture, or whether there is a long antecedent sequence of slowly developing stone craft. We will have to find this out by patient searches.

A later set of assemblages can also be recognized, which are still of lower Pleistocene age (i.e. 1.5-0.7 m.y.). These involve the addition of a variety of new types to the total artifact repertoire, a propensity for assemblages to vary in composition from one site to the next, and higher artifact densities. The lower Acheulean and the developed Oldowan Industries of middle and upper Bed II, Olduvai, fall into this set as does the Karari Industry of East Rudolf.

How do the South African and North African occurrences compare with this apparent sequence? Having examined, by courtesy of C.K. Brain and P.V. Tobias, parts of the collections from Swartkrans and from Sterkfontein Extension site, I would venture the opinion that both of these belong morphologically with the later set of East African Plio-Pleistocene assemblages. This is in accord with M.D. Leakey's findings (1971) and with earlier reports by Robinson and Mason (1962). I do not wish to use the morphological matching to suggest a relative date for these assemblages, since we are all trying to get away from that kind of circular procedure.

Unfortunately we have no complete assemblages from the Plio-Pleistocene of North Africa which were recovered by excavation and which include a fair sample of both core tools and flakes etc. In this region as in East Africa there seem to be both pre-biface and biface-containing industries, but there is no means of knowing whether the change occurred at a similar time. The abundance of spheroids at Ain Hanech, coupled with the presence of bifaces in an immediately overlying layer (Balout, 1955) suggests similarities to the Developed Oldowan.

Function

We have as yet no direct evidence of the functions of early stone tools, but there is strong circumstantial evidence for associating them with some activities which we can surmise would have been facilitated by their use. At both Olduvai and Koobi Fora, the early artifacts form scatters coincident with patches of broken-up mammal bones which would seem to constitute evidence for the cutting up and consumption of animals ranging in size from rodents to pachyderms. It is hard to conceive of a large carcase being dismembered by smallish primates without cutting tools, so that tools may fairly be regarded as an integral part of an adaptive complex which also involved hunting and food sharing. In this connection it should be pointed out that there has been a growing awareness of the tendency for butchery to involve small comparatively simple tools (Clark and Haynes, 1969). To be useful, a sharp or pointed piece need only be large enough to be held between index finger and thumb with the point or edge projecting: that is to say, sharp pieces from 10 to 15 mm. in diameter are potentially useful. This realization received dramatic reinforcement during fieldwork at Lake Rudolf. In our presence, a young Shangilla pastoralist found himself without a metal knife while confronted by a fresh lion-killed antelope carcase. Spontaneously he tapped off a very small flake from a lava cobble and proceeded to slit the skin covering a cannon bone, which he then peeled and cracked open to obtain marrow. Clearly the minute flakes used would have been equally effective for cutting articular sinew. From this and related observations (e.g. Gould, 1968) it emerges that the small sharp flakes and flake fragments, which by convention we label as waste or debitage, may well have had crucial adaptive importance. Perhaps it is significant that this is in fact the preponderant class of material in all the early stages.

It seems unlikely that any of the early stone artifacts was actually fashioned as a weapon. However, if sticks and branches were modified for use as spears or digging-sticks, then presumably the sharp flakes would have served to notch and whittle, while the stouter, jagged chopper edges may have been effective for hacking. It is not inconceivable that bark trays such as those found at Kalambo Falls could have been made with the use of flakes and core tools.

In the regrettable absence of more direct evidence the matter can also be viewed in another way – the known stone tool kit of Plio-Pleistocene sites would be quite adequate to perform all the essential tasks of tropical, non-agricultural peoples, namely to butcher carcases and to make spears, digging-sticks and containers. These are integral parts of human adaptation.

Tradition and culture history

Distinctive features of stone artifact assemblages can be attributed to differences in the traditions or cultures of the hominids that made them. Clearly before this is done it is desirable to distinguish features which may have been induced largely by *differences in raw material*, and differences which may reflect *varied activities* by the same people at different times and places. The distinctiveness of the Shungura industries *vis-à-vis* Olduvai and Koobi Fora may be an example of differences induced by contrasting raw materials, which therefore cannot be interpreted as necessarily indicative of either cultural or developmental stage differences. There are differences also between the Olduvai Developed Oldowan and the Sterkfontein industry that could as well be due to the influence of material as to cultural difference *per se*.

The dichotomy between Acheulean and Developed Oldowan

industries in Bed II at Olduvai cannot be explained in terms of raw material. A lively and as yet unresolved debate continues about the relative merits of several possible models which might help account for the observed pattern (see Isaac, 1972). Distinct cultural groups, perhaps corresponding to species differences, are one possibility (M.D. Leakey, 1971, pp. 269-73). Others have suggested differentiation of activities (e.g. Clark, 1970, pp. 85-6).

Transport

All the important Plio-Pleistocene archaeological sites involve the transport of some materials prior to their being discarded at the sites. Full details of the systems have not been worked out, but in most cases the distances involved need not be more than a few kilometres. The quantities at sites range from a few kilograms to perhaps a hundred or so. These are guesses, since total weights have been worked out for very few sites. Since we do not know any of the critical variables, such as how many hominids worked, and for how long, we cannot yet work out the minimum number of hominid trips that might have been needed – with and without containers to augment the amount carried at one time.

A very early 'factory site' was excavated at Olduvai by Marie-Lou Harms working in conjunction with Dr M.D. Leakey. D. Stiles carried out laboratory analysis and has reported on this material (Stiles *et al.*, 1974).

Bone refuse and diet

Many of the early sites at Olduvai and the two excavated sites in the Lower Member of the Koobi Fora Formation consist of coincident patches of stone artifacts and scatters of broken bones. The conclusion seems inescapable that the same hominids who made the artifacts concentrated the bone. It also seems virtually certain that the bone was the residue discarded after the consumption of meat. These sites provide us with positive evidence that at least some tool-making Plio-Pleistocene hominids were partially carnivorous; but what we do not know at these or other sites is to what degree vegetable and gathered foods were also important. I have argued elsewhere that the evidence is at least consistent with the notion that tropical hominids have always had a two-pronged opportunistic subsistence strategy involving both hunting and foraging, as reported for !Kung, Ba Twa, Hadza, Australian aborigines, etc. (Isaac, 1971; Lee and DeVore, 1968). I continue to regard this as highly likely.

The excavated archaeological sites of the Shungura Formation lack significant bone concentrations, as does the site of FxJj 10 at Koobi Fora; but these cases cannot be used as proof of meat-free diets, since they are just as likely to be due to poor preservation of bone.

Mary Leakey's report on the Olduvai sites is as usual the most important source of evidence (M.D. Leakey 1971, Ch.9). It emerges that the early hominids were eclectic in their tastes, and bone remains range from mice to elephants. At most sites medium-sized antelopes predominate in the remains, as they do in the fauna itself when it is on the hoof (Table 3). The notion that these sites involved mainly small species and young animals has not been sustained.

There is also a small number of Plio-Pleistocene sites where the partly dismembered carcase of a single large animal has been found with artifacts scattered around. These are indistinguishable from sites termed butchery sites by the archaeologists. In the KBS Tuff (East Rudolf) a hippo carcase is represented at the site of HAS, while at Olduvai FLK N an elephant and a deinothere are present at different levels. At present it is hard to tell the extent to which the meat involved in these cases was acquired by hunting as opposed to scavenging. Schaller, Kruuk and others have shown that there is no fixed distinction between hunters and scavengers amongst large carnivores. On this and other grounds I am inclined to think that the hominids were hunters, although they may also have pirated and scavenged other animals' kills.

Recent field studies of non-human primates have shown that some other species, notably chimpanzees and baboons, are predatory and carnivorous. However, meat appears as an occasional, opportunistic extra in diet rather than a regular component, and the prey species are all much smaller than the primate predator. The archaeological evidence from East Africa strongly suggests that by 2 to 2½ million years ago some hominids, at least, were eating meat regularly and included prey as large or larger than themselves. I would join Washburn and others in regarding this as a highly significant adaptive shift (e.g. Washburn and Lancaster, 1968; Campbell, 1966; Pilbeam, 1972, etc.).

Dr Mary Leakey has shown that some changes occur in the character of bone refuse between Bed I and upper Bed II (1971, pp. 248-56). Notable points of contrast include: a rise in the ratio of artifacts to bone fragments (Figure 4); an increase in the degree to which the bone is broken up and rendered unidentifiable; a change in species composition, with very large animals being very slightly better represented in the later sites: in particular the extreme predominance of bovids drops from 70-80% in Bed I, to 40-50% in upper Bed II, while equids and hippos become more conspicuous components; the first known instances of successful decimation of animal herds occurs in upper Bed II (*Antidorcas recki* at SHK, and *Pelorovis* at BK).

We do not yet have sufficient data to judge whether the rather slight and subtle changes observed at Olduvai reflect widespread progressive shifts or local adjustments. There is bone associated with the Karari industry at East Rudolf, but studies are not yet far enough

Table 3 **Representation of Macro-Mammals on Lower Pleistocene living floors in East Africa. Percentages are not yet available for the East Rudolf (Koobi Fora) sites, or for the smaller animals at Olduvai**

	Selected Sites *Olduvai Bed I after M.D. Leakey, 1971, p.257*							*Koobi Fora Lower Member*	
	DK	FLK NN 3	FLK Zinj	FLK N 6	FLK N 5	FLK N 1-2	FLK II Deino	KBS	HAS
	%								
Bovidae (Antilopes)									
Equidae	3	4	7	p	2	3		—	—
Suidae	12	12	8	15	9	8		p	
Primates	4	—	5	—	p	p		—	—
Hippopotamidae	2	—	—	p	p	p		p	
Rhinocerotidae	1	—	—	—	—	—		—	—
Proboscidea	1	—	—		p	—		—	—
Griaffidae	1	—	p	p	—	p		p	—
Hare and/or Pɒrcupine	p	p	p	p	p	p		p	—
Micro-mammals	—	p	p	p	p	p		—	—
Snakes and Lizards	p	p	p	p	p	p		—	—
	1407	274	596	473	922	527			

Note: p = present. Percentages recalculated to exclude carnivores, micromammals and reptiles.

advanced for comment on its implications.

I find myself unable to assess the significance of comparative data from other regions. The Transvaal cave sites yield hominids in association with an abundance of other animal bones, but in no case does the evidence appear compelling that the hominids were the principal bone-concentrating agency. Brain (1970) has provided convincing arguments that at Swartkrans, leopards were involved in the emplacement of at least some of the hominid bones. Investigations are currently in progress at Makapansgat which should help to clarify the mode of accumulation involved there (Tobias *in litt.*).

In Morocco, the very early sites are largely devoid of significant bone accumulations. Bone was associated with the artifacts at Ain Hanech and included *Anancus, Elephas*, rhinoceros, *Stylohipparion, Equus, Hippopotamus, Omochoerus, Libytherium, Giraffa, Bubalus, Bos, Gazella, Oryx, Numidocapra*, etc. (Balout, 1955, p.163). Unfortunately it is not clear to what extent these constitute food refuse associated with the artifacts.

Spatial configurations and ecological opportunities

I have recently reviewed aspects of this evidence and will offer only a very brief commentary here (Isaac, 1972). Traces of the life and death of early hominids are not evenly scattered over the ancient landscape. Once we have distinguished between effects due to life patterns and effects due purely to preservation differences, we can attempt to learn about ecology from the observed configurations.

The first point to stress is that we have an extremely biased sample from the Plio-Pleistocene in East Africa. As yet no site is known which can inform us regarding hominid activities on the hills and uplands: all our data concern the alluvial plains and shoreline marshes of sedimentary basins.

Within the sedimentary basins the archaeological material is not evenly distributed; there is commonly a widespread, low density scatter of artifacts, and then there are concentrated patches of discarded artifacts. Eventually we will get round to systematic studies of the dispersed material and may learn much from it. However, for the moment, one is obliged to restrict comments to the meaning and location of the concentrated patches. These are indistinguishable from vestiges that in later periods are known as camp-sites, and they seem to indicate that the movements of Plio-Pleistocene hominids were organised around a home base. This is a distinctive feature of human behaviour *vis-à-vis* other hominoids, and has its closest parallels in social carnivores, birds and social insects (see concluding section). The sizes of the early sites seem to be very similar to the sizes of later Pleistocene sites, namely 5 to 20 metres in diameter.

Comparative studies suggest that while sites occupy very diverse settings, the artifact concentrations tend to be associated with stream channel situations (see Isaac, 1975, p.517). Even sites that are on a flood plain soil substratum are often immediately adjacent to channels (e.g. Koobi Fora FxJj 11 and 20, Omo FtJj 2 etc.). The association appears to become more pronounced after about 1 to 1½ million years ago. There has been some discussion of the reason for this site location pattern (Isaac, 1966, 1972; M.D. Leakey, 1971:259). I tend to think that one important factor has been the propensity of trees and bushes to be distributed as ribbons fingering out along channels into the edaphic grasslands of the basins. These gallery strips would have provided shade, cover, fruiting trees and bushes – and something to climb when predators came. It is almost a metaphysical point, but there is some interest in the fact that hominids, while colonizing the savannah, may have preferred to keep their home bases in strips of woodland that extended out into more open country, rather like tourists transporting themselves into Hilton hotels in alien lands! In this connection it is perhaps significant that the only horizon at the Omo where artifact concentrations have been found in large numbers is Member F (Coppens, Chavaillon and Beden, 1973; Merrick *et al.*, 1973). The horizons are associated with indications that the normal axial hydrographic pattern of the proto-Omo river may have broken down into a braided, anastomosing network of smaller stream courses (Heinzelin, pers. comm.).

In summary, the palaeoenvironmental reconstructions of the basins that preserve Plio-Pleistocene archaeological traces suggest a mosaic of diverse habitats: beaches, reed beds, swamps, edaphic grassland, savannah, riverine woodland and bush, some gallery forest. All we know for certain is that at least two species of hominids were active at least from time to time amongst this varied stock of opportunities. We do not know whether the presence of either or both was seasonal. By stressing some habitats rather than others one could reinforce arguments in favour of seed-eating, rhizome eating or hunting – but I strongly suggest that it was the *diversity of resources* that may have been attractive. Hominid adaptation as we know it from later times has flexibility and opportunism as its hallmark. Very likely this began early in human evolution.

Geography and chronology

The best dated Plio-Pleistocene traces of hominids come from the savannah[3] country of Eastern Africa, where locally conditions of preservation were optimal, and where perhaps also conditions of life were particularly favourable. The most prolific sources of fossils are still the various Transvaal cave sites, which are also in savannah country *sensu lato*. Although not well dated they certainly fall within

3. The term savannah is used to cover vegetation that is neither desert nor forest.

the range 4 to 1 million years. Other occurrences within Africa that may be of this age range include the Chad fossil and the Maghreb artifacts (Ain Hanech and *Civilisation du galet amenagé* of Biberson, 1961). All of these are in areas that are environmentally intermediate: that is, not forest or desert.

Distribution maps of African prehistoric remains commonly show a plethora of 'Pebble culture' (more or less equivalent to 'Oldowan') occurrences including sites in Central Africa, West Africa and all over the Sahara. Most of the plots represent undated, typologically designated surface collections. Given the improbability of the survival of recognizable artifacts for one or more million years, without their being encased in a sedimentary formation, most of these records must be discounted. The absence of confirmed and dated finds of this age in the forested zones of the Congo basin and of West Africa cannot be interpreted since suitable deposits have not been located and searched. However within East Africa there are indicators that the optimal zone of early hominid occupation lay more in the drier east than in the moister west. Extensive prospecting on partially fossiliferous exposures of great thickness from Plio-Pleistocene deposits in the Western Rift has not revealed hominids or stratified artifacts (e.g. Bishop, 1971). It seems inconceivable that these could have been as well represented as in the Eastern Rift. The only possible exception is the locality of Kanyatsi where de Heinzelin (1960) found artifacts that may be of Plio-Pleistocene age.

Outside Africa there are a very few artifactual or fossil traces of Plio-Pleistocene hominid presence that are more than 0.7 million years old (i.e. the age of the Matuyama-Brunhes palaeomagnetic boundary and a convenient base for the 'Middle Pleistocene'). These include 'Ubeidiya in Israel which is probably ~ 0.6-0.8 million years old (Horowitz *et al.*, 1973; Bar-Yosef, pers. comm.). The Djetis and Trinil faunal zones of Java which possibly span from $1\frac{1}{2}$ to $\frac{1}{2}$ million years ago (Jacob, 1972; Isaac, 1972; Pilbeam, 1975) and perhaps the Grotte du Vallonet near Nice.

For what it is worth then, available archaeological data is consistent with a tropical distribution of Plio-Pleistocene hominids, perhaps centred in Africa and extending into South East Asia. Within Africa the hominids may well have been predominantly savannah forms.

Archaeology and models of human evolution

It has become fashionable for all kinds of research workers to present models intended to elucidate the process by which the early hominids became differentiated. To mention but a few: Lancaster (1967) wrote from the stance of primate studies; Fox (1967) tackled the questions from the viewpoint of a social anthropologist; Reynolds (1966 and 1968) used chimpanzee studies as a basis for suggestions; and Jolly

(1970) offered a very specific seed-eating model inspired by patterns in comparative anatomy and by his interpretation of the development of masticatory mechanisms. More or less comprehensive models have been put forward by human biologists such as Washburn (1960, 1965, 1968b); Campbell (1966) and Pilbeam (1972). These latter are all in my view convincing in their broad outlines. All share the practice of treating anatomy, diet, tool involvement and behaviour as interrelated parts of an integrated system of adaptation. These versions draw in a general way on the main features of the archaeological record, but do not treat it very specifically. In effect, the only discipline which has not yet had a fling at articulating a hominid differentiation model is archaeology. I venture to offer the sketch of one, because archaeologists may have a vantage point that can lead to improved reconstructions. One of the most distinctive aspects of human evolution has been the development of self-recording behaviours. The great apes, for all their intricacy and interest, leave no archaeological record.

I find it easiest to approach the model-building proposition by way of a comparison of human behaviour with the behaviour of man's closest living relatives, the African apes (Figure 5). Clearly the most relevant materials for comparison on the human side are the living-arrangements of peoples not dependant on agriculture. Amongst the apes, the chimpanzee is closest, for reasons of ecology and also of phylogeny, on the evidence of biochemistry. The comparison of behaviours defines the challenge involved in seeking to make models: it is done without any intention to imply that human behaviour is derived from chimp behaviour. However, it seems certain that behaviour patterns that are prominent in man but absent or very weakly expressed in other primates must have been developed during the evolutionary divergence of the hominids. The chimp studies provide a means of preparing such a list as a basis for discussion. Table 1 sets out an oversimplified summary of features that I would judge to have particular relevance. I have underlined items for which direct physical evidence can be sought, while those which have some parallels amongst social carnivores are marked with an asterisk. Let me turn now to the Plio-Pleistocene record, and see what we know about the position of at least some hominids with regard to the points of contrast.

1. Some hominids were fully upright bipeds (Napier, 1967; Robinson 1972).
2. Most hominids had slightly larger brain/body weight ratios than the apes, and some had reached a condition intermediate between apes and men: brain size 600-800 ccs. with small to moderate body size.
3. Teeth and the masticatory mechanisms had been rearranged, including loss of large canines.

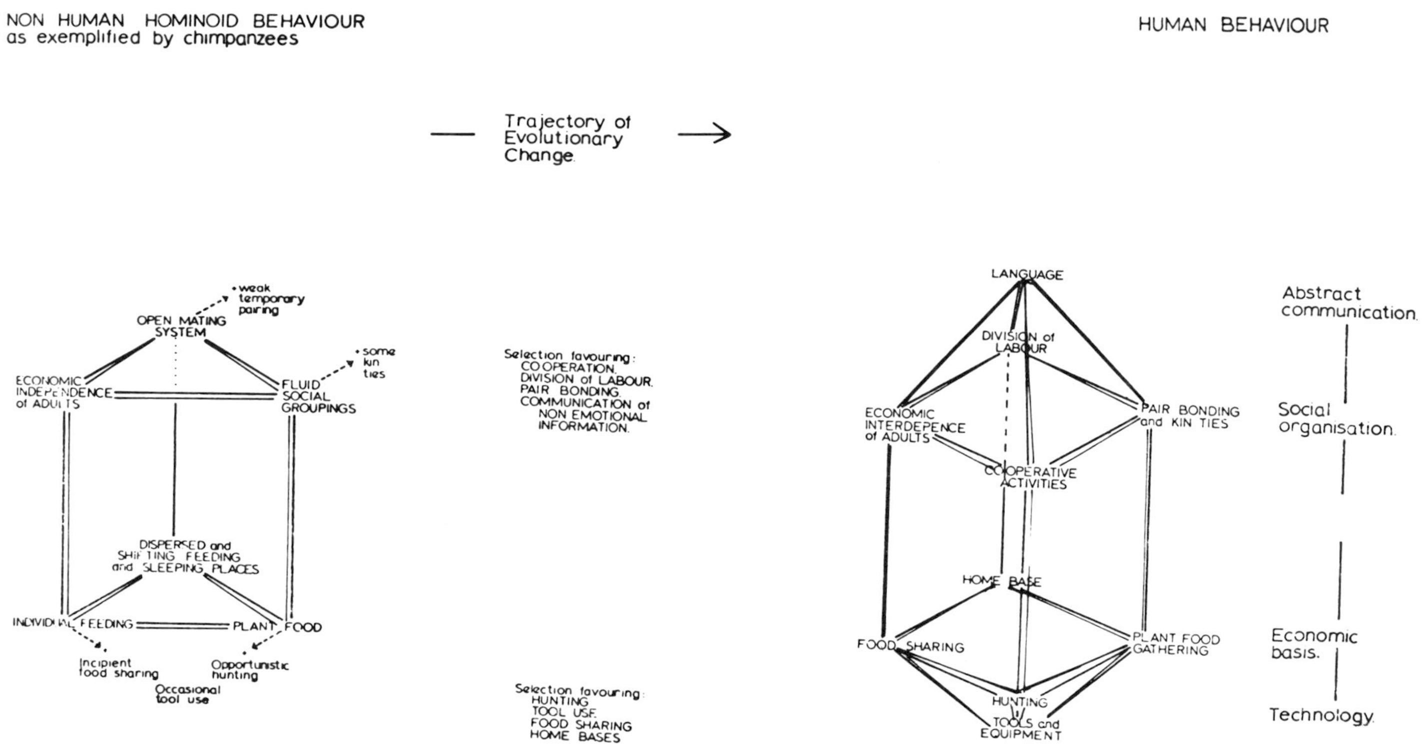

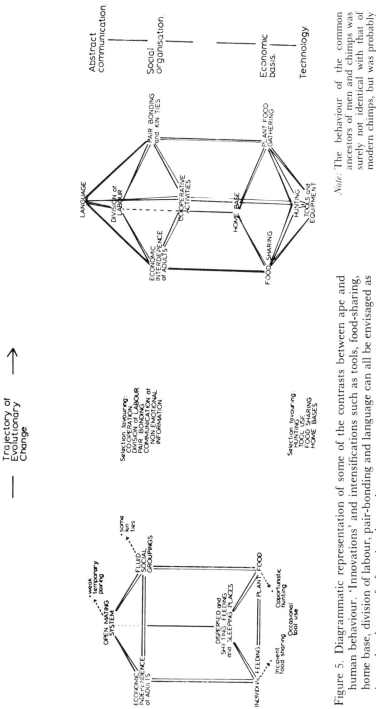

Figure 5. Diagrammatic representation of some of the contrasts between ape and human behaviour. 'Innovations' and intensifications such as tools, food-sharing, home base, division of labour, pair-bonding and language can all be envisaged as interrelated parts of a functional complex.

Note: The behaviour of the common ancestors of men and chimps was surely not identical with that of modern chimps, but was probably more like it than modern human behaviour.

4. Infancy may have been even more prolonged than in the apes (Mann, 1968).
5. Some hominids were extensively involved in tool manufacture, but we do not know to what degree they were dependent on equipment.
6. Significant quantities of meat were eaten and this derived from animals far larger than any hunted by other primates.
7. Concentrated patches of discarded artifacts and food refuse strongly suggest home base behavioural arrangements, and food sharing to some degree.
8. The known extent of ecological and geographic distribution *may* not have been much greater than that of several other primate species.

Fragmentary as the evidence is, it strongly suggests the existence, by the Plio-Pleistocene, of some hominids which had already diverged from the last common ancestor with an ape, to the point where a whole series of adaptive novelties had become firmly established. To find parallels for some of the traits, one has to turn not to other primates but to social carnivores, or even social insects. Some hominids had become free-ranging, striding bipeds, using tools (and weapons?), hunting large animals and carrying at least part of the meat back to camps for sharing. But this is not at all the same as saying that these hominids were men in the way we understand the term today. With Jane Lancaster (1967) I am inclined to think that we are dealing with traces of an original adaptive system that was perfectly successful in its day, and which has no living counterpart. One variant of it happens to have been transformed by further evolution into the human situation which thereby has features in common with it.

If the basics were established by 2 to 3 million years ago, what has happened since? Palaeoanthropology can fairly readily document the following changes:

1. Further enlargement, and presumably continued reorganization, of the brain.
2. Increased complexity of tools and equipment with regard to both the number of designs and the degree of precision in execution.
3. The augmentation of art, ritual and symbol systems.
4. Great increases in ecological and geographic range.

It is also tempting to surmise that the development of human levels of capability in communication ('language') has been extensively post-Pliocene, though I am inclined to guess that the early hominids already had rudimentary sound communication signal systems beyond those of other primates. Of course the enlargement of the brain has in part been connected with language and association.

I suggest therefore that one can conveniently divide the continuum of human evolution into two phases. Probably the first involved shifts in the basic systems of locomotion and subsistence, plus two new ingredients – tools and foodsharing. This led to a pattern of adaptation which in hindsight we see as protohuman, but which is probably better termed 'early hominid', since it was probably a non-human system that was effective in its own right. As I envisage it, the early hominid adaptive pattern created a situation in which, during the Pleistocene, natural selection favoured the exaggeration of certain qualities that facilitate making a living by being an opportunistic, food-sharing hunter and forager. These qualities include communication and information exchange, restraint, cunning, economic and social insight, plus ability to augment anatomy with diverse equipment.

Now these suggestions are speculative in that we have no direct information on the stages by which man's linguistic capabilities developed. However it seems reasonable to me to suggest that the main phase of selection for this capacity has been since the Plio-Pleistocene. I and others have argued that there is archaeological evidence of a critical threshold in design complexity that was crossed in the upper Pleistocene, and which may have been related to an analogous threshold in linguistic efficacy (Isaac, 1972).

The existence of pair-bonds between human males and females, and the incorporation of family modules into social and economic structures, have been universal characteristics of our species. Since there is no direct fossil evidence we really do not know whether this arrangement in some degree was primitive to the basal hominoid stock, whether it was part of the first early hominid adaptive pattern, or whether it has been a middle Pleistocene development. Since it could easily have been functionally interconnected with food sharing and division of labour I would surmise its development during the first adaptive shift.

The divergence of the hominid lineage(s) from the last common ancestor with one or more pongid lineages lies in the time range prior to that on which the attention of this essay is focussed. We have no archaeological evidence and very little fossil evidence regarding either the steps by which the transformation proceded, or the environmental context of the population involved. If one follows some biochemists (e.g. Sarich and Wilson, 1968) then one infers that the divergence occurred no more than 4 to 8 million years ago; while if one accepts *Ramapithecus* (= *Kenyapithecus*) as an ancestral hominid, then the point of divergence was at least 15 million years ago (e.g. L.S.B. Leakey, 1962; Simons and Pilbeam, 1965). It seems to me that the Plio-Pleistocene pattern of skeletal and archaeological traces (3-1½ m.y. BP) represents a situation which could equally well have been derived by either a shortish period of relatively fast evolutionary charge, or by a long, period of slower, perhaps sporadic development. To decide finally between these rival hypotheses, we badly need more complete *Ramapithecus* fossils and an interpretable series from the time-span between 10 million years and 4 or 5 million years ago.

In accounting for the origins of the first adaptive shift, it has been customary to invoke as causes more or less drastic environmental changes such as a Pliocene drought (Ardrey, 1961, and many others), or dramatic dietary specializations such as hunting or seed-eating (Jolly, 1970). However, as research progresses, it becomes increasingly apparent that there has probably not been any great environmental trauma in the late Tertiary of Africa. The continent seems to have supported throughout this time a fluctuating mosaic of forest, woodland, savannah, grasslands and steppe. It is an exaggeration to think of a Pliocene decimation of continuous Miocene forests. The most dramatic faunal change in Africa appears to have occurred 4 to 5 million years ago and to relate more to intercontinental connections than to climatic change (Maglio, in press). Similarly the view expressed by Jolly (1970, p.19) that almost all grasslands and savannahs are recent artifacts of man can be specifically disproved even from the fragmentary pollen records now available (Kendall, 1969; Livingstone, 1967, 1971; Bonnefille, 1972; Van Zinderen Bakker and Coetzee, 1972). It seems to me that deterministic environmental factors of these kinds are not only undocumented, they are unnecessary as explanations. If one accepts that evolution is a consequence of mutation and natural selection and that it is a restless opportunistic process (cf. Simpson 1949) then it does not seem difficult to accept that the normal pressures of ecological competition could transform the versatile behavioural system of ancestral hominids into the novel early hominid pattern. It is widely believed that the process involved extensive feedback amongst the several subsystems, thus: hunting facilitated food-sharing since meat was more readily carried than any other common food stuff; missiles, weapons and tools facilitated the killing and butchering of larger and larger animals; bipedalism facilitated weapon use, the carrying of food for sharing, and long range mobility; gathered vegetable foods remained as a staple and as an insurance policy against failure in the hunt, so that division of labour (and pair-bonding?) gave stability to the system; bags and baskets facilitated food-sharing and division of labour, etc. It can thus be argued that savannah *sensu lato* constituted a vacant ecological niche for an animal at the hominoid grade, capable of basing its subsistence on a combination of hunting and foraging. Opportunism is the hallmark of mankind as we see the species in ethnography and history, and I would suspect that it was important, perhaps crucial from start to finish in human evolution.

Clearly Mio-Pliocene patterns of hominid life and the circumstances of evolutionary divergence of men and apes need to be identified and studied before we will *know* about the actual history of what happened. But before the data are gathered, I would be ready to bet that we will find a steady trajectory of change, guided by evolutionary processes involving opportunistic exploitation of diverse microenvironments, rather than dramatic causation through occupation of a restricted habitat and/or sudden adoption of a radically different diet, whether chosen or imposed. Archaeology does not as yet contribute anything substantial to the problem of species divergence within the Hominidae. At Olduvai, Omo, East Rudolf and Swartkrans there seem to be at least two species of hominid with overlapping habitats. These formations each contain artifacts but, as Mary Leakey (1967, p.442) has pointed out the attribution of the tools and camp sites to one or the other or both hominid species is a matter of intuition. Hindsight makes us feel sure that the ancestors of *Homo sapiens* would have been amongst those involved with tools, hunting and food-sharing – but can we be sure that these traits were not part of a primitive hominid adaptive pattern shared by both species? We will need much more data on artifacts and fossil distribution before anything beyond an intuitive answer can be offered. Clearly the general model for hominid divergence presented above can accommodate internal differentiation between lineages which placed uneven emphasis on the exploitation of the multitude of subsistence opportunities presented by savannah mosaics. In default of a detailed late Tertiary fossil record we do not yet known whether the divergence took place between ecologically differing sympatric populations, or was initially related to geographic isolation which later broke down, leading to a pattern of overlapping ranges such as that we seem to observe in the sedimentary basins of East Africa. Both hominid species were by our standards powerful, grinding chewers; but in one species this condition seems to have been more marked than in the other. Whether this contrast really relates to dietary differences, patterns of tool use, or to other factors remains to be determined.

Epilogue

In concluding this review of archaeological information on the activities of early hominids, I would like to pay tribute to those who took the lead in establishing the kinds of enquiry with which this essay has been concerned. In South Africa both Raymond Dart and John Robinson looked beyond the morphology of bones to evidence that would indicate aspects of the behaviour and ecology of the australopithecines. In East Africa Mary and Louis Leakey long since recognized the opportunity afforded by well-preserved occupation sites, and steadily pushed back the time span covered by carefully excavated documents. Without their pioneering efforts and patient research, there would have been but little data to review. It was Louis and Mary who introduced me to this field, and under their tutelage many of the ideas expressed above began to germinate. Then over the past four years I have been directly engaged in research into the intriguing problems of the Plio-Pleistocene through a partnership extended to me by Richard Leakey, an old campaign friend. This work is done with the benefit of continual interchange amongst members of an interdisciplinary team. Many of the lines of thought developed have their origins in discussions with my colleagues Sherwood Washburn, J. Desmond Clark, F. Clark Howell, past and present students of Berkeley and with my wife, who works with me, argues with me, draws the pictures and corrects the spelling. My research is largely supported by the National Science Foundation.

Figure 6. The site of KBS after the excavation of a trial trench in 1969.

Figure 7. Part of the old ground surface at KBS re-exposed by excavation. Discarded artifacts and broken bone is scattered over this surface to form a patch or 'occupation' site.

Figure 8. The hippo bones and stone artifacts eroding out of the top of the KBS tuff, at the site of HAS.

Figure 9. Broken bone on the old ground surface at KBS: a large rib fragment, several antelope teeth and (top left) a portion of hippo tusk.

Figure 10. A polyhedron (core-tool) being exposed on the floor at KBS.

Figure 11. A small sharp flake being lifted out of its position in the KBS tuff at the site of HAS.

References

Arambourg, C. (1950) Traces possibles d'une industrie primitive dans un niveau Villafranchien de l'Afrique du Nord. *Bull. Soc. préhist. française* 47, 350.

Ardrey, R. (1961) *African Genesis*. London.

Balout, L. (1955) *Préhistoire de l'Afrique du nord*. Paris.

Biberson, P. (1961) *Le Paléolithique inférieur du Maroc Atlantique*. Rabat.

Bishop, W.W. (1959) Kafu, stratigraphy and Kafuan artifacts. *S. Afr. J. Sci.* 55, 117-21.

Bishop, W.W. (1971) Late Cenozoic history of East Africa in relation to hominoid evolution. In Turekian, K.K. (ed.), *Late Cenozoic Glacial Ages*. 493-528. New Haven and London.

Bonnefille, R. (1972) *Associations polliniques, actuelles et Quaternaires en Ethiopie (Vallées de l'Awash et de l'Omo)*.

Brain, C.K. (1970) New finds at Swartkrans Australopithecine sites. *Nature* 225, 1112-18.

Butzer, K.W. and Isaac, G. Ll. (eds.) (1975) *After the Australopithecines*. Proceedings of Burg Wartenstein symposium 58, *Stratigraphy and patterns of cultural change in the middle Pleistocene*. The Hague.

Campbell, B.G. (1966) *Human Evolution: an Introduction to Man's Adaptations*. Chicago.

Chavaillon, J. (1967) La préhistoire éthiopienne à Melka Kontouré. *Archéologie* Nov.-Dec., 56-63.

Chavaillon, J. (1970) Découverte d'un oldowayen dans la basse vallée de l'Omo (*Ethiopie*). *Bull. Soc. préhist. française* 67, 7-11.
Chavaillon, J. (1976) Evidence for the technical practices of early Pleistocene hominids: Shungura Formation, Lower Valley of the Omo, Ethiopia. In Coppens, Y. *et al.* (eds.), 565-73.
Clark, J.D. (1970) *The Prehistory of Africa*. London.
Clark, J.D. and Haynes, C.V. (1969) An elephant butchery site at Mwanganda's Village karonga, Malawi, and its relevance for palaeolithic archaeology. *World Archaeology* 1, 390-411.
Coppens, Y., Chavaillon, J. and Beden, M. (1973) Resultats de la nouvelle mission de l'Omo (campagne 1972). Découverte de restes d'hominidés et d'une industrie sur eclats. *C.R. Acad. Sci.* Paris (Série D).
Coppens, Y. *et al.* (eds.) (1976) *Earliest Man and Environments in the Lake Rudolf Basin: Stratigraphy, Paleoecology and Evolution*. Chicago.
Curtis, G.H. and Hay, R.L. (1972) Further geological studies and potassium-argon dating at Olduvai Gorge and Ngorongoro Crater. In Bishop, W.W. and Miller, J.A. (eds.), *Calibration of Hominoid Evolution*, 289-301. Edinburgh.
Dart, R.A. (1957) The Makapan australopithecine osteodontokeratic culture. In Clark, J.D. (ed.), *Proceedings of the Third Panafrican Congress on Prehistory, Livingstone: 1955*, 161-71.
Fox, R. (1967) In the beginning: aspects of hominid behavioural evolution. *Man* 2, 415-33.
Gould, R.A. (1968) Chipping stone in the outback. *Natural History* 77, (2), 42-9.
de Heinzelin, J. (1960) Le paléolithique aux abords d'Ishango. *Exploration du Parc National Albert* Fasc. 6, 10-11. L'Institut Belge pour l'Encouragement de la Recherche Scientifique Outre-Mer.
Horowitz, A., Siedner, G. and Bar-Yosef, O. (1973) Radiometric dating of the 'Ubeidiya Formation, Jordan Valley, Israel. *Nature* 242, 186-7.
Howell, F.C. (1960) European and northwest African Pleistocene hominids. *Current Anthropology* 1, 195-232.
Isaac, G. Ll. (1966) New evidence from Olorgesailie relating to the character of Acheulian occupation sites. In Cuscoy, L.D. (ed.), *Actas del V Congreso Panafricano de Prehistoria y de Estudio del Cuaternario*, Vol. 2, 135-45. Publicaciones del Museo Arqueológico Santa Cruz de Tenerife, 6.
Isaac, G.Ll. (1967) The stratigraphy of the Peninj Group – early middle Pleistocene formations west of Lake Natron, Tanzania. In Bishop, W.W. and Clark, J.D. (eds.), *Background to Human Evolution*, 229-57. Chicago.
Isaac, G.Ll. (1971) The diet of early man: aspects of archaeological evidence from lower and middle Pleistocene sites in Africa. *World Archaeology* 2, 278-98.
Isaac, G.Ll. (1972) Comparative studies of Pleistocene site locations in East Africa. In Ucko, P.J. and Dimbleby, G.W. (eds.), *Man, Settlement and Urbanism*, 165-176. London.
Isaac, G.Ll. (1975) Middle Pleistocene stratigraphy and cultural patterns in East Africa. In Butzer, K.W. and Isaac, G.Ll., (eds.), 495-542.
Isaac, G.Ll., Leakey, R.E.F. and Behrensmeyer, A.K. (1971) Archaeological traces of early hominid activities east of Lake Rudolf, Kenya. *Science* 173, 1129-34.
Isaac, G.Ll. and Curtis, G. (1974) The age of early Acheulian industries:

evidence from the Peninj Group, Tanzania. *Nature*, 249, 624-7.

Isaac, G.Ll., Harris, J.W.K. and Crader, D. (1976) Archaeological evidence from the Koobi Fora Formation. In Coppens, Y. *et al.* (eds.).

Jacob, T. (1972) The absolute date of the Djetis Beds at Modjokerto. *Antiquity* 182, 148.

Jolly, C. (1970) The seed-eaters: a new model of hominid differentiation based on a baboon analogy. *Man* 5, 5-26.

Kendall, R.L. (1969) An ecological history of the Lake Victoria Basin. *Ecological Monographs* 39, 121-76.

Lancaster, J.B. (1967) The evolution of tool-using behaviour. *Amer. Anthrop.*, 70, 56-66.

Leakey, L.S.B. (1962) A new lower Pliocene fossil from Kenya. *Ann. Mag. nat. Hist.* 13, 689-96.

Leakey, L.S.B. (1968) Bone smashing by late Miocene Hominidae. *Nature* 218, 528-30.

Leakey, M.D. (1967) Preliminary summary of the cultural material from Beds I and II Olduvai Gorge, Tanzania. In Bishop, W.W. and Clark, J.D. (eds.), *Background to Evolution in Africa*. 417-42. Chicago.

Leakey, M.D. (1970a) Early artifacts from the Koobi Fora area. *Nature* 226, 228-30.

Leakey, M.D. (1970b) Stone artifacts from Swartkrans. *Nature* 225, 1222-25.

Leakey, M.D. (1971) *Olduvai Gorge* Volume 3. *Excavations in Beds I and II, 1960-1963.* London.

Lee, R.B. and DeVore, I. (eds.) (1968) *Man the Hunter*. Chicago.

Livingstone, D.A. (1967) Postglacial vegetation of the Ruwenzori Mountains in Equatorial Africa. *Ecological Monographs* 37, 25-52.

Livingstone, D.A. (1971) Speculations on the climatic history of mankind. *Amer. Sci.* 59, 332-7.

Maglio, V.M. (1975) Pleistocene faunal evolution in Africa and Eurasia. In Butzer, K.W. and Isaac, G. Ll. (eds.), 419-76.

Mann, A.E. (1968) The palaeodemography of *Australopithecus*. Unpublished doctoral dissertation, University of California, Berkeley.

Merrick, H.V. *et al.* (1973) Archaeological sites of early Pleistocene age from the Shungura Formation, Lower Omo valley, Ethiopia. *Nature* 242, 572-5.

Napier, J.R. (1967) The antiquity of human walking. *Sci. Amer.* 216, 56.

Pilbeam, D.R. (1972) *The Ascent of Man*. New York and London.

Pilbeam, D.R. (1975) Trends in middle Pleistocene hominid evolution. In Butzer, K.W. and Isaac, G.Ll. (eds.), 809-56.

Reynolds, V. (1966) Open groups and hominid evolution. *Man* 1, 441-52.

Reynolds, V. (1968) Kinship and the family in monkeys, apes and man. *Man* 3, 209-23.

Robinson, J.T. (1972) *Early Hominid Posture and Locomotion*. Chicago.

Robinson, J.T. and Mason, R.J. (1962) Australopithecines and artifacts at Swartkrans. *S. Afr. archaeol. Bull.* 17, 87-125.

Sarich, V.M. and Wilson, A.C. (1968) Immunological time scale for hominid evolution. *Science* 158, 1200.

Schaller, G.B. and Lowther, G.R. (1969) The relevance of carnivore behaviour to the study of early hominids. *S. W. J. Anthrop.* 25, 207-41.

Simons, E.L. and Pilbeam, D.R. (1965) Preliminary revision of the Dryopithecine (Pongidae, Anthropoidea). *Folia primat.* 3, 81-152.

Simpson, G.G. (1949) *The Meaning of Evolution*. New Haven.

Speth, J.D. (1972) Mechanical basis of percussion flaking. *American Antiquity* 37, 34-60.
Stiles, D.N., Hay, R.L. and O'Neil, J.R. (1974) The MNK chert factory site, Olduvai Gorge, Tanzania. *World Archaeology* 5, 285-308.
Tobias, P.V. (1967) Cultural hominisation among the earliest African Pleistocene hominids. *Proc. Prehist. Soc.* 13, 367-76.
Tobias, P.V. and Hughes, A.R. (1969) The new Witwatersrand University excavation at Sterkfontein. *S. Afr. archaeol. Bull.* 24, 158-69.
Van Zinderen Bakker, E.M. and Coetzee, J.A. (1972) Reappraisal of late Quaternary climatic evidence from tropical Africa. *Palaeoecology of Africa* 7, 151-81.
Washburn, S.L. (1960) Tools and human evolution. *Sci. Amer.* 203, 3.
Washburn, S.L. (1965) An ape's eye-view of human evolution. In DeVore, P.L. (ed.), *The Origin of Man*, 89-96. New York, private circulation.
Washburn, S.L. (1968a) *The Study of Human Evolution.* Condon Lectures, Oregon State System of Higher Education, Eugene, Oregon.
Washburn, S.L.J. (1968b) Behaviour and the origin of man. *Proc. Roy. Anthrop. Inst.* 1967, 21-7.
Washburn, S.L. and Lancaster, C.S. (1968) The evolution of hunting. In Lee, R.B. and DeVore, I. (eds.).

Postscript (March 1977)

In the three years since this paper was written, new data have become available which both advance archaeological knowledge and call for revisions. Only a few selected points can be dealt with here. New references are given as a supplementary bibliography.

The date of $2\frac{1}{2}$ million years for the KBS tuff and the KBS site has been seriously challenged by Curtis *et al.* (1975), who obtained consistent K-Ar age determinations of 1.6 + 0.06 m.y. in the type area (Area 105) and of 1.82 + 0.04 m.y. in Area 131. Fitch *et al.* (1976) have defended their $2\frac{1}{2}$ m.y. result, while adjusting it from 2.61 + 0.02 to 2.42 + 0.01. Hurford *et al.* (1976) report fission track results of 2.44 + 0.08 on zircon crystals from the Area 131 outcrops formerly classified as KBS tuff. Palaeontological and geological considerations have lead Brown, Howell and Eck (in Bishop (ed.), 1977) to favour the revised dating of Curtis *et al.* Equally an independent palaeontological inquiry by J.M. Harris and T. White (in preparation) has led them to conclude that the fauna from strata below the so called KBS tuff of Area 131 is more or less equivalent in age to, or, slightly older than, Member G of the Shungura Formation and Bed I at Olduvai. Other palaeontological data are claimed to contradict this. Palaeomagnetic data cannot settle the dispute (Hillhouse *et al.*, 1977). In short, the situation as regards the age of the KBS tuff remains uncertain. Both geo-chronologists and palaeontologists need to do more work to resolve the contradictory indications of different data sets. However, at present the K-Ar dates of Curtis *et al.* and the palaeontological results of Harris and White seem to me to be the most promising indicators of age. I see these as putting the balance of probability in favour of an age of 1.6-1.8 m.y. for the KBS industry which is discussed in this paper.

The Karari Industry has been formally defined by Harris and Isaac (1976) and reports on the KBS Industry and sites have been published (Isaac *et al.* 1976, Isaac 1976).

It appears that the archaeological record of the Shungura Formation extends back into Member E, 2.0-2.2 m.y. (announcement by J. Chavaillon at Nice, September 1976). Isaac and Crader (in press) have undertaken a careful review of the evidence for early hominid meat eating and have come up with a positive conclusion, though a rather more cautious one than is presented in this paper. Specifically it now seems likely that scavenging was more important for early hominids than is implied in this paper.

Additional References

Bishop, W.W. (ed.) (1977) *Geological Background to Fossil Man in East Africa.* Edinburgh.

Curtis, G. *et al.* (1975) Age of KBS Tuff in Koobi Fora Formation, East Rudolf, Kenya. *Nature* 258, 395-8.

Fitch, F. *et al.* (1976) $^{40}Ar/^{39}Ar$ dating of the KBS Tuff in Koobi Fora Formation, East Rudolf, Kenya. *Nature* 263, 740-4.

Harris, J.W.K. and Isaac, G.Ll. (1976) The Karari Industry: Early Pleistocene archaeological evidence from the terrain east of Lake Turkana, Kenya. *Nature* 262, 102-7.

Hurford, A. *et al.* (1976) Fission-track dating of pumice from the KBS Tuff, East Rudolf, Kenya. *Nature* 263, 738-44.

Hillhouse, J.W. *et al.* (1977) Additional results on palaeomagnetic stratigraphy of the Koobi Fora Formation, east of Lake Turkana (Lake Rudolf), Kenya. *Nature* 275, 411-15.

Isaac, G.Ll. (1976) Plio-Pleistocene artifact assemblages from East Rudolf, Kenya, in Coppens *et al.* (eds.).

Isaac, G.Ll. and Crader, D. (in press) Diet and adaptation amongst Pliocene and early Pleistocene hominids: evidence from the ground. In Teleki, G. and Harding, R. (eds.), *Human and Primate Predation.* New York.

W.W. Bishop

Geochronological framework for African Plio-Pleistocene Hominidae: as Cerberus sees it

Explanation of the title

Geochronology. It is axiomatic that geological considerations cannot be divorced from any chronology (whether biologic or isotopic in origin). Geochronology is a union between partners that are both essential for time-based correlations.

Framework. Firm correlations between local sequences of strata, and their biological content, can only be effected by using all available lines of evidence to establish cross-struts. Care is needed to see that such links are firmly founded and not merely tenuous straws (see geomorphological dating below).

Cerberus. This fabled three-headed dog that guards the portal to 'plutonic' realms is used to illustrate the need for a three-pronged approach to geochronology.

East Africa

The Gregory Rift, from the Omo valley southwards to the vicinity of Olduvai Gorge, contains unique sequences of hominid-bearing strata in the Plio-Pleistocene time range. The geological evidence from that area reveals both advantages and disadvantages for the study of hominid evolution.

Advantages

1. *Law-of-superposition.* By the classical law-of-superposition, the relative situations of hominid fossils in rock sequences, and inferentially through time, have been established within numerous local and usually well exposed East African successions. Even if isotopic dates were not available, an evolutionary tree with 'squeeze-box time' running along its notional trunk and branches could be

constructed with hominids clinging to their correct stratigraphic positions.

2. *Geological mapping.* With a basis in geological mapping correlations have been made, aided by air and satellite photography and controlled by ground survey, between adjacent stratigraphic sections. The Gregory Rift mapping has been assisted by the presence of good marker horizons, in the form of time synchronous tephra or more usually deposits derived from and dominated by tephra. These are also virtually time-synchronous. *Tephrochronology* is concerned with the establishment of chronosequences of geological events based on the unique characteristics of tephra layers (individual primary volcanic ash-fall or flow units) (Thorarinsson, 1954, 1969; Westgate, 1974). Throughout the Rudolf Basin, at Olduvai Gorge and to a lesser extent in the Baringo Basin, mapping has been assisted by the presence of such 'tuff' marker beds although in many cases the source volcano lay outside the area of study and frequently could not be located.

3. *Potassium-argon dates.* In East Africa many lavas, together with sediments from predominantly volcanic sources and including some tephra, are potassium rich and have been dated by potassium-argon methods (whole rock and single mineral ^{40}K-^{40}Ar, $^{40}/^{39}$ and step heat). Olduvai witnessed the first application of ^{40}K-^{40}Ar to the dating of rocks as young as Pleistocene by Evernden and Curtis (1961, 1965) in the Berkeley dating laboratory of the University of California. These dates were fortunately keyed into the mapped strato-geometry of Hay. At Omo the work of Brown benefited from the detailed stratigraphic framework established by Heinzelin and others; at East Rudolf the chronometry of Fitch and Miller had the advantage of the Iowa State University mapping programme directed by Vondra and the more specific study of the 'tuffs' by Findlater. Harvard University teams mapping south and west of Lake Rudolf obtained dates from commercial laboratories. In the Baringo district detailed mapping was carried out for the Kenya Government by research teams directed by Bishop and King, based at Bedford College, University of London, for which dating was undertaken at the Cambridge University laboratory by Miller and the Institute of Geological Sciences by Snelling. In the combined results for the whole Gregory Rift the detailed mapping is integrated with numerous isotopic dates obtained from several laboratories. Although the coverage is still incomplete this constitutes a most formidable exercise in Plio-Pleistocene calibration.

4. *Palaeomagnetic polarity studies* and the development of a Plio-Pleistocene 'palaeomagnetic polarity time-scale' (Cox, 1969; Cox *et al.*, 1963; Watkins, 1972). The work of Brock at East Rudolf and Brock and Cox at Olduvai Gorge has already yielded consistent results (Brock and Isaac, 1974). These provide cross-checks for the potassium-argon data but additionally the palaeomagnetic polarity time-scale may be used independently to provide dates derived from

the presence of transition horizons. Palaeomagnetic data are now eagerly awaited from Omo (see Howell, this volume; Brown and Shuey, 1975; Brown, 1975) in the hope that they may help to solve some problems involved in reconciling the correlation of the sequences at Omo and Rudolf suggested by fossil mammal assemblages with that indicated by potassium-argon dates.

The fact that differences in correlation exist between these two well-documented successions from areas only 50 miles apart in the same present-day basin has several possible interpretations. One is that this is the first occasion on which mammalian fossil assemblages and suggested lineages of fossil genera have been viewed against such a closely spaced 'washboard' of time lines. If this proves to be the root of the problem, or at least a contributory factory, it has exciting implications for the study of mammalian and hominid evolutionary changes through time.

Remanent magnetism may provide the solution by allowing characteristic polarity patterns to be compared. In addition, recognizable transitions of polarity at epoch/epoch or epoch/event boundaries provide a very refined method of 'dating'. In the Baringo area a thorough sampling recently carried out by a Liverpool University team, of the long section of lava units from circa 14 m.y. to late Pleistocene, should yield important palaeomagnetic data and also increase the accuracy of dates for lavas bracketing the fossiliferous sedimentary formations. It will also confirm the position of the Plio-Pleistocene mammal-bearing sedimentary units within a long, well-controlled sequence.

5. *Fission track dates.* These have been little used in the Gregory Rift area although early work at Olduvai was undertaken by Fleischer (Fleischer *et al.*, 1965). There is a tremendous potential for cross-checking potassium-argon dates (particularly on sanidines from pumices) against glass shards (representing fractured bubble walls) from the same tephra source. Such material has yielded consistent sequences of fission-track ages from New Zealand particularly in the range from 2.0 to 0.2 m.y. (Seward, 1973).

6. *Comparative studies of recent environments and processes.* The patchwork of rift environments is worthy of mention as a further advantage. The whole graben is, and has been for 16 or 17 million years, a negative 'sump' region into which sediments have been decanted (including fossils and, towards the end of the period, artifacts as an integral part of the sediment). Later phases of recurrent fault movement or the initiation of grid faults have exposed certain sediments to erosion and scientific observation. Volcanic activity broke out intermittently but persistently, sealing sedimentary basins, diverting drainage lines and forming fresh catchments for water and sediment. Volcanicity has been an important factor in providing the basis for most of the isotopic dating methods referred to above. In addition it contributed burial materials in the form of tuffs (both

primary fall-out and secondary derivatives) that provided geochemical environments favouring the preservation and mineralisation of bone (e.g. carbonatite ash from the pre-rift volcanoes Napak or Rangwa), which helped to preserve bones of Miocene mammals, including primates. Modern analogues occur in the form of carbonate-rich tephra from Ol Doinyo Lengai.

This similarity between present-day and past volcanic products illustrates the function of the rift as a 'laboratory'. So many different local environments occur that analogues for past situations are seldom difficult to find. No study illustrates this better than taphonomy although much remains to be done in this developing field. However, some 'burial laws' are already beginning to emerge thanks to the studies of Behrensmeyer (this vol.) and Hill (Hill and Walker, 1972) in rift environments both ancient and modern.

Disadvantages

1. *Limited sample size.* The long sequences of superimposed fossil-bearing units outlined above have advantages from the point of view of dating hominid material but they have one major disadvantage. No large sample of hominid remains referable to one genus or one species has been found in, or on, a single stratum. Thus inferred variations within a taxon must be traced through time without the palaeontologist being able to study variability in an association from the same area even approximating to a sample of a population from a single time-plane. Frequently only scanty and disarticulated remains are found although they can sometimes be assigned to one individual.

2. *Facies faunas and life and death assemblages.* Fossil-bearing formations, members and beds can be traced over 30 or 40 miles (as for instance in the Omo valley and at East Rudolf) with the aid of reliable tephra, tephra-derived, or other marker horizons. However, change of facies may result in the sampling of 'facies faunas' representing different local environments of broadly equivalent age. Taphonomy plays an important role in helping to interpret such deposits. It is also important in showing the extent to which mammalian fossils, including hominids, have become 'bedfellows' only after death by being transported into one sedimentary environment although representing animals favouring different habits during life.

South Africa

In South Africa there are the Makapan, Sterkfontein, Swartkrans and Taung sites (this order has no significance except that it is alphabetical).

Advantages

1. *Accumulation.* Once caves in the dolomitic limestone are in communication with the surface they provide repositories where under the influence of gravity, water, mammalian and human agency, bones of animals that lived and died in the vicinity are accumulated.

2. *Chemical environment.* A limestone cave favours the preservation of bone structure. Although some distortion may occur owing to compaction or through roof falls, infiltration of carbonate into the breccia matrix and the formation of travertine layers assist rapid consolidation favouring the survival of bone and tooth.

3. *Comparative studies.* The existence in the same area of similar modern caves permits studies to be undertaken of the various processes involved in sediment or bone accumulation and mineralization.

4. *Sites.* The caves represent localized accumulations of bone from which large numbers of hominid remains have been recovered – e.g. over 600 specimens from Swartkrans represent at least 70 individuals (Brain, pers. comm.). Unfortunately, the time over which this number of specimens accumulated is not known. Nevertheless, it may be argued that once a cave is open to the surface, particularly if the cave mouth area is attractive as a lair or habitation, infill is probably rapid. The fill includes biological and other material which falls or is washed in, roof fall, travertine and interstitial carbonate, together with animal remains and other items brought in. Some phases of infill have been recognized from changes in the sedimentation pattern. However, such accumulations are probably the nearest that a palaeontologist studying Plio-Pleistocene hominids approaches to having a large sample from a 'population' as they possibly span only limited periods of time. It is necessary to add a further *caveat* that the possibility of secondary solution and later infill cannot be ignored in a limestone area.

Disadvantages

1. *Cave bias.* A cave fill may sample only a biased representation of the total biomass that lived in the cave area. Bias may be in the direction of selective eating and collecting habits or of preferences for a life style in or near caves. However, 'pit fall' mechanisms probably serve to redress some of this otherwise selective sampling.

2. *Stratigraphic isolation.* The former caves are now represented by masses of bone-bearing breccia that are stratigraphically isolated entities. They are volumes, rather than layers, of rock separated by virgin dolomite or by erosion from any surviving remnants of an original cave system or related deposits. The infills of individual caves have been analysed most elegantly by sedimentological or stratigraphic investigations (Brain, 1958, this vol.; Butzer, 1974).

However, they cannot be linked by normal stratigraphic procedures into even local sequences.

3. *Temporal isolation.* The caves are isolated in time as well as in space. As yet no isotopic dating technique or other dating method *independent of the fossils themselves* has been successful despite persistent efforts to explore every possibility.

Correlation between the individual cave sequences and faunas is therefore dependent upon comparison of fossil assemblages typical of the cave environments of accumulation. This involves elimination of purely local ecological differences and use of stage-of-evolution as the criterion for establishing relative age. Some 'second-hand' dates have been derived by correlating the cave assemblages with other mammalian sequences already calibrated isotopically. This becomes particularly difficult when it involves extrapolation across distances of 2500 km. or more (e.g. from Sterkfontein to Olduvai Gorge); from the southern part of a continental mass (latitude 26°S) to a more central situation almost on the equator (latitude 3°S). There are additionally the problems referred to above of relating the South African cave assemblages to East African open plain, lake shore or riverside 'mixed' assemblages.

Dating and correlation

It is important to differentiate with care between these two terms. Dating should be retained for the establishment of dates, measured in potassium-argon decay years or radiocarbon years etc. Correlation may be effected by use of lithological sequence, biological content, palaeomagnetic characteristics or by comparing isotopic dates established by similar methods. Correlation may yield 'second hand dates' but these should not then be re-used for further dating.

Cerberus

The relationship between stratigraphy, isotopic dating methods and biometry can best be illustrated by reference to Cerberus as in Figure 1 (see also Bishop, 1973). Only when information from all sources is related to a mapped stratigraphic sequence can reliable geochronology be practised.

An alleged geomorphological dating method

In a recent *Nature* paper Partridge (1973) attempts to use a geomorphological approach to derive dates for the opening of four South African caves which contain hominid-bearing cave deposits.

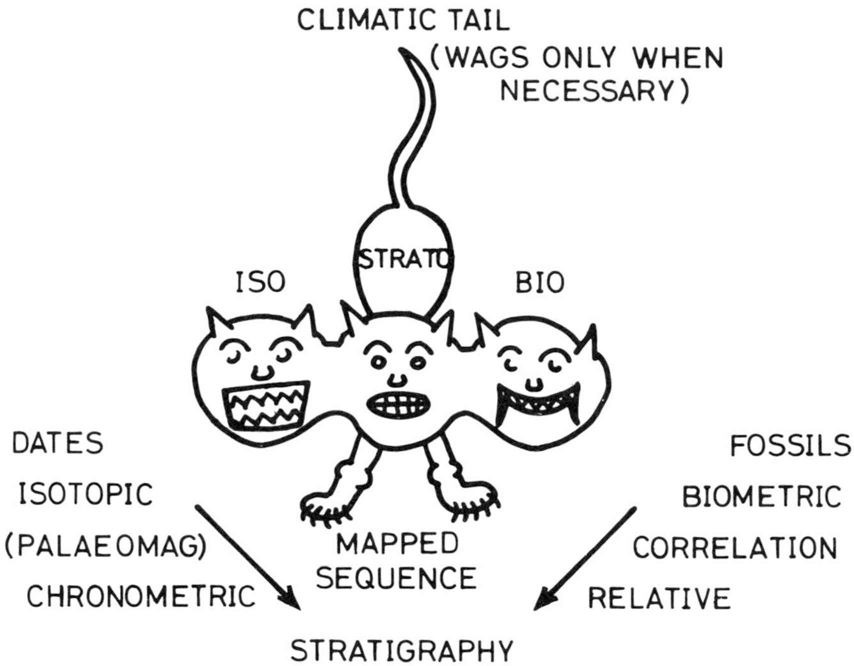

Figure 1. Cerberus, the dating dog.

This has not been referred to above as it is not a viable 'dating' method. The three major assumptions on which the method is based all have inherent problems.

Assumption 1 requires that a geomorphological datum, the African erosion cycle of L.C. King (1962), is a well established morphological feature throughout Southern Africa; occurs and is recognizable near each of the hominid-bearing localities; can be dated by extrapolation from its time of inception at the coast (in this case about 100 m.y.); was developed at a relatively constant rate; and has remained virtually unmodified since its initial planation.

Various comments on L.C. King's findings given by B.C. King (1958), Holmes (1965), and De Swardt (1974) are not repeated here. Where surfaces correlated with the African Surface by L.C. King have been assigned a limiting age, by dating overlying sediments or lavas, the dates are not in accord with ages extrapolated from inferred time of initiation of the cycle at the coast (Bishop, 1966). It can be shown that considerable modification of such surfaces has occurred even in the last 12 to 15 million years.

Assumption 2 concerns migration of nickpoints related to L.C. King's Post African I cycle (dated as leaving the coast during Burdigalian times – about 20 m.y.). De Swardt also criticises the validity of this approach. Partridge assumes that headward erosion along three river systems (two major tributaries of the Limpopo flowing to an Indian Ocean base-level and a tributary of the Orange river flowing to the South Atlantic) progressed at a sufficiently constant rate during the Post African I cycle to permit comparisons between the different rivers. The length of each section of river downstream from a cave situation is compared with total stream length in order to derive a measure of time elapsed.

Assumption 3 involves the establishment of time lapsed in widening the valley to produce cavern opening in the period since the nickpoint was opposite the cave site. Partridge lists further assumptions involving rectilinear valley flanks, down cutting of the channel and regular retreat of rectilinear valley flanks. However, it is not certain that all the caves opened as a result of valley wall retreat as opposed to widening of joints communicating with the surface of an interfluve.

Assumption 1 calls for a number of subjective judgments but, apart from noting the critical comments referred to above, these are not considered here. The problems raised by Assumptions 2 and 3 are sufficient to invalidate the method. For instance, recent studies of modern erosion rates for rivers and slopes (e.g. Douglas, 1969; Gibbs, 1967; Young, 1969), and recorded in various text books) make clear the variables involved. Widely different rates are obtained depending upon the interplay of climate, aspect, slope and substrate.

Past erosion rates as recorded in the geological column are more difficult to quantify. However, attempts have been made which provide 'guestimates' ranging from 0.1 to 100 $m.^3/km.^2/year$ (Clark and Jager, 1969; Ruxton and McDougall, 1967. Dury, 1972, cites further references to relevant work).

Other variables include change in ground cover while a slight change in climate in a semi-arid area grossly changes the sediment yield (Douglas, 1967). Similar effects may be induced through removal of vegetation, however this is brought about. Variations in lithology, even those which are very local and not recorded in Partridge's assignment of his river profiles to four broad divisions of substrate, can greatly alter rates of headward erosion.

In brief, the variation observed in the parameters controlling the migration of nickpoints and valley flanks is so great that the geomorphologically derived dates cited by Partridge are meaningless. One would welcome a dated sequence of South African hominid-bearing caves to set alongside the East African hominid chronostratigraphy. However, this attempt at geomorphological dating seems to be a case of the wish becoming father to the thought.

It is particularly unfortunate that in two recent papers Professor Tobias accepts Partridge's dates as having 'implications' for the study of South African hominids (1973a, b). In his *Nature* paper (1973a) he refers to the dates as only estimates. However, in an abstract prepared for the IX INQUA Congress (Tobias, 1973b) they are quoted as if they were firm and reliable ages.

Tobias's concern over problems raised by the young geomorphological age of the Taung skull and his ensuing discussion of taxonomic implications seem unnecessary. The most likely explanation for the young 'date' at Taung is that the locality is on a different river system from the Transvaal sites. The river flows over a contrasting substrate and through a series of different morphological settings to an Atlantic rather than an Indian Ocean base-level. Tobias also includes South African localities and specimens in his figures illustrating 'hominid temporal distribution' and 'hominid populations at different times' (Tobias, 1973a). These have no meaning if geomorphological 'dating' contributes to their notional time-base. His phyletic tree similarly lacks a time-scale for those branches on which the Taung problem child and other South African specimens are placed.

Only in so far as they are based on re-interpretation of observed morphology of the South African specimens are Professor Tobias' conclusions well founded. Correlations based on stage-of-evolution of the mammal faunas may help in assigning what Tobias himself calls 'purely relative faunal dates' (Tobias, 1973a). This has been the basis of the correlations suggested by Maglio (1972) and by Cooke and Maglio (1972). However, the suggestion by Tobias that the hominids themselves can be used in support of the geomorphological ages seems particularly unfortunate.

The hominid collections from both East and South African localities have different attributes. The East African area is one of extensive fossiliferous formations whereas in South Africa one has localised fossil 'sites'. Nevertheless both regions are valuable in different ways:

1. The South African caves yield large samples of hominids from deposits having a small vertical thickness. It seems probable that the main hominid-bearing strata within these cave fills span comparatively short periods of time. They are often separated from the original opening of each cave by variable and in some cases possibly long periods, represented by sediments barren of fossils. In contrast the East African horizons provide only limited numbers of hominids from each locality although these are firmly localised in respect of environment, stratigraphic setting and age of deposition. The South African accumulations are probably the nearest that a palaeontologist studying Plio-Pleistocene hominids approaches to having a large sample from a 'population' spanning only a limited period of time.
2. The East African hominids are related to a well established, stratigraphically controlled chronology and yield unique information concerning possible evolutionary lineages. Conversely the South African cave fills and their contained hominids must still be considered as undated.

Acknowledgment

I gratefully acknowledge helpful discussions of the problems outlined in this last section with Dr Robert Brain, Dr Karl Butzer, Professor Basil Cooke, Professor Phillip Tobias and Dr Martin Williams.

References

Behrensmeyer, A.K. (this volume) The habitat of Plio-Pleistocene hominids in East Africa; taphonomic and microstratigraphic evidence.

Bishop, W.W. (1966) Stratigraphical geomorphology. In Dury, G.H. (ed.), *Essays in Geomorphology*, 139-76. London.

Bishop, W.W. (1973) The tempo of human evolution. *Nature* (London) 244, 405-9.

Brain, C.K. (1958) The Transvaal ape-man-bearing cave deposits. *Mem. Transv. Mus.* 11, 1-131.

Brain, C.K. (this volume) Some aspects of the South African Australopithecine sites and their bone accumulations.

Brock, A. and Isaac, G. Ll. (1974) Palaeomagnetic stratigraphy and chronology of hominid-bearing sediments east of Lake Rudolf, Kenya. *Nature* (London) 247, 344-8.

Brown, F.H. (1975) Radiometric dating and palaeomagnetic studies of Omo Group deposits. In Coppens, Y. *et al.* (eds.), *Earliest Man and Environments in the Lake Rudolf Basin: Stratigraphy, Paleoecology and Evolution*. Chicago.

Brown, F.H. and Shuey, R.T. (1975) Preliminary magnetostratigraphy of the Lower Omo Valley, Ethiopia. In Coppens, Y. *et al.* (eds.), *Earliest Man and Environments in the Lake Rudolf Basin: Stratigraphy, Paleoecology and Evolution*. Chicago.

Butzer, K.W. (1974) Palaeoecology of South African Australopithecines: Taung Revisited. *Current Anthropology*. 15, 367-426.

Clark, S.P. and Jager, E. (1969) Denudation rate in the Alps from geochronological and heat flow data. *Amer. J. Sci.* 267, 1153-60.

Cooke, H.B.S. and Maglio, V.J. (1972) Plio-Pleistocene stratigraphy in East Africa in relation to proboscidean and suid evolution. In Bishop, W.W. and Miller, J. (eds.), *Calibration of Hominoid Evolution*, 303-29. Edinburgh.

Cox, A. (1969) Geomagnetic reversals. *Science* 163, 237-45.

Cox, A., Doell, R. and Dalrymple, G.B. (1963) Geomagnetic polarity epochs and Pleistocene Geochronometry. *Nature* (London) 198, 1049-51.

De Swardt, A.M.J. (1974) Comments upon Partridge's paper on Geomorphological dating. *Nature* (London) 250, 683.

Douglas, I. (1967) Man, vegetation and the sediment yields of rivers. *Nature* (London) 215, 925-8.

Douglas, I. (1969) The efficiency of humid tropical denudation systems. *Trans. Inst. Br. Geogr.* 46, 1-16.

Dury, G.H. (1972) Some current trends in geomorphology. *Earth Sci. Rev.* 8, 45-72.

Evernden, J.F. and Curtis, G.H. (1961) Age of Bed I, Olduvai Gorge, Tanganyika. *Nature* (London) 191, 478-9.

Fleischer, R.L. *et al.* (1965) Fission track dating of Bed I, Olduvai Gorge. *Science* 148, 72-4.

Gibbs, R.J. (1967) The geochemistry of the Amazon river system. Part I: The factors that control the salinity and the composition and concentration of the suspended solids. *Bull. geol. Soc. Amer.* 78, 1203-32.

Hill, A.P. and Walker, A. (1972) Procedures in vertebrate taphonomy: notes on a Uganda Miocene fossil locality. *J. geol. Soc. Lond.* 128, 399-406.

Holmes, A. (1965) *Principles of Physical Geology*. London.

King, B.C. (1958) The geomorphology of Africa. *Science Progress* 15, 672-81; 16, 97-107.

King, L.C. (1962) *The Morphology of the Earth*. London.

Maglio, V.J. (1972) Vertebrate faunas and chronology of hominid bearing sediments east of Lake Rudolf, Kenya. *Nature* (London), 239, 379-85.

Partridge, T.C. (1973) Geomorphological dating of cave openings at Makapansgat, Sterkfontein, Swartkrans and Taung. *Nature* (London) 246, 75-9.

Ruxton, B.P. and McDougall, I. (1967) Denudation rates in northeast Papua from potassium-argon dating of lavas. *Amer. J. Sci.* 265, 545-61.

Seward, D. (1973) Some aspects of the sedimentology of the Wanganui Basin. Ph.D. thesis, Victoria University of Wellington, New Zealand.

Thorarinsson, S. (1954) *The eruption of Hekla 1947-8.* Part 2: *The tephra fall from Hekla on 29 March 1947.* Reykjavik.

Thorarinsson, S. (1969) A Pleistocene Ignimbrite in Thorsmork. *Natturufraedingurinn* 39, 135-55.

Tobias, P.V. (1973a) Implications of the new age estimates of the early South African hominids. *Nature* (London) 246, 79-83.

Tobias, P.V. (1973b) New African evidence on hominid phylogeny. *Abstracts*, IX INQUA Congress, 369-70. Christchurch, New Zealand.

Watkins, N.D. (1972) Review of the development of the geomagnetic polarity time-scale and discussion of prospects for its finer definition. *Geol. Soc. Amer. Bull.* 83, 551-74.

Westgate, J. (1974) A bibliography of tephrochronology. IX INQUA Congress, Christchurch, New Zealand. Printing Services, University of Alberta.

Young, A. (1969) Present rate of land erosion. *Nature* (London) 224, 851-2.

H.B.S. Cooke

Faunal evidence for the biotic setting of Early African Hominids

Introduction

At another Wenner-Gren conference in 1962 the writer attempted to review the Pleistocene mammal faunas of Africa (Cooke, 1963) and included lists of the genera and species then known. These lists are in need of surprisingly few corrections, but there are numerous additions demanded by new studies, principally at sites little explored or unknown a mere decade ago. Notable is the work in the Lake Rudolf region which was the focal point of a workshop conference (1974); the volumes recently published (Coppens *et al.*, 1976) contain excellent faunal lists for Omo and East Rudolf that need not be repeated here. Both the Omo and the East Rudolf areas comprise successions of strata that span the period from about 1.0 to 4.5 million years ago, overlapping the Olduvai sequence on the one hand and the Kanapoi deposits on the other. Figure 1 gives a simplified outline of the major stratigraphic units, with a time scale based on radiometric and palaeomagnetic determinations.

At Olduvai much new geological work has refined the stratigraphy and palaeogeography (Hay, 1971). Extensive explorations in the Lake Baringo area have brought to light a number of sedimentary units, many of them fossiliferous; although their faunas are not yet adequately known, some preliminary lists have been published (Bishop, 1972). The Baringo sequence is particularly important in spanning much of the former gap between the Miocene site of Fort Ternan, and the now well-known Pleistocene/later Pliocene (the base of the Pleistocene is here taken at approximately 2.0 m.y. and of the Pliocene at 5.5 m.y.). As the yield of hominids is still unfortunately limited, these faunas will not be discussed here. Kanapoi and Lothagam likewise have furnished only very fragmentary hominids, important as they are, and the faunas are still incompletely worked out, so it is felt that ecological consideration would be premature.

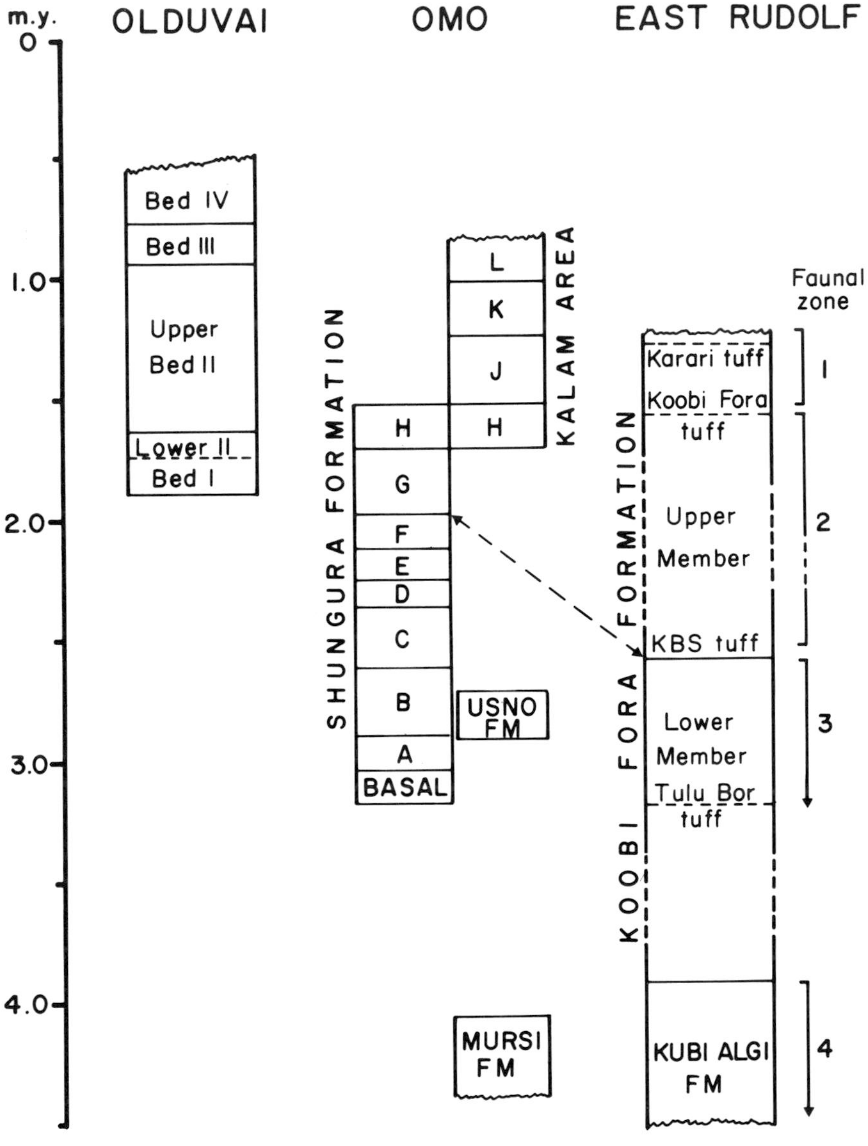

Figure 1. Stratigraphic units and provisional radiometric/palaeomagnetic correlation of some East African Plio-Pleistocene strata. The arrowed broken line shows the correlation of the KBS tuff suggested by some elements of the fauna.

Environment and habitat

Africa has a wide variety of climates, vegetation and topography which provides a considerable range of habitats, from almost rainless deserts to dense evergreen forest where precipitation may exceed 80 inches (2,000 mm.) a year. To a large extent the climate is reflected in the vegetation, so a vegetation map (Figure 2) is a useful guide to the general distribution of the major habitats. The true tropical evergreen forest is limited to the equatorial belt west of the highlands flanking the western rift and does not extend across the elevated plateau of East Africa. However, evergreen forest also occurs in the high mountains as a part of the montane communities that are an important feature of the African scene, providing habitats different from those of the region. Between the tropical forest and the desert lies a vast area of savannah, varying from a forest-savannah mosaic where the rainfall is above about 55 inches (1,400 mm.), through open woodland with *Isoberlinia, Julbernardia* and *Brachystegia*, to *Acacia*-wooded grassland, bushveld (or thornveld), terminating in dry grass steppe with scattered thorn trees. In the cooler upland areas of South

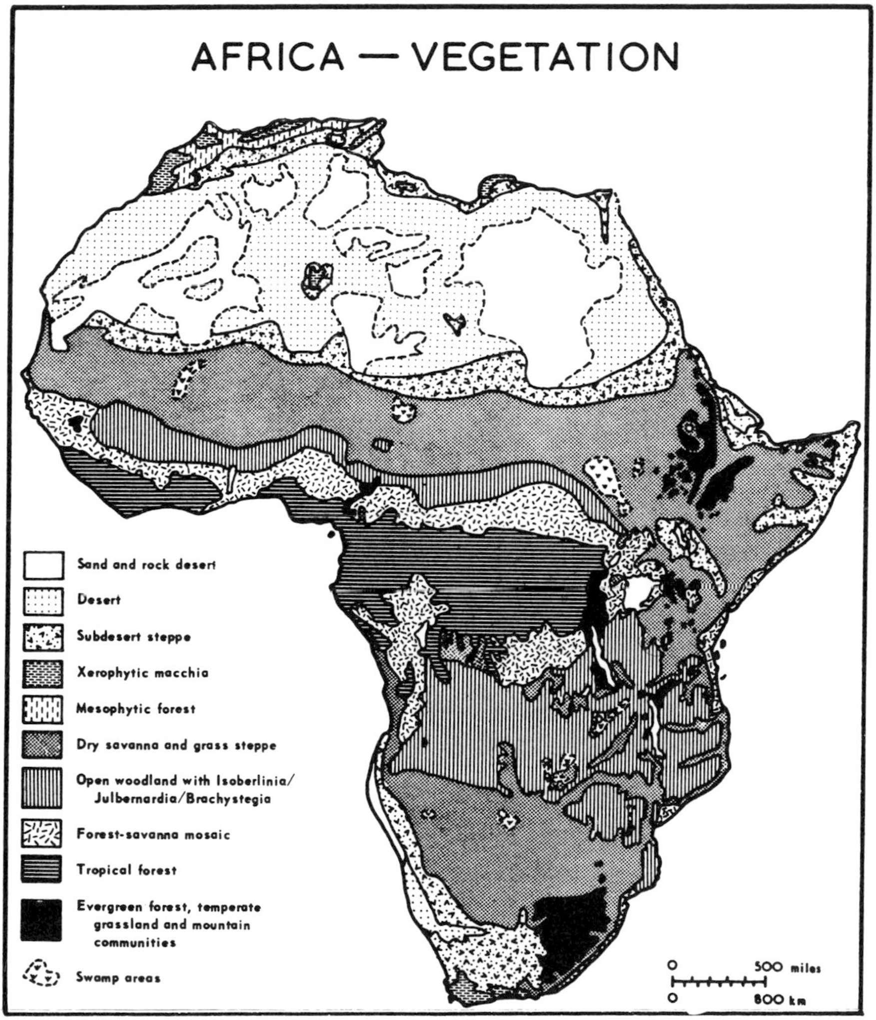

Figure 2. The vegetation of Africa.

Africa and in Ethiopia, temperate mixed grassland occurs, with scattered trees or bush, the latter well developed along the streams. Indeed, the occurrence of bush or gallery forest along watercourses is a very characteristic feature of the African landscape, carrying the vegetation of a more humid environment into the drier areas. In hilly country, the steep-sided ravines also offer protected settings for the development of heavy bush or forest and these furnish shelter for suitably adapted animals. This extensive and varied savannah is the home of the great bulk of the ungulate population and of the predators and scavengers that live upon them. Even the drier areas are surprisingly well populated as long as surface water is available throughout the year.

Although the various game reserves in Africa do have characteristics of their own, the general cross-section of mammals represented in them is fairly similar. This is a reflection of the wide range of particular conditions under which the majority of the herbivores and carnivores will survive, or even flourish. Among the larger mammals there are relatively few genera and species that are clear 'indicators' of very specific environments and so the problem of interpreting the fossil record is rendered difficult. It is thus necessary to look at the total assemblages and to glean what little can be inferred from the associations. In this connection the distribution maps of Dorst and Dandelot (1969) are particularly useful, as also are their comments on the habitats favoured by the living species. Undoubtedly the small mammals are more restricted in their environmental demands but as yet data for their evaluation are limited, and in the case of extinct species it is difficult to know which of the living species is the best analogue. The inferences that follow are thus tentative and subject to modification as new data come to light.

East Rudolf

For the East Rudolf area four faunal zones have been established by Maglio (1972), numbered with 1 as the youngest and 4 as the oldest. His paper includes a good faunal list, which will be supplemented in the new East Rudolf conference volume already mentioned above. Zone 4, the *Notochoerus capensis* zone, has a Kanapoi-type fauna but so few taxa have been identified that its ecological setting is not clear.

Zone 3, the *Mesochoerus limnetes* zone, has an abundant and varied fauna indicating broadly a mixed thornbush and grassland environment, not as dry as at present and accompanied by riverine bush or gallery forest. Among the non-human primates *Theropithecus oswaldi* is moderately plentiful and is most probably a denizen of open country like its modern cousins. However, some colobines also occur and would demand at least continuous strips of forest along the river courses. In this zone the bovids are not plentiful but one third of those found are reduncines, which have a high water requirement. An impala, *Aepyceros* sp., is also relatively plentiful and its preference for areas with bush or cover, together with a reluctance to move far from water supplies, would favour the existence of open acacia woodland. Alcelaphines and antelopes are rarer and do not suggest extensive grassland in the immediate vicinity. The white and black rhinoceroses are both present, but rare, and this would accord with the environment depicted above. The suids are all forms with moderately low-crowned molars, probably with a bush-pig-like habit and reluctance to move far into open or dry country. Two different hippopotami are present, one of them perhaps more a land-based browser than an aquatic type. Carnivores are relatively rare, but they are generally poor environmental indicators as they tend to range where food is available and can move long distances to water if necessary. An otter, *Lutra* sp., is amongst the fossils from this zone and demands substantial streams and a good supply of fish.

In Zone 2, the *Metridiochoerus andrewsi* zone, the fauna as a whole shows a shift towards slightly drier conditions with more grassland in the vicinity, indicated by an increase in the alcelaphine bovids and diminution in the impala population. *Oryx* occurs and suggests drier conditions as well. However reduncines remain dominant in the bovid fauna, requiring plentiful water and adequate cover. Colobines would seem to demand strips of forest. A vervet monkey is also found, but the normal habitat of this type is savannah rather than forest. The very large suid for which the zone is named has some phacochoerine features in its skull architecture and has high-crowned teeth obviously adapted to grazing. *Mesochoerus* is still plentiful but the third molars are more elongate and somewhat higher crowned than in zone 3, possibly in response to the demand for adaptation to a wider range of diet, including some grass.

Zone 1, the *Loxodonta africana* zone, does not suggest any great environmental change, as the bovid spectrum is much the same as in zone 2. Many of the changes may be evolutionary rather than ecological. Riverine bush and some forest are still required but the grassland must have dominated the area, much as it does today.

Omo

Correlation between the Omo and East Rudolf areas is based primarily on radiometric dating, supported by palaeomagnetic stratigraphy. The faunal assemblages are affected by physical and ecological differences not yet fully evaluated but there is some suggestion of disparity between the faunal and radiometric correlations (see Figure 1). The Mursi Formation has a Kanapoi-like fauna and is of similar date (older than 4.05 m.y.) but no ecological interpretation is possible at present. The Shungura Formation has a very good palaeomagnetic record which makes the earlier radiometric dates below Member C seem too old, and the latest evaluation is given by Brown (1975). The top of the main Shungura sequence is roughly contemporary with Bed II at Olduvai. Still higher horizons are present in the Kalam area with an age of less than 1.0 m.y.

Faunal zonation at Omo is still tentative and has not been published. The first apparent change lies within member C and there is another change within member G, but the changes are not abrupt. Faunistically the Usno Formation, which is geographically separated from the main sequence, belongs within member B and the faunal horizons are estimated to be about 2.9 m.y. (Brown, 1975). The taxa represented in the Shungura below G constitute a rather different spectrum from those present at East Rudolf, inhibiting good correlations. Although generalizations are difficult to make, the overall impression is of a wetter environment, although not far from open grassland and thornbush. Much of the material is very fragmentary and associated skeletons are rare, so the presence of elements that have been transported into the area cannot be excluded.

Of the primates, colobines represent only a small proportion and are most abundant in the Usno Formation (Eck, 1975). *Theropithecus*, on the other hand, makes up about 85% of the primate material and the commonest species is *T. brumpti*, as compared with *T. oswaldi* at East Rudolf. It may have had a different ecological niche as it almost disappears above G with the incoming of a strong grassland-dominated fauna, including true horses (*Equus* sp.). Hipparionid equines occur throughout, showing steady dental evolution, and they continued to co-exist with *Equus*. As the hipparionids were presumably grazers, they provide possible evidence for the occurrence of grassland at no great distance even below G. Both *Ceratotherium simum* and *Diceros bicornis* occur throughout the Shungura sequence, so suitable thornbush and scrub were present in the area.

Of the bovids, about one third of the specimens represent an impala, which favours a mixed thorn-scrub environment not far from water, and there is also a modest representation of the water-loving reduncines, especially abundant in members B, E and G (Gentry, 1975). The boselaphine-like *Tragelaphus nakuae* is dominant in members C, D and E, but dwindles in F and G; its habitat is unknown but may be inferred to be somewhat like that of the kudu, which favours moderately open, bushy terrain. Kudu itself is absent until member F but moderately plentiful in F and G. Above G there is a change to an Olduvai-like fauna, with a diminution of the reduncines and the eland, and the disappearance of *Tragelaphus nakuae*. Thus the bovid fauna does not suggest the proximity of grassland and it is possible that *Hipparion* at this stage was also an occupant of the open scrub and thornbush. If grassland was present it may have been wet rather than dry. The suids were mainly bush-pig-like with brachyodont molars which, however, increased in size and complexity during the

Shungura. One variety of *Notochoerus* became progressively more warthog-like in its dentition and implies increasing opportunities for grazing from D upward. Above G there is a marked change in the suid fauna with the arrival of advanced forms, like '*Afrochoerus*', that seem to have been derived from the East Rudolf complex. The carnivora, although of particular interest on account of links with the South African cave breccias, are unhelpful in the ecological picture, as are the three different hippopotami.

In summary, then, the faunal evidence favours an environment essentially of reasonably well-watered open bush and thornveld, with localized areas of wet grassland, and denser bush along the watercourses. In G there is a rather rapid swing towards a drier, or more contrasting, environment with open grassland not far away.

Olduvai

A faunal list for Olduvai was given by Leakey in 1965 and, although it requires some amendment, is the best overall assessment available. A distinct 'faunal break' in the middle of Bed II was recognized and the meticulous stratigraphic work of Hay (1971) has shown that it marks a period of faulting that led to the draining of a large lake that dominated Bed I times. The earlier fauna is a balanced one typical of a mixed thornbush and scrub environment, with some grassland elements such as *Equus*. The suids from Bed I belong to a *Mesochoerus* very similar to *M. limnetes*. They were probably bush-pig-like in habits but there are some features of the teeth that resemble those of the forest hog *Hylochoerus* and they may have had a similar liking for woodland thickets. There is also a dwarf *Phacochoerus* (*P. modestus*) at the top of Bed I, more adapted for grazing, and it persists to Bed IV. Above the faunal break the small *Mesochoerus* is replaced rather abruptly by the larger *M. olduvaiensis*, already present at an earlier time in the Lake Rudolf area and presumably entering the Olduvai area as an immigrant as the environment favoured it. Also above the faunal break is the large phacochoerine '*Afrochoerus*', together with other suids well adapted to a diet of harsh grasses. At the same time there is a change in the species of grazing alcelaphines represented, although little change in abundance. *Diceros* replaces *Ceratotherium*, and the presence of bush as well as grassland is indicated by eland and large bovines. The faunas of Bed III and Bed IV are poorly known, but there are some species that seem smaller than their earlier representatives, perhaps indicating a harsher environment.

The fauna of Peninj, although scanty and not studied in detail, has a broad resemblance to that of the upper part of Bed II (above the faunal break) and probably reflects a generally similar environment of grassland and thornscrub not far from water.

The South African cave breccias

The fauna of the South African cave breccias was discussed by Ewer and Cooke (1964) and little has altered since then to require serious changes in the relative chronology. At that time the combined faunal list totalled about 150 species and today it is closer to 170. Most of this addition is due to the recognition of further elements in the faunas, particularly in unpublished work by the writer on the complex of sites at Bolt's Farm and that at Gladysvale not far away, as well as new material from Taung. However, there has also been a fair amount of revision and it seems timely to give here a full list of the identifications as they appear at the moment (Table 2). The writer is indebted to D.H.S. Davis and J.J. Meester for the data on the Bolt's Farm microfauna and to Q.B. Hendey for the revision of the section on the carnivores. Work on the bovids of Sterkfontein and Swartkrans by Elizabeth Vrba has been helpful in the present table (see Vrba, 1974), and Brain (1976) has separated the two component faunas at Swartkrans.

It is difficult to separate entirely the problems of relative age and of ecological factors. Taung is at present on the dry fringe of the Kalahari, Makapansgat in the well-watered hills of the northern Transvaal, and the remaining sites on the undulating dolomite area near the Witwatersrand ridge west of Johannesburg, with an adequate but strongly seasonal rainfall. It is obvious from the Table that each of the sites has a substantial number of species that are at present known only from that locality and these are of little value in the assessment of relative age. It is perhaps surprising that there are a number of species that occur at nearly all the sites (notably *Cercopithecoides williamsi, Parapapio jonesi, Elephantulus langi, Myosorex robinsoni, Mystromys hausleitneri, Otomys gracilis, Cryptomys robertsi, Procavia antiqua, P. transvaalensis*, and *Equus capensis*), so these are not time-sensitive species but do form a characteristic part of the total assemblage.

One method of indicating the mutual affinities of the various faunal assemblages is shown in Table 1. This is an analysis which selects for each site the number of species also present at at least one other site. The number of these species present at each of the other sites is then expressed as a percentage of the number at the 'control' site (which is at the left of the Table). The Table can only be read horizontally; for instance, of the 38 species at Makapansgat that also occur elsewhere, 75% are represented also at Sterkfontein but only 45% at Kromdraai.

As Bolt's Farm includes some dozen separate pockets of breccia, it does not represent a single age but overlaps in part with Sterkfontein and in part with Swartkrans. The table confirms the faunal resemblances between Sterkfontein and Makapansgat as a 'pair' and between Swartkrans and Kromdraai as another 'pair' with little

Table 1 Faunal affinities of cave breccias

The abbreviations are as in Table 2. Figures in brackets on the left are numbers of species at that site which are shared with one or more other sites. The figures in the table are percentages of those species that occur also at the site under which the percentage appears. The table reads only in a horizontal sense.

		Ta	Mk	St	Sw*	Swa	Swb	Kr	BF	Gv
Ta	(22)	100	68	55	59	36	27	45	64	32
Mk	(40)	38	100	75	70	48	35	48	58	25
St	(41)	29	78	100	63	54	39	63	54	29
Sw*	(46)	20	52	50	100	—	—	74	63	26
Swa	(31)	19	55	48	—	100	52	68	42	26
Swb	(30)	17	40	33	—	57	100	67	60	30
Kr	(44)	25	48	52	89	52	48	100	64	27
BF	(48)	35	48	44	71	44	52	56	100	40
Gv	(26)	31	58	54	65	54	46	58	77	100

*Swartkrans fauna undifferentiated as only part has been divided by Brain (1976) into a and b.

obvious separation. Taung has closer resemblances to Makapansgat than to any of the others (except to the 'intermediate' mixture of Bolt's Farm), and there can be little doubt that it belongs essentially with Makapansgat and Sterkfontein; it is certainly not younger than Swartkrans and Kromdraai, as has been suggested, although it could possibly occupy a bridging position between the Mk-St and Sw-Kr pairs. In view of the probable time span involved, the overall faunal resemblances are more striking than the differences.

In Table 2 an attempt has been made to indicate, in shorthand form, the general habitat preferences of the various species that can reasonably be assessed. This is an over-simplification of the picture but may be useful. Although there is some indication that Taung has more species favouring fairly dry conditions, this is not a very strong trend and does not suggest an arid environment. Rather, for Taung, the overall picture is one of dry grassland with rocky areas and scrub, or even localized bush in sheltered situations. Makapansgat has a fauna suggesting rather more bush than at the other Transvaal sites, but the dominant impression is of grassland and thornscrub with water nearby. Sterkfontein, Swartkrans and Kromdraai have a similar impression, with less call for bush than at Makapansgat. This general setting is widespread in southern Africa in areas with substantial differences in rainfall and the fauna associated with it is also widespread. The minor differences would be difficult to detect in the fossil assemblages, even if the spectrum were not dependent on the selectivity of predators, whether carnivore or human, or on the whims and successes of the sharp-eyed owls.

Table 2 Faunas of South African cave breccias

Key
Ta – Taung; Mk – Makapansgat Limeworks; St – Sterkfontein; Sw – Swartkrans a,b; Kr – Kromdraai; BF – Bolt's Farm area; Gv – Gladysvale; Hab. – Habitat; F – Forest; B – Bush; T – Thornbush or scrub; G – Grassland; R – Rocky; S – Sandy; V – Variable; D – Dry; W – Water requirement; x – except, when used with habitat indicator.

PRIMATES	Ta	Mk	St	Sw	Kr	BF	Gv	Hab.
Homo sp.				a,b				
Paranthropus robustus				a	x			
Australopithecus africanus	x	x	x					
Cercopithecoides williamsi	x	x	x	b	x	x		B
Dinopithecus ingens				a				
Papio robinsoni				a	x	x	x	V
Papio angusticeps					x			
Papio izodi	x							
Papio wellsi	x							
Parapapio antiquus	x							
Parapapio jonesi	x	x	x	a	x			
Parapapio broomi		x	x			x		
Parapapio whitei	x	x	x			x		
Theropithecus darti		x						GB/R
Theropithecus danieli				a				GB/R
Gorgopithecus major					x			
INSECTIVORA								
Nasilio cf. *brachyrhyncha*	x			x	x	x		GD
Proamblyşomus antiquus					?	x		G?
Chrysotricha hamiltoni		x						S?
Chlorotalpa spelea			x	?				F/B?
Erinaceus broomi						x		G?
Elephantulus broomi		x				x		DGT?
Elephantulus antiquus		x	x	x	x	x		DGT?
Elephantulus sp.		x						
Elephantulus or *Nasilo* sp.	x			x		x		DG?
Macroscelides sp.	x	x						D
Mylomygale spiersi	x		?					
Crocidura taungsensis	x							DGT?
Crocidura cf. *bicolor*			x		x	x	x	DGT?
Suncus infinitesimus		x	x				x	VxD
Suncus cf. *varilla*		x	x	x	x	x		S
Suncus sp.		x	x	x	x			
Myosorex robinsoni		x	x	x	x	x		B?
Diplomesodon fossorius		x						
CHIROPTERA								
Rhinolophus cf. *capensis*	x	x				x		Cave
Myotis sp.						x		Cave
LAGOMORPHA								
Pronolagus cf. *randensis*		x						R/BG
Lepus sp.	x			b		x		GT

Table 2 (continued)

RODENTIA	Ta	Mk	St	Sw	Kr	BF	Gv	Hab.
Pedetes gracile	x							
Pedetes cf. *caffer*						x		V
Mystromys antiquus	x							G/B?
Mystromys hausleitneri		x	x	x	x	x	x	
Mystromys darti		x						
Mystromys sp. nov. (Davis)	x			x	x	x		
Tatera leucogaster				x	x	x		VS
Tatera cf. *brantsi*	x		x		x			VxD
Desmodillus auricularis						x		V
Grammomys cf. *dolichurus*		x			x			F/B
Dasymys bolti				?		x		
Dasymys sp. nov. (Davis)	x					x	x	
Dasymys cf. *incomtus*		x	x					B/W
Arvicanthis sp.			x			x		V
Pelomys cf. *fallax*		x	?					BW
Lemniscomys cf. *griselda*		x						GT
Rhabdomys cf. *pumilio*		x	x					V
Aethomys cf. *namaquensis*		x	x					R
Rattus debruyni	x					x	x	T
Mastomys cf. *natalensis*	x	x	x					G
Zelotomys sp.		x						V
Mus cf. *minutoides*		x	x					
Mus cf. *major* (Broom ms.)						x		
Acomys cf. *cahirinus*		x						VxD
Dendromus antiquus	x							GT?
Dendromus cf. *mesomelas*		x	x					GT
Dendromus spp.	x	x		x	x	x	x	GT?
Malacothrix cf. *typica*	x			x		x		DGT
Malacothrix (?) *makapani*		x						
Steatomys pratensis		?		cf	cf	x		GT
Otomys gracilis	x	x	x	x	x	x	x	RV
Otomys cf. *saundersiae*						x		RV
Otomys sp. nov. (Davis)						x		RV?
Otomys campbelli	x							RV?
Xenohystrix crassidens		x						
Hystrix makapanensis		x						
Hystrix cristata			x					V(D)
Hystrix africaeaustralis		x		a,b		cf	x	V
Petromus minor	x							
Gypsorhychus darti	x							
Gypsorhychus minor	x							
Gypsorhychus makapani		x						
Cryptomys robertsi	x	x	x	x	x	x	x	V
Heterocephalus sp.		x						V
CARNIVORA								
Canis cf. *mesomelas*	x					x		GT
Canis mesomelas pappos		?	x	a,b	x			
Canis terblanchei					x			
Canis brevirostris			x					
Lycaon atrox					x			VxF
Lycaon sp.				b				VxF

Table 2 (continued)

CARNIVORA	Ta	Mk	St	Sw	Kr	BF	Gv	Hab.
Vulpes pulcher				a	x			
Vulpes sp.		x						VD
Otocyon recki				b		cf		GB?
Ictonyx sp. nov. (Cooke)						x		V
Mellivora cf. *sivalensis*				b				V
Suricata cf. *suricatta*						x		V(D)
Aonyx cf. *capensis*						x		W
Herpestes mesotes					x			WB
Herpestes cf. *sanguineus*				b	x			VR
Herpestes sp.						x		
Crossarchus transvaalensis					?	x		B
Cynictis penicillata				b				VGT
Cynictis penicillata brachyodon		x						
Euryboas silberbergi			x	x				
Euryboas cf. *lunensis*			x					
Euryboas nitidula				a				
Hyaenictis forfex				a				
Crocuta crocuta ultra				a,b	x			VxF
Hyaena cf. *brevirostris*		x						
Hyaena brunnea	?							V(D)
Hyaena brunnea dispar				a,b	?			
Hyaena hyaena makapani		x						
Hyaena bellax					x	x	x	
Proteles cristatus				b	x	x		GT(D)
Proteles transvaalensis				a	x			
Felis spelaeus						x		
'Felis' crassidens					x			
Panthera aff. *leo*			x	b	x	x	?	VxF
Panthera pardus incurva			x	a,b	x			VF/B
Dinofelis barlowi		x	x	a	?	x	?	
Dinofelis piveteaui					x			
Magantereon gracile			x					
Magnatereon eurynodon				x	x			
Homotherium problematicus		x						
'Machairodus' transvaalensis						x		
TUBULIDENTATA								
Orycteropus cf. *afer*		x						VSxF
PROBOSCIDEA								
cf. *Elephas recki* (stage 1)		x	x			x		BG?
HYRACOIDEA								
Procavia cf. *capensis*						x		VRxF
Procavia antiqua	x	x	x	a,b	x	x		R?
Procavia transvaalensis	x	x	x	a,b	x		x	R?
Gigantohyrax maguirei		x						
PERISSODACTYLA								
Hipparion steytleri		x		a	x	x		G?
Equus burchelli					?	?	?	G

Table 2 (continued)

PERISSODACTYLA	Ta	Mk	St	Sw	Kr	BF	Gv	Hab.
Equus quagga				a,b	x			G
Equus plicatus						x	?	G?
Equus capensis		x	x	a,b	x	x		G?
Ancylotherium hennigi		x						
Ceratotherium simum		x						GT
Diceros bicornis		x					x	TB
SUINA								
Potamochoeroides shawi	x	x				x	x	B?
Metridiochoerus andrewsi				a		x		G
Notochoerus capensis	x							G
Phacochoerus modestus				b	x	x		G
Hippopotamus amphibius		x						W
GIRAFFIDAE								
Giraffa camelopardalis		x						BTxF
Sivatherium maurusium		x		b				
BOVIDAE								
cf. *Tragelaphus strepsiceros*		x		a,b	x			BW
cf. *Tragelaphus scriptus*				b	x	x		F/BW
cf. *Tragelaphus angasi*	x	x	x	a				BGW
cf. *Taurotragus oryx*				b	x	x	x	GB(D)
cf. *Syncerus caffer*	x	x	x	a	x	x		BTxD
Cephalophus parvus	x							B?
cf. *Cephalophus monticola*		x						F/B
cf. *Kobus leche*							x	Swamp
Kobus ellipsiprymnus				b				BW
Redunca darti		x	x	a				
cf. *Redunca arundinum*		x	x					GBxD
cf. *Redunca fulvorufula*		x						GBR
cf. *Hippotragus niger*				b				GBW
Hippotragus cf. *equinus*			x		x		x	GTW
cf. *Hippotragus gigas*		x						
cf. *Damaliscus lunatus*						x	x	G(B)
cf. *Damaliscus dorcas*				b		x	x	G(B)
Damaliscus or *Parmularius* sp.		x	x	a	x			
Damaliscus sp. (cf. *niro*)				b		x	x	
Rabaticeras porrocornutus				a,b				
cf. *Alcelaphus buselaphus*							x	G(B)
cf. *Alcelaphus lichtensteini*						x	x	GB
Alcelaphus spp.		x	x	a,b	x	x	x	G(B)
Megalotragus sp.		x	x	a,b	x	x	x	G(T)?
cf. *Connochaetes taurinus*		x	x	a,b	x	x	x	G(T)
Connochaetes sp.			(x)					
Oreotragus major	x	x		a,b				RT/B?
Oreotragus oreotragus				b				RT/B?
Ourebia cf. *ourebia*				b				
cf. *Raphicerus campestris*		x		b	x	x		GT
Pelea capreolus				a,b	x			

Table 2 (continued)

BOVIDAE	Ta	Mk	St	Sw	Kr	BF	Gv	Hab.
cf. *Aepyceros melampus*		x						T/BG
cf. *Antidorcas australis*				b		x	x	G
Antidorcas recki			(x)	a	x	x	x	G?
Antidorcas bondi			?	b	?			
Gazella vanhoepeni		x						G?
Gazella sp.		x	(x)	a		x	x	G?
Makapania broomi		x	(x)	a		x	x	GT?

Bracketed designations for Sterkfontein are based on the writer's identifications in an old privately-owned collection, now unfortunately lost. The Kromdraai fauna is mainly from 'B' but is not differentiated.

Acknowledgments

In preparing this account the writer has drawn freely upon the papers presented at the East Rudolf Basin Conference (Coppens *et al.*, 1975) and is indebted to many authors whose valuable contributions do not happen to be cited by name in the References. Use has been made of other papers by Beden, Coppens, Harris, Hooijer, Howell and Meave Leakey in particular, to all of whom the writer is much indebted. Financial support from the Wenner-Gren Foundation for Anthropological Research is gratefully acknowledged.

References

Bishop, W.W. (1972) Stratigraphic succession 'versus' calibration in East Africa. In Bishop, W.W. and Miller, J.A. (eds.), *Calibration of Hominid Evolution*, 219-46, Edinburgh.

Brain, C.K. (1976) A re-interpretation of the Swartkrans site and its remains. *S. Afr. J. Sci.* 72, 141-6.

Brown, F.H. (1975) Radiometric dating and palaeomagnetic studies of Omo group deposits. In Coppens, Y. *et al.* (eds.).

Cooke, H.B.S. (1963) Pleistocene mammal faunas of Africa, with particular reference to southern Africa. In Howell, F.C. and Bourlière, F. (eds.), *African Ecology and Human Evolution*, 65-116. Chicago.

Coppens, Y. *et al.* (eds.) (1976) *Earliest Man and Environments in the Lake Rudolf Basin: Stratigraphy, Paleoecology and Evolution*. Chicago.

Dorst, J. and Dandelot, P. (1969) *A Field Guide to the Larger Mammals of Africa*. Boston.

Eck, G.G. (1975) Cercopithecoidea from Omo group deposits. In Coppens, Y. *et al.* (eds.).

Ewer, R.F. and Cooke, H.B.S. (1964) The Pleistocene mammals of southern Africa. In Davis, D.H.S. (ed.), *Ecological Studies in Southern Africa*, 35-48. The Hague.

Gentry, A.W. (1975) Bovidae of the Omo group deposits. In Coppens, Y. *et al.* (eds.).

Hay, R.L. (1971) Geologic background of Beds I and II: Stratigraphic summary. In Leakey, M.D. (ed.), *Olduvai Gorge: Excavations in Beds I and II, 1960-63*, 9-18. London.

Leakey, L.S.B. (1965) *Olduvai Gorge 1951-1961: Fauna and Background*, 7-78. London.

Maglio, V.J. (1972) Vertebrate faunas and chronology of hominid-bearing sediments east of Lake Rudolf, Kenya. *Nature* 239, 379-85.

Vrba, E. (1974) Chronological and ecological implications of the fossil Bovidae at the Sterkfontein Australopithecine site. *Nature* 250, 19-23.

PART III
ANATOMICAL EVIDENCE

J. Wallace

Evolutionary trends in the early hominid dentition

> A fossil tooth or bone is certainly a dull and uninspiring object if it is looked at in the wrong way (I am tempted to let out the secret that even professional students of fossils do not always look at them in the right way.) The wrong way is to look at fossils as something dead and petrified, to measure and describe them as if they were pieces of rock, to compare them bit by bit and to slap new names on those that look a little different, with never a thought for the processes and meanings behind those differences. (Simpson 1951)

In this paper I attempt to dissect out some of the morphogenetic and selective mechanisms that underlie the bumps and grooves and nooks and crannies of early hominid teeth, in the hope of re-creating some aspects of the life of the individuals.

Incisors and premaxillary form

The pattern of wear on early hominid upper incisors changes with age. In the early stages not long after eruption, the incisal surface, viewed in profile, is seen to have a slight upward, inward bevel. With advancing age and continuing abrasion by dietary grit, the incisal surface becomes worn flat (Figure 1). A flat, horizontally worn incisal surface is evidence of an edge-to-edge (better surface-to-surface) occlusion (Weidenreich, 1937; Hojo, 1954; Begg, 1965).

Some individuals developed a surface-to-surface incisor bite earlier than others. For example, SK 852 + SK 839, a *Paranthropus* child from Swartkrans, had a surface-to-surface bite of the deciduous incisors before KNM-ER 808, the East Rudolf specimen recently attributed to *Homo* by Leakey and Wood (1973). The di^1's of KNM-ER 808 are worn with an upward, inward bevel, whereas those of SK 852 + SK 839 are worn flat. Since the M^1's of KNM-ER 808 but not of SK 852 + SK 839 had erupted (occlusal attrition facets are present on M^1 in the

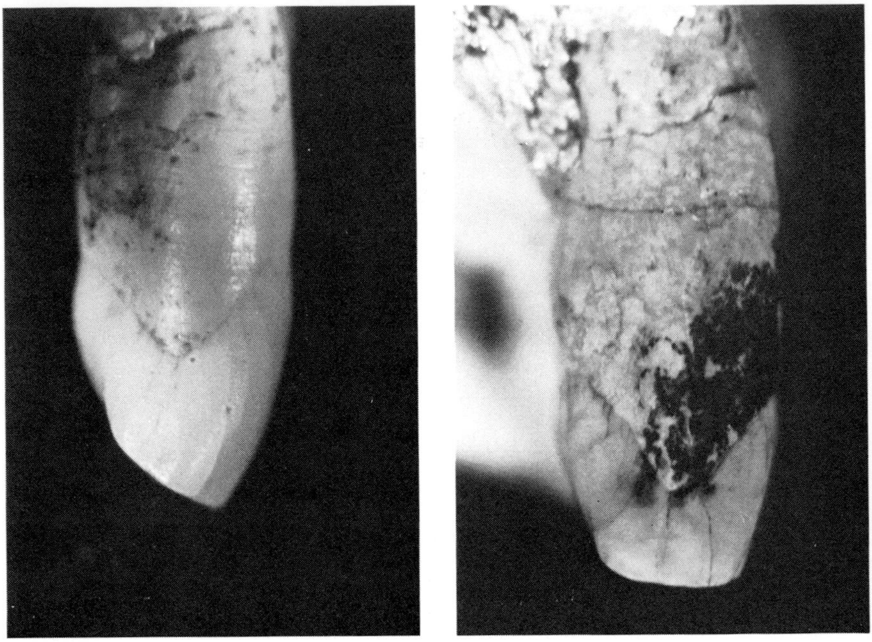

A B

Figure 1. Incisal wear planes: with age the incisal surface of upper incisors becomes worn flat. A. SK 2 (I^1). B. SK 65 (I^1).

former but absent in the latter), a surface-to-surface incisor occlusion appeared earlier in life in the *Paranthropus* child. And for another example, in this case in the permanent dentition, we find that the I^1's of Olduvai Hominid 5 are worn flat, in contrast to those of the Sterkfontein *Australopithecus*, Sts 52a + b, which are bevelled upward and inward. Since OH 5 and Sts 52a + b are the same dental age, as judged by the eruption stage of the third molars, a surface-to-surface incisor bite developed earlier in OH 5.

Why? Probably because OH 5 has a flatter maxilla and more vertically implanted incisors (Tobias, 1967). The incisors most likely erupted almost directly into an edge-to-edge relationship with the lowers. In Sts 52a + b, on the other hand, the incisors rooted in a prognathous maxilla erupted obliquely downward and forward; in such a position the incisal surface became worn with an upward, inward bevel. A flat, anteriorly compressed maxilla carrying vertically set incisors predisposes to early development of a surface-to-surface incisor bite. Since in modern man vertically implanted upper incisors are common in orthognathous jaws and proclined ones in prognathous jaws (Hasund and Ulstein, 1970), and since *Australopithecus* is more prognathous than *Paranthropus* (Robinson, 1956), we can conclude that a surface-to-surface bite developed earlier in life in *Paranthropus* than in either *Australopithecus* and early *Homo*

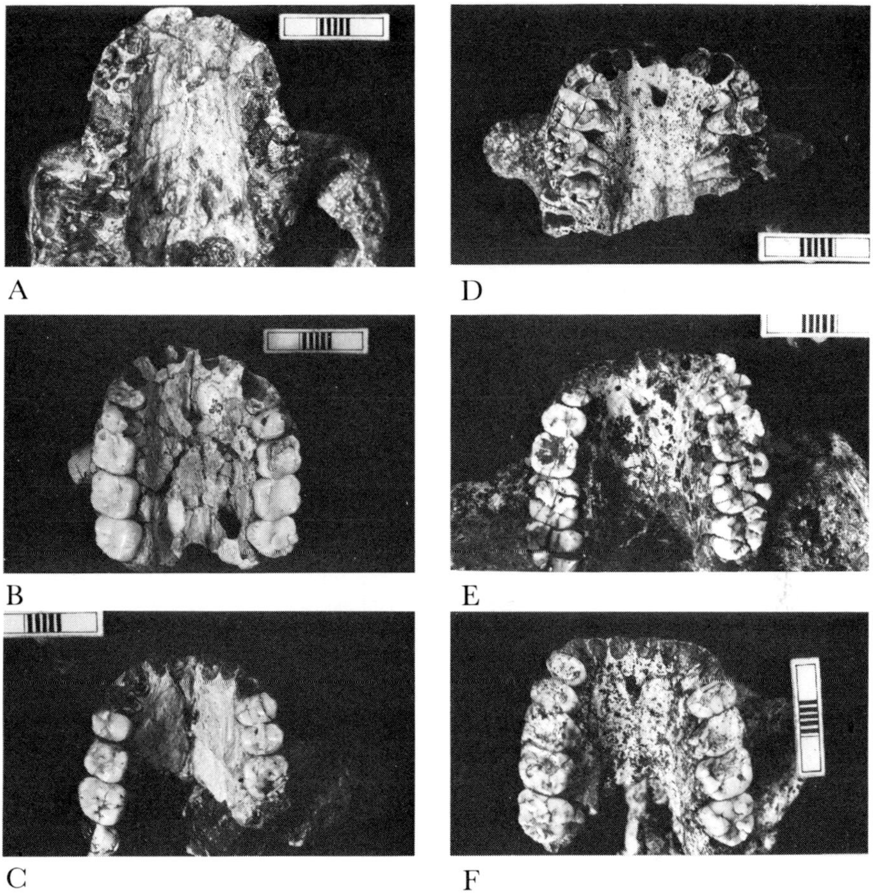

Figure 2. Anterior dental arcade: in *Australopithecus* the maxilla is convex anteriorly. In *Paranthropus* the maxilla is flattened; the alveolar margin runs more or less straight across from one canine alveolus to the other. A. Sts 5. B. Sts 53. C. Sts 17. D. SK 12. E. SK 79. F. SK 46.

because *Paranthropus* had a flatter maxilla with more vertically implanted incisors (Figure 2).

Thus far a causal chain has been constructed linking incisor wear, incisor proclination and maxillary prognathism. It remains now to uncover the cause for the maxillary prognathism. We focus on the premaxilla because this is the bone that develops between the maxillae and the bone that supports the upper incisors. Early in the third foetal month the premaxilla loses its independence and 'fuses' with the maxilla.[1] In extant apes, in contrast, the premaxillary suture may persist facially into late foetal life and in some individuals until

1. More accurately the suture is lost not by fusion but by 'overgrowth of a secondary heavily trabecularized network of bone' that arises from the buccal face of the canine alveolus (Kraus and Decker, 1960).

late childhood (Krogman, 1930). In a comparative study of the premaxilla in primates Montagu (1935) found that the suture remained open for a longer period in long-snouted than short-snouted forms. This correlation between facial profile and age of obliteration of the premaxillary suture holds true for modern man. In a series of foetal and neonate skulls, Montagu found that the premaxillary suture remained open longer in Negroes than in Caucasoids; an observation that led him to the conclusion that this probably accounts for the pronounced prognathism of the Negro.

Variation amongst the early hominids in incisor wear planes, incisor inclination, maxillary profile, and age of appearance of a surface-to-surface bite most likely reflects variation in age of 'fusion' of the premaxilla. The premaxilla was lost earlier in ontogeny in *Paranthropus* than in *Australopithecus* and *Homo*.

More evidence for this hypothesis is found in an analysis of the upper pre-canine diastema. This is the gap between the upper lateral incisor and the canine through which the premaxillary suture runs in its passage from the palate onto the face. The width of the diastema may reflect variation in timing of sutural obliteration. For example, early closure of the suture might result in a small diastema or the absence of a diastema as is often seen in modern man, whilst late fusion with a longer period of growth so that I^2 is carried forward away from $\underline{C}$ might account for the wide diastema of apes.

Pithecanthropus IV has a diastema – the alveolar septum between

Figure 3. Canine overbite and guidance in Taung: the facets on the lingual slope of the apex and distal incisal ridge of the d$\underline{c}$ and on the buccal slope of the mesiobuccal ridge of the mesiobuccal cusp of dm_1 indicate that the upper canine guided the lower teeth into centric occlusion.

the lateral incisor and canine measures 5-6 mm. (Weidenreich, 1945). In his description of the maxilla, Weidenreich was impressed by the 'very pronounced facial and alveolar prognathism', and as to the slope of the incisors, he remarked: The teeth must have continued in the same prognathous direction of the naso-alveolar clivus.' The diastema, the prognathism, and the excessive length of the palate, suggest that in Pithecanthropus IV 'fusion' of the premaxilla was delayed.

Taung has an upper pre-canine diastema (Figure 3). The *Paranthropus* child, OH 3, from upper Bed II, Olduvai, does not have a diastema: a di^2-facet is present on the mesial surface of the $d\underline{c}$. Rather than being in the middle third of the mesial surface, the facet is found in the buccal third on the mesial buccal angle. A mesial facet in this position suggests that the $d\underline{c}$ was rotated.

Distally rotated, permanent upper canines have been found in *Paranthropus* but not in *Australopithecus*. *Paranthropus* specimens with rotated $\underline{C}$'s are: SK 48, SK 845, SK 1590b, SK 83, KNM-ER 816a, OH 5 (Tobias 1967) and KNM-CH 1 (Figure 4). There has been some post-mortem displacement of the SK 845 canine, but it is certain that the canine erupted into a rotated position because the distal facet on the $\underline{C}$ is on the distal lingual ridge and the mesial facet on the P^3 occupies the buccal border of the mesial surface. In the isolated upper

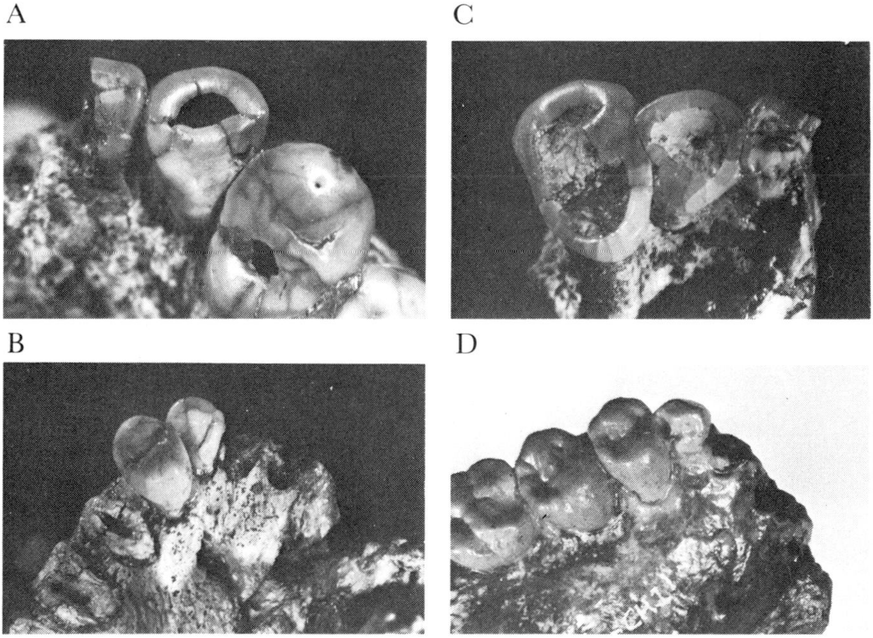

Figure 4. Distal rotation of *Paranthropus* upper canines: the upper canine instead of facing lingually faces distolingually A. SK 845. B. SK 48. C. SK 1590b. D. KNM-CH 1 (cast).

canine of KNM-ER 816a, the distal facet occupies the distallingual ridge and the mesial surface is devoid of a facet for I^2. Neither of the two *in situ* upper canines from Sterkfontein (Sts 52a + b and TM 1512) are rotated in their alveoli. Most likely distally rotated upper canines are a result of early closure of the pre-maxillary suture. To accommodate itself to a shortened, compressed anterior arch, the upper canine of *Paranthropus* was forced during its eruption to rotate distally. The presence in *Paranthropus* but not in *Australopithecus* of distally rotated upper canines is additional evidence for the hypothesis that the premaxilla was 'lost' earlier in ontogeny in *Paranthropus*.

The incisal and premaxillary complex of *Ramapithecus* is more like that of a hominid than a pongid: maxillary prognathism is reduced, upper incisors tend to be vertically emplaced, and there is a small upper pre-canine diastema. In his diagnosis of *Ramapithecus punjabicus* (based on YPM 13799), Lewis wrote: 'The roots indicate that the incisors more nearly approached the vertical than is the case in the Simiidae known hitherto; the attendant slight prognathism is hominid.' He continued: 'The dental arch is very much compressed. The nearest approach to a diastema occurs between the alveoli of the canine and second incisor, which are separated by a scant 2 mm. – no more than in many human specimens, and insufficient to produce a diastema between the crowns' (Lewis 1934).

The Fort Ternan *Ramapithecus* (KNM-FT 45+46) has an abbreviated premaxillary region, a feature which 'very clearly places *Ramapithecus wickeri* apart from contemporary species of *Dryopithecus*' (Walker and Andrews, 1973). Compared to its Indian relative, *R. wickeri* appears to have a wider diastema (Walker and Andrews, 1973, Figure 3).[2] Presumably the premaxilla 'fused' with the maxilla earlier in *R. punjabicus* than *R. wickeri*. *R. punjabicus* appears to be 2-4 million years more recent than *R. wickeri* (Bishop *et al.*, 1969; Simons *et al.*, 1971; Conroy and Pilbeam, 1973). Perhaps there was a phylogenetic trend towards early loss in ontogeny of the premaxilla.

If there was a trend we would expect evidence of it amongst the australopithecines. *Paranthropus* from Swartkrans postdates *Australopithecus* from Sterkfontein type locality (Ewer and Cooke 1964, Cooke 1963),[3] and as set out previously, the differences in maxillary profiles, incisor inclinations, and rotated canines point to the conclusion that the premaxilla was lost earlier in ontogeny in *Paranthropus*. The simplest explanation of these observations is that there is indeed a phylogenetic trend toward early loss of the premaxilla. Whether we project upward in time from *Ramapithecus* or backward in time from *Paranthropus*, the trends intersect. In foetus after foetus, year after year for at least 10 million years natural

2. Andrews (1974) reports that the upper canine has a large mesial facet made by the lower canine which is evidence that a diastema was present.

3. I ignore the 'absolute dates' of the South African cave deposits (Partridge, 1973), because of doubts on the validity of the dating technique (Bishop, 1974).

selection was at work fusing the premaxilla to the maxilla earlier and earlier in ontogeny.

This is not to say the rate of 'fusion' was constant. Lewis (1934) gives the width of the I^2-$\underline{C}$ interalveolar septum in *R. punjabicus* as 2 mm. In *Australopithecus* the width of the septum is not appreciably different: in 7 maxillae septal width ranges from 1.2 to 2.4 mm., with an average of 1.7 mm. (Robinson, 1956). Perhaps during the long interval that divides *Ramapithecus punjabicus* from *Australopithecus africanus* the evolutionary change in rate of 'fusion' was very slow, in which case it accelerated rapidly in the comparatively short interval that separates *Australopithecus* from *Paranthropus*. In 13 maxillae of the Swartkrans *Paranthropus*, Robinson (1956) reports the septal width ranged from 0.2 to 1.7 mm. with a mean of 0.7 mm.

As a working hypothesis, I see three stages in the evolution of the premaxillary complex in the *Ramapithecus-Paranthropus* lineage: an initial short period of (say) 1 to 2 million years of intense selection during the time *Ramapithecus* was diverging from the dryopithecines; a long intermediate period of some 8 to 9 million years characterized by a relative relaxation in selection for early fusion; and a final, short period, akin to the initial one, of intense selection for early fusion that marked the emergence of *Paranthropus*.

Phylogenetic trends, besides having direction and rates, usually involve a progressive improvement in the performance of a task (Simpson, 1950). Early closure of the premaxillary suture results in vertically implanted upper incisors that early in life wear into a surface-to-surface occlusion. Such an occlusion enhances crushing. The earlier this occlusion appears, the longer the individual has an incisor crushing mechanism. Thus in functional terms the trend from *Ramapithecus* to *Paranthropus* was characterized by early development of incisor crushing, not long after eruption.

Canines, premolars and molars

The path the lower molars describe from the time they leave centric occlusion until the time they return (c. 1 sec.) is called the masticatory cycle (Hildebrand, 1936; Beyron, 1964; Murphy, 1965; Ahlgren, 1966, Figure 5). The angle at which the lower molars engage the uppers in the grinding phrase of the cycle depends upon the height of the upper canine, premolar and molar cusps. If these cusps are high and projecting, they guide the lower molars upward and into the centric position along a steep, vertical path. Conversely, if the cusps are so low that guidance is absent, the lower molars come into centric occlusion along a more horizontal path (Shepherd, 1960; Koivumaa, 1961; Ingervall, 1972). Guidance may be absent initially following eruption of genetically low-cusped teeth, or it may be lost after eruption by abrasion levelling the cusps. Lacking guidance, the lower molars are

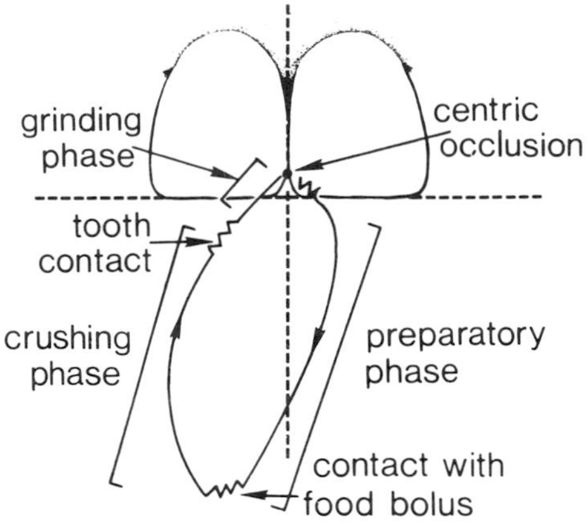

Figure 5. The masticatory cycle: the angle the lower molars engage the uppers in the grinding phase depends upon the height of the upper cusps (coronal projection).

free to follow a transverse shearing path in their sweep across the upper molars.

In modern man the deciduous and permanent upper canines usually erupt into an overbite relationship with, respectively, the deciduous, first lower molar and the permanent, lower anterior premolar. More precisely, the lingual slope of the distal incisal ridge of $d\underline{c}$ overlaps the buccal slope of the mesiobuccal ridge of the protoconid of dm_1, and the lingual slope of $\underline{C}$'s distal incisal ridge overlaps the buccal slope of the mesiobuccal ridge of P_3's buccal cusp (Zeisz and Nuckolls, 1949; Wheeler, 1965). This overlapping relationship predisposes to canine guidance; that is, to mutual contact of these upper and lower ridges during ascent into centric occlusion.

The Taung $d\underline{c}$ has an attrition facet running the length of the lingual slope of the apex and distal incisal ridge, which in centric occlusion is seen to overlie an equally elongate facet on the buccal slope of the mesiobuccal ridge of the dm_1 protoconid. Unquestionably, the dc of Taung erupted into overbite, and at the time of death canine guidance was present (Figure 3).

The *Paranthropus* child from Swartkrans, SK 852 + SK 839, had a surface-to-surface $d\underline{c}/dm_1$ occlusion, since the dm_1-facet on the $d\underline{c}$ is not on the lingual slope of the distal incisal ridge but rather on its incisal surface which is worn flat, and the $d\underline{c}$-facet on dm_1 is not on the buccal slope of the mesiobuccal ridge but on the occlusal surface of the mesial marginal ridge. Hence the $d\underline{c}$ of SK 852 + SK 839 at the time of death was not functioning as a cuspal guide; the lower deciduous molars were free to follow a horizontal, transverse shearing path across the upper molars.

The question arises whether the *Paranthropus* dc erupted into overbite and functioned initially as a guide. In SK 64 and SK 3978 buccal $d\underline{c}$-facets are present on the dm_1's, which indicates that the $d\underline{c}$

had erupted into overbite. However, in dentally older *Paranthropus* children (SK 62, SK 61, KNM-ER 1477, and SK 852)[4] $d\underline{c}$-facets are absent from the buccal slopes of the mesiobuccal ridges of the dm_1 protoconids, but present on the occlusal surface of the mesial marginal ridges, which is certain evidence that the dc in these individuals was not guiding the lower deciduous molars into centric. From this cross-sectional study the ontogeny of the $d\underline{c}/dm_1$ occlusion of *Paranthropus* may be inferred. Probably the $d\underline{c}$ acted as a cuspal guide for a short period after eruption until abrasion by dietary grit levelled the apex, unlocked the overbite, eliminated the guidance and established a surface-to-surface occlusion.

The age at which canine guidance was lost in *Paranthropus* is uncertain; on the present evidence it seems that the loss occurred after the dm_2's had made occlusal contact but before the M 1's had erupted occlusally. (Attrition facets are present on the dm_2's of SK 64 and SK 3978 but absent from the M 1's of SK 61, SK 852 + SK 839 and KNM-ER 1477.)

Since SK 61, SK 852 + SK 839 and KNM-ER 1477 are dentally younger than Taung (the M 1's of Taung are worn), it follows that these *Paranthropus* children acquired the potential for transverse grinding or shearing earlier than *Australopithecus* from Taung.[5]

Did the permanent, upper canine of *Paranthropus* erupt into overbite and function as a guide? As evidenced by the fine enamel scratches on the buccal face of the canine and premolar, the $\underline{C}$ and P_3 of SK 55a + b had erupted fully and were functional at the time of death. There is no buccal C-facet on the P_3. Slightly older individuals (SK 857, SK 831 and SK 6 + SK 100), as judged from occlusal wear, also lack buccal $\underline{C}$-facets on their P_3's. The recently erupted *Paranthropus* P_3 of KNM-ER 1178b (a distal dm_2-facet is present) lacks a buccal but has an occlusal $\underline{C}$-facet, indicating that the upper canine did not erupt into overbite, but rather occluded surface-to-surface with P_3. None of the dentally old individuals of *Paranthropus*, that is those with dentine exposed on the P_3's (SK 23, SK 858, SK 14001, SK 74a, SK 30, SK 72 and SK 1593), have buccal $\underline{C}$-facets. Although it is certain that guidance was absent in these individuals, it is impossible to determine from a study of tooth wear whether the upper canine erupted into overbite and functioned initially as a guide. However, from the specimens available, it seems that canine guidance in *Paranthropus* having been lost in childhood did not re-appear in adolescence with the eruption of the permanent upper canine. Once aquired in childhood the potential for transverse grinding remained until death.

Not so for *Australopithecus* and *Homo*. Buccal $\underline{C}$-facets are present on

4. Assignment to *Paranthropus* is based on the degree of molarization of the dm_1's (see Robinson, 1956).

5. Had Taung lived abrasion probably would have eliminated the guidance before the $d\underline{c}$ was shed, since the dentally older East Rudolf *Homo*, KNM-ER 820 (Leakey and Wood, 1973) has a surface-to-surface $d\underline{c}/dm_1$ occlusion.

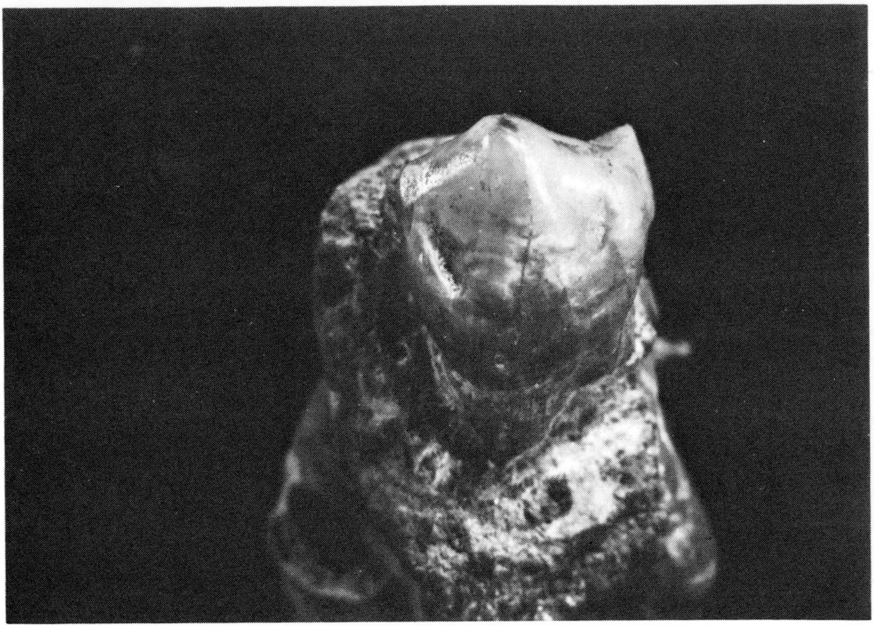

Figure 6. Evidence of canine overbite and guidance: a $\underline{C}$-facet is seen on the buccal slope of the mesiobuccal ridge of the buccal cusp of P_3 (Sts 49).

the P_3's of Sts 52a + b, Sts 39, OH 7, OH 16, and KNM-ER 806 (Figure 6). Undoubtedly, the permanent, upper canine of these individuals erupted into overbite and functioned as a guide. In dentally older individuals, those with dentine exposed on the P_3's (KNM-ER 992, Sts 36 and Sts 7), the occlusal surface of the premolars are worn flat and buccal $\underline{C}$-facets are absent, suggesting that they had a surface-to-surface $\underline{C}/P_3$ occlusion. Studied cross-sectionally, these 8 specimens suggest that in *Australopithecus* and *Homo* cuspal guidance was present from the time the permanent upper canine erupted until abrasion by dietary grit lowered the crowns and eliminated the guidance. The age when guidance was lost is uncertain. In OH 16 it was still present at the time the M 3's first made occlusal contact (the M_3 of OH 16 has a single attrition facet, indicating that at the time of death the third molars had just made occlusal contact). In KNM-ER 992 all the cusps of M_3 are faceted but dentine had not been exposed. On the basis of these two specimens it appears that guidance was lost not long after the third molars erupted occlusally. *Paranthropus*, as we have seen, lost canine guidance as a child, before the permanent first molars had erupted.

Why did *Paranthropus* lose canine guidance earlier in life than *Australopithecus* and *Homo*? One possibility is that *Paranthropus* had more grit in its food, with the result that the $d\underline{c}$'s wore out of overbite into a surface-to-surface occlusion at a faster rate. That seems improbable for three reasons. First, Taung and SK 63 + SK 89 + SK 90 + SK 91, which are dentally the same age, as judged from the eruption stage of the permanent, first molars, have dentine exposures on their deciduous molars almost identical in size, suggesting that the rates of abrasion and hence the amounts of grit in their diets were similar. Secondly, enamel microchipping which is a measure of abrasion by fine particles of sand and soil in the diet is not appreciably different in *Paranthropus* and *Australopithecus* from South Africa (Wallace, 1973). Finally, relative differences in rates of abrasion cannot be invoked to explain the absence of buccal $\underline{C}$-facets on the recently erupted P$_3$'s of *Paranthropus* nor account for their presence on the P$_3$'s of *Australopithecus* and *Homo*.

The most likely reason *Paranthropus* lost canine guidance at an early age is that the upper canines were genetically short – shorter incisocervically than those of *Australopithecus* and *Homo*. Relative height of the deciduous, upper canine may be inferred from the size and position of the d$\underline{c}$-facet on dm$_1$. As seen from the teeth in occlusion and confirmed from the pattern of wear, the d$\underline{c}$-facet on the Taung dm$_1$ consists of two parts: a mesial third made by contact with the apex of the upper canine and a distal two-thirds made by contact with the distal incisal ridge of the upper canine. In the two Swartkrans *Paranthropus* dm$_1$'s with buccal d$\underline{c}$-facets (SK 64 and SK 3978), only the mesial part of the facet is present; the distal two-thirds of the mesiobuccal ridge is free of faceting. Thus the overbite was less in SK 64 and SK 3978 than in Taung, probably because the d$\underline{c}$ was shorter incisocervically in the *Paranthropus* specimens.

More evidence that *Paranthropus* possessed short d$\underline{c}$'s is found in the morphology of the deciduous, lower first molar. The mesial marginal ridge of *Paranthropus* dm$_1$'s is thickened and expanded lingually, resulting in a 'squaring-off' of the mesiolingual corner, a re-alignment of the anterior fovea and mesial marginal ridge at a right angle to the occlusal surface, and closure of the lingual end of the anterior fovea (Figure 7). Together these features give to the dm$_1$'s of *Paranthropus* a more molarized appearance than is seen in the dm$_1$'s of *Australopithecus* and *Homo* (Sts 24, TM 1516, Taung, and KNM-ER 820).

As noted previously the d$\underline{c}$/dm$_1$ occlusion in early hominids changes with age: progressive abrasion levels the cusps, unlocks the overbite, eliminates the guidance, and results in a surface-to-surface bite where the d$\underline{c}$ flattened by wear comes to occlude with the occlusal surface of the mesial marginal ridge of dm$_1$. Development of a surface-to-surface d$\underline{c}$/dm$_1$ occlusion, as evidenced previously, occurred earlier in life in *Paranthropus* than Taung. The expanded mesial marginal ridge of the dm$_1$ increases the occlusal table for crushing, and may be regarded as a morphological adaptation to genetically short dc's which early on in life wear out of overbite into a surface-to-surface occlusion.

This leads to the hypothesis that molarization of dm$_1$ is a correlated

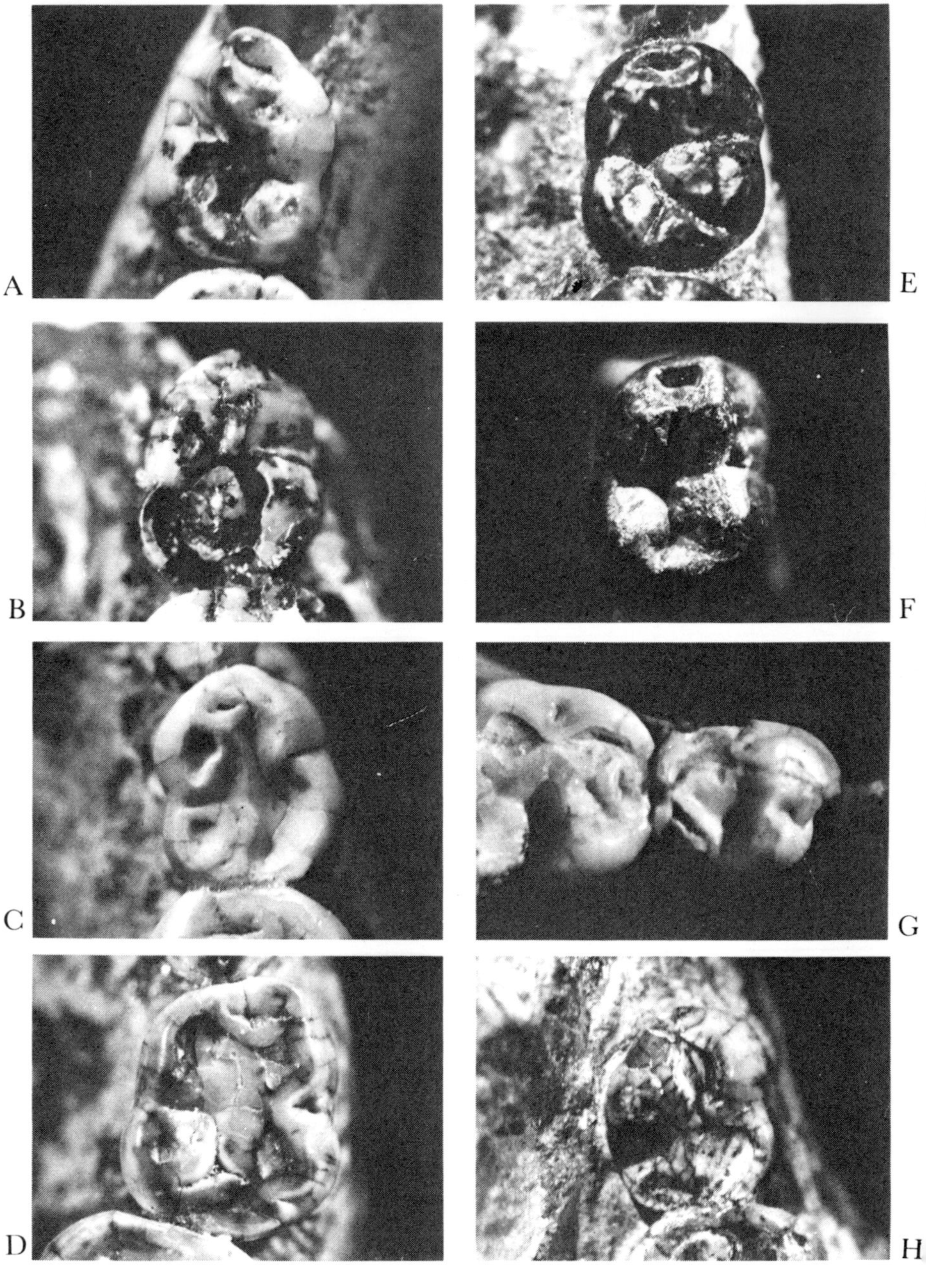

Figure 7. Molarization of dm_1: note variation in mesial marginal ridge morphology. Lingually the mesial marginal ridge is thicker and more elevated in *Paranthropus* dm_1's than in those of *Australopithecus* (Taung and Sts 24). A. SK 3978. B. SK 852. C. SK 63. D. SK 61. E. TM 1536. F. TM 1601. G. Taung. H. Sts 24.

genetic change accompanying incisocervical reduction of $d\underline{c}$. This hypothesis finds its test in Taung, where we would predict from the late persistence of an overbite that elongate $d\underline{c}$'s and less molarized dm_1's would co-occur. Indeed the correlation is found. Taung possesses a sharp, pointed $d\underline{c}$ apex and a less molarized dm_1.

In the permanent dentition the absence of buccal $\underline{C}$-facets on the recently erupted *Paranthropus* P_3's of SK 55a + b, SK 857, SK 831, SK 6 + SK 100, and KNM ER 1178b suggests that these individuals had incisocervically short C's. Conversely, the presence of buccal $\underline{C}$-facets on the P_3's of *Australopithecus* (Sts 52a + b and Sts 49) and *Homo* (OH 7, OH 16 and KNM-ER 806) indicates that the $\underline{C}$'s of these individuals were longer and more projecting. In OH 7, which is dentally older than SK 55a + b, the $\underline{C}$-facet covers the incisal third of the buccal surface of the P_3.

Regrettably, a metrical comparison of height of unworn maxillary canines from Swartkrans and Sterkfontein is precluded by the fact that every upper canine from Sterkfontein is worn. However, as Robinson's (1956) measurements testify, unworn mandibular canines from Swartkrans are lower than homologues from Sterkfontein. It seems reasonable to infer this was true also for the maxillary canines. Speaking of unworn $\underline{C}$'s of the Swartkrans *Paranthropus* Robinson (1956) said: 'In no case is the apex a sharp point.' Even allowing for the slight abrasion on the upper canines of Sts 52a + b – wear which is

A B

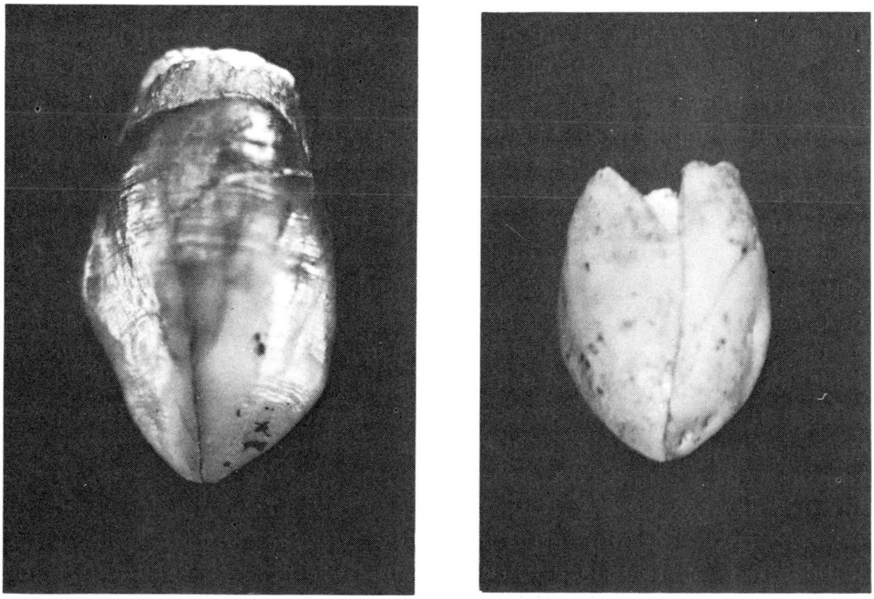

Figure 8. Upper canine cusps: the cusp of MLD 11 (*Australopithecus*) tends to be sharper and more projecting than that of SK 92 (*Paranthropus*). A. MLD 11. B. SK 92.

confined to the lingual face of the cusp and not to the tip – the apex is seen to be sharper than apices of unworn Swartkrans *Paranthropus* $\underline{C}$'s. The permanent, upper canines of SK 92, SK 85 + SK 93 and MLD 11 are unerupted, and thus ideal for comparison of cusp heights. The pointed apex of the Makapansgat *Australopithecus* $\underline{C}$ stands sharply in contrast to the low rounded apices of the *Paranthropus* specimens (Figure 8). I suspect that the difference in canine height reflects a difference only in cusp height; that is, variation in canine height amongst the specimens involves only the apex.

From this analysis of canine occlusion we can conclude that compared to *Australopithecus* and *Homo, Paranthropus* lost canine guidance early in life because the upper canines were genetically short. This does not necessarily mean that *Paranthropus* had a transverse grinding masticatory stroke, because, as noted previously, the grind angle is governed not only by the height of the upper canine but also by the height of the cusps on the cheek teeth; that is, the premolar and molar cusps act as guides. Accordingly, we would predict that low cusped canines would be coupled with low cusped cheek teeth. And, indeed, this is what we find.

Referring to the buccal and lingual cusps on *Paranthropus* P^3's, Robinson (1956) remarked: 'Neither has sharp apices in any of the specimens to hand, the cusps being low and bluntly rounded. When only very slightly worn no traces remain of apices.' Of the *Paranthropus* M^1, Robinson (1956) said: 'The cusps are all relatively low and rounded. When entirely unworn there may be a moderate apex to each cusp but after the slightest wear the cusps are low, rounded tubercles.' I compared Sterkfontein and Swartkrans premolar and molar homologues that were unerupted and homologues from these two sites that were almost identically worn. Although unmeasured, it was apparent from inspection that *Paranthropus* cheek teeth from Swartkrans had lower cusps. Moreover, in *Paranthropus* cheek teeth dentine is seen first *after* the cusps are levelled, whereas in *Australopithecus* cheek teeth dentine is seen *before* the cusps are reduced to the level of the occlusal base. The most likely reason, consistent with the above, is that *Paranthropus* cheek teeth have genetically lower cusps.

Low molar cusps predispose to a guidance-free occlusion at eruption or early loss of guidance not long after eruption by dietary grit wearing down the low cusps. As inferred from the eruption of the permanent, first molars, SK 63 + SK 89 + SK 90 + SK 91 from Swartkrans and Sts 24 from Sterkfontein were, at the time of death, approximately the same dental age. The M_1 of Sts 24 has a facet on the buccal slope of the mesiobuccal ridge of the mesiobuccal cusp. In SK 63 + SK 89 + SK 90 + SK 91 the homologous facet (confirmed by occluding the upper and lower molars) is found not on the buccal slope but on the occlusal surface of the mesiobuccal ridge. This means that in the *Australopithecus* specimen M^1 erupted into over-bite and acted as a guide. But in the *Paranthropus* specimen M^1 did not erupt into overbite and did not act as a guide. In OH 7, the type specimen of *Homo habilis*, M^2-facets occupy the buccal slopes of the M_2. Buccal M^2-facets are absent from the M_2's of SK 55a + b. This *Paranthropus* specimen is dentally younger than OH 7 (the dm 2's had not yet been exfoliated), and there is no doubt that the M 2's had erupted since occlusal attrition facets are present on the distal cusps of the M_2. Clearly, the M^2 in OH 7 but not in SK 55a+b erupted into overbite and functioned as a guide during chewing. This is not surprising since as seen earlier the two specimens differed in canine overbite. The M_2 of OH 16 has a small dentine exposure on the protoconid and M^2-facets on the buccal slopes of the buccal cusps. None of the dentally younger *Paranthropus* specimens (those without dentine exposures such as, SK 1, SK 55a+ b, SK 843 and SK 6 + SK 100) with M_2's in occlusion have buccal M^2-facets. Even if it be supposed that the M^2 had erupted into overbite in these individuals, molar guidance (if indeed it ever was present) was lost earlier in life than in *Australopithecus* and *Homo* specimens. Present evidence suggests that *Paranthropus* molars did not erupt into overbite and the guidance was absent from the time of eruption until death. The reason, most likely, is that *Paranthropus* had genetically low molar cusps.

Ramapithecus (KNM-FT 45 + 46, YPM No. 13799, YPM 13906, GSI No. 18068, GSI D-118/119, YPM 13814, and YPM 13833) has lower and broader molar cusps than contemporary species of *Dryopithecus* (Lewis, 1934, 1937; Leakey 1962; Simons, 1968).[6] And as one might predict *Ramapithecus* has a low canine. Comparison with the Rusinga Island specimen of *D. africanus* reveals that the Fort Ternan *Ramapithecus* has a lower, less projecting upper canine, and less of a canine overbite (Andrews, 1971). It seems reasonable to conclude that, compared to the dryopithecines, *Ramapithecus* had the potential for a more transverse grinding or shearing masticatory stroke due to its lower canine and cheek teeth cusps.

Again, whether we project upward in time from *Ramapithecus* or backward from *Paranthropus*, the trends for low canine and cheek teeth cusps intersect. *Ramapithecus* seemingly is at the beginning of a trend for reduction in cusp height that was to culminate some 10 million years later in *Paranthropus*.

Canine and cheek teeth apparently evolved *pari passu*: indeed no functional advantage would be gained if cusp height reduced in canines but not in cheek teeth, or conversely if reduction occurred only in the height of the cheek teeth cusps. This functional interrelationship of canines and cheek teeth suggests that cusp height in early hominids was a morphogenetic field, in some way under unitary genetic control. We can only speculate as to the

6. The Ngorora M^2 is low-cusped as L.S.B. Leakey noted (in Bishop and Chapman, 1970). This is a genetic character; the lowness of the cusps is not due to wear.

developmental mechanism underlying reduction in cusp height. Perhaps the cervical loop (the junction of the inner and outer enamel epithelium) shifted its direction of growth from a downward to a more lateral direction, resulting in a splaying-out of the inner enamel epithelium. This might explain why low cusped cheek teeth tend to have broad occlusal bases. The expansion of the occlusal base may be a pleiotropic effect of genes controlling cusp height.

It is not improbable that breadth, length and height of a cusp are controlled by a single gene complex. Earlier we noted the probable genetic correlation of height of the dc cusp apex and molarisation of dm_1, as well as the possibility that facial profile, incisor implantation, incisor wear planes, diastemata, rotated canines, and age of appearance of a surface-to-surface incisor bite are secondary and tertiary effects of one morphogenetic process: suppression of the premaxilla. No doubt there are other developmental processes or morphogenetic fields in the early hominid dentition that await detection. Identification of these morphogenetic units simplifies our understanding of how the genetic basis underlying a *Ramapithecus* dentition was transformed into one like that of *Paranthropus*.

The key is that genes can effect the rate and timing of developmental processes. Individual genes by controlling patterns of differentiation can affect whole morphological units. Acceleration or retardation of a developmental pathway may result in a structure that had once appeared late in ontogeny now appearing earlier; or, depending on the rate and magnitude of the ontogenetic alteration, the structure may not even appear. Selection of such growth rates results in phylogenetic changes apparent in the adults (Haldane, 1932; De Beer, 1958). If we are to understand the logic, the plan, the how and why behind the cluttered morass of adult anatomy, we must turn to the child and to the study of embryonic and growth processes. And so it is with phylogeny: the 'causes' of phylogeny are to be found in ontogeny. Indeed, phylogeny is but a sequence of changing ontogenies; ontogeny recapitulates ontogeny, with variations in the rates of growth (De Beer, 1958).

The major phylogenetic trend in dental function from *Ramapithecus* to *Paranthropus* involved an ontogenetic alteration in growth rates. Dental and cranio-facial growth was accelerated in ontogeny so that a crushing-grinding occlusion would appear not long after the teeth had erupted. The genetic mechanism underlying this trend may have been very simple. For example, the flat face, the vertically implanted incisors, the flat incisal wear planes, the early development of a surface-to-surface incisor bite, and the rotated canines of *Paranthropus* may owe to nothing more than the introduction by genetic recombination of one or two alleles that accelerated the mitotic rate of osteoblasts in the premaxillary region. There is no need to invoke a multitude of mutations to account for the dental variation amongst the early hominids, or for the transformation of a *Ramapithecus* to an *Australopithecus* or an *Australopithecus* to a *Paranthropus*.

Origin of the hominids

The question here is why crushing and grinding was selected in *Ramapithecus* and not at all or to a lesser extent in contemporary species of *Dryopithecus*. The obvious (and simplest) answer is that *Ramapithecus* was eating harder, tougher foods; foods that had thicker outer coverings than those eaten by the early apes. An oval masticatory cycle coupled with incisors capable of powerful crushing can be regarded as an adaptation for breaking into, cracking apart, or splitting open hard, tough foods. Conversely, a vertical masticatory cycle might be interpreted as an adaptation for slicing and piercing either softer foods or fewer foods with thick outer coverings. In the evolution of the gorilla and chimpanzee, cusp height increased over that of the early dryopithecines (Pilbeam, 1972). This suggests, in the light of the functional relationship between cusp height and mastication, that a slicing-piercing form of mastication was being selected in the gorilla and chimpanzee lineages.

These pongids apparently evolved a masticatory mechanism for more effective slicing and piercing, whereas hominids from the time of *Ramapithecus* to *Paranthropus* became more proficient at crushing and grinding. The reason most likely is that the early chimpanzees and gorillas living in the forest and feeding mostly in the trees ate fewer foods with thick outer coats, whilst early hominids living on the ground found a wider variety of food items, most of which had thick outer coverings.[7] A crushing-grinding mode of mastication seemingly would be more effective than a slicing-piercing one not only for releasing nutrients locked beneath fibrous coats of seeds, nuts and fruits, but also for freeing those encased in chitinous exoskeletons and cornified integuments, such as found in invertebrates, and small amphibians, reptiles and mammals.

Jolly (1970) has suggested that the early hominids ate mostly 'small, hard objects' identified as seeds, because 'only seeds of grasses and annual herbs are widespread enough in open country to be a likely staple'. Perhaps seeds were present year round when and where *Ramapithecus* originated, but I think it unlikely this was true for the later representatives of this lineage. Dr R.A. Lubke of the Department of Botany of the University of Witwatersrand tells me that grass seeds today are available for two, or at most three, months of the year. If

7. Implicit in this hypothesis is the assumption that *Ramapithecus* lived on the ground, at least for most of its life. Preliminary examination of the teeth of *D. africanus*, *D. nyanzae* and *R. wickeri* suggested those of *Ramapithecus* had been more worn by dietary grit than by tooth-to-tooth contacts, whereas the converse seemed to be the case for *Dryopithecus*. *Ramapithecus* apparently had more dirt in its food presumably because it spent more time feeding on the ground. This hypothesis might be tested by counting the number of replicated scratches per unit area of enamel. Hopefully the individuals might be placed on a relative scale of time spent in the trees (or on the ground).

conditions on the South African highveld today are similar to those of the past, seeds probably were not present year-round. Of course, we cannot exclude the possibility that seeds were eaten. Indeed, seed eating seems likely – but only when seeds were in season. In other words, seeds probably were a selective factor, but not, I think, *the* selective factor. The selective factor was the ability to crush and grind effectively: to chew anything and everything edible they could get their hands on to stay alive. What was selected was efficient crushing and grinding. The lineage became specialized in intra-oral crushing and grinding of food.

Sterkfontein Homo

At Sterkfontein the Sts and TM fossils were found in the eastern end of the cave. Because the type specimen of Broom's *Plesianthropus* were found here, the eastern end of the Sterkfontein cave was called the Type Site. Eighteen m. west of the type quarry, miners had exposed a pocket of breccia that came to be called the West Pit. It was here in 1955 that Brain found the first Sterkfontein stone tools, a discovery which prompted Robinson to excavate the West Pit breccia. To the enlarged West Pit Robinson gave the name Sterkfontein Extention Site.

In the Extension breccia Robinson found a dm^1-dm^2-M^1 (SE 255), an M^2 (SE 1508), a lingual half of a probable M^2 (SE 1579), a $\underline{C}$ (SE 1937), and a lingual half of a P^3 (SE 2396). Robinson (1962) assigned these teeth to *Australopithecus*, save for SE 2396 which is catalogued as ? *Homo* ? *erectus* (Telanthropus). Tobias (1965) noted that the M^1 of SE 255 was small and approached the homologues of *H. habilis* rather than those of *Australopithecus* from the Sterkfontein Type Site and Makapansgat. Because of the small size of the M^1 and the P^3 (SE 255 and SE 2396), the reduction of the metacone in the M^2 (SE 1508), and the median position of the lingual ridge in the SE 1937 $\underline{C}$ – characters not seen in the Sts and TM specimens from the type site – I tentatively classify the Se hominids not as *Australopithecus* but as *Homo*. The only tooth class at present shared by the Sterkfontein and Swartkrans *Homo* is the P 3: both the SK 18a P_3 and the Se 2396 P^3 are small and have thin enamel.

Swartkrans Homo

In early 1949, Robinson found at Swartkrans a mandible bearing the left M_1-M_2-M_3 and the right M_2-M_3 (SK 15), an isolated P_3 (SK 18a) believed to belong to the mandible, and a proximal end of a radius (SK 18b) presumed to be from the same individual. The buccal half of an isolated P_4 (SK 43) was found at the same time and catalogued as belonging to the SK 15 mandible. Two months after these discoveries an incomplete mandibular corpus with a right M_1-M_2 (SK 45), and a palate with the stump of an I^2 and a fragmented P^3 (SK 80) were unearthed. The SK 15 mandible was described as the remains of a human-like creature, *Telanthropus capensis* (Broom and Robinson, 1952). In 1953 Robinson referred SK 18a, SKb, SK 45 and SK 80 to *T. capensis*, and in 1961 he sank *T. capensis* and transferred all the specimens to *H. erectus*.

In 1970 R.J. Clarke observed that SK 847, a cranial fragment with a left M^3, articulated perfectly along a break with the SK 80 maxilla. Moreover, a portion of a left temporal (SK 846b) could be brought into union with SK 847. The combined cranial complex of SK 80/847/846b was classified as *Homo* sp. (Clarke *et al.*, 1970). Clarke and Howell (1972) compared the cranial morphology of SK 80/847/846b with other Swartkrans hominids, adducing evidence that, contrary to Wolpoff (1971), this specimen is not a small, robust australopithecine but an early member of the genus *Homo*.

I now describe dental observations which support the assignment of SK 80/847/846b to *Homo* rather than to *Paranthropus*. The pattern of

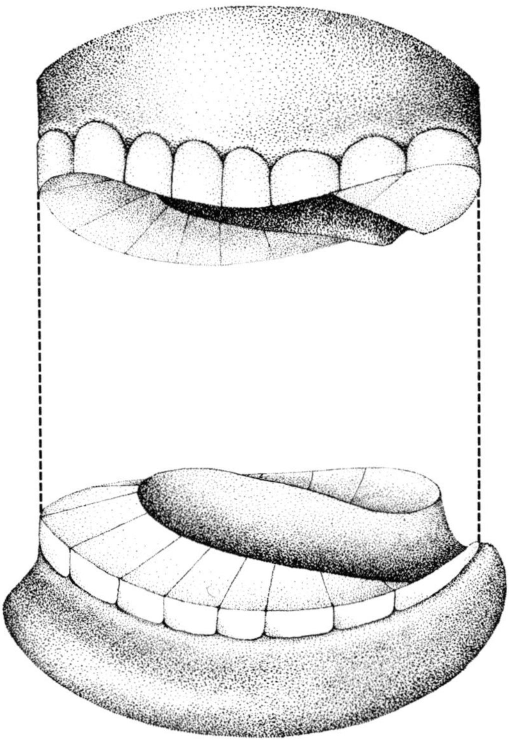

Figure 9. Helicoidal occlusal plane: the mesial zone is pitched bucally in the lower jaw, whereas in the upper jaw it is pitched lingually. The distal zone is pitched lingually in the lower jaw, and buccally in the upper jaw.

wear on the M^3 of SK 80/847/846b is unique among early hominid specimens from South Africa. The tooth is worn more on the buccal than the lingual half of the occlusal surface, and the first dentine exposure is on the mesiobuccal cusp. In all other South African early hominid M^3's sufficiently worn for this character to be discerned, the *lingual* half of the occlusal surface is more abraded than the buccal half, and the first dentine exposure is on the mesiolingual cusp. Murphy (1959) found that in Australian aborigines dentine is usually exposed first on the mesiolingual cusps of M^1 and M^2, but on the mesiobuccal cusp of M^3.

The pattern of wear seen on the M^3 of SK 80/847/846b is part of a helicoidal occlusal wear plane (Campbell, 1925; Moses, 1946; Ackermann, 1963). In a helicoidal or 'twisted' occlusal plane two zones can be distinguished, a mesial and a distal. The mesial zone includes the first molar and the mesial third of the second molar, whilst the distal zone embraces the distal two-thirds of the second molar and the whole of the occlusal surface of the third molar. The wear slopes of the two zones differ. In the mandible the mesial zone is bevelled downward and outward ('pitched bucally'), whereas the distal zone is bevelled downward and inward ('pitched lingually'). In the maxilla the pitch is reversed (Figure 9). Thus in an helicoidal plane, the buccal half of M^3 would be more worn than the lingual half. The helicoidal occlusal plane is a reflection of differences in width between upper and lower dental arches. In the mesial zone the upper arch is wider than the lower (positive overjet); at the place of transition, the pas helicoid, both arches are equally wide (0 overjet); and distally

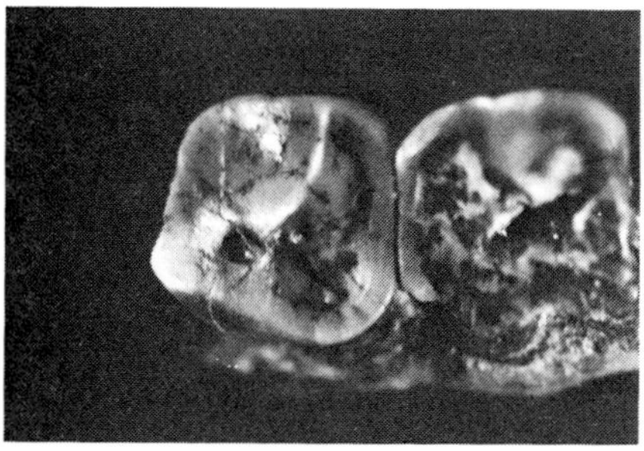

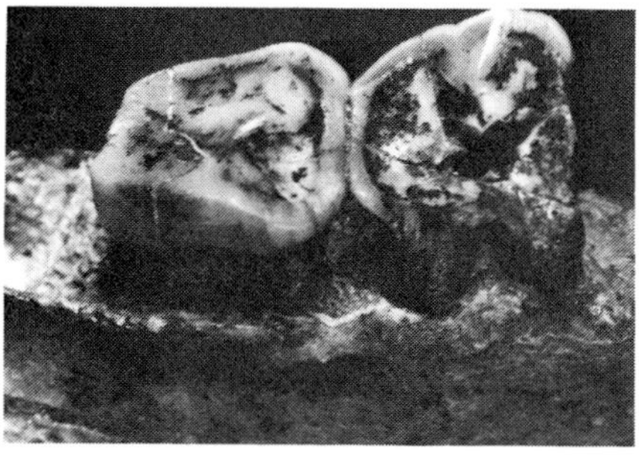

Figure 10. Helicoidal occlusal plane in SK 45: Note the buccal pitch on M_1 and the pas helicoid on M_2.

in the region of the third molar, the upper is narrower than the lower dental arch (negative overjet).

The only other South African early hominid specimen with a helicoidal occlusal wear plane is SK 45. In the M_1 the occlusal surface of dentine slopes bucco-cervically some 45° from a narrow strip of lingual enamel to reach the buccal enamel line. Mesiobuccally, the wear has passed on to the anterior root. In the M_2 the mesial third of the occlusal surface slopes buccocervically as does the M_1, but the distal two-thirds of the occlusal surface is worn flat. The buccal pitch and pas helicoid are shown in Figure 10.

Close study under the binocular microscope reveals that the distinctive micro-gouging of occlusal enamel on the M^3 of SK 80/847/846b is identical to that on the M_2 of SK 45. Moreover, the stain and colour of the jaw bones are almost identical. Because of these similarities – helicoidal occlusal planes, micro-gouging of occlusal enamel, and staining and colour of the jaw bones – I believe SK 45 and SK 80/847/846b belonged to the same individual.

Day and Leakey (1973) note that KNM-ER 730, a specimen they attribute to *Homo*, has a helicoidal occlusal wear plane.

A unique pattern of wear is seen in SK 15. The three buccal cusps and the mesiolingual cusp of the M_1 have almost equally sized dentine exposures, a feature which is not seen in any other Swartkrans M_1. In the M_2 of the SK 15 dentine has appeared almost simultaneously on the hypoconid and hypoconulid. In all other Swartkrans M_2's, the exposure on the hypoconid appears before that on the hypoconulid, as judged from the substantial size difference between these dentine exposures.

The molars of SK 15 are relatively smaller than those of *Paranthropus* and appear to have thinner enamel (Robinson 1953). The mesial surfaces of the left M_1 and the right M_2 of SK 15 are carious. These are the only two South African early hominid teeth with approximal caries. Clement (1956) who described the lesions said they were typical of those associated with 'the breakdown of the contact point and the subsequent interproximal impaction of food debris'. The presence in SK 15 but absence in other Swartkrans hominids of approximal caries suggests that SK 15 had a relatively rapid rate of approximal attrition. Another comparison illustrates the high rate of approximal attrition in SK 15. The M_2's of SK 23, SK 34 and SK 15 are at a similar stage of occlusal wear, but relative to M_2 and M_1 of SK 15 is much more worn approximally. This apparent rapid loss of approximal enamel suggests that SK 15 has thinner enamel than *Paranthropus*. Observations on the broken molars of KNM-ER 808, a specimen assigned to *Homo* (Leakey and Wood, 1973), confirms my suspicion that dentally early *Homo* is distinguished from *Australopithecus* and *Paranthropus* by possession of smaller teeth with thinner enamel.

Sterkfontein, Makapansgat, and Taung Australopithecus

Robinson (1967) classifies the Sterkfontein (Sts and TM̆), Makapansgat and Taung specimens as *Homo*. I do not, because they lack the complex of dental features found in the Swartkrans *Homo*, and (this is the more important reason) there is no evidence that they made stone tools. Stone tools have not been found in the Type quarry, nor in the grey breccia of Makapansgat, nor at Taung. I suspect, based on comparison with the well-dated Omo hominid teeth, that the Sterkfontein, Makapansgat, and Taung specimens represent populations from which *Paranthropus* and *Homo* evolved. The test of this hypothesis turns on the date of Sterkfontein, Makapansgat and Taung, relative to the KBS tuff and the East Rudolf stone tools. Until reliable dates are forthcoming we are left with suspicions and hunches based only on morphology as to the genetic relationship of these specimens to those at the Sterkfontein extension site, Swartkrans, Omo, East Rudolf and Olduvai.

Origin of Homo

For at least 10 million years hominids had relied on their teeth for 'chewing'. At some time between 2.5 and 3 million years ago, a dentally 'gracile' australopithecine, perhaps much like those at Sterkfontein and Makapansgat, discovered a better, a more efficient way of 'chewing', namely stones. This hominid who substituted sharpened stones for his teeth to split apart the tough outer coverings of foods was the first *Homo*, the first hominid to escape from selection for reduction of cusp height and early fusion of the premaxilla.[8] Now largely removed from teeth, selection focused on the brain, and as the record attests the brain began to blossom (Tobias, 1971, this volume; Holloway, this volume).

The origin of *Homo* – the origin of stone tools – was a response, I believe, to the challenge of finding a more effective method than teeth for penetrating the skin/bone/muscular body wall of animals. Stones were the dissecting instruments, albeit crude, for bashing brain boxes to gain the brain; for cracking rib cages to uncover the heart and lungs; for smashing long bones to expose the marrow, for slicing the thick-skinned anterior abdominal wall to lay bare the kidneys, liver, spleen and stomach contents; and for sawing the tough, fibrous joint ligaments to free a limb for transport to home base.

8. The diastema of Pithecanthropus IV might be interpreted as a consequence of a relaxation in selection pressure.

Other populations of gracile australopithecines maintained the status quo, doing what their ancestors had done before: crushing and grinding food with their teeth. Selection intensified both for early fusion of the premaxillary suture and low cusps with the result there emerged a creature we recognize as *Paranthropus*. For at least a million years two hominid lineages co-existed: one (*Paranthropus*) was crushing and grinding the food inside the mouth with teeth, the other (*Homo*) was crushing and grinding the food mainly outside the mouth with stone tools.

Extinction of Paranthropus

The most recent specimen of *Paranthropus* at Olduvai is OH 3 from upper Bed II, bearing an estimated date of 1 m.y. (Hay, 1971). The Peninj and Chesowanja *Paranthropus* fall within the time range of 1-1.5 m.y. (Carney *et al.*, 1971; Isaac, 1967). *Paranthropus* probably became extinct without issue at *c.* 1 m.y. The beginning of the end of *Paranthropus* coincides with the appearance of *Homo erectus* and the Acheulian (Leakey, 1971; Isaac, 1972). By this time (1.5 m.y.), *Homo* had, we may surmise, increased in number, expanded in body size to equal or exceed *Paranthropus*, and habitually hunted and butchered large animals with stone tools such as hand-axes and cleavers. Organized hunting had now become a way of life for *Homo*, and one of the prey was *Paranthropus*. *Homo*, whose appearance on the African landscape probably brought *Paranthropus* into existence, now a million years later brought extinction. Teeth, a beautiful, functionally integrated set of teeth, a product of 14 million years of evolution, could not compete with an expanded brain and a hand that held a tool.

Acknowledgments

I am deeply grateful to Dr C.K. Brain, Mr R.E.F. Leakey, Prof. P.V. Tobias, Prof. F.C. Howell, and Mr F.T. Masao for permission to examine the fossil hominids in their care. This work was supported by the Wenner-Gren Foundation for Anthropological Research.

References

Ackermann, F. (1963) The helicoid principle in human dental occlusion and articulation. *Int. Dent. J.* 13, 532-57.

Ahlgren, J. (1966) Mechanism of mastication: a quantitative cinematographic and electromyographic study of masticatory movements in children, with special reference to occlusion of the teeth. *Acta. Odont. Scand.* 24 (Suppl. 44), 1-109.

Andrews, P. (1971) *Ramapithecus wickeri* mandible from Fort Ternan, Kenya. *Nature* 231, 192-4.
Andrews, P. (1974) Personal communication.
Begg, P.R. (1965) *Orthodontic Theory and Technique*. Philadelphia.
Beyron, H. (1964) Occlusal relations and mastication in Australian aborigines. *Acta. Odont. Scand.* 22, 597-678.
Bishop, W.W., Miller, J. and Fitch, F. (1969) New potassium-argon age determinations relevant to the Miocene fossil mammal sequence in East Africa. *Amer. J. Sci.* 267, 669-99.
Bishop, W.W. and Chapman, G.R. (1970) Early Pliocene sediments and fossils from the northern Kenya rift valley. *Nature* 226, 914-18.
Bishop, W.W. (1974) Personal communication.
Broom, R. and Robinson, J.T. (1952) Swartkrans Ape-Man, *Paranthropus crassidens*. *Trans. Mus. Mem.* No. 6.
Campbell, T.D. (1925) *Dentition and Palate of the Australian Aboriginal*. Adelaide.
Carney, J., Hill, A., Miller, J.A. and Walker, A. (1971) Late australopithecine from Baringo district, Kenya. *Nature* 230, 509-14.
Clarke, R.J., Howell, F.C. and Brain, C.K. (1970) More evidence of an advanced hominid at Swartkrans. *Nature* 225, 1219-21.
Clarke, R.J. and Howell, F.C. (1972) Affinities of the Swartkrans 847 hominid cranium. *Amer. J. phys. Anthrop.* 37, 319-35.
Clement, A.J. (1956) Caries in the South African ape-man: some examples of undoubted pathological authenticity believed to be 800,000 years old. *Brit. Dent. J.* 101, 4-7.
Cooke, H.B.S. (1963) Pleistocene mammal faunas of Africa, with particular reference to southern Africa. In Howell, F.C. and Bourlière, F. (eds.), *African Ecology and Human Evolution*, 65-116. Chicago.
Conroy, G.C. and Pilbeam, D. (in press) *Ramapithecus*: A review of its hominid status. In *Antecedents of Man and After* (ed. R.H. Tuttle), Proc. IX Int. Cong. Anthrop. Ethnol. Sc.
Day, M.H. and Leakey, R.E. (1973) New evidence of the genus *Homo* from East Rudolf, Kenya. I. *Amer. J. phys. Anthrop.* 39, 341-54.
De Beer, G.R. (1958) *Embryos and Ancestors* (3rd ed.). Oxford.
Ewer, R.F. and Cooke, H.B.S. (1964) The Pleistocene mammals of southern Africa. In Davies, D.H.S. (ed.), *Ecological Studies in Southern Africa*, 35-48. The Hague.
Haldane, J.B.S. (1932) The time of action of genes and its bearing on some evolutionary problems. *Am. Nat.* 66, 5-24.
Hasund, A. and Ulstein, G. (1970) The position of the incisors in relation to the lines NA and NB in different facial types. *Amer. J. Orthodont.* 57, 1-14.
Hay, R.L. (1971) Geologic background of Beds I and II. In Leakey, M.D.
Hildebrand, Y. (1936) Studies in mandibular kinematics. *Dental Cosmos* 78, 449-58.
Hojo, M. (1954) On the pattern of the dental abrasion. *Okaj. Folia anat. Jap.* 26, 11-30.
Ingervall, B. (1972) Tooth contacts on the functional and non-functional side in children and young adults. *Arch. Oral. Biol.* 17, 191-200.
Isaac, G.L. (1967) The stratigraphy of the Peninj Group/Early Middle Pleistocene formations west of Lake Natron, Tanzania. In Bishop, W.W. and Clark, J.D. (eds.), *Background to Evolution in Africa*. Chicago.

Isaac, G.L. (1972) Chronology and tempo of cultural change during the Pleistocene. In Bishop, W.W. and Miller, J.A. (eds.), *Calibration of Hominoid Evolution*, 381-40. Edinburgh.

Jolly, C.J. (1970) The seed-eaters: a new model of hominid differentiation based on a baboon analogy. *Man* 5, 126.

Koivumaa, K.K. (1961) Cinefluorographic analysis of the masticatory movements. *Suom. Hammaslaak Toim.* 57, 306-36 (quoted from Ingervall, B., 1972).

Kraus, B.S. and Decker, J.D. (1960) The prenatal inter-relationships of the maxilla and premaxilla in the facial development of man. *Acta. Anat.* 40, 278-94.

Krogman, W.M. (1930) Studies in growth changes in the skull and face of anthropoids. *Am. J. Anat.* 46, 315-53.

Leakey, L.S.B. (1962) A new lower Pliocene fossil primate from Kenya. *Ann. Mag. Nat. Hist.* 4, 689-96.

Leakey, M.D. (ed.) (1971) *Olduvai Gorge*, Volume III: *Excavations in Beds I and II, 1960-1963.* London.

Leakey, R.E.F. and Wood, B.A. (1973) New evidence of the genus *Homo* from East Rudolf, Kenya II. *Amer. J. phys. Anthrop.* 39, 355-68.

Lewis, G.E. (1934) Preliminary notice of new man-like apes from India. *Amer. J. Sci.* 27, 161-79.

Lewis, G.E. (1937) Taxonomic syllabus of Siwalik fossil anthropoids. *Amer. J. Sci.* 34, 139-47.

Montagu, M.F.A. (1935) The premaxilla in the primates. *Quart. Rev. Biol.* 10, 32-59 and 181-200.

Moses, C.H. (1946) Studies of wear, arrangement and occlusion of the dentition of humans and animals and their relationship to orthodontia, periodontia and prosthodontia. *Dental Items* 68, 953-99.

Murphy, T.R. (1959) The changing pattern of dentine exposure in human tooth attrition. *Amer. J. phys. Anthrop.* 17, 167-78.

Murphy, T.R. (1965) The timing and mechanism of the human masticatory stroke. *Arch. Oral Biol.* 10, 981-93.

Partridge, T.C. (1973) Geomorphological dating of cave openings at Makapansgat, Sterkfontein, Swartkrans and Taung. *Nature* 246, 75-9.

Pilbeam, D. (1972) Evolutionary changes in the hominoid dentition through geological time. In Bishop, W.W. and Miller, J.A. (eds.), *Calibration of Hominoid Evolution*, 369-80. Edinburgh.

Robinson, J.T. (1953) *Telanthropus* and its phylogenetic significance. *Amer. J. phys. Anthrop.* 11, 445-501.

Robinson, J.T. (1956) *The dentition of the Australopithecinae. Trans. Mus. Mem.* No. 9.

Robinson, J.T. (1960) An alternative interpretation of the supposed giant deciduous hominid tooth from Olduvai. *Nature* 185, 407-8.

Robinson, J.T. (1961) The australopithecines and their bearing on the origin of man and of stone tool-making. *S. Afr. J. Sci.* 57, 3-13.

Robinson, J.T. (1962) Australopithecines and artifacts at Sterkfontein, Part 1: Sterkfontein stratigraphy and the significance of the extension site. *S. Afr. arch. Bull.* 17, 87-107.

Robinson, J.T. (1967) Variation and taxonomy of the early hominids. In Dobzhansky, T., Hecht, M.K. and Steere, W.C. (eds.), *Evolutionary Biology*, Volume 1, 69-100. New York.

Shepherd, R.W. (1960) A further report on mandibular movement. *Aust. Dent. J.* 5, 337-42.

Simons, E.L. (1968) A source for dental comparison of *Ramapithecus* with *Australopithecus* and *Homo. S. Afr. J. Sci.* 64, 92-112.

Simons, E.L., Pilbeam, D. and Boyer, S. (1971) Appearance of *Hipparion* in the Tertiary of the Siwalik Hills of North India, Kashmire and West Pakistan. *Nature* 229, 408.

Simpson, G.G. (1950) Some principles of historical biology bearing on human origins. In *Cold Spring Harbour Symposia on Quantitative Biology, Origin and Evolution of Man*, XV, 5566.

Simpson, G.G. (1951) *Horses: The Story of the Horse Family in the Modern World Through Sixty Million Years of History.* New York.

Tobias, P.V. (1965) New discoveries in Tanganyika: their bearing on hominid evolution. *Curr. Anthrop.* 6, 391-411.

Tobias, P.V. (1967) *Olduvai Gorge*, Volume II: *The Cranium and Maxillary Dentition of Australopithecus (Zinjanthropus) boisei.* London.

Tobias, P.V. and Hughes, A. (1969) The new Witwatersrand University excavation at Sterkfontein. *S. Afr. arch. Bull.* 24, 158-69.

Tobias, P.V. (1971) *The Brain in Hominid Evolution.* New York.

Walker, A. and Andrews, P. (1973) Reconstruction of the dental arcades of *Ramapithecus wickeri. Nature* 244, 313-14.

Wallace, J.A. (1973) Tooth chipping in the australopithecines. *Nature* 244, 117-18.

Weidenreich, F. (1937) The dentition of *Sinanthropus*: a comparative odontography of the hominids. *Paleont. Sinica.* 10, 1-180 and 1-121.

Weidenreich, F. (1945) Giant early man from Java and South China. *Anthrop. Pap. Am. Mus. Nat. Hist.* 40 (1), 1-134.

Wheeler, R.C. (1965) *Dental Anatomy and Physiology* (4th ed.). Philadelphia.

Wolpoff, M.H. (1971) Is the new composite cranium from Swartkrans a small robust australopithecine? *Nature* 230, 398-401.

Zeisz, R.C. and Nuckolls, J. (1946) *Dental Anatomy.* St. Louis.

M.H. Day

Functional interpretations of the morphology of postcranial remains of early African hominids

Introduction

Since the initial discoveries of South African early hominid remains at the Transvaal sites of Taung, Sterkfontein, Swartkrans and Kromdraai, a number of sites in East Africa have provided a great deal of new material. These sites include Olduvai Gorge, Tanzania; North Kenyan sites such as Lothagam, Kanapoi, Chesowanja, Chemeron, and East Rudolf; the Omo region, and, most recently, Hadar, both in Ethiopia. Amongst this comparative wealth of fossil remains a steadily increasing number of postcranial bones have been recovered that have added greatly to knowledge of the morphology of the limbs of early hominids. These bones have provided functional and taxonomic insights that were previously either doubtful or simply lacking. The functional insights have, however, often led to suggestions as to the locomotor capabilities of the early hominids, capabilities often themselves regarded as *a priori* taxonomic criteria. The dangers of circularity of argument are obvious here but they have not always been heeded.

A preliminary functional interpretation of previously unknown postcranial bones is most easily accomplished by comparative anatomical methods; this involves the identification in modern forms of homologous structures, and combinations of structures whose functional significance is known from field or laboratory observations on the living. Naturally since the anatomy of modern man is better known than that of any other living primate it forms the principal basis of most comparative studies of related hominids; but even here detailed knowledge of the biomechanical basis of stance, gait, joint movement and muscular activity is restricted both in range and in depth. There is commonly a lack of precision in the use of words and phrases such as 'upright', 'bipedal' and 'manipulative ability' that clouds discussions since the meaning of these terms often appears to relate to a comparison with the modern human condition. Thus early hominid locomotor abilities tend to be described in terms that suggest 'imperfect' adaptations by comparison with *Homo sapiens*, an attitude that is unacceptable in other fields of biology and recalls the Platonic concept of the 'ideal type'.

It is my feeling that a change of attitude in this area may prove rewarding if the fossils are analysed from the viewpoint of the evidence that they show of early hominid adaptation to the early hominid environment. Here the new fields of local palaeoecology and palaeogeography that are being explored by some members of the East Rudolf expedition have great promise. Only a detailed knowledge of the environmental problems that beset the early hominids will lead to reasonable functional interpretations of the skeletal remains that we have.

What we should seek is the modal phenotype of each of the groups to which we have access from the fossil record, accepting that geographic and temporal variation may well have progressed to the level of subspeciation many times in the Pleistocene history of the Hominidae. Whether or not this variation has left a record imprinted on fossil bones and teeth is a continuing problem, while the total numbers of available fossils remain a tiny sample of the populations from which they were drawn.

With this in mind it is my purpose to review the spectrum of early hominid postcranial remains, in terms of their functional adaptations, as determined from the viewpoint of anatomy assisted at times by the statistical treatment of numerical data – well aware that true metrical comparisons should be made with comparable fossils and not only with modern counterparts.

The upper limb girdle

The scapula

This, the most fragile of the upper limb girdle bones, is seldom preserved for examination in the hominid record.

Sts 7

A small fragment of hominid scapula, including the glenoid, is known from Sterkfontein and has been described (Broom, Robinson and Schepers, 1950). It is badly crushed and not fully developed from the matrix. It consists of a broken glenoid with a small portion of the spine; part of the acromion was present originally but has become lost. In a discussion of the specimen, Robinson (1972) emphasized the limitations imposed by the poor state of this specimen, and strongly questioned the suggestion that this scapula fits into the brachiating locomotor group (Oxnard, 1968) on the grounds that critical data are unavailable on the fossil. No reconstruction of this scapula has been published. Campbell (1967) appears to conclude that this fragment suggests 'some degree of brachiation in the ancestry of hominids'. Oxnard (1968) finally draws two possible but alternative conclusions, both of which he regards as unlikely. One is that considerable reassessment of the locomotor pattern of *Australopithecus* may be necessary since it has been generally thought that forms ancestral to man had not exhibited 'those highly specialized features associated in the arboreal gibbon and orang-utan with effective arm suspension'. The alternative conclusion is that 'the fragment does not belong to *Australopithecus* but to some other ape living at the same time'.

The scapular fragment from Sterkfontein is anatomically inadequate and poorly preserved; the missing parts are unrestored and the scanty metrical data often consist of 'best estimates'. Upon this shaky edifice ideas have been put forward as to the possible locomotor category of the genus *Australopithecus*. In my view discussions such as those outlined above tend to confuse important issues rather than to clarify them.

KNM-ER 1500(0) (Leakey, 1973, Day, 1978a)

A left-sided fragment of scapular glenoid with preservation of the infraglenoid tubercle. A gracile bone associated with the remainder of an australopithecine partial skeleton. Few useful locomotor conclusions can be drawn from this fragment alone.

The clavicle

MLD 20 (Boné, 1955)

Examination of this 'clavicular' fragment reveals that it is neither hominid nor clavicular. It seems most likely to be an equid phalanx (Walker, pers. comm.). It should be removed from the hominid fossil record.

OH 48

Two clavicles have been reported from Bed I deposits at Olduvai Gorge (Leakey, 1960). This appears to be an error since only one specimen is known (OH 48). This clavicle has been reconstructed and compared with a large number of modern clavicles belonging to *Homo sapiens, Pan, Gorilla* and *Pongo* as well as a series of fossil clavicles from Willey's Kopje, Nakuru and Pin Hole Cave. It was possible to match the Olduvai clavicle with a single modern human clavicle in terms of general morphology with the sole exception of a smooth groove situated postero-inferiorly at the medial end. It is possible that this was caused by pressure from the subclavian vessels and the brachial plexus. Canonical analysis of 10 clavicular dimensions did not separate this clavicle significantly from modern human groups. Unfortunately the angle of clavicular torsion, used by Ashton and Oxnard (1964) in their analyses of shoulder girdle function, is not available on this specimen. Since both ends are missing, neither of the points needed for determining this angle are present. In addition, radiographic analysis shows the shaft to be internally fractured in many places so that the longitudinal integrity of the bone is not assured. Locomotor suggestions based on the 'torsion' angle of this fossil (Oxnard, 1969) should, therefore, be regarded with caution.

Speculations upon the functional anatomy of the early hominid shoulder girdle must remain cautious since the material gives little or no clue to posture or usage. Key joints such as the sternoclavicular joint and the acromioclavicular joint, are quite unknown, while the form of the only clavicle known suggests that its function did not differ significantly from that known in modern man. The sheer size of the clavicle, however, is of interest, since it is proportionately very much larger than the adult remains attributed to *Homo habilis*, such as the OH 8 foot and OH 35 tibia and fibula. While it may be 'man-like' in size and shape, no australopithecine clavicle is known with which to compare it.

The arm

The humerus

Sts 7

A well preserved head of a right humerus with a crushed surgical neck and part of the shaft is known from Sterkfontein (Broom, Robinson and Schepers, 1950). The head is well rounded with prominent muscular markings for the short scapular muscles and a deep intertubercular groove for the long head of biceps. It has been reassessed recently (Robinson, 1972) and compared with a number of other humeri. Functional conclusions would seem to be limited to the possession of free ranging shoulder movement with well developed stabilizing short scapular muscles and a powerful biceps brachii.

Sts 14

A fragment of humerus shaft that is doubtfully hominid (Boné and Dart, 1955; Boné, 1955); of little or no value for functional assessment.

TM 1517

A distal end of humerus that is well known as part of the hypodigm of

Paranthropus robustus, (Broom and Schepers, 1946; Le Gros Clark, 1947; Straus, 1948). Both Broom and Le Gros Clark believed it to be very similar to that of modern man. Straus took a contrary view and saw many pongid features in the specimen; he also felt that the lower end of the humerus was of 'extremely limited value in taxonomic and phylogenetic studies' and that its structure was unable to predict the 'structure and usage of the forelimb'. Robinson (1972) 'agrees basically' with Straus's conclusions. McHenry (1972) published the results of a multivariate analysis of measurements taken from a group of hominoid humeri into which the TM 1517 humerus was interpolated. The results were consistent with the hypothesis that locomotor groups can be distinguished by this method and that TM 1517 fell with the bipeds.

Kanapoi

A lower end of humerus. A comparative study of this specimen (Patterson and Howells, 1967) including a discriminant function analysis concluded that the Kanapoi specimen was even more 'manlike' than TM 1517 from Kromdraai and quite unlikely to be of the same lineage since, although 'earlier' in time, it is more hominine. Unfortunately the Transvaal sites are in my view still not reliably dated, despite recent work (Partridge, 1973).

Examination of this fossil has disclosed no features that indicate a particular form of locomotion such as knuckle-walking, brachiation or terrestrial quadrupedalism; indeed it is hard to point to a single anatomical feature or group of features not well known in modern man. Functionally it must be nearly identical with the modern human condition. This opinion based upon morphology is borne out by a metrical analysis conducted by McHenry (1972); using both ratios and raw data he concluded that the Kanapoi humerus bears a close resemblance to man and fell in the bipedal locomotor category.

KNM-ER 739 (Fig. 1)

This humerus was recovered in 1970 and reported by Leakey (1971). It consists of the lower end and the greater part of the shaft lacking only the head and surgical neck; it has been described by Leakey, Mungai and Walker (1972). In brief it is a long and robust humerus with many powerful muscular markings. The complete lower end discloses a well rounded capitulum and an olecranon fossa that lacks any feature that would indicate specialisation for knuckle-walking. Its length must raise the question of arborealism but its sheer size would appear to rule out brachiation as an habitual mode of locomotion, suggesting that any arboreal traits are merely evidence of a relatively recent common ancestry with more arboreal forms. The muscular marking for deltoid is massive, that for brachioradialis very large and

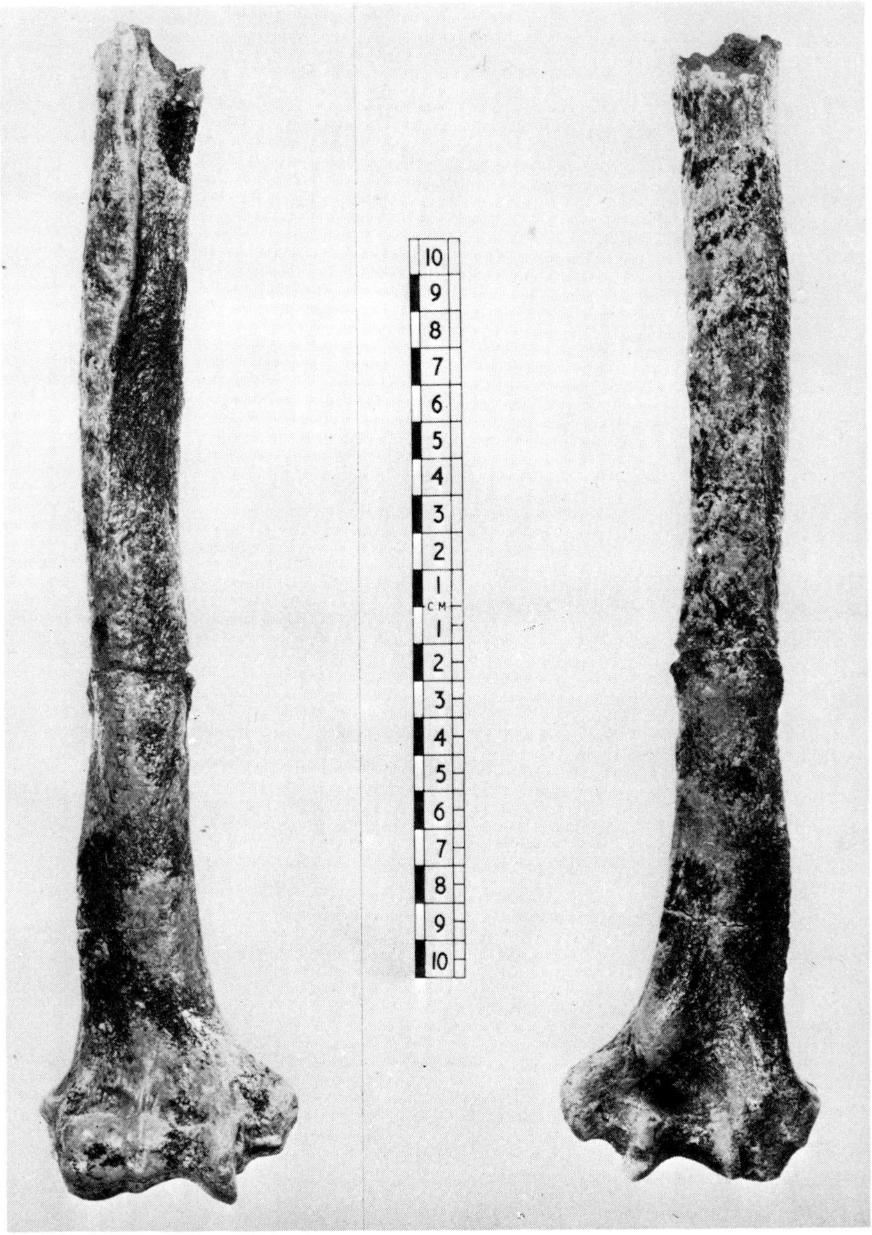

Figure 1. KNM-ER 739: a right hominid humerus from East Rudolf. L. Anterior aspect. R. Posterior aspect.

the common flexor and extensor origins are very pronounced. Abduction of the shoulder was clearly a powerful movement, flexion of the elbow as well as pronation and supination were free and powerful, and the superficial flexor and the extensor groups of the forearm were strong, indicating powerful extrinsic hand musculature.

The total combination of morphological features shown by this humerus would seem to be outside the range of that known for *Homo sapiens* and probably also of the genus *Homo*. A recent assessment of the humeral fragment, following a multiple discriminant function analysis of 18 dimensions taken upon the fossil and upon comparative samples from *Homo sapiens, Gorilla gorilla* (♂ and ♀), *Pongo pygmaeus* (♂ and ♀), *Pan troglodytes* and *Pan paniscus*, has shown the morphological uniqueness of the fossil (McHenry 1973). Wisely the question of habitual bipedalism coupled with that of the possible manipulative use of the forelimb in this form has been left open. However, no knuckle-walking functional affinities seem to be apparent in this fossil.

KNM-ER 740 (Leakey, 1971)

A fragment of the distal end of an adult left humerus with part of the shaft and part of the epicondyle. It has a shallow olecranon fossa with no knuckle walking specialization. This fossil is similar to ER 739 but from a smaller individual.

KNM-ER 1473 (Leakey, 1973)

The head of an adult right humerus with some erosion of the articular surface. Part of the greater tuberosity is present with part of the supraspinatus insertion, part of infraspinatus insertion and the subscapularis insertion. There is a very broad intertubercular groove. The head is hemispherical and all of the anatomical neck is present. The surgical neck is eroded away. Functional information is limited to the evidence for a freely mobile shoulder joint with good evidence of stabilizing rotator-cuff musculature.

KNM-ER 1500(l) (Leakey, 1973)

A small supracondylar fragment of humerus with very little anatomical detail. Its only significance is that it forms part of a truly associated australopithecine partial skeleton.

KNM-ER 1504 (Leakey, 1973)

A fragment of the distal end of an adult humerus. It has a shallow olecranon fossa, divided trochlear and capitular fossae and a prominent medial epicondyle. It is smaller than ER 739 but similar in shape.

KNM-ER 1591 (Leakey, 1973)

A right humeral shaft fragment, that lacks both head and distal ends, associated with a trochlear fragment. Functional deductions are limited.

No hominid humeral remains are known from Olduvai Gorge, Tanzania.

The forearm

The radius

SK 18b

A proximal radial fragment known from Swartkrans (Broom and Robinson, 1949) that was attributed to '*Telanthropus capensis*'. Subsequently this fossil was given 'euhominid' status and transferred to *Homo erectus* (Robinson, 1953) without detailed comparison of comparable material from this taxon. It is simply stated to be 'as in modern hominids'. Examination discloses it to be an adult left radial head and neck and part of the shaft bearing a well marked radial tubercle. This tubercle has a rough posterior portion for the tendon of biceps and a smooth anterior portion for the play of the tendon in pronation and supination. The neck has a well defined 'tide-mark' for the reflection of the synovial membrane while the head is rounded and recessed for the compound movement of pronation and supination in flexion or extension. The size of the radial tubercle suggests a powerful biceps brachii with functions both as a supinator in flexion and as an auxiliary flexor of the elbow.

Sts 68

This unpublished proximal end of radius from Sterkfontein is very dubiously hominid. The head is asymmetrically set on the shaft, the rim of the head is very thin and the radial tuberosity although damaged appears to be markedly dimpled. It is possible that it belongs to a fossil baboon. It is not mentioned in a recent reappraisal of hominid postcranial remains from this area (Robinson 1972).

OH 49 (unpublished)

A section of the mid-shaft of a right radius that has recently been recognized as hominid. It was recovered in 1960 from the floor that produced Olduvai Hominids 7 and 8. It is approximately 90 mm. long, gently curved, bears a sharp interosseous border, a clear marking for pronator teres insertion and the oblique lines of the anterior surface. It would appear to have functional characters, such as they are, identical with those of modern man.

KNM-ER 803 (Leakey, 1972; Day and Leakey, 1974)

A very similar fragment to OH 49; part of the left mid-shaft region bearing the pronator teres insertion. Functionally appears identical with that of modern man.

KNM-ER 1500(e) (Leakey, 1973; Day, 1976a)

Head, neck and a short length of shaft of a right radius. Small, gracile rounded neck with capitular depression. Part of an australopithecine partial skeleton.

KNM-ER 1500(k) (Leakey, 1973; Day, 1976a)

Fragment of right radius shaft, lower one-third, sharp interosseous border, flattened ventral surface, oval proximal section. Part of an australopithecine partial skeleton.

The ulna

TM 1517

A small fragment associated with the humerus of the same number from Kromdraai. Described by Broom (in Broom and Schepers, 1946) and discussed by Le Gros Clark (1947) and Robinson (1972). This tiny scrap of ulna shows no significant features that would indicate any functional differences from that of modern man. Although it is small it appears to fit the humeral fragment and should probably be considered in association with it as a functional complex.

Omo Locality 40(40-19) (Howell and Wood, 1974)

This almost complete ulna recovered in 1971 is somewhat crushed but its anatomy is generally well preserved. It was recovered from a layer that underlies a tuff dated at 2.04 m.y. BP. In the preliminary description of the ulna it has been stated that the fossil resembles modern human ulnae in many respects but not in all; features that depart from the human condition include its length, dorso-ventral shaft curvature, cross-sectional shaft profile, some features of the muscle attachment patterns and the shape of the ulnar head. The length is said to fall within the ranges of both *Gorilla* and *Homo*, the curvature index falls outside the human range but within that of the 'knuckle-walkers'. Overall the functional implications of these differences are said to point to an elongated forearm with some adaptations 'not unlike those seen in modern knuckle-walkers' yet it is wisely suggested that the morphological and functional evidence seen in the specimen are insufficient to infer that it is an arboreal form in process of adapting to terrestrial life.

Features of the Omo ulna that would argue strongly against 'knuckle-walking' are the 'set' of the articular surface of the upper end in relation to the shaft and the relative weakness and lack of buttressing of the coronoid process. Both *Gorilla* and *Pan* ulnae show a marked obliquity of 'set' of the upper end and prominent well-buttressed coronoid processes to help withstand weight-transfer through the upper limb to the ground.

In addition, the Omo ulna shows a notably weak hollow for the play of the radial tuberosity suggesting that biceps brachii may not have been large.

Detailed functional considerations must await its full description but it appears to possess none of the terrestrial adaptations of the baboon ulna and few of those of the 'knuckle-walking' great apes. In both these respects it resembles the ER 739 humerus and shares with that humerus some adaptations that may simply indicate a common arboreal ancestry.

KNM-ER 803(c) (Leakey, 1972; Day 1976a)

A broken section of left ulna whose general features are similar to those of modern man. It has a prominent interosseous border, a supinator crest and a well marked hollow for the play of the tuberosity of the radius. This ulna is part of an associated skeleton attributed to the genus *Homo* (Day and Leakey, 1974).

KNM-ER 1500(b) (Leakey, 1973; Day 1976a)

The olecranon process, coronoid process and the trochlear notch are all present on the proximal end of a right ulna. The fragment is small and gracile and bears insertions for triceps on the olecranon and for supinator on a crest. Functionally it is unremarkable but morphologically the upper end bears a general resemblance to the Omo ulna. The ER 1500 partial skeleton is regarded as australopithecine.

The hand

TM 1562

Described by Broom and Schepers (1946) and referred to by Le Gros Clark (1947 and 1967) as hominid, this capitate is small and well preserved. Le Gros Clark's conclusion that this bone has a 'human appearance' has been challenged (Lewis, 1973). In a detailed comparative study of the wrist, but working from a cast of the relevant fossil, Lewis concludes that none of the 'essentially human specializations associated with the precision grip were realized in the Sterkfontein capitate'. Even further he asserts that the lack of 'progressive hominoid features' in the australopithecine bone argues for a relatively recent separation of the australopithecine and African great ape lines – a bold conclusion to draw from the cast of one fossil capitate and comparative studies without metrical analysis.

SK 84 and SK 85

These two metcarpals, a first and a broken fourth, were described by Napier (1959). The first was allocated to '*Paranthropus*' and the fourth to '*Telanthropus*'. The fourth metacarpal could not be distinguished morphologically or functionally from that of *Homo sapiens* but the first metacarpal was distinctive in a number of ways. Short, curved, with a beaked distal articular surface and pronounced sesamoid grooves, it was said to be pongid in many respects. In essence Robinson (1972) agrees with Napier's assessment.

A multivariate analysis (Rightmire, 1972) relating to the Swartkrans thumb metacarpal has shown that Discriminants 1 and 2 (accounting for 90.5% of the total variance) place the fossil nearest to the *Homo sapiens* centroids. Discriminant 3 (accounting for only 8% of the total variance and said to be based mainly on size alone) separates the various genera and allies the fossil with *Pan*.

As Rightmire (1972) notes, Discriminant 1 does not disperse the known locomotor groups in a fashion that reflects pollical capability, and this would seem to indicate that the selected dimensions are less functionally relevant than would have been desirable.

SKW 14147

A perfect fossil fifth metacarpal from Swartkrans has been described recently (Day and Scheuer, 1973). In almost all respects it is similar to its modern human counterpart differing only in some morphological details of the base that do not appear to affect its function. Lack of known comparative material from *Australopithecus* or *Homo erectus* coupled with minor differences between the fossil and the modern series has led to its allocation to *Hominidae* (*gen. et sp. indet*) for the present. However, that there was a hominid creature at Swartkrans at least capable of a power grip seems to be indicated by the find.

TM 1517 (Figures 2 and 3)

Of the TM 1517 assemblage, specimens (e), (f), (h), (k) and (n) are identified here as foot bones while (i), (j), (m) and (o) are regarded as hand bones.

(h) This was described (Broom and Schepers, 1946) as a broken second metacarpal of the left side. Doubts expressed by Day and Scheuer (1973) concerning its correct identification have been reinforced. We feel that it may be a third or fourth metatarsal of the right side belonging to either a baboon or even a carnivore. The

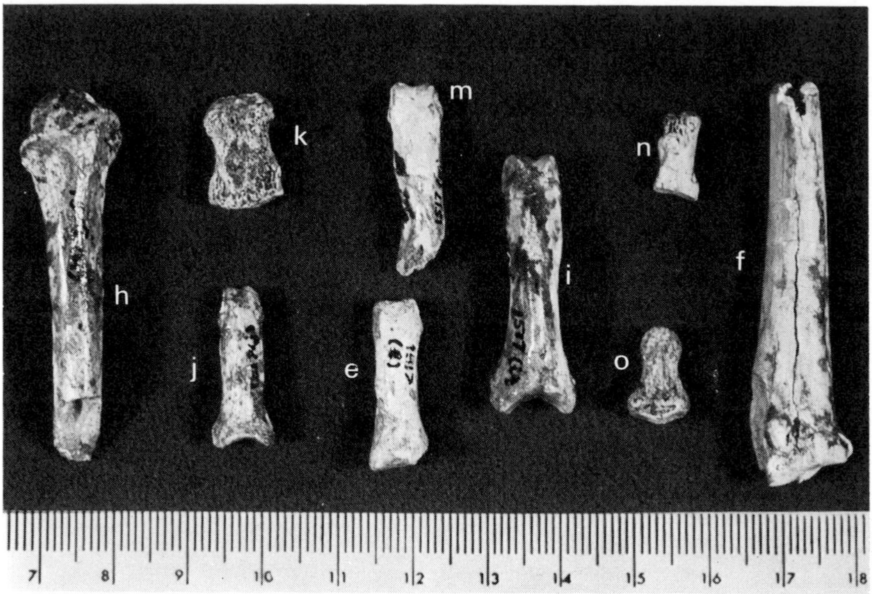

Figure 2. Part of the TM 1517 assemblage from Kromdraai:
(e) dorsal view; (f) medial view; (h) dorsal view; (i) dorsal view; (j) dorsal view; (k) ventral view; (m) dorsal view; (n) dorsal view; (o) dorsal view. See text for details.

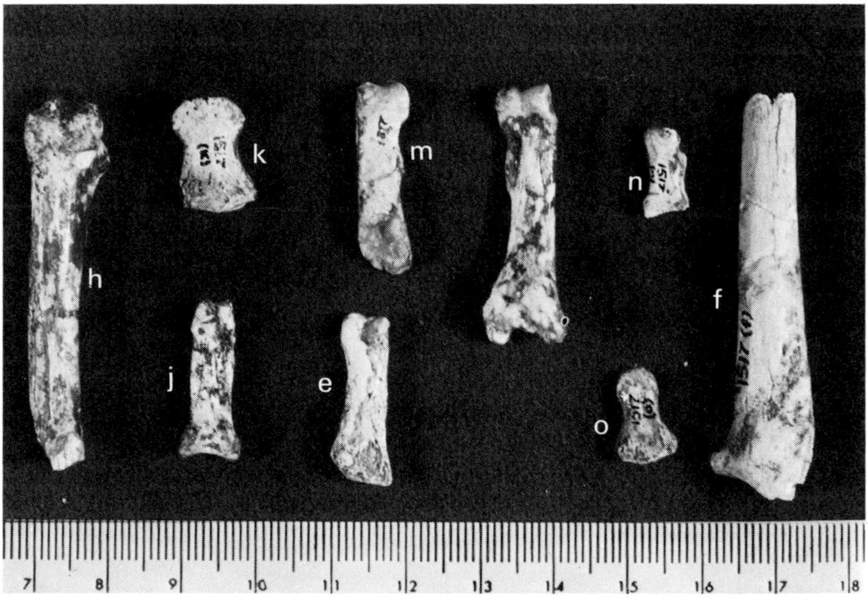

Figure 3. Part of the TM 1517 assemblage from Kromdraai:
(e) ventral view; (f) lateral view; (h) ventral view; (i) ventral view; (j) ventral view; (k) dorsal view; (m) ventral view; (n) ventral view; (o) ventral view. See text for details.

proximal fragment illustrated in Broom and Schepers (1946) is now missing from the fossil.

(i) This appears to be a proximal phalanx of a large baboon on account of the large dorsal tilt of its base. Here I agree with Krantz (1960). It was attributed to *Paranthropus robustus* (Broom and Schepers, 1946; Plate XIII, Figures 157, 170, 171, 173, 176, 179, 182).

(j) This appears to be a proximal phalanx of *Papio (=Parapapio) angusticeps* as suggested by Broom and Schepers (1946). I agree with them on the basis of the tilt of the base alone.

(m) This appears to be a broken proximal phalanx of a baboon. The configuration of the head and the positions of the muscle attachments are such that this diagnosis cannot be excluded, but the baboon-like tilt of the base cannot be shown since the bone is broken.

(o) This appears to be a terminal phalanx of the hand. It has no clear-cut diagnostic features other than a concave dorsal surface. This feature is not typical of baboon phalanges but is known in hominid phalanges such as those of modern man and in the Olduvai hand. Whether or not this feature alone, of an isolated phalanx, is sufficient evidence to make a hominid attribution seems to be very doubtful. This bone is figured by Broom and Schepers (1946), plate XII, Figure 156, and recorded in the legend to the figure as a distal phalanx of toe of *Plesianthropus transvaalensis*. This is almost certainly an error since this bone bears the Transvaal Museum number 1517 (o) and is part of the hypodigm of *Paranthropus robustus*. In the text it is stated to come from Kromdraai (Broom and Schepers, 1946: 118).

The Olduvai hand bones (OH 7 a-o)

During 1960 a number of hand bones were recovered from site FLKNN I Olduvai Gorge, Tanzania. Of the original 21 bones or bone fragments 15 were identified as hominid and described (Napier, 1962). The remainder were not identified as hominid; some of these have subsequently been shown to belong to fossil baboons while others have been rejected as unidentifiable fragments. Of the group described, 7 are juvenile middle and terminal phalanges, 2 are adult proximal phalanges, 3 are carpal bones of uncertain age, 1 is a second metacarpal base of uncertain age and 2 are fragments of proximal phalanges of uncertain age. There is some reason to believe, however, from their disposition, colour and degree of fossilization, that the carpal bones and the base of the second metacarpal may relate to the juvenile material.

Having identified the bones as hominid, Napier regarded them all as belonging to one taxon, later termed *Homo habilis* (Leakey, Tobias and Napier, 1964), apparently on the basis of Occam's principle rather than morphological similarity since the adult and juvenile proximal phalanges are very different in form. The use of the principle of economy of hypothesis, while philosophically correct, has very real

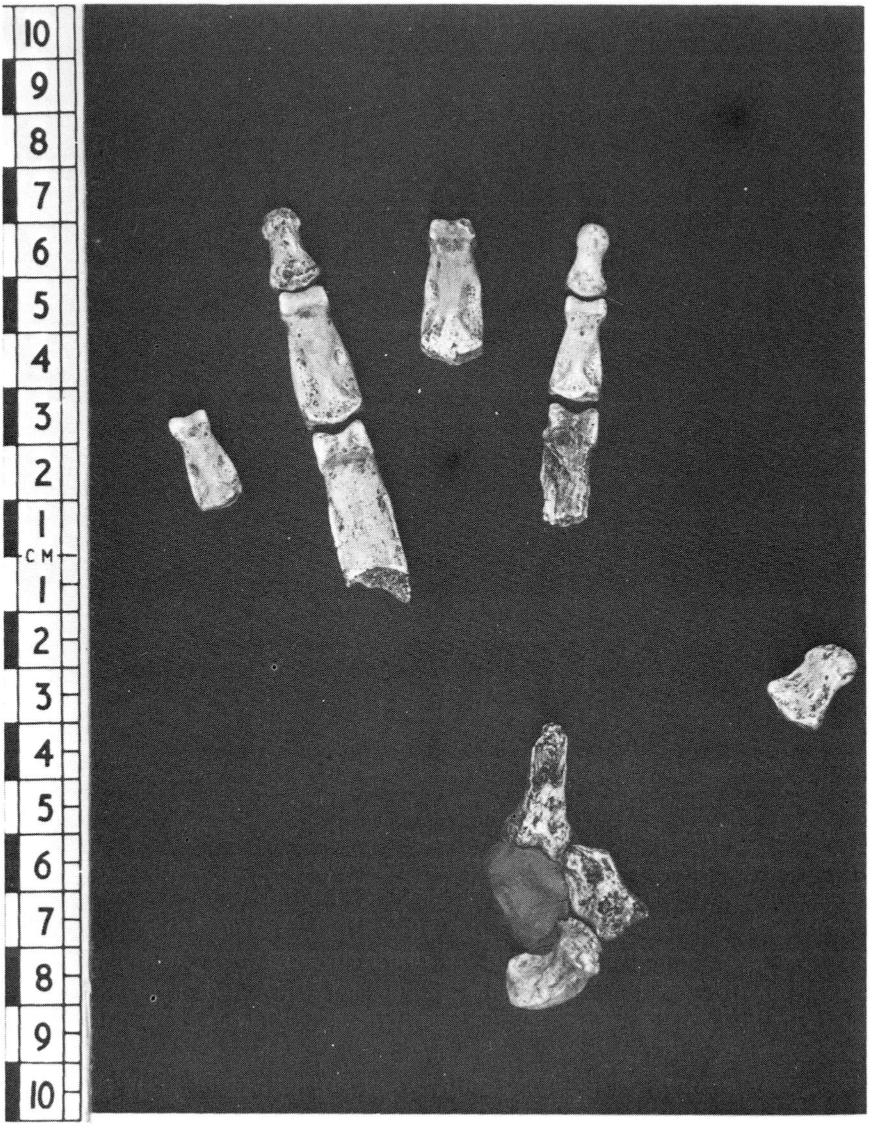

Figure 4. An articulation of the Olduvai Hominid 7 hand: ventral view.

drawbacks in a field situation at a palaeontological site. The FLKNN I living floor yielded the remains of many genera including non-hominid fossil primates. In view of this it would seem proper to question the taxonomic unity of the hand assemblage most carefully.

The two bones that stand out as morphologically distinct are the two adult proximal phalanges; very similar in form, they are both heavily curved dorsoventrally and bear remarkable ridges for the attachment of fibrous flexor sheaths, which leads to a guttered

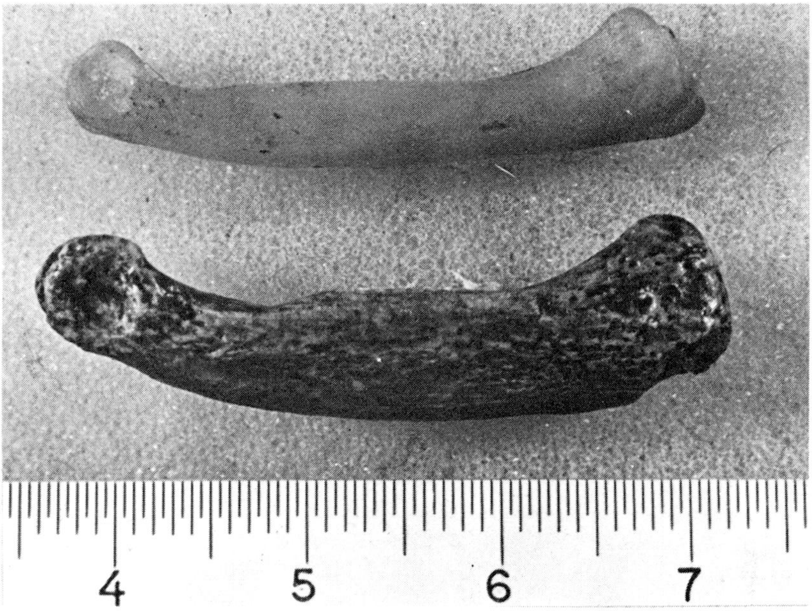

Figure 5. Lateral view of one of the Olduvai adult proximal hand phalanges (j) below compared with a corresponding phalanx from *Colobus polykomos,* above.

appearance of the ventral aspect. In addition, they have disproportionately small heads in relation to their bases. The general features of these bones suggest arboreal adaptation and the nearest modern primate seems to be *Colobus polykomos*. Among the fossil primates examined none has provided a match so far; even the giant *Paracolobus chemeroni* skeleton known from Kenya has almost every bone preserved except its hand phalanges.

It is of particular interest that Oxnard (1972a), employing an ingenious and, I believe, valid use of the stressed plastic profiles method, concludes that these phalanges are highly arboreally adapted. It seems, therefore, that the two adult proximal phalanges in this assemblage are taxonomically distinct from the juvenile group on morphological grounds and that they are most likely to belong to a non-hominid primate.

The carpal bones comprise a right trapezium and scaphoid, and a left capitate that is severely damaged. The trapezium bears a broad saddle surface for the first metacarpal and can be articulated with the scaphoid and the second metacarpal base. The saddle surface suggests that the thumb was capable of a wide range of movements at this joint including rotation, movements essential for the performance of both the power and precision grip postures. The two damaged proximal phalanges (i and h) seem likely to belong with the juvenile group. They are broad and stout with well developed trochlear distal ends.

The four middle phalanges (d, e, f and g) form a set of distinctive morphology; stout, bottle-shaped in outline and bearing marked depressions for flexor digitorum superficialis insertions. Because of their overall similarity and their relative sizes it is assumed that they belonged to one juvenile hand. Comparisons with a known series of modern human hands suggests, on the basis of the tilts of the heads, that this is part of a right hand. The three terminal phalanges, in particular that of the thumb, are broad and spatulate.

In summary, I think that the juvenile bones and those of uncertain age come from one hominid (possibly one individual) while the two adult bones come from another primate that was far more arboreally adapted (Day, 1976b). Functionally, the juvenile hand had powerful fingers, flat nails and a thumb capable of rotation out of the plane of the palm.

Omo 18-1970-1848

An adult intermediate phalanx reported by Coppens (1973) and allocated to the third finger of the left hand. Preliminary inspection suggests several similarities to the Olduvai intermediate phalanges, while a comparison of the published measurements shows the Omo specimen to be generally a little larger than the largest Olduvai specimen, which is, of course, immature. Consideration of the tilt of the head and the size of the phalanx suggests that it most probably belongs to the second digit of the left hand.

KNM-ER 164 (Leakey, 1972; Day and Leakey, 1974)

A composite specimen, still partly embedded in matrix, consisting of two proximal phalanges, a fragment of the shaft of a third phalanx and the head of a metacarpal in articulation with the base of the shorter phalanx. Similar to modern human phalanges and different from those from Olduvai in that they are long and straight. Functional deductions would be premature.

When all the known early hominid upper limb material is viewed as a group, several points stand out clearly. The first is that virtually nothing is known about the upper limb girdle. The scapular remains (Sts 7 and KNM-ER 1500 (1)) are very poor specimens indeed, while no clavicular remains are known from East Rudolf and those from South Africa can be discounted. This leaves OH 48 as the sole example of an early hominid clavicle, but at least this was taken from a well-dated living floor (1.75 m.y. BP). Whichever of the early hominids this clavicle derives from, and its taxonomic allocation is not clear to me, its functional characters appear to be similar to those of *Homo sapiens*.

Arm remains are more plentiful but none are known from Olduvai.

All three of the Transvaal fragments are small; despite the attribution of TM 1517 to *A. robustus* it is functionally similar to the humerus of man. The other humeral remains from Sterkfontein are not very revealing, merely suggesting free-ranging shoulder movement. The East African humeral remains are more numerous; the Kanapoi fragment is similar to TM 1517 and even more manlike than this fragment. The most important group of humeral remains includes KNM-ER 739, 740, 1473 and 1504, a group with several features in common. The best example (KNM-ER 739) is very robust, well muscularized and unique in its metrical features. It shows no affinity, however, with modern primate quadrupedal or knuckle-walking humeri, although it may still show some arboreal traits. The remaining East Rudolf humeri (KNM-ER 1500 and 1591) are not yet fully examined but KNM-ER 1500 is known to be part of a single fragmentary hominid partial skeleton.

The forearm is represented by both radial and ulnar remains. The radii are very fragmented and include two poorly diagnostic shaft fragments (OH 49 and KNM-ER 1500), one upper end (Sts 68), and a shaft fragment that is part of a single skeleton attributed to *Homo* on other grounds (KNM-ER 803). In functional terms none of these radial fragments differs significantly from that of man but detailed comparative studies remain to be completed.

The ulna is better known, being represented by the Omo ulna (Omo 40-19) and the East Rudolf ulna (KNM-ER 803) attributed to the genus *Homo* as part of the partial skeleton. These two ulnae show distinctive features that are probably both functionally and taxonomically significant. The remaining ulna fragments (TM 1517 and KNM-ER 1500) are less helpful.

The hand bones known are scanty apart from the group found at Olduvai which have been culled here to provide a more acceptable reconstruction than that which was possible when using the whole assemblage. The Omo phalanx has very clear similarities to the Olduvai intermediate phalanges. East Rudolf has provided little hand material but the KNM-ER 164 phalanges are very modern in appearance. From South Africa almost all the TM 1517 'hand' material appears to be non-hominid or to belong to the foot whereas the SKW 14147 fifth metacarpal is clearly hominid but less certainly hominine. Similarly, of the Swartkrans hand bones, one, the fourth metacarpal head, appears hominine, while the first metacarpal has some distinctive features. Functionally what we know of the early hominid hand appears to indicate powerful finger flexion and at least a power grip; as yet there is no certainty of a precision grip in these creatures.

The vertebral column

SK 853

An immature first lumbar vertebra attributed to *H. erectus* (Robinson, 1972).

SK 854

An axis vertebra attributed to *Paranthropus* (Robinson, 1972).

SK 3981 (a and b)

Two adult vertebrae said to resemble their Sts 14 equivalents. Vertebra (a) is stated to be a twelfth thoracic and (b) a fifth lumbar. A lumbar lordosis is suggested by their anatomy (Robinson, 1970).

Sts 14

A single vertebral column consisting of 15 thoracic and lumbar vertebrae. Examination of the vertebrae from Sterkfontein suggests strongly that this individual possessed a well-marked lumbar lordosis – a neglected point of great significance in relation to the discussions that still continue concerning the evidence for upright posture and bipedal gait in relation to the pelvis of this specimen (see below).

So far the only discussion of all of these vertebrae has centred on their taxonomic allocation; SK 854, SK 3981 (a) and (b) have been allocated to *Paranthropus* while SK 853 is allocated to *Homo erectus* (Robinson, 1972). A functional analysis of these early hominid vertebrae is needed.

KNM-ER 164 (Leakey, 1972; Day and Leakey, 1974)

Two vertebrae are known from East Rudolf, a seventh cervical and a first thoracic, found in articulation and retained so by matrix. They are small and provisionally appear to resemble modern human vertebrae. Detailed comparisons and a functional analysis must await their further development and study.

The lower limb girdle

The only early hominid pelvic girdle remains known are those from Sterkfontein, Swartkrans and Makapansgat. None have been recovered from Olduvai and none from East Rudolf despite special searches.

Sts 14

The most complete early hominid pelvic remains known are those from Sterkfontein. It is upon this pelvis that much locomotor speculation has been based. Broom, Robinson and Schepers (1950) considered that its features were consistent with upright posture and bipedal gait. This belief was supported by Le Gros Clark (1967). However, as late as 1967 it was stated that this pelvis had some quadrupedal features (Zuckerman *et al.*, 1967).

Recent examination of this pelvis discloses that the current reconstruction contains anatomical errors, particularly on the left side – errors that preclude the accurate measurement of many pelvic dimensions (Day, 1973). The principal difficulty lies in the position of the left pubis which is obliquely placed and astride the midline. The reconstructed acetabulum is not round, and the pubis, ischium and ilium are all separated here by plaster infill. Correction of this reconstruction would shorten the 'pongid' relative pubic length and resolve the difficulty concerning this dimension (Robinson, 1972).

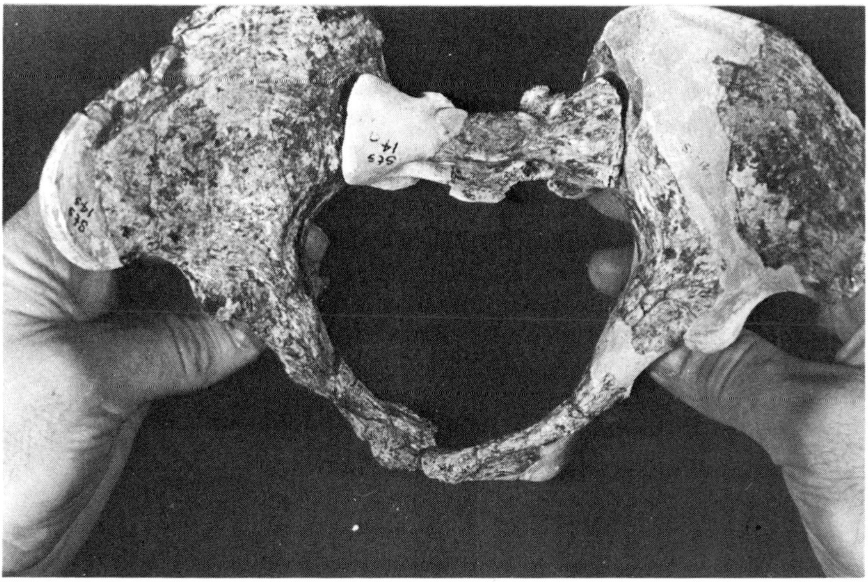

Figure 6. The Sts 14 pelvis viewed from above to show the incorrect reconstruction of the left side and the damaged and distorted condition of the right side.

A recent study (Zuckerman *et al.*, 1973) was based on a reconstructed secondary cast of the right side of this pelvis and a wide range of prosimian, cercopithecoid, ceboid and hominoid comparative material. A series of measurements was taken on the reconstruction and on the comparative material and extensively treated by means of multivariate statistical methods. The results obtained were inconclusive since, in the analyses of features related to weight-bearing, *Australopithecus* was said 'in general to be like man', whereas in features relating to muscle-pulls, '*Australopithecus* tends to contrast with man and agrees with many sub-human Primates, and especially the great apes'.

Sts 65

A group of fragments (not all of which are hominid) including a hominid right ilio-pubic fragment that contains part of the acetabulum and shows an anterior inferior iliac spine, a pectineal line, an ilio-psoas groove, a raked iliac pillar, an S-shaped iliac blade and a small auricular surface with a pre-auricular groove. This latter point, in association with others, suggests that the Sts 65 pelvis belonged to a female.

SK 50 (Broom and Robinson, 1950)

This badly crushed pelvic fragment discloses only a few anatomical features of note; a backwardly directed ilium, a small acetabulum and an iliac pillar raked forward. There seem to be few anatomical measurements that can be taken safely on this fossil.

TM 1605 (Robinson, 1972)

An iliac fragment that resembles SK 50 in some respects is known from Kromdraai. No detailed study has been published.

SK 3155 (b)

An adolescent pelvic specimen showing a complete but small acetabulum, a backward extension of the ilium, an S-shaped iliac blade and an anterior inferior iliac spine. The SK 3155 (b) pelvis has been described and assigned to the genus *Homo,* possibly even to the species *Homo erectus* (Brain, Vrba and Robinson, 1974). This view has not been accepted by McHenry (1975) who finds its anatomy to be essentially australopithecine. I favour the latter view since SK 3155 (b) is quite unlike the only previously known *Homo erectus* pelvis (Olduvai Hominid 28; Day, 1971), and a subsequent specimen with the same anatomical characters from East Turkana, – KNM-ER 3228 (Leakey, 1976).

The group of early hominid pelvic remains, as well as other material from Makapansgat, shares a group of features apparently typical of these early hominids. These anatomical features indicate to me an upright stance and a bipedal gait, but perhaps not a gait of precisely modern human character.

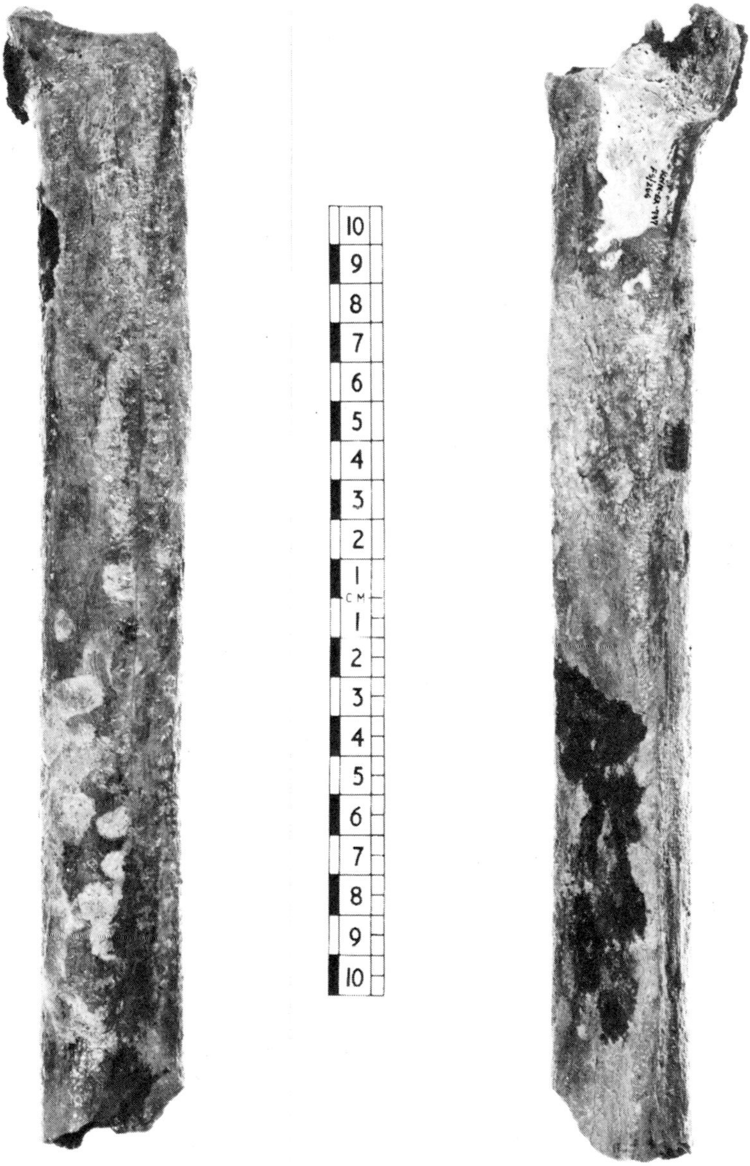

Figure 7. KNM-ER 736 left femur shaft. It is broken across proximally just above the base of the lesser trochanter (left anterior view, right posterior view).

The thigh

The femur

There are now 16 or 17 early hominid femoral specimens known from East Rudolf (Day, in prep.) as well as one from Olduvai, two from

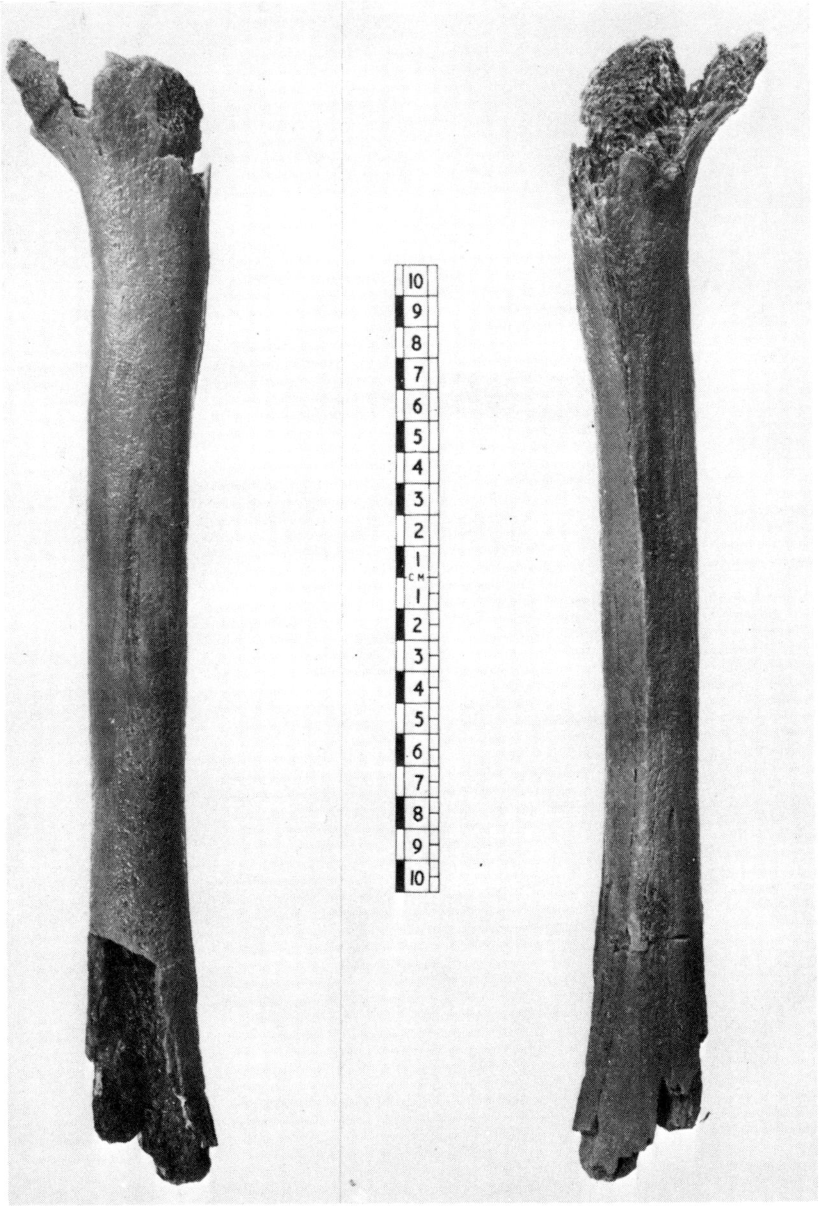

Figure 8. KNM-ER 737 left femur shaft, attributed to the genus *Homo* (left anterior view, right posterior view).

Swartkrans and three from Sterkfontein.

Of the Sterkfontein specimens I agree with Walker (1973) that Sts 14 is of little or no value on account of its poor state of preservation (Day, 1973). In this paper Walker has also confirmed the group of features that distinguish australopithecine femora, including a small head, low neck angle, long and compressed neck, lack of flare of the greater trochanter and the lack of an inter-trochanteric line. Some of these features had formerly been discounted as being within the modern human range (Lovejoy and Heiple, 1972). However, Walker does not confirm, from the East Rudolf series, that the lesser trochanter is laterally placed in these forms. What remains clear is that no single modern human femur has yet been found that possesses the *combination* features now well known in these early hominids, although at least one has come close to this combination (Wolpoff, pers. comm.).

An earlier assertion that the SK 82, SK 97 and OH 20 femora do not possess femoral tubercles (Day, 1969) should be withdrawn in the light of criticism (Robinson, 1972) and examination of all the originals. However, I maintain that the 'trochanteric line' in these specimens is very weak indeed and is more like a synovial reflection (Lovejoy and Heiple, 1972) than a ligamentous attachment. The clear upper attachment of the ilio-femoral ligament shown on pelves SK 3155 (b) and SK 50 would seem to relate to the transverse band of this ligament alone. (The extraordinary development of the femoral tubercle in KNM-ER 1472 must be of interest in this respect.)

Among the East Rudolf femoral collection there are six specimens that do not appear to have clear australopithecine features: KNM-ER 736, KNM-ER 737, KNM-ER 803, KNM-ER 999, KNM-ER 1472 and KNM-ER 1481 (a). KNM-ER 999 is a massive femur with relatively modern human characters (Day and Leakey, in press) while 803 and 737 have marked similarities to the Peking femora and Olduvai Hominid 28 (Day 1973). KNM-ER 1472 and 1481 are of tremendous interest since they have a mixture of features some of which are modern human and others that are not (Day *et al.*, in prep.). Five of these specimens have been or will be attributed to the genus *Homo* while KNM-ER 736 has been attributed to *Australopithecus*; I feel that it has greater affinity with the massive KNM-ER 999 and should be attributed to the genus *Homo*.

From the morphology of all of these femora two groups appear to emerge, an australopithecine group and an '*erectus*-like' group, both of which have bipedal characters. These patterns of femoral morphology tend to blur in the two early femora KNM-ER 1472 and KNM-ER 1481 (a). The nature of the fine distinctions of gait that may exist between these groups seems to me to be obscure at present, but the clear morphological differences between the australopithecine femora and the '*erectus*-like' femora seem likely to have been reflected in function to some degree.

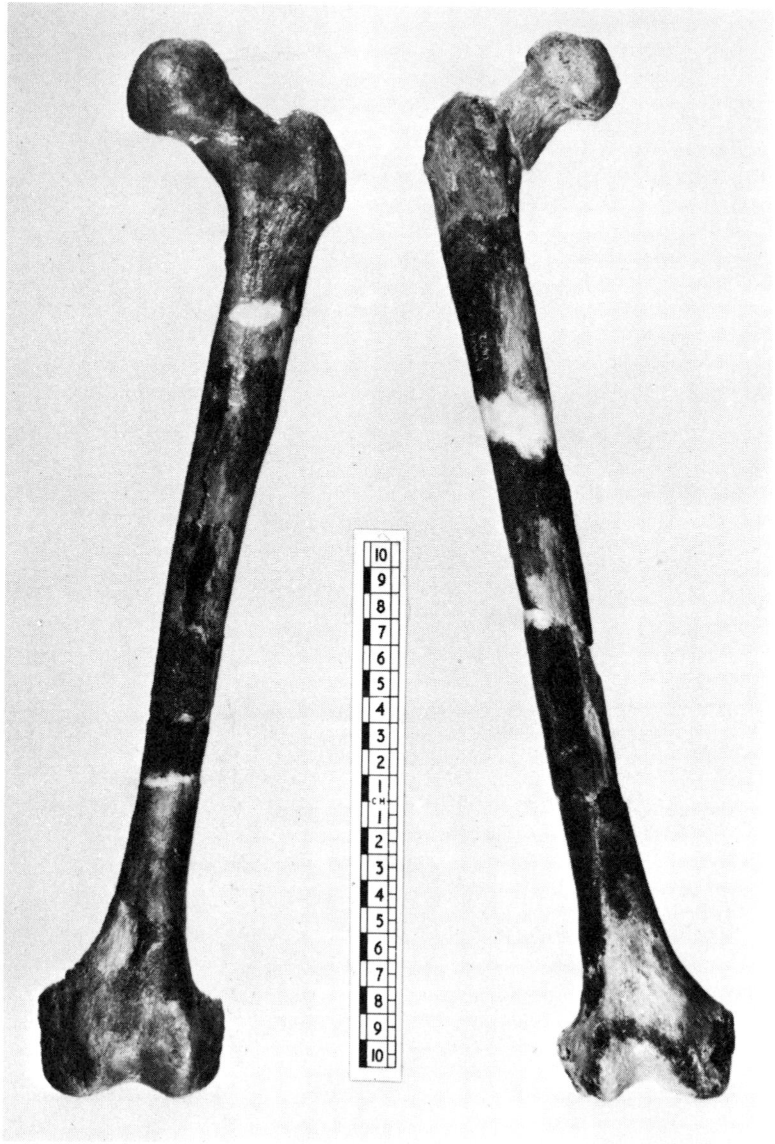

Figure 9. KNM-ER 1481 (a) left femur (left), anterior view, and KNM-ER 1472 right femur (right), anterior view.

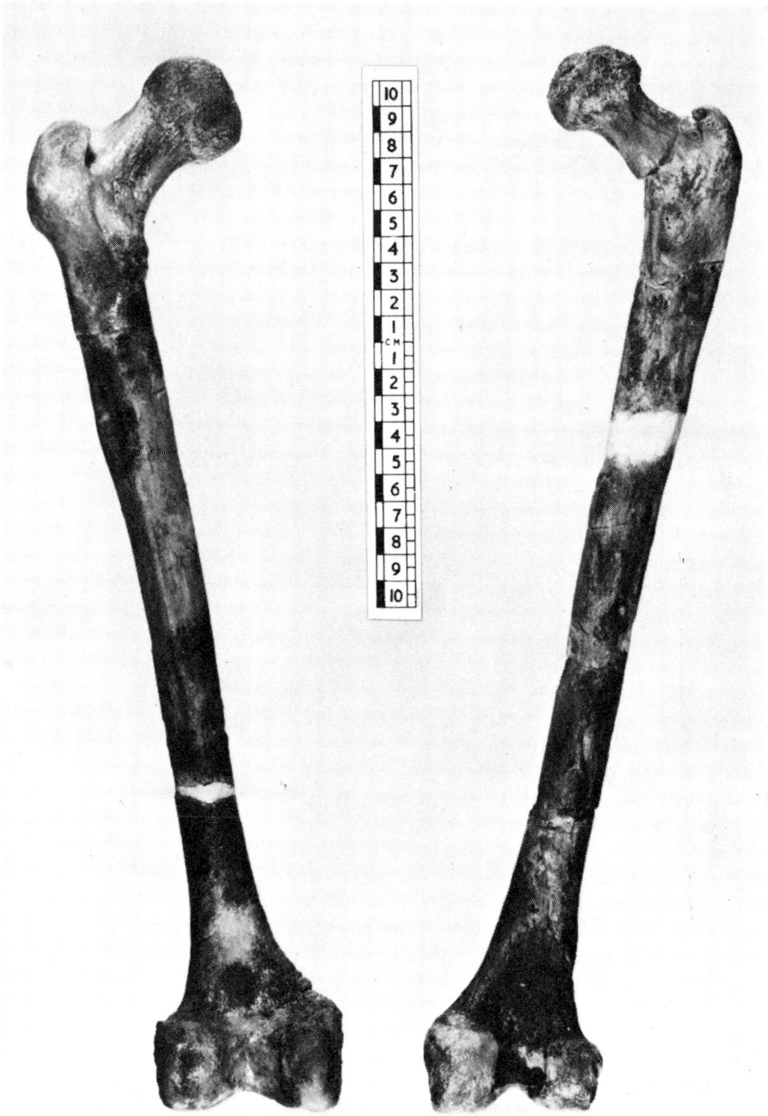

Figure 10. KNM-ER 1481 (a) left femur (left), posterior view, and KNM-ER 1472 right femur (right), posterior view.

The leg

No leg bones are known from the South African sites.

OH 35

The Olduvai tibia and fibula (Davis, 1964) form a pair and articulate well together. Davis concluded that they belonged to a hominid who was well adapted to bipedalism at the ankle but less well adapted at the knee; while an habitual bipedal plantigrade primate, this form was said to have a gait that may well have differed considerably from that of modern man.

It is of great interest that these bones can be reasonably articulated with the talus of the Olduvai foot from a nearby site, without suggesting that they all belong to one individual. A recent reappraisal

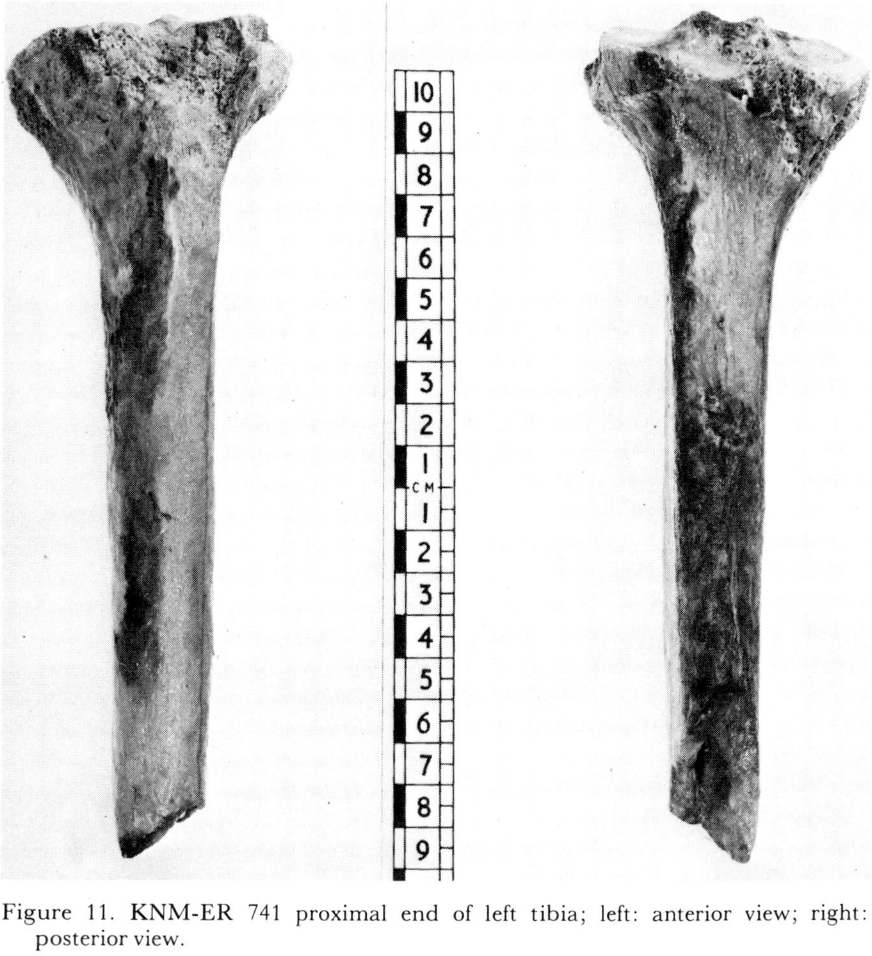

Figure 11. KNM-ER 741 proximal end of left tibia; left: anterior view; right: posterior view.

of these bones (Day, 1974) has questioned the previous interpretation of the anatomy of the upper end of the tibia (Davis, 1964) and thus detracts from the view that the knee of this form was less well adapted for bipedalism (see also Lovejoy, this volume).

Perhaps the most confusing group of postcranial material yet recovered from East Rudolf is the tibial and fibular fragments, KNM-ER 741, 803 (b), 813 (b), 1471, 1476 (b and c), 1481 (b, c and d), 1500 (a and h). Considerable anatomical analysis, metrical comparison and biomechanical investigation will be needed to elucidate the tibial and fibular anatomy of these early hominids. The following tentative conclusions are open to revision.

KNM-ER 741 (Figure 11)

An upper end of tibia, provisionally allocated to *Australopithecus* (Leakey, Mungai and Walker, 1972), shows, however, many features similar to those known in *Homo*.

KNM-ER 803 (b) (Leakey, 1972; Day and Leakey, 1974; Day, 1976a)

A tibial shaft that is part of an associated skeleton allocated to *Homo* on other grounds (Day and Leakey, 1974).

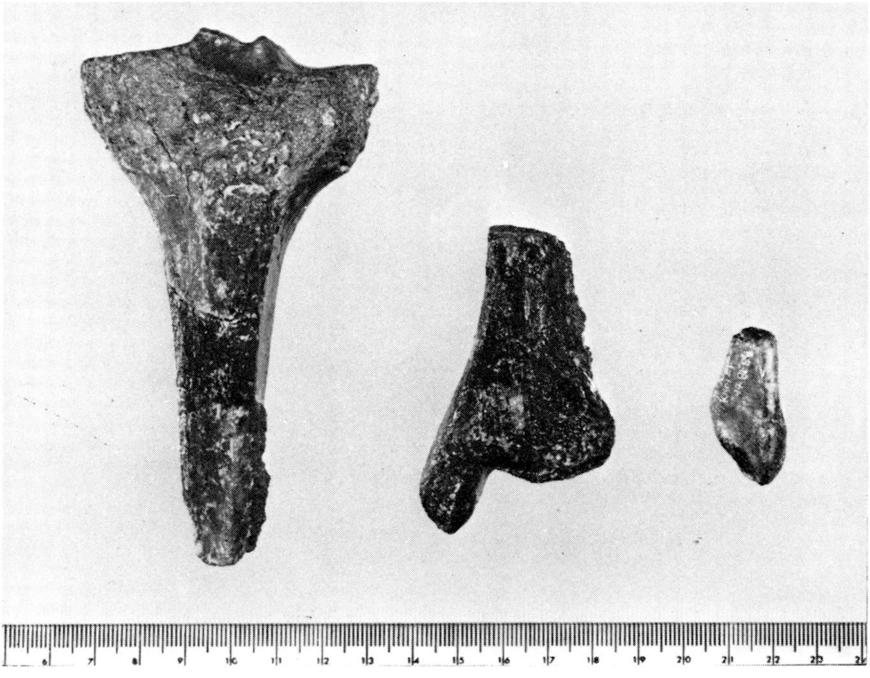

Figure 12. KNM-ER 1481: (*b*) proximal end of left tibia, (*c*) distal end of left tibia, (*d*) distal end of fibula. Anterior views.

KNM-ER 813(b)

Possibly part of a tibial shaft but equally possibly part of a femur shaft. Associated with a talus, KNM-ER 813(*a*), attributed to *Homo* (Wood, 1973).

KNM-ER 1471 (Leakey, 1973)

Proximal end and proximal shaft of a tibia whose detailed anatomy is almost identical with that of modern man.

KNM-ER 1476(b and c) (Leakey, 1973)

Proximal end and proximal shaft of a left tibia; the mid-shaft of a right tibia. Small, gracile, similar to OH 35 and KNM-ER 1500.

KNM-ER 1481(b, c and d) (Leakey, 1973) (Figure 12)

Parts of a tibia and fibula associated with the femur of the same number. The femur has been allocated to the genus *Homo*.

KNM-ER 1500(a and h) (Leakey, 1973)

(a) The upper one third to one half of a left tibia. Small, gracile and very similar to OH 35.
(h) Broken lower end with a keeled trochlear surface.
(KNM-ER 1500 is an associated skeleton attributed to *Australopithecus* on other grounds) (Day, 1976a).

Other than to say that all of this leg material seems to be bipedally adapted, functional conclusions are reserved. Study of the tibiae in conjunction with the known femora is most likely to provide functional information in relation to the knee joint.

The foot

TM 1517 (Figure 13)

An incomplete talus from Kromdraai (Broom and Schepers, 1946), discussed in detail by Le Gros Clark (1947) and Robinson (1972). A metrical study (Day and Wood, 1968) showed similarities between the Olduvai talus and this bone, and also their difference from modern human and pongid tali.

The remaining postcranial foot bones in the TM 1517 assemblage are (e), (f), (k) and (n); (h) has been referred to previously with the hand material.

(e) was figured by Broom and Schepers (1946) as a proximal

Figure 13. TM 1517 talus from Kromdraai: dorsal view.

phalanx of the toe of *Plesianthropus transvaalensis* (Plate XII, Figure 155 and legend to Figures). This is almost certainly an error since the bone is now part of the Kromdraai assemblage under the Transvaal Museum number 1517, as part of the hypodigm of *Paranthropus robustus*, and was said to have been found at Kromdraai (Broom and Schepers, 1946, p. 118; Musgrave, 1970). In any event it does not seem to be anatomically distinct from a baboon phalanx.

(f) This bone appears to be undescribed. It is the shaft and base of a second right metatarsal, this attribution being made on the basis of the side-to-side flattening of the shaft, the tilt of the articular surface of the base, the configuration of its lateral and medial articular facets, and the inferior buttressing of the shaft as it approaches the base. Its overall length would have been greater than its counterpart in the Olduvai foot and it would be large for a modern baboon metatarsal, although no foot material is known from the larger fossil baboons from the Transvaal deposits. Further comparisons must be made before a firm attribution of this metatarsal can be made.

(k) This bone seems to be undescribed. It appears to be the terminal phalanx of a left great toe that is complete in its length but it is somewhat eroded ventrally particularly at the base. It is broad, flattened dorsoventrally and waisted. The unguicular tuberosity is well marked and the attachment for flexor hallucis longus distinct. It is hard to determine any tilt of the shaft with respect to the base. It does, however, possess one feature that may be of considerable significance, that is the presence of a marked degree of torsion similar to that described in the Olduvai Hominid 10 terminal phalanx (Day and Napier, 1966) and so far only observed otherwise in modern man. Clearly further investigation is warranted but there are some clear-cut features in this terminal phalanx that point towards its hominid nature and perhaps to bipedal functional affinities.

(n) This bone appears to be undescribed. It is a fragmentary intermediate phalanx of toe that has lost its base and part of its head. There are insufficient features remaining to make a taxonomic attribution.

OH 8 (Figure 14)

The Olduvai Hominid 8 foot remains the most convincing single piece of direct palaeontological evidence for early hominid bipedalism: twelve bones found on a land surface within a square foot that articulate perfectly to form a clearly recognizable functional complex (Leakey, 1960; Day and Napier, 1964). The lack of divergence of the hallux is indisputably shown by the presence of a joint between metatarsals I and II. The metatarsal robusticity pattern with

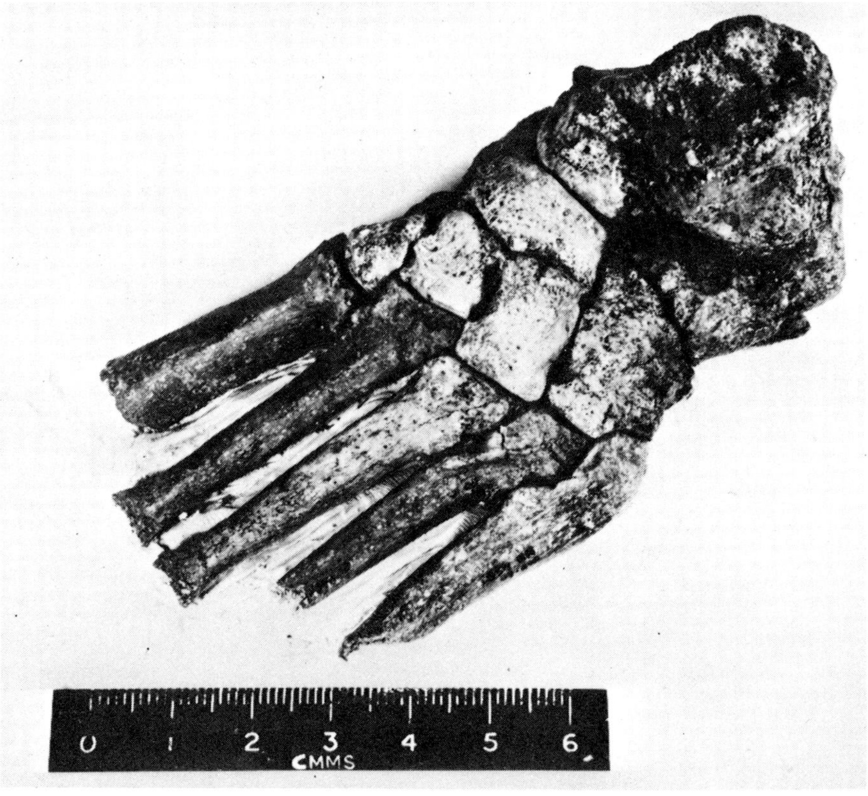

Figure 14. An articulation of the Olduvai Hominid 8 foot.

preponderance of I and V is of human bipedal character as are the arch formations and the evidence for their static and dynamic support. In short this is a non-prehensile, plantigrade, propulsive bipedal foot.

OH 43

Two metatarsals, recently recognized, from the FLKNN I assemblage. They are a left third and a left fifth metatarsal, both without heads. Very similar in form and size to the Olduvai metatarsals, they indicate the presence of a second individual on this floor.

OH 10

A terminal phalanx of the right hallux (Day and Napier, 1966; Day, 1967) shows features that indicate its use in propulsive bipedalism. A metrical study supported the morphological analysis. Criticisms of the statistical conclusions (Oxnard, 1972b) have been answered (Day, 1974).

KNM-ER 803 (e,f,j,k,l,m,q)

A group of foot bones that form part of a partial skeleton (Day and Leakey, 1974), including a third left metatarsal. The bones are very similar to their modern human counterparts in both form and size.

KNM-ER 813 (a)

A well preserved talus with many modern human features (Leakey, 1972; Leakey and Wood, 1973). A recent metrical study (Wood, 1973) shows the bone to have modern human functional affinities.

KNM-ER 997 (Leakey, 1972)

A third left metatarsal less its head. Base similar to that of OH 8 but the shaft is longer.

KNM-ER 1464 (Leakey, 1973)

A perfect right talus with mixed features some of which recall the Olduvai talus and others the KNM-ER 813 talus. It seems likely that this talus should be attributed to the genus *Homo*.

KNM-ER 1476 (a) (Leakey, 1973)

A left talus, very similar to the Olduvai talus (OH 8).

KNM-ER 1500 (Leakey, 1973; Day, 1976a)

A third metatarsal base, similar to the Olduvai third metatarsals (OH 8). Part of the partial skeleton that has been attributed to *Australopithecus* on other grounds.

Discussion

Any attempt to summarize the whole range of early hominid postcranial material in terms of function is almost certainly doomed to failure. However, some points seem to emerge from this review.

In the most general terms two patterns of postcranial morphology seem to be apparent in the material available; one of these can be termed australopithecine and the other hominine. Of the australopithecine group, variability in size is clear and may relate to the so-called robust and gracile forms. Nonetheless in terms of morphology it appears that these sub-groups have much in common, and it seems that suggestions of widely differing forms of locomotion in the two sub-groups are not well supported. Both appear to be capable of upright posture and bipedal locomotion; neither shows clear anatomical evidence of quadrupedalism or of 'knuckle-walking' in the style of modern pongids.

The functional relationships of the hominine group of material appear to be clearly with those of man; indeed it is hard to point to a distinctive feature in this material that could in itself suggest marked functional difference in terms of locomotion between the fossil and modern human remains.

Not all of the material mentioned here can be allocated with certainty since some of it is incomplete and other specimens show a mixture of features. The latter point is not necessarily unexpected since some of the more recent finds are from early deposits that may even be approaching the levels at which the two principal groups diverged, if only two groups there were! Only new finds from earlier levels will help to resolve this problem.

Finally, this reappraisal has served to eliminate a number of fossil bones from the hominid record; this alone may help to clarify the position and facilitate future locomotor investigations.

Acknowledgments

It is a pleasure to record my gratitude to the Wenner-Gren Foundation for Anthropological Research for the support of this work. In addition I would like to thank the Royal Society of London and the Boise Fund for their support. I am very grateful to my colleagues Dr. Louise Scheuer, Dr. Alan Walker and Dr. Bernard Wood for assistance and for helpful discussions. I must thank R.E.F. Leakey, Director of the National Museums of Kenya, and the Government of Kenya for permission to study materials in their care. I must also thank Dr. C.K. Brain, Director of the Transvaal Museum, for his kindness in allowing me to study the collection in his care, and also Professor P.V. Tobias for the same courtesy.

References

Ashton, E.H. and Oxnard, C.E. (1964) Functional adaptations in the primate shoulder girdle. *Proc. Zool. Soc. Lond.* 142, 49-66.

Boné, E.L. (1955) Une clavicule et un nouveau fragment mandibulaire *d'Australopithecus prometheus. Palaeontologica Africana*, 3, 87-101.

Boné, E.L. and Dart, R.A. (1955) A catalog of the australopithecine fossils found at the Limeworks, Makapansgat. *Amer. J. phys. Anthrop.* 13, 621-4.

Brain, C.K., Vrba, E.S. and Robinson, J.T. (1974) A new hominid innominate bone from Swartkrans. *Ann. Transv. Mus.*, 29, 55-66

Broom, R. and Robinson, J.T. (1949) A new type of fossil man. *Nature* (London), 164, 322-3.

Broom, R. and Robinson, J.T. (1950) Note on the pelves of fossil ape-men. *Amer. J. phys. Anthrop.* 8, 489-94.

Broom, R., Robinson, J.T. and Schepers, G.W.H. (1950) Sterkfontein ape-man, *Plesianthropus. Transv. Mus. Mem.* 4, 1-117.

Broom, R. and Schepers, G.W.H. (1946) The South African fossil ape-men: the Australopithecinae. *Transv. Mus. Mem.* 2.

Campbell, B.G. (1967) *Human Evolution, 1-272* London.

Clark, W.E. Le Gros (1947) Observations on the anatomy of the fossil Australopithecinae. *J. Anat.* (London) 81, 300-33.

Clark, W.E. Le Gros (1967) *Man-apes or Ape-men?* New York.

Coppens, Y. (1973) Les restes d'hominidés des formations Plio-Villafranchiennes de l'Omo en Ethiopie (Récoltes 1970, 1971 et 1972). *C.R. Acad. Sci.* (Paris) 276, 1823-6.

Davis, P.R. (1964) Hominid fossils from Bed I, Olduvai Gorge, Tanganyika: a tibia and fibula. *Nature* (London) 201, 967-8.

Day, M.H. (1967) Olduvai Hominid 10, a multivariate analysis. *Nature* (London) 215, 323-4.

Day, M.H. (1969) Femoral fragment of a robust australopithecine from Olduvai Gorge, Tanzania. *Nature* (London) 221, 230-3.

Day, M.H. (1971) Postcranial remains of *Homo erectus* from Bed IV, Olduvai Gorge, Tanzania. *Nature* (London) 232, 383-87.

Day, M.H. (1973) Locomotor features of the lower limb in hominids. *Symp. Zool. Soc. Lond.* 33, 29-51.

Day, M.H. (1974) The interpolation of isolated fossil foot bones into a discriminant function analysis: a reply. *Amer. J. phys. Anthrop.* 41, 233-6.

Day, M.H. (1976a) Hominid postcranial remains from the East Rudolf succession: a review. In Coppens, Y. *et al.* (eds), *Earliest Man and Environments in the Lake Rudolf Basin: Stratigraphy, Paleoecology and Evolution.* Chicago.

Day, M.H. (1976b) Hominid postcranial material from Bed I, Olduvai Gorge. In Isaac, G.L. and McCown, E.R. (eds.), *Human Origins: Louis Leakey and the East African Evidence*, Menlo Park, Cal.

Day, M.H. and Leakey, R.E.F. (1974) New evidence of the genus *Homo* from East Rudolf, Kenya (III). *Amer. J. phys. Anthrop.* 41, 367-80.

Day, M.H. *et al.* (in prep.).

Day, M.H. and Napier, J.R. (1964) Fossil foot bones. *Nature* (London) 201, 969-70.

Day, M.H. and Napier, J.R. (1966) A hominid toe bone from Bed I, Olduvai Gorge, Tanzania. *Nature* (London) 211, 929-30.

Day, M.H. and Scheuer, J.L. (1973) SKW 14147: A new hominid metacarpal from Swartkrans. *J. human Evol.* 2, 429-38.

Day, M.H. and Wood, B.A. (1968) Functional affinities of the Olduvai Hominid 8 talus. *Man* 3, 440-55.

Howell, F.C. and Wood, B.A. (1974) Early hominid ulna from the Omo basin, Ethiopia. *Nature* (London) 249, 174-6.

Krantz, G.S. (1960) Evolution of the human hand and the great hand-axe tradition. *Kroeber Anthrop. Soc. Pap.* 23, 114-28.

Leakey, L.S.B. (1960) Recent discoveries at Olduvai Gorge. *Nature* (London) 188, 1050-2.

Leakey, L.S.B., Tobias, P.V. and Napier, J.R. (1964) A new species of the genus *Homo* from Olduvai Gorge. *Nature* (London) 202, 7-9.

Leakey, R.E.F. (1971) Further evidence of lower Pleistocene hominids from East Rudolf, North Kenya. *Nature* (London) 231, 241-5.

Leakey, R.E.F. (1972) Further evidence of lower Pleistocene hominids from East Rudolf, North Kenya. *Nature* (London) 237, 264-9.

Leakey, R.E.F. (1973) Further evidence of lower Pleistocene hominids from East Rudolf, North Kenya, 1972. *Nature* (London) 242, 170-3.

Leakey, R.E.F. (1976) New hominid fossils from the Koobi Fora formation in Northern Kenya. *Nature* (London) 261, 574-6.

Leakey, R.E.F., Mungai, J.M. and Walker, A.C. (1972) New australopithecines from East Rudolf, Kenya (II) *Amer. J. phys. Anthrop.* 36, 235-51.

Leakey, R.E.F. and Wood, B.A. (1973) New evidence of the genus *Homo* from East Rudolf, Kenya II. *Amer. J. phys. Anthrop.* 39, 355-68.

Lewis, O.J. (1973) The hominoid os capitatum, with special reference to the fossil bones from Sterkfontein and Olduvai Gorge. *J. human Evol.* 2, 1-11.

Lovejoy, C.O. and Heiple, K.G. (1972) Proximal femoral anatomy of *Australopithecus*. *Nature* (London) 235, 175-6.

McHenry, H.H. (1972) Postcranial skeleton of early Pleistocene hominids. Ph.D. dissertation, Harvard University.

McHenry, H.H. (1973) Early hominid humerus from East Rudolf, Kenya. *Science* 180, 739-41.

McHenry, H.H. (1975) A new pelvic fragment from Swartkrans and the relationship between the robust and the gracile australopithecines. *Amer. J. phys. Anthrop.* 43, 245-62.

Musgrave, J.H. (1970) An anatomical study of the hands of Pleistocene and Recent man. Ph.D. Thesis. Cambridge University.

Napier, J.R. (1959) *Fossil metacarpals from Swartkrans. Fossil Mammals of Africa*, 17. British Museum (Nat. Hist.), London.

Napier, J.R. (1962) Fossil hand bones from Olduvai Gorge. *Nature* (London) 196, 409-11.

Oxnard, C.E. (1968) A note on the fragmentary Sterkfontein scapula. *Amer. J. phys. Anthrop.* 28, 213-18.

Oxnard, C.E. (1969) A note on the Olduvai clavicular fragment. *Amer. J. phys. Anthrop.* 29, 429-32.

Oxnard, C.E. (1972a) Functional morphology of primates: some mathematical and physical methods. In Tuttle, R. (ed.), *The Functional and Evolutionary Biology of Primates*. Chicago.

Oxnard, C.E. (1972b) Some African fossil foot bones: a note on the interpolation of fossils into a matrix of extant species. *Amer. J. phys. Anthrop.* 37, 3-12.

Partridge, T.C. (1973) Geomorphological dating of cave openings at Makapansgat, Sterkfontein, Swartkrans and Taung. *Nature* (London) 246, 75-9.

Patterson, B. and Howells, W.W. (1967) Hominid humeral fragment from early Pleistocene of Northwestern Kenya. *Science* 156, 64-6.

Rightmire, G.P. (1972) Multivariate analysis of an early hominid metacarpal from Swartkrans. *Science* 176, 159-61.

Robinson, J.T. (1953) *Telanthropus* and its phylogenetic significance. *Amer. J. phys. Anthrop.* 11, 445-501.

Robinson, J.T. (1970) Two new early hominid vertebrae from Swartkrans. *Nature* (London) 225, 1217-19.

Robinson, J.T. (1972) *Early hominid posture and locomotion*. Chicago.

Straus, W.L., Jnr. (1948) The humerus of *Paranthropus robustus*. *Amer. J. phys. Anthrop.* 6, 285-311.

Walker, A.C. (1973) New *Australopithecus* femora from East Rudolf, Kenya. *J. human Evolution*. 2, 545-55.

Wood, B.A. (1973) A *Homo* talus from East Rudolf, Kenya. *Proc. Anat. Soc. Gt. Br. Ire.*

Zuckermann, S. *et al.* (1967) The functional significance of certain features of the innominate bone in living and fossil primates. *Proc. Anat. Soc. Gt. Br. Ire.* 101, 608.

Zuckerman, S. *et al.* (1973) Some locomotor features of the pelvic girdle in primates. *Symp. Zool. Soc. London*. 33, 71-165.

B.A. Wood

An analysis of early hominid fossil postcranial material: principles and methods

The wealth of new material presents a suitable opportunity to reflect on the analytical concepts that are at present used in the interpretation of early hominid postcranial fossils. In any analysis, to ensure the most perceptive and useful results, the problem has to be tackled in a logical order. The interpretation of hominid fossils is really no different from that of other palaeontological material, and it may be profitable to examine the principles and methods used in these general studies to see how they may be applied to hominid postcranial remains. If this is done, it becomes apparent that disagreements that exist between hominid palaeontologists about postcranial material may reflect differences in approach rather than fundamentally divergent views on interpretation. Evidence will be put forward which indicates that functionally relevant variables, rather than being cardinal in phylogenetic studies, may in fact provide proportionately less information than other variables about the important patristic[1] component of overall affinity.

Prior to the discovery of the first postcranial material from the South African cave sites in 1936 (Broom and Schepers, 1946), early hominid postcranial material was limited to that found at Trinil, Indonesia, in 1892 and 1900 (Dubois, 1892, 1932, 1934) and at Choukoutien, China, between 1927 and 1936. (Editorial in Nature, 1932; Davidson Black, 1933; Weidenreich, 1938, 1941). Discussion about this material centred on the status of the Trinil femora and this debate has recently been reviewed (Day and Molleson, 1973). The South African material itself received very uneven attention. Debates took place in the journals over the pelvic and humeral remains yet two proximal femoral fragments, found in 1949, remained unconsidered until discussed by Napier (1964). It may be that the difficulties and uncertainties of deciding whether a bone was hominid or not deterred some workers. Fragmentary, and even quite complete, specimens can

1. For definitions of patristic, cladistic, etc. see Cain and Harrison (1960).

be misleading and careful examination by experienced morphologists continues to reveal cases of misidentification. Recent examples are some of the South African fossils (Wolpoff, 1973), and the femur from Kedung Brubus (Hooijer, *in litt.*).

Until a decade ago there was still relatively little postcranial evidence and maximum use was made of often incomplete specimens to gain insight into the locomotor patterns of early hominids. In the last decade, however, the available evidence has increased in both quantity and quality; there are now forty-six specimens from Olduvai Gorge, Tanzania and from Koobi Fora, Kenya, alone. More complete material is being discovered and a welcome development is the growing number of cases where postcranial bones are found together and can be considered, with varying degrees of certainty, as components of a single individual.

A coincidental, but very relevant, change had also been taking place in the field of statistical analysis. The growth and refinement of multivariate techniques and the increase in the capacities of electronic computers have been eagerly exploited by the interpreters of fossil postcranial material in the search for a greater functional understanding of the fossils (Day, 1967; Patterson and Howells, 1967; Day and Wood, 1968; Oxnard, 1969; Zuckerman, 1970; Rightmire, 1972; Zuckerman *et al.*, 1973; Day, 1973; Wood, 1974a). Biomechanical and stress analysis have also been utilized to study fossil material, the former by Preuschoft (1971) and the latter by Oxnard (1973), but their use has been more limited than that of metrical analysis. This concentration on a functional approach may have led to the comparative neglect of both the taxonomic considerations of postcranial fossils and of comparative anatomical studies, but an exception to the latter is the work of Lewis (1972a, b, 1973).

Before embarking on the task of analysing the wealth of recently discovered material, it is perhaps worth considering whether we have been tackling the analytical problems in the correct order. Though analysis of locomotor function has achieved a primacy over other studies, such as the assessment of affinity and phyletic arrangement, it is quite possible that functional questions are being asked at too early a stage in the analysis of fossils and that their place in relation to taxonomic and other studies needs revision. What follows is a review of the principles and methods of research and an attempt to clarify the apparently wide differences in the interpretation of early hominid postcranial fossils.

Classification was defined by Simpson (1961) as the 'ordering of organisms into groups (or sets) on the basis of their relationships', and taxonomy as the 'theoretical study of classification, including its bases, principles, procedures and rules'. This process of ordering must proceed in the proper sequence. The first stage is the acceptance that the fossils should be treated as samples of larger populations.

Therefore, unless we are to revert to typological studies, we have to investigate whether fossils are so alike that it is probable that they come from similar original populations and should therefore be considered together as a group. The process of grouping similar fossils as a morphotype is distinct from the subsequent identification of that group as a taxon, giving it a label that is no longer neutral and allocating it to a place in a hierarchic classification. The second part of this process, in the post-Darwinian period, has phylogenetic connotations, the first part has not.

In 1960 Cain and Harrison recognized the difference between the two stages and proposed that the first, the sorting of similar fossils into groups, be called 'arrangement' and the latter process 'classification'. What must be stressed is that the criteria used for 'arrangement' are morphological, for the morphology of fossils is all that remains. If evidence about chromosomes, blood enzymes and protein structure were available it would be admissible too. This confinement to morphology does not mean that it has to be investigated in traditional ways. Trabecular patterns on skiagrams and complex optical analyses to describe shape are both examples of how modern techniques are helping to extract the maximum amount of information out of the fossils. There are many modern instances of the inadequacy of behavioural data for this initial arrangement process. When animals of various types adapt to similar habitats, their superficial similarities can and have been misleading. Thus while trabecular pattern in the femoral neck can contribute to a functional interpretation of a fossil form, it is the morphological evidence, and not the functional inferences made from it, that are admissible in this initial sorting process.

Perhaps it is this confusion about the relevance of morphological and functional evidence that has led to misunderstandings about the studies of Lovejoy, Heiple and others (1970, 1972, 1973, this volume). At the risk of misrepresenting them, I suggest that they make two general points in these reports. First, that certain Plio-Pleistocene fossils, including femoral, pelvic and talar material, have a morphology that is not unusual in a widely based modern human comparative sample. Secondly, that if morphological differences do exist they represent no impediment to these fossil forms having a similar locomotor pattern to that of modern man. They claim also that the differences in femoral and pelvic morphology in modern man are the result of modifications to an enlarged pelvic birth canal.

Their first point is very relevant. Quite often, large samples are used to back up statements that a structure does or does not occur in modern man, but these samples are taken from geographically and racially homogeneous collections and fail to reflect any intra-specific variation in modern man. The inclusion by Lovejoy and his co-workers of Amerindian material in the *Homo sapiens* sample has strengthened our comparative data base, and perhaps the inclusion of more African and Asian specimens would be helpful also. As long ago as 1758 Linnaeus believed that there were sub-species of modern man (indeed *Homo sapiens americanus* was one of them) and it may be that further work will reveal more geographically distinct morphological features, whether due to genetic, nutritional or environmental reasons, than have hitherto been accepted.

Given a comprehensive comparative sample, the fact that individual variables of single fossils or groups of fossils lie within the range of modern man does not exclude the possibility that they are morphologically distinct overall. The absence of overlapping distributions for all variables between two closely related, but different, animals is the exception rather than the rule – the chimpanzee and gorilla are a good example. The importance of quantifying in an objective way visually apparent differences, and the frailty of univariate methods for assessing overall morphological affinity, have led to the use of multivariate methods of analysis. There are two kinds of such analyses. The first is the simple, but elegant, estimate such as the Coefficient of Racial Likeness (Pearson, 1926) and modifications of it (Penrose, 1954) and the Mean Character Difference (Cain and Harrison, 1958). The second kind takes account of the correlations or covariances between many variables to calculate either a distance statistic, for example the D^2 of Mahalanobis (1936), or a smaller number of uncorrelated linear functions than there were original variables. These linear functions or axes can then be used to investigate the relationships between the fossils (Rao, 1948, 1952). Fuller descriptions of these methods can be found elsewhere (Blackith and Reyment, 1971; Rao, 1971; Oxnard, 1973).

These techniques are not without their critics and controversy about their use in this initial arranging process is centred around three points. First, are the results of such multivariate methods relevant for this purpose at all, and do the risks of their misinterpretation outweigh their advantages? Second, is it right to weight against correlated variables as some of these methods do? Third, should *a priori* judgments be made about the variables leading to their being weighted in the analyses?

The relevance of multivariate methods to anthropological problems has been reviewed by Oxnard (1968) and more recently by Kowalski (1972). Their judgments are that these methods are valuable (provided that they are used in the right context), though there are still unsolved, and perhaps insoluble, difficulties with their use. For instance, Kowalski quotes Rao who showed that samples that are significantly different on univariate testing may in fact produce an insignificant result when multivariate techniques are applied. How much of this difference is due to the inclusion of irrelevant variables and how much is due to the elimination of correlation inherent in the multivariate method is difficult to assess. It does however indicate that multivariate techniques are unlikely to produce spurious separations.

Some techniques are certainly more robust than others. Dunn and Varady (1969) have shown that one of the distance statistics, Hotellings T^2, is very sensitive to unequal covariance matrices, whereas Reyment (1969), investigating the effect of such inequality on Mahalanobis's D^2 statistic, has shown it to be much less affected by such differences. A possible source of misinterpretation has also been discussed by Oxnard (1972). He pointed out that the results of Canonical Analysis may be misleading if considered on their own, but showed that when single cases are being investigated, if the results of distance statistics and the Canonical Analysis are considered together, the risk of misclassification will be minimized. Given their judicious use in the right situation, and the assessment of affinity is undoubtedly one such situation, multivariate methods are preferable to univariate ones and constructive criticisms of their use should not deter workers from continuing to experiment with their application.

The second problem, of whether correlated variables should be treated independently, is just as controversial as the first. Adanson (1763), Sneath (1961) and Sokal and Sneath (1963) all claim that it is the very fact that variables are correlated that leads to separation between groups and that it is the establishment of this grouping that is the essence of taxonomy. This is expressed in a different way by Gilmour (1937, 1951) when he says that the most 'natural' grouping is that about which most propositions can be made, i.e. which has the greatest number of variables correlated. In contrast are the views of Cain and Harrison (1958, 1960) who say that of a group of variables that are necessarily correlated, only one is applicable in the assessment of overall affinity. Their definition of necessary correlation is not entirely clear and its application to single fossils is problematical but their general meaning is plain enough.

The decision to retain or exclude all but one correlated character is a most complex one. To be set against the danger of exaggerating differences between forms is the fact that it is the change in the pattern of correlations between variables that is responsible for changes in shape between different animals. Indeed the examination of the major and subsequent axes of a correlation matrix by Principal Component Analysis is a way of investigating these differences (Jolicoeur and Mosimann, 1960). Whatever the defects of methods that seek to allow for correlated variables they are always likely to be conservative in their assessment of affinity, which is at least erring on the side of caution.

There is little guidance from general palaeontological studies about the third problem, whether there should be *a priori* weighting of variables in the initial arrangement of fossils into morphotypes. Weighting of variables has been widely debated in the context of assigning to taxa a place in a hierarchical classification, and this will be discussed later, but only Cain and Harrison (1958) have discussed it in relation to the assessment of overall affinity. They came to the proper conclusion that as many characters as possible should be used, but included the caveat about correlated variables discussed above. Lovejoy (this volume) contends that only variables that have a satisfactory bio-mechanical interpretation should be included. Though there are those who argue that such considerations should influence the valency of variables when phylogeny is being studied it is clear that the initial grouping must be done without initial bias or weighting of the variables.

As an illustration of the principles and methods outlined above, the 'arrangement' of early hominid proximal femoral remains will be considered. The relevant specimens are SK 82 and SK 97 from Swartkrans (Napier, 1964), OH 20 from Olduvai Gorge (Day, 1969) and KNM-ER 738 (Leakey, 1971; Leakey, Mungai and Walker, 1972) KNM-ER 1463, KNM-ER 1465, KNM-ER 1503 and KNM-ER 1505 (Leakey, 1973a).

Napier (1964) put forward morphological and metrical evidence that SK 82 and 97 had a head and neck morphology unlike that of modern man. OH 20 fitted closely to the same morphological pattern (Day, 1969) and subsequent finds from Koobi Fora have established that there are now seven similar fragments, which among themselves are not very variable (Wood, 1976). The data of Napier and of Wood are in agreement and their comparative samples embrace Caucasian, African and a few Asian bones. These data indicate that the bones of the smaller-statured Bushmen are generally no nearer to the fossil femora than the larger Caucasians, suggesting that allometry is unlikely to account for the morphological differences seen in these comparatively small fossil femora. The results of a Canonical Analysis using variables taken on the femoral neck (Day, 1973) confirm that these fossil femora are distinct from those of modern man and are a homogeneous group themselves.

Having established that a group exists, questions about gait pattern and its place in man's phylogeny can then be posed. However, it is fundamental that these questions be asked *about* the group rather than that they be given consideration in the *formation* of the group. In an attempt to see whether a more widely drawn modern human sample would vitiate the distinctiveness of these early femora an extensive programme of data collection has been initiated by the author.

Three more fossil specimens which include the femoral neck region were found in the Koobi Fora area in 1972; they are KNM-ER 1481, KNM-ER 1472 and KNM-ER 1475 (Leakey, 1973b; Day *et al.*, 1974). They do not fit into the homogeneous morphotype of the other early hominid femora and so there must have existed two hominid femoral morphotypes in the Plio-Pleistocene, one resembling that of modern man and the other more distinctive. Once more it is essential to understand that this decision has been made independently of functional and phylogenetic considerations.

It remains to consider the rest of the classification process and the phylogenetic and functional interpretation of hominid postcranial bones.

When the monophyletic conception of man's evolution went unchallenged and the 'single-species' concept was seemingly well-founded, the classification of postcranial fossils was relatively simple. The basic decision was whether hominid status could be given to the fossil. Once included in the Hominidae it would have been allocated to *Australopithecus* if it looked very different from the equivalent bone in modern man, and to *Homo* if it was more similar to modern man. In difficult cases some workers have even suggested a time barrier as the deciding factor for generic attribution; Campbell (1972) has proposed that an arbitary line be drawn at 2 million years – older fossils would be *Australopithecus*, younger would be *Homo*.

While doubting whether hard-won chronological data are most profitably used in this way there is no doubt about the appropriateness of their use in phylogenetic studies. If it is assumed, for the sake of argument, that two morphotypes of femoral hominid fossils do exist, it is fundamental to a phylogenetic interpretation to know whether they were synchronic (existed at the same time) or allochronic (existed at different times). The latter situation is compatible with either an ana- or clado-genetic descent; the former situation, however, effectively excludes an anagenetic pattern of evolution in the Hominidae. From Koobi Fora there is now evidence that the two early hominid femoral morphotypes were approximately synchronic and we must assume that either they belonged to a single polytypic species or to separate lineages evolving side by side; the cranial and dental evidence supports the latter concept.

In order to collate cranial and postcranial evidence certain assumptions must be made about their association at various sites. The first that must be made is that the majority of the cranial and postcranial remains at Swartkrans in South Africa belong to the same group of animals. This assumed association is not without its hazards, especially now that the heterogeneous nature of the breccia is being revealed (Butzer, 1971; Brain, this volume), but without it we cannot ensure that the phylogenetic interpretation of postcranial material is not worked out in isolation from other fossil evidence. For, while evidence about associated cranial fossils should not influence decisions about the existence of postcranial morphotypes, all evidence can justly be considered when phylogeny is being studied. If the association of the femoral morphotype and 'robust' australopithecine skulls and jaws at Swartkrans is accepted, the coexistence of similar cranial and postcranial material at Olduvai Gorge, OH 5 (Tobias 1967) and OH 20, and at Koobi Fora, KNM-ER 406 (Leakey, Mungai and Walker 1971) and KNM-738 etc., lends support to this hypothesis.

The second early hominid femoral morphotype, more closely resembling modern man, has been found in horizons at Koobi Fora where a cranial morphotype, distinct from the 'robust' australopithecines, has also been found (Leakey, 1973b; Wood, 1976). It is likely, but as yet only conjectural, that these cranial and postcranial materials are related, and in fact both have been provisionally assigned to *Homo* (Leakey, 1973a, 1974).

There is evidence to support this dual lineage hypothesis from another postcranial bone, the talus. A talus, KNM-ER 813, from Koobi Fora (Leakey, 1972; Leakey and Wood, 1973) has been found to be similar to modern human tali (Wood, 1974a). Tali from two other sites, OH 8 from Olduvai Gorge (Day and Napier, 1964) and TM 1517 from Kromdraai (Broom and Schepers, 1946) are quite similar to one another and are both less like modern man than the East Rudolf talus (Day and Wood, 1968; Wood, 1974a) and thus parallel the situation seen in the femora.

The apparent existence of two parallel lineages of hominids, the postcranial evidence for which has been detailed, poses problems in the classification of fossil bones that are poorly represented in the fossil record – the ulna Loc 40-19 from Omo is a case in point (Howell and Wood, 1974). All one can do is to examine the morphology of the bone, see if and how it deviates from the modern human pattern, judge subjectively how significant any departures in morphology are and then decide into which postcranial morphotype, or none of them, it fits best. The initial classification is necessarily provisional; more fossil or comparative data may cause it to be modified. It could be argued that cases such as these should not be classified, but left with their N_1 names only (Simpson, 1963). However, as long as other workers treat the proposed classification as a working hypothesis, which it is, no harm is done.

The hypothesis that postulates two postcranial morphotypes is, like most hypotheses about hominid evolution, easier to propose than to refute. In the future, if it is discovered that such a morphological dichotomy as has been described for femora and tali is not found in all other postcranial bones, it does not necessarily mean the demise of the hypothesis. Among many modern primates the ratio of inter- to intra-group variability differs from bone to bone. It happens to be quite high for tali and femora, yet it is low for ulnae. It is thus conceivable that for some bones, especially small bones, there may be little morphological difference between the proposed lineages, and thus in these cases a detailed taxonomic attribution is impossible (Day and Scheuer, 1973).

The limited phyletic reconstruction that has been attempted has relied solely on phenetic differences assessed visually and confirmed metrically. Apart from negatively weighting correlated variables the multivariate methods have included no other *a priori* weighting of the variables. There are those such as Adanson (1763), Gilmour (1937) and Sokal and Sneath (1963) who claim that this should always be the way to assemble classification schemes. Cain and Harrison (1960) proposed a method designed to eliminate the convergent component of phenetic affinity; what remained after modifications would therefore be the basis of a phyletic classification but Sokal and Sneath (1963) claim that attempts to eliminate convergence can only ever be partly successful.

It has also been claimed that variables that can be given a biomechanical or functional interpretation are somehow more relevant for assessing the patristic relationship than other non-functional variables. For example, Le Gros Clark (1964) felt that a fossil that showed signs of a functional modification that is well advanced in a modern group should be more closely associated with that group than other fossils, but in practice this is by no means justifiable in every case. The contrary view is expressed by Cain and Harrison (1960). They claim that one of the components of overall affinity that must be removed in order to reveal phyletic information are those variables that relate to similar adaptations to an ecological niche and are therefore convergent; an example would be the parallel development of an upright posture in a savannah situation. A passage from their paper may be very relevant as a guide to the phyletic interpretation of postcranial material: 'Those characters in two forms which are different but appear on functional analysis to be responses to the same functional or ecological demand are good indicators that the two forms are not closely related, and probably not derivable from one another.' This passage emphasizes that the crucial decision is the initial one about the existence of more than one synchronic postcranial morphotype. It also demonstrates that functional similarity between the two forms argues as much, if not more, for their phyletic separation than it does for their phyletic unity.

The relegation of the consideration of functional interpretations to last is only an indication of the place they should take in the narrow context of the process of classification. However, in terms of the task of relating the evolution and progress of the hominids to their environment these are probably the most important aspect of the investigation of postcranial hominid fossils.

Locomotor capabilities of fossils can be investigated by either absolute or relative methods. Absolute methods rely on the assessment of the fossil bones' ability to withstand simulated loading situations; an example is the work of Preuschoft (1971) on the biomechanical vector analysis of the cross-sectional profiles of large or miniature long bones.

Relative methods involve the comparison of the fossil material with data from modern bones of a known locomotor category. One such method is photoelastic analysis which matches the reaction of the fossil to stress situations with that of modern bones (Oxnard, 1973). A second method uses metrical analysis to identify features of modern bones that are believed to relate to various broad functional roles, and then examines the degree and development of these features in the fossil. This method has been developed over many years by the Birmingham Group and its latest application is to the pelvis (Zuckerman *et al.*, 1973). A third method is based on metrical analysis and has been developed by Day (Day, 1967; Day and Wood, 1968, 1969; Day, 1973; Wood, 1973). It is based on the interpretation of multivariate statistical techniques and can best be explained by reference to a specific case, the analysis of fossil hominid tali.

Groups of modern primate tali belonging to several locomotor categories, including modern bipedalism, were submitted to Canonical Analysis. Of the linear functions or axes generated only those that were able to discriminate between bipeds and the other groups were considered relevant for this particular problem. Then, by applying the variable weightings of the relevant axes to the fossil data, a process which is mathematically quite proper (Gower, 1968), the behaviour of the fossil on the axes is an indicator whether it is likely to have belonged to a biped or a quadruped. The assignment of the fossil to a place within any of the modern locomotor groups is not sufficient evidence that it belongs to that modern population: Oxnard (1972) has recently pointed out that distance statistic values have to be consulted before more definite statements can be made. This method is most useful, and its power of discrimination greatest, in a situation where there are a number of relevant modern locomotor forms to examine (Wood, 1973).

The application of these methods of relative functional analysis is made more difficult by the apparent existence of two hominid postcranial morphotypes. Interpretations of the morphological features of the 'robust' australopithecine material have indicated that it also was adapted for bipedalism, if not actually a habitual biped (Robinson, 1972; Day, 1973; Zuckerman *et al.*, 1973). It is apparent that only one of the morphotypes has a modern representative in *Homo sapiens*. Even so, the partial expression of the features of the only extant biped in a fossil bone is *a posteriori* no guarantee that the fossils necessarily belong to a stage in the evolution of the modern morphotype rather than belonging to the now unrepresented one.

Often apparently homologous structures are used as an indication of a functional similarity. An example is the association of a high angle of torsion of the head in modern human tali with the modern human-type gait. Its presence in a fossil talus has been considered by some (Lisowski, 1967) to indicate a gait pattern similar to modern man's. However, when Richard Owen (1843) introduced the concept of homology into biology he based it on structure and not function; to paraphrase De Beer (1971), 'a structure is homologous because of what it *is*, not because of what it *does*'. In fact the talar head has a high angle of torsion in *Colobus* (Wood, 1973), a form with a locomotor pattern very different from that of modern man. From this it is not surprising that examples of possible misinterpretations of the function of homologous structures can be found in the narrower category of hominid bipedalism (Wood, 1974b). The way to see that confusions of this sort are reduced to a minimum is to investigate a much wider range of comparative material. This will enable those features that are truly specializations to be identified.

Far from the importance of classical comparative anatomical studies declining, with the increasing use of more sophisticated statistical methods of discrimination, the existence of a firm basis of comparative anatomical data is as essential now as it was at any time in the past.

Acknowledgments

I would like to thank M.D. Leakey, R.E.F. Leakey and Dr C.K. Brain for allowing me to examine fossils in their care. I am especially grateful to my teacher, Michael Day, who originally introduced me to these studies and has since provided wise guidance. Professor Glenister and Dr L. Scheuer kindly read the manuscript and suggest many improvements. Miss Janice Wicks typed the text.

References

Adanson, M. (1763) *Familles des plantes*, Vol. 1. Paris.

Black, D. (1933) Fossil man in China. *Geol. Mem.*, Ser A, 11 (2), 63-109.

Blackith, R.E. and Reyment, R.A. (1971) *Multivariate Morphometrics*. London.

Broom, R. and Schepers, G.W.A. (1946) The South African fossil ape-men: the Australopithecinae. *Trans. Mus. Mem.* 2, 73-5.

Butzer, K.W. (1971) Another look at the australopithecine cave breccias of the Transvaal. *Amer. Anthrop.* 73, 1197-201.

Butzer, K.W., this volume.

Cain, A.J. and Harrison, G.A. (1958) An analysis of the taxonomist's judgment of affinity. *Proc. Zool. Soc. Lond.* 131, 85-98.

Cain, A.J. and Harrison, G.A. (1960) Phyletic weighting. *Proc. Zool. Soc. Lond.* 135, 1-31.

Campbell, B.G. (1972) Conceptual progress in physical anthropology: fossil man. *Annual Rev. Anthrop.*, Vol. 1, 27-54.

Clark, W.E. Le Gros (1964) *The Fossil Evidence for Human Evolution*. 2nd ed., Chicago.

Day, M.H. (1967) Olduvai Hominid 10: a multivariate analysis. *Nature* 215, 323-4.

Day, M.H. (1969) Femoral fragment of a robust australopithecine from Olduvai Gorge, Tanzania. *Nature* 221, 230-3.

Day, M.H. (1973) Locomotor features of the lower limb in hominids. *Symp. Zool. Soc. Lond.* 33, 29-51.

Day, M.H., this volume.

Day, M.H., Leakey, R.E.F., Walker, A.C., and Wood, B.A. (1974) New hominids from East Rudolf, Kenya (1). *Amer. J. phys. Anthrop.* (n.s.) 42, 461-76.
Day, M.H. and Molleson, T.I. (1973) The Trinil femora. In Day, M.H. (ed.), *Human Evolution*, 127-54. London.
Day, M.H. and Napier, J.R. (1964) Hominid fossils from Bed I, Olduvai Gorge, Tanganyika: fossil foot bones. *Nature* 201, 967-70.
Day, M.H. and Scheuer, J.L. (1973) SKW 14147: A new hominid metacarpal from Swartkrans. *J. human Evol.* 2, 429-38.
Day, M.H. and Wood, B.A. (1968) Functional affinities of the Olduvai Hominid 8 talus. *Man* 3, 440-55.
Day, M.H. and Wood, B.A. (1969) Hominoid tali from East Africa, *Nature* 222, 591-2.
De Beer, G. (1971) *Homology, an Unsolved Problem*. London.
Dubois, E. (1892) Paleontologische onderzoekingen op Java. *Versl. Mijnw.*, Batavia, 3, 10-14.
Dubois, E. (1932) The distinct organization of Pithecanthropus of which the femur bears evidence, now confirmed from other individuals of the described species. *Proc. K. ned. Akad. Wet.* 35 (6), 716-22.
Dubois, E. (1934) New evidence of the distinct organization of Pithecanthropus, *Proc. K. ned. Akad. Wet.*, 37, No. 3: 139-45.
Dunn, O.J. and Varady, P.D. (1966) Probabilities of correct classification in discriminant analysis. *Biometrics* 22, 908-24.
Editorial (1932) The Peking Man. *Nature* 130, 53.
Gilmour, J.S.L. (1937) A taxonomic problem. *Nature* 139, 1040-2.
Gilmour, J.S.L. (1951) The development of taxonomic theory since 1851. *Nature* 168, 400-2.
Gower, J.C. (1968) Adding a point to vector diagrams in multi-variate analysis. *Biometrica* 55, 582-5.
Howell, C. and Wood, B.A. (1974) Early hominid ulna from the Omo basin, Ethiopia. *Nature*, 249, 174-6.
Jolicoeur, P. and Mosimann, J.E. (1960) Size and shape variation in the Painted Turtle: a Principal Component Analysis. *Growth* 24, 339-54.
Kowalski, C.J. (1972) A commentary on the use of multivariate statistical methods in anthropometric research. *Amer. J. phys. Anthrop.* (n.s.) 36, 119-31.
Leakey, R.E.F. (1971) Further evidence of lower Pleistocene hominids from East Rudolf, North Kenya. *Nature* 231, 241-5.
Leakey, R.E.F. (1972) Further evidence of lower Pleistocene hominids from East Rudolf, North Kenya, 1971. *Nature* 237, 264-9.
Leakey, R.E.F. (1973a) Further evidence of lower Pleistocene hominids from East Rudolf, North Kenya, 1972. *Nature* 242, 170-3.
Leakey, R.E.F. (1973b) Evidence for an advanced Plio-Pleistocene hominid from East Rudolf, Kenya. *Nature* 242, 447-50.
Leakey, R.E.F. (1974) Further evidence of lower Pleistocene hominids from East Rudolf, North Kenya, 1973. *Nature* 248, 653-6.
Leakey, R.E.F., Mungai, J.M. and Walker, A.C. (1971) New australopithecines from East Rudolf, Kenya. *Amer. J. phys. Anthrop.* (n.s.) 35, 175-86.
Leakey, R.E.F., Mungai, J.M. and Walker, A.C. (1972) New australopithecines from East Rudolf, Kenya (II), *Amer. J. phys. Anthrop.* (n.s.) 36, 235-52.

Leakey, R.E.F. and Wood, B.A. (1973) New evidence of the genus *Homo* from East Rudolf, Kenya (II). *Amer. J. phys. Anthrop.* (n.s.) 39, 355-68.
Lewis, O.J. (1972a) Osteological features characterizing the wrists of monkeys and apes, with consideration of this region in *Dryopithecus (Proconsul) africanus*. *Amer. J. phys. Anthrop.* (n.s.) 36, 45-58.
Lewis, O.J. (1972b) The evolution of the hallucial tarso-metatarsal joint in the Anthropoidea. *Amer. J. phys. Anthrop.* (n.s.) 37, 13-33.
Lewis, O.J. (1973) The hominoid Os Capitatum, with special reference to the fossil bones from Sterkfontein and Olduvai Gorge. *J. hum. Evol.* 2, 1-11.
Linnaeus (1758) *Systema Naturae*, 10th ed., Stockholm (quoted in Campbell, C. (1962) The systematics of man. *Nature* 194, 224-31).
Lisowski, F.P. (1967) Angular growth changes and comparisons in the primate talus. *Folia primat.* 7, 81-97.
Lovejoy, C.O., this volume.
Lovejoy, C.O. and Heiple, K.G. (1970) A reconstruction of the femur of *Australopithecus africanus*, *Amer. J. phys. Anthrop.* (n.s.) 32, 33-40.
Lovejoy, C.O. and Heiple, K.G. (1972) Proximal femoral anatomy of *Australopithecus*. *Nature* 235, 175-6.
Lovejoy, C.O., Heiple, K.G. and Burstein, A.H. (1973) The gait of *Australopithecus*. *Amer. J. phys. Anthrop.* (n.s.) 38, 757-80.
Mahalanobis, P.C. (1936) On the generalized distance in statistics. *Proc. nat. Inst. Sci. India* 2, 49-55.
Napier, J.R. (1964) The evolution of bipedal walking in the hominids. *Archs. Biol.* (Liège) 75, 673-708.
Owen, R. (1843) *Lectures on Comparative Anatomy and Physiology of Invertebrate Animals*. London.
Oxnard, C.E. (1968) Primate evolution: a method of investigation. *Amer. J. phys. Anthrop.* (n.s.) 28, 289-302.
Oxnard, C.E. (1969) Evolution of the human shoulder: some possible pathways. *Amer. J. phys. Anthrop.* (n.s.) 30, 319-32.
Oxnard, C.E. (1972) Some African fosssil foot bones: a note on the interpolation of fossils into a matrix of extant species. *Amer. J. phys. Anthrop.* (n.s.) 37, 3-12.
Oxnard, C.E. (1973) *Form and Pattern in Human Evolution: Some Mathematical, Physical and Engineering Approaches*. Chicago.
Patterson, B. and Howells, W.W. (1967) Hominid humeral fragments from Early Pleistocene of Northwestern Kenya. *Science* 156, 64-6.
Pearson, K. (1926) On the coefficient of racial likeness, *Biometrika* 18, 105-17.
Penrose, L.S. (1954) Distance, size and shape. *Annals Eugenics* 18, 337-43.
Preuschoft, H. (1971) Body posture and mode of locomotion in early pleistocene hominids. *Folia primat.* 14, 209-40.
Rao, C.R. (1948) The utilization of multiple measurements, in problems of biological classification. *J. Roy. Stat. Soc.*, Series B, 10, 159-93.
Rao, C.R. (1952) *Advanced Statistical Methods in Biometric Research*. New York.
Rao, C.R. (1971) Taxonomy in anthropology. In Hodson, F.R. *et al.* (eds.), *Mathematics in the Archaeological and Historical Sciences*, 19-29.
Reyment, R.A. (1969) Some case studies of the statistical analysis of sexual dimorphism. *Bull. Geol. Instn. Univ. Uppsala* n.s. 1, 97-119.
Rightmire, G.P. (1972) Multivariate analysis of an early hominid metacarpal from Swartkrans. *Science* 176, 159-61.

Robinson, J.T. (1972) *Early Hominid Posture and Locomotion*. Chicago.

Simpson, G.G. (1961) *Principles of Animal Taxonomy*. New York.

Simpson, G.G. (1963) The meaning of taxonomic statements. In Washburn, S.L. (ed.) *Classification and Human Evolution*, 1-31. Chicago.

Simpson, G.G., Roe, A. and Lewontin, R.C. (1960) *Quantitative Zoology*. New York.

Sneath, P.H.A. (1961) Recent developments in theoretical and quantitative taxonomy. *Syst. Zool.* 10, 118-39.

Sokal, R.R. and Sneath, P.H.A. (1963) *Numerical Taxonomy*. San Francisco.

Tobias, P.V. (1967) *The Cranium of Australopithecus (Zinjanthropus) boisei*. London.

Weidenreich, F. (1938) Discovery of the femur and the humerus of *Sinanthropus pekinensis*. *Nature* 141, 614.

Weidenreich, F. (1941) The extremity bones of *Sinanthropus pekinensis*. *Paleontologia Sinica*, New Series D, 5, 1-151.

Wolpoff, M.H. (1973) Posterior tooth size, body size, and diet in South African gracile australopithecines. *Amer. J. phys. Anthrop.* (n.s.) 39, 375-94.

Wood, B.A. (1973) Locomotor affinities of hominoid tali from Kenya. *Nature* 246, 45-6.

Wood, B.A. (1974a) Evidence on the locomotor pattern of *Homo* from early Pleistocene of Kenya. *Nature* 251, 135-6.

Wood, B.A. (1974b) Olduvai Bed I postcranial fossils: a reassessment. *J. human Evol.* 3, 373-8.

Wood, B.A. (1976) Remains attributable to *Homo* in the East Rudolf succession. In Coppens, Y. *et al.* (eds.), *Early Man and Environments in the Lake Rudolf Basin: Stratigraphy, Paleoecology and Evolution*, 490-506. Chicago.

Zuckerman, S. (1970) *Beyond the Ivory Tower*. London.

Zuckerman, S., Ashton, E.H., Flinn, R.M., Oxnard, C.E. and Spence, T.F. (1973) Some locomotor features of the pelvic girdle in Primates. *Symp. Zool. Soc. Lond.* 33, 71-165.

A.L. Zihlman

Interpretations of early hominid locomotion

Introduction

The investigation of early hominid locomotion spans three issues: the origin of hominid bipedalism, the nature of australopithecine bipedal adaptation, and possible transitions between Plio-Pleistocene hominids and modern *Homo sapiens*. On what configuration of anatomy and behaviour did selective pressures operate? How can these pressures explain the different patterns of locomotion? Can different patterns be deduced from the evidence? Obviously these questions focus on functional analysis at a specific time, the Plio-Pleistocene, as well as anatomical and behavioural changes over long intervals. This paper is concerned primarily with the australopithecine adaptation. I am using 'australopithecine' to include all Plio-Pleistocene hominids prior to *Homo erectus*; my use of the generic term *Australopithecus* refers to both robust and gracile forms.

As interest in early hominid locomotion has grown, many and sometimes conflicting conclusions have been drawn from research on particular aspects of the problem. Some workers correlate observed morphological differences with two presumed locomotor adaptations within the genus, encompassing australopithecines and modern man; still others claim that *Australopithecus* moved differently from any extant man or beast.

One reason for this confusion is the state of the fossil material. Although 60 to 70% of the body weight is involved in locomotion (Grand, 1977), less than 10% of early human fossils belong to the locomotor skeleton (Robinson, 1972). Compared with skulls and teeth, fragmentary femora, tibiae, tarsal bones and the like are infrequent, and joints and long bones are rare. The relatively small sample allows widely divergent interpretations.

Another source of conflict is the difficulty in sorting out fine points of difference between closely related species; all Plio-Pleistocene hominids were bipedal. Naturally, theoretical frameworks of investigators differ and influence their methods of approaching the fossils. Finally, problems of dating, of establishing correct sequences of morphological change and determining whether bones and teeth found together actually go together – these difficulties and uncertainties produce still more controversy.

Each of the few limb bones found has been studied exhaustively. A configurational approach attempts to interrelate morphological and behavioural aspects of adaptation. So joints, limb alignment, muscle mechanics – the entire animal, and the milieu in which it functions, must be considered. The comparative and functional analyses presented in this paper will show that *Australopithecus* evolved a unique bipedal adaptation.

A behavioural-evolutionary framework

Wherever possible, fossils should be studied as if they are *living* organisms. A configuration emerges from three kinds of information: (1) the relation of locomotion to environmental context of the species; (2) the correlation of locomotor behaviour with morphology using information from free-ranging primates; (3) analysis of the total limb and joint system – the whole animal. What is the role of each source of information for achieving a configurational analysis, and how does each source relate specifically to *Australopithecus*?

Environment and locomotion

For *Australopithecus* as for all mammals, locomotion is the most significant whole body activity and is therefore a major aspect of its way of life. Bipedalism is the basis for the hominid adaptation – for freeing the hands for tool use, carrying and throwing objects – and must be studied not just for its own sake, but for its role in the total species adaptation.

Configurational analysis considers species adaptation in its environmental setting. Australopithecines seem to have been primarily forager/gatherers, ranging widely over the open savannah, using tools to obtain a variety of foods. (The way of life of *Australopithecus* as presented here is developed more fully elsewhere). This adaptive complex included the ability to run and to carry gathered plants and small animals that had been caught and killed, as well as tools and defensive objects (rocks, sticks). Distances could be great between food, raw material, water, and camp-sites, and various terrains – sandy, hilly, rocky, muddy, perhaps marshy – had to be negotiated. *Australopithecus* used areas around lakes and rivers but was adapting to open country. What is crucial here, and often overlooked, is the firm relationship between these adaptive needs and the evolution of bipedal posture and locomotion.

Anatomical and behavioural correlates: generic level of adaptation

Plio-Pleistocene hominids made similar adaptations in ecology, cultural level, diet and locomotion. *Australopithecus* inhabited the savannah, used tools for food-gathering and defence, and had large molar and premolar teeth, reduced canines, a small brain, and pelvic, femoral and foot structures appropriate for bipedalism. Even if there was more than a single species, common phylogeny and similar environments provide sufficient bases for pursuing their adaptive pattern at the generic rather than the specific level.

Correlates between morphology and behaviour may be difficult to establish with fossil bones alone. Even in living animals studied in their environmental setting, considerable motor variability may be observed in the same species. Both social and locomotor behaviour may change according to environment with no corresponding anatomical change, as in *Presbytis entellus* (Grand, 1968). Furthermore, locomotor-environmental correlation may not be apparent – for example, several species of *Cercopithecus* monkeys coexist in the African rain forests: they vary in colour and size but little in musculoskeletal anatomy, yet motor behaviour varies from species to species (Schultz, 1970; Gartlan and Struhsaker, 1972). On the other hand, anatomical differences may occur in similar environments: the genus *Macaca* varies from the long-tailed small crab-eating macaque to the large stocky tail-less Japanese macaque, yet both live in trees.

Admitting these variables and ambiguities at the species level in living forms available for investigation, one can appreciate why, in making deductions from the fossil record alone, it is sounder to generalize about the locomotor adaptation of the Plio-Pleistocene hominids at the generic level.

Anatomical complex: interrelationship of parts

In a configurational approach to the locomotor anatomy of a species, the whole limb must be studied so that the functional complex of a single part will not be distorted. One joint cannot be examined isolated from what is known of others. This is particularly important for evolving lineages where joints may vary in their rate of change or within a limb, one joint may lag relative to two others. Correct extrapolation from one joint to another (in both living and fossil forms) is not always possible. For example, to reconstruct the knee joint position accurately within a bipedal system, information on the total limb is needed; the morphology of the proximal tibia provides some information; the distal femur, its bicondylar angle, size and orientation of the condyles affects position; in the proximal femur the amount of torsion of the head and neck relative to the shaft and to the distal end contribute to knee position; and, finally, the acetabulum, if placed more medially or laterally, will affect knee joint position (Hall, 1965; Lovejoy and Heiple, 1970; Heiple and Lovejoy, 1971; Preuschoft, 1970, 1971; Jenkins, 1972). The position of hip and knee joints ultimately influences the position of the foot (Gregory, 1912). Therefore, to reconstruct the orientation of the knee joint (and thus the foot) with reasonable certainty at least two of these four elements are necessary.

The value of configurational analysis of anatomical complexes is further illustrated by comparison of howler and spider monkeys of the New World. If the *entire* upper limb is viewed holistically – with comparison of shoulder, elbow and wrist joints – two structural patterns are apparent; observations in the wild of total body postures and behaviour of howler and spider monkeys clearly demonstrate two distinct motor styles (Grand, 1968 (ms); Lewis, 1971).

In contrast, if comparison of upper limbs is accomplished by matching bones isolated from the limb configuration – *only* scapulae, *only* humeri or *only* radii or ulnae – then the differences between the two are not particularly marked. In multivariate analysis of primate scapulae those of spider and howler monkeys cluster (Stern and Oxnard, 1973), and one might be led to conclude incorrectly that they express similar locomotor adaptations. Similarly in *Australopithecus* bony structures cannot be isolated from each other nor can gait be interpreted from the isolated pieces. The entire bone, joint and whole limb must be incorporated into a comparative functional analysis in order for a pattern to emerge.

One way to discover a pattern is the application of functional, biomechanical analysis to the lower limb of *Australopithecus*. Structural features may then be explained functionally in terms of relative *mechanical* efficiency and so contribute to understanding locomotor change (Gregory, 1912; Schaeffer, 1947; 1950). *Australopithecus* needed to walk long distances over variable terrain to seek widely dispersed resources; they had to carry this extra weight (females had to carry infants as well), to run after small animals and to throw objects at predators. Selection worked toward overall efficiency in a variety of behaviour patterns, and until these were fully developed, there may have been an effective if mechanically inefficient stage (Schaeffer, 1950).

Unique configuration of australopithecine locomotion

Configurational analyses, as summarized below, demonstrate that the configuration of the hip, knee and ankle joints and foot in *Australopithecus* was unique (Preuschoft, 1971; Jenkins, 1972; Zihlman and Hunter, 1972; Zihlman, 1973; n.d.). Other studies have interpreted fossils of the australopithecine locomotor system similarly, although expressed in a variety of ways: 'transitional', 'not fully human', 'intermediate', 'unique', and so on. These studies include those of Washburn (1951, 1963) on the form and function of the hip joint musculoskeleton; Le Gros Clark (1947, 1955) on the South African innominates, distal femur and talus; Mednick (1955) on internal organization and split-line patterns of innominate bones and hip joint function; Davis (1964) on the Olduvai tibia and fibula; Day and Napier (1964) on the Olduvai foot; Day and Napier (1964) on the pelvic and femoral fossils from South Africa and available material from East Africa. Recently Oxnard (1972, 1973) using biometrics on fossil innominates and tali concluded that the fossil pattern is unique.

Stress analysis

Preuschoft's approach (1970, 1971) to the study of posture and locomotion examines the shapes of bones relative to the stresses placed on them. This method depends upon consideration of interrelationships between bone, joint and muscle, because stresses in bones are determined by relative forces of muscles acting on them and by length of lever arms, as well as by points of application and directions of external forces; these latter are dependent upon body posture and locomotor pattern. The shapes of skeletal elements and mechanical stressing can be investigated by theoretical mechanical analysis. This type of analysis has three stages: (1) calculation of shapes of bones which would provide the highest stresses with minimum material; (2) investigation of mechanically important characters of the fossils; and (3) results of above investigation are compared with optimal shapes which have been found by theoretical analysis (Preuschoft, 1971, p.210).

Based on analyses of the leg and foot bones of apes and humans, it was possible to determine where stress in the lower extremities occurs. Important mechanical features of the fossils were determined and compared to results in living forms. The following fossils were included in the study: the distal phalanx of a right big toe bone from Olduvai (Day and Napier, 1966); the Olduvai foot (Day and Napier, 1964); Olduvai tibia and fibula (Davis, 1964); and the distal femora from Sterkfontein (Le Gros Clark, 1947; 1967).

From stress analyses Preuschoft concluded that the australopithecine foot was a terrestrial non-prehensile one; the big toe could not be completely abducted; toes were short with rather weak long flexors (1972, p.217). Certain features of the fossil talus (such as the horizontal angle of the neck) and the calcaneus are intermediate between apes and humans but more similar to the latter. The tibia is not curved as in pongids, but is straight in its longitudinal axis; it was adapted to stresses which are also typical for modern man (1971, p.235).

A displacement of the centre of gravity backwards (in a dorsal direction), possibly caused by lordotic curvature of the lumbar and cervical sections of the vertebral column, theoretically placed the line of gravity behind the knee joint. This situation is indicated by the powerful upper limbs of the fossil hominids (1971, p.236). Furthermore, analysis of force distribution on the tibia and fibula suggests that the knees were not adducted into a midline as they are in modern man. But since the proximal tibia is absent, this cannot be proved. Interestingly, Preuschoft concluded from study of the South African distal femora that neither the adducted (valgus) position of the knee joint which exists in modern man nor its abducted (varus) position in apes occurred in this fossil; thus an intermediate or unique pattern may be present for this feature.

Cineradiographic analysis

Jenkins (1972) used cineradiography to study bipedalism in chimpanzees in order to document joint movements, posture and alternating motions of the limb from the midline. Pelvic orientation and vertical and lateral oscillation of pelvic position were measured at specific phases of gait. Movements of the femur, excursion of the knee joint, amount of ankle motion and foot position were all noted.

This study provides a contrast with human locomotion and is a refinement over early significant research by Elftman (1944). Components of human gait (pelvic rotation, pelvic tilt, hip and knee flexion, knee and ankle interactions and lateral displacement of the pelvis) were recognizable in chimpanzee gait although the total pattern was very different. For example, in chimpanzees the flexed hip and knee joints during stance phase were not placed under the trunk, whereas in modern man extended hip and knee joints are aligned under the pelvis. Internal rotation occurred when the hip was flexed, rather than during hip extension as in modern man. Pelvic tilt was reversed; the pelvis was lifted on the side of the swinging limb rather than tilting on the supporting side as it does in *Homo sapiens*. A major dissimilarity between the gaits was abducted femoral excursion (movement around the midline) of chimpanzees compared to the straight line femoral excursion in humans. Femoral flexion and extension relative to the pelvis are the same during both bipedal and quadrupedal locomotion in chimpanzees; their bipedalism is essentially a quadrupedal limb movement with the trunk relatively upright without the supporting body weight.

In the study of fossils, Jenkins suggests that femoral excursion in *Australopithecus* was intermediate, that is, the knees would have been more adducted than in chimpanzees but less than in modern man. This is based on the relatively shallow acetabulum of SK 50 innominate and the femoral head margin of the SK 82 proximal femur which is intermediate between ape and man. The greater flaring of the iliac blade may also be explicable in terms of a more abducted femoral excursion in the fossil (1972, p.879).

This conclusion raises the possibility (also suggested from the previously cited study) that the functional significance of the high bicondylar angle in the Sterkfontein distal femur as reconstructed by Heiple and Lovejoy (1971) may *not* be the same as for modern man. Therefore, the issue of whether the knees of the australopithecines were together (adducted) in a midline position as Heiple and Lovejoy have stated remains open for discussion.

Joint reconstruction analysis

Biomechanical analysis of three-dimensional models of fossils provides the opportunity for analysing bone/joint/muscle relationships and for evaluating the results in terms of adaptation. The first study on the Makapan ilium positioned in the Dart Bushuman pelvic reconstruction analysed the meaning functionally of its less curved ilium compared to that in *Homo sapiens* (Zihlman and Hunter, 1972). The other study on the hip joint of the Swartkrans innominate (SK 50) and the proximal femur (SK 97) reconstructed mass and position of major muscle groups of the hip joint, and compared these features in the fossil relative to quadrupedal apes and bipedal humans (Zihlman, 1974).

Specific features were then viewed in a wider context: the contribution of hip rotation and abduction to efficiency of motor behaviours and how they worked in the fossil and how mass distribution, size and orientation of muscle groups affect overall motor efficiency of the fossils.

Muscular development and planes of joint motion underlie the total motor adaptation. In bipedal hominid locomotion, hip and knee extension, hip rotation and abduction and ankle extension are important. The large muscles are one-joint rather than two-joint (Haxton, 1947): gluteus maximus, quadriceps femoris for hip and knee extension, respectively; gluteus medius and minimus for rotation and abduction, and soleus for ankle extension.

Bones also reflect changes in motion, line of weight-bearing and size and position of muscles. The ilium, for example, once long and narrow, is now short and broad; it once had no curvature and was oriented in one plane of movement but is now curved and motion in three planes is possible. One feature affected by the reorientation of the ilium is the position of the muscle fibres attaching on the anterior part of the ilium. The shortened and broadened ilium positions these muscles to produce hip joint rotation in hominids. Also, the long femoral neck of SK 97 and the flared ilium of SK 50 and MLD 7 indicate that abduction and rotation were well developed in

Australopithecus; the long lever arm of gluteus medius and gluteus minimus show that a great deal of torque (rotational force) was produced by contraction of these muscles. Interestingly, torque was reduced in the evolution from *Australopithecus* to *Homo*.

Given the crucial role of abduction and rotation in gait efficiency in hominid bipedalism as well as the marked rotational force postulated in *Australopithecus*, hip joint motion can be assumed as integral to the locomotor adaptation of these early hominids. From an evolutionary perspective, what factors might explain its reduction in evolution? In answering this question it is necessary to specify how this motion element fits into the australopithecine motor repertoire and body transport mode.

First, if *Australopithecus* had short lower limbs, then more torque would maximize stride; as the legs became longer and so stride was longer, less torque per step sufficed. Reduction of the lever arm of gluteus medius and gluteus minimus increased speed and arc of movement with each muscle contraction and a longer step using less energy was possible (Zihlman and Hunter, 1972).

Second, if *Australopithecus* had longer arms and a relatively *massive upper trunk*, then more force was necessary to adjust trunk and upper limbs over the supporting foot. (This is some evidence that limb proportions in *Australopithecus* may have been unlike those of modern man or modern apes (Zihlman, 1967; McHenry, 1974).) Reduction in mass of the upper body would reduce the amount of muscle force of gluteus medius and gluteus minimus needed to align the trunk over the supporting foot and to overcome resistance in moving forward.

Third, the position of the abductors and their long lever arm in *Australopithecus* would tend to lower hip joint pressure and so reduce the load on the hip joint and femoral head (Lovejoy, this volume). This feature would be adaptive if distribution of body mass were different in *Australopithecus* with relatively more weight present in the upper part of the body than in the pelvis and lower limbs.

Fourth, if the knees were not aligned in the same way in the fossil and in modern man, as suggested by Jenkins and Preuschoft, then perhaps more torque was necessary for placing one foot in front of the other in a midline position; modern man solves this problem by torsion of the femur which cants the distal femora (knee joints) into the midline. The fossil would have used muscle energy to achieve what in modern humans is accomplished by bony configuration.

Total configuration of the lower limb: summary

The australopithecine lower limb configuration appears to be unique in joint alignment, muscle mechanics and gait pattern. Stresses acting on the leg, ankle and foot and the distal femur show that joint alignment and weight-bearing were different for the fossils compared to living hominoids. These features in the knee and ankle joints support conclusions that the hip joint also functioned differently. The alignment of the lower limb joints was distinctive in the fossils, and the mechanism of hip rotation-abduction performed by gluteus medius and gluteus minimus was not fully human.

Functional/biomechanical analyses can provide a basis for interpreting adaptive change. Certain anatomical changes eventually increased effectiveness of motor behaviour: change in pattern of weight-bearing and line of gravity through joints leading to development of an adducted knee position; increase in length and mass of the lower limbs with decrease in mass of upper limbs and trunk reflecting the distribution of mass throughout the body; decreased lever arm length of rotator-abductor hip joint muscles as measured by increased curvature of the anterior part of the ilium and decrease in femoral neck length.

Issues in locomotor studies

Since bipedal locomotion marks the origin of the hominid family, gait of modern man provides a necessary, though not exclusive, basis for the interpretation of previous bipedal patterns. However, different conclusions have been reached from similar studies because the perspective and approach of investigators varies. The view I present, that pelvic (internal) rotation is performed by muscle action and is critical for locomotor efficiency, is one basis for the conclusion that the nature of early hominid bipedalism is unique and less mechanically efficient (though effective) than later bipedalism (Zihlman and Hunter, 1972; Zihlman, 1974). A contrasting view maintains that hip rotation does not result from muscle action and that australopithecine bipedalism was at least as efficient as that of modern man, if not more efficient (Lovejoy *et al.*, 1973).

Opposed views of lower limb recovery action is a reason for these differing conclusions. By definition, pendulum action occurs when the muscles relax and the limb swings forward without muscular effort. The Weber brothers in 1836 first maintained that the swing of the human lower limb was automatic. However, Steindler (1955), Kummer (1962) and others, on theoretical grounds, stated that the human lower limb could not act as a pendulum. More recently Basmajian (1967), using electromyography, demonstrated that iliopsoas, the primary hip flexor in gait, is active when the swing phase begins and the limb swings forward; this movement is therefore initiated by a burst of muscular activity. By definition, then, the lower limb is not a pendulum. Since the pendulum interpretation does not apply to human gait (nor to the gait of quadrupeds), it cannot be a basis for extrapolation to the fossils. The pendulum concept probably does not apply to other animals either. Recently Dagg and DeVos examined the possibility that the front legs in eight species of artiodactyls act as pendulums in a slow walk. They found that 'a front leg swings forward about twice as fast as it would if it swung freely like a cylindrical pendulum, *so that muscles play an important role in pulling the leg forward even in a slow walk*' (1968a, 110; my italics).

It was assumed for some time that the upper limbs also swing by pendular rather than muscular action, in rhythm contra-lateral to the forward-swinging lower limb. Arm swing, however, is controlled by muscle action, as first maintained by Elftman (1939) and later demonstrated electromyographically (Basmajian, 1967). Even if pendular movement of both upper and lower limbs occurs under the ideal conditions of the smooth support surface of the laboratory, it remains questionable whether this would hold true outside such conditions.

Interpretation of the significance of internal rotation at the hip joint follows from one's views on pendulum action of the lower limb. Although Lovejoy maintains that rotation is simply initiated by ground reaction at toe-off, direct and indirect evidence demonstrate that muscle action is responsible. Elftman, in contrast to Lovejoy, asserts that the ground reaction does *not* produce accelerations of the body; instead ground reaction *reflects* the accelerations due to muscle action and to gravity and is an accurate measure of them (1954:433). Laboratory studies on human gait viewed in isolation may obscure the importance of rotation; its significance takes on greater meaning if diverse comparative studies are examined.

For one, laboratory studies on human gait, including electromyography, show that gluteus medius and gluteus minimus contract for 40% of stance phase when one foot supports body weight (Scherb, 1952; Basmajian, 1967). The anterior fibres of these muscles are the only possible internal rotators (Duchenne, 1949; Elftman, 1954; Basmajian, 1967; Ducroquet, 1968), although Basmajian points out that this was not accepted for some time. Their posterior fibres act as abductors to control lateral pelvic tilt. Abduction and rotation together balance the trunk by realigning it over the supporting foot and thereby promote smooth forward progression (Saunders *et al.*, 1953). The amount of rotation with each step as measured in the laboratory is small (average is 8° according to Levens *et al.*, 1948), but with increased speed or with adjustment to uneven terrain, pelvic rotation is significantly increased (Eberhart *et al.*, 1954; Murray *et al.*, 1966; Inman, 1967).

Second, arm motion lends support to muscle action of internal rotation. The swinging arms aid in regulating body rotation by reversing the rotational force from the supporting hip joints on to the supporting limb. This rhythm suggests that the rotational force generated in forward movement is powerful, and more so than presumably could occur without muscle action; the arms are needed to counteract rotation and transfer it evenly to the other limb.

Third, internal rotation at the hip joint (with assistance from knee and ankle motion) positions feet in the midline. In human gait effective positioning of the foot under the centre of gravity is an active rather than a passive movement, especially critical on uneven ground, and it permits even transfer of body weight to the other limb with minimal lateral deviation – a motion contributing to efficient gait and so critical that it must be under muscular control. Arboreal primates have well-developed internal rotatory abilities at the hip joint, because it is fundamental for placing one foot in front of the other along the surface of a branch.

Since the basis for Lovejoy's conclusions on human gait, and therefore on australopithecine gait, rest upon the application of the lower limb acting as a pendulum, his conclusions are doubtful. In all phases of human gait muscular control rather than pendular action is the basis for motion.

Limitations of non-configurational methodologies

Comparison of bony shapes without reference to joints, to the whole limb or entire animal gives little sense of dynamics or motion. Although suitable as an initial step, comparison of features of bones alone can be taken only so far. Unless a pattern rather than a single bony feature is studied, extrapolation into the evolutionary dimension is necessarily incomplete. This non-configurational approach is limited in three ways: (1) contradictory results ensue; (2) little sense of variation is achieved; and (3) sufficient functional information for evolutionary interpretations is missing.

There is a range of opinions based on the same material, such as the australopithecine innominate bones. Le Gros Clark (1955) on the one hand, concludes that Sterkfontein and Swartkrans were intermediate in pelvic shape between apes and man; Oxnard (1973) using biometrics reaches a similar conclusion. On the other hand, Zuckerman also using biometrics maintains 'that in the bulk of characters, the australopithecine bones resemble those of the ape' (1966:107). Similarly, piecemeal comparisons such as the length of the 'true ischium' lend themselves to disagreements, and measurements alone will not settle them.

If the features of the australopithecine innominates – the small acetabulum, the long part of the smooth ischium, the less curved ilium, the small sacroiliac joint, are examined as a whole, a unique total pattern emerges, *even if* any specific feature can be duplicated in a living form.

Unless a configurational approach is taken, it is difficult to decide which features are attributable to functional differences and which to normal variability of size, age and sex. For example, lumping may occur when the bones are in fact part of different motor styles, as in the howler and spider monkey scapulae. Or, splitting may occur when there is a similar pattern but when variability of ischial length and acetabulum size is due to size differences, as in the Swartkrans and Sterkfontein innominates.

Comparison alone of isolated parts – the ilium, ischium, proximal or distal femur, or whatever – is an incomplete way to establish information on gait. Without consideration of joints and muscular relationships, how a joint functions cannot be established. Functional or biomechanical analyses which are based on relations between bones, joints and muscles need to be carried out to determine adaptive change.

Another limitation of non-configurational methods is that they neglect the comparative dimension and rely too heavily on information from *Homo sapiens*. As with shapes, laboratory studies on human gait by themselves are of limited value in interpreting evolutionary change. Conditions under which clinical experiments are carried out do not represent those under which hominid gait evolved. Evolutionary processes did not act upon shod feet walking on smooth laboratory surfaces; it is impossible to answer evolutionary questions by non-evolutionary methods. A variety of ecological challenges required extensive joint and muscle activity to facilitate effective locomotor and other behaviours, and thus formed the basis for selection. Laboratory experiments have not duplicated such conditions.

Results from laboratory studies can give distorted pictures of muscle action in gait. For example, some studies maintained that gluteus maximus does not contract during walking in the laboratory and (by extrapolation) this muscle is not of particular importance in normal gait. That this conclusion is distorted is relatively obvious because gluteus maximus is the largest single muscle in the human body and has changed markedly in mass and position during evolution, as Washburn (1951) correctly emphasized. In spite of this, Zuckerman (1966) concluded that this muscle is not significant in gait and by implication in human evolution.

Scherb (1952), Basmajian (1967, 1972) and others have shown that this muscle does contract during locomotion especially when the centre of gravity is shifted. Therefore, when carrying weight, going up and down hills, sitting down and getting up – in postural adjustments which occur frequently in normal activities – gluteus maximus is active. Its multiple functions make it essential for normal human movement and account for its change in evolution (Stern, 1972).

Present issues and future research

Problems remain concerning speciation and lineage number and details of ecological, cultural, dietary and locomotor adaptations.

Those involving the locomotor skeleton are: the nature of structural and functional refinements in locomotion in evolution from *Australopithecus* to *Homo sapiens*; the number of gait patterns within the genus; and body size and distribution of mass throughout the body.

Australopithecine walking was a unique motor pattern and the origin of a familial character. This pattern is worth evaluation in itself and later forms in terms of mechanical efficiency, it is possible to reconstruct what was involved in evolution from *Australopithecus* to *Homo sapiens*. These early hominids had become irreversibly bipedal, and their motor behaviour was refined in subsequent evolution.

The issue of australopithecine bipedalism is often seen in terms of 'striding', and the measure of australopithecine 'humanity' was whether it could stride. Unfortunately, that word has induced simplistic analysis of all changes in the pelvis and lower limb and disregard of necessary motor variability and flexibility. (A similar problem is illustrated by using 'brachiation' as an exclusive description of gibbon locomotion.) Gait and stride are altered with variations in velocity, terrain, and the stature, age, size and health of individuals (Ducroquet, 1968; Murray *et al.*, 1966). This kind of variation has also been elegantly demonstrated for several species of artiodactyl (Dagg and DeVos, 1968a; 1968b). It is unlikely that striding would well describe walking over rocky or sandy terrain. In addition, motor elements crucial in walking or striding are also essential in a variety of other behaviours, such as running and throwing. In the evolution of *Australopithecus* to *Homo sapiens*, striding would not have been selected for *per se* except as part of a larger pattern of bipedal behaviour.

An important question confronting researchers is the degree of locomotor variability and gait difference among the early hominids. Although Robinson (1972) and others have supported the idea of two patterns, other studies have concluded that one pattern existed (Zihlman, 1971; Lovejoy *et al.*, 1973). With recent discoveries of many long bones from East Rudolf, these specimens can be studied to determine range of variability among them and how it compares to specimens from other areas. Next, the question is to what is the variability attributable – to locomotion or to size, age, health, etc. of the individuals or to adaptive differences among populations. Day (1976) and Wood (1976) discuss the East Rudolf specimens, and Wood proposes that one lineage of hominids may be very modern very early in locomotor adaptation.

The issue of variability is further confused by locomotor categories. The Plio-Pleistocene hominids may represent several experiments with bipedalism, and so there may be several patterns. More is known about the category for Old World monkey 'quadrupedalism' than about hominid 'bipedalism'. But terms do not exist to differentiate slightly different bipedal styles with very different biomechanical effects.

For sorting out specific differences in fossils, extensive studies on free-ranging primates are needed to provide information on ecology, locomotor variability and the anatomical correlates that exist within a genus and within a species. Comparative laboratory studies will give data on elements of motor behaviour. Electromyographic studies on humans should be carried out which attempt to duplicate a variety of surfaces, with the subjects carrying weights and without shoes, in order to obtain data on muscle action and joint motion under variable conditions. Reconstruction and analyses of fossil joints wherever possible will help assess functional and biomechanical change in hominid evolution.

Crucial to understanding postcranial, as well as cranial, anatomy are correct estimates of body size for *Australopithecus*. Many estimates of body size by weight have been made, and large differences have been postulated for the two species (Robinson, 1962). Body size is more than just the weight itself; more important is how the mass is distributed throughout the body. Motor patterns correlate with how body weight is concentrated in the segments at distances from the 'centre of mass' (Grand, 1977).

Mass distribution was probably unique in *Australopithecus* and may have been similar in both species even if body size was different. That limb proportions in the early hominids were similar to apes or to humans cannot be assumed. It is essential to assess correctly the distribution of weight in various parts of the body is in order to understand the evolution of the postcranial skeleton and its role in providing an efficient behavioural system. The changes in relative weight of body parts in *Australopithecus* would have affected hip abduction and rotation, joint alignment and pattern of weight-bearing specifically, and locomotor efficiency generally. Selection pressures which affect the distribution of mass to ensure the most efficient movements are not confined to the pelvis and lower limbs but affect most body parts. Because so much of body mass is devoted to locomotion, modifications in the skeleton and particularly in the pelvis would appear to relate primarily to changes in locomotion from *Australopithecus* to *Homo sapiens* and only secondarily to other factors, such as changes in the birth canal.

It is gratifying that considerable attention is now focused on the postcranial skeleton. Although few, these bones warrant extensive study, and Robinson's book (1972) is an important step in this direction. The issues are far from settled; there is much to learn about the australopithecine body, and many techniques must be applied to reach these ends. Doubtless more fossils will further this endeavour by providing more information as a basis for reaching new insights.

Acknowledgments

I wish to thank Dr. C.K. Brain and Professor P.V. Tobias for permission to study the South African hominid fossils, and Alun Hughes, Brian Hume and Elizabeth Voight for their assistance during my study. For thoughtful comments I thank Dr. Jerry Lowenstein, Kathleen Smith, Alis Temerin, Professor S.L. Washburn and Dr. Norma Wikler. Special thanks are due Dr. Ted Grand for valuable discussion and criticism.

This research has been made possible by grants from the Wenner-Gren Foundation for Anthropological Research; its support is gratefully acknowledged.

References

Basmajian, J.V. (1967) *Muscles Alive: Their Functions Revealed by Electromyography*. Baltimore.

Basmajian, J.V. (1972) Biomechanics of human posture and locomotion: perspectives from electromyography. In Tuttle, R. (ed.), *Functional and Evolutionary Biology of Primates*, 292-304. Chicago.

Dagg, A.I. and DeVos, A. (1968a) The walking gaits of some species of Pecora. *J.Zool.* (London) 155, 103-10.

Dagg, A.I. and De Vos, A. (1968b) Fast gaits of pecoran species. *J. Zool.* (London) 155, 499-506.

Davis, P.R. (1964) Hominid fossils from Bed I, Olduvai Gorge, Tanganyika: A tibia and fibula. *Nature* 201, 967-8.

Day, M.H. (1976) Hominid postcranial remains from the East Rudolf succession. In Coppens, Y. *et al.* (eds.), *Earliest Man and Environments in the Lake Rudolf Basin: Stratigraphy, Paleoecology and Evolution*, 507-21. Chicago.

Day, M.H. and Napier, J.R. (1964) Hominid fossils from Bed I, Olduvai Gorge, Tanganyika: Fossil foot bones. *Nature* 201, 968-70.

Day, M.H. and Napier, R.J. (1966) A hominid toe bone from Bed I, Olduvai Gorge, Tanzania. *Nature* 211, 929-30.

Duchenne, G.B. (1949) *Physiology of Motion*. Trans. and ed by E.B. Kaplan. Philadelphia.

Ducroquet, R., Ducroquet, J. and Ducroquet, P. (1968) *Walking and Limping: A Study of Normal and Pathological Walking*. Philadelphia.

Eberhart, H.D., Inman, V.T. and Bresler, B. (1954) The principal elements in human locomotion. In Klopsteg and Wilson (eds), *Human Limbs and Their Substitutes*, 437-71. New York.

Elftman, H. (1939) The function of the arms in walking. *Hum. Biol.* 11 (4), 529-35.

Elftman, H. (1944) The bipedal walking of the chimpanzee. *J. Mammal.* 25, 67-70.

Elftman, H. (1954) The functional structure of the lower limb. In Klopsteg and Wilson (eds.), *Human Limbs and Their Substitutes*, 411-36. New York.

Gartlan, J.S. and Struhsaker, T.T. (1972) Polyspecific associations and niche separation of rain-forest anthropoids in Cameroon, West Africa. *J. Zool.* (*Lond.*) 168, 221-66.

Grand, T. (1968) Functional anatomy of the upper limb: Biology of the howler monkey (*Alouatta caraya*). *Bibl. Primat.* 7, 103-25. Basel.

Grand, T. (1977) The distribution of tissues and the weight of limb segments in *Alouatta, Macaca* and *Canis*. *Amer. J. phys. Anthrop.*, in press.

Grand, T. (ms.) Techniques of linear progression along arboreal supports.

Gregory, W.K. (1912) Notes on the principles of quadrupedal locomotion and on the mechanism of the limbs in hoofed mammals. *Ann. N.Y. Acad. Sci.* 22, 267-94.

Hall, M.C. (1965) *The Locomotor System: Functional Anatomy.* Springield, Illinois.

Haxton, H.A. (1947) Muscles of the pelvic limb: a study of differences between bipeds and quadrupeds. *Anatomical Record* 98, 337-47.

Heiple, K.G. and Lovejoy, C.O. (1971) The distal femoral anatomy of *Australopithecus*. *Amer. J. phys. Anthrop.* 35, 75-84.

Inman, V.T. (1967) Conservation of energy in ambulation. *Arch. phys. Med. and Rehabil.* 48, 484-8.

Jenkins, F.A. (1972) Chimpanzee bipedalism: cineradiographic analysis and implications for the evolution of gait. *Science* 178, 877-9.

Kummer, B. (1962) Gait and posture under normal conditions with special reference to the lower limbs. *Clin. Orthop.* 25, 32-41.

Le Gros Clark, W.E. (1947) Observations on the anatomy of fossil Australopithecinae. *J. Anat.* 81, 300-33.

Le Gros Clark, W.E. (1955) The os innominatum of the recent Ponginae with special reference to that of the Australopithecinae. *Amer. J. phys. Anthrop.* 13, 19-27.

Le Gros Clark, W.E. (1967) *Man-apes or Ape-men?* New York.

Levens, A.S., Inman, V.T. and Blosser, J.A. (1948) Transverse rotation of the segments of the lower extremity in locomotion. *J. Bone Jt. Surg.* 30A (4), 859-72.

Lewis, O.J. (1971) The contrasting morphology found in the wrist joints of semibrachiating monkeys and brachiating apes. *Folia primat.* 16, 248-56.

Lovejoy, C.O. (1974) The biomechanics of stride and their bearing on the gait of *Australopithecus*. *Yrbk. phys. Anthrop.* 17, 147-61.

Lovejoy, C.O. and Heiple, K.G. (1970) A reconstruction of the femur of *Australopithecus africanus*. *Amer. J. phys. Anthrop.* 32, 33-40.

Lovejoy, C.O., Heiple, K.G. and Burstein, A. (1973) The gait of *Australopithecus*. *Amer. J. phys. Anthrop.* 38, 757-80.

McHenry, H. (1974) Stature estimates for early hominids. *Amer. J. phys. Anthrop.* 40, 145 (abstract).

Mednick, L.W. (1955) The evolution of the human ilium. *Amer. J. phys. Anthrop.* 13, 203-16.

Murray, M.P., Kory, R.C. and Sepic, S.B. (1966) Comparison of free and fast walking patterns of normal men. *Amer. J. phys. Med.* 45, 8-24.

Napier, J.R. (1964) The evolution of bipedal walking in the hominids. *Arch. Biol.* 75, suppl., 673-708.

Oxnard, C.E. (1972) Some African fossil foot bones: a note on the interpolation of fossils into a matrix of extant species. *Amer. J. phys. Anthrop.* 37, 3-12.

Oxnard, C.E. (1973) *Form and Pattern in Human Evolution.* Chicago.

Preuschoft, H. (1970) Functional anatomy of the lower extremity. In Bourne, G. (ed.), *The Chimpanzee*, 3, 221-94.

Preuschoft, H. (1971) Body posture and mode of locomotion in early Pleistocene hominids. *Folia primat.* 14, 209-40.

Robinson, J.T. (1972) *Early Hominid Posture and Locomotion.* Chicago.

Saunders, J.B. de C.M., Inman, V.T. and Eberhart, H.D. (1953) The major determinants in normal and pathological gait. *J. Bone Jt. Surg.* 35, 543-58.

Schaeffer, B. (1947) Notes on the origin and function of the artiodactyl tarsus. *Amer. Mus. Novit.* 1356.

Schaeffer, B. (1950) Functional evaluation of adaptive morphological characters. *Amer. J. phys. Anthrop.* 8, 281-94.

Scherb, R. (1952) *Kinetisch-Diagnostische Analyse von Gehstorungen. Stuttgart.*

Schultz, A.H. (1970) The comparative uniformity of the Cercopithecoidea. In Napier, P. and Napier, J.R. (eds.), *Old World Monkeys,* 39-51. New York.

Steindler, A. (1955) *Kinesiology.* Springfield, Illinois.

Stern, J.T., Jr. (1972) Anatomical and functional specializations of the human gluteus maximus. *Amer. J. phys. Anthrop.* 36, 315-40.

Stern, J.T. and Oxnard, C.E. (1973) Primate locomotion: some links with evolution and morphology. *Primat.* 4 (11), Basel.

Washburn, S.L. (1951) The analysis of primate evolution with particular reference to the origin of man. *Cold Spring Harbor, Symp. Quant. Biol.* 15, 67-78.

Washburn, S.L. (1963) Behaviour and human evolution. In Washburn, S.L. (ed.), *Classification and Human Evolution,* 190-203. Chicago.

Wood, B.A. (1976) Remains attributable to *Homo* in the East Rudolf succession. In Coppens, Y. *et al.* (eds.), *Earliest man and Environments in the Lake Rudolf Basin: Stratigraphy, Paleoecology and Evolution,* 490-506. Chicago.

Zihlman, A.L. (1967) The question of body size in *Australopithecus.* Amer. Anthrop. Assoc. Meetings, Washington, DC.

Zihlman, A.L. (1971) The question of locomotor differences in *Australopithecus. Proc. 3rd int. Cong. Primat.,* Zurich 1970, vol. 1, 54-66, Basel.

Zihlman, A.L. (1974) A model for the interpretation of the hip joint of *Australopithecus* based on specimens from Swartkrans. *J. phys. Anthrop.* 40, 157.

Zihlman, A.L. and Hunter, W.S. (1972) A biomechanical interpretation of the pelvis of *Australopithecus. Folia primat.* 18, 1-19.

Zuckerman, S. (1966) Myths and methods in anatomy. *J. Roy. Coll. Surg. Edinb.* 11, 87-114.

Ralph L. Holloway

Problems of brain endocast interpretation and African hominid evolution

Introduction

From the point of view of my current research on the evolution of the hominid brain, at least as represented by the African specimens, this conference is much too early! If anyone is reading this paper with the hope of finding a simple, or precise answer to either brain evolution or the taxonomic affinities of the African hominids, they are going to be disappointed. I find myself not *less* confused by the work I have done on the older and new specimens, but *more* so. Part of the problem, of course, lies in the tendency of most palaeoanthropologists, who have never seen an endocast, let alone studied one, to be preoccupied with the cranial capacity determinations made, and the possible statistical relationships among these crude numbers. I am not claiming any particular innocence for myself in this matter – my own recent publications (1970a + b; 1972a + b; 1973a + b) have certainly tried to make a picture from this crude parameter also, albeit with a number of caveats. The contributions to this volume include efforts to show taxonomic affinities between fossils on the basis of dental and jaw dimensions and the postcranial fragments, with but a polite glance at how the endocranial values fit or do not fit. Yet there are at least two points that any freshman or sophomore college student who had read G.G. Simpson's *Meaning of Evolution* could point out:

1. Evolution is *opportunistic.*
2. Evolution is *mosaic.*

Put another way, structure and function are guided by behavioural impetus and there is no *a priori* reason why dentition X could not be guided by behavioural set A or B, or that dentitions X and Y could not be guided by behavioural set A or B. In other words, different brain organizations with the same outward manifestation such as gross size could direct the same anatomical complexes of dentition and locomotory organization, or different organizations could be guided by the same brain organization.

Maybe the teeth of the South African hominids we used to think of as *Australopithecus africanus* and *A. robustus* are very similar, perhaps even the two sexes of a single species (although I do not agree with this position). Their brains do not appear similar in morphological pattern. The teeth of the so-called *A. robustus* South African forms are not identical to those of OH 5, but the endocranial casts of the two do seem identical (Holloway, 1972a).

One may argue that the dental remains of the two Omo specimens collected by Clark Howell and his team are very like certain of the teeth from both East and South Africa. The endocranial cast of his 338-s specimen, however, is almost unique in shape, and matches nothing very closely that I have seen before, of any size. The new, sensational ER 1470 skull discovered by Richard Leakey's team is so far unmatched by any other endocranial fragment, except possibly by OH 16, and supposedly there are 1.3 million years between them.

I am going to take the 'devil's advocate' position in this paper that until we know more about the variation of endocranial casts and their adaptive significance, any taxonomic assessment or anagenetic evolutionary scheme which pretends to be holistic is simply that ... a pretension. My reasons for this skepticism are many. The basic reason of course is that we do not yet have any really decent evidence for the endocasts, and therefore no secure basis for talking about brain behavioural adaptation in hominid evolution that can possibly put closure on problems of taxonomic affinities or lines of evolutionary descent.

I hope this position of skepticism or devil's advocacy will not be misinterpreted. My own bias is that we will learn considerably more from the endocasts than previously, and that perhaps they will even be useful in both taxonomic and functional problems. Some beginning analyses, utilizing multivariate statistical techniques, have been initiated, but only on a pilot basis. It is already clear that discriminant analysis can, with 100% accuracy, classify endocasts of *Pan paniscus*, *P. troglodytes*, *Gorilla gorilla*, gracile and robust australopiths, habilines, and *Homo erectus* into their respective groups by using at least six crude measurements. This is based on small sizes, however, and further analyses must await larger samples of the comparative base, the pongids. Once this is achieved, other techniques can be tried.

In addition, I am presently involved in reconstructing endocasts of no less than five *Homo erectus*, of all the Solo crania, except 6 and 11 which could be endocast complete, of Omo 338-s, and of ER 1470. I only mention this to point out that much work is still in progress, germane to this paper, that cannot be included at this time.

Materials and methods: A hard look

I will not concern myself in this paper with the overall problems that exist in the study of brain evolution. These have been published elsewhere (Holloway, 1966a + b; 1968, 1969; 1970c; 1972b) and are, I hope, familiar. Rather, I would like to discuss some of the 'nitty-gritty' problems that attend the endocranial remains of almost all of the African hominids.

1. *Problems of a comparative base*

First of all, the problem is very great, because the base does not exist. There are a few scattered pongid endocasts here and there in various museums and laboratories, but nothing approaching a decent sample for any taxon. Work is currently under way in my laboratory to correct this situation, and I now have endocasts from some thirty-five gorillas, twenty-five chimpanzees (*Pan troglodytes*), and eight pygmy chimpanzees (*Pan paniscus*). While there is ample data for investigation of volumetric variation (e.g. Tobias's 1971 compilations), very few data exist on endocast dimensions, indices, proportions, morphological variations, or actual brain: body weight variability.

Nothing, and I would emphasize *nothing*, is known about behavioural and neural structural variation, whether it be for the outside endocranial form, or for the internal organization.

The measurement of these endocasts and mathematical analyses by both univariate and multivariate techniques are currently under way, as well as a programme continuing to enlarge the sample size by additional endocasting.

Minimally, one can say that the African hominid endocasts known so far are not identical to any pongid endocasts in form, whatever the coincidence of gross sizes. Just to give one simple example of the state of our knowledge, let me leave you to ponder a simple question: What is the range of variability in cerebellar form within a single taxon of pongids? I have stated (Holloway, 1972) that the cerebellum of the splendid SK 1585 specimen from Swartkrans appeared quite advanced, perhaps more so than in the so-called gracile *A. africanus* forms. There is no fully objective basis for saying so, whatever my intuitions, experience or predispositions, until there is a firm comparative base showing how the cerebellar morphology varies in the endocasts of living species.

Still, none of the pongid endocasts I have made shows either a frontal lobe or a temporal pole with a shape like that of any of the hominids. The volumes of course overlap, at least for the South African forms and the Omo 338-s specimen, but not the form. With experience, it is easy to distinguish between chimpanzee and gorilla endocasts, even ignoring size, but the various indices and proportions show almost total overlapping. In other words, there are *Gestalten* of morphological attributes perceptible (at least to my eye) which distinguish chimpanzee and gorilla yet so far are not expressed mathematically.

My point here is simply that a base of data for comparison does not exist with respect to *either* (1) a large enough sample with reasonable variability, *or* (2) mathematical expression of morphological patterns discriminatory for each taxon. A truly effective scientific study of the hominid endocranial specimens will not be possible until a more secure base exists, and any arguments about taxonomic affinities based on gross brain size or this or that particular morphological feature are simply premature.

2. *Problems of hominid specimens*

The most obvious difficulty, of course, is the small number of specimens. But sample size alone is not the only problem, and perhaps a few observations about those available are necessary. Consider, for example, the so-called robust australopiths. What exactly is available in terms of endocasts? Actually, only two (OH 5 and SK 1585) are really available in such a condition as to permit fairly accurate reconstruction, volume determination, and examination of surface morphology. Of these, we really accept the SK 1585 as robust because (a) it comes from Swartkrans, (b) it has a volume of 530 ml. and (c) it looks almost exactly like OH 5. As I have observed elsewhere (Holloway 1972, 1973) the OH 5 endocast may not be reconstructed entirely correctly, since the anterior tips of the temporal lobes are clearly too anterior, and the whole endocast was probably a bit longer. The only other specimen giving a half-way decent endocast is the KNM-ER 732, from which the whole posterior segment is missing. Neither KNM-ER 732 nor OH 5 yields satisfactory surface details. The massive KNM-ER 406 is filled with matrix, and the KNM-ER 407 base and vault fragments are extremely distorted, making reconstruction almost impossible.

The South African endocasts are not without obstacles to clear-cut interpretation either, despite their gem-like appearance. The Taung specimen is an infant or young child, thus it does not provide us with an accurate picture of adult morphology. Sts 60 lacks important segments, namely the cerebellar and occipital pole region, as well as the anterior trip of the temporal lobe. Type 3 from Sterkfontein, showing the double-valeculated fracture, and beautifully preserved gyral and sulcal relief in the frontal region, is distorted through at least *three* major planes, making reconstruction extremely difficult. The major specimen for overall morphology of the gracile australopith (aside from the dentition, which it lacks) is Sts 5 or 'Ms. Ples'. The endocast is totally unlike any other known hominid endocast. The cerebellar and temporal lobes defy description, and not a single gyral or sulcal marking remains. The volume is secure at 485 ml., but it does not help us with understanding form, nor does it resemble any other specimen from either South or East Africa.

The two specimens from Makapansgat, MLD 37/38, and MLD 1 are of course incomplete. MLD 37/38 is still solid, and also a source of controversy between Professor Tobias and myself as far as the volume is concerned. I believe this can be solved, but there is no endocast for this specimen, and to make one would destroy the original specimen. The MLD 1 occipital fragment has yielded a nice posterior endocast portion, which shows no affinity to any of the other specimens, either South or East African, and could be considered either gracile or robust. On the basis of biasterionic breadths, I would be more inclined to consider it *A. robustus*. Sts 19/58 gives a beautifully detailed demi-basal portion, and all the dimensions, and the partial endocast method, suggest a small volume, 436 ml. (Holloway, 1970a + b). The remaining specimens, such as Sts 17, 26, 71, are either very immature, distorted, or too fragmentary really to help.

What about the East African hominids? OH 7 is composed of the parietals only, and does not provide any certain surface details. As we are all aware, it is still a controversial specimen as far as volume and taxonomic status are concerned (see for example Tobias, 1964, 1966, 1971; Holloway, 1965, 1966b, 1970b, 1973a; Wolpoff, 1969, 1970). There is no frontal, no occipital, no base, no temporals, no cerebellum. Yet it is the type for the taxon, *Homo habilis*, and I still agree with Professor Tobias's (1966, 1971) estimates of its large volume, as I will explain later. OH 13 is too incomplete and OH 24 is too distorted to give anything but crude estimates of approximate volume. Indeed, the value of 590 ml. seems large compared to the smallish cranial dimensions, such as lambda-bregma, bregma-asterion, etc. On the endocast, the temporal tips are smallish, partly attributable to the crushing of the basal fragments and their subsequent reconstruction, so beautifully carried out by Ron Clarke. The temporal tips seem small in relation to the rest of the reconstruction, however, and this is one of the puzzling characters which leaves me with a sense of disquietude about my reconstruction. Perhaps the endocast should be smaller, but I fail to see how it could be small enough to fit the present distribution of the South African gracile forms, about 450 ml. However striking the similarities between OH 24 and Sts 5 in terms of the frontal torus, and concavity of the face, the temporal tips of the OH 24 endocast are not like those of Sts 5; in addition, Sts 5 lacks the maxillary dentition, and I find it difficult to equate the two crania in this region. Finally, the endocranial reconstruction of OH 13 is admittedly fragmentary, but the temporal fragment of the left side, as well as the shape of the parietal bossing on the right side, suggest a pattern *not* found thus far in any of the South African endocasts. Now one may argue that the reconstruction of both OH 13 and OH 24 could be smaller (or even larger), yielding values not all that different from South African forms. Such an argument, however, overlooks the morphological differences just noted. Until we have complete or otherwise less fragmentary endocasts from both East and South Africa, I think that any application of 'Occam's razor' to link the South and East African gracile forms as subspecies of a single species, is hardly a conservative position: rather, it is one that ignores morphology for what amounts to fictional values based on a simplistic wish for a neater picture. OH 12 from Bed IV is clearly small (although there are problems of reconstruction), and it is particularly difficult to fit to any simple one-line scheme of anagenesis (Holloway, 1973a). OH 16, 'George', has yet to be described, but from my close examination and measurements, it clearly needs considerable reconstruction, as Dr Walker can well attest. Nevertheless, in terms of the frontal region, which probably requires the least reconstruction, it matches very closely, both in morphology and dimensions, the KNM-ER 1470 endocast! The present OH 16 has been likened to 'a few bits of bone floating in a sea of plaster'. Without labouring the point, it is clear from the meandering positions of the temporal lines that something is wrong, as is the fact that a portion of the sagittal suture can be found about 1 cm. to the right of sagittal midline. On the other hand, the frontal region probably requires the least reconstruction, and it is in this region that a strong resemblance to ER 1470 can be found. For example, the breadth of the frontal lobes, at roughly the minimal frontal diameter region, just anterior to the anterior limit of the third inferior frontal convolution, or Broca's cap, is about 70 mm. on OH 16, and about 65 mm. on ER 1470. The form of the frontal lobes appears the same, i.e., broad and squarish, rather than pointed. To this writer, there are a number of features on the ER 1470 cranium that do not suggest a *Homo erectus* morphology, particularly in the supramastoid region, which suggests a flaring in shape reminiscent of OH 5. In addition, the height of the cortex of ER 1470 is not at all suggestive of the platycephalic disposition of usual *Homo erectus* endocasts. It is tempting, of course, to go beyond these simple observations, and predict the likely status of this exciting cranium, but until the formal description is published, I would only warn that the endocranial morphology will be as least as important as its endocranial volume, which I am afraid will be the most important attribute in most minds.

In other words, for the entire hominid assemblage from Olduvai Gorge, only two specimens are really complete and undistorted enough to give accurate, dependable volumes and some idea of endocast morphology: OH 5, and the beautifully prepared OH 9 from Bed II, which, thanks to Dr Walker's skill, has provided the best endocast of the lot. Incidentally, however much the cranium may suggest an affinity with the *Homo erectus* fossils from Indonesia, the endocast of OH 9 is very different from any of the six *Homo erectus* specimens I am currently reconstructing in both temporal and cerebellar lobe morphology.

I wish I could discuss at greater length the sensational new ER 1470 endocast, but at the time of writing I can only comment briefly on the endocast I prepared with Dr Walker's help. The endocast is 752 ml. in volume, and although the specimen is considerably distorted, I do not believe it will make any significant difference in the volume. The endocast has a peculiar mixture of features. The frontal lobe is very reminiscent of those of *Homo erectus*, but the rest of the endocast, particularly the occipital and parietal lobes, is not. The similarity to OH 16 has already been mentioned. Lest there be any remaining doubt about its large size in such an early context, the KNM-ER 1590 specimen, of which I was able to add a number of fragments this past summer, will probably prove to be larger, although without any decent morphology of the surface.

The Chesowanja specimen, KNM-CH 1, about which a minor controversy exists (Walker, 1972; Szalay, 1971) does not provide enough endocast material to give any affinities. The size, however, should no longer be a matter of controversy. My own dimensional analysis shows it to be most comparable to the OH 5 specimen.

Figure 1 shows a sketch of the orbital and temporal surface with corresponding dimensions for the Sts 5, OH 5, and Chesowanja specimen. As the figures show, there is no basis for claiming a larger volume for Chesowanja. Of course, these measurements are crude only, as there are no secure landmarks to measure.

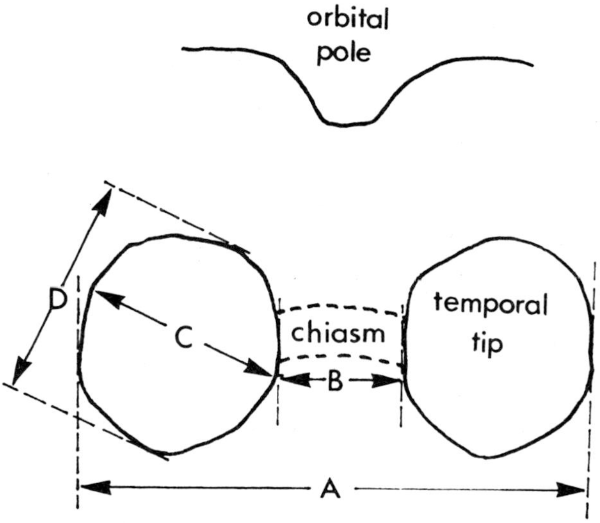

Figure 1. Diagram of basal portion of endocast, showing dimensions as follows:

Dimension	OH 5	Chesowanja	STS 5
A	78.5 mm.	79 mm.	79.3 mm.
B	20.5 mm.	20.5 mm.	20.6 mm.
C	33.7 mm.	31.1 mm.	36.2 mm.
D	35.5 mm. (approx.)	27.4 mm.	27.0 mm.

I have purposely been very discursive in this section, for which I hope the reader will forgive me. The point is, obviously, that there are almost no decently complete specimens, without attending ambiguities of one sort or another, upon which to make a safe mensurational or morphological analysis for any taxonomic or adaptational purpose.

The recent spate of discoveries in East Africa may indeed have provided us with beautiful teeth, jaws, and limb bones, but the questions of brain evolution have very little reliable evidence to pursue.

3. *Problems of method*

It is beyond the scope of this paper to detail the exact methods utilized for each specimen. It must suffice to note that while each specimen requires its own idiosyncratic methodology, they can be lumped according to overall method. The following is based mainly on a previous publication (Holloway, 1973b) but amended here to include more recent work on the 1973 summer's research (see also Holloway, 1970a, b, and 1972a for fuller discussion of the South African specimens). Table 1 lists the various specimens and the methods used, with an admittedly subjective evaluation of the reliability of the method. Method A refers to direct water displacement either of a full endocast, or of a hemi-endocast with minimal plasticene reconstruction, as for example in SK 1585 or the Taung specimen. As Table 1 shows, the OH 24 volume is listed as being determined by this method. This is perhaps misleading, as the reconstruction did involve a small amount of plasticene addition, but it *did* require a considerable realignment of three main sections of the original endocast, as described in the 1973b publication. I have already commented on my uneasy feelings about this reconstruction. Method B refers to a volume determination based on Tobias's (1967, 1971) descriptions of the partial endocast method, where the full volume is extrapolated by ratios of the part to the whole in comparison with known volumes and dissections. It should be pointed out that this method requires much more testing with larger samples before we can be certain about its accuracy. For example, the use of the *Homo erectus* I parietal tunnel in relation to the whole used what I regard as a highly inaccurate total volume of about 750 ml. I believe the total volume of *Homo erectus* I to be closer to 940 ml. This would increase, I think, the estimated total volume of OH 7. It is important to repeat these partial endocast studies. It would be interesting to learn what the partial method might give for OH 7, if a parietal tunnel from ER 1470 were used.

Method C involves extensive plasticene reconstruction of about half of the total endocast. Obviously, this latter method, and to some extent A, require a sort of 'feel' on the part of the 'reconstructor' and

Table 1

Specimen	*Region*	*Taxon*	*Capacity* (ml)	*Method*	*Evaluation*
Taung	South Africa	*A. africanus*	440*	A	1
Sts 60	South Africa	*A. africanus*	428	A	1
Sts 71	South Africa	*A. africanus*	428	C	2–3
Sts 19/58	South Africa	*A. africanus*	436	B	2
Sts 5	South Africa	*A. africanus*	485	A	1
MLD 37/38	South Africa	*A. africanus*	435	D	2
MLD 1	South Africa	?	500 ± 20	B	3
SK 1585	South Africa	*A. robustus*	530	A	1
OH 5	East Africa	*A. robustus*	530	A	1
OH 7	East Africa	*H. habilis*	687	B	2
OH 13	East Africa	*H. habilis*	650	C	2
OH 24	East Africa	*H. habilis*	590	A	2–3
OH 9	East Africa	*H. erectus*	1067	A	1
OH 12	East Africa	*H. erectus* (?)	727	C	2–3
ER 406	East Africa	*A. robustus*	510 ± 10	D	2
ER 732	East Africa	*A. robustus*	500	A	1
ER 1470	East Africa	*H. sp.*?	752	A	1
ER 1813	East Africa	*A. africanus* (?)	509	A	1
ER 1805	East Africa	?	582	A	1

*Estimated adult value. Actual specimen = 404 ml.

also a certain amount of 'faith' on the part of the audience. I am convinced that small additions of reconstruction, as in Method A, give highly accurate results, because the additions are easily placed following the form already existing, with very little variation possible. Method C, however, does raise problems, and I can be wholly sympathetic if the audience's 'faith' turns into outright skepticism! This is very much the case with the East African hominids, particularly OH 12 and OH 13. With the Indonesian specimens, this method has fewer drawbacks, because those specimens appear to be remarkably homogenous, and one can model one upon another. Still, Method C probably does get within 10-15% of the true value. It is interesting that this method, at least in reconstructions I have carried out, comes so close to Professor Tobias' figures based on Method B.

Method D uses the formula of MacKinnon *et al.* (1956), $V = f\ \frac{1}{2}(LWB + LWH)$, where *f* is determined from other complete endocasts of the same taxon, or those most closely related, as in the case of ER 406, and MLD 37/38. The '*f*s' appear to be specific or distinct for each taxon, including those on the extant pongid endocasts measured thus far. This is interesting, and must be applied to larger samples to ascertain the variation, since it offers some hope of calculating cranial capacities very accurately, with 2%, from radiographs, and of course can help in reconstructing. The '*f* s' vary from about .43 to .51, each taxon (e.g., *G. gorilla, P. troglodytes, P. paniscus, Homo sapiens, H. erectus, A. africanus*, etc.) being reasonably distinct. Indeed, it suggests to me that some of my reconstructions, particularly of OH 24, may be incorrect.

Finally, each reconstruction shown in Table 1 is weighted by a crude scale of 1 to 4, for confidence of the resulting volume, 1 being the highest.

Dimensional stability and measurement

The South African endocasts are rarities, in that most other hominid specimens must be moulded in liquid latex, and then reconstructed. In the South African specimens, such as Taung, Sts 60, or SK 1585, nature has done the first part, as accurately as possible. The major problems encountered when using latex are two-fold: (1) to retrieve the cured mould without damaging the specimen, and (2) to retain as perfectly as possible the original dimensions. For example, Sts 5, due to prior preparation with shellac, is now exfoliating from the inner table of bone, making any further endocasting impossible. 'Admold' latex offers no separation problems providing the specimen is fully fossilized, and that the surface of the bone is hardened and not exfoliating. Recent or extant specimens offer no difficulty here, and preparation of the fossil specimens with thin coats of 'Butvar' overcomes any problem of adherence between the cured latex and the bony table.

Once the first problem is taken care of, the problem of stability of dimensions must be considered. In making whole endocasts, extracted through the foramen magnum, or some small opening, the cured latex must be as thick as possible for rigidity, yet thin enough to permit collapse and retrieval. Once out of the cranium, the semi-rigid latex shell can be filled with plaster, usually under water to equalize as much as possible the hydrostatic pressure acting between the liquid plaster inside and the water from without. The larger the latex shell, the more care must be taken. This method has been checked numerous times on the endocasts made so far, by measuring particular points on the extracted and rigid shells before and after filling with plaster. The distortion, if any, is usually under 1%.

For those fossils with incomplete crania, such as most of the East African hominids, it is possible to pour the plaster keeper while the latex is still in the skull, provided there are some glue joints which can then be dissolved, and the cranial fragments removed one at a time. This was done with ER 1470 and the 338-s cranial fragments, for example. The resulting endocast portions are then dimensionally perfect.

None of the early reports on endocast volumes has ever mentioned, in any suitable detail, how the author has checked the volumes for accuracy. For example, the endocast volume of the Broken Hill ('Rhodesian Man') cranium is reported to be 1280 ml. (Smith, 1928, in Pycraft *et al.*). The original endocast, at the BMNH, M 16975, gave an average water displacement of 1308 ml. In checking the dimensions of this cast against the original specimen, the measurements agreed perfectly. Indeed, filling the original specimen with water, after making the cranium water-tight, gave readings of 1305+ ml. (A fuller description of this finding is in preparation.) I might add that almost all of the *Homo erectus* fossils from Indonesia are giving significantly different values from those published (e.g. Tobias, 1971). All of the reconstructions made for the African hominids have first been checked for dimensional accuracy, whether based on the original latex casts, or on plaster replicas. In no case has error been greater than 1.0%.

Another source of inaccuracy may be attributed to a certain increase in volume relating to glue joints. Consider, for example, an ellipsoid whose volume is

$$V = 1/6\,\pi\, abc$$

(This volume of an ellipsoid is not a perfect estimate for volume of a brain endocast, but usually approaches it within 15%.)

Per cent error can be determined as

$$\%\ \text{error} = \frac{V_2 - V_1}{V_1} \times 100$$

or

$$= \frac{(a \pm \Delta a)\ (b \pm \Delta b)\ (c \pm \Delta c) - abc}{abc}$$

If the breaks in the cranium are in one plane only, the error reduces to,

$$\frac{\Delta a}{a},\ \text{or}\ \frac{\Delta b}{b},\ \text{or}\ \frac{\Delta c}{c}$$

depending on the plane. Taking *a* as the distance between frontal and occipital poles, and *b* as maximum width, usually on the superior part of the temporal lobe, and *c* as the height from vertex to the bottom of the temporal lobes, the largest error will occur with glue joints in the sagittal and horizontal planes, particularly the latter, since height is normally the least measurement.

Table 2 gives some idea of the possible volume errors under a variety of conditions, based on some actual endocast dimensions applied to the formula for an ellipsoid. As can be seen, even with cracks in all three planes, accumulating to 1.0 mm. each, the error is around 1%. None of the specimens I have worked on thus far suggests errors of this magnitude, except possibly OH 5. Fortunately, the error will be in the greatest dimension, A-P length, and will not radically effect Tobias's estimate of 530 ml. (1967). It should be apparent, then, that reconstruction error will be approximately proportional to the amount of reconstruction required, and the principal axis of reconstruction, i.e., length, width, or height. The more the

Table 2 Some sample volume changes based on formula for an ellipsoid (V = 1/6 *abc*. *a* = length, *b* = width, *c* = height).

Specimen	*Actual vol. (ml.)*	*a*	*b*	*c*	*Calc. vol. (ml.)*	*Added vol. (ml.)*	*% increas*
Taung	404	11.7	8.6	8.3	437	—	—
	(+ Δa)	*11.8*	8.6	8.3	441	4.	0.99
	(+ Δb)	11.7	*8.7*	8.3	442	4.69	1.1
	(+ Δc)	11.7	8.6	*8.4*	442	4.87	1.2
	($\Delta a + \Delta b + \Delta c$)	*11.8*	*8.7*	*8.4*	451	14.00	3.4
	(+ $2\Delta a$)	11.9	8.6	8.3	444	7	1.7
OH 9	1067	16.8	12.8	10.8	1216	—	—
	(+ Δa)	*16.9*	12.8	10.8	1223	7	0.65
	(+ Δb)	16.8	*12.9*	10.8	1225	9	0.84
	(+ Δc)	16.8	12.8	*10.9*	1227	11	1.03
	($\Delta a + \Delta b + \Delta c$)	*16.9*	*12.9*	*10.9*	1224	28	2.62

reconstruction lies towards the centre of the specimen, rather than towards any extremity, the more potential error is possible. This is why I have less faith in the reconstruction of OH 24, for example, than in OH 13. Again, each specimen requires special consideration beyond the limitations of this paper. It should suffice to note that these kinds of considerations must be rigidly adhered to, and should explain, I hope, some of my discontent with the materials available to date. None of the Olduvai or East Rudolf specimens is really complete enough, with the exception of OH 9 and ER 406, to give unquestionable determinations of volume. Unfortunately, 406 merely sits in its coffin.

Significance of the endocranial volumes

I am sorry if the preceding sections have seemed unduly pedantic, but if both evolutionary and taxonomic questions are to utilize the evidence from endocasts, it is necessary to understand the present limitations of the data at hand. In this section I would like to continue my devil's advocacy a while longer, because I am convinced the data at present raise a number of intriguing questions.

Why bother with endocasts? I have already reviewed this question at length (Holloway, 1972) and here wish only to outline why correct volumes rather than crude estimates are necessary.

First of all, we cannot be sure that volumes *per se* have any really significant *valence* in taxonomic determinations. This does not mean that they do not, only that we are not really certain. There seems to be an inherent faith in most of us that the brain always underwent an increase in size during hominid evolution, with neither reversibility in size, or significant variations in relative brain size. The possibility that various Neanderthals' brain volumes might be larger than modern *Homo sapiens'* is merely an unexplained minor embarrassment.

Naturally those fossils should be re-investigated. Tables 3 and 4 show some crude indices which are suggestive of possible shape reversals.

If the date for the KNM-ER 1470 skull is indeed 2.9 million years, and if the newer estimates of the Taung specimen have any validity (Partridge, 1973; Tobias, 1973), a number of intriguing questions present themselves. If the Taung is to be considered a member of the

Table 3 Some crude indices for endocranial casts

Specimens	*vol.* *ml.*	D arc / L arc	D arc / L arc	L / H	H^3 / V
Taung	404	1.13	1.48	1.41	1.41
STS 60	428	1.00	1.35	1.40	1.29
STS 5	485	1.08	1.39	1.42	1.27
OH 5	530	1.47	1.37	1.45	1.20
SK 1585	530	1.73	1.42	1.43	1.37
ER 732	506	1.06	1.42	1.48	1.13
OH 24	590	1.01	1.29	1.40	1.32
OH 13	650	1.17	1.49	1.48	1.16
OH 9	1067	1.05	1.31	1.55	1.18
OH 12	727	1.11	1.41	1.60	0.97
HE I	943	1.10	1.33	1.59	1.02
II	815	1.06	1.35	1.53	1.08
IV	900	1.00	1.31	1.64	.94
VI (1963)	855	1.05	1.33	1.68	.97
VII (1965)	1059	1.07	1.41	1.65	.92
VIII (1969)	1004	.98	1.25	1.61	1.00
ER 1470	752	1.04	1.37	1.36	1.30
Omo 338s	427	1.02	1.37	1.54	1.03

Table 4

Specimens		*vol.* *(ml.)*	D arc / L arc	D arc / Larc	L / H	H^3 / V
Pan paniscus (n = 8)						
	Av.	325	.99	1.33	1.46	1.04
	Range	284-363	.97-1.01	*1.28-1.37*	1.36-1.54	.86-1.21
Pan trog. (n=29)						
	Av.	394	.96	1.28	1.47	1.09
	Range	334-474	.88-1.01	*1.20-1.34*	1.39-1.59	.95-1.23
Gorilla gorilla (n=36)						
	Av.	498	.98	1.26	1.53	1.04
	Range	383-625	.94-1.04	1.19-1.33	1.39-1.67	.85-1.24
Homo sapiens (n=4)						
	Av.	1442	1.10	1.43	1.40	1.25
	Range	1324-1586	1.04-1.14	1.39-1.46	1.35-1.46	1.11-1.42

A. robustus lineage rather than *africanus* (e.g. Tobias, 1973), and with a date of 0.8 million years, it suggests both reversibility in brain size and multiple species living contemporaneously over a long period of time.[1] My estimate of 440 ml. for the adult volume (404 on the actual immature specimen; Holloway, 1970a) differs from Tobias's (1971) value of 500 by a considerable margin; and I fail to understand the experimental or other basis for Tobias's retention of the 500 ml. value.

Purely on the basis of endocranial volumes, and assuming the parameter has considerable taxonomic merit, the present values suggest no less than four hominid groups in East and South Africa, these being roughly contemporaneous. First, the South African gracile australopiths, including Sts 5, 60, 71, 19/58, Taung, and MLD 37/38, with endocranial volumes of 428 to 485 ml. Second, the robust forms from both East and South Africa, including OH 5, ER 406, 732, and SK 1585, with values of 500 to 530 ml. Third, the Olduvai Bed I and II hominids, such as OH 7, 13, 24, and possibly 16 ('George'), referred to *Homo habilis*, with values ranging from 590 to 687 ml. The fourth possibility is ER 1470 from E. Rudolf, and possibly also ER 1590, with ER 1470 having a volume of 752 ml. In fact, I suspect, as does Dr. Walker, that OH 16 and ER 1470 might be the same line of hominid, which puts a strain on the concordance between absolute dates and the fossils.

There are, of course, other possibilities. The first, and most obvious, is that we have only sampled a very small portion of the range of variability in the fossils with regard to the so-called Olduvai habilines and the South African gracile australopiths, and ER 1470 type. A second possibility, which I believe highly improbable, is that sexual dimorphism can account for the differences between South African gracile and robust forms, and between ER 1470 and the habilines from Beds I and II at Olduvai. However, if ER 1470 is 752 ml., and the values of 590 to 687 ml. are accurate for Bed I and II hominids (OH 7, 13, 24), 590 ml. (OH 24) and 650 ml. (OH 13) might be taken as low female values, and 687 ml. as a low male, with OH 16 probably around 700 ml. This assumes a dimorphism over 10%, and with ER 1470 still 10% larger than other males (i.e. OH 7 and 16). It also assumes we have sampled mainly the extremes. A third possibility might be that we are sampling different groups, but only at subspecific or demic levels, again with the exception of the robust group. This view would be analogous to comparing, say, human pygmies from the Congo with tall tribes in East Africa, the only significant difference being that of body size, and thereby brain: body relationships might be the same. These problems are not going to be thoroughly settled without more specimens, hopefully more intact

1. As became clear during the conference, there was no agreement about Partridge's dates or the methods used to arrive at them, nor could anyone agree that Taung was a robust australopith.

than the present ones, associated with post-cranial remains to give more reliable estimates of body size, and absolute dates. Thus far, the endocranial morphological variation has no meaningful significance and cannot be utilized with any confidence.

A fourth possiblity is that there was a sort of adaptive radiation of hominids in the late Pliocene and early Pleistocene, as I suggested in my reply to Tobias in 1966 (Holloway, 1966). I suspect that a number of natural experiments were going on among different hominid groups entering into a basically new adaptive strategy which involved procurement of high-protein flesh on a more constant basis than observed for either baboons or chimpanzees. The major variables operating would have been: (1) efficiency of bipedal locomotory development; (2) dentition; (3) organization of brain and social behaviour; (4) body size and ecological niche width, meaning the relationship between body size and protein availability. With respect to the latter interrelationship, there exists a clear possibility of transient and temporary reversals of body size, limited essentially by the pattern and distribution of proteinaceous resources.

Here of course I am clearly speculating, but the enormous size of OH 9, and appearance and disappearance of large fauna at various times in the palaeontological record, makes it an intriguing possibility. I have always believed that the robust australopiths did become victims, so to speak, once some critical threshold was reached for the further growth of body size among the immediate ancestors of *Homo erectus* types. That is, the newly emerging hominid types, at the end of the Pliocene, were *not* in some terrible competition for resources until one line passed a critical size state which required an additional source of protein for continued evolution of both brain and body size. The differences in dentition and locomotor anatomy suggest, at least to me, that gracile and robust forms, both in East and South Africa, need not have been always in a competitive state.

It is for these above reasons, and particularly in relation to the other variables I have discussed elsewhere (e.g. Holloway, 1972b, 1970c) such as duration of growth and length of post-natal dependence, endocrine-target tissue interactions, sexual dimorphism, social behaviour, etc., that I stress the need for highly accurate volumes and body size figures. I am convinced that that knowledge will be an important key to our understanding of the dynamics of hominid evolution, and the interrelationships between hominid taxa.

Table 6 shows a number of possible brain: body weight relationships which are of interest because they indicate that the likely relative brain size was within human limits, thus yielding 'Progression indices' (Stephan, 1972) within the known range for modern *Homo sapiens*. The equation used is the so-called 'basal insectivore' regression line of $\log_{10} h = 1.632 + 0.63 \log_{10} k$, as determined by Bauchot and Stephan (1969). We do not have any exact indications of body weights for the hominids, so the figures in Table 6 are meant

Table 5 A numbers game with brain-body double-log relationships based on a general formula of h = bk^{x}

Brain weight	*Body weight (lb.)*			*Slope*
450 ml. (*A. africanus*)	40	50	60	
930 ml. (*Homo·erectus*)	83	103	123	1.0
1361 ml. (*Homo sapiens*)	123	150	180	1.0
450	40	50	60	
930	115	143	180	.6
1361	198	>200	>250	.6
1361	150			1.92
930	123			1.92
450	85–86			1.92
My favorite:				
450	*c.* 50 lb.	slope = 1.0		
775	*c.* 84 lb.	slope = .6		
930	*c.* 114 lb.	slope = 1.75		
1361	*c.* 140 lb.			

only to show a range of possibilities. For example, for a gracile australopith to have the same encephalization coefficient, or 'progression index', as a chimpanzee, it would require a body weight of 100 lb., which does not appear likely on the basis of the known postcranial fragments.

I have watched with ever-growing curiosity an increasing spate of publications which attempt to plot brain weights against body weights in double-logarithmic style, or which try to plot endocranial capacity against time. Obviously, such attempts are premature until we have facts: accurate volumes, body weights, and dates. Still, it seems like a growing popular sport, and I would like to add some further possibilities for thought on the matter.[2] If you take double-log graph paper, using 450, 930, and 1361 ml. as reasonably accurate means for gracile *Australopithecus, Homo erectus*, and *Homo sapiens* respectively, and beginning with the first taxon by assigning a range of reasonable body weights, say 40 to 60 pounds, you can draw a number of lines of varying slope to the successively higher cranial capacities for the two species of *Homo*. You can draw lines with slopes equalling .6, 1.0, and 2.4 (and all values in between) which do not seem unreasonable. Table 5 shows a number of such possibilities, with resulting body weights based on each particular slope assumption. Of course, the different slopes have significantly different meanings in terms of allometric growth and brain: body relationships through time, and thus, one would suspect, quite different statements

2. Part of the stimulus for this discussion comes from a conversation with Dr Pilbeam at the Conference. See Pilbeam and Gould, 1974.

Table 6 Some possible brain-body rations and 'progression indices', based on Stephan's (1972) formulation, using a basal insectivore line (see text)

Specimens	*Brain size (ml.)*	*Assumed body weight (lb.)*	*Brain: body ratio*	*Progression index*
Gracile				
A. africanus	Av. = 442	40	1.41	21.4
		50	1:62	18.7
		60	1:51	16.9
Robust				
A. africanus		50	1:43	22.30
		60	1:51	19.88
		75	1:64	16.9
		110	1:94	12.8
Homo sapiens	Av. = 1361	150		28.8
Homo erectus	Av. = 930	92	1:45	26.6
	930	125	1:61	22.0

about selection pressures could result. The tendency in most publications is to follow 'Occam's Razor' as a guide, and try to connect points by a line with only one slope, whether it be 1.0 or 0.66. Of course, one could just as easily construct a line with slope .66 from the australopith average of 442 ml. to the 930 ml. average of *Homo erectus*, and from there, a slope of either 1.0, or 2.4, for example, to the 1,361 ml. average for *Homo sapiens*, depending on which body weight value one chooses for the australopith taxon. One could also reverse these slopes, or approach the problem from the top down, so to speak (see Figure 2).

This is, of course, a game of demifictional numbers, and while we do expect scientists' minds to travel in straight lines, must we be so certain that the hominids' brain evolution did the same thing? As one possibility, I have put 'my favourite' in the table. I hope my points are obvious. First of all, a slope of .6, retained as a constant throughout hominid evolution, will result in impossibly high body weights for modern *Homo sapiens*. This suggests strongly that hominid evolution has departed from the usual .6 slope relationship seen in almost all other vertebrate, and particularly mammalian, groups. Secondly, of course, this exercise should demonstrate how important the question of body weights became for the hominids. A very significant key indeed to the actual evolutionary dynamics between and within lineages rests upon these relationships between brain volumes and body weights through time.

Minimally, I think the endocranial casts of both the South and East African hominids show the following:

1. Reorganization toward a human pattern as reflected in the non-pongid shape of the temporal lobe, the orbital surface of

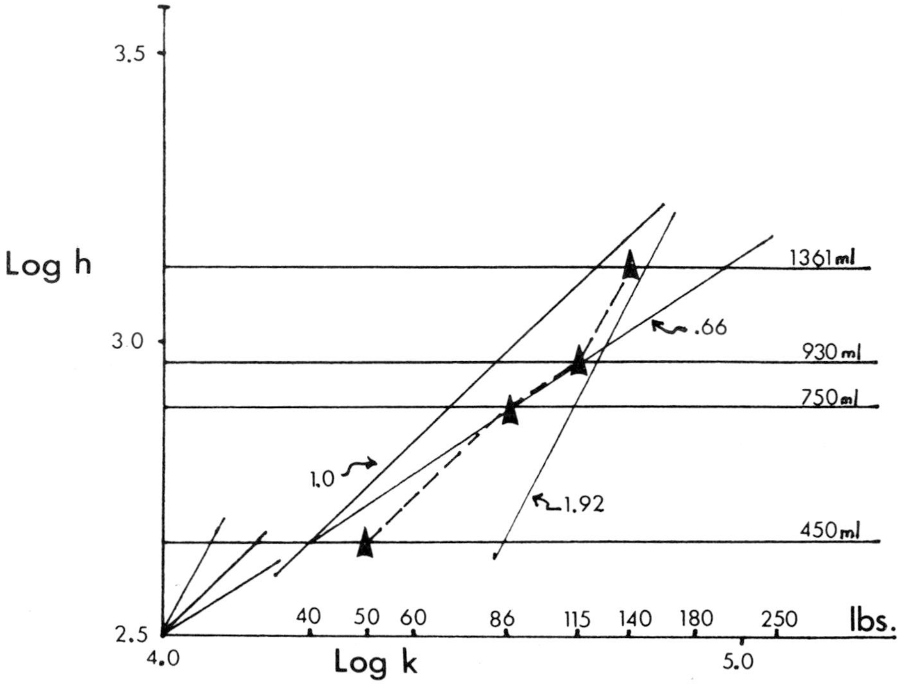

Figure 2. A double-log (base 10) graph showing some possible regression lines, depending on assumptions of body-weight, and an allometric growth equation of exponential form, $h = bk$, or, $\log_{10} = \log_{10} + \log_{10}$, where h = cranial capacity in ml. k = body weight in grams, and x = slope of the line. The average for gracile australopithecines is taken as 450 ml, *Homo erectus* as 930 ml. (based on my own unpublished determinations of 6 endocasts), and 1361 ml. as the average for modern man based on Tobias (1971). A slope of 0.66 is usually regarded as the best slope for all mammals (e.g., Stephan, 1972). The point of this diagram is to show that a number of possibilities exist, but that the general slope of 0.66, if maintained throughout hominid evolution, results in body weights for modern *Homo* that are too heavy. Most slope possibilities suggest genuine selection for heavier brains. It should be realised that a number of alternative lines can be drawn. For example, the line of slope = 1.0 is based on a 40 pound body weight for the gracile Australopithecine. Shifting that line over to 50 or 60 pounds would give more realistic body weights for *Homo erectus* and modern man. The composite line through the triangles has three different slopes, indicating changing selection pressures for allometric growth relationships through time. Another limitation to keep in mind is that the basal values for brain weight come from three different types of populations, the higher values coming from Asian fossils, and a world-wide average for modern man.

the frontal lobe, the expanded and more distinct shape of the third inferior frontal gyrus, the expansion of inferior parietal surface and posterior position of any lunate sulcus, and brain sizes consistently larger than apes, particularly when body size is taken into consideration. *This reorganization is present for all possible taxa, regardless of the morphological variation among endocasts.*

2. The more 'advanced' hominids of East Africa, such as ER 1470,

all of the Olduvai hominids, including OH 9 and OH 12 (VEK IV), show an idiosyncratic morphological pattern that, while similar to known *Homo erectus* endocasts from Asia, in particular Indonesia (I-VIII), are noticeably different, particularly in the temporal, occipital, and cerebellar regions. The significance of these differences is *unknown, either* with respect to taxonomic affinity, or functioning. This suggests the possibility, if not probability, of different taxonomic placement at the specific level from *Homo erectus* (in the Asian sense); and some independent parallel evolution.

3. While more accurate estimates of body sizes are necessary, some of the estimates, e.g. Lovejoy and Heiple (1970), suggest brain:body ratios close to modern human values (i.e. 1:46), and 'progression indices' as defined by Stephan (1972), within known modern human values (see Holloway, 1973b) (on the other hand, see Tobias, 1967; Leutenegger, 1973). If this can be corroborated by additional specimens and estimations, it suggests that body-size, and, one supposes, its fit as an adaptive parameter to ecological context, was an important focus of past selection pressures.
4. However similar the dental and postcranial remains may be in the East and South African hominids, aside from the robust australopith specimens, the endocranial casts studied thus far suggest different morphological patterns in East and South African 'gracile' specimens. Whether these differences indicate functional (behavioural) differences is open to question and must await further research. *Nevertheless, these differences should caution those palaeoanthropologists who are tempted to draw simple correlations between bipedalism, dentition, diet, competition for resources, and the impossibility of sympatric or overlapping species utilizing the same ecological zones. This applies also to the robust lineage(s).*
5. There is nothing in the morphological appearance of the endocasts of any of the East or South African hominids which can be taken to rule out behavioural adaptations involving bipedalism, coordinated use of the hands to make stone tools to standardized patterns, hunting, or a primitive communications system based on symbols. Nor can these features prove the presence of any of these adaptations.
6. Regarding the question of mosaic evolution, the evidence provided by the endocranial remains of the African hominids indicates that brain evolution has been an important variable from the beginning, and not something which evolved later than other morphological components, i.e., the dentition, locomotory skeleton, etc. The evolution of the human brain has thus been an important aspect throughout *all* of hominid evolution, the latter stages probably involving more the relationship between brain and body size (i.e., allometric growth), than basic reorganization.

Conclusion

It should be apparent by now that the evidence provided by the endocranial casts processed so far is ambiguous. The range of morphological variations is great, and there is no good comparative base against which we can assess this variability. Similarly, we are not able to justify any functional observations, or behavioural adaptations, on the basis of endocasts beyond a speculative level. Two major possibilities arise in interpreting the significance of the endocasts: (1) either the range of variation is very great in the early hominids, more so than in any pongid endocasts, and we must rely on the teeth, cranial, and postcranial remains for taxonomic assessment; or (2) the variation of endocasts is significant regardless of how similar the rest of the anatomy is. On a number of occasions now, I have listened to my colleagues argue about the hominid remains as if the only variable operating during hominid evolution were the teeth. Teeth among present *Homo sapiens* are far less varied than their diets and Dr Walker will attest to the strange and 'improper' stomach contents he has found during his autopsies of many different animals in East Africa. It is almost as if none of the early hominids ever had a brain in his cranium; only teeth. One might reply that at least with jaws and teeth and limb bones we are on safer ground in interpreting structure, function, and behaviour. I wonder. If we are so much better off with these lines of evidence and can ignore the brain, why all the controversy? Admittedly, the study of the hominid endocasts is really only at a beginning stage, and much remains to be done in this area. I must admit, however, from what I have seen so far, that perhaps in the early stages of hominid evolution, i.e., up to a *Homo erectus* stage, there was more taxonomic variability than present 'lumpers' care to see, and I find myself more open to the possibility of an adaptive radiation of early hominids within the Pliocene. But until I have studied these remains further, I prefer to leave this simply as a caveat.

Acknowledgments

In working on this material, I have been very fortunate to have had the cooperation and encouragement of those more directly responsible for finding the primary material. I am particularly grateful and indebted to Professor P.V. Tobias who made my entry into endocasts possible; to Dr C.K. Brain who allowed me the first thrill of preparing the original SK 1585 specimen; to the late Dr L.S.B. Leakey, Dr Mary Leakey, and to R.E.F. Leakey for their kindness, cooperation and hospitality during my studies in Nairobi; to F.C. Howell for his cooperation and kindness in endocasting the Omo 338-s specimen; to Carole Orkin, Elizabeth Voight, John Harris, and Margaret

Leakey for all their understanding and patience, and to Alan Walker for his encouragement, hospitality, and facilities.

This work has been carried out under the auspices of NSF grants G2300, and GS-29231, to which organization I am extremely grateful. Finally, my thanks and appreciation to Kate McFeeley who helped so much with this manuscript.

References

Bauchot, R. and Stephan, H. (1969) Encephalisation et niveau évolutif chez les simiens. *Mammalia* 33, 225-75.

Brace, C.L. (1973) Sexual dimorphism in human evolution. *Yb. phys. Anthrop.* 16, 31-49.

Holloway, R.L. (1973a) New endocranial values for the E. African early hominids. *Nature* 243, 97-9.

Holloway, R.L. (1973b) Endocranial capacities of the early African hominids and the role of the brain in mosaic evolution. *J. human Evol.* 2, 449-59.

Holloway, R.L. (1972a) New Australopithecine endocast, SK 1585, from Swartkrans, S. Africa. *Amer. J. phys. Anthrop.* 37, 173-86.

Holloway, R.L. (1972b) Australopithecine endocasts, brain evolution in the Hominoidea, and a model of hominid evolution. In Tuttle, R. (ed.), *Functional and Evolutionary Biology of the Primates*, 185-204. Chicago.

Holloway, R.L. (1970a) Australopithecine endocast (Taung specimen 1924): a new volume determination. *Science* 168, 966-8.

Holloway, R.L. (1970b) New endocranial values for the Australopithecines. *Nature* 227, 199-200.

Holloway, R.L. (1970c) Neural parameters, hunting, and the evolution of the human brain. In Noback, C.R. and Montagna (eds.), *The Primate Brain*, 299-310. New York.

Holloway, R.L. (1969) Some questions on parameters of neural evolution in primates. *Ann. N.Y. Acad. Sci.* 167, 332-40.

Holloway, R.L. (1966a) Cranial capacity, neural reorganization and hominid evolution: a search for more suitable parameters. *Amer. Anthrop.* p.68, 103-21.

Holloway, R.L. (1966b) The Olduvai Bed I hominine capacity: a reply to Prof. Tobias. *Nature* 210, 1108-11.

Holloway, R.L. (1965) Cranial capacity of the hominine from Olduvai Bed I: some confirmatory evidence. *Nature* 208, 205-6.

Lovejoy, C.O. and Heiple, R.G. (1970) A reconstruction of the femur of *Australopithecus africanus*. *Amer. J. phys. Anthrop.* 32, 32-40.

MacKinnon, I.L., Kennedy, J.A. and Davies, T.V. (1956) The estimation of skull capacity from Roentgenologic measurements. *Amer. J. Roentg., Rad. Ther. & Nucl. Med.* 76, 303-10.

Partridge, T.C. (1973) Geomorphological dating of cave openings at Makapansgat, Sterkfontein, Swartkrans, and Taung. *Nature* 246: 75-9.

Pilbeam, D. and Gould, S.J. (1974) Size and scaling in human evolution. *Science* 186, 892-906.

Pycraft, W.P., Smith, G.E., et al. (1928) *Rhodesian Man and Associated Remains*. London: British Mus. Nat. Hist.

Stephan, H. (1972) Evolution of primate brains: a comparative anatomical investigation. In Tuttle, R. (ed.) *Functional and Evolutionary Biology of the Primates*. Chicago, Aldine, 155-74.
Szalay, F.S. (1971) Biological level of organization of the Chesowanja robust Australopithecine. *Nature* 234: 229-30.
Tobias, P.V. (1973) Implications of the new age estimates of the early South African hominids. *Nature* 246, 79-83.
Tobias, P.V. (1971) *The Brain in Hominid Evolution*. N.Y., Colombia University Press.
Tobias, P.V. (1967) *Olduvai Gorge: The Cranium and Maxillary Dentition of Australopithecus (Zinjanthropus) boisei*. Vol. 2. Cambridge, Cambridge University Press.
Tobias, P.V. (1966) The distinctiveness of *Homo habilis*. *Nature* 209, 953-7.
Tobias, P.V. (1964) The Olduvai Bed I hominines with special reference to cranial capacity. *Nature* 202, 3-4.
Walker, A. (1972) Chesowanja Australopithecine. *Nature* 238, 108-9.
Wolpoff, M. (1970) Taxonomy and cranial capacity of the Olduvai hominid 7. *Nature* 227, 747.
Wolpoff, M. (1966) Cranial capacity and taxonomy of Olduvai hominid 7. *Nature* 223, 182-3.

Postscript

Needless to say, much has happened in the three years since this Conference was held. New specimens, such as ER 1805, ER 1813, ER 1590 and most recently, ER 3732 and ER 3733 have been found, and endocasts prepared, except for ER 3733. The samples for extant pongids have been significantly increased: *Pan paniscus*, N=40; *Pan troglodytes*, N=33; *Gorilla, N*=39. In addition newer analyses, utilizing polar-coordinate-stereoplotting apparatus devised by Drs. Alan Walker and D. Oyen, are in progress, analysing some 300+ data points for the dorsal surface alone of each endocast. Pilot analyses are in progress on the sagittal, horizontal, 20° and 40° (anterior and posterior) transects using discriminant analysis. Radial distances to the same homologous center point (in between frontal and occipital poles) are allometrically related to volume of endocast, with r=approx. .96 for most points, but the residuals appear to be taxon-specific, giving correct classifications of roughly 90% for each transect. The groups are: (1) *Pan paniscus* (N=5), (2) *Pan troglodytes* (N=5), (3) *Gorilla* (N=5), (4) *Homo erectus*, Indonesia (N=5), (5) *Homo erectus*, China (N=4), (6) *Homo sapiens soloensis* (N=5), (7) *Homo sapiens sapiens* (N=5), (8) *Austrolopithecus africanus* (N=4), (9) *Aust. robustus* (N=3), with ER 1470, ER 1813, ER 1805, and OH 9 as unclassified. All variables are allometrically corrected, and in general ER 1470 is classified as either *Homo erectus* or *A. robustus*, ER 1813 as *Austrolopithecus africanus*, ER 1805 mostly as *Gorilla* (!), and OH 9 always as *Homo erectus*, depending on choice of variables and whether the solution is 'direct' (all variables simultaneously), or step-wise. Misclassifications are usually between contiguous groups, i.e., *Pan troglodytes* into *Pan paniscus*, or vice versa, and the Indonesian into Chinese (or vice versa) groups. In misclassifications, the 2nd highest probabilities are always in the correct group, at reasonably high classification levels, viz., 30-45%.

It should be pointed out that to date, no attempts have been made to analyse eigenvalues or coefficients for *functional* interpretations. In other words these pilot studies are only being used to test the applicability of the date and procedures for taxonomic classification.

Since 1974, an enormous amount of data and their analyses have been performed on the endocasts, much of it reported in the recent U.I.S.P.P. Conference in Nice, September 1976, and which cannot be mentioned here for reasons of space limitations. I regret that the question of allometry was not discussed in more detail in this paper, as I believe a reasonably good synthesis between allometry and 'neural reorganization' can be made, and that certain of the measurements on the endocasts suggest that *residuals* from allometrically corrected data are taxon specific.

By and large, the problems discussed in this particular paper remain, as does my own 'devil's advocacy' position demonstrated herein. Consequently I have chosen to allow the contribution to remain intact, but I would caution the reader to examine more carefully the paper presented in Colloquium VI, 'The Oldest Hominids', of the IX Congress of the U.S.I.P.P., Nice, September 13-18, 1976, for more details of the progress made in the study of endocasts, the problem of allometry, and the functional aspects of hominid brain evolution.

C.O. Lovejoy

A biomechanical review of the locomotor diversity of early hominids

In the analysis and reconstruction of the locomotor pattern of early Pleistocene hominids, there would appear to be two questions of primary importance:

1. To what extent is the morphology of available australopithecine post-cranial samples indicative of a bipedal gait?
2. Are there indications of multiple locomotor patterns among australopithecine populations, especially with regard to the frequent separation of these populations into allomorphic groups?

In this presentation I should like to restrict discussion to the former of these two problems, because if it can be shown that available samples are all equally indicative of a fully bipedal, striding gait (of a type generally similar to that found in modern man) the second question is immediately obviated.[1] It should be noted that the subject of this paper is not the taxonomic separation of early Pleistocene hominids, but only whether differences in gait pattern can be detected between allomorphs recognized at present. Before turning to a discussion of the available specimens, it would seem advisable to consider the nature of the evidence in a more general way and to present three propositions

1. The definition of 'stride' can be approached in two ways. It may be defined on the basis of energy expenditure and gait efficiency (Lovejoy, 1973) but this would require extensive analysis of the available australopithecine materials and would require assumption of a more anatomical definition. The word is used here, therefore, to mean the ability (1) to walk bipedally, successively placing each foot closely under the centre of gravity; (2) to stabilize the pelvis against rotation by an abductor mechanism adequate to eliminate large trunk shifts; (3) to utilize the principle of the compound pendulum for the lower extremity so that the advance of each limb in swing phase can be accomplished mostly by gravity (with minimal muscle contraction for accelerations and decelerations). The definition also includes the ability to run at speeds faster than normal or walking gait. If the above three requirements are met, then running would have to be considered an equally well-established part of the adaptive strategy of *Australopithecus*.

Figure 2. The amount of trunk flexion required of modern man in order to obtain a suitable position for quadrupedal locomotion. Such flexion, however, results in a lengthening of the gluteus maximus to 120% of its approximate physiological length, resulting in a 20% reduction of its force capacity (cf. Figure 1). Note that the lengthening is actually greater than this since the hip joint must also be flexed slightly.

locomotion, the normal range of motion of the hip in the sagittal plane is from about 20° of extension (from the neutral position) to about 90° of flexion. We approximated the length of the maximus in a human skeleton at these two positions, using a metric tape-measure, and assuming that the centroid of the origin of gluteus maximus lay near the lateral border of the sacrum at the level of the third sacral foramen, and that the centroid of insertion lay mid-way down the gluteal ridge of the femur. The extended position gave a length of 21 cm., and the flexed position a length of 15 cm. Assuming that the maximus is significantly active over this excursion, a reasonable assumption would be (for the purpose of this demonstration) that its physiological length would lie at the midpoint of the two lengths or 18 cm. This is reasonable since this length occurred in this specimen at about 30° of hip flexion – a position in which the force output of the maximus would be substantial in fast walking, running, jumping, etc. In order to determine the most likely optimal length in the quadrupedal position, we may turn to the chimpanzee in which the mid-point of normal range of motion in the hip is about 90° of flexion. Figure 2 shows our projected difference between optimal (physiological) maximus lengths in the bipedal and quadrupedal positions. In order to attain the quadrupedal position from the bipedal one, a trunk flexion of 45° is required. This results in an increase in the length of the maximus to about 120%. Reference to Figure 1 indicates that this results in a 20% reduction in force capacity.

If all muscles about the hip, shank, and foot were also considered, it is clear that quadrupedal gait in an animal adapted to bipedalism could only result in rapid fatigue, so much so that it would almost preclude the use of quadrupedal locomotion over significant distances. Thus while it can never be asserted that early Pleistocene hominids did not occasionally rest on their knuckles, climb trees to obtain food or escape predators, or infrequently utilize some form of quadrupedal scramble (Kay, 1973; Kortlandt, 1973; Robinson, 1972; Sarich, 1971; Washburn, 1967; 1968), it can be said with some certainty that whenever the evolution of bipedalism was significantly advanced among early hominids, alternative forms of locomotion would have been rapidly eliminated from their primary adaptive strategy. Because the adaptations to bipedalism are so substantial in *Australopithecus* we have little choice but to presume that this early hominid rarely if ever moved quadrupedally.

2. *The phenotypic plasticity of bone tissue*

A second issue which requires considerable attention in the study of early hominid locomotor patterns is the problem of phenotypic plasticity in bone and its effect upon skeletal morphology. Since we shall shortly be discussing the australopithecine tibia, a discussion of the phenotypic variability of this bone would appear useful. The diaphyseal form of the tibia is an extremely variable trait among and between modern human populations. In particular, the form of the shaft at its midpoint has been given considerable attention for decades. The shape of this region can be grossly expressed by means of the mid-shaft index (mediolateral diameter/anteroposterior diameter x 100). This index varies in modern populations from below 50 to over 100 (Lovejoy, 1970). More important, however, are the extreme variations in the actual distribution of cortical bone in the tibia. In Figure 3 an Amerindian tibia (mid-shaft cross section) has been superimposed upon that of a Euro-american. The Amerindian specimen differs substantially from the latter by virtue of its more elliptical form, its more elliptical medullary canal, and the strong pillar of bone on its posterior surface (the 'posterior pilaster'). Yet the actual amount of bone in these two specimens, when normalized for maximum length, is practically identical. We have recently been able to show that the striking differences in these tibial shafts are primarily the result of phenotypic remodelling; they are an expression of the bone's response to the loading patterns that each suffered during life.

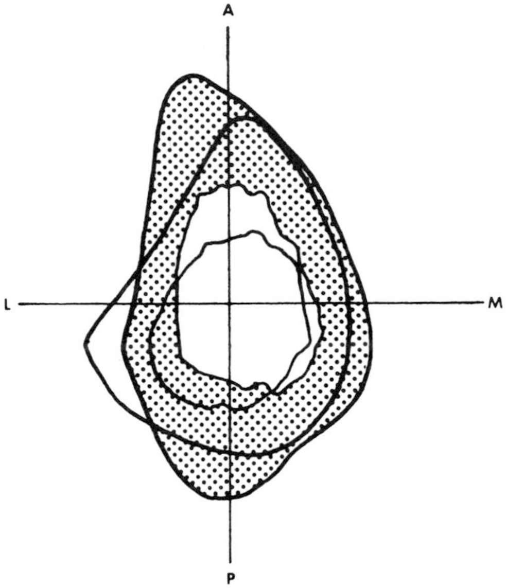

Figure 3. Mid-shaft cross section of a platycnemic tibia (shaded) superimposed upon that of a euricnemic tibia. The mediolateral axis was defined in each case as the transverse axis of the tibio-talar joint (L-M). Note the elliptical form of the platycnemic bone, including its medullary canal, and the posterior extension of the cortex (the posterior pilaster). The platycnemic bone is stronger in torsion and anteroposterior bending; the euricnemic is stronger in medio-lateral bending (Lovejoy, 1970).

This remarkable capacity of bone tissue to respond to the specific external loads placed upon it during life can also be illustrated by the recent experimental evidence provided by Burstein *et al.* (1972). In these tests a hole was drilled near the femoral midshaft in a series of test animals. Dynamic testing of these femora before healing demonstrated a marked reduction in torsional and bending strength. When healing was allowed to proceed for 8 weeks, however, the complete strength of the bone was restored. Of particular interest are the data obtained when a silastic plug was inserted into the hole immediately after drilling. This prevented the bone from correcting the defect by a simple filling of the hole with new bone tissue. Yet after a period of 8 weeks, dynamic testing of these femora again showed that all stress-concentrating effects of the drill hole (which was of course still present) had been removed by the remodelling process. Thus the bone had developed a system of transmitting forces around the drill hole and of avoiding its stress-concentrating effects.

The phenotypic plasticity of bone as demonstrated both in the marked variation of skeletal elements among and between modern human populations and in such experimental procedures as those outlined above should be a central consideration in the interpretation of fossil material. In fact these data should form the basis of a general principle: that the morphology of any bone is generally a reflection of the individual loading conditions which it suffered during life and except in cases where pathological processes are in evidence, its form should be considered the strongest and most economical structural arrangement of bone material possible within the limits of the primary genetic design parameters.

How, then, are labile variations such as shaft form to be treated in the analysis of fossil samples? For the most part, they should not be used to suggest locomotor or phyletic relationships, except in those instances in which the mechanical significance of a particular pattern of bone distribution is clearly understood. The wide variation in the shape and form of the bones of modern man implies significant shaft remodelling in response to comparatively minor environmental variables such as postural habits, differences in substrate, ranges of skeletal motion, resting positions, etc. We must therefore not place undue importance on these kinds of variations when attempting to elucidate what may be considered more general adaptations of the skeleton, i.e., gait pattern. As an example, the interpretation of the shape of the femoral neck comes to mind, especially with reference to its considerable variation among australopithecine femora thus far recordered. There would appear to be no reasonable basis on which to suggest that the remodelling capacity of early hominids was any less evolved than that of modern man. Thus it may also be assumed that femoral neck cross sections in these early hominids are specific expressions of individual loading patterns. Differences in the cross-sectional form of the femoral neck in *Australopithecus* and modern man are therefore insufficient grounds on which to suggest differences in primary gait pattern without careful mechanical analysis. This is especially true because there *are* significant differences in some mechanical parameters which would be expected to affect neck shape (e.g., length of the neck, neck-shaft angle, etc.) but which themselves are not necessarily indicative of differences in gait pattern.

We know that the intense phenotypic plasticity of bone tissue will correct constantly during life for the specific loads imposed upon a bone. Thus while the pattern of bone distribution may be considered *reflective* of the kinds of stresses that a bone suffered during life, it cannot, by definition, be considered less than adapted to such stresses. Where careful mechanical analysis can be applied to variations in the distribution of cortical bone (and the arrangements of trabecular bone), it may be possible to identify the particular loads reflected by the patterns (Lovejoy, Burstein and Heiple, 1976). Until such time as these kinds of analyses are performed, however, suggestions that variations in bone distribution constitute *a priori* indications of differences in gait pattern between two or more populations should not be considered valid.

3. *The interpretation of statistical distance studies*

The application to skeletal elements of such techniques as multivariate and canonical analysis has recently received strong criticism on purely procedural grounds (Kowalski, 1972) and we would like to stress what we regard as additional limitations of these techniques. Two central issues in their application are the measurements employed and the interpretation of the results of their statistical comparison. With regard to the latter it must always be remembered that the product of a multivariate analysis is a statistic. The numerical distances obtained are not necessarily related to either functional or phyletic distances. As such they must be considered only preliminary evidence and conclusions with respect to such problems as the taxonomic status or locomotor pattern of a fossil must await more substantive kinds of analysis.

The types of measurements employed in statistical studies often tend to also limit their validity. They are often employed without full consideration of such parameters as body weight and mechanical correlation. An example of the latter can be found in the magnitude of the bicondylar angle and the depth of the patellar groove. Reference to Figure 4 demonstrates that an increase in the depth of this groove is a requirement in femora with high bicondylar angles. Yet assessment of these two features would normally be entered independently in a multivariate formula. That is, while the features can be adaptively related by means of a biomechanical interdependency, the landmarks which would be used in their metric assessment are not clearly related and would not necessarily be correlated. Yet any statistical distances obtained would in reality be reflective of only one primary adaptive difference – valgus of the knee joint during locomotion.

While the above example *is* amenable to simple mechanical interpretation, numerous other dimensions often used in statistical comparisons of samples may reflect mechanical correlations which are more obtuse and thereby much more difficult to identify. In fact, it is very probable that most metrically assessable characters are interrelated, and without careful biomechanical interpretation and appropriate weighting, the issue of mechanical correlation of characters will greatly limit the value of these techniques.

As we pointed out earlier, the phenotypic plasticity of bone must also be considered with respect to statistical analysis. African pongid tibias are often platycnemic. Metrically therefore the Amerindian tibia can be more similar to the pongid than to the Euro-american. In this particular case (and we suspect also in numerous other cases) the use of this trait in a statistical analysis would not group the two populations of bipedal hominids apart from that of the quadrupedal pongid, but would instead group the Amerindians with the chimpanzee and separate these from the Euro-americans! To summarize, the tibial loading patterns suffered during both bipedal and quadrupedal locomotion probably share numerous similarities but the loading pattern is at the same time so highly variable that it may differ substantially in two populations with identical primary locomotor patterns.

4. *The null hypothesis*

Almost all students of early hominid locomotion are now agreed that the australopithecines exhibit substantial adaptations to bipedalism (Dart, 1949; 1957; 1958; Day, 1969; Day and Napier, 1964; Le Gros Clark, 1947; 1964; Napier, 1964; Preuschoft, 1971; Robinson, 1972; Schultz, 1969; Walker, 1973; Zihlman, 1971). Most disagreements centre around the *degree* of their bipedal adaptation. In a series of earlier papers we have pointed out that while there are differences in the lower limb skeletons of *Australopithecus* and modern man, these are not reflective of differences in primary gait patterns but are for the most part the result of specializations of the modern hip and thigh to allow the free passage of term foetuses with unusually large crania. In the remainder of this presentation we will review some of those skeletal differences which have been suggested to reflect differences in gait pattern. In doing so we shall review the evidence in light of the following null hypothesis:

> All australopithecine populations, including those presently divided into separate hypodigms (e.g., gracile and robust and/or *Australopithecus* and *Homo*) were equally capable of an upright striding gait similar to that of modern man. Those morphological features which are known to differ in *Australopithecus* and modern man are reflections of greater encephalization in the modern foetus, and not to differences in primary gait pattern.

The substantial degree to which the australopithecine postcranial skeleton resembles that of modern man fully justifies this approach.

In conjunction with the above null hypothesis, those general principles enumerated earlier may now be restated as corollaries of the hypothesis:

1. The restrictive nature of bipedalism implies that only bipedalism may be considered as a primary gait pattern in *Australopithecus*.
2. Features of unknown mechanical significance (especially those attributable to phenotypic plasticity) which differ in *Australopithecus* and modern man do not necessarily reflect differences in gait pattern and should not be assumed to do so without careful biomechanical analysis.

3. Statistical distances obtained in the comparison of skeletal elements from man and *Australopithecus* cannot be considered to reflect differences in gait pattern unless accompanied by biomechanical demonstrations of the significance of each trait employed in the analysis.

5. The lower limb skeleton of Australopithecus *and modern man*

The foot of *Australopithecus* is now represented by several samples. These include the almost complete foot from Olduvai (OH 8), the incomplete talus from Kromdraai (TM 1517), and new specimens from East Rudolf (Leakey, 1972; 1973). The strong similarities between all of these specimens and modern tarsals has been generally recognized, although it has been suggested that some features preclude a gait pattern similar to modern man. As far as we can detect, however, they do not differ from modern specimens in any significant detail, when the range of variation in modern man is fully considered.

As an example, the 'horizontal axis of the talar neck' has been given some attention by several workers (Day and Napier, 1964; Day and Wood, 1968; Robinson, 1972). This angle is 28° in OH 8 and 32° in TM 1517 (Day and Wood, 1968). A sample of modern specimens used by Day and Wood for comparison had a mean value of 19° and a standard deviation of 3.4°. Thus both australopithecine specimens lie about 3 standard deviations from the mean *of this particular sample.* A primary problem, of course, is the variability of this metric in various populations of modern man. The normal Amerindian talus frequently displays a marked divergence of the talar neck. Of the six specimens illustrated in Figure 5 three have talar neck angles which equal or exceed those of OH 8 and TM 1517. (It was impossible to measure the angle of the talar neck in a suitably reproducible manner; I therefore have not included a metrical analysis of this feature.) They also exceed the angle in the newer East Rudolf specimen, KNM-ER 813. Thus the range of variation among the modern specimens illustrated is greater than that of the australopithecine samples. Several other features of the talus are illustrated in Figure 5. Note that the length of the talar neck varies substantially, as does its angle of torsion. Indeed, the range of variation in these Amerindian specimens exceeds that of available australopithecine samples in the prolongation of the trochlea onto the talar neck, and the degree to which the lateral sustentacular facets, the posterior extension of the sub-articular shelf (including the degree to which the groove for flexor hallucis longus is developed), the extension of the medial malleolar surface of the trochlea onto the talar neck, and the degree to which the lateral malleolar surface is extented in the form of a shelf. For all of the above

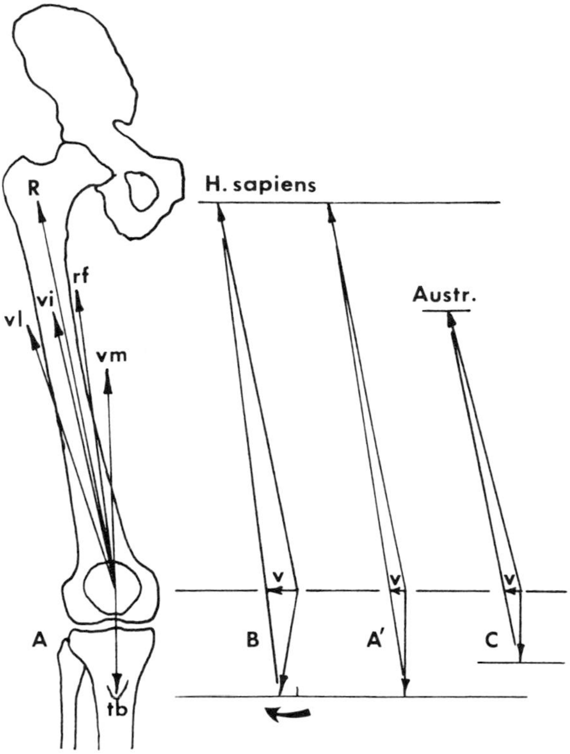

Figure 4. Some factors affecting mediolateral stability of the patella. The four muscles of the quadriceps group (vi; vl; vm; rf), when contracting, tend to pull the patella in the direction R. The patellar tendon inserts at the tibial tuberosity (tb). During contraction the patella tends to be displaced laterally (v). A and A′: modern man; B: modern man with tibia in external rotation; C: *Australopithecus*. The bicondylar angle increases v while a deep patellar groove tends to prevent dislocation. For details see Heiple and Lovejoy (1971).

features there exist no significant differences between australopithecine and modern human tali.

To return to the angle of the talar neck, one additional point seems worth discussing. Many students have assumed that a high talar neck angle is directly related to divergence of the hallux (Straus, 1963). This would appear highly doubtful on several grounds:

1. Three joint surfaces separate the talar neck from the hallux. Very slight alterations in the form of these would have a more significant effect than the angle of talar neck divergence.
2. Barnett measured the talar neck angle in a number of primates and found it to be unrelated to divergence of the hallux. The rhesus monkey, baboon, and orang-utan had values similar to those of modern man (Barnett, 1955).

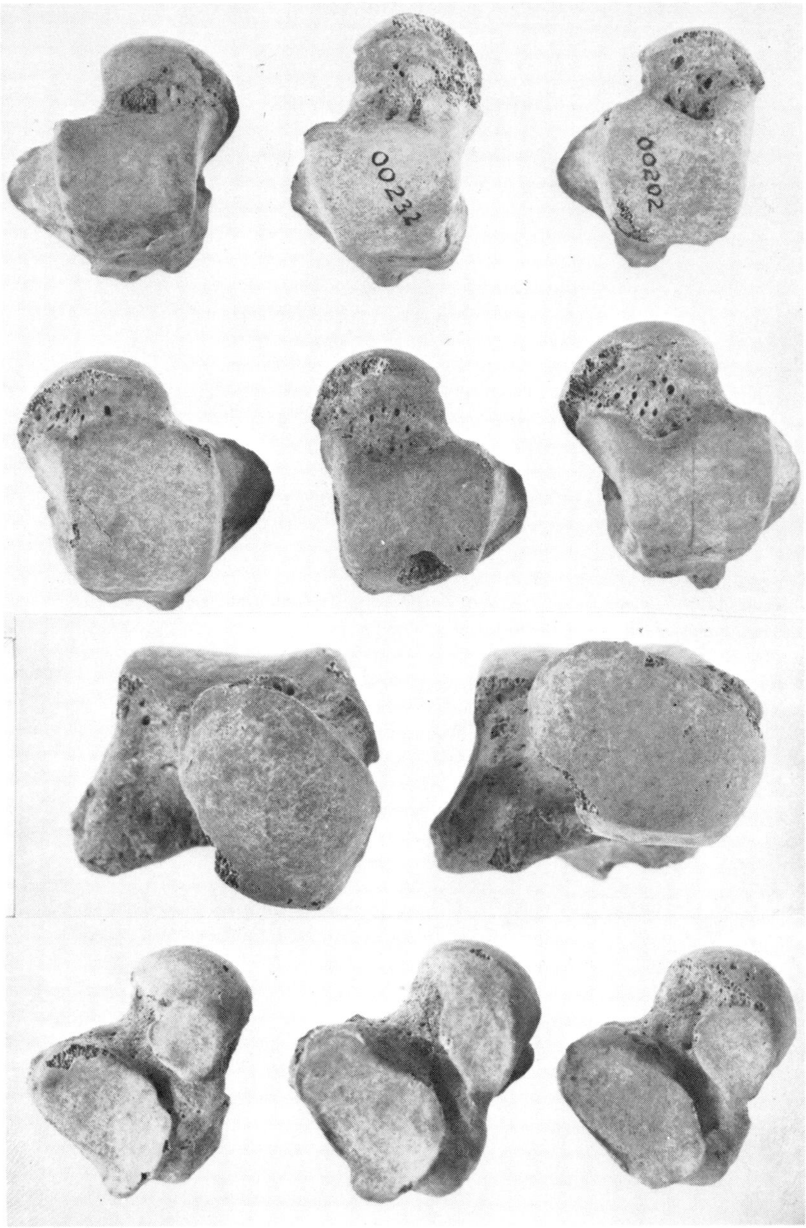

Figure 5. Some normal variations in the Amerindian talus (all specimens are from a single population). The first two rows show substantial variations in the length of the talar neck, its angle with the trochlea, the anterior prolongation of the trochlea, and the projection of the lateral fibular facet. The third row shows variation in the angle of torsion of the talar neck. The bottom row shows variations in the anterior and middle sustentacular facets. Note that the specimen on the extreme right does not have an anterior sustentacular facet.

3. The talar neck angle is very high in the infant foot (Trotter has estimated an average of 35°) and it is therefore likely that this metric varies strongly with relatively minor variations in its mechanical environment during development.

For some time the australopithecine tibia was known on the basis of only one specimen (OH 6), and the conclusions of Davis with regard to this specimen have been widely quoted, especially his comments regarding the knee joint (Davis, 1964).

His original suggestion that the distal portion of OH 6 was essentially identical to the modern human tibia, but that the proximal end of the bone was indicative of 'incomplete adaptation to bipedal gait', can now be given closer scrutiny. While we agree that the form of the distal articular surface of OH 6 is similar to the modal condition of modern man (including an articular surface essentially perpendicular to the long axis of the bone), we do not agree with Davis' conclusions regarding the proximal portion of the bone. We have elsewhere argued (Lovejoy, 1976) that the large, posterior, vertical ridge on the proximal portion of OH 6 is the upper portion of the spiral (=soleal) line – a feature shared by many modern specimens. Both in numerous *Homo sapiens* and in OH 6 the spiral line descends vertically, shifting medially as it approaches the region of flexor digitorum longus. In modern man the relationship of these muscles is highly variable (Vallois, 1938) and OH 6 is therefore not a particularly unusual specimen.

A central issue in posterior tibial morphology, of course, is the implication of the spiral line – whether it is simply depicting the margin of popliteus or is indicative of a tibial origin of the soleus. African pongid tibias are in general very similar to those of modern man in the morphology of the posterior compartment. Almost identical dispositions of the spiral line, flexor digitorum longus origin, popliteus origin and tibialis posterior origin can be found in moderate samples of human and African pongid tibias. *Homo sapiens* specimens, however, are in general more rugose in this region and the rugosity of OH 6 clearly implies that its spiral line is fully homologous with a tibial origin of the soleus. A new speciman, recently discovered by Leakey *et al.* (1972) provides considerable evidence with respect to the above issues because its proximal morphology is almost completely intact. It has a deep groove for the flexor digitorum longus and while the tibialis posterior region is too weak for clear definition, the line of the interosseous membrane can be readily palpated and indicates a modern disposition of this muscle. In addition it is clearly fully modern in morphology. It has an angle of retroversion (based upon the medial condyle) well within the range of modern man (Table 1). Its angle of torsion is likewise well within the modern range (Table 1).

When the range of variation in modern man is considered, there would appear to be no morphological feature of significance which

Table 1 Metric parameters of KNM-ER 741 and modern tibias

Specimen	*Angle of torsion***	*Angle of inclination**
KNM-ER 741	20–26°	17°
Amerindians: (N = 50)		
$\overline{X}$	18.7	17.3
S.D.	6.1	3.8

*Based upon the medial condyle only. Therefore it is defined as the angle between the centroidal axis of the shaft and the plane of the medial condyle.

**Because the australopithecine specimen was incomplete, the transverse axis of the tibio-talar joint could not be determined. Therefore only an estimated range is provided for this specimen.

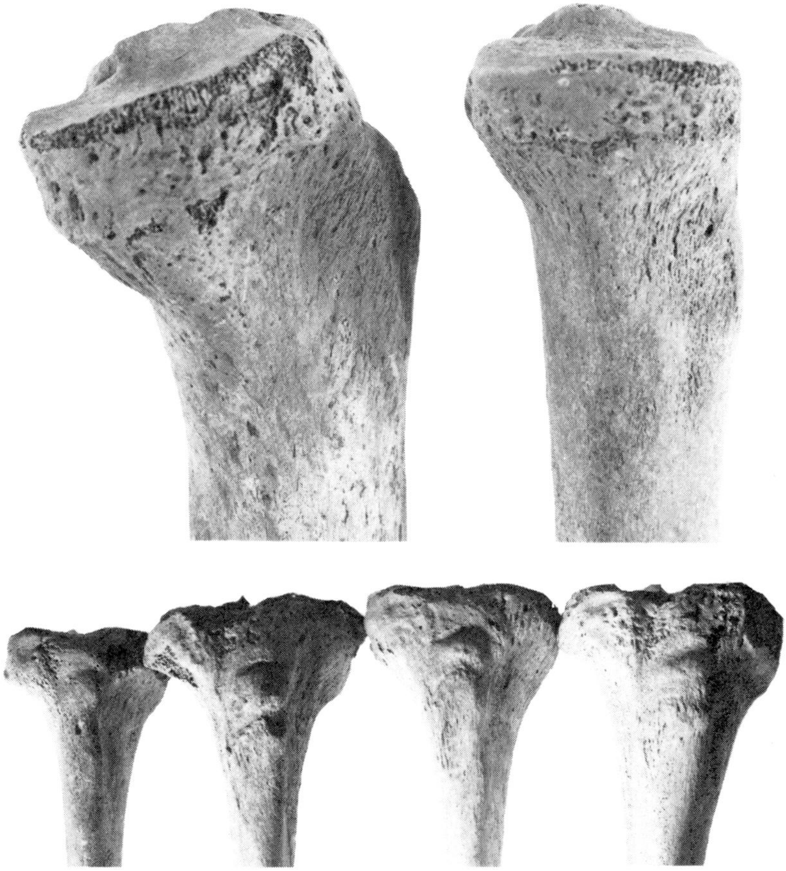

Figure 6. Variation in the Amerindian tibia. The two top specimens illustrate marked differences in the degree of proximal retroversion. The degree of retroversion shown by the specimen on the left is well within the range of variation of the chimpanzee. The bottom row illustrates differences in the form of the tibial tuberosity. It varies from a narrow ridge on the far left to an extremely broad and undefined area of the bone (extreme right).

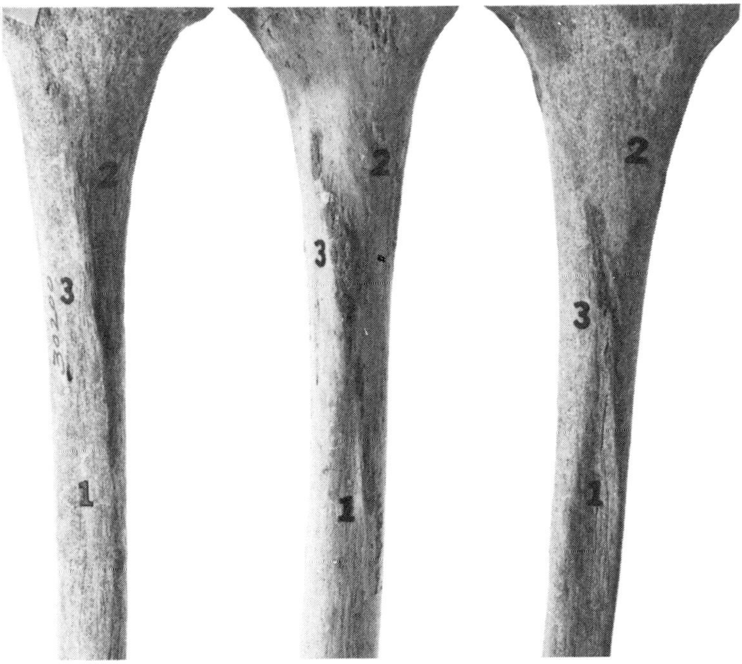

Figure 7. Variations in the posterior compartment of the Amerindian tibia. 1: area of origin of flexor digitorum longus; 2: area of origin of popliteus; 3: area of origin of tibialis posterior. Note the division of the spiral line in the Amerindian specimen on the far right and the course of the superior portion of this line.

can be used to distinguish australopithecine and modern tibias. Figures 6 and 7 show some variations among modern tibias including different expressions of the patellar tuberosity and posterior compartment. The range of variation provided by a single Amerindian population is sufficient to incorporate the australopithecine traits thus far observed. In addition, the similar disposition of the muscle impressions of the posterior compartment, the virtual identity of the distal joint surface of OH 6 and those of modern tibias, the similarity of KNM-ER 741 to modern specimens in proximal retroversion and torsion, all fail to justify rejection of the null hypothesis set forth above.

In addition to the above observations it may also be pointed out that the australopithecine specimens show degrees of platycnemia typical of many modern human populations. KNM-ER 741 also shows the distinct posterior pilaster often associated with this feature in the modern tibia. We have recently pointed out that both the elliptical cross-sectional form and posterior pilaster often associated with this feature in the modern tibia. We have recently pointed out that both the elliptical cross-sectional form and posterior pilaster associated with platycnemia are phenotypic adaptations of the tibia to pronounced torsional and anteroposterior bending loads (Lovejoy *et*

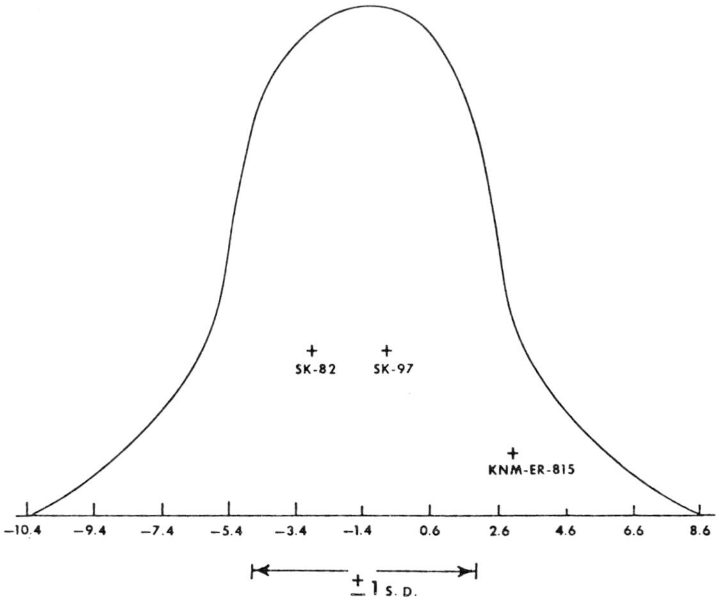

Figure 8. Normal curve fitted to 96 Amerindian femora measured for position of lesser trochanter relative to the medial border of the femoral shaft. Mean of the human sample was -1.4 mm.; S.D. = 3.6 mm. The position of the australopithecine specimens (measured by identical methods) is indicated. Note the similarity in range of variation. For details see Lovejoy and Heiple (1972).

al., 1976). These tibias thus indicate that plantarflexion was heavily expressed among australopithecines – a conclusion strongly supported by the disposition of the muscles of the posterior compartment and the tibial origin of the soleus.

A number of features of the australopithecine femur have been suggested to comprise evidence of its incomplete adaptation to a bipedal gait, but none of these appear to have withstood closer scrutiny. Both the form and position of the lesser trochanter are well within the range of variation of their position in modern man. The more recent East African specimens confirm that *Australopithecus* was equally as variable as modern man in expression of this feature (Figure 8). Walker has pointed out that of five specimens now available in which the development of the inter-trochanteric line can be observed, none shows a very pronounced expression of this trait. Although Day has suggested that this rugosity is related to the tension of the ilio-femoral ligament, several considerations tend to dispute such a suggestion, including the absence of any expression of the trait in numerous modern specimens (Lovejoy and Heiple, 1972). It is more likely that the development of the line is age-related and that the available australopithecine specimens are generally too young to show a pronounced development of this feature. The well-developed

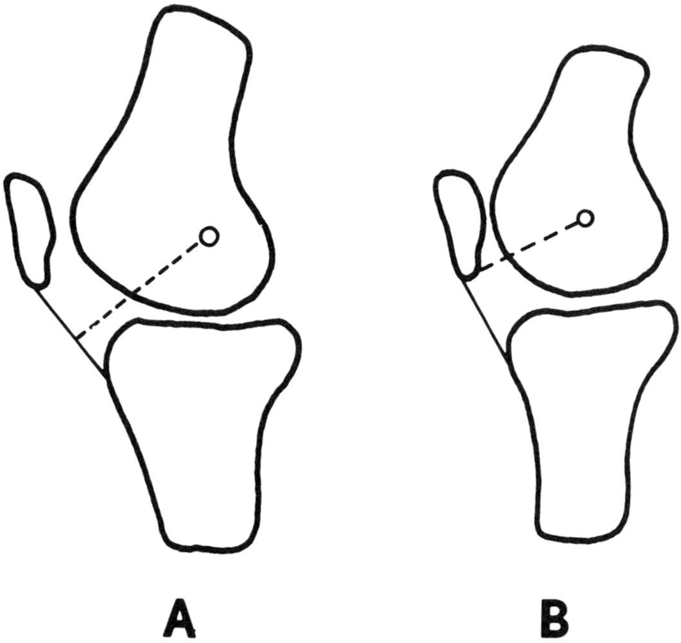

Figure 9. Two lateral projections of the knee joint during extension. A: the normal human knee (after Zimmer, 1968). B: the chimpanzee knee during bipedal gait (after Jenkins, 1972). Note the distinct elliptical form of the lateral condyle of the human compared to the circular form of the chimpanzee. The elliptical form of the human projects the patella more anteriorly relative to the instant centre of the knee joint (approximated here by assuming sliding joint motion) (Frankel and Burstein, 1970), resulting in a 20% increase in the lever arm of the quadriceps (drawn to same scale).

anterior inferior iliac spine is a more certain indicator of the presence of a well-developed ilio-femoral ligament (Robinson, 1972).

A distinct obturator externus groove is detectable in almost all of the proximal femoral samples thus far recovered (Day, 1969; Robinson, 1972). It serves as an indication that the obturator externus tendon was closely applied to the posterior aspect of the femoral neck – a condition only explicable by consistent full extension of the femur.

The form of the intercondylar notch is similar to its condition in modern humans. The attachments of the anterior and posterior cruciate ligaments do not differ from their condition in modern man (Robinson, 1972). The form of the lateral femoral condyle is, like that of *H. sapiens*, elliptical and unlike that of quadrupedal primates in which it is circular. This is indicative of a specialized restriction of maximum true cartilage contact only during full extension of the knee (Heiple and Lovejoy, 1971). A second effect of this elliptical form is an increase in the length of the lever arm of the quadriceps femoris during the latter phases of knee extension. This may be seen in Figure 9. The elliptical form of the condyle projects the line of action of the patellar tendon anteriorward, resulting in a longer lever arm for the patellar tendon. This is a crucial adaptation since extension of the knee by the quadriceps is a primary source of impulse during bipedal gait (Lovejoy *et al.*, n.d.).

The bicondylar angles of available femoral samples are all significantly above the range we observed in a limited sample of quadrupedal primates (Heiple and Lovejoy, 1971). In fact the mean value for the bicondylar angle in *Australopithecus* (including the newer East African specimens) is above that of modern man. A deep patellar groove and high lateral condylar lip are likewise present in all known australopithecine distal femoral samples, indicating a complete adaptation to the prevention of patellar dislocation which may result from valgus of the knee during bipedal locomotion (Figure 4).

The neck-shaft angles of a number of australopithecine femora are now available. Their mean value lies considerably below that of most modern populations, although the great variation in modern man indicates that moderate variations in this angle do not critically affect individual gait pattern. The net mechanical effect of a lower neck-shaft angle is an increase in the distance between the greater trochanter and the hip joint, and the lower mean value of this angle among australopithecine femora is thus commensurate with their significantly greater morphological and biomechanical neck lengths (Table 2).

As we have pointed out elsewhere, the femur is perhaps the most distinctive bone of the australopithecine lower limb, in that it tends to reflect differences from modern man, not with respect to gait pattern,

Table 2 Metric parameters of Australopithecine and modern femora

Specimen	*Bicondylar angle* (1)	*Neck-shaft angle* (2)	*Maximum length* (3)	*Max. diam. fem. head* (4)	*Bio. neck length* (5)	(5)/(3) x 10^3	(4)/(3) x 10^3
SK 97	—	118°	—	37	67	—	—
SK 82	—	120°	—	34	64	—	—
Sts 14	—	118°	—	31	53	—	—
OH 20	—	115°	—	—	—	—	—
KNM-ER 993	15°	116°	—	—	—	—	—
KNM-ER 815	—	115°	—	—	—	—	—
Sts 34	15°	—	—	—	—	—	—
TM 1513	14°	—	—	—	—	—	—
Reconstructions:							
Sts 14: Robinson			310	31	53	189	111
Sts 14: Lovejoy & Heiple			280	31	53	171	100
KNM-ER 993/OH 20: Walker			366	36	72	197	100
Amerindians: (N = 50)							
$\bar{X}$	10.5°	128°	450	45	68	151	100
S.D.	1.3	3.6	29	3.4	5.3	7	4.4

but rather in response to the degree of encephalization of the population and its commensurate effects upon the pelvo-femoral complex. Thus *Australopithecus* has a longer femoral neck, lower neck-shaft angle, and a slightly greater bicondylar angle. As pointed out above, most australopithecine specimens have to date shown only a minimal flare of the greater trochanter and a relatively weak expression of the intertrochanteric line while numerous other features are shared with modern man but not with quadrupeds. Together all of these features may be said to comprise the total morphological pattern (Le Gros Clark, 1964) or total biomechanical pattern (Lovejoy, 1975).

The consensus of most authors is that the ilium of *Australopithecus* is very similar to that of modern man (Dart, 1949; 1957; 1958; Le Gros Clark, 1967; Robinson, 1972). Its general morphological pattern is clearly hominid, and the available specimens are very similar to the modern human ilium. This includes a large and distinct retroauricular part, a prominent anterior inferior iliac spine, a deep sciatic notch, a clearly defined ilio-psoas groove, and a well-defined ischial spine. Robinson, however, has suggested that the auricular surface of Sts 14 (the only adult specimen in which it is preserved) is smaller than that of *H. sapiens*. He bases his opinion upon the breadth of the auricular surface in this specimen (29.5 mm.) (1972). The same measurement in a small sample of *H. sapiens* measured by Schultz (1930) yielded a mean value of 62 mm. Robinson has estimated body size in Sts 14 at approximately 40-60 lbs. This would mean an identical weight/auricular surface ratio for Sts 14 and modern man were the latter to have weighed from 80-120 lbs. This is of course very probable.

A number of authors have pointed out that a more pronounced lateral iliac flare characterized australopithecine specimens relative to modern man (Le Gros Clark, 1967; Lovejoy *et al.*, 1973; Lovejoy, 1974; Robinson, 1972; Zihlman, 1967). Such lateral flare increases the horizontal distance from the acetabulum to the lateral-most extent of the iliac crest. It is thus commensurate with a long femoral neck as discussed above. Together these features provide a greater lever length for the abductor muscles.

Most authors are now agreed that a clearly defined iliac pillar is present in adult australopithecine ilia (Dart, 1957; 1958; Day, 1959; Zihlman, 1967; Lovejoy *et al.*, 1973). Its development in the adolescent ilia, MLD 25 and MLD 7, is equal to that of modern ilia of equivalent osteological age. Both we and Robinson have pointed out, however, that it tends to be slightly more anteriorly situated than in most modern ilia. This is a result of the greater lateral flare of the australopithecine ilium (Lovejoy *et al.*, 1974).

An additional feature which differs from the typical modern condition is the anterior prolongation of the anterior superior spine. As we have previously pointed out, this is also a result of the greater iliac flare of australopithecine ilia. Such flare places the anterior-most

Table 3 Relative ischial length in *Australopithecus* and *Homo sapiens*

Observer	*Metric*		Sts 14	SK 50	*Modern man* N	mean	S.
Schultz (1969)	Acetabulum diameter / Functional ischial length	x 10^2	80	67	24	67.6	–
Robinson (1972)[2]	Acetabulum diameter / Functional ischial length	x 10^2	87	62	40	68.4	4.
Lovejoy *et al.* (1973)	Iliac height / Functional ischial length	x 10^2	47	–	25	48	3.

point on the ilium in a more posterior position unless compensation is made by an extension of its anterior portion. Such compensation (in the form of an extension of the anterior superior spine) assures a similar placement of the inguinal ligament and sartorius. The degree to which this extension is expressed would be largely dependent upon body size and the degree of lateral iliac flare. This would account for the more pronounced expression of the feature in SK 50 relative to Sts 14.

The earlier literature has consistently suggested that the australopithecine ischium was longer than that of modern man. We have elsewhere pointed out that this opinion was based upon the improper use of a non-functional measurement, and that the use of a measure which reflects *functional* length results in similar ischial lengths in *Australopithecus* and modern man. Robinson has also recently employed a revised measure (1972), but has concluded that while the ischial length of Sts 14 is similar to that of modern man, that of SK 50 is significantly longer. Table 3 reveals, however, that this conclusion is not based upon acceptable statistical grounds (the SK 50 length is well within two standard deviations from the mean of a small modern sample). In addition the table shows that the results of work by other researchers confirm a similar ischial length in SK 50 and modern man.

6. *The total biomechanical pattern of* Australopithecus

The preceeding review of the lower limb skeleton of *Australopithecus* has revealed that most features of biomechanical significance lie well within the range of variation of modern man. While this is indeed true of every individual trait discussed above, populational differences do emerge between the lower limbs of *Australopithecus* and *H. sapiens*. Those features which appear to differ are restricted to the hip joint (i.e., proximal femur and ilium). Australopithecines have lower neck-

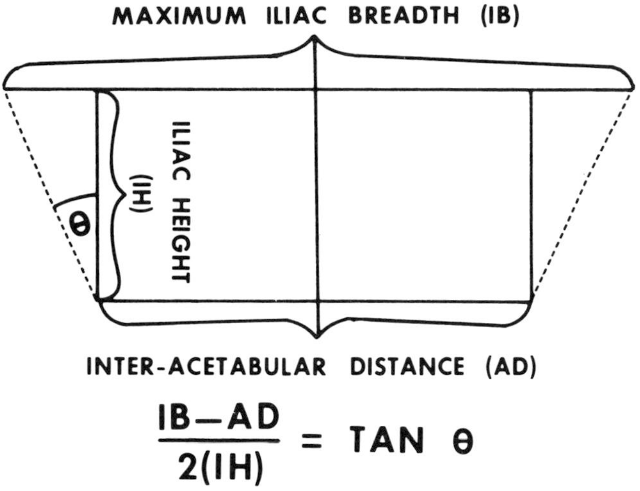

Figure 10. Method by which lateral flare was assessed in the Amerindian pelvis. Angle theta was defined as the degree of flare. For details, see Lovejoy (1975).

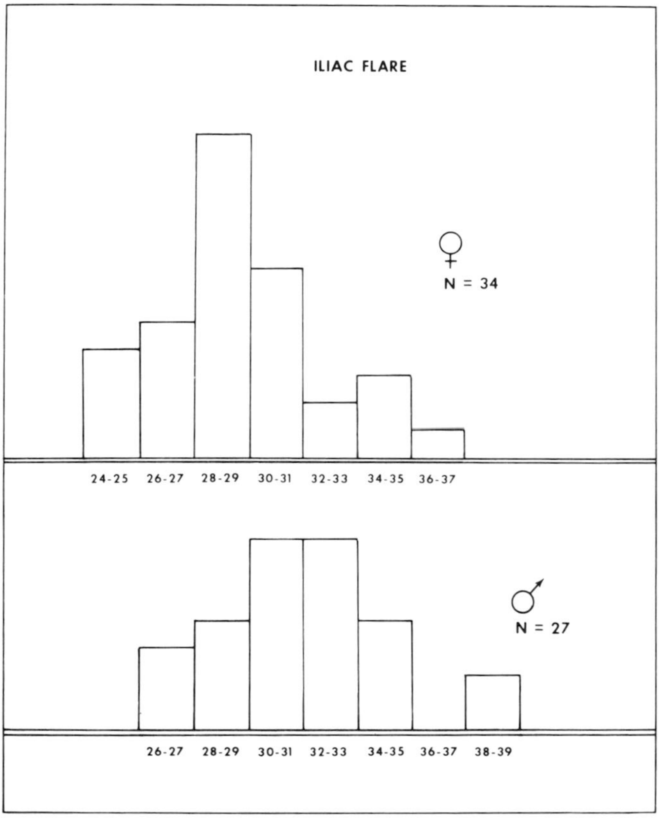

Figure 11. Results of the metrics described in Figure 10 applied to 34 female and 27 male Amerindian pelves. The male mean was 31° and that of the females was 28°. The populations differ significantly (P = .001; t-test).

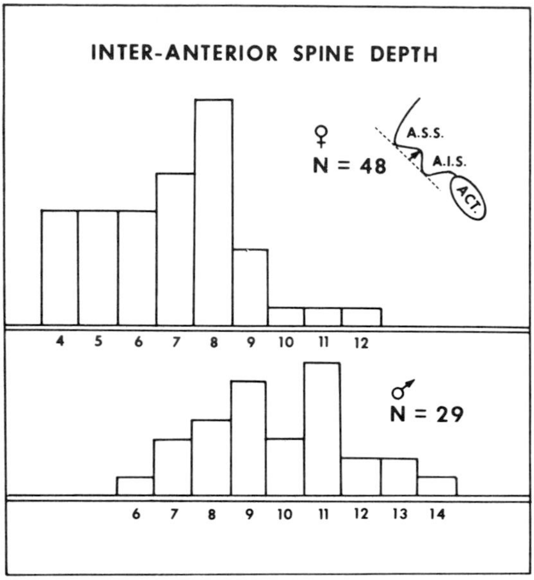

Figure 12. Sexual dimorphism in the protrusion of the anterior superior spine. The metric used has been illustrated by the inset. The results of its application to 48 female and 29 male Amerindian innominates is shown. The populations are significantly different (P = .001; t-test).

shaft angles, longer femoral necks, greater lateral iliac flare, more protuberant anterior superior spines, and a more anterior position of the iliac pillar. We have related this complex of features to a combination of a completely bipedal gait and relatively narrow interacetabular distance (Lovejoy *et al.*, 1973). The mechanical factors which determine the pressure upon the articular cartilage of the femoral head are primarily three: body weight; the length of its lever arm (the distance between the centre of the hip joint and the line of action of body weight during stance phase); and the length of the abductor lever arm (the right angle distance between the line of action of the abductors and the centre of the hip joint). The relationship of the last two factors in affecting hip joint pressure is shown in Figure 13.

The interacetabular distance of *Australopithecus* was almost certainly smaller (relative to body size) than that of modern man. This shorter distance would mean a shorter lever arm for body weight during stance phase and would thus lower joint reaction force in the hip. At the same time the relative narrowness of the pelvic canal allows a greater length for the abductor lever arm (without increase in overall pelvic breadth). This also lowers joint reaction force. The difference in these two dimensions between modern man and *Australopithecus* accounts for all of the known morphological differences of their hip joints. The longer lever length of the abductors in *Australopithecus* is

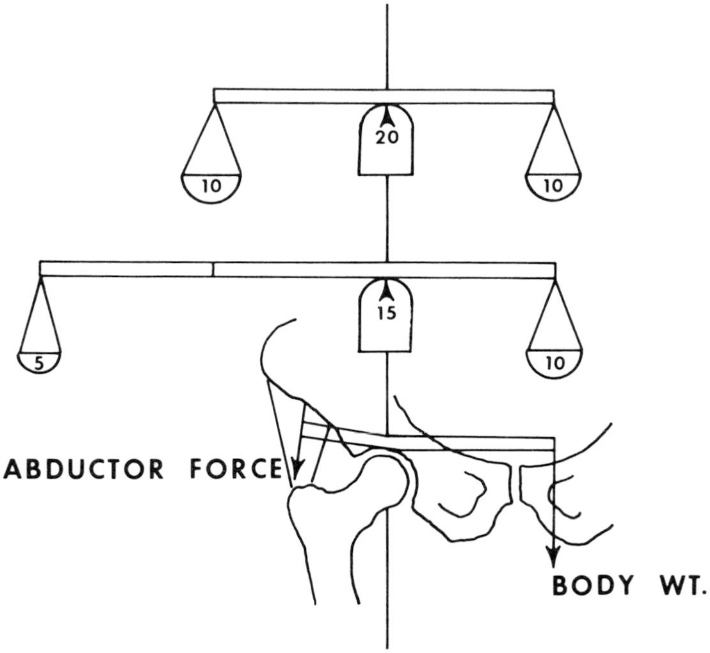

Figure 13. The effects of alterations of the lever lengths of body weight and the abductors. In the uppermost diagram, two equal weights are balanced by virtue of equal distances from the fulcrum. The force on the fulcrum is 20 lbs. In the second diagram, one of the weights has been halved but is still in balance by virtue of its doubled lever length. The force on the fulcrum is now 15 lbs. Note in the third diagram that increase in femoral neck length and iliac flare decrease fulcrum (hip joint) pressure while an increase in interacetabular distance makes it greater.

obtained via the longer femoral neck, lower neckshaft angle, and greater lateral iliac flare. As pointed out above, the latter modification requires morphological adjustments to retain basic muscular and mechanical relationships (more protuberant anterior superior spine; more anterior position of the iliac pillar) (Lovejoy *et al.*, 1973).

We have recently tested this hypothesis by reviewing the expression of these features in modern man with respect to sexual dimorphism. We hypothesized that males would display a more australopithecine-like hip complex than females, since the necessity of a large interacetabular distance for facile parturition would not be as strongly expressed. A sample of Amerindian pelves revealed that males have greater lateral iliac flare (Figures 10 and 11) and more protuberant anterior superior spines (Figure 12). In addition, Walker has pointed out that males have lower neck-shaft angles, the difference being as great as 3° between the means of the sexes (1973).

Finally, the problem of femoral head size in *Australopithecus* should be given some consideration. Throughout the earlier literature it was assumed that the femoral head of *Australopithecus* was relatively smaller than that of modern man and this might at first be expected in light of its lower joint reaction force (Lovejoy *et al.*, 1973). For equal body weights in two individuals, a lower joint reaction force would result in lower pressures upon the articular cartilage of the hip joint. This would compensate for a relatively smaller femoral head. Although the morphological features which differentiate australopithecines and modern man are clearly indicative of lower joint reaction forces in *Australopithecus*, the evidence available at present does not support the conclusion that the femoral head of *Australopithecus* was smaller than modern man's. Until recently, only three samples were available for which femoral head diameter was known: Sts 14, SK 82, and SK 97. The former of these is an extremely small individual and in light of this, its femoral head diameter of 31 mm. is not small (Table 2). The remaining two specimens are proximal fragments only, and normalization for stature is therefore not possible. Reference to Table 2 demonstrates that when normalized by femoral length the probable head diameter of ER 993 is also not small compared to modern man. A simple answer to this apparent contradiction lies in the assumption of equal body weights (relative to femoral length) in *Australopithecus* and modern man, and in equal degrees of physical activity in these two hominids. Forces on the femoral head increase substantially during active locomotor activity. It is not an unattractive hypothesis to suggest that the level of physical and locomotor activity in australopithecines of the lower Pleistocene savannahs would be significantly greater than that of recent populations of modern man. It is also not unlikely that the muscularity and body mass of australopithecines was significantly greater (relative to stature) than that of recent human populations. Both of these factors would tend to *increase* hip joint pressure while the more advantaged position of the abductors in *Australopithecus* would tend to *lower* hip joint pressure. The net effect of both would probably result in femoral head/femoral length ratios similar to those of modern man. At present, this seems the most economical hypothesis available.

In summary, the total biomechanical pattern of the australopithecine lower limb is fully commensurate with a bipedal striding gait similar to that of modern man. All of those features of biomechanical significance which differ in these two taxa are accountable by their differing degrees of response to fetal encephalization. In addition there would appear to be, at present, no basis for phyletic or mechanical division of australopithecine lower limb samples into two or more allomorphic groups. Rather, the range of variation of australopithecine tarsals, tibias, femurs, and innominates is exceeded with remarkable ease by normal variation in modern man. In light of the great temporal and geographical differences in the provenance of these specimens, the null hypothesis, as stated above, cannot be rejected.

Acknowledgments

I wish to thank Dr K.G. Heiple, Dr A.H. Burstein, and Dr M.H. Wolpoff for their valuable discussions and criticisms; Dr Michael Day for a cast of OH 20 and Dr Alan Walker for a cast of his reconstruction of the australopithecine femur based on KNM-ER 993 and OH 20. I wish also to thank Brad Thornton, Terry Calhoun, Richard Meindl and Richard Larson for measurements of the Amerindian skeletal material. The photographs are by Larry Rubens.

References

Barnett, C.H. (1955) Some factors influencing angulation of the neck of the mammalian talus. *J. Anat. (London)*, 89, 225-30.

Burstein, A.H. *et al.* (1972) Bone strength: the effect of screw holes. *J. Bone Jt. Surg.* 54A, 1143-56.

Davis, P.R. (1964) Hominid fossils from Bed I, Olduvai Gorge, Tanganyika: a tibia and fibula. *Nature* 201, 967-70.

Dart, Raymond (1949) Innominate fragments of *Australopithecus prometheus. Amer. J. phys. Anthrop.* 7, 301-34.

Dart, R. (1957) The second adolescent (female) ilium of *Australopithecus prometheus. J. Palaeont. Soc. India* 2, 73-82.

Dart, R. (1958) A further adolescent ilium from Makapansgat. *Amer. J. phys. Anthrop.* 16, 473-9.

Day, M.H. (1959) *Guide to Fossil Man.* London.

Day, M.H. (1969) Femoral fragment of a robust australopithecine from Olduvai Gorge, Tanzania. *Nature* 221, 230-3.

Day, M.H. and Napier, J.R. (1964) Hominid fossils from Bed I, Olduvai Gorge, Tanganyika: fossil foot bones. *Nature* 201, 967-70.

Day, M.H. and Wood, B.A. (1968) Functional affinities of the Olduvai Hominid 8 talus. *Man* 3, 440-55.

Day, M.H. and Leakey, R.E.F. (1973) New evidence of the Genus *Homo* from East Rudolf, Kenya. I. *Amer. J. phys. Anthrop.* 39, 341-54.

Frankel, V.H. and Burstein, A.A. (1970) *Orthopaedic Biomechanics.* Philadelphia, Pa.

Heiple, K.G. and Lovejoy, C.O. (1971) The distal femoral anatomy of *Australopithecus. Amer. J. phys. Anthrop.* 35, 75-84.

Jenkins, F.A. Jr. (1972) Chimpanzee bipedalism: cineradiographic analysis and implications for the evolution of bipedal gait. *Science* 178, 877-9.

Kay, R. (1973) Humerus of robust *Australopithecus. Science* 182, 396.

Kortlandt, A. (1972) *New Perspectives on Ape and Human Evolution.* Stichting Voor Psychobiologie, Amsterdam.

Kowalski, C.J. (1972) A commentary on the use of multivariate statistical methods in anthropometric research. *Amer. J. Phys. Anthrop.* 36, 119-32.

Leakey, R.E.F. (1970) Fauna and artifacts from a new Plio-Pleistocene locality near Lake Rudolf in Kenya. *Nature* 226, 223-7.

Leakey, R.E.F. (1971) Further evidence of lower Pleistocene hominids from East Rudolf, North Kenya. *Nature* 231, 241-5.

Leakey, R.E.F. (1972) Further evidence of lower Pleistocene hominids from East Rudolf, North Kenya, 1971. *Nature* 237, 264-9.

Leakey, R.E.F. (1973) Further evidence of lower Pleistocene hominids from East Rudolf, North Kenya, 1972. *Nature* 242, 170-3.

Leakey, R.E.F. (1973a) Evidence for an advanced Plio-Pleistocene hominid from East Rudolf, Kenya. *Nature* 242, 447-50.

Leakey, R.E.F.,· Mungai, J.M. and Walker, A.C. (1971) New australopithecines from East Rudolf, Kenya. *Amer. J. phys. Anthrop.* 35, 175-86.

Leakey, R.E.F., Mungai, J.M. and Walker, A.C. (1972) New australopithecines from East Rudolf, Kenya (II). *Amer. J. phys. Anthrop* 36, 235-51.

Leakey, R.E.F. and Wood, B.A. (1973) New Evidence of the Genus *Homo* from East Rudolf, Kenya. II. *Amer. J. phys. Anthrop.* 39, 355-68.

Le Gros Clark, W.E. (1947) Observations on the anatomy of the fossil Australopithecinae. *J. Anat. (London)* 81, 300-13.

Le Gros Clark, W.E. (1964) *The Fossil Evidence for Human Evolution* (2nd ed.). Chicago.

Lovejoy, C.O. (1970) Biomechanical methods for the analysis of skeletal variation with an application by comparison of the theoretical diaphyseal strength of platycnemic and euricnemic tibias. Ph.D. thesis, University of Massachusetts, Amherst.

Lovejoy, C.O. (1974) The gait of australopithicines. *Ybk. Phys. Anthrop.* 17, 147-61.

Lovejoy, C.O. (1975) Biomechanical perspectives on the lower limb of early hominids. In Tuttle, R.H. (ed.), *Primate Morphology and Evolution*, 291-326. The Hague.

Lovejoy, C.O. and Heiple, K.G. (1970) A reconstruction of the femur of *Australopithecus africanus*. *Amer. J. phys. Anthrop.* 32, 33-40.

Lovejoy, C.O. and Heiple, K.G. (1972) Proximal femoral anatomy of *Australopithecus*. *Nature* 235, 175-6.

Lovejoy, C.O., Heiple, K.G., and Burstein, A.H. (1973) The gait of *Australopithecus*. *Amer. J. Phys. Anthrop.* 38, 757-9.

Lovejoy, C.O., Burstein, A.H. and Heiple, K.G. (1976) The biomechanical analysis of bone strength: A method and its application to platycnemia. *Amer. J. Phys. Anthrop.* 44, 489-506.

Lovejoy, C.O., Johanson, D.C., Heiple, K.G. and Burstein, A.H. (n.d.) Biomechanical implications of the Afar knee joint. In manuscript.

Napier, J.R. (1964) The evolution of bipedal walking in the hominids. *Archives Biologie* (Liège) 75, 673-708.

Preuschoft, H. (1971) Body posture and mode of locomotion in early Pleistocene hominids. *Folia primat.* 14, 209-40.

Robinson, J.T. (1972) *Early Hominid Posture and Locomotion*. Chicago.

Sarich, V.M. (1971) In Dolhinow, P. and Sarich, V.M. (eds.), *Background for Man: Readings in Physical Anthropology*, 60-81. Boston.

Schultz, A.H. (1930) The skeleton of the trunk and limbs of higher primates. *Human Biology* 2, 303-438.

Schultz, A.H. (1969) Observations on the acetabulum of primates. *Folia Primatologica* 11, 181-99.

Sigmon, B.A. (1975) Functions and evolution of hominoid hip and thigh musculature. In Tuttle, R.H. (ed.), *Primate Morphology and Evolution*, 235-52. Mouton.

Straus, W.L. (1963) The classification of *Oreopithecus*. In Washburn, S.L. (ed.), *Classification and Human Evolution*, 146-77. Chicago.

Trotter, M. (1966) Osteology. In Anson, B.J. (ed.), *Morris' Human Anatomy*, 133-315. New York.

Vander, A.J., Sherman, J.H. and Luciano, D.S. (1970) *Human Physiology: The Mechanics of Body Function*. New York.

Vallois, H.V. (1938) Les méthodes de mensuration de la platucnémie: étude critique. *Bulletin et Memoir Societie de Anthropologie Paris, Series 8*, 9, 97-108.

Walker, A.C. (1973) New *Australopithecus* femora from East Rudolf, Kenya. *Journal of Human Evolution*, 2, 545-55.

Washburn, S.L. (1967) Behaviour and the origin of man. *Proc. Roy. Anthrop. Soc.* 21-7.

Washburn, S.L. (1968) In Rothblatt, B. (ed.), *Changing Perspectives on Man*, 193-206. Chicago.

Wolpoff, M.H. (1973) Posterior tooth size, body size, and diet in South African gracile australopithecines. *Amer. J. phys. Anthrop.* 39, 375-94.

Zihlman, A.L. (1967) Human locomotion: a reappraisal of the functional and anatomical evidence. Ph.D. thesis, University of California, Berkeley.

Zihlman, A.L. (1971) The question of locomotor differences in *Australopithecus*. *Proceedings of the 3rd International Congress of Primatology*. Basel.

Zimmer, E.A. (1968) *Borderlands of the Normal and Early Pathologic in Skeletal Roentgenology* (trans S.P. Wilk). 3rd ed. New York.

Richard G. Van Gelder

The voice of the missing link

At the close of the conference, one of the participants kindly remarked to me that I had served as a 'link to reality'. If my comments served this function, I would then presume that I spoke as or for the 'missing link'. The study of living mammals undoubtedly produces as many imaginative hypotheses as does palaeontology, but with the better opportunities to confirm or deny them, the invalid ones may not long persist.

My perspective of the conference was limited to the areas in which I have some experience, namely mammalian ecology, population, behaviour, and systematics. I can offer no ready solutions to the existing palaeoanthropologic problems except in the guise of indicating what may be errors of concept or approach, or alternative hypotheses. The application of the tools of neontology to the hominid fossils is valid only so long as the users are aware of the nature of the tools and the validity of the applications.

Mann (1975) correctly points out the difficulty of ascertaining the sexes of the fossils on the basis of the limited material available. However, even the tacit acceptance of the idea that there was sexual dimorphism in early hominids or that the larger form was the male can be questioned. There are some whole orders of mammals, whales and lagomorphs, in which the females average larger than the males. Even within families in which the rule is for larger males, there may be exceptions. Among the primates, even, spider monkeys are a group in which the females average larger than the males. In the carnivora the spotted hyena females are larger than the males, although generally in this order males are larger than females. My point here is merely that there are variations in sexual dimorphism within groups, and when working with fossils about whose life-styles so little is known, the exceptions must be borne in mind and must be appropriately considered.

Mann's demonstration that the eruption of the permanent molars in the South African fossil hominids occurred in the same sequence as in modern *Homo sapiens* essentially provides another datum for confirming the placement of South African fossils in the Hominidae. However, I take exception to some of Mann's extrapolations from his data.

First of all, the fact that the sequence of the eruption of the molar teeth is the same as in *H. sapiens* does not mean that the time interval between eruptions is necessarily the same. The presence of wear on the first molars before the eruption of subsequent ones in youthful hominids suggests only that the early need for the full array of molars was not as great as it is in modern chimpanzees. While I agree that this would suggest that there was a long period of maternal dependence, as Mann indicates, I would not attempt to equate the concept of relatively long dependence with actual years. To go on with this extrapolation to suggest an age of sexual maturation is, I feel, even more dangerous. The age of menarche in Europe and North America, for example, has changed considerably over the past 150 years, possibly as a result of improved nutrition during the winter. The data from captive chimpanzees do not conform with those from wild animals, as Goodall (pers. comm. 1971) has stated that the development rate of wild chimpanzees in the Gombe Stream Reserve is approximately half that of captive animals and that adolescence in the females is reached at about age 13. Her earlier assumption of menarche at nine years (Goodall, 1971, p.179) was erroneous in that it was extrapolated from data on captive animals and was not gained from the known age of wild individuals that began menstruation. Finally, sexual maturity (i.e. the physiological ability to reproduce) in many mammals occurs earlier than full skeletal maturation; actual reproduction may be delayed either by social factors, especially in males, or several years of adolescent sterility in the females. Goodall (pers. comm. 1971) also suggested this for chimpanzees.

The assumption that the need for the transmission of learned behaviour from one generation to the next may have been a pressing factor in the evolution of early hominids is reasonably valid, but it is not confined to hominids as a group, and it is possible to continue to learn while remaining in the group after skeletal, dental, and reproductive maturity.

The determination by Mann of age at death is permeated with a high degree of possible error. First, as I have pointed out, his placing of years on the times of eruption of the molar teeth is subject to numerous questions, some of which he has already raised. To complicate matters further, he has utilized tooth wear as a functional correlative of time. Those who have worked with mammals other than primates, as well as those who have worked with primates, are always conscious that the degree of wear varies not only with individuals within a population but between populations as well. Further, the assumption that the rate of wear on the first molar provides a chronological constant for ascertaining the amount of wear on subsequent molars is questionable in several aspects, including the disregard of the high probability that some change in diet occurred with increasing age. Considering the multitude of variables that exist, Mann's construction of histograms showing the age of death cannot really be considered as such, but at best can only be taken as a frequency distribution of tooth wear without any precise chronology. The mean ages of death presented are, as might be expected, comparable to some populations of *Homo sapiens* and are actually higher than those reported in the fifteenth and sixteenth centuries by Malthus.

To my mind, to extrapolate further from these data to the social organization of the South African early hominids is unwarranted. Since virtually nothing is known with any degree of certainty concerning their food habits, and the longevity and maturation times are open to question, I do not see what useful purpose is served by attempting to establish any particular social structure for them. While Mann presents the possibility of a social structure like chimpanzees, I see no reason why equal credence could not be given to a gorilla-type social structure, a baboon-type social structure, a wild-dog-type social structure, or even a hyena-type social structure. The data on growth and maturity of African elephant females (Smith and Buss, 1974) are very close to those postulated by Mann for the South African hominids, and the life span is also similar. Postulating an elephant-type social structure for the hominids might be equally valid or invalid. In short, it seems to me that the application of ethological data from Recent mammals to the early hominids of South Africa is far too premature.

Wolpoff (this volume) has analysed some of the concepts of taxonomy and their applicability to palaeoanthropology. Although he correctly states that the biological basis for the definition of species is one that defies testing at present for fossil material, he is mistaken to think that morphology 'plays little role in the definition of species'. In the actual practice of mammalian systematics, it is rare that there is knowledge of biological reproductive isolation between the species studied, and conclusions are based largely on morphology. The description of the species is generally based on morphology. In essence, the difference between palaeoanthropologic taxonomy and neontologic taxonomy is the amount of knowledge available about the specimens. The neontologist often has the opportunity to obtain additional material from areas where specific distinctions may fail. He generally, but not always, has more, and more complete, material at his command. Where there is a paucity of material, however, the neontologist is in much the same position as the palaeoanthropologist, and the description of a species is based largely on morphology as an estimate of whether or not the degree of difference that the taxonomist sees is, in his opinion, great enough to preclude interbreeding with the closest forms.

The palaeoanthropologist must also estimate whether or not the morphological differences between two specimens or samples are of the same magnitude as those observed in living species. The problem is that the spectrum of species available as analogues among the living mammals provides one with almost any example one wishes. There are species that are virtually indistinguishable skeletally that we know are good species. There is sexual dimorphism so great that we are fairly certain that, had we only fossils, we would be likely to classify the males and females in different species. We know that in many taxa the isolating mechanisms are behavioural, rather than morphological. We know that there are some species that are allopatrically distributed and others that are sympatric.

What Wolpoff has demonstrated is the danger of applying to fossil material some of the techniques of taxonomy that have developed from large samples and more refined systematics. The pooling of specimens has inherent dangers of subjectivity to which are later applied the objective criteria of statistics. For example, Wolpoff regards the canine breadth of South African gracile hominids to be bimodal, yet the coefficient of variation for the pooled 'sexes' is about 11. This is approximately one-half the coefficient of variation that is derived for the same measurement in the pooled sample of maxillary canine breadth in the data Wolpoff presents for gorillas, but it is about equal to the coefficient of variation that exists in each sex – about 9 for males and 8 for females. Considering that a greater span of time probably exists for the sample of the South African specimens than for the gorillas, one would tend to expect more variation in the pooled sample. The point here is not whether or not there are two sexes represented in this fossil material, but merely that data may be selected – either consciously or unconsciously – to demonstrate whatever point of view one wishes. In fact, if Wolpoff had grouped the South African gracile specimens in the same size-class intervals as he did the gorillas, the bimodality would disappear.

The tables of measurements of teeth that Wolpoff presents at the end of his paper are equally useful to point to some of the shortcomings that may result from inappropriate use of statistics. The high coefficient of variation figures would tend to warn the taxonomist from using these characters. One could even use Wolpoff's data to show that, because there is overlap in the measurements between the gorilla, the orangutan, and the chimpanzee in every measurement, the three should be considered taxonomically indistinguishable, lumped into the same genus or species, and recognized only as subspecies. This is a conclusion that even the most extreme taxonomists seem not to have suggested.

Neontologists generally isolate as best they can the several influences on variation by analysing a population in view of the sex, age-classes and geographic derivation of the individuals. When these influences on morphology are eliminated, the remaining variation is considered individual variation that results from the spectrum of genetic arrays that are present in the more narrowly defined population. Taxonomically useful variation generally ranges from coefficients of variation of 2 or 3 up to 10, and most neontologists would be wary of using higher ones in their conclusions. The high figures presented by Wolpoff's table led me immediately to suspect that, even in those that are analysed by separating the sexes, obscuring variants were present. These, I have found, include the multiplying of two linear dimensions (length and width) to determine 'crown area' – which of course is not representative of the actual surface area, as it presumes both that the teeth are rectangular and that the surfaces are flat. Secondly, the samples are not drawn from a single geographic population, but over the total expanse of the range of the species, thus introducing geographic variation that is further biased by unequal numbers from different localities. Lastly, specimens of varying age-classes are presented. Pilbeam (pers. comm.) has informed me that when specimens of gorillas are segregated by age-class, sex, and geography, and when the linear dimensions are considered separately, the coefficients of variation conform much more with the amounts generally found in similarly restricted samples of other mammals.

The palaeoanthropologist, of course, must also deal with another cause of variation that most neontologists ignore – time. Rarely is a palaeontological sample composed of animals that were contemporaneous in the neotological sense. This complicates analysis further in much the same fashion as geographic variation might. An additional handicap to the palaeontologist is that the preserved material may not be the material in which taxonomic distinction shows.

Despite all of these drawbacks to analysis, I do not mean to imply that the techniques of systematics are not applicable to these materials. I mean only to advise caution in their use.

In the search for measurable differences and similarities between the fossils available, grouping of specimens can be made within some definable parameters. Under existing statistical procedures, it is assumed that a single specimen drawn at random from a population will fall within one standard deviation of the mean of that population in about two-thirds of such samplings, and within two standard deviations of the mean in about 95% of such samplings. Inasmuch as any fossil came from a biological population and may be considered a random sample, certain assumptions can be made about its nature in relation to any other specimen, or random sample, and statistical probabilities may be applied.

It is possible, for example, to construct the standard deviation for a single specimen by assuming a particular coefficient of variation. It is then possible to evaluate the statistical probability that a second specimen may have been drawn from the same statistical sample. The multiple assumptions that have to be made, however, including that the specimen may be representative of the mean, the low extreme, or the high extreme, or that the population actually had the amount of variation assumed, tend to point up once more the dangers of the applications of statistics to materials of this sort. Before individual specimens are lumped for the purposes of analysis, it would be advisable to make a check of this sort at least to obtain some estimate of the probability that the grouping itself is valid.

Essentially, Wolpoff has demonstrated that an attempt to apply statistics to small samples by making them larger may not be productive. The techniques that he has employed have found application in neontological investigations, but the material selected for comparison must be appropriate to the sample. Comparisons must be made utilizing equivalents of presumed age, presumed sex, and presumed biological, geographical, and temporal samples. From Wolpoff's data, one could conclude that a maxillary canine from a South African robust hominid that measured 9.2 mm. could equally well have come from a gracile hominid from South Africa, an East African '*Homo*', an East African 'robust', or modern man, or from a chimpanzee or gorilla. At this stage of the art, it would seem that the discernable morphological differences in the individual teeth or other parts are as valid as or more valid than measurements in allocating speciments to particular morphs, as Campbell (this volume) indicates.

Campbell's analysis of the relationship, categories, and lineages of the African hominids has an anthropocentric subjectivity that seems to pervade much of primatology today. From a broader zoological perspective, I tend to give much less 'weight' to the importance of many of the characters, real or presumed, of the fossil hominids. From my naive point of view, the differences between the South African fossils allow for almost *any opinion* of relationships that one desires. Certainly differences exist, but many are of the same magnitude as (or even less than) those one may find between males and females of some living species of mammals, between geographic races of a given species, or between species within the same genus. Considering the limitations of the existing material and the similarities, however, I think generic distinction would not be granted by most systematists with a wide range of experience with taxa of living mammals. By the same token, a number of neontologists would tend to include the current families Pongidae and Hominidae within a single family.

The use of a generic level by Campbell for the arrival of species at a new adaptive plateau should be based on the morphological adaptations that evolve in response to the exploitation of that plateau. Within the living genus of primates *Cercopithecus* there are both grassland and forest species without sufficient morphological adaptation to warrant generic distinction. Where morphological adaptations to the grassland existence have occurred, a generic distinction is recognized, as in *Erythrocebus*. I see no reason to utilize presumed environments for the fossil species as criteria for what seems an arbitrary generic distinction, unless there are morphological or proved behavioural distinctions to warrant them. The adaptive zone that the Plio-Pleistocene hominids achieved was bipedalism. When this occurred, or what the locomotion of *Ramapithecus* was, is not yet known. In much of evolution, of course, the rise of new groups or the exploitation of new environments takes place with the animals whose existence was marginal (either geographically or biologically), while the mainstream of evolution persists in the old environmental niche, or evaporates with it. With some degree of morphologic adaptation to permit success of the new environment or different exploitation of the old one, a new spectrum of selective pressures comes into play. We know, or assume, only a small part of the selection that seems to have taken place, mainly involving a general change of molar size and a change in cranial capacity, and probably a refinement of bipedalism.

The great weight that Campbell gives, following Huxley, to language and technology as criteria for the genus *Homo* are characters that are not now perceptible in the fossils, and are representative of the anthropocentricity to which I previously referred. The subjectivity of taxonomic levels for fossils requires that a reviser or arranger of the taxa states his criteria. With only one living species within the genus *Homo*, it would seem appropriate that the criteria for subspecies, at least, be established and stated for the living forms and that the systematics of the fossils be evaluated on that basis.

The extensive and detailed analyses of the faunal elements at the hominid sites by Behrensmeyer (this volume) and Cooke (this volume) provide some indication of the environments that may have prevailed in the regions where the fossils were formed. As the sites are fluvial and lacustrine, the least presumptious conclusion is that the early hominids were attracted to these areas by a need for water. Most of the animals, likewise, are either aquatic or belong to groups whose recent representatives, at least, are water-dependent. Despite Behrensmeyer's statistical analysis, I would be reluctant to draw conclusions concerning habitat preference for the hominids. The general picture that the faunal remains suggest is not unlike that seen in many parts of eastern and southern sub-Sahara Africa today, and there is no way of telling which specific elements of the environments, if not all, were being used by the hominids. One could also draw the conclusion that they did not normally inhabit the sites where the fossils are found but were drawn there only during times of extreme drought, at which time one might likewise excpect a higher mortality. Until data are available concerning the cause of death of the hominids, it would also seem premature to suggest that the *Australopithecus* were either more numerous in the fluvial sites or preferred them. More of their fossils have been found there (so far) but why this is so is not indicated by the data. In regard to the environments for the early hominids, I would raise a general question that may have some bearing on where they lived or desired to live.

Assuming that they were diurnal, as most but not all primates are, where did they spend the night? All of the savannah and other ground-dwelling primates seek refuge in trees or heights at night. The females and young and smaller male great apes take refuge in trees at night, but these are essentially forest dwellers. Baboons, patas monkeys, and vervets that inhabit tree savannahs do not spend the night on the ground.

It would seem that if the early hominids inhabited open country they might require some form of protection from nocturnal predators. Except for Taung, one or more large felids, hyenids, or canids is present at each of South African sites. The same is probably true for the East African sites. Climbing trees at night or seeking refuge on cliff-faces or in caves would be logical assumptions for the early hominid's means of protection at night without presuming the construction of thorn shelters, fences, and/or the construction of weapons or the use of fire. To what extent have the palaeoecologists considered the availability of night roosts near the fossil sites?

Because of the relative abundance of teeth preserved, there has been a tendency to look at the possibility of different foods and eating patterns as major selective forces in the evolution of the hominid lineages. The exploitation of food sources by omnivores may not put strong selection on the morphology of teeth. If the early hominids required protection against predators at night, the selective pressures for living in a region that provided refuges would be high, as would the selective pressures for utilizing tools and fire for protection, when these were achieved, as permitting these hominids to venture farther into environments that were previously extremely hazardous to them at night.

In view of the general excellence of the papers presented, I have largely limited my comments to some of the extrapolations that have been made from existing data. The study of the ancestry of man is a relatively new field, as is evolution as a whole. Considering the conceptual changes that have been caused by the successive discoveries of more fossils, the imaginative and resourceful uses of the discoveries in other sciences for chronology, and the increasing numbers of investigators and opportunities for research in this area, it is not surprising that the picture has increased in complexity. If the history of other fields of biology is a guide, palaeoanthropology has progressed into a middle-ground of unclarity, and the more accurate determination of the evolution of the hominids awaits more materials and study.

References

Behrensmeyer, A.K., this volume.
Campbell, B.G., this volume.

Cooke, H.B.S., this volume.
Goodall, J. van Lawick (1971) The behaviour of free-living chimpanzees in the Gombe Stream Reserve. *Animal Behaviour Monographs* 1, 165-311.
Mann, Alan (1975) *Palaeodemographic Aspects of the South African Anstralopithecines*. Pennsylvania Publications in Anthropology No. 1.
Smith, N.S. and Buss, I.O. (1974) Reproductive ecology of the female African elephant. *Journal of Wildlife Management* 37 (4), 524-34.
Wolpoff, M.H., this volume.

J.T. Robinson

Evidence for locomotor difference between gracile and robust early hominids from South Africa

The concern of this paper is to discuss the evidence bearing on the locomotor habit of early hominids from South Africa, with special reference to possible differences between gracile and robust forms. The literature has tended strongly to the tacit or overt assumption that whatever is found to be true of the locomotor habit of the gracile form will also apply to the robust form and vice versa. This is simply one aspect of the general tendency for authors to write as though statements made about any aspect of one type of early hominid holds for the other also, as though the 'australopithecines' were a clearly defined group of hominids with rather uniform characteristics distinct from those of other hominids.

Although there is still some discussion going on as to whether indeed two validly different forms of early hominid existed, the fairly extensive information now available, or emerging, continues to present to me the appearance of two distinct sets of morphological features among early hominids. So far no one, in my opinion, has presented a biologically acceptable argument that combines these two sets of features into a single meaningful pattern, thereby demonstrating that a single lineage only existed. Indeed, at the conference from which this volume stems, one of the strongest previous supporters of the single-species hypothesis seemed no longer to believe it probable. On the contrary, the evidence now seems stronger than ever that at least two distinct lineages existed. Failing to differentiate between the two groups in discussion is a fruitful source of confusion and almost certainly of error also. So it is no more than prudent to make clear in discussion to which form reference is being made.

During discussion in the last days of the conference it became clear that a considerable degree of unanimity existed among those present that the so-called robust early hominid of South and East Africa,

Paranthropus (=*Australopithecus robustus* of most recent authors), is indeed a very distinct form deserving generic distinction from other early hominids. This point of view has long seemed reasonable to me (e.g. Robinson, 1954, 1967, 1972). Although there was some sympathy for the point of view that the remaining early hominids all belonged in the genus *Homo*, some believed that it might be wiser at present to retain such forms as the typical gracile early hominids of South Africa and some of the smaller-brained East African forms in a separate genus *Australopithecus*, from which probably the larger-brained early hominids of the genus *Homo* arose.

I shall, however, continue to use the classificatory scheme first proposed by me in 1954 and modified slightly in 1965, 1966, 1967 and 1972, in which two genera only are employed, *Paranthropus* and *Homo*. As is set out in detail elsewhere (especially Robinson, 1972) the reason for this is that the basic adaptation of the gracile early hominids seems to me in principle the same as that of later forms of *Homo*, but distinctly different from that of *Paranthropus*. Moreover, it seems to me that the emergence of *Homo*, in the sense used here, was an evolutionary event of inestimable importance, representing the emergence of a new kind of organism with a new kind of evolutionary mechanism as compared to *Paranthropus* and all other known prehominid organisms whatsoever, with their 'genes + natural selection' evolutionary method. In short, the emergence of *Homo* represents a major step in the evolution of evolution itself, bringing into existence a new mode of evolution of colossal potential, but one whose difficulties are at present causing man serious problems. To pursue this point, however, will take us too far afield from the theme of this paper; it is mentioned simply to indicate the significance that seems to me to lie in careful appraisal of early hominid classification.

When I first began studying postcranial aspects of the early hominids I inclined to the belief that little would distinguish gracile and robust forms with respect to locomotor habit. Further study led to a very different conclusion, however (Robinson, 1972); locomotor habit seems to have differed very considerably in the two forms. Postcranial material is much more useful for determining locomotor habit than is cranial material; unfortunately cranial material is by far the more common in fossil deposits. Small sample size is a real difficulty when comparing postcranial remains of early hominids. The picture is, however, brighter than it might seem. Locomotor habit in mammals is always a very important aspect of the basic adaptive pattern of a species – perhaps it is more logical to say genus. So it is a reasonable conclusion that the elements making up the locomotor adaptation are under close natural selection control. That is to say one will not find in a species, at one time level, individuals adapted quite differently with respect to locomotion. For example, if a very small sample of a population – even one specimen – gives clear indication of a power-oriented propulsive mechanism, it is not reasonable to suppose that a larger sample would turn up some individuals with a clearly speed-oriented propulsive mechanism. This fact makes up somewhat for very small sample sizes, provided that one is concerned with really significant locomotor differences: one cannot expect to detect modest differences in the same basic locomotor adaptation from very small samples. Of course, larger samples are always preferable to small ones; the point being made is that detection of significant locomotor differences should not be regarded as impossible at present because sample sizes are very small.

Cranial evidence

The cranium is only modestly affected by posture; the chief evidence for posture and locomotor habit comes from the occiput, particularly its nuchal plane. In quadrupedal higher primates the nuchal plane rises to, or almost to, lambda, hence there is little or no occipital plane. Moreover lambda is situated relatively high up the skull, being about as high above the Frankfort Plane as are the brow ridges. In the first phase of the evolution of erect bipedal posture (Robinson, 1972) the nuchal plane becomes re-oriented to a more nearly horizontal position and occupies a relatively much smaller portion of the total external area of the occipital bone. This re-orientation also involves re-positioning of the foramen magnum in a slightly more anterior position. The changed relation between occipital and nuchal planes and the re-orientation of the nuchal plane are, however, far more obtrusive changes accompanying erect bipedalism than are the changed position of the foramen magnum and occipital condyles.

Both the gracile *Homo africanus* (=*Australopithecus africanus*) and the robust *Paranthropus* (=*Australopithecus robustus*) have the re-oriented nuchal plane of the occiput. In both the reorientation is complete, with inion approximately in the Frankfort Plane. Both therefore also have a well developed occipital plane of the occiput. This evidence indicates that both forms had undergone at least some specific adaptation for erect bipedalism, but does not allow distinction to be made between them regarding the nature or degree of bipedalism. To the small extent that cranial evidence does reflect bipedalism, it provides no basis for differentiating between robust and gracile early hominids in this respect.

Postcranial evidence

The burden of demonstrating locomotor habit thus lies with the postcranial material, scanty as it is. Interpreting locomotor habit from fossil skeletal material is obviously extremely difficult. It is well known that closely related living primates with very similar skeletons may nevertheless be dissimilar in locomotor behaviour. Especially in primates, the locomotor behavioural repertoire may be extensive, and dissimilar animals may do similar things and similar animals may do dissimilar things. There are other problems. All muscle fibres do not contract at the same speed and whether a muscle contains more or less of one or the other type will materially affect what it does and how it does it. This problem is different from that of pennateness of the muscle, which is also important. The scar of attachment of a muscle is not an accurate guide to the volume of the muscle whose tendon attached there, except in very broad terms. Knowledge of these aspects of the locomotor apparatus thus lie entirely or almost entirely outside of the grasp of the palaeontologist. Comparison with the closest living forms can be of some help, but may also be considerably misleading.

Normally the palaeontologist simply has some of the skeletal bones alone to study, but even here hazards are present that may not always be obvious. It has been said, for example, by a number of authors that the ischium is similar in length in the two early hominids, great apes and man – the implication, or explicit conclusion, being that my use of ischium length to differentiate between *Paranthropus* and *Homo africanus* is invalid. Walker (1973) has examined the femur of *Australopithecus* and states that, apart from size, he can find no real differences in femoral anatomy among the early hominids. Such studies or statements leave the general reader with the impression, intended or not, that many studies have shown that there are no differences between *Paranthropus* and *Homo africanus*. This impression is misleading. It is fallacious to argue, for example, that because functional ischial length in most pongids greatly overlaps in absolute size those of modern man and *Paranthropus*, therefore the difference cannot be of significance and the ischium cannot be used to differentiate them. The functional length of the ischium represents the maximum moment arm length of the hamstrings. In considering locomotion, the length of the lever being moved by the hamstrings also has to be taken into account. So have the hamstrings themselves – but we have already seen that this information is not available to the palaeontologist. However, the relation in length between the functional ischial length and the length of the lower limb is of considerable importance because this tells one a good deal about the structural or biomechanical framework within which those muscles operated and this gives one more information about locomotion than does study of either the ischium or the femur alone. This illustrates the fallacy – to which Zihlman (this volume) also draws attention – of considering one bone at a time rather than attempting to see the whole pattern into which it fits.

Because the usual evidence available to the human palaeontologist consists of bones, there is another temptation – that of using biomechanical approaches only to the problems of interpreting the fossils. Often insufficient evidence is available for proper biomechanical analysis and so assumptions are made which may in fact be very far from correct, but the conclusions reached by this pathway are treated as though they are established conclusions. This is unwise, not only because some of the assumptions made may be – and in some cases demonstrably are – incorrect, but also because the approach ignores all that other evidence already mentioned concerning muscle physiology, size, structure, behavioural flexibility, and so on. Clearly, in the circumstances our conclusions must be over-simplifications and the danger is that so often this seems not to be realised. It would be prudent to bear in mind the comment by Lord Ashby (1971) (italics mine):

> But the framework of concepts in science owes its coherence and strength to the fact that those who build it *do not try to comprehend reality: they build from abstractions and simplifications*. So it is evident to anyone who has done basic research that the problems to be tackled cannot be defined by persons outside the discipline, and that *the solutions obtained are valid only within the framework of the discipline*.

If it is true that science in general is built on abstractions and simplifications, then how much more must it be true in palaeontology where most of the basic data available to the neontologist are seldom or never available. Perhaps we would be wiser to treat our conclusions about early man as interesting exercises in detection and deduction rather than to cover them over with the elaborate guise of great truths and be ever ready to sally forth with lance and mace to defend to the death our own particular mental jugglings with the few facts available. It is particularly unwise to pile assumption upon assumption, put the precarious result through a computer and then claim to have proved this or disproved that.

There is a modest range of postcranial material bearing on locomotor difference between the two forms of early hominid. The key evidence in my opinion – and that which started my thinking in the direction of locomotor difference and away from my original assumption that there would be no difference of significance – is the difference in absolute and relative length of the ischium. As used here ischial length is measured, along the central axis of the ischial shank or body, from the centre of the acetabulum to the distal extremity of the ischial tuberosity. This length closely approximates the maximum moment arm of the hamstrings in moving the lower limb around its fulcrum in the acetabulum. It is a pelvic dimension with obvious functional importance. The measure of ischial length used by Washburn (1963) and Zihlman (1971) seems to me to have no functional significance.

The most significant relevant specimens are Sts 14 from Sterkfontein and SK 50 from Swartkrans. Both innominates are present in Sts 14 and both ischial bodies are essentially complete but have suffered some damage to the tuberosity surface. SK 50, a right innominate, has the ischial body well preserved but most of the tuberosity surface is missing. However, enough is preserved to leave only very minor uncertainty about the length of the bone.[1] One other *H. africanus* ischium is known; this is MLD 8 from Makapansgat, the right ischium of a juvenile individual. This specimen is well preserved but the tuberosity epiphysis, which had not yet fused, is missing. Two other juvenile innominate specimens from Makapansgat (MLD 7 and 25) have no part of the ischium present, nor had the only other adult *H. africanus* innominate known – Sts 65 from Sterkfontein. Other than SK 50, one *Paranthropus* innominate is known, TM 1605 from Kromdraai. It also has none of the ischium preserved. The ischium of the early hominids is thus represented by the very small sample of two adult ischia of one individual and one juvenile ischium of *H. africanus* and one adult ischium of *Paranthropus*. The lengths of these adult ischia are given in Table 1.

Table 1

	N	*Mean*	*Standard Pop. Range (Mean ± 3 sd)*
Pan	10	79.9	55.7 – 104.1
Pongo	10	74.3	48.4 – 100.2
Gorilla	10	119.3	67.1 – 171.5
H. sapiens	40	80.6	58.4 – 102.8
Paranthropus	1	(69.0)	–
H. africanus	1	(45.0)	–

Dimensions are in millimetres. The samples of *Pan, Pongo, Gorilla* and *H. sapiens* contain equal numbers of males and females.

From Table 1 it is clear that in absolute length the ischia of *Paranthropus* and of *H. sapiens* fairly closely correspond with the mean values for *Pongo* and *Pan*. The *H. africanus* ischium, however, is distinctly small, falling a little outside of the estimated standard population ranges for man and the three pongids. Ischial length and general body size are highly correlated, however (Steudel, 1974), and a good deal of evidence suggests that there was an appreciable difference in robusticity between *H. africanus* and *Paranthropus* (Robinson, e.g. 1972). Difference in absolute length of ischium by itself does not necessarily prove that there is a real functional

1. Since this was written I have seen, by courtesy of Dr. D.C. Johanson, the left innominate of AL-288-1 from Hadar. It closely resembles the Sts 14 innominates and has the ischial tuberosity perfectly preserved. It has a small distal extension of the tuberosity I had not anticipated, making the ischial length of Sts 14 slightly longer (51) than I had assumed. Recalculation of results shows this correction makes no difference to my conclusions, which are supported also by the above specimen.

difference in ischium length in this case. Comparison must be made with some other dimension in the same individual. Because of damage to the SK 50 specimen few of the measurements that are possible on Sts 14 can be made on SK 50. The most suitable is acetabulum diameter, even though the SK 50 acetabulum has suffered some warping. As the entire acetabulum is present, however, and the warping is not complex, it seems to me that the right order of magnitude of size can readily be estimated. I have used two estimates; one is my best estimate of the actual size and the other is a larger estimate which tends to minimize differences between *Paranthropus* and *H. africanus* ischial lengths in order deliberately to err on the conservative side. Acetabular width in higher primates also has a high correlation, and is approximately isometric, with body size (Steudel, 1974). Proportionate length of ischium can now be determined by using the index acetabular width x 100/ischial length. Results are set out in Figure 1. The three pongids form a compact group; the differences between their means are not significant where p=.001. The difference between *H. sapiens* and the pongid nearest it (*Pongo*) is significant where p = .001. The SK 50 values are almost exactly intermediate between the means for *H. sapiens* and *Pongo* and within the standard population ranges of both of them. The Sts 14 value falls very far from those of SK 50, on the opposite side of the *H. sapiens* mean and right outside the upper end of the standard population range of the latter. Indeed, the distance separating SK 50 and Sts 14 is as great as the entire, rather extended, standard population range for *H. sapiens*. Moreover, the separation between the two early hominid specimens is somewhat greater than the distance separating the lowest standard population value (*Pan*) and the highest (*Pongo*) for the

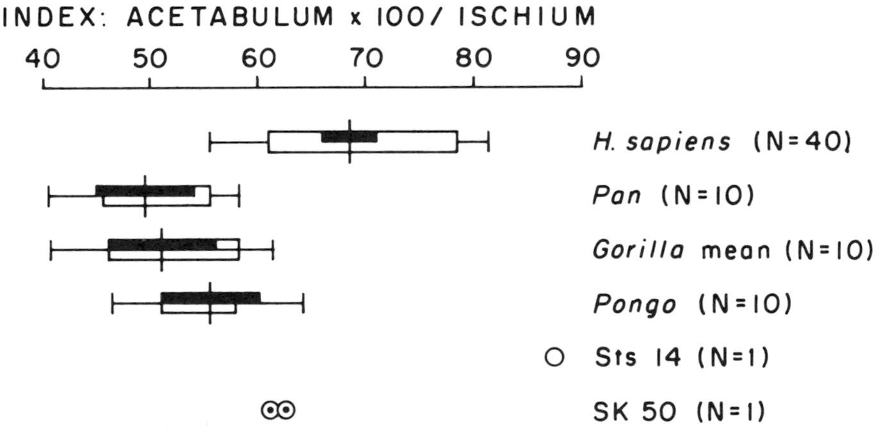

Figure 1. The relationship of ischium and acetabulum size expressed as the index acetabulum width x 100/ischium length for some hominoids. Centre line in each bar indicates the sample mean, the enclosed space indicates observed sample range, the total length is the standard population range (mean ± 3 SD) and the black rectangle is the confidence interval for the mean where p = .001.

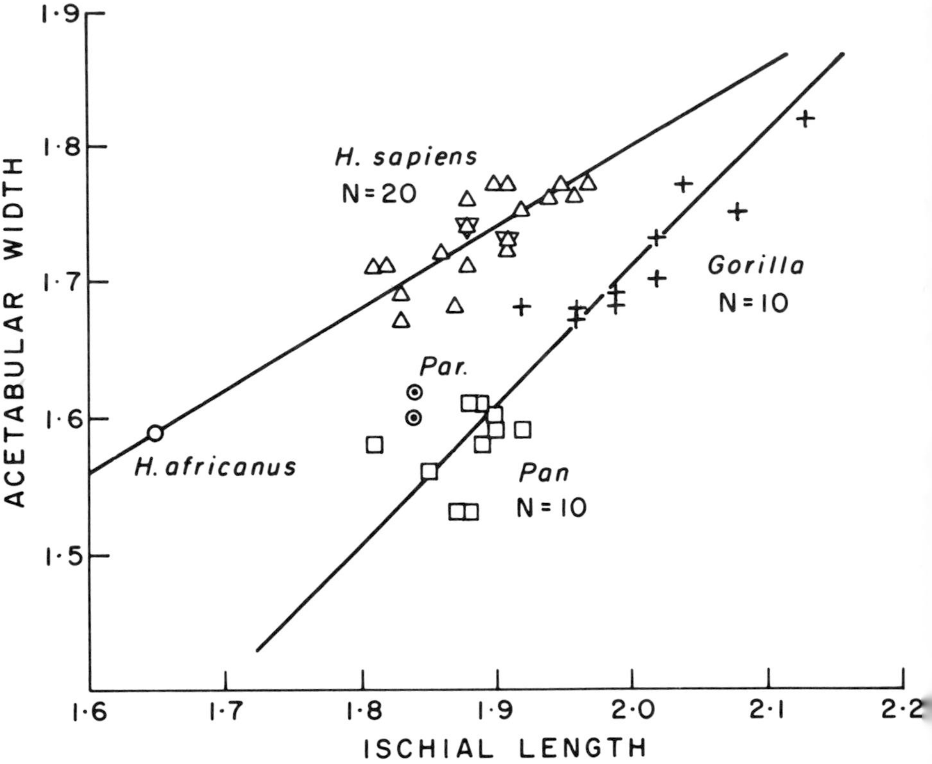

Figure 2. Logarithmic bivariate plot of acetabular width against ischial length.

entire pongid sample. It is worth pointing out that all specimens involved in these samples were measured by me and therefore a uniform measuring technique applies to them.

The relationship between acetabulum width and ischial length is set out differently in Figure 2. This is a logarithmic bivariate plot showing *H. africanus* (Sts 14) and *Paranthropus* (SK 50) as well as samples of individuals of *H. sapiens, Pan* and *Gorilla*. The individuals of *H. sapiens* cluster along one line while those of *Pan* and *Gorilla* cluster along another. *H. africanus* appears to be on the same line as *H. sapiens* while *Paranthropus* appears to be more nearly on the pongid line. To simplify the diagram, fewer comparison points were included than were actually available.

The difference between the two early hominid specimens is therefore clearly very considerable. Unfortunately the SK 50 and Sts 14 values are not mean values for *Paranthropus* and *H. africanus* respectively but values for single individuals. If it is assumed that the two individuals happen by chance to represent opposite extreme values for the populations from which they came, then conceivably they could have belonged to the same population as shown in Figure 1, although this seems unlikely from Figure 2. The chance that the only two specimens known would happen to be the two opposite absolute extremes for the same population is very small indeed. But clearly this is not the only evidence bearing on whether the two specimens could belong to the same population. There are morphological differences other than the ischial difference, such as appreciably greater forward extension of the iliac blade in *Paranthropus*, slightly different orientation of the acetabulum relative to the iliac blade, and different morphology in the region where the anterior inferior iliac spine abuts on the acetabular margin. Moreover, the adolescent ischium from Makapansgat (MLD 8) has so short an ischial shank that the adult is likely to have had an ischium no longer than that of Sts 14. This evidence considerably reduces the chance that the Sts 14 individual is an extreme variant. In addition, there is the long series of differences in cranial morphology between *Paranthropus* and *H. africanus*; it has led most workers to accept that they belong at least to different species, and apparently now many are prepared to accept separate generic status. This morphological evidence, along with the relatively large separation between SK 50 and Sts 14 in Figures 1 and 2, makes it reasonable to treat the two specimens as representative individuals from two different species. The difference in relative ischial length between the two is considerable: in Figure 1 SK 50 falls in the lower end of the relative size distribution for pongids and in the *upper* end of that for modern man, while Sts 14 falls below the *lower* end of the distribution for modern man and is thus ultra-human in this respect.[2]

There is a complication in that *H. sapiens* has a larger acetabulum relative to its body size than is the case in any of the other species. The fact, however, that the Sts 14 and SK 50 acetabula are of comparable size minimizes this difficulty. This problem, moreover, is overcome if one turns to the functional significance of the ischial body length: this relates to the length of the lower limbs rather than to the size of the acetabulum, which was used here simply as a means, present on the same innominate specimen as the ischium, for judging the relative length of the ischial body. The ischial tuberosity region is the area of origin of the hamstring muscles and the distance from the centre of the acetabulum to the end of the tuberosity represents the maximum possible length of the moment arm for the hamstrings in extending the lower limb at the hip joint. One may note in passing that in the earlier discussions on early hominid locomotion the notion was current that Sts 14 has a very long ischium. This sprang from the measure of ischial length being used; the distance from the acetabular margin to the nearest edge of the ischial tuberosity (Washburn, 1963; Napier, 1964; Zihlman, 1971, uses a very similar measure). It is difficult to see why this was chosen as a measure of ischial length as it seems to have

2. The new value of ischial length for Sts 14 gives an index value of 77 instead of 87. This places Sts 14 in the upper end of the modern human range rather than making it ultra-human.

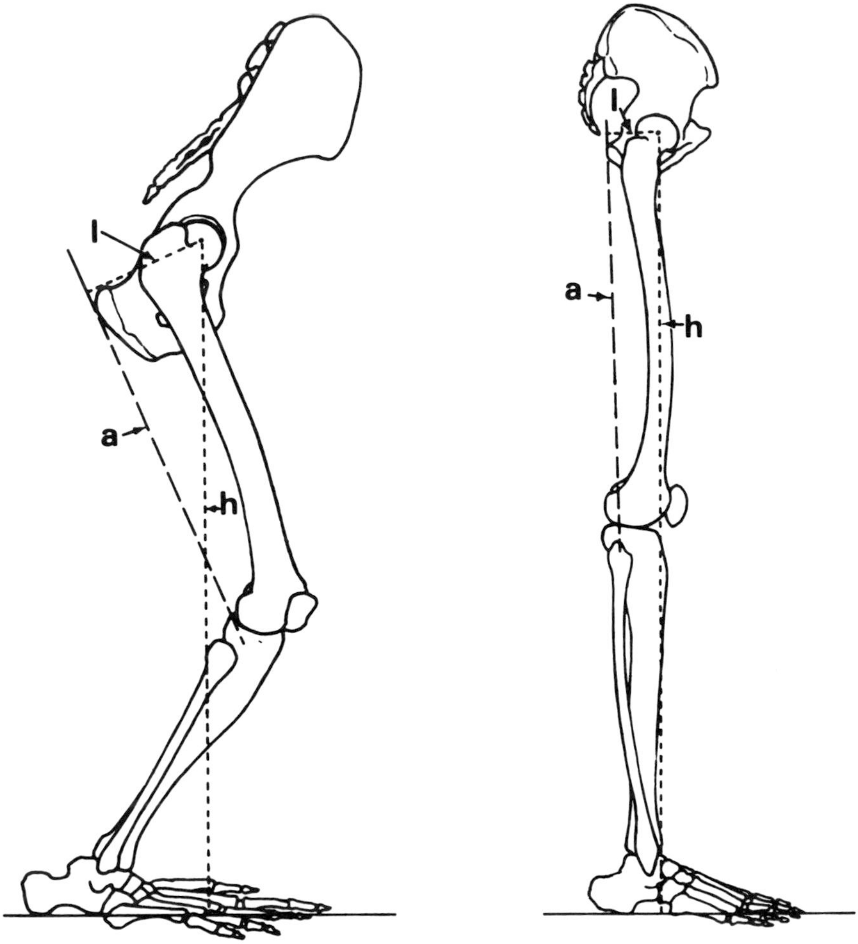

Figure 3. Pongid and human pelvis and lower limb drawn to same size (not scale). *l* indicates the moment arm of the hamstrings *a*, and *h* is the length of the lever being moved by the hamstrings. The very different ratio of *l:h* in the two is readily apparent.

no functional meaning and does not represent a constant fraction of any functional measure; nor is it the usual measure of ischial length used osteometrically by physical anthropologists.

Returning to the point at issue; one of the very important functions served by the ischium is as the origin of the hamstring muscles. The moment arm (power arm) of the hamstrings is the vertical distance from the line of function of the hamstrings to the centre of the acetabulum (Figure 3). The length of this arm varies with the position of the limb but it cannot exceed the ischial length; the power arm and ischial length coincide when the limb is in an early part of the stance phase. One other measure is necessary in order to evaluate ischial length and that is the length of the lever being moved by the hamstrings, which is the distance from the fulcrum (acetabulum) to the ground (Smith and Savage, 1956). The ratio between the moment arm length and the lever length determines the mechanical advantage the hamstrings have in extending the limb at the hip. In pongids, where the ischium is long and the lever is short because the already relatively short lower limb is used in a flexed position, thus further reducing lever length, this ratio varies from about 1:4 in early stance phase to about 1:5·5 in late stance phase as the moment arm shortens (Robinson, 1972; Robinson, Freedman and Sigmon, 1972). In modern man the comparable figures are 1:10 to 1:13. The significance of the difference here is emphasized by the finding of Smith and Savage (1956) that the ratio for the main propulsive muscle of the forelimb of the hairy armadillo (*Dasypus*), a powerful digger, is 1:4, while the equivalent for the fast-running horse (*Equus*) is 1:13. The propulsive mechanism of the armadillo forelimb is strongly power oriented, that of the horse is strongly speed oriented and the ratios involved are of the same order of magnitude as those of pongid and man. The elongation of the human lower limb is an important aspect of his locomotor habit, contributing among other things to capacity to stride and to conservation of energy, allowing him to walk or jog along distances, as well as to the ability to move the foot rapidly through a relatively long distance when need arises.

The significance of ischial length can therefore more easily be judged in relation to lower limb length, which is roughly twice the length of the femur. Whole femora are, unfortunately, very rare in the fossil record. Sts 14 has a substantial portion of the left femur present, though somewhat poorly preserved. In conjunction with the distal end of a femur from the same site but probably a different individual (TM 1513), the length of this femur has by various means been conservatively estimated at 310 mm. (Robinson, 1972). Lovejoy and Heiple (1970), using other techniques, estimated the length to be 276 mm., but this is almost certainly much too short as it would not allow the Sts 14 femur to be completed with the distal morphology known from TM 1513 and Sts 34 from the same site (Robinson, 1972).

Walker (1973) has argued that the TM 1513 specimen must have come from a larger femur than the Sts 14 specimen and estimates the original length of the latter at only 250 mm. As Steudel (1974) has pointed out, however, Walker estimates the three known *H. africanus* proximal femoral fragments as belonging to smaller femora than the two *H. africanus* distal fragments that he discusses. This suggests the possibility that he expects smaller distal ends in relation to proximal ends than is actually the case. After much careful comparison, I do not believe TM 1513 is too large for Sts 14. The beautiful gracile femoral distal end of femur found in the Afar triangle by Dr C.D. Johanson (Johanson and Taieb, this volume) very kindly shown to me in the original, is a little smaller than TM 1513. Yet its anatomical characteristics appear to me to offer no grounds for reducing at all my estimate of 310 mm. for the original length of Sts 14. Moreover, at least one of the femora now known from East Africa that is of comparable shaft thickness to Sts 14 was noticeably longer than 310 mm.; thus the latter may actually be an underestimate rather than an overestimate.

Using the apparently conservative length of 310 mm. for Sts 14 and doubling it to approximate lever length for this individual, gives a moment arm: lever length ratio of 1:13.8. Even if the value of 276 mm., which seems to me clearly to be a serious underestimate, is used the ratio is 1:12.3. In order to reduce the amount of uncertainty involved in this estimation of lever length, one may use instead the ratio between ischium length and femur length. Using mean values, except for Sts 14, the ratios are as follows:

H. sapiens	5.2
Pan	3.6
Pongo	3.4
Gorilla	3.4
Sts 14	6.9*

* This becomes 6.1 on the new ischium length estimate.

From these figures it seems clear that the lower limb of *H. africanus* had elongated to at least the extent found in modern man and that the relation of hamstring power arm to lever length was such that the propulsive mechanism was at least as speed-oriented as in modern man, or possibly even more so.

The case of SK 50 is less easy to decide because the two femora known from the same site (SK 82 and SK 97), although much better preserved than that of Sts 14, are proximal ends that are much less complete than that of Sts 14. They are too incomplete to allow length estimates that are any more than guesses. Lovejoy and Heiple (1970) estimated the femoral bicondylar length for *Paranthropus* using the technique employed for Sts 14 and obtained a figure of 315 mm. Their technique, however, requires fairly accurate figures for two characters – interacetabular distance and shaft obliquity (the method is very sensitive to variation in the latter), neither of which are known for any *Paranthropus* individual. Both values simply have to be guessed at and the guesses must be based on the assumption that *Paranthropus* will have resembled *H. africanus* in morphology. This is not a safe assumption since most of the *Paranthropus* anatomy known is different from that of *H. africanus*. Nevertheless, if one uses their estimate, the ischium length: femur length ratio is 4·6, which is intermediate between pongids and man and distinctly less than the 6·9 for Sts 14. However, the value of 4·6 should not, in my opinion, be taken seriously because it was based on a series of assumptions that are unsupported.[3]

3. Since the above was written femur KNM-ER 1463 has become available from Late Turkana and is, in my opinion, of *Paranthropus*. It has only a small amount missing

One of the most obtrusive features of the *Paranthropus* femora as compared to that of Sts 14 is that although head size is much the same in both taxa (see Robinson, 1972, in connection with head size for the Sts 14 femur), shaft thickness is much greater in the *Paranthropus* specimens. A proximal end of femur from Olduvai attributed to *Paranthropus* (Day, 1969) also has a thick shaft. The thick shaft implies greater weight to be supported. In a study on the relative thickness of long bones and vertebrae in primates, Schultz (1953) concluded that slender-shafted long bones tend to be long and thick-shafted ones short. If the early hominids also fell into this general primate pattern, then one would expect the relatively robustly shafted *Paranthropus* femora (see Robinson, 1972, figs. 71, 72, and 84) to be shorter than that of Sts 14. If this was so, then the relatively long ischium of *Paranthropus* (SK 50) would mean that the propulsive mechanism was considerably more power-oriented than was the case in Sts 14. Conversely, one could estimate the length of femur necessary for SK 50 to give it a propulsive mechanism as speed-oriented as that of Sts 14. This turns out to be 476 mm., which value falls near the upper end of the range for modern man. This seems a most improbable figure, unless one makes the assumption that *Paranthropus* had an extremely large body size, a point not supported by other evidence (Robinson, 1972). Both of these lines of argument thus suggest that the lower limb of *Paranthropus* was relatively not as elongate as that of Sts 14. Thus, the long ischium means that the propulsive mechanism was considerably more power-oriented than that of Sts 14 or of modern man, but not quite as much as in living pongids.

It is worth noting here a paper by Jenkins (1972) in which, among other topics, he discusses the shape of the articular surface of the femoral head in some hominoids and the light this throws on the normal range of movement of the femur relative to the innominate bone. He concludes that the head articular surface in *Paranthropus* is intermediate in its characteristics between that of man and the chimpanzee and strongly suggests that *Paranthropus* did not use the lower limbs with the knees as much adducted (valgus position) as in modern man. In both of the *Homo africanus* femoral distal ends from Sterkfontein, the relatively great femoral shaft obliquity (the so-called bicondylar angle) and the relatively high lateral lip of the patellar groove argue clearly in favour of a well-developed valgus position in this form. If Jenkins' line of argument is sound, then it provides additional evidence that the gait and locomotion of *Paranthropus* and of *Homo africanus* were noticeably different, a conclusion in harmony with that already drawn from the evidence of the ischium and lower limb length relationship.

---

at each end and I estimate the length to have been 290 mm. This and the ischium of SK 50 gives a ratio of 4.2; of course it would be far preferable to have both values from the same individual.

If Sts 14 is strongly speed-oriented with respect to the propulsive mechanism as we argued earlier, then it is very unlikely indeed that other individuals of the same species would have power-oriented propulsive mechanisms. So in spite of small sample sizes, the locomotor difference indicated by them almost certainly reflects differences between *Paranthropus* and *H. africanus* generally, rather than differences merely between two individuals. A number of femora are known from East Africa but these have not yet been described. Moreover there is much more of a problem assigning them to their correct taxa than is the case in South Africa.

The fully elongated – perhaps even ultra-long – lower limb of Sts 14 implies the capacity to stride. This, in turn, implies a compact, arched and relatively inflexible foot to help provide the firm push-off that is necessary for striding. The foot of *H. africanus* is not known from South Africa. However, a foot of a suitable sort is known from Bed I at Olduvai. This has been attributed to *H. habilis*. It seems to me that the Bed I material attributed to this taxon cannot be distinguished from *H. africanus* as belonging to a distinct lineage. For this reason, and because the elongated lower limb of Sts 14 would require such a foot, I consider the Olduvai specimen to represent *H. africanus* (Robinson, 1972). A very interesting feature of this foot has been pointed out by Day and Wood (1968), namely that in spite of having had a fully adducted hallux and a generally rather low level of flexibility, the talar horizontal neck angle is large and ape-like. This was compensated for by having the talar head articular surface turned toward the foot midline so that it is not symmetrical about the neck axis. This condition apparently represents an intermediate condition between a more pongid-like state and that in *H. sapiens*, though functionally the foot was much more like that of *H. sapiens*.

Fortunately there is at least one talus of *Paranthropus* (TM 1517) from Kromdraai. This also has the large and ape-like horizontal neck angle seen in the Olduvai foot (28° in the latter and 32° in the former) but in this case the head articular surface is not asymmetrically placed about the neck axis but is extensive and symmetrically placed. This surface thus extended from an ape-like position round into a man-like position. This represents an evolutionary stage earlier than that of the Olduvai foot; a compromise between an ape-like grasping foot with abducted hallux and a man-like foot with fully adducted hallux. Presumably the *Paranthropus* foot, as represented by the Kromdraai talus, was more flexible than the Olduvai foot and had a hallux that could be adducted but that was not habitually adducted; see also Le Gros Clark, 1947; Day and Napier, 1964; and Day and Wood, 1968, Robinson, 1972. Such a foot would not be suitable for striding and hence would presumably not be associated with an elongated lower limb. This evidence supports the conclusion reached with respect to the propulsive mechanism – *Paranthropus* had a distinctly more power-oriented propulsive mechanism than had *H. africanus*.[4]

Very little evidence of the hand is available for early hominids. A thumb metacarpal of *Paranthropus* from Swartkrans is short, powerful and curved. It was distinctly more pongid-like than man-like (Napier, 1959; Rightmire, 1972) and seems to have been capable of gripping with power but had poor manipulative precision. Additional evidence from Kromdraai and Olduvai suggests the possibility that the *Paranthropus* hand was long, powerful and had a short thumb. No satisfactory evidence of the hand of *H. africanus* is available; a capitate bone from Sterkfontein led Broom (in Broom and Schepers, 1946) and Le Gros Clark (1947) to the conclusion that it is more man-like than ape-like.

The best evidence for locomotor difference between *H. africanus* and *Paranthropus* is that the former had an ultra-hominid ischium with respect to relative length, while the latter had a much more ape-like ischium. Coupled with evidence from the femur there are reasonable grounds for concluding that *H. africanus* had a fully elongated, man-like, or even ultra-man-like lower limb and speed-oriented propulsive mechanism. *Paranthropus*, on the other hand, appears to have had a lower limb proportionately somewhat longer than that of pongids (though probably a long upper limb) but shorter than that of either *H. sapiens* or *H. africanus* and, therefore, a much more power-oriented propulsive mechanism than *H. africanus*. *H. africanus*, though lacking some of the refinements of modern man, seems to have had essentially the same locomotor pattern – that of a fully erectly bipedal, striding ground-dweller. It seems to have differed from modern man more in the upper limb than in the pelvis and lower limb.

Paranthropus apparently had a curiously mixed combination of characters. The arrangement of the nuchal plane of the occiput, probably the spinal column and certainly the iliac portion of the pelvis and probably the sacrum, were those of an erect biped, including evidence for lateral balance control having been well established. But then the lower part of the pelvis, specifically the ischium, the length of the lower limb and the foot, were distinctly more ape-like. One must presume that some behaviour significant to its way of life required a power-oriented propulsive apparatus and flexible foot even though this conflicted to some extent with the requirements of erect bipedalism. By far the most logical reason for needing power orientation of the propulsive apparatus, a reasonably flexible foot with an abductable hallux and a powerful grasping hand is that

4. In the years since this was written several morphometric studies on fossil and modern tali have appeared. The latest (African fossil tali: further multivariate morphometric studies, by Lisowski, Albrecht and Oxnard, *Amer. J. phys. Anthrop.* 45, 5-18, 1976) concludes that the Kromdraai and Olduvai tali are closer to extant pongid tali than to that of modern man, a conclusion consistent with the argument presented here.

Paranthropus, as well as spending much time on the ground, was still climbing trees – presumably to sleep, and perhaps also some of its feeding may have been done in trees. I have elsewhere (Robinson, 1972) set out more fully an evolutionary scheme accounting for the evolution of erect bipedalism in which this compromise between quadrupedal climbing and erect bipedalism in *Paranthropus* is given a logical place which fits also with the evidence for a primarily herbivorous (as distinct from omnivorous or carnivorous) dietary habit. Such schemes must inevitably be oversimplified, but the one I have presented seems to provide a good deal of insight into the sequence and course of the changes that led from an ape-like forest-dweller to early man of the savannah and also some of the major selection factors that lay behind those changes.

Acknowledgments

I wish to acknowledge with particular gratitude very helpful discussions with and other assistance from my friend and colleague Dr Karen L. Steudel, in connection with this paper. I wish also to thank the conference organiser, Dr Clifford Jolly, and its sponsors, the Wenner-Gren Foundation for Anthropological Research and the National Science Foundation, for making my participation possible.

References

Ashby, Eric, Lord (1971) Science and antiscience. The Bernal Lecture, 1971. *Proc. Roy. Soc. Lond.* B, 178, 29.

Day, M.H. (1969) Femoral fragment of a robust australopithecine from Olduvai Gorge, Tanzania. *Nature* 221, 230.

Day, M.H. and Napier, J.R. (1964) Fossil foot bones. *Nature* 201, 969.

Day, M.H. and Wood, B.A. (1968) Functional affinities of OH 8 talus. *Man* 3, 429.

Jenkins, F.A. (1972) Chimpanzee bipedalism: cineradiographic analysis and implications for the evolution of gait. *Science* 178, 877.

Le Gros Clark, W.E. (1947) Observations on the anatomy of the fossil Australopithecinae. *J. Anat.* (London) 81, 300.

Lovejoy, C.O. and Heiple, K.G. (1970) A reconstruction of the femur of *A. africanus*. *Amer. J. phys. Anthrop.* 32, 33.

Napier, J.R. (1959) Fossil metacarpals from Swartkrans. *Fossil Mammals of Afr.* 17. London, British Museum (Natural History).

Napier, J.R. (1964) The evolution of bipedal walking in the hominids. *Arch. de Biol.* (Liège) 75: suppl. 673.

Rightmire, A.P. (1972) Multivariate analysis of an early hominid metacarpal from Swartkrans. *Science* 176, 159.

Robinson, J.T. (1954) The genera and species of the Australopithecinae. *Amer. J. phys. Anthrop.* 12, 181.

Robinson, J.T. (1965) *Homo habilis* and the Australopithecines. *Nature* (London) 205, 121.
Robinson, J.T. (1966) The distinctiveness of *Homo habilis*. *Nature* (London) 209, 953.
Robinson, J.T. (1967) Variation and the taxonomy of the early hominids. In Dobzhansky, T., Hecht, M.K. and Steere, W. (eds), *Evolutionary Biology*, 69. New York.
Robinson, J.T. (1972) *Early Hominid Posture and Locomotion*. Chicago.
Robinson, J.T., Freedman, L. and Sigmon, B.A. (1972) Some aspects of pongid and hominid bipedality. *J. human Evol.* 1, 361.
Schultz, A.H. (1953) The relative thickness of the long bones and the vertebrae in primates. *Amer. J. phys. Anthrop.* 11, 277.
Smith, J.M. and Savage, R.J.G. (1956) Some locomotory adaptations in mammals. *J. Linn. Soc. (Zool.)* 42, 603.
Steudel, K.L. (1974) *Primate Locomotion: a Study of Pelvic Function in Living Primates and Fossil Hominids by Multivariate Statistics*. PhD Thesis, University of Wisconsin, Madison.
Walker, A. (1973) New *Australopithecus* femora from East Rudolf, Kenya. *J. human Evol.* 2, 545.
Washburn, S.L. (1963) Behaviour and human evolution. In Washburn, S.L. (ed.), *Classification and Human Evolution*. Viking Fund Publications in Anthropology, no.37.
Zihlman, A.L. (1971) The question of locomotor differences in *Australopithecus*. *Proc. 3rd int. Congr. Primate.*, Zurich, 1, 54.

PART IV

THE INTERPRETATION OF HOMINID DIVERSITY

M.H. Wolpoff

Analogies and interpretation in palaeoanthropology

Introduction

It is my view that palaeoanthropology is a science, based on the underlying paradigm of the Synthetic Theory of Evolution. As in any other science, conceptual changes are made as one hypothesis replaces another. Hypotheses are testable statements of causal frameworks which must, at least in theory, be refutable. It is the process of refutation, rather than verification, which leads to the replacement of one hypothesis by another, and the purpose of hypothesis testing is to attempt refutations. In sum, what makes one hypothesis more desirable than another is the process of refutation, rather than a probabilistic calculation of likelihood, which in any event is probably impossible in any formal sense (for a contrary view see Pilbeam, this volume). In dealing with the ancient remains of hominids, many hypothesis cannot be directly tested through experiment. Consequently, it is often necessary to test expectations by analogies with living species for which much more information is known.

The purpose of this paper is to discuss the use of primate analogies in the interpretation of hominid phylogeny. From the outset, it should be understood that it is not my intent to decide or arbitrate taxonomic issues. Rather, I hope to raise certain problems concerned with the use of *any* analogies between fossil and living taxa, and will suggest some parameters which limit phylogenic interpretations for fossil samples. The specific discussion will concern Pliocene and lower Pleistocene hominids.

Nature of the fossil record

A collection of fossils comprises a unique type of biological sample, with characteristics that cannot be matched by a sample of living specimens, however collected. To begin with, fossil specimens are representative of once living biological populations.[1] However, the specimen is not the population, and consequently cannot be expected to exhibit the biological parameters of the population. Of course, some characteristics of a fossil specimen are undoubtedly shared by all members of the population, but it is equally likely that other characteristics show variation within the population. From a single specimen, it is impossible to prove which specific characteristics are invariant, and which are not. Moreover, there is no direct way to determine the accuracy of any variation estimator (i.e. a statistic to estimate sample variation for a feature), when applied to the biological population from which the specimen was sampled.

While the specimen was drawn from a living population, one cannot assume that it exhibits the mean or modal characteristics of that population. Actually, this assumption *seems* quite reasonable. Single specimens are usually expected to represent the population mean, since this appears to utilize the fewest assumptions. However, if a random sample of one is drawn from each of a large number of differing populations, the mean of the sample set will estimate the grand mean of all specimens from all populations, and not the mean of population means; the variance of this set will estimate the grand variance of all specimens, and not the variance of population means; and the range of the sample set will estimate the total range for all specimens, and not the range of population means. In biological terms, this suggests that *single samples from populations within the same taxon cannot be used to estimate the mean, variance, or range of any individual population, but can only be used to derive such estimators for the taxon as a whole.*

This point is important to consider when analysing fossil sample variation. The sample of 20 or more mandibles from East Turkana has a sample range which estimates the total range of all 20 populations represented, and not just the range of the 20 means. This sample range, then, would best be compared with the total range of 20 human populations, and not the range of the 20 population means, if one desired to compare the sample with modern man. To put this another way, a sample is used to estimate the parameters of a 'real' entity. In this case, the entity estimated by a fossil sample is a group of populations rather than a single one. The descriptive statistics of the sample estimate the descriptive statistics of this group, and as the sample gets larger this estimation becomes better. If the fossil sample is actually a hodgepodge of different species, then the sample statistics will increasingly approximate the statistics that would result from mixing populations of different living species. Conversely, if the fossil

1. Population here is used consistently in the sense of a local mendelian population: the individuals of a given locality which form a single breeding community. Population boundaries are sometimes ill-defined. However, as Coon once said, cities still exist as distinct entities even though people live and travel between them.

sample represents a single, although possibly polytypic species, then the sample statistics approximate the statistics that could be calculated from a multi-populational sample of a living polytypic species. Obviously, this whole discussion only refers to samples drawn from what are already established as very similar groups. If one wished to compare the difference between ER 818 and 992 with the variation in modern man, the question is not whether the same amount of variation occurs in a single population, or between a number of population averages, but whether the variation occurs within the total range of a number of human populations equal to the number of identifiable individuals found in the timespan including these two specimens.

Another unique characteristic applies to fossil specimens in hominoid palaeontology. With very few exceptions, *no two fossil specimens can ever be assumed to be drawn from the same biological population.* The few exceptions in hominid fossils occur in the upper Pleistocene where at certain sites such as Shanidar and L'Hortus it appears possible that part of the fossil sample was drawn from a single population. However, only one exception to this generalization is known to me for the Pliocene and lower Pleistocene hominids. The circumstances of deposition for the South and East African specimens do not allow any other assumption. Therefore, a collection of fossil specimens, even from the same layer at a particular site, does not necessarily comprise a sample from a single biological population.

It is unfortunate that the *statistical* term for such a collection is a 'population', because 'population' used in this statistical sense does not have the same meaning as 'population' in the biological sense. The Sterkfontein sample is not a population. The sample from FLK-NN1 at Olduvai is not a population. The sample from the Koobi-Fora tuff at East Turkana is not a population. In these samples, one can only assume that each specimen was drawn from a different biological population. In terms of actual biological relationship, it is possible that two specimens found 'cheek to jowl' in the Swartkrans cave are less closely related to each other than perhaps respectively to specimens found on the same floor at Olduvai. In point of fact, a palaeoanthropologist cannot make either assumption on the basis of proximity. Of course, it is possible that two specimens from the same site were actually drawn from the same population, but this is impossible to verify and consequently cannot be assumed.

The combination of these unique characteristics of fossil samples suggests certain limitations. The most important of these is that it is not possible to estimate directly the parameters (mean, variance, range) of individual biological populations. These parameters can only be estimated for *samples* which represent collections of populations. Such collections may be taxonomically distinct as geographic races, subspecies, species, genera, and so on, but the one thing they are *not* is distinct as single biological populations. In other words, it is not usually possible to deal with fossils at the populational level.

This does not mean that sites cannot be analysed at a level beyond the description of individual specimens, nor that collections cannot be compared with each other. All specimens at a site, in an area, or even on a continent, are identical at *some* taxonomic level. It is for the observer to determine what this level is, so that taxa at the same level can be compared with each other. The only valid comparisons are between like taxa: subspecies to subspecies, species to species, genus to genus. There is nothing sacrosanct about a collection of specimens from a certain level at a given site unless they are to be compared with an equivalent taxonomic unit. If a taxon is spread over a wide geographic range, it is neither necessarily correct nor necessarily incorrect to 'lump' together all specimens over this range for purposes of comparison. This depends entirely on the taxonomic units compared. If, for instance, a subspecies occurs in both South and East Africa, it is not necessarily incorrect to use a collection of all specimens in the subspecies for comparison with all specimens in another subspecies over its entire geographic range. In fact, the collection of all specimens in such a subspecies found in South Africa can only be properly compared with all specimens in another subspecies, or in the same subspecies, in a similarly limited geographic area. Similarly, a segment of a lineage recognized as taxonomically distinct on the subspecies level can be properly compared to a similar time segment, recognized as distinct at the subspecies level, on another lineage. On the other hand, it does not always seem reasonable to compare temporal subspecies when the time depths or geographic ranges of the samples are significantly different. The point is that in valid comparisons, like entities must be compared. The nature of fossils limits the like entities that can be determined and thus utilized.

Taxonomic levels

The really difficult problem for the palaeoanthropologist lies in determining the taxonomic level of a given sample or collection. There are a number of reasons why this problem is particularly difficult. Modern taxa are defined for living populations. This is not just a matter of convenient definition. The practice of modern taxonomy is part of the science of systematics, and its methods of operation are derived directly from the Synthetic Theory of Evolution. At the species level, definitions are not arbitrary, nor are they decided upon by general consensus. A species is a genetic entity whose boundaries are defined by actual or potential reproductive behaviour. Both above and below the species level the definitions of taxonomic entities are more arbitrary, and at these levels consistency with empirical observation, and consensus thinking amongst the workers, become much more important in taxonomic considerations. Below the species level, taxonomic definitions depend heavily upon morphological variation. Most workers recognize subspecies as samples which show no more than 25% overlap (75% of the individuals in one differ from all – e.g. 97% – individuals in the other). Often, the coefficient of difference (difference between the means divided by the sum of the standard deviations) is used in this determination. The size of this coefficient necessary to establish subspecies is empirically determined. Differences in excess of values between 1.3 and 1.5 have been found to correspond with subspecific variation as determined by other criteria in a wide range of vertebrate taxa by a number of authors (Mayr, 1969, pp. 188-93). Such methods for determining subspecies, of course, are only valid when comparing samples within the same species.

Above the species level morphological differences also play a predominant role. However, other data that clarify phylogenetic relationship are utilized, so that most workers define a genus as a group of species more closely related to each other than to any other species, separated from other genera by a decided gap. Some authors further suggest that the member species occupy a similar 'adaptive plateau'. While it appears that workers differ in the operational definitions used to delineate genera, the important point is that a genus consists of species (*not* populations or individuals) related to each other and morphologically separated from other species. In sum, for categories both above and below the species level, species are a crucial part of the definition. This suggests that species determination should be undertaken prior to any other taxonomic considerations.

Because species are entities based on reproductive behaviour, the problem is that *fossil species can never be determined with certainty*. This is not a practical limitation based on the fact that there is only a limited amount of evidence, or on the problem of evolutionary continuity over time. Rather, it stems from the concept of species itself since reproductive behaviour cannot be directly observed in fossils.

In time depth, it is the lineage rather than the species that takes on evolutionary significance. A lineage is a group of ancestral-descendent populations which are actually or potentially interbreeding at any point in time, and which are reproductively isolated from other lineages. Each lineage evolves separately from all others, and has its own unique evolutionary tendencies. At a given point in time, a lineage is a species. However, the concept of lineage is a more realistic description of the evolutionary process. The species is a time-restricted portion of a lineage for which the process of evolution is frozen.

Seen this way, problems of fossil sample interpretations resolve into the question of whether branching or continuous evolution has occurred between samples (it is extremely unlikely to find evidence of a lineage in the process of branching, and probably impossible to verify even if fossils from a segment in time during which branching was occurring were found). Branching evolution could lead to differences on the subspecific, specific, or generic level (and ultimately higher levels). Similarly, continuous evolution leads to taxonomic distinctions on these levels. In this case, however, taxonomic distinctions are entirely arbitrary divisions of a genetically continuous evolving lineage, and are done for our terminological convenience rather than because they correspond to actual distinct entities.

It might seem quite justifiable to stop using the terms 'subspecies', 'species', and 'genus' as descriptions of segments of a single continuously evolving lineage, and rather reserve them to describe living taxa and the result of branching evolution in fossil samples. In practice, however, geographic and temporal divisions are usually impossible to distinguish when samples are found at different sites since precise contemporaneity usually cannot be established.[2] Even at a single locality, what appears to be a succession of temporal taxa may be the result of migration and geographic variation. Over limited time periods, the geographic and temporal components of variation seem to merge as the result of necessary limitations to the fossil record. Consequently, it is an arbitrary but practical decision to apply the same criteria in classifying distinctions due to continuous evolution as are applied to classifying distinctions due to branching evolution.

We are left, then, with the concepts of subspecies, species, and genus to describe variation due to branching evolution, whether in the past or at the present time. These concepts are also used for practical reasons to describe variation along a continuously evolving lineage. The problem comes from the lineage definition itself, and consequently from the species definition. How can lineages be accurately separated from each other in the fossil record, given that reproductive behaviour cannot be directly observed? It is desirable to maintain equivalent definitions, to whatever extent is possible, since to do otherwise would create an unassailable distinction between past and present evolutionary change which could only serve to obscure and confuse the study of evolution as an ongoing process.

Use of the morphospecies concept, as recently suggested by several authors, does not really establish equivalency between taxonomic divisions of fossil and living organisms, although its use is tempting. Grouping fossil specimens into what Delson (this volume) describes as

2. This point cannot be overemphasized. The IB tuff at Olduvai and the I_2 tuff at Omo are both dated radiometrically to about 1.8 million years. However, this does not mean that hominid samples at these levels of the respective sites are in any sense contemporary. Even if both radiometric dates are correct and are exactly 1.8 m.y., the probable error of the dates is great enough so that the samples could be separated by as much as a quarter of a million years. This is a considerable time span which might well be longer than the entire South African hominid sequence, and is five times longer than the time which Brain (1967) estimates it took for the Swartkrans cave to fill.

a 'morphologically relatively uniform sample' eliminates many of the problems implicit in applying the species concept to palaeontological data. Furthermore, the approach always 'works', in the sense that once discriminating criteria are established, the criteria will successfully discriminate specimens. However, there is a disturbing circularity in applying the morphospecies concept within a group of obviously related specimens: any variable sample can be divided into subsamples on the basis of some criteria whether or not the subsamples have any biological reality. Once divided, the subsamples can be shown to be different on a level of statistical significance, and if the sorting criteria themselves are continuous over a long temporal span, the appearance of separate lineages results. In a given situation there may indeed have been separate lineages that were successfully sorted and accurately determined. However, if the sorting criteria turn out to be size based, sex based, or ecologically based, in a single polytypic lineage, the fact that they can be consistently and accurately applied does not bespeak of biologically 'real' results. In sum, the morphospecies concept will tend to establish phylogenetic distinctions whether or not they actually occurred. The fact that both the closest living ecological counterparts of the early hominids and the most closely related descendent species are both polytypic suggests adequate reason to suspect that the early hominids themselves formed one (or perhaps more) polytypic species. At least, this possibility cannot be dismissed. The results of applying morphological sorting criteria to a polytypic species can be seen in the biological 'hodgepodges' resulting from most modern human 'racial' taxonomies.

This is not meant to downgrade the importance of morphology in dealing with either fossil or living organisms. No one wishes to lump baboons together with apes, and morphological sorting is necessary to avoid such gross mistakes. The real problems only arise after these initial determinations are made and the relevant questions concern how many baboon or how many ape lineages occurred. Morphology plays a special but restricted role in the definition of living species. When morphology is used in the recognition of living species, it is used to infer reproductive isolation, and not simply to establish some arbitrary 'degree' of difference. In general, the palaeoanthropologist usually has more information at his disposal than the morphology of the individual fossils in a sample.

Analogy and interpretation

It seems to me that the remaining course is to establish correspondence between taxa of the living and the dead. The serious problems really only arise in determining criteria for *differentiating* lineages (not for *defining* them since lineages actually exist whether or not our definitions successfully distinguish them). Both subspecies and genus definitions are arbitrary, are based on the recognition of distinct lineages, and utilize morphological comparisons which can be directly applied to either fossil or living samples.

Reproductive isolation can only be established for fossil samples by analogy to living species. Perhaps 'established' is a misleading word, since the suggestion of reproductive isolation between two fossil samples is a hypothesis that can never be validated or refuted with complete certainty, and in many cases even with reasonable accuracy. A basic decision must be made at the onset. Are *any* analogies between fossil and living taxa valid? Analogies raise some very real problems. Fossil and living samples are not equivalent. There is no way of drawing a sample from living organisms that is statistically equivalent to a fossil sample for at least two reasons. First, the time-depth is not available for living samples. Second, no information is available concerning population parameters for the fossil populations represented by the fossil specimens. In other words, not only is the analogy not exactly equivalent, but we can never be sure that the living taxon is actually analogous. If these problems are serious enough to prevent any analogies between living and fossil taxa, there is no way to deal with fossil specimens in an evolutionary framework. Conversely, in order to apply an evolutionary framework to the analysis and understanding of fossil samples, analogies must be made despite these limitations but with clear recognition of them and with calibration of the uncertainty that they necessarily introduce. In other words, these limitations do not make palaeontology impossible but rather to some extent uncertain.

The uncertainty is a function of the samples studied. There is very little uncertainty in suggesting that the taxa represented by baboons and cats at a site are distinct lineages. Similarly, there is very little uncertainty in assuming that the number of orbits in a fossil hominid is invariant in the population it represents. Yet it should be pointed out that what gives these interpretations a high degree of probability is the analogy drawn between the variation observed in or between the samples and the variation observed in or between known taxa of living organisms. Experience with living organisms suggests that the more similar the samples, the less certain we can be that lineage determinations are accurate.

In fossil samples that are similar enough so that the question of whether or not they belong to the same lineage does not have an obvious answer, the same criteria must be applied that would be applied to living species if the species category is to have as equivalent a meaning as possible. *Since reproductive behaviour cannot be observed, it must be inferred from the data available.* One way of approaching this inference is by analogy to variation known to occur in living organisms. Two general approaches are possible: comparison with variation that occurs within a known species, and comparison with variation that occurs between known closely related species. These comparisons use living species as a model to delimit the amount of genetic variation that occurs both within a protected gene pool and between protected gene pools. The model does not indicate what actually occurred in the past, but rather approximates limits on what to expect. One must recognize that interpretive limits set by analogy are probabilistic, and are not necessarily correct. There is no way of identifying fossil lineages with certainty.

The differences which occur between populations in a polytypic species provide a model for the amount of genetic variation which can occur within a protected gene pool. Comparisons are most useful when made between fossil taxa and the most closely related living taxa, both genetically and ecologically. In fossil hominids, there is really no need to choose between ecological similarity and genetic relationship. Both should be used in calibrating a scale of expected genetic variation since one is interested in establishing a range of possible limits and not a set of absolute criteria. Comparison of variation within a supposed fossil species and a living species does not 'prove' whether or not the fossil species has been correctly identified. If the fossil sample is more variable than the living species in certain features, it becomes more probable that the fossil sample consists of more than one species, temporal or geographic. If, on the other hand, the fossil sample shows less variation in certain features, it suggests only that *speciation cannot be established on the basis of those features*. It does not necessarily mean that speciation has not occurred, but only that it cannot be demonstrated.

Some additional points must be considered in such a comparison. The features used must be sufficiently numerous in the fossil sample to give a true indication of its variation. However, the best represented characteristics are not necessarily useful in distinguishing taxa. The optimum situation occurs when the fossil sample consists of sympatric taxa. In the case of sympatric closely related taxa, a species level difference should result in well defined character displacement in at least some adaptive features as the result of competition. Such features yield the optimum information when compared with a living species, if present in sufficient number. Clear morphological gaps are more likely to be found between adaptive features of closely related sympatric species than between adaptive features in closely related allopatric species.

Finally, there is the problem of the equivalence between geographic variation in living species and temporal variation in a fossil sample. Basically, one is interested in comparing like entities as much as possible. Since population level parameters are generally unavailable for fossils, no comparisons with single living populations are really valid. The best chronological control for fossil hominids is the situation where several specimens appear on the same living floor. One cannot assume that a single population is represented. On the other hand, temporal contemporaneity is fairly well established, so that the variation within such a sample can be validly compared with the variation in a locally restricted set of living populations. However, it must be remembered that the parameters of the fossil sample estimate the mean, variance, and range of all the specimens from all populations samples, and thus must be compared with the grand mean, variance and range for the set of living populations – *not* with the mean, variance, and range of the population means. Unfortunately, in instances of several specimens from the same living floor presently known, the sample size is too small to give a reasonable estimate of variation in any feature. In other words, no comparison can be made in practice. The next possibility is to use a fossil sample of specimens found at different sites at what appears to be the same time level. In this instance, there is no way to separate geographic from temporal variation and there really is no chronological control. Given the probable error for radiometric dates, a necessary part of the dating technique, what appears to be radiometric contemporaneity can in actuality represent a time span many times longer than the upper Pleistocene, and is in no sense temporally equivalent to a generation of living organisms. This is a theoretical problem that is not likely to be solved by sophistication of known radiometric techniques. At least part of the uncertainty in the radiometric dates is irrespective of problems in contamination and deposition of the samples, or association with the biological material, but rather is a necessary consequence or the probabilistic nature of radioactive decay. The theoretical and practical equivalency of geographic and temporal variation in fossil samples is a limitation which is not likely to disappear in the foreseeable future, if ever. Consequently, the equivalence problem is not between geographic and temporal variation, but is rather between geographic variation in living species, and variation in fossil species for which the geographic and temporal components are indistinguishable in theory and fact. This limitation makes the comparison of geographic variation in living taxa and variation in fossil sample from several sites more palatable. Under these circumstances there is no advantage to using specimens from only one site when the same taxon is present at other sites.

There is no way of judging with certainty if the equivalence is entirely valid, or of determining the amount of uncertainty in conclusions drawn from the analogy. Yet, if the goal of making comparisons between equal categories is to be maintained, *geographically variant populations of a living species comprise the sample which is best comparable to a fossil collection.* They are surely a better sample for comparison than a single biological population, or a sample of several living species lumped together. These considerations raise one final problem. What sample is comparable to a collection dated radiometrically to a 'given' time period? If this collection does not make up the entirety of a fossil taxon, there are no guidelines to determine what modern sample to compare it with. Similarly, comparison with collections dated at different time levels may be far from equivalent in time spans actually represented. In addition to the point that such comparisons usually have very limited sample sizes, the uncertainty in the dating procedure alone makes it virtually impossible to compare equivalent entities.

This is not to say that collections from different times should not be compared with each other. Such a comparison is particularly valuable if the collections come from different levels at the same site, or levels which can be directly related to each other stratigraphically, if the sample size is large enough to estimate reasonably the range, variance, and mean of the populations represented by the sample. However, even in this case there is the problem of equivalence in time span between collections in each of the levels compared. In all, it is difficult to pick reasonably equivalent samples for comparison under these conditions, if the goal is to detect speciation.

Given these limitations, there appears to be a more useful approach to the whole problem of choosing analogous comparisons. The purpose of the comparison is to help establish whether a fossil sample seems to include more than one species. The comparison is between internal variation within the fossil sample, and internal variation known to occur within a protected gene pool. It seems reasonable, then, for the fossil sample to consist of all specimens which there is reason to hypothesize might belong to a single species. The most equivalent living sample to compare this with would be all specimens known to belong to a single protected gene pool, within the limitations of close genetic relationship and ecological similarity. Should such a comparison show less variation for the available features in the fossil sample, it follows that those features cannot be used to establish multiple species *within* the fossil sample. On the other hand, if the fossil sample variation exceeds the modern model, it is more likely that geographic or temporal speciation has occurred within it. At this point available dating information, whether absolute or relative, becomes important since any information helping to suggest whether the speciation is geographic or temporal bears strongly on the question of the number of lineages under observation. It is also at this point that the question of how much geographic variation is observed between fossil samples becomes relevant. It does not seem to me that anything less than the total variation (mean, variance) in the protected gene pool of a living species can be used for an appropriate comparison. The parameters estimated from the fossil sample apply to the distribution characteristics of the taxon as a whole. For features with a large sample size, the number of populations represented cannot be assumed to be different from the size of the sample and whether the observed variation in this fossil sample is geographic or temporal cannot be resolved.

A second strategy of comparison uses the amount of difference known to occur between closely related but separate species. This is especially appropriate when variation *between* the species exceeds variation *within* either species. Then it is clear that the analogous model from living species consistently calibrates a distance yardstick for which more variation occurs between protected gene pools than within them. The best comparison is with differences occurring between two living species closely related to each other, chosen either because of their close genetic relationship or apparent ecological similarity to the fossil sample. If the hypothesis tested is that two fossil samples belong to different species, the probability of the hypothesis is increased if the difference between the samples exceeds that between living species, and decreased if the differences are less. If different species seem the more likely explanation, then temporal and geographic information, within the limits that can be determined for the fossil sample, can be introduced again to help determine the number of fossil lineages involved. As in the previous case, the best units for comparison are the total samples for the hypothesized fossil species. Geographic and temporal information is introduced at a later stage of analysis to help partition variation into geographic and temporal components.

These analogies provide the best way to interpret morphological variation and difference in very similar samples of fossils. In the end, however, it is impossible to judge the accuracy of taxonomic determinations for fossil samples. Yet, if no analogies are made, it is not even possible to begin.

There are three other factors useful in establishing similarity between fossil taxa. First, one can look for evidence of similarity in adaptation in both the functional morphology of the specimens, and in the ecology suggested by the functional morphology and the environment at the sites where the samples are found. Second, the existence of morphologically intermediate specimens provides a direct indication of whether gene flow was occurring. Both of these factors gain particular importance if the taxa were sympatric, since in sympatric species we can expect the clearest evidence of character displacement, such as adaptive difference and morphological gaps in adaptive characteristics. Third, if information concerning temporal variation is available, one would expect that separate but similar species will become more dissimilar over time, with a greater difference between means and less overlap of ranges, as a result of the separation in gene pools. Separate lineages, as already discussed, evolve independently with their own evolutionary role and tendencies (Simpson, 1961). Again, the expectation is that the differences will become more pronounced if the taxa are sympatric.

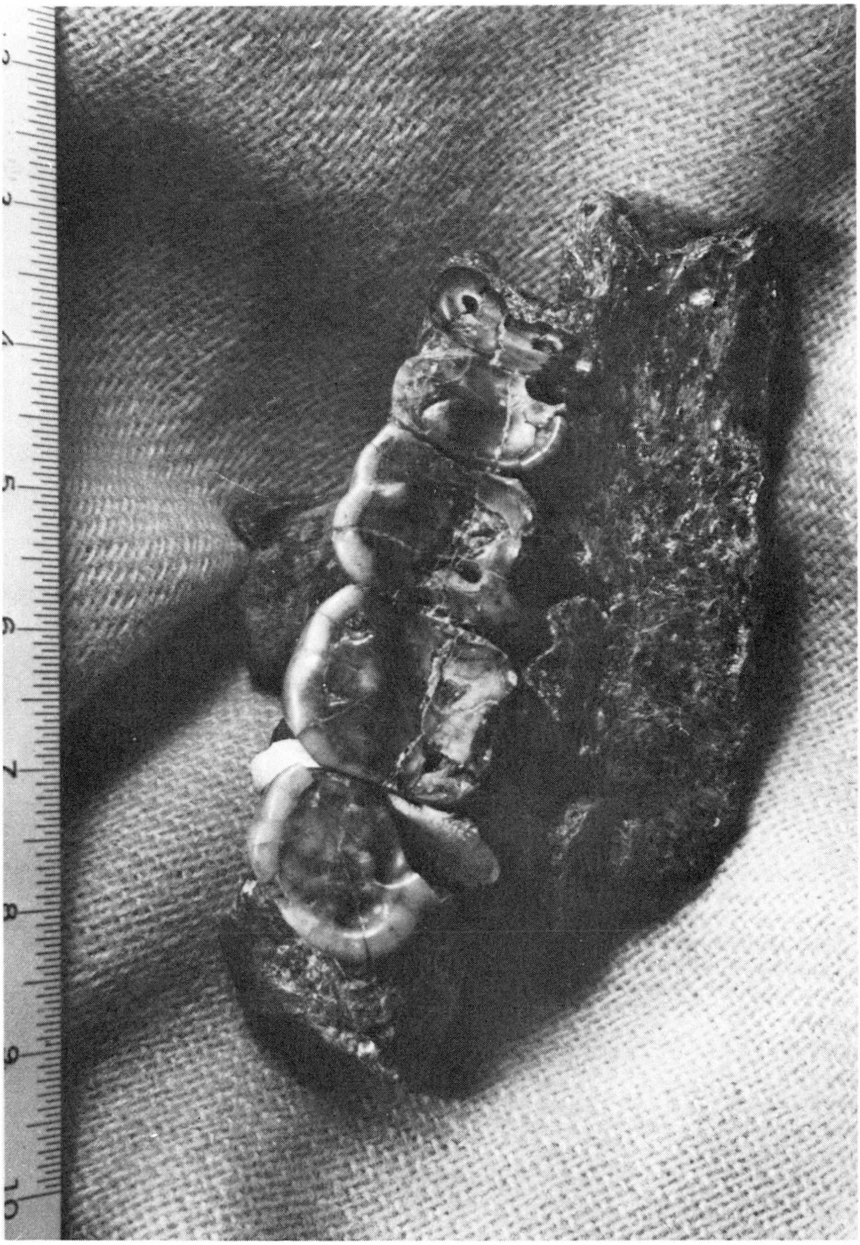

Figure 1. The MLD 9 maxilla.

Early hominids

Most problems of speciation in the hominid fossil record centre about the African early hominids, dated from Pliocene and lower Pleistocene deposits. I do not intend to propose a new taxonomy for these hominids, nor to defend strongly any of the taxonomies already suggested. Instead, I wish to apply the principles discussed, with the intent of illuminating the *problems and limitations* which accompany any reconstruction of evolutionary history and associated taxonomy for this sample. The terms used to refer to the various collections of samples are not meant to have taxonomic meaning at any particular level. I use the term 'australopithecine' to refer to all early hominids previous to *Homo erectus*. Thus in some views the term refers to a single lineage with only one species, and in other views the term refers to the Pliocene-lower Pleistocene representatives of an entire hominid family.

The first problem in treating these hominids is to decide what constitutes a proper sample for comparison. Objections are raised from time to time against lumping the specimens from a site together, as well as to lumping the specimens from a number of sites together. These objections raise the very valid possibility of confusing taxa. Yet, taxa are easily confused when closely related and represented largely by fragmentary material. The taxa must be recognized, first at the species level and later at other levels, before they can be sorted. The Null Hypothesis tested in palaeoanthropology is the hypothesis of no difference. A sample of even two specimens from the same living floor may actually represent two species. Discovering two separate species in a large sample presents exactly the same problems as recognizing them in a small one, but is much easier since the statistics used to estimate the range and variance for comparison with known species will be more accurate. In other words, if only one species is present it

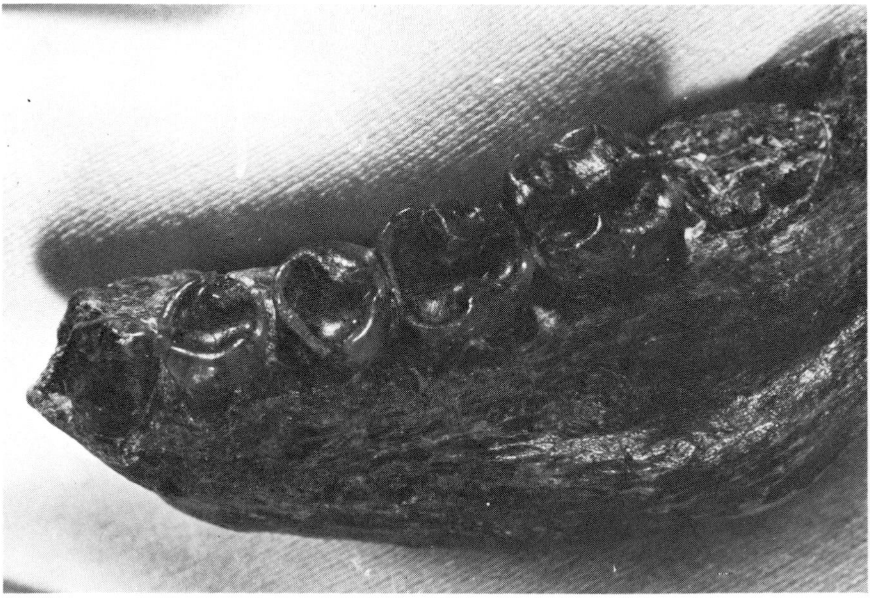

Figure 2. The MLD 40 mandible, courtesy of C.L. Brace.

does not matter if various sites are lumped together to test the Null Hypothesis, and if more than one species is present the test of the hypothesis will be more accurate in the larger sample. I would suggest that this point can be sustained even if a single phenon, or morphologically uniform sample (see Delson, this volume), at a given site, rather than all the specimens at that site, are considered. Is it really true, as Delson (this volume) suggests, that 'it actually seems more likely that specimens of a given phenon from a single locality will in fact be more closely related biologically than specimens chosen at random from that same phenon (or taxon)'? It seems to me that this is precisely the assumption that cannot be made, especially when considering a taxon that was probably both wide-ranging and polytypic. The actual evidence from the sites themselves suggests the presence of widely different populations at various times even within what almost all workers would call the same phenon. For instance at Makapan, the posterior teeth of the MLD 9 maxilla show deep grooved wear (Figure 1) but only on the lingual side of the teeth. Such wear is probably the result of chewing hard particles, at least during initial crushing, in an anterior-posterior direction. In the MLD 40 mandible there is also cupping wear, but in this specimen (Figure 2) a groove involving several teeth is not formed. Instead, individual teeth are cupped, sometimes in an anterior-posterior direction but in other cases in a lateral direction. If hard particles caused the cupping wear, as is likely, the food bolus was much smaller and the jaw motion more strongly lateral during anterior contact. Finally, the wear on

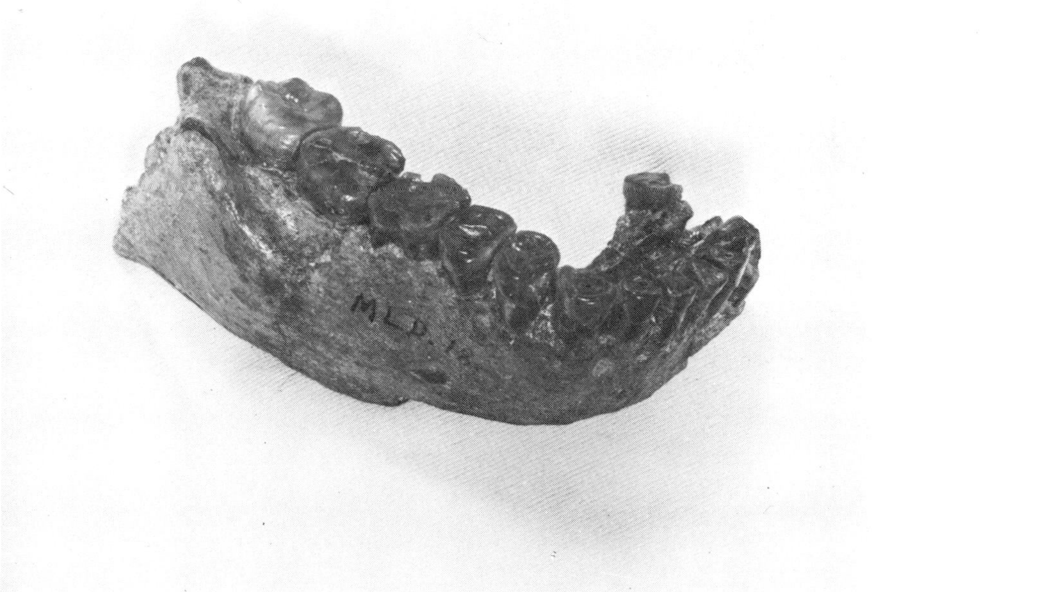

Figure 3. The MLD 18 mandible, courtesy of C.L. Brace.

mandible MLD 18 (Figure 3) is flat rather than cupped. There is little differential wear between the teeth, all worn to the same level. Such wear results from a diet without large abrasive particles but requiring extensive grinding. The point to this is that at a single locality, a single phenon samples specimens (and by inference populations) with different dietary and masticatory habits. Equivalent wear variation occurs at Sterkfontein and Swartkrans. For instance, the SK 46 maxilla shows cupping wear similar to MLD 40, while the SK 23 mandible has flat wear with less cupping. Why should we assume that all the Makapan specimens of the same phenon are more closely related to each other than they are to specimens of the same phenon from other sites? Given the variety of different adaptive patterns that occur in members of the same phenon at a single site, there is no reason to believe that specimens at a given site represent, in any sense, a genetically continuous local population sampled over time.

I propose to construct samples according to the most widely accepted schemes, but with the goal of maximizing sample size. The South African 'gracile' sample refers to the sample from South Africa often placed in the taxon designated '*Australopithecus africanus*', and the South African robust sample refers to the specimens associated with '*Paranthropus robustus*'. The East African gracile sample consists of the various specimens which have been placed in '*Homo*' from East Africa (with the confirmed presence of *Homo erectus* just below the Okole tuff at Turkana, it is possible that the latter specimens are taxonomically distinct), and the East African robust sample includes specimens from the area placed in '*Australopithecus*'. These are not my taxonomic designations and it is not my purpose to either defend or refute them.[3] In addition, using these four taxa does not imply that I believe the taxonomic distinctions between them are necessarily on the same level. They are convenient because they correspond to the various hypotheses that have been suggested to explain early hominid evolution. The hypotheses fall into two general categories. The first is that the entire sample reflects variation in one lineage which broadly gave rise to *Homo erectus*. The second is that at least two separate lineages occur in this period. The first gave rise to later forms of the genus *Homo* while the other(s) became extinct. Almost all variations of this second hypothesis are based on a form of Robinson's Dietary Hypothesis. The former lineage is seen as an omnivore and hunter utilizing culture and depending on it, while the latter lineage is viewed as primarily vegetarian, likely cultureless or utilizing only rudimentary tools, and stable and unchanging evolutionarily over this period. This lineage is viewed as incompletely or inefficiently bipedal.

3. The taxonomic designations are generally specimen-specific in East Africa and site-specific (e.g., everything from Sterkfontein is considered gracile) in South Africa. These are defensible in the same sense as any taxonomic designation for a sample: all specimens in *any* sample are the same at some taxonomic level. The question is to determine which level, and then possibly to sort the sample into lower level taxa.

Differences in the second hypothesis concern whether or not the South African gracile sample is part of the lineage giving rise to *Homo erectus*. According to Robinson (1972) and Tobias (1973) it is, while according to R.E.F. Leakey (1973) it generally is not, although some isolated specimens from South Africa might be in the ancestral lineage.[4] Further, there is some disagreement about the level of taxonomic difference between South and East African robust samples. Some workers suggest a species and others a subspecies distinction. The question I wish to consider is what limitations the available data place on these hypotheses.

Before analogies with living primates are discussed, it should be noted that the question of level of taxonomic distinction between these groups does not have an obvious answer for good reasons. Fossil taxa, particularly for similar samples, cannot be delineated with certainty. These four samples show a great deal of similarity, morphologically and adaptively, regardless of the level of taxonomic difference which is ultimately thought to distinguish them. This is why careful workers have honest disagreements about the interpretation of this very large sample of fossil hominids.

The similarities in the samples concern common features in both their evolutionary grade and adaptation. All known specimens are characterized by large faces and small crania, when compared with later hominids. Either absolutely or compared with estimates of body size, the posterior dentition is quite large – actually within the range of variation of gorillas (Wolpoff, 1973a). The large posterior dentition and the mechanics of the anteriorally situated masseter attachment, selecting for maximum vertical occlusal force, lead to an inordinately large temporalis (Wolpoff, 1974). A significant component of the diet included foods requiring heavy mastication. At the same time, the absolute size and the morphology of the anterior dentition are *Homo erectus* like. While these features show variation within the samples, and between them, they serve to distinguish these from later hominids (Wolpoff, 1973b). A recent analysis shows that all available evidence indicates the locomotion was bipedal and striding. No locomotor differences between the samples could be established (Lovejoy, Heiple, and Burstein, 1973). The question of culture is more difficult to ascertain, because no evidence can ever 'prove' whether or not the early hominids presently known made and used the tools found at early hominid sites, nor whether the tool making activity was part of a more extensive pattern of learned behaviour than characterizes

4. With the recent evidence, a rather different interpretation of this hypothesis would allow for tool use and bipedal striding as Pliocene adaptations in a single, polytypic australopithecine lineage. Speciation, according to this model, took place in the basal Pleistocene with the hyper-robust specimens of East Africa utilizing rather different resources from the developing non-opportunistic hunting adaptation of the remaining taxon. It might be the very adaptability allowed by tool use that resulted in the increasingly divergent dietary adaptations of the two lineages.

pongids like chimpanzees. Almost all authors believe that the gracile samples in South and East Africa made tools and exhibited cultural behaviour. The main argument against tool making in the robust samples seems to be that at all sites where robust specimens are found with tools, 'evidence of a more advanced hominid can be found'. Whether or not this is true is debatable, especially given the presence of tools at Chesowanja where *only* a robust specimen has been found. However, even on other grounds, the argument itself is not convincing. Some members of a sample will always look 'more advanced' than others, and the fact remains that the robust specimens are usually but not always found with tools, as is true of the gracile sample. More relevant evidence comes from the demonstration that the robust sample shows delayed molar eruption timing when compared with pongids (Mann, 1968), indicating a long period of growth and maturation, and by inference of learning. Given these data, it is likely that all early hominids made tools and in general utilized much more learned behaviour than any pongid. *The point is that there is no evidence suggesting a difference in cultural behaviour between the samples.*

Additional evidence of similarity is found in the presence of numerous intermediate specimens. Since the combined size distributions for all teeth except the canines are continuous and fundamentally unimodal, there is continuous variation between gracile and robust samples. Although the sample of crania is much

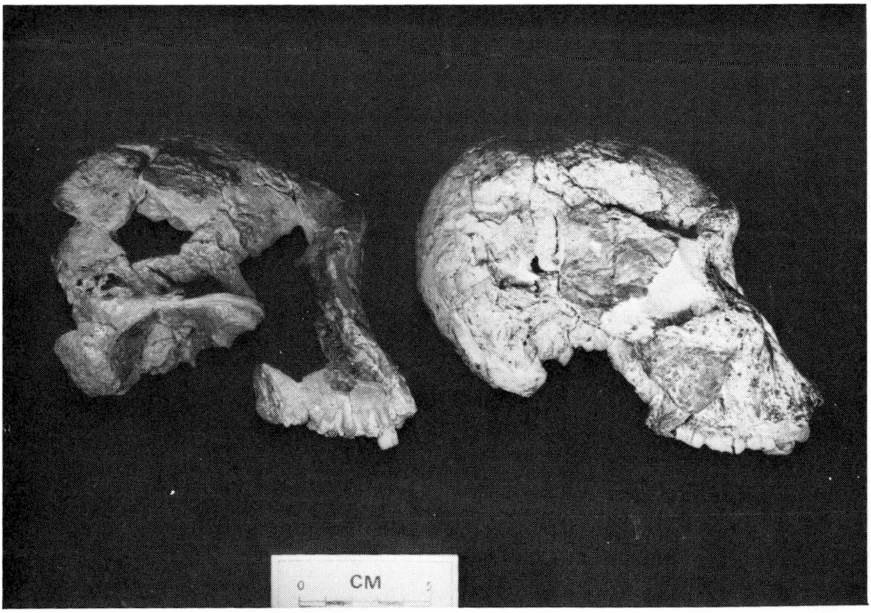

Figure 4. Comparison of Sts 71 and a cast of ER 732 in side view. These crania are very similar in general form and proportion, although one is considered a female robust specimen (ER 732) and the other a male gracile (Sts 71).

more limited, the same continuity of variation exists. For instance, OH 24 is the most complete cranium of a '*Homo*' specimen from Olduvai. ER 732 has been suggested as a female of the East Rudolf robust australopithecine sample when compared with ER 406 (Leakey, 1972). OH 24 and ER 732 are very similar to each other, although the supraglenoid and supramastoid areas of 732 are somewhat more pneuminized. Similarly in South Africa, several of the Sterkfontein crania such as MLD 1 and Sts 17 show evidence of having had a sagittal crest (Wolpoff, 1974) and crania such as Sts 71 have very anterior zygomatics (see Figure 4). At Swartkrans, small crania such as SK 80/847 are very similar to crania found in the Sterkfontein sample. The point is that the continuity in variation between these samples could be interpreted to show that gene flow occurred between them, although it could also be the result of overlapping ranges in genetically distinct but very similar lineages, or the result of the samples being mixed.

In sum, the morphological evidence suggests that prior to the appearance of *Homo erectus* the Plio-Pleistocene hominids, whatever the number of taxa they represent, occupy a similar adaptive grade, sharing the very characteristics that make them different from both pongids and later hominids. This fundamental similarity must be taken into account by any taxonomic argument, not so much because it means that the specimens are morphologically similar, but rather because it imposes an ecological restriction on any multiple lineage hypothesis. If there are multiple lineages in these closely related primates, the more similar the species are at any given time in their adaptive pattern (as reflected by functional morphology) the more the overlap of their fundamental niches. Should two such species live in the same area, there would necessarily be great overlap between their realized niches and consequently competition would be expected. While there is a variety of possible consequences to such competition, the point is that one of these consequences should occur if a multiple lineage hypothesis is correct in areas where both are found.

Given these grade similarities, the problem is to determine the level of difference between pre-*Homo erectus* samples, and then to analyse the taxonomic implications that these differences suggest. Comparisons are limited by what is available. In the australopithecine sample, the only fragments that are present in sufficient number to allow comparisons between samples that have statistical significance (i.e. accurately represent the taxon from which it was drawn) are teeth and jaws. Other comparisons can and should be made, but their significance is much more difficult to establish since it is unlikely that characteristics with small sample sizes accurately indicate the parameters of the taxon from which they were drawn. It is of some interest to determine what conclusions can be drawn from features represented by adequate sample size. Actually, there is some reason to believe that the dental comparisons will give useful data. The proponents of separate early hominid lineages uniformly suggest an underlying dietary and adaptive difference between them. Sympatry has been apparently established at a few sites, such as FLK-NN1 at Olduvai where cranial fragments of a robust australopithecine are on the same living floor as the juvenile parietals, mandible, and hand of a gracile specimen. The two proposed lineages are known to be allopatric, and in a few places observably sympatric, for a very long time period in East Africa. At E. Turkana they are found in the same habitats (Behrensmeyer, this volume). If the lineages were truly separate, one would expect the adaptive differences between them to become greater over time. This has been suggested by some workers who assert that the lineage ancestral to *Homo* shows evolutionary change while the robust australopithecines remain static and unchanging, although these assertions seem to ignore the implications of specimens such as ER 1470 and Chesowanja, both of which combine a large calvaria with a robust australopithecine dentition and face. The Kromdraai individual, TM 1517, may also be a late large-brained robust australopithecine specimen. In any event, dental differences, particularly in the size of the posterior teeth, are adaptive to differences in diet so that one might expect dietary differences as extensive as those suggested for early hominids to be reflected in posterior dental size, particularly in competing lineages. Such differences do appear with the appearance of *Homo erectus*; the discussion here concerns problems prior to this time.

Since it is apparent that whatever the level of taxonomic difference between the pre *Homo erectus* early hominid samples, they are very similar in functional morphology, it is necessary to rely on analogy to judge the level of taxonomic difference. The purpose in making analogies is twofold: to see if the variation in the individual samples, or in the entire sample, is greater than that which normally occurs within modern species; and to determine whether the differences between the samples are as great as those between the modern species. In the later comparison, the gorilla and the chimpanzee are particularly useful, since their dietary difference is much less than that suggested for the australopithecines (Jones and Pi, 1971) while the body size difference is about the same as that suggested for gracile and robust australopithecines in South Africa by Robinson (1972). However, in the former comparison there are problems regarding which species are appropriate.

Variation within the australopithecine dental samples can be compared with variation within known species of living primates, as these present the only models of how much variability actually occurs within protected gene pools (species). Which modern species make the most valid analogies? Living baboons are probably the closest ecological counterparts to the early hominids. They are adapted to the same type of niche, and are divided into polytypic populations which are spread over all of Sub-Saharan Africa. Because they are not cultural, there is more reason for local morphological distinctions to arise in adaptive response to local environmental differences. In early hominids, where the efficiency of cultural adaptation was at a much lower level than in modern hominid populations, it is likely that a similar pattern of locally distinct populations in a widespread polytypic terrestrial species occurred. In sum, the most reasonable ecological analogy for early hominids is with modern baboons. There is no reason to expect that early hominid variation would be in any way analogous to arboreal cercopithecines or colobines, given the great difference in niches utilized.

At the present time, baboon taxonomy is in a state of flux, mainly as the result of applying different species concepts to the definition of baboon species. However, if the interbreeding population concept of species is used, I have determined that *baboons are consistently more variable than any partitioning of the early hominid sample (including the sample of all Plio/Pleistocene hominds) for every tooth*, as measured by both the coefficient of variation and the range statistic shown in the appendix.

Some might argue that in spite of the ecological reasons for using a baboon analogy, the use of the most variable living primate might prejudice the study. What, then, are the alternatives? Delson (this volume) finds the use of cercopithecoids acceptable, but suggests using an apparently terrestrial fossil monkey species (*Mesopithecus pentelici*). Unless there is no alternative, I do not believe that any fossil species are useful in constructing and testing hypotheses based on analogy, because the definition of any other fossil species involves the same problems that have been discussed. Using another fossil species for an analogy would make the conclusions an entire order of magnitude more uncertain because by doubling the necessary assumptions, the error probabilities are squared (e.g. if two assumptions are both thought to be 60% certain, using them together lowers the probability of certainty to 36% – .6 × = .36).

Tooth-by-tooth comparisons ignore the possibility of systematic proportional differences in this sample. Such differences do appear, but I believe they are the result of marked sexual dimorphism in the canines and differing sex rations in the sample. Table 1 shows the distribution of canine breadth in the four australopithecine samples, and for australopithecines as a whole. These are compared with the canine breadth distribution in a large sample of modern man. Table 2 gives the same data for canine breadth distribution in the gorilla and the chimpanzee. The australopithecine distribution is very clearly bimodal, with very little overlap between the modes, in both mandible and maxilla. A bimodal distribution occurs for each of the individual samples, when sample size is large enough to show it. The modes in the individual samples are the same, and it is likely that this bimodality is the result of sexual dimorphism. The sample of modern man is clearly unimodal. The chimpanzee sample is bimodal, but the modes overlap greatly so that many females extend into the male

Table 1 Australopithecine canine breadth distribution

Maxillary canine breadth (mm)

	South African gracile n=16	*Robust n=12*	*East African 'Homo' n=5*	*Robust n=4*	*All lower Pleistocene specimens n=46*	*Modern man n=288*
6.5–6.9						1
7.0–7.4						3
7.5–7.9						33
8.0–8.4	1	2			3	84
8.5–8.9	3	5		1	9	81
9.0–9.4	5	5	2	1	13	49
9.5–9.9	1	0	0	1	2	27
10.0–10.4	4	5	0	1	10	5
10.5–10.9	0	2	0	0	2	5
11.0–11.4	1	1	0	0	2	
11.5–11.9	0	0	2	0	2	
12.0–12.4	1	1	0	0	2	
12.5–12.9			1		1	

Mandibular canine breadth (mm)

	South African gracile n=8	*Robust n=10*	*East African 'Homo' n=9*	*Robust n=9*	*All lower Pleistocene specimens n=36*	*Modern man n=349*
6.0–6.4						2
6.5–6.9						18
7.0–7.4			1		1	66
7.5–7.9	0	0	0	1	1	88
8.0–8.4	0	2	1	1	4	87
8.5–8.9	1	4	1	0	6	53
9.0–9.4	3	2	3	2	10	24
9.5–9.9	1	0	1	0	2	10
10.0–10.4	1	1	1	3	6	1
10.5–10.9	1	1	0	2	4	
11.0–11.4	1	0	1	0	2	
12.0–12.4						
12.5–12.9						

range. Only in the gorilla distribution are the modes as clearly defined as in the australopithecine sample. There is apparently little overlap of male and female distributions in both cases. Such sexual dimorphism likely accounts for the often quoted average difference observed between anterior tooth size in gracile and robust samples. Actually, the ranges of the anterior teeth overlap almost completely in the observed samples (see appendix). However, it appears that the robust samples have proportionally more females, so that the *averages* are different. If male and female specimens are weighted equally, the average canine and central incisor areas are about the same, and the

Table 2 Pongid canine breadth distribution

	Maxilla (mm)		*Mandible (mm)*	
	Chimpanzee	*Gorilla*	*Chimpanzee*	*Gorilla*
6.0–6.9				
7.0–7.9	1		2	
8.0–8.9	20		21	1
9.0–9.9	24	1	22	14
10.0–10.9	19	15	17	27
11.0–11.9	17	21	23	7
12.0–12.9	9	11	6	4
13.0–13.9	9	3	4	13
14.0–14.9	1	8	3	17
15.0–15.9		12	1	12
16.0–16.9		15	0	3
17.0–17.9		8	1	1
18.0–18.9		4		1
19.0–19.9		1		
20.0–20.9		1		

lateral incisor areas are bigger in the robust samples. It should be emphasized that this identity of anterior tooth size in the gracile and robust samples, weighing males and females equally in the samples, is not an artifact of comparing isolated teeth.

It is often claimed that the important aspect of anterior tooth size is its relative relation to the posterior teeth, which can only be seen in complete jaws. It has been traditional to use the ratio of canine size to third premolar size to demonstrate this difference. Actually, I do not believe that this ratio (or any similar one) is particularly useful in discerning a functional pattern since it is apparent that the anterior and posterior teeth respond to rather different selective pressures. However, if we make comparisons of such ratios, the result is again complete overlap between the samples. Male robust australopithecines such as SK 83 and SK 876 have a relative canine size as large as male gracile australopithecines (see Figures 5 and 6). In sum, the evidence whether considered for the entire sample or for particular individuals simply does not support the notion of significant absolute or relative anterior tooth size difference while in the posterior teeth the baboon analogy does not suggest that differences are sufficient to demonstrate multiple lineages. However, it is possible that a hominoid rather than a cercopithecoid analogy should be used.

The appendix presents data for the area of each tooth separately, and for the summed posterior areas, for each of the samples. Data are further collected into total gracile and robust samples, total South and East African samples, the total combined sample, and the combined sample without the East African specimens attributed to '*Homo*', which corresponds to the distinction which R.E.F. Leakey makes

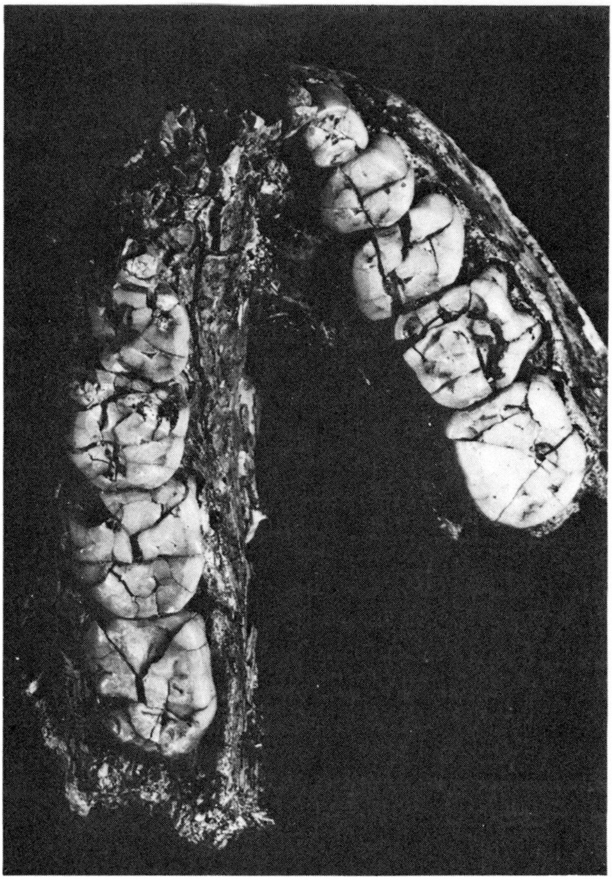

Figure 5. The SK 876 mandible showing the very large canine (right).

between the genera *Australopithecus* and *Homo* but which includes only a few specimens attributable to *Homo erectus*. For purposes of comparison, data are also given for a worldwide sample of modern man, chimpanzees, orangs, and gorillas. Data for the latter are given by sex and for the combined sample.

Two measures of variation are presented, the coefficient of variation and the range presented as a percentage of the sample mean. The coefficient of variation is calculated for all samples above two, but really does not have much meaning for small sample sizes. In considering the four samples of gracile and robust australopithecines in South and East Africa separately, almost all very high coefficients (above 20) occur for small sample sizes. The exceptions to this are M^3 variation in the South African gracile sample and likely I^2 variation in the South African robust sample, although in the latter case the sample size is below 10.

Considering gracile and robust australopithecines in South and

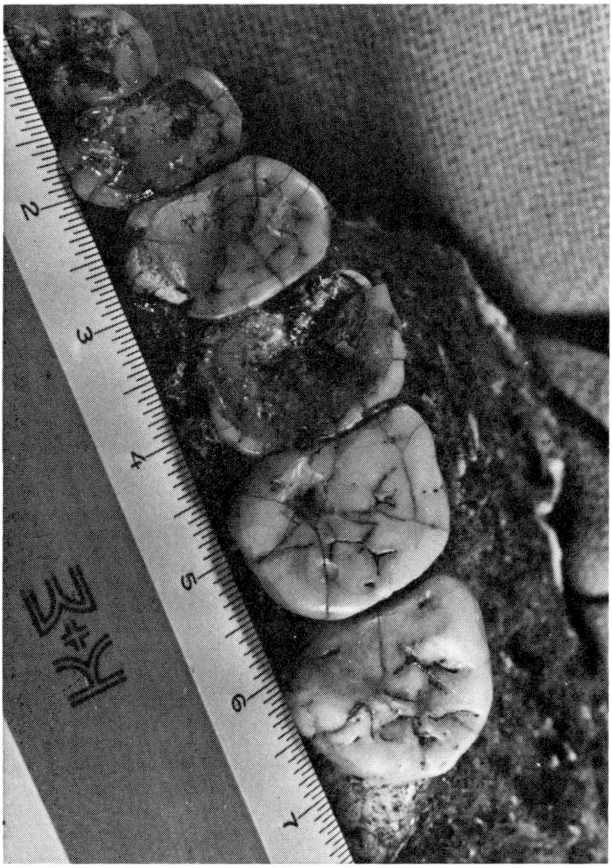

Figure 6. The SK 83 maxilla, showing the very large canine.

East Africa as four separate samples, in most cases the coefficient of variation for the postcanine teeth of these samples is greater than those for the chimpanzee. In many cases, coefficients of variation exceed those for the gorilla. This occurs for all the mandibular cheek teeth of the East African robust sample, the first two mandibular molars of the other three samples, and almost all the maxillary cheek teeth of the East African gracile sample. When the total australopithecine sample is considered, all of the cheek teeth expecting P_3 exceed the gorilla in the coefficient of variation. P_3 is not comparable between hominids and pongids in any event. Where large samples of the maxillary lateral incisor are available, these also exceed the gorilla in variation. These data can be interpreted to suggest either that some of the samples, especially those from East Africa, might include more than one species, or that the australopithecines are more variable than living gorillas. In comparison with modern man, the most variable of the living primates used excepting the anterior dentition, the mandibular cheek teeth of the East African robust sample which generally show the least genetic variation, P_3, M_1, and M_2 are more variable than the modern human sample. The maxillary sample sizes are too small to draw meaningful comparisons. In considering the total australopithecine sample, all of the mandibular cheek teeth are more variable than modern man, as measured by the coefficient of variation. Every one of the individual samples is more variable than modern man in at least a few teeth, but it is apparent that the variation in the total sample is mostly due to variation in the East African robust sample.

In sum, the coefficient of variation shows that each sample is more variable than the African apes in some respects, and that the East African robust sample is the most variable of the four. If this is the result of 'lumping' together different time periods, the partitioning of this variation into gross temporal components must await a final dating of the East Rudolf sequence since this is where the bulk of the material comes from. However, there is another point to be considered. Is the coefficient of variation the best measure of variability for these samples? There is some reason to believe it may not be. The distribution curves from tooth areas at each site are not normal, and in fact for canines they are not even unimodal. In general, the curves are flatter and more widely distributed than a true normal distribution so that it takes a much larger sample size to estimate the true variance than the 'rule of thumb' sample size of 15 that is generally applicable to a normal distribution.

A second measure of sample variation may be considered: the range. Table 3 presents indexes of the sample range divided by the

Table 3 Table of range/mean index

	Man	*Chimpanzee*	*Gorilla*	*Pongo*	*Australopithecine*
I^1	85.2	99.4	98.9	87.5	*47.0*
I^2	127.5	77.8	113.2	94.5	*77.9*
C	109.6	138.0	175.0	150.0	*85.2*
P^3	98.1	60.7	92.8	74.3	*86.4*
P^4	102.6	83.6	70.2	75.1	*82.2*
M^1	112.5	61.7	76.7	72.0	*74.0*
M^2	117.8	83.4	94.7	85.2	*89.0*
M^3	124.2	127.2	115.8	89.6	*89.9*
P^3–M^3	80.0	55.8	76.6	54.9	*64.6*
I_1	105.1	102.7	103.8	74.3	*39.6*
I_2	110.2	85.0	95.9	79.8	*40.6*
C	76.0	133.1	155.9	126.1	*52.1*
P_3	101.0	76.9	92.0	97.9	*82.1*
P_4	134.1	60.2	86.0	93.5	*92.9*
M_1	75.1	58.6	80.1	84.2	*95.9*
M_2	113.3	73.2	82.3	101.8	*84.1*
M_3	110.7	123.8	108.6	100.1	*110.3*
P_3–M_3	59.7	57.5	80.5	64.0	*70.7*

mean. The table shows that this index is greater than that of modern man in the combined australopithecine sample for only one tooth, M_1. Other values are less than those for modern man, and are about the same as for the gorilla sample. None of the values for the individual australopithecine samples exceed any of the living primates. The total range of the individual samples fits within the expectation of ranges within modern hominoid species while the distribution of variation within that range does not.

The data for australopithecine range and variance, in other words, are borderline between confirming and refuting the Null Hypothesis, in that they are borderline between clearly exceeding and clearly falling within the limits of variation known to occur within modern taxa. The fact that the analogy with modern taxa is a somewhat uncertain procedure, since it is possible that the analogy is not completely valid, does not help to clarify the situation. Moreover, cercopithecoids and hominoids provide different conclusions. Were the observed australopithecine variation 25% higher or lower, the situation would be much easier to interpret.

A rather different approach might be to attempt to decide between two different hypotheses. In this case, the two hypotheses are the Null Hypothesis, and the hypothesis that a given sample is actually the mixture of two (or more) different species. It is possible to estimate the expected sample variation under the second hypothesis by using gorillas and chimpanzees. The gorilla and chimpanzee are the two most closely related of the living hominoids. They have diets which are similar, although not identical – surely more similar than the dietary difference for australopithecines proposed by the Dietary Hypothesis. Their geographic ranges partially overlap, and when sympatric they occupy restricted and non-overlapping realized niches to avoid competition. In other words, in many respects they fit the same sort of ecological model that is often proposed for australopithecine species. Delson's suggestion (this volume) to compare chimpanzees and orangs does not approximate the constraints of the australopithecine problem. These modern apes are allopatric, and consequently are not subject to the disruptive selection that would result from competition.

According to dates from Omo, the postulated australopithecine phena have been separated for long enough so that even slight differences in selection would have led to significant morphological difference over the time period represented by the bulk of the sample. While we cannot be positive about how long gorillas and chimpanzees have been separated, most evidence indicates over 10 million years, so that the differences between them can be taken as a direct measure of the differences in selection acting on them. It does not appear that this difference in selection is particularly great. Their body size difference is the same as that suggested for the australopithecines by Robinson (1972). Therefore, a mixed sample of chimpanzee and gorilla

Table 4 Statistics for a mixed sample of gorillas and chimpanzees

	Mean	*N*	*Range (R)*	*CV*	*R/M*
I^1	135.0	403	6.0–203.7	20.0	102.0
I^2	89.5	379	48.1–152.0	19.6	116.1
C	246.8	455	78.0–620.4	42.9	219.8
P^3	134.5	727	66.0–203.7	36.2	150.1
P^4	125.5	704	56.1–230.6	36.3	139.0
M^1	177.0	722	83.7–325.8	32.6	136.8
M^2	190.8	743	76.8–416.2	40.9	177.9
M^3	163.6	662	51.7–385.8	43.6	204.2
P^3–M^3	927.5	309	409.2–1557.3	33.0	123.8
I_1	68.0	417	29.5–122.4	18.5	136.6
I_2	88.0	421	41.6–131.6	18.8	102.3
C	190.7	485	77.4–432.0	39.3	185.9
P_3	150.2	595	58.5–301.9	39.4	162.1
P_4	117.9	595	51.6–229.5	35.3	150.9
M_1	170.2	605	77.1–310.6	31.3	137.2
M_2	205.6	601	74.8–398.0	37.5	157.2
M_3	192.1	553	31.0–409.8	42.4	197.2
P_3–M_3	865.4	351	380.8–1586.6	36.8	139.3

dentitions provides a model for the variation which should occur in a sample mixture of two species more similar in diet and ecology than has been proposed for the australopithecines. Table 4 presents the data for a mixed chimpanzee and gorilla sample. In most cases the coefficients of variation are about double those for the total australopithecine sample, and in all cases they greatly exceed this sample. Were a mixed dental sample of chimpanzees and gorillas found as fossils, the range and variance comparisons would unequivocally show that the sample was not consistant with the Null Hypothesis. Using analogy to create models of variation based on the Null Hypothesis and the hypothesis of different but closely related taxa, the combined australopithecine sample is not midway between the expectations, but rather conforms more closely to the Null Hypothesis, although by no means confirming it.

Three possible conclusions can be drawn from these data.

1. The australopithecines consist of one lineage that when sampled over its entire time span shows slightly more variation in some respects than living hominoid species and instead approximates baboons. Should this be true, partitioning into time periods is necessary to determine whether there is a temporal component to the variation. This is not possible at the present time for much of the sample.
2. The australopithecines consist of at least two separate lineages. If this is true, the data suggests that both lineages occur in all four samples. Since I have found that there are no distinct bimodalities in the dental distributions, excepting canine size

Table 5 Tooth area difference in percent ($\frac{\text{Maximum} - \text{Minimum}}{\text{Minimum}}$ x 100)

	Averages for 8 Human Populations			*Australopithecines*			*Gorilla*		*Pongo*
	Max	*Min*	Δ	*All robust vs. graciles*	*'Homo' vs. remaining sample*	*East vs. South Africa*	*Gorilla vs. chimpanzee*	*Male vs. female*	*Male vs. female*
I^1	78.1	64.0	22.0	–12.1	–11.9	13.2	11.8	18.4	23.2
I^2	58.7	47.4	24.3	15.5	1.8	–1.2	16.3	20.1	24.4
C	90.1	68.5	31.5	–11.1	–16.5	1.8	97.3	105.9	83.5
P^3	8.35	63.9	30.7	20.2	14.9	–4.4	107.0	14.2	21.0
P^4	83.5	65.4	24.3	30.9	25.7	–5.5	113.6	12.2	20.2
M^1	149.5	109.3	36.8	15.8	14.4	1.2	94.0	11.1	20.1
M^2	142.2	101.5	40.1	6.9	14.2	1.8	133.8	14.0	22.2
M^3	123.9	89.5	38.4	8.3	27.7	7.5	144.8	18.6	28.1
P^3–M^3	576.0	466.0	23.6	16.1	9.4	25.1	106.0	15.9	19.4
I_1	47.1	31.8	31.1	2.7	–7.3	9.4	–6.1	15.9	23.4
I_2	47.4	38.6	22.8	–12.3	–6.9	–2.7	12.9	20.2	23.8
C	77.7	52.0	36.0	–9.8	–4.4	–0.4	70.5	95.0	23
P_3	65.9	55.4	19.0	6.1	8.8	6.0	124.7	34.3	35.3
P_4	71.6	60.2	18.9	37.8	35.7	18.0	109.0	16.1	21.4
M_1	140.0	109.2	28.2	16.7	21.8	–1.7	93.6	12.2	19.6
M_2	134.0	95.5	40.3	17.0	25.1	3.6	128.7	15.4	24.2
M_3	131.7	90.2	46.0	25.3	32.8	7.0	154.5	20.7	28.1
P_3–M_3	524.0	457.0	14.7	25.7	29.3	12.2	122.2	20.4	21.3

which appears to show sexual dimorphism, only non-dental features can be used to separate the lineages within each sample. No non-dental features are present in sufficient number to make this possible at the present time. Although there are hints of some differences in the small samples, the lineages are much more similar than chimpanzees and gorillas.

3. Dental data are not taxonomically relevant to the question of how many lineages occur. If true, it would imply that the adaptive difference is not as great as has been suggested if there is more than one lineage coexisting over the long time span prior to the appearance of *Homo erectus*.

All three of these possible conclusions raise questions which must be answered in an evolutionary framework. The most important contradiction, yet to be resolved, is why, if the second or third possibilities are correct, there is not a greater adaptive difference between the two lineages than can be observed. If the first possibility is correct why does the observed variation exceed modern hominoid species, albeit slightly? It is possible to suggest answers to both of these questions, but if the answers are not suggested in the form of testable hypotheses there is no way to decide between them.

One further possibility is to observe the differences between the four samples. These can be compared with mean differences between modern taxa which gives an expectation of how much difference occurs between protected gene pools. The relevant difference is between the most similar and closely related taxa, gorillas and chimpanzees. Comparison can also be made with the difference which occurs between modern hominid populations, giving an expectation of how much difference can occur within a protected gene pool. Table 5 presents indexes of mean differences between the extremes of 8 human populations, and between chimpanzees and gorillas. Various australopithecine sample comparisons are made. The comparison of all robust vs. graciles tests that taxonomic division suggested by Robinson, while the comparison of East African 'Homo' vs. the remaining sample tests the taxonomic division suggested by R.E.F. Leakey. All comparisons show differences less than occur between human populations except P 4. In other words, for the most part the separation of australopithecine taxa is at about the population level when compared to man. When comparison is made to the pongid differences, chimpanzees and gorillas are usually many times more different than the australopithecine comparisons. At what taxonomic level are these differences relevant? Mayr (1969) suggests the coefficient of difference as a means of recognizing subspecies. A coefficient above 1.3, at the minimum, suggests subspecies difference for a wide range of vertebrates. Table 6 gives this coefficient for a number of comparisons. The coefficients for the human populations are slightly above the subspecies level for only 3 teeth. The species

Table 6 Coefficient of difference values $\left(\frac{\bar{X}_1 - \bar{X}_2}{\sigma_1 + \sigma_2}\right)$

	All robust vs. graciles	*South African robust vs. gracile*	*'Homo' vs. remaining sample*	*Extremes for 8 modern group averages*	*Gorilla vs. chimpanzee*
I^1	–0.5	0	–0.4	0.6	0.3
I^2	0.4	0.6	0.0	0.5	0.4
C	–0.3	–0.3	–0.4	0.8	1.0
P^3	0.7	0.8	0.4	0.8	2.6
P^4	1.0	0.9	0.8	1.1	3.0
M^1	0.5	0.3	0.5	1.4	2.9
M^2	0.2	0.0	0.4	1.3	3.0
M^3	0.2	0.0	0.6	0.8	2.6
P^3–M^3	0.7	0.7		0.8	2.8
I_1	0.1	0.4	–0.3	1.3	–0.2
I_2	–0.7	–0.5	–0.4	0.8	0.4
C	–0.4	–0.4	–0.1	1.4	0.9
P_3	0.2	0.0	0.3	0.8	2.3
P_4	0.9	0.7	0.8	0.8	2.6
M_1	0.5	0.1	0.7	1.1	2.8
M_2	0.5	0.1	0.7	1.6	3.1
M_3	0.6	0.2	0.8	1.4	2.8
P_3–M_3	0.9	0.8		0.6	3.0

level of difference can be determined for hominoids by the pongid comparison. Every one of the australopithecine comparisons is below the subspecies level.

The same three possibilities can be drawn from these data.

1. A single lineage could be represented with sample differences at or below the subspecies level.
2. Two or more lineages are present and each sample has a mixture of both so that the sample comparisons are not valid.
3. Dental evidence is not relevant to the problem.

Conclusions

As I suggested at the beginning of this work, the purpose of this discussion is not to settle issues, but to raise them. It seems to me that some information can be drawn from the analysis of australopithecine variation by use of analogy with living hominoids. This information, however, is in the form of limitations to the possible taxonomic interpretations, and the problems which these interpretations must solve in a testable manner.

The first problem is whether the analogies are valid. The living hominoids are the closest genetic relations to the australopithecines, although they are not the closest in terms of their ecological adaptation. A model for populational differences in dental selection applicable to australopithecines might better be derived from baboons. There is some uncertainty introduced to the comparisons based on the choice of models, although it is probably not possible to estimate how much. In addition, there is the problem of whether the modern samples represent enough different populations for valid comparisons, since the total australopithecine sample reflects variation in populations equal in number to the sample size.

The second question is whether dental variation is taxonomically relevant in distinguishing early hominid lineages. If it is not, there is still some information that can be gained because the dietary hypothesis, as presently stated, predicts that dental differences will occur. Consequently, if there are two or more lineages, and their adaptive difference is not reflected by the dentition, this suggests that the adaptive difference is much less than that which can be observed between the gorilla and chimpanzee in terms of diet and dental preparation of foods.

If dental variation is taxonomically relevant, one of two possibilities seem likely. The australopithecines may be represented by one lineage with more dental variation than occurs within living hominoids, though significantly less variation than occurs when living hominoid species are mixed. This could be the result of temporal and geographic variation, body size variation between populations reflecting differing adaptive responses to the environment, and considerable sexual dimorphism within populations. If so, it must ultimately be possible to partition the variation into these categories. If only one lineage is present, the question of sample composition becomes much less important. The weakest point of this hypothesis is the amount of variation present in the combined sample. Yet, it is apparent that the great amount of variation is not simply characteristic of the combined sample, but is also characteristic of smaller samples morphologically sorted (e.g. the robust phenon from East Africa). Whether the amount of dental variation present is 'too much' for a single taxon is not obvious, as it would be if the variation was either as small as occurs in chimpanzees or as large as occurs in the combined sample of chimpanzees and gorillas. Certainly, if the early hominids follow a baboon-like pattern of variation, there is not 'too much' variation. However, the point is that the conclusion depends on the analogy used, and thus to some extent it depends on the original assumptions that one chooses to make.

On the other hand, it is possible that two lineages, or more, are present. In this event, the dental evidence indicates that each sample used is likely mixed. It will probably not be possible to sort specimens on the basis of dental evidence alone, since whatever differences occur are much less than those that separate closely related and ecologically similar living pongid taxa. The weakest point of the multiple lineage hypothesis is the problem of grade similarity, suggesting a common, specific and rather unique adaptive niche for all the early hominids. If it is impossible to establish clear adaptive differences based on hominid morphology, the ecological reconstructions for the various sites are equally inconclusive. Butzer (this volume) reviews the South African sites, and suggests that the only evidence for a dietary hypothesis would have to come from the hominids themselves, since it cannot be established for ecological comparisons of the sites. Behrensmeyer, in analysing the ecological circumstances of the East Turkana hominid occurrences (this volume), establishes that specimens assigned to 'Australopithecus' and 'Homo' both occur in all of the ecozones she was able to distinguish. This pattern suggests that if sympatry did occur, there would have been competition over limiting resources in a number of different realized niches. While there is no foreseeable circumstances under which sympatry could be absolutely proved, the continuous mixture of two or more early hominid phena at numerous sites strongly suggests it. The alternative explanation is to suggest subtle ecological preferences, unidentifiable at the present, acting to keep populations of distinct but extremely similar hominid species separate in a variety of different niches that both species occupy. There is no basis to assume the latter is correct, and I believe that there is no point to making more assumptions than is necessary in any analysis that necessarily rests on unavoidable assumptions.

The weakness of the multiple lineage hypothesis results from these factors. Hominid species which are closely related, very similar ecological and in terms of their functional morphology, and indistinguishable in those elements of behaviour that can be inferred, would be subject to the competitive exclusion principle, especially if in competition in a variety of different realized niches. The expected results are extinction of one, geographic separation, or ecological and adaptive separation. None of these *seems* to have occurred prior to the appearance of *Homo erectus*. However, the demonstration that one of them has in fact happened, would go a long way towards making the multiple lineage hypothesis more credible. The dietary hypothesis provided such a demonstration, but as presently started it predicts far more extensive and consistent morphological differences than can be actually observed.

In sum, whether or not the dental evidence is taxonomically relevant, if there are separate australopithecine lineages they are much more similar dentally than has usually been supposed. Given the other grade similarities observed in the non-dental remains, it is probably going to be extremely difficult, in the foreseeable future, to resolve convincingly from dental evidence alone the question of how many australopithecine lineages occurred.

Acknowledgments

I am deeply indebted to C.K. Brain and E. Voigt of the Transvaal Museum, P.V. Tobias and A. Hughes of the Department of Anatomy, University of the Witwatersrand, and M.D.M. Leakey, M.D. Leakey, and R.E.F. Leakey of the National Museums of Kenya, Centre for Prehistory and Palaeontology for permission to examine the fossil hominid material in their possessions, and for the help and encouragement given to me during my visits. I am grateful to the Cleveland Museum of Natural Science for use of the Hamann-Todd collection. Finally, I thank T. White, L. Greenfield, C. Madden, and R. Glenn Northcutt for help in preparing this manuscript. Research for this study was supported by NSF grant GS-33035, a grant from the American Philosophical Society, and a Rackham Research grant.

Appendix (pp. 495-502)

Statistical tables for fossil and living hominoid samples. The statistics calculated are the sample mean, size (N), observed range, coefficient of variation (CV), and the index of the observed range divided by the mean. All australopithecines were measured by the author except those from Omo which were reported by Howell (1969) and Coppens (1970, 1971). The sample of modern humans was reported by Wolpoff (1971), and the pongid sample by Mahler (1973). The samples consist of material known in 1974. Since that time, a *Homo erectüs* cranium has been discovered at East Turkana in beds equivalent in age to mid-Bed II at Olduvai. The '*Homo*' sample probably includes a mixture of later, true *Homo erectus* specimens (ER 807, 820 992) with earlier australopithecine material.

	Gorilla (both sexes)					Pongo (both sexes)				
	Mean	N	Range	CV	R/Mean	Mean	N	Range(R)	VC	R/Mean
Maxilla										
I^1	139.2	289	66.0–203.7	18.5	98.9	159.3	72	104.8–244.2	17.0	87.5
I^2	91.8	311	48.1–152.0	19.2	113.2	72.8	92	45.4–144.2	19.7	94.5
C	278.8	349	132.5–620.4	35.2	175.0	183.8	103	92.7–386.4	34.8	150.0
P^3	174.3	406	101.0–262.7	13.8	92.8	129.2	126	88.2–184.2	15.5	74.3
P^4	162.3	404	116.6–230.6	12.1	70.2	121.3	125	74.5–165.6	14.5	75.1
M^1	224.1	409	154.0–325.8	11.5	76.7	161.3	138	110.3–226.4	14.6	72.0
M^2	256.9	409	172.9–416.2	13.2	94.7	170.4	134	99.4–244.5	16.2	85.2
M^3	223.3	363	127.3–385.8	15.3	115.8	154.4	112	89.4–227.7	18.8	89.6
P^3–M^3	1042.0	243	759.2–1557.3	12.6	76.6	721.0	54	563.1–958.7	13.4	54.9
Mandible										
I_1	66.6	279	29.5–93.6	18.4	103.8	82.4	84.	52.2–113.4	182	74.3
I_2	91.1	297	44.2–131.6	19.5	95.9	89.8	94	64.4–136.1	17.6	79.8
C	221.0	324	87.4–432.0	31.2	155.9	152.8	101	88.3–280.9	32.8	126.1
P_3	191.9	362	125.3–301.9	18.3	92.0	146.3	129	92.0–235.2	22.5	97.9
P_4	148.2	362	102.1–229.5	14.4	86.0	126.2	132	79.5–197.5	17.9	93.5
M_1	208.7	374	143.4–310.6	11.8	80.1	154.1	129	112.9–242.6	15.1	84.2
M_2	262.3	370	182.2–398.0	13.0	82.3	176.6	133	112.4–292.1	16.9	101.8
M_3	252.5	335	135.6–409.8	15.2	108.6	170.0	110	105.7–275.9	19.3	100.1
P_3–M_3	1062.0	233	732.2–1586.6	13.4	80.5	755.9	62	553.2–1036.9	14.6	64.0

Appendix (continued)

	Gorilla female					Gorilla male				
	Mean	N	Range (R)	CV	R/Mean	Mean	N	Range (R)	CV	R/Mean
Maxilla										
I^1	124.5	103	66.0–179.8	17.6	91.4	147.4	186	82.8–203.7	16.3	82.0
I^2	81.4	114	48.1–117.6	19.0	85.4	97.8	197	52.2–152.0	19.0	102.0
C	168.1	132	132.5–227.5	13.2	56.5	346.2	217	243.9–620.4	16.3	108.8
P^3	159.7	149	101.0–223.5	11.0	76.7	182.3	257	136.2–262.7	12.7	69.4
P^4	150.6	145	115.5–199.3	10.6	54.9	168.9	259	134.6–230.6	10.9	56.8
M^1	209.2	147	145.0–275.4	9.9	58.0	232.5	262	175.6–325.8	10.6	64.6
M^2	235.9	149	172.9–309.7	11.1	58.0	268.9	260	193.2–416.2	11.9	82.9
M^3	199.6	132	127.3–292.4	13.5	98.9	236.8	231	174.2–385.8	12.8	89.4
P^3–M^3	945.1	86	759.2–1203.3	9.4	47.0	1095.1	157	844.7–1557.3	10.9	65.1
Mandible										
I_1	60.4	98	36.0–86.0	17.6	82.8	70.0	181	29.5–98.6	16.7	98.7
I_2	80.5	104	45.1–120.0	19.9	93.0	96.8	193	44.2–131.6	16.6	90.3
C	135.8	110	87.4–202.8	12.8	85.0	264.8	214	180.0–432.0	16.1	95.2
P_3	156.6	124	125.3–218.9	11.7	59.8	210.3	238	149.9–301.9	12.6	72.3
P_4	133.9	123	102.1–174.9	11.4	54.4	155.5	239	115.6–229.5	13.1	73.3
M_1	193.0	126	143.4–238.8	9.6	49.4	216.6	248	163.2–310.6	10.7	68.1
M_2	238.2	127	182.2–304.3	10.4	51.3	274.9	243	200.2–398.0	11.5	72.0
M_3	221.7	111	135.6–273.0	11.9	62.0	267.7	224	206.1–409.8	12.6	76.1
P_3–M_3	936.7	80	732.2–1111.0	8.6	40.4	1127.4	153	897.3–1586.6	10.9	61.1

	Modern man (both sexes)					Australopithecine (total sample)				
	Mean	N	Range (R)	CV	R/Mean	Mean	N	Range (R)	CV	R/Mean
Maxilla										
I^1	66.7	244	42.0–98.8	15.3	85.2	79.6	13	66.4–103.8	14.6	47.0
I^2	50.1	235	21.6–85.5	17.8	127.5	50.6	25	33.9–73.3	21.2	77.9
C	71.9	283	40.8–119.6	14.8	109.6	89.1	27	68.9–144.8	19.3	85.2
P^3	73.0	315	36.4–108.0	17.5	98.1	123.1	49	77.4–183.7	16.0	86.4
P^4	69.5	318	38.5–109.8	18.4	102.6	140.4	58	93.5–208.9	18.4	82.2
M^1	126.3	488	42.0–184.1	15.4	112.5	187.6	72	133.3–272.1	15.6	74.0
M^2	118.1	450	56.0–195.1	17.6	117.8	223.9	48	157.8–359.0	15.6	89.9
M^3	102.6	331	45.5–172.9	20.1	124.2	231.3	47	144.3–345.3	19.1	86.9
P^3–M^3	504.0	164	370.0–710.0	13.5	80.0	916.0	15	726.0–1354.6	15.8	64.6
Mandible										
I_1	33.2	226	16.9–51.8	16.9	105.1	37.4	16	29.3–44.1	11.2	39.6
I_2	41.0	249	22.4–67.6	14.8	110.2	49.7	14	39.7–59.9	10.9	40.6
C	57.9	311	36.5–80.5	14.5	76.0	79.5	24	59.8–101.2	14.8	52.1
P_3	59.4	390	36.0–96.0	14.7	101.0	118.1	38	85.0–182.0	16.4	82.1
P_4	64.9	409	39.6–126.6	17.0	134.1	141.9	41	96.0–227.9	25.0	92.9
M_1	127.3	558	83.6–179.2	12.6	75.1	191.4	59	130.7–314.2	17.6	95.9
M_2	119.9	529	67.5–203.3	15.7	113.3	229.5	59	136.9–333.0	18.7	84.1
M_3	116.4	448	59.5–188.3	17.9	110.7	242.2	59	150.8–418.0	21.3	110.3
P_3–M_3	496.0	216	353.0–64.90	11.0	59.7	962.5	19	660.0–1340.0	17.4	70.7

Appendix (continued)

	Chimpanzee (both sexes)					Australopithecines (without East African gracile)				
	Mean	N	Range (R)	CV	R/Mean	Mean	N	Range (R)	CV	R/Mean
Maxilla										
I^1	124.5	114	73.0–196.8	21.9	99.4	76.4	9	66.4–85.9	9.4	25.5
I^2	78.9	68	58.5–119.9	16.2	77.8	50.8	20	33.9–73.3	21.7	77.5
C	141.3	106	78.0–273.0	30.2	138.0	887.2	24	68.9–127.1	15.9	66.7
P^3	84.2	321	60.8–111.9	11.9	60.7	126.1	40	92.0–183.7	15.0	72.7
P^4	76.0	300	56.1–119.6	12.0	83.6	145.5	48	99.6–208.9	17.1	75.1
M^1	115.5	313	83.7–154.9	9.9	61.7	192.0	59	143.4–272.1	15.3	67.1
M^2	109.9	334	76.8–168.5	13.6	83.4	227.4	42	177.7–359.0	15.2	79.7
M^3	91.2	299	51.7–167.7	18.5	127.2	234.6	44	177.0–345.3	18.3	71.8
P^3–M^3	505.8	66	409.2–691.5	12.1	55.8	921.14	14	762.0–1354.0	16.1	64.3
Mandible										
I_1	70.9	138	49.6–122.4	18.1	102.7	36.7	12	29.3–40.9	11.0	31.6
I_2	80.7	124	41.6–110.2	12.4	85.0	48.7	10	39.7–59.9	12.0	45.2
C	129.6	161	77.4–249.9	27.2	133.1	78.9	20	65.6–101.2	14.0	45.1
P_3	85.4	233	58.5–124.2	13.4	76.9	119.4	33	85.0–182.0	16.7	81.3
P_4	70.9	233	51.6–94.3	11.9	60.2	147.5	35	104.0–227.9	23.8	84.0
M_1	107.8	231	77.1–140.3	10.6	58.6	199.8	45	144.0–314.2	16.3	85.2
M_2	114.7	231	74.8–158.7	11.8	73.2	237.5	49	155.0–333.3	17.1	75.1
M_3	99.2	218	31.0–153.8	16.3	123.8	252.8	49	175.3–418.0	19.3	96.0
P_3–M_3	477.9	118	380.8–655.6	10.5	57.5	986.1	17	775.0–1340.0	17.0	57.3

	South African gracile					South African robust				
	Mean	N	Range (R)	CV	R/Mean	Mean	N	Range (R)	CV	R/Mean
Maxilla										
I^1	81.9	2	77.9–85.9		9.8	73.1	4	66.4–83.3	10.2	23.1
I^2	43.9	6	33.9–51.8	15.3	40.8	55.5	9	39.0–73.3	24.2	61.8
C	92.1	7	74.3–127.1	18.7	57.3	86.9	13	70.1–111.3	15.0	47.4
P^3	112.7	15	92.0–129.2	8.6	33.0	132.3	22	103.4–158.6	12.3	41.7
P^4	120.2	13	99.6–161.0	14.3	51.1	151.9	30	112.5–181.0	12.0	45.1
M^1	176.5	21	143.4–219.5	11.1	43.1	193.8	33	153.6–261.3	13.3	55.6
M^2	222.4	20	177.7–288.0	12.7	49.6	224.0	20	180.8–294.1	12.3	50.6
M^3	227.4	17	177.0–317.7	21.6	61.9	228.8	22	147.0–289.3	13.4	62.2
P^3–M^3	834.0	5	811.0–863.0	2.7	6.2	899.6	7	762.0–973.0	7.9	23.5
Mandible										
I_1	34.3	4	29.3–40.8	16.4	33.5	36.9	4	35.8–39.2	4.3	9.2
I_2	51.7	5	46.0–59.9	12.0	26.9	47.8	3	46.2–50.3	4.5	8.6
C	84.8	7	70.1–101.2	13.9	36.7	75.5	9	65.6–97.2	13.6	41.9
P_3	116.0	10	94.6–143.9	12.9	42.5	116.1	18	85.0–153.4	15.3	58.9
P_4	117.3	8	108.0–137.5	8.3	25.1	137.0	17	104.0–182.0	14.2	56.9
M_1	187.7	14	153.1–247.0	15.5	50.0	195.5	23	144.0–244.9	12.0	51.6
M_2	221.6	14	191.5–277.2	13.1	38.7	229.2	23	155.0–278.4	13.5	53.8
M_3	224.8	12	175.3–263.5	14.0	39.2	240.4	23	181.6–304.0	14.8	50.9
P_3–M_3	863.2	6	775.0–953.0	9.6	20.6	981.4	7	902.0–1076.0	6.7	17.7

Appendix (continued)

	East African gracile					East African robust				
	Mean	N	Range (R)	CV	R/Mean	Mean	N	Range (R)	CV	R/Mean
Maxilla										
I^1	86.7	4	73.0–103.8	20.1	35.5	77.03	3	68.4–81.8	9.7	17.4
I^2	49.9	5	35.3–62.4	21.4	54.3	50.6	5	42.1–56.1	11.6	27.7
C	104.4	3	81.9–144.8	33.6	60.2	79.7	4	68.9–90.0	10.8	26.5
P^3	109.8	9	77.4–143.5	16.9	60.2	147.2	3	122.2–183.7	22.0	41.8
P^4	115.8	10	93.5–144.2	12.0	43.8	173.3	5	150.9–208.9	14.3	33.5
M^1	167.8	13	133.3–196.0	11.9	37.4	245.1	5	216.8–272.1	8.5	22.6
M^2	199.2	6	157.8–238.0	14.6	40.3	311.3	2	263.5–359.0		30.7
M^3	183.7	3	144.3–225.1	22.0	44.0	284.4	5	227.8–345.4	14.9	41.4
P^3–M^3	842.0	1				1215.5	2	1077.0–1354.0		22.8
Mandible										
I_1	39.6	4	34.2–44.1	11.2	25.0	39.0	4	34.2–40.9	8.3	17.2
I_2	52.3	4	49.7–57.0	6.9	14.0	42.3	2	39.7–44.9		12.3
C	82.5	4	59.8–100.0	20.3	48.7	76.2	4	63.8–85.9	12.3	29.0
P_3	109.7	5	96.9–127.6	11.8	28.0	138.2	5	108.1–182.0	20.8	53.5
P_4	108.7	6	96.0–123.9	10.2	25.7	189.7	10	137.6–227.9	15.9	47.6
M_1	164.1	14	130.7–202.3	12.5	43.6	233.5	8	165.1–314.2	17.9	63.9
M_2	189.9	10	136.9–234.9	16.4	51.6	272.0	12	182.0–333.0	18.5	55.5
M_3	190.3	10	150.8–235.2	15.1	44.4	297.3	14	212.9–418.0	17.5	69.0
P_3–M_3	762.5	2	660.0–865.0		26.9	1178.5	4	972.0–1340.0	14.4	31.2

	Gracile Australopithecine					Robust Australopithecine				
	Mean	N	Range (R)	CV	R/Mean	Mean	N	Range (R)	CV	R/Mean
Maxilla										
I^1	85.1	6	73.0–103.8	16.4	36.2	74.8	7	66.4–83.3	9.5	22.6
I^2	46.6	11	33.9–58.1	19.0	51.9	53.8	14	39.0–73.3	21.0	64.8
C	95.8	10	74.3–144.8	23.5	73.6	85.2	17	68.9–111.3	14.5	49.8
P^3	111.6	24	77.4–143.5	12.0	59.2	134.1	25	103.4–183.7	13.8	59.9
P^4	118.3	23	93.5–161.0	13.2	57.0	154.9	35	112.5–208.9	13.1	62.2
M^1	173.2	34	133.3–219.5	11.5	49.8	200.5	38	153.6–272.1	15.2	59.1
M^2	217.0	26	157.8–288.0	13.6	60.0	231.9	22	180.8–359.0	17.1	76.8
M^3	220.8	20	144.3–318.5	22.5	78.9	239.1	27	147.0–345.3	16.3	82.9
P^3–M^3	835.0	6	811.0–863.0	2.4	6.2	969.8	9	762.0–1354.0	17.3	61.0
Mandible										
I_1	36.9	8	29.3–44.1	14.9	40.1	37.9	8	34.2–40.9	6.9	17.7
I_2	52.0	9	46.0–59.5	9.5	26.7	45.6	5	39.7–50.3	8.4	23.3
C	83.9	11	59.8–101.2	15.5	49.3	75.7	13	63.8–97.2	12.7	44.1
P_3	113.9	15	94.6–143.9	12.4	43.3	120.9	23	85.0–182.0	18.2	80.2
P_4	133.6	14	96.0–137.5	9.6	36.5	156.5	27	104.0–227.9	22.3	79.2
M_1	175.9	28	130.7–247.0	15.6	66.1	205.3	31	144.0–134.2	16.1	82.9
M_2	208.4	24	136.9–277.2	16.0	67.3	243.9	35	155.0–333.0	17.7	73.0
M_3	209.1	22	150.8–280.4	16.4	62.0	261.9	37	181.6–418.0	19.2	90.3
P_3–M_3	838.0	8	660.0–953.0	12.0	35.0	1053.1	11	902.0–1340.0	13.8	41.6

Appendix (continued)

	All South Africa					All East Africa				
	Mean	N	Range (R)	CV	R/Mean	Mean	N	Range (R)	CV	R/Mean
Maxilla										
I^1	76.1	6	66.4–85.9	10.2	25.6	82.3	7	68.4–103.8	17.0	42.9
I^2	50.9	15	33.9–73.3	24.4	77.4	50.3	10	35.3–62.4	16.2	53.9
C	88.7	20	70.1–127.1	16.2	64.3	90.3	7	68.9–144.8	27.6	81.4
P^3	124.4	37	92.0–158.6	13.6	53.5	119.2	12	77.4–183.7	22.6	89.2
P^4	142.3	43	99.6–181.0	16.2	57.2	134.9	15	93.5–208.9	24.4	85.5
M^1	187.0	54	143.4–261.3	13.3	63.0	189.3	18	133.3–272.1	21.5	73.3
M^2	223.2	40	177.7–294.1	12.3	52.2	227.2	8	157.8–359.0	27.7	88.6
M^3	228.2	39	177.0–317.7	17.2	61.7	246.6	8	144.3–345.4	26.3	81.5
P^3–M^3	872.0	12	762.0–973.0	7.3	24.2	1091.0	3	842.0–1354.0	23.4	46.9
Mandible										
I_1	35.6	8	29.3–40.8	11.4	32.3	39.3	8	34.2–44.1	9.2	25.2
I_2	50.3	8	46.0–59.9	10.4	27.6	49.0	6	39.7–57.0	12.5	35.3
C	79.6	16	65.6–101.2	14.6	44.7	79.3	8	59.8–100.0	16.4	50.7
P_3	116.0	28	85.0–153.4	14.2	59.0	123.4	10	96.9–182.0	20.9	69.0
P_4	130.7	25	104.0–182.0	14.7	59.7	159.3	16	96.0–227.9	29.6	82.8
M_1	192.6	37	144.0–247.0	13.3	53.5	189.4	22	130.7–314.2	23.7	96.9
M_2	226.3	37	155.0–278.4	13.3	54.5	234.7	22	136.9–333.0	25.2	83.6
M_3	235.0	35	175.3–304.0	14.7	54.8	252.7	24	150.8–418.0	27.3	105.7
P_3–M_3	926.8	13	775.0–1076.0	10.1	32.5	1039.8	6	660.0–1340.0	25.0	65.4

References

Brain, C.K. (1967) Procedures and some results in the study of Quaternary cave fillings. In Bishop, W.W. and Clark, J.D. (eds.), *Background to evolution in Africa*, 285-301. Chicago.

Coppens, Y. (1970) Les restes d'hominidés des séries inférieures et moyennes des formations plio-villafranchiennes de l'Omo en Ethiopie. *C.R. Acad. Sci.*, Serie D, 271, 2286-9.

Coppens, Y. (1971) Les restes d'hominidés des séries supérieures des formations plio-villafranchiennes de l'Omo en Ethiopie. *C.R. Acad. Sci.*, Serie D, 272, 36-9.

Howell, F.C. (1969) Remains of hominidae from Pliocene/Pleistocene formations in lower Omo basin, Ethiopia. *Nature* 223, 1234-9.

Jones, C., and Pi, J.S. (1971) Coparative ecology of *Gorilla gorilla* (Savage and Wyman) and *Pan troglodytes* (Blumenbach) in Rio Muni, West Africa. *Biblio. Primat.* 13.

Leakey, R.E.F. (1972) Further evidence of lower Pleistocene hominids from East Rudolf, North Kenya, 1971. *Nature* 237, 264-9.

Leakey, R.E.F. (1973) Evidence for an advanced Plio-Pleistocene hominid from East Rudolf, Kenya. *Nature* 242, 447-50.

Lovejoy, C.O., Heiple, K.G. and Burstein, A.H. (1973) The gait of *Australopithecus*. *Amer. J. phys. Anthrop.*, 38, 757-80.

Mahler, P. (1973) Metric variation and tooth wear patterns in the dentition of *Gorilla gorilla*. Ph.D. Thesis, University of Michigan; University Microfilms, Ann Arbor.

Mann, A. (1968) The palaeodemography of *Australopithecus*. Ph.D. Thesis, University of California at Berkeley. University Microfilms, Ann Arbor.

Mayr, E. (1969) *Principles of Systematic Zoology*. New York.

Robinson, J.T. (1972) *Early Hominid Posture and Locomotion*. Chicago.

Simpson, G.G. (1953) *The Major Features of Evolution*. New York.

Tobias, P.V. (1973) Implications of the new age estimates of the early South African hominids. *Nature* 246, 79-83.

Wolpoff, M.H. (1971) *Metric Trends in Hominid Dental Evolution*. Case Western Reserve University Studies in Anthropology 2. Cleveland.

Wolpoff, M.H. (1973a) Posterior tooth size, body size, and diet in South African gracile australopithecines. *Amer. J. phys. Anthrop.* 39, 375-94.

Wolpoff, M.H. (1973b) The evidence for two australopithecine lineages in South Africa. *Ybk. phys. Anthrop.* 17, 113-39.

Wolpoff, M.H. (1973c) Sexual dimorphism in the australopithecines. Publication of the IXth International Congress of Anthropological and Ethnological Sciences.

Wolpoff, M.H. (1974) Sagittal cresting in the South African australopithecines. *Amer. J. phys. Anthrop.* 40, 397-408.

D. Pilbeam

Recognizing specific diversity in heterogeneous fossil samples

Apart from the rather intractable nature of much of the data, agreement about the course of human phylogeny has been more than a little hampered by a failure on the part of many of us to be sufficiently careful in outlining our hypotheses verbally, and in distinguishing between 'empirical' or 'verbal' hypotheses, and 'quantitative' or 'numerical' hypotheses. Only when they are explicitly articulated can empirical hypotheses be couched in the quantitative form generally necessary for their further evaluation (Pilbeam and Vaisnys, 1975). Perhaps as important is the need to enumerate ways in which each of our hypotheses might be refutable, and which kinds of evidence we would accept as disproving them.

Before tackling the problem of heterogeneity the most sensible course might be to review what is usually meant by homogeneity. Homogeneity can be defined both genetically and phenotypically. Homogeneous biological populations are those that are relatively panmictic (Mayr, 1963); continuous, non-dimorphic traits in such populations generally have probability density distributions that are normal or at least unimodal (Pilbeam and Zwell, 1972). Genetically, all interbreeding populations up to the level of species are, in this sense, at some level more or less homogeneous. They comprise compatible genotypes, clustering around an average or mean state, with progressively fewer genotypes departing from the average condition. Infraspecies populations in different geographical areas may be on average different one from another, yet viewed collectively each species will tend to be more or less homogeneous.

Medium and large mammals, because of their size and mobility, generally exhibit genetic homogeneity over areas of 10^5 or 10^6 sq.km. Populations of the same species inhabiting contiguous areas of similar size generally resemble one another in many features, although they may differ in some traits; rarely do adjacent populations show very marked differences, unless separated by barriers significant enough to affect gene flow. It seems unlikely that allopatric infraspecies populations connected by even moderate gene flow would become or remain very different over major periods of time (10^3 or 10^4 years).

Genetic homogeneity within a species is generally reflected in phenotypic homogeneity in most characters. In the case of polygenic traits, many are approximately normally distributed within species populations. However, because of sexual dimorphism in body size, certain characters will have bimodal distributions, although within sexes most of those features will be distributed in a unimodal and generally normal manner; traits such as body weight, femur diameter, and – in many mammals – canine size, will be distributed in this way with distinct peaks for males and females. But, even in very dimorphic species, certain traits will be unimodally and nearly normally distributed for the sexes considered together; brain volume, and linear and areal measurements of cheek teeth are examples of such characters (Pilbeam and Zwell, 1972).

Although many traits of genetically homogeneous species and intraspecies populations will be normal (and therefore in certain combinations multivariate normal), many of course will not be. It is possible nevertheless to obtain some estimate of the degree of non-normality usually to be expected in genetically homogeneous populations.

Populations of a species are rarely if ever ideally genetically homogeneous. Heterogeneity due to migration between contiguous areas and subsequent hybridization might be quite common. However, over lengthy periods of time, species populations are likely to remain relatively homogeneous. It is probably rare for two infraspecies populations, originally geographically distinct and therefore genetically different, to mix without significant introgression occurring within a relatively brief time period. Human populations often provide exceptions to this general rule.

In a purely descriptive sense, genetic heterogeneity can be said to exist within a particular area when two or more (generally related) species are present in that area. In such a case, in a sample containing more than one species, phenotypes will generally not be distributed in a way that is normal or multivariate normal, including those traits where normality or unimodality is typical even in strongly sexually dimorphic species. In many characters there will be little or no overlap, and distributions will be non-normal and often markedly bimodal. Cases are known where genetically rather similar species may be geographically contiguous or overlapping with little or no hybridization. In such instances, character divergence (Mayr, 1963) or displacement (Brown and Wilson, 1956) may occur in areas of sympatry, and so after a certain time sympatric populations of two species will become genetically and phenotypically more different from each other than their allopatric populations; the sympatric 'sample' will thus be more heterogeneous. However, this phenomenon is by no means universal and there are cases among mammals, including primates, where related species may be sympatric without significant hybridization, yet in a number of phenotypic characters remain or become quite similar. Species of *Cercopithecus* and *Macaca* illustrate this point well.

It is also generally possible to differentiate between populations of different species on the basic of morphology and proportions ('shape'), while populations of the same species can generally not be so easily distinguished. Thus, the contiguous populations of large and small baboons (*Papio c. cynocephalus* and *P. c. ursinus*), found in Zambia (Hill, 1970; Freedman, 1963) are both clearly baboons; such shape differences between them as there are can be interpreted as due to scaling or allometry (Gould, 1966; Freedman, 1962). However, both baboons can be readily distinguished from, say, the similarly-sized patas monkey or gelada baboon on the basis of many shape features that are unrelated to size.

Thus, the sources of genetic and phenotypic heterogeneity in particular living biological populations or aggregations are those due to sexual, infraspecies, and interspecies differences. However, in reconstructing past populations from palaeontological data, another factor must be considered: time.

Few fossil 'samples' actually include animals that lived at the same time. Even fossils from a single unit such as a 'living floor', or a thin sandstone lens representing a stream channel, probably rarely samples periods of less than about 10^2 or 10^3 years. There are, no doubt, exceptions to this. A group of ungulates may, for example, drown at the same time and be preserved as a sample; some living floors may also contain large numbers of animals killed at or about the same time. In both cases, the fossil sample may well contain animals from a genetically homogeneous biological population.

A species lineage, or infraspecific population lineages within it, may be evolving. Traits of fossils sampled from such a lineage or lineages over a significant period of time will probably not be distributed in a manner typical of living forms. However, certain features may still exhibit a unimodal distribution, albeit more variable than usual, particularly if evolution is slow and approximately constant.

Time is thus a difficult factor for the palaeontologist to cope with. However, it is sometimes possible to obtain samples from a rather restricted time range; from a lens deposited rapidly by a channel, for example; or from interglacial deposits that may collectively span no more than 1 or 2×10^4 years (Wright, 1972). This will keep the amount of heterogeneity due to time to a minimum. It is also possible, given sufficiently reliable stratigraphy or calibration, to note whether or not there are significant changes through time within sets of individuals sufficiently similar to be considered part of one lineage. Thus, specimens of the East African early Miocene pongid *Dryopithecus africanus* may well have remained dentally and gnathically stable for 2×10^6 years or more (Pilbeam, 1970). Segments of the

North American Eocene prosimian lineages classified as *Notharctus* species also probably exhibited stability over periods of 1 or 2 × 10^6 years. Indeed, it has been argued that lineages may exhibit during their evolution long periods of relative stasis, punctuated by brief periods of rapid change (so-called 'punctuated equilibrium') (Eldredge and Gould, 1972). However, it is clear that there are also many examples of periods during which steadier, more constant rates of evolution are typical ('phyletic gradualism') (Gingerich, 1972). Given sufficient sample sizes, appropriately distributed stratigraphically, it is often possible to tell whether there is or is not much change through time in an inferred species lineage.

In assessing heterogeneity in fossil populations it is important whenever possible to have samples or aggregates that are drawn from a relatively restricted geographical area, in order to keep variation due to infraspecies population mixing to a minimum, and also from a relatively restricted time range. Samples from different time periods can be pooled if little or no change is apparent in the traits under analysis.

As Wolpoff (above) has pointed out, each fossil is most likely a unique sample from a local breeding population or deme, although occasionally whole samples almost certainly do come from a single homogeneous local population. It has been argued that this 'constraint' must be taken into account in assessing variability in fossil assemblages. However, most museum collections of living forms that are used as reference populations to provide estimates of species or infraspecies population variability are subject to similar constraints. For example, collections of *Galago crassicaudatus* almost certainly sample almost as many demes as there are bushbabies in the collection.

In living species made up of many demes, there will generally be, on average, morphological differences between demes; variability within different demes is generally subequal. In human hunter-gatherer populations, and probably in other primate species that are relatively heterophenogamous, average demic differences are often relatively slight over quite wide areas (Yellen and Harpending, 1972). Also, for most continuously distributed traits, distributions of demic means are unimodal and close to normal, and these samples of means have low variances (as expressed by their coefficients of variation). Thus, a sample of mean endocranial volumes from eight African *Homo sapiens* populations (Martin and Saller, 1959) yield a V of less than 7; V's for endocranial volume in single *Homo sapiens* populations are generally much higher (Ashton and Spence, 1958).

If each fossil comes from a different deme, the fossil sample mean will be the best estimator of the mean of the demic means; the sample variance will reflect the spread of the means. Thus if a fossil assemblage shows high variability in one trait, or if, when several traits are considered together (thus taking into account 'shape') the fossil dispersion matrix is heterogeneous as compared to those derived from a single population, we may conclude that more than one species is being sampled. Even if, strictly speaking, we can know little about variability within 'fossil' demes, we can know a great deal about variability within a past species made up of demes.

Determination that samples are heterogeneous, particularly because of the presence of more than one related or similar species lineage, follows by comparison of trait distributions in the sample to those in appropriate living species. (The terms 'related' or 'similar' are used because most workers can, for example, sort perissodactyls from carnivores, bovids from suids, and cercopithecines from colobines, given appropriate parts.) Living species naturally do not provide us with rigid standards for comparison, yet it is possible to tell whether a fossil aggregate is more or less variable than, or as variable as, some, most, or all living species. Also, it is often possible to demonstrate whether the kind of variability observed in a sample is typical or atypical of extant forms. If a sample is shown to be more variable than might be expected, the possible sources of variability – temporal, sexual, infraspecific, specific – can then be evaluated.

The important point to establish is the likely presence of more than one species in a fossil assemblage. If fossils are sampled from, say, two species, these species may have been quite different in certain traits, and similar in others. It is important not to be too rigid in making comparisons based on analogy. The fact that two fossil hominids may not be, in cheek tooth size, as different as gorilla and chimpanzee could very well be irrelevant, particularly if dental morphology and proportions are as different, and endocranial volume and post-cranial morphology more different! We have no idea which differences between *Pan* and *Gorilla*, which mainly involve size rather than allometrically corrected shape (Giles, 1956; Pilbeam and Gould, 1974), are features necessary to maintaining species distinction. It would certainly be dangerous to conclude that size differences are the main ones separating related sympatric species. Species of the fossil ape genus *Dryopithecus* are found together in Miocene localities even though some of them were not particularly different in size. Among living cercopithecoids, size overlap between sympatric species is very common.

Methodologically, it is easiest to begin an analysis with characters that are approximately normally distributed even in sexually dimorphic populations (Pilbeam and Zwell, 1972). As noted before, good examples of such traits are brain volumes and cheek tooth areas; following this, relative variability of single measurements can be assessed using either the coefficient of variation or, better, the variance of the log measurements; departures from normality (kurtosis and skew) can be tested. Comparisons of multivariate variability between fossil assemblages and 'standard' living samples can be made quite easily, for example, by comparing dispersion matrices using Wilkes'

Lambda criterion (Tatsuoka, 1971). Whether or not the 'scatter' of individuals in hyperspace is typical of homogeneous populations can be assessed by looking at the set of interindividual distances, for example, by such a simple method as the Mann-Whitney U-test (Zwell, pers. comm.).

Multivariate comparisons are important because they permit analyses of relationships between variables. Thus, in most sexually dimorphic populations males have larger cheek teeth, on average, than females, and also larger brains. It will be readily apparent if two subsets within a sample segregate under multivariate analysis because one has large teeth and small brains, the other small teeth and large brains.

Collectively, such analyses enable one to state whether or not, and by how much, a fossil aggregation is more variable than certain specified living species, and also whether the variability is of a different kind than might be expected within a species. It is then often possible to segregate a fossil (or living) assemblage into more than one 'kind', 'morph', or 'type'. This can be done, and most frequently is done, intuitively; however, a variety of quantitative techniques are available for sorting individuals into subsamples (Principal Components and Principal Coordinates Analysis are two of the best known methods). Once this is accomplished, the question then becomes what the subsets represent. Are they different sexes of a dimorphic species? Or are they infraspecies populations? (This would be perhaps less likely if the differences apparently persisted through time.) Or are they sampled from separate species lineages(Decisions on these matters are again made on the basis of analogy with living forms (Pilbeam and Vaišnys, 1975). Thus, if two subsamples are significantly more different in attributes considered singly or collectively than would reasonably be expected if they represented different sexes or infraspecies populations, then the most reasonable conclusion is that they probably represent distinct species.

The thorny problem of Pliocene and early Pleistocene hominids (those between 5 m.y. and, possibly, 1 m.y.) can now be tackled. There is a considerable amount of material, mostly jaws and teeth, of these early hominids. South African specimens come from sites, some of which may span up to 10^5 years or more (Butzer, 1971, above; Brain, above), where calibration has proved difficult; there is as yet no accepted dated stratigraphic scheme, the main problem being the total lack of radiometric age determinations. The expanding East African early hominid sample is, on the other hand, very well calibrated (Bishop and Miller, 1972). Three relatively long sequences are known, the Omo River region in Ethiopia, the area east of Lake Rudolf in Kenya, and Olduvai Gorge in Tanzania.

Disagreements over taxonomy abound. Hominids have been classified into one, two, or more species lineages; nomenclatures too may be widely divergent, but this is less important than agreeing on the number of lineages. Although the bulk of the material found up to the 1950s came from South Africa, the more recently recovered East African hominids are superior for settling at least the question of the number of species lineages sampled. This is because, in a relatively restricted geographical area, sequences are well calibrated and yield relatively large samples of hominids that are as heterogeneous as any late Cenozoic hominids. They span the time from more than 4 m.y. to less than 1.5 m.y. (Bishop and Miller, 1972). At Olduvai they are sampled mainly from deposits 1.85 to some 1.6 m.y. old; at the Omo they are concentrated between 2.5 and 3 m.y. and between 1.6 or 1.7 and 2 m.y.; at East Rudolf they are abundant between 1.5 and around 2 m.y. (Whatever the exact age of the KBS tuff at East Rudolf, faunal material from above the tuff is probably not much older than 2 m.y.) Thus, there is a fairly good East African hominid sample from 2 m.y. or a little less to 1.5 m.y. or a little more, mostly consisting of jaws and teeth, with some cranial and postcranial remains. Little or no change in known parts can be observed through this time period.

In many features this assemblage shows high variability (Pilbeam and Zwell, 1972; Pilbeam and Vaišnys, 1975). Thus, cheek teeth are, in the main, very significantly more variable in linear and areal dimensions than those of other primate samples, including species that are highly sexual dimorphic (for example, *Papio* and *Gorilla* species) or infraspecifically variable (*Homo sapiens*). Multivariate analyses indicate the same conclusion. The overall pattern of variation also appears to be different from that typical of living mammals; forms with large cheek teeth have small anterior dentitions, small brains, and, apparently, postcranials that are rather morphologically distinct from those of individuals with larger and (externally) contrasting brains, small cheek teeth, and large (relatively and/or absolutely) incisors and canines. The sample can be segregated into at least two groups exhibiting little or no overlap in a number of characters, and few measurable changes through time. This much is generally agreed.

However, interpretations vary. Variability in these hominids is greater than, and different in kind from, that due to sexual dimorphism or variability within contiguous infraspecific populations in most if not all mammals. From these observations I, along with many others, deduce that more than one species lineage is being sampled. Conversely, it is possible to assume *a priori* that only one 'cultural' hominid lineage can ever have existed (the 'single species hypothesis'); the high variability is then accepted, viewed as a peculiarity of these early hominids (Brace, 1967; Wolpoff, 1971). The problem with this hypothesis as an explanation of the data is that there is no obvious way in which it can potentially be refuted since the data are initially assumed to belong to only one lineage.

At this point it is worth making a few general comments about hypothesis testing. Without being too rigid, one can distinguish between at least two classes of hypotheses; what have been called 'verbal' or 'empirical' hypotheses (also, 'propositions'), and 'quantitative' or 'numerical' hypotheses (Pilbeam and Vaišnys, 1975). As an example, a verbal hypothesis might be: 'Only a single hominid species lineage is being sampled between 2 and 1.5×10^6 years ago; this lineage changed relatively little during that time, and its genetic variability was insignificantly different from that of related polytypic, strongly sexually dimorphic primates living today.' Assuming this proposition (or set of propositions) to be correct, a series of quantitative statements or hypotheses can be generated; for example: 'The probability density distribution of M_1 lengths should be close to normal, as it is in most related living species, with specified mean and variance, μ and σ^2.' The verbal proposition can then be assayed by 'experiments' on these quantitative hypotheses.

There are various ways of testing such quantitative hypotheses. One involves setting up a 'null hypothesis' (H_0), generally so that an observed sample value, or difference between sample values, is assumed due to chance alone, because the parametric value or difference under H_0 is actually zero. A test is then selected (for example, t- or F-), and a rejection level chosen (usually the .05 level). If the calculated test statistic exceeds the value of the statistic expected to occur *by chance alone* only 5% of the time, then H_0 is said to be rejected at that probability level. Strict adherents of null hypothesis testing methods would argue that H_0 can only be disproved, never confirmed, by an experiment or test.

Many workers would consider this an unduly rigid approach. A second 'school' of hypothesis testing points out that there are two kinds of errors that can be made: rejecting H_0 when it is true (so-called Type I error) and accepting H_0 when it is false (Type II error). This school prefers to take two hypotheses, test both against the data, and make a choice between them. In many ways, this is superior to a strict null hypothesis approach because it treats hypothesis testing not so much as a restrictive choice between two outcomes ('false' or 'unconfirmed'), but as a means by which hypotheses can be adjusted and modified by data and experiments. This corresponds more closely to the way in which both scientific inference and the human mind operate.

A third approach is that adopted by the so-called Bayesians (Thomas Bayes was an eighteenth-century clergyman and statistician). Bayes derived the relation:

$$p(H/D) = \frac{p(D/H) \cdot p(H)}{p(D)}$$

where H is the hypothesis, D the data, p(H/D) the probability of H given D (what we would like to find out), and so on; p(H) is the probability of the hypothesis based on information before the data, D, are utilized – the prior or *a priori* probability. The way in which such a probability is assigned can be rather subjective, depending on 'feelings' or 'intuition', and hence Bayesians are sometimes dismissed as 'unscientific', particularly by those who would view 'probability' strictly as a quantitative relation between the frequency of a particular event in a class and the frequency of all possible events of that class. However, there is a more general definition of probability (Baierlein, 1971, p.15): 'A quantitative relation, between a hypothesis and an inference, corresponding to the degree of rational belief in the correctness of the inference, given the hypothesis', which brings us closer to the basis of scientific methodology, concerning belief in the truth of statements.

Bayes' relation can be modified (Pilbeam and Vaišnys, 1975) in order to compare two hypotheses (H_1 and H_2) with respect to a single data set (D). Thus:

$$\frac{p(H_1/D)}{p(H_2/D)} = \frac{p(H_1)}{p(H_2)} \quad \frac{p(D/H_1)}{p(D/H_2)}$$

Hence, we calculate the *relative* probability of the two hypotheses given one set of data, by multiplying what is a kind of likelihood ratio by the ratio of prior probabilities. If we wish to be conservative, or pass no judgments in favour of either hypothesis, $P(H_1)/p(H_2)$ can be set at 1; or, alternatively, at any value we deem reasonable.

Again, it should be emphasized that there is a real contrast in approach here. The null hypothesis 'school' is interested in deciding whether or not to reject H_0 (regardless of the fact that H_0 is rarely true!), whereas the other 'schools' are concerned with adjusting a hypothesis and a set of data, or with comparing several hypotheses, in order to strengthen rational beliefs. The Bayesian approach is seen by some as a further refinement permitting considerable scientific flexibility. Having evaluated quantitative hypotheses in some way, we can proceed back to our original empirical hypotheses.

Many times we behave as though these two distinct classes of hypotheses were equivalent. Thus, we talk about testing verbal 'null' hypotheses; it is frequently claimed that the 'single species hypothesis' is a 'null' hypothesis (comparable to a statistical H_0 of no parametric difference) because it is the 'simplest' hypothesis. But in what way is it 'simple', other than the purely trivial sense in which one is 'simpler' than two, or two simpler than three? On the contrary, considering all I know *a priori* about the hominid fossil record, nature, biology, etc., I could very well argue that the hypothesis to be disproved ought to be one invoking several species to explain the observed data. But why stake all on the formal analysis of only one hypothesis? Why not evaluate several? After all, that is what I do at an informal or 'intuitive' level all the time.

However, if it can be agreed that uniformitarian comparisons, as long as they are made flexibly, are appropriate for evaluating palaeontological data, then it can be stated with reasonable confidence that, on the basis of present knowledge, hominids in East

Africa around 1.75 ± .15 × 10^6 years ago were significantly more heterogeneous than one would expect were they sampled only from different sexes or contiguous populations within a single species lineage.

Acknowledgments

I would like to thank Stephen Gould, Carol Pilbeam, Rimas Vaišnys, and Michael Zwell for stimulating and provocative discussions.

References

Ashton, E.H., and Spence, T.F. (1958) Age changes in the cranial capacity and foramen magnum of hominoids, *Proc. Zool. Soc. Lond.* 130, 169-81.

Baierlein, R. (1971) *Atoms and Information Theory*. San Francisco.

Bishop, W.W. and Miller, J.A. (eds.) (1972) *Calibration of Hominoid Evolution*. Edinburgh.

Brain, C.K., this volume.

Brace, C.L. (1967) *The Stages of Human Evolution*. Englewood Cliffs, N.J.

Brown, W.L. and Wilson, E.O. (1956) Character displacement. *Syst. Zool.* 5, 49-64.

Butzer, K.W. (1971) Another look at the australopithecine cave breccias of the Transvaal. *Amer. Anthrop.* 73, 1197-201.

Butzer, K.W., this volume.

Eldredge, N. and Gould, S.J. (1972) Punctuated equilibria: an alternative to phyletic gradualism. In Schopf, T.J.M. (ed.), *Models in Paleobiology*, 82-115. San Francisco.

Freedman, L. (1962) Growth of muzzle length relative to calvaria length in *Papio*. *Growth* 26, 117-28.

Freedman, L. (1963) A biometric study of *Papio cynocephalus* skulls from Northern Rhodesia and Nyasaland. *J. Mammal.* 44, 24-43.

Giles, E. (1956) Cranial allometry in the great apes. *Hum. Biol.* 28, 43-58.

Gingerich, P.D. (1976) Paleontology and phylogeny: patterns of evolution at the species level in early Tertiary mammals. *Amer. J. Sci.* 276, 1-28.

Gould, S.J. (1966) Allometry and size in ontogeny and phylogeny. *Biol. Rev.* 41, 587-640.

Hill, W.C.O. (1970) *Primates* Vol. VIII. New York.

Martin, R. and Saller, K. (1959) *Lehrbuch der Anthropologie*. Stuttgart.

Mayr, E. (1963) *Animal Species and Evolution*. Harvard.

Pilbeam, D. (1970) Tertiary Pongidae of East Africa: evolutionary relationships and taxonomy. *Peabody Mus. Bull.*, 31.

Pilbeam, D. and Gould, S.J. (1974) Size and scaling in human evolution. *Science*, 186, 892-901.

Pilbeam, D. and Vaišnys, J.R. (1975) Hypothesis testing in paleoanthropology. In Tuttle, R.H. (ed.), *Paleoanthropology, Morphology and Paleoecology*, 3-13. The Hague.

Pilbeam, D. and Zwell, M. (1972) The single species hypothesis, sexual dimorphism, and variability in early hominids. *Yb. phys. Anthrop.* 16, 69-79.

Tatsuoka, M. (1971) *Multivariate Analysis.* New York.

Wolpoff, M.H. (1971) Competitive exclusion among lower Pleistocene hominids: the single species hypothesis. *Man* 6, 601-14.

Wolpoff, M.H. this volume.

Wright, H.E. (1972) Interglacial and postglacial climates: the pollen record. *Quat. Res.* 2, 274-82.

Yellen, J. and Harpending, H. (1972) Hunter-gatherer populations and archaeological inference. *World Arch.* 4, 244-53.

E. Delson

Models of early hominid phylogeny

Fifty years or more after Dart's original recognition and description of *Australopithecus*, we are at last learning enough to propose meaningful hypotheses about the evolutionary history of these early hominids. New sites are being discovered at the rate of nearly one per year, some are producing new specimens at a prodigious speed and interpretive studies of function and variation are providing the data base from which evolutionary studies must build. Today there are at least three major schools of thought about the pattern of evolution and the related systematic placement of the early hominids, as well as a number of variants or nearly discarded prior hypotheses. The purpose of this conference has been to consider the present state of our knowledge of selected aspects of early hominid palaeobiology and to look ahead toward new problems and strategies for their solution. I will try to follow this course with regard to phylogeny and systematics, first briefly describing the main theoretical models of early hominid evolution and then considering how some new trends in general evolutionary and phylogenetic thought may be applied to them. The aim is to determine whether present hypotheses can be tested and compared so as to select the most reasonable and likely among them. I have previously argued (Delson and Andrews, 1975) and still consider that Hominidae should include all living Hominoidea, with Homininae for *Homo* and related fossils, but in the spirit of this conference, I will here use 'hominid' in its more familiar restricted sense.

Competing models of early hominid evolution

Perhaps the most recent interpretation of the phylogeny of early hominids to be strongly championed is that known as the single-species hypothesis. The basic conclusion of this school is that the observed variation among Plio-Pleistocene hominids can best be explained as regional and temporal variability within one presumably culture-bearing species. The brunt of the presentation of this viewpoint has been borne by Brace and Wolpoff, with numerous papers outlining the hypothesis and investigating aspects thereof (e.g. Brace, 1973; Brace, Mahler and Rosen, 1973; Wolpoff, 1968, 1970, 1971a, 1971b, 1971c, 1973, 1975 and this volume). The argument rests on two central postulates: (1) the cultural nature of hominid adaptation; and (2) a rather high degree of variation in early hominids by comparison with variation in the same characters in modern man and modern pongids. In dealing with the first point, Wolpoff (1971c, p.601) wrote that 'because of cultural adaptation, all hominid species occupy the same, extremely broad, adaptive niche. For this reason, allopatric hominid species would become sympatric (leading to) the continued survival of only one hominid lineage'. In that paper, Wolpoff argued that in both canine and summed cheek-tooth size (area), the ranges for 'gracile' and 'robust' australopiths[1] overlapped broadly and were comparable in variability to those of a broad series of modern human populations. Brace (1973) later suggested that sexual dimorphism within a given australopith population might be expected to be larger than that in a single *H. sapiens* population, being more comparable perhaps to that in larger non-human primates. He also indicated that absolute dental size does not clearly distinguish the 'gracile' Sterkfontein form from the 'robust' Swartkrans variety (although the latter argument is weakened when one realizes the 'Telanthropus' mandibles SK 15 and SK 45 were included in the comparisons). Finally, Wolpoff has indicated (1) that there is most probably moderate sexual dimorphism in canine area among australopiths and that it may be possible to sex isolated teeth, albeit with some uncertainty (1975); (2) that absolute size of cheek teeth (P3-M3) in 'gracile' australopiths from South Africa broadly overlaps that in gorillas of much larger body size (1973); and (3) that the absolute dental size differences between 'graciles' and 'robusts' may not be as great as previously thought, with coefficients of variation for pooled samples being only moderately higher in most variates than those for samples divided taxonomically by other authors (this volume). It must be emphasized that the latter two points, namely the large absolute size of 'gracile' australopith cheek teeth and their metrical similarity to those of 'robusts', are observations of great value previously overlooked by many authors. It may also be noted that the origin of the single-lineage idea derives from studies of the South African fossils, with East African specimens discussed only in some of the latest contributions.

The other, by far more common, view of australopith evolution

1. The term 'australopith' is used here, rather than 'australopithecine', as it carries no connotation of the existence of a subfamily (or tribe) 'Australopithecinae'. 'Gracile' and 'robust' are quoted here because the former, as smallish animals of moderate to heavy build, with cheek teeth absolutely as large as those of gorillas, may not fit the usual image of gracility.

recognizes at least two lineages of early hominids. Distinctions can be drawn between 'schools' on the basis of the number of lineages recognized, which this conference has shown to be still an open question, or of other features. I consider the most meaningful basis for comparison to be each model's determination of the character complexes likely to be found in the common ancestor of the known 'graciles' and 'robusts'. In one view, espoused mainly by Robinson (1954, 1956, 1961, 1967, 1971, 1972, this volume; Robinson and Steudel, 1973), the characters observed in 'robust' australopiths or *Paranthropus* are considered to correspond best with those expected in a common ancestor. In his studies, Robinson has attempted to show that the 'robust' form is more ape-like than the 'gracile' in a number of characters, especially in the post-cranial skeleton, the larger cheek teeth, lower skull vault and small brain, while being 'hyper-hominid' in certain other features, such as ischial length, premolar molarization and especially the greatly reduced anterior dentition relative to cheek-tooth size. The dietary model which Robinson proposed to explain these differences suggested that the 'robust' forms were pongid-like vegetarians, while the 'graciles' and their *Homo* descendants incorporated a steadily increasing percentage of hunted or scavenged meat in their diets, with concomitant reduction of the gnathic apparatus required. In his more recent work (since 1967), Robinson has advocated the formal inclusion of *Australopithecus* in the genus *Homo*, while retaining *Paranthropus* for the known 'robust' forms and the presumed much earlier common ancestors of both lineages.

In opposition to this view is the model advocated, in one form or another, by most researchers. This recognizes the distinctions between 'robust' and 'gracile' forms drawn by Robinson and others, but holds that the latter morph represents less divergence away from the ancestral pattern while nonetheless leading broadly to later hominids. On the other hand, the 'robust' forms are seen as a younger, derived offshoot following a separate evolutionary course and leaving no known descendants. The variants in this model depend on the recognition of more than one variety of 'gracile' australopith, such as *Homo habilis* or the taxon represented by KNM-ER 1470 and 1590, etc. Similarly, formal classification schemes vary among supporters of this model, depending upon both taxonomic philosophy and the number of different morphological types recognized (2, 3 or 4). Such authors as Campbell (1972, this volume), Howell (1967, 1972, this volume), Howells (1973), Jolly (1970), R.E.F. Leakey (1973a, 1973b, this volume), Pilbeam (1972, 1973, this volume), Pilbeam and Gould (1974), Szalay (1975), Tobias (1967, 1973a, 1973b, this volume) and Walker (1976) represent a sampling of opinions and interpretations. Some nearly agree with Robinson taxonomically but prefer an *A. africanus*-like ancestor, others accept numerous independent lines from a basically 'gracile' but unspecified common ancestor. Further comment on some views will be presented at relevant points below. At present, having hastily reviewed the state-of-the-art, it is possible to look farther afield.

New developments in systematic methodology

During the past decade, two schools of systematic philosophy have arisen in opposition to certain views and methods of the 'New Systematics' of the 1940s, which today may be called the accepted or 'classical' school ('evolutionary' to its practitioners; see Hull, 1970 or Simpson, 1975). The 'numerical' or phenetic approach has been concerned with computational reduction of large masses of observational and metrical data in order to indicate the relative similarity among samples without *a priori* weighting of observations. On the other hand, the cladistic or 'phylogenetic' approach has been to concentrate on the distinction between 'derived' versus 'ancestral' characters in the assessment of relationships, which method has been developed along with a number of more controversial, though minor, points. Each of these schools has valuable techniques and methods which can profitably be integrated into the 'evolutionary' approach; the latter in turn must be more widely infused into certain branches of palaeontological study. Forsten's 1973 study, for instance, applies them to *Hipparion*, which exhibits numerous similarities with the australopiths. The application of such methods to the models discussed above may enable us to see ways of testing certain hypotheses and suggest new directions for future, more intensive research.

It is always dangerous to try to isolate one part of a hypothesis or model to test in a short review, because both sides of the argument may feel cheated by the lack of space allowed. Nonetheless, I think it fair to say that proponents of the single-lineage hypothesis, having made a set of assumptions about culture-bearing hominids, spend a majority of their writings in discussion of metrical attributes (i.e., size) of specimens and the overlap between the groups compared. Multi-lineage models, on the contrary, appear to rest on considerations of proportions and 'observational morphology', not directly based on metrical comparisons. It seems best to begin with a consideration of the single-lineage model, primarily because it is the simplest.

Metrical phenetics and the single-lineage hypothesis

Multivariate analyses

Out of the numerous studies employing a 'numerical taxonomic' approach have developed new types of computational methods which may be applied to metrical and other quantifiable data. Also valuable has been the realization that these methods must be applied carefully, that the most appropriate statistic should be used to test the precise hypothesis under consideration (see Kowalski, 1972; Pilbeam and Vaišnys, 1975), and that care must be taken with samples of small size added in to the analysis either initially or afterward (see Oxnard, 1972; Andrews and Williams, 1973). The study by Brace, Mahler and Rosen (1973) may in part illustrate a failure to consider these *caveats*.

In a multivariate discriminant function analysis of fossil and modern hominid mandibular tooth areas, these authors found that Olduvai Hominid 13 always grouped with their *Homo erectus* sample, while OH 7 fell with *Australopithecus* (or with 'gracile' rather than 'robust' forms when that distinction was made). This was interpreted to mean that the linking of OH 7 and OH 13 in the taxon *Homo habilis* could not be substantiated. They did *not* mention certain aspects of these results which render the outcome more equivocal. First, in any discriminant function analysis, the test is inappropriate unless it can be assumed that the unknowns actually were drawn from one of the reference populations. For this reason, the technique is excellent for determining sex and often race. But the question to be investigated here was precisely whether the two fossils belonged to *either* of the 'given' populations, so that a discriminant function was perhaps not the best approach to use. Moreover, their Tables 7 and 8 show that OH 13 was always much further (in terms of the D^2 statistic) from the group mean of *H. erectus* than other specimens listed, while OH 7 was further from the mean of *A. africanus*, although not the furthest from the mean when all australopiths were pooled. This may reflect the composite nature of the combined sample, revealed in the clearer results of the test in which 'graciles' and 'robusts' were separated. The results of this second test would also tend to reject the single-lineage hypothesis on the authors' own criteria, but they discount this conclusion as premature because of sampling problems. Unfortunately, this is true of the whole exercise. The lack of discussion of the 'inconvenient' D^2 values exemplifies the ease with which statistical results may be only partly interpreted and conclusions thus altered. Further, the problem of cranial capacity, dealt with in more detail by Pilbeam and Vaišnys (1975), is not considered at all. It must finally be added that while I disagree with those who claim that use of the computer to analyse 'inoffensive early hominid dental data' is 'statistical overkill' (Brace *et al*., 1973, p.64) – I would emphasize that the more sophisticated the techniques utilized in any field of study, the greater must be the care taken not to misuse them.

Another aspect of the problem is that the data of both Brace (1973) and Wolpoff (see below) do not reveal a major difference in absolute size between the 'gracile' and 'robust' early hominids, especially those from South Africa. On this point, their data clearly support their interpretations. But the main reason for separating the two forms dentally has not been one of absolute size difference, but one of proportion within individual specimens (see Robinson, 1971; Robinson and Steudel, 1973), a point which is little discussed by the single-lineage advocates. Wolpoff has discussed canine size, posterior tooth size and for this conference all tooth sizes, but without mention of Robinson's claims of major differences in the proportion of anterior and cheek teeth, especially of C and P3. Robinson's latest dental study (Robinson and Steudel, 1973) reiterated this distinction with the aid of a multivariate analysis, although again utilizing discriminant functions instead of a less 'canalized' technique such as cluster analysis. Wolpoff's data in this volume do not reveal a great distinction between South and East African 'gracile' and 'robust' australopiths in the ratio of C to P3 tooth areas. This, however, may be due to the inclusion of all available isolated teeth, where, as Robinson has long maintained, this comparison applies only to teeth derived from single individuals. The main value of considering all available specimens is obviously to increase sample size, which is important in certain analyses, but not meaningful in the consideration of intra-individual proportions. The examination of individuals, even in limited numbers, does support the comparisons drawn by Robinson in both South and East Africa.

Models of variation in early hominids

The matter of sample size and selection is of great importance in the study of variation. In response to Wolpoff's (1971c) review summarized above, Shaklee (1973) argued that the comparison of two samples by means of a *t*-test may yield quite different results depending on sample size and internal variation among other factors. Thus, with a larger sample, or with less variable features chosen, Wolpoff's finding of no significant difference between hominid populations in molar tooth size might be reversed. Bilsborough (1972) further noted that Wolpoff has compared variation in australopiths from part of one continent to that in modern (or later fossil) populations from a much larger area (and with very different cultural patterns), thus possibly biasing the comparison: less variability in the modern populations chosen would result in the australopiths appearing more variable, in opposition to Wolpoff's argument. The matter of the 'best' or most reasonable model to use in the evaluation of variability in fossil hominid populations is one which Wolpoff has explicitly discussed only once (this volume). As the choice of model will strongly influence the significance of the results and their effect on the hypothesis under consideration, it is important to consider this matter further.

Wolpoff (this volume) makes several points which indicate his views on the choice of a model for comparing variation in fossil samples. First, he argues that no two fossils can be assumed to have belonged to a single biological population, except in the case of certain late human burials or other rare cases. This is, of course, true not only of human palaeontology, but for all fossils as well as most museum collections. Vertebrate palaeontologists and other zoologists have long accepted this reasoning. There seems little need to discuss it at length today; one need merely employ the usual cautionary procedures and assumptions.

In direct opposition to Bilsborough's comment, Wolpoff argues that 'single population samples from populations within the same taxon cannot be used to estimate the mean, variance or range of any individual population, but can only be used to derive such estimators for the taxon as a whole'. More specifically, he reasons that a sample of N fossil individuals should be compared metrically to N modern populations, not to N modern individuals of one (local) population. Following directly from this is Wolpoff's further hesitation to utilize fossils from only one site to estimate the statistical parameters of a sample. He suggests employing all the available fossils grouped together, as this will have no effect other than to increase the sample size, for sampling is already being done from the total universe of populations of the taxon. If specimens from one site were no more likely to be related biologically than those from different sites, this argument might be partially valid, but it actually seems more likely that specimens of a single phenon[2] from a single locality will in fact be more closely related biologically than specimens chosen at random from that same phenon (or taxon), even if they did not belong to an single breeding population at a particular time. Furthermore, if the prior step of only comparing N fossils with N populations is accepted (and I feel this needs more rigorous mathematical and biological proof), the next step only holds true if the comparison is made between the fossils and modern populations. If fossils from one locality or group of localities, all identified as belonging to a single phenon, are compared to an equivalent number of fossils from one or more sites of another phenon, the problem may diminish if not vanish. In fact, a sample from one site may be compared to a sample from another site if both contain sufficient individuals to provide a 'reasonable estimate' of their respective population parameters (but how many is a 'reasonable' number?), or the pooled sample from a number of sites may be compared with a similar pooled sample. This is especially useful if it is known that only one species is represented at the site(s) used as a standard of comparison. It may even be possible

2. The term 'phenon' is used here in the sense of Mayr (1969) (not that of the numerical taxonomists) to designate a morphologically relatively uniform sample. As will be seen below, specimens may be sorted into phena, or morphs, and then grouped into taxa in successive stages of a study. Obviously, one does not wish seriously to compare tooth size in large pigs and small elephants, for example, just to show that they can overlap, nor is the comparison of the more metrically and morphologically similar teeth of peccaries, phenacodonts and dryopiths of any value. Hence the assumption that phena (or members of single species, genera, etc.) are being compared.

to employ skeletons of modern mammals in this way, but this involves the problem of the equation of temporal and geographic variation treated well by Wolpoff and which I do not wish to discuss at greater length.

Having thus suggested an escape from part of Wolpoff's problem, we can turn to why he did not take such a route, which depends on the taxonomic choice of model. Wolpoff argues that the modern 'baboons are probably the closest ecological counterparts to the early hominids', but rejects them because of their great variability in favour of the modern pongids and hominids, less ecologically comparable but taxonomically closer to australopiths. Moreover, discussion during the course of the conference revealed an attempt to restrict comparison to those groups which are phyletically closest to the animals under study, in order to maximize genetic similarities underlying morphological variation. I agree that comparison is best between closely related forms, but suggest that cercopithecids are close enough to hominids to be used. Moreover, if we are to use fossil populations as models, we must seek situations in which only one species is 'known' to be present in the sample. The African dryopith samples of the Early Miocene would be eminently useful in this case, but they suffer from the same problem as the early hominids – how many species are to be recognized in the samples? (see Andrews, 1974). In fact, modern baboons today are in the same boat, with the results of genetic, behavioural and morphologic studies indicating the possibility of all 'savannah' baboons – *Papio (Chaeropithecus)* – being part of an enormously polytypic single species with semi-restricted gene flow in certain areas (Jolly and Brett, 1973). On the other hand, there are some fossil monkeys which meet both requirements: single taxon at a site (not true of Plio-Pleistocene African forms) and apparent open-country adaptations. The most interesting of these for our purposes is *Mesopithecus pentelici* (Delson, 1973, 1975a).

This species is known mainly from southern Europe and south-western Asia during the Turolian mammal age (*c.* 10-5 m.y.). Most localities are in the southern Balkans and associated with an open-country but not intensely arid fauna. A second species referred to this genus, *?M. monspessulanus*, appears to have evolved from *M. pentelici* at the end of the Miocene and continues in approximately the same range through the Pliocene, but with a possible decrease in terrestrial adaptations. This change might in part be due to the spread at this time of the sympatric, large, highly terrestrial *Dolichopithecus ruscinensis*, possibility also derived from *M. pentelici*. Each of these species is known mainly from the sample at its type locality, with smaller numbers of individuals referred from several other localities; *M. pentelici* is the sole cercopithecid at the localities in which it occurs (Delson, 1974). Neither species is polytypic as now understood, but part of the polytypy of australopiths results from the unwarranted pooling of dissimilar phena in Wolpoff's tabulations.

Table 1 Estimators of variability in molar area of *Mesopithecus* species

Taxon / *Locality*	M^1 Area *Mean*	*N*	*CV*	*RMI*	M^2 Area *Mean*	*N*	*CV*	*RMI*	M^3 Area *Mean*	*N*	*CV*	*RMI*
M. pentelici												
Pikermi	46.09	27	7.7	33.3	54.35	26	7.4	26.7	47.16	25	10.1	36.6
all	46.51	30	7.8	33.2	54.70	32	7.1	21.5	46.96	29	9.6	36.8

	M_1 Area *Mean*	*N*	*CV*	*RMI*	M_2 Area *Mean*	*N*	*CV*	*RMI*	M_3 Area *Mean*	*N*	*CV*	*RMI*
M. pentelici												
Pikermi	40.11	23	7.7	27.4	48.72	34	7.8	30.6	57.46	32	9.0	38.6
other	41.20	10	11.7	36.4	53.07	9	5.4	17.3	63.27	9	6.0	20.5
all	40.44	33	9.2	37.1	49.63	43	8.1	30.6	58.73	41	9.2	37.8
?M. monspessulanus												
Montpellier					39.73	5	10.8	29.8	52.54	6	9.3	23.2
other					42.10	5	14.1	35.5	51.90	4	13.3	32.0
all					40.91	10	12.2	36.7	52.29	10	10.3	31.8
Mesopithecus spp.												
all					47.99	53	11.3	50.1	57.47	51	10.4	48.6

In order to provide material for comparison with that supplied by Wolpoff on early hominid dental size, calculations of tooth areas were made for the upper and lower molars of these species, grouped in a number of ways. Most data are provided for *M. pentelici*, which has both the largest sample sizes and was probably ecologically most similar to the early hominids. Table 1 lists the mean values (M), sample sizes (N), coefficient of variation (CV = 100 sd/m), and range-mean index (RMI = 100 R/M) for each sample. As regards the CV, Simpson, Roe and Lewontin (1961) note that values between 5 and 10 (especially 5-7) may be average for *linear* variates in a homogeneous sample, while higher values (above 15 for many workers) *tend* to indicate heterogeneity. As this study is made on *areal* variates, a higher score would be expected, especially for the cercopithecids: because of the shape of these teeth, the area was calculated from the formula $\frac{1}{2}$(anterior breadth + posterior breadth) × length.

Interpretation is made more difficult because Wolpoff provides no data on specimens from a single site, but Table 1 reveals that for the six molar teeth, samples of 25 to 34 Pikermi *M. pentelici* have CVs ranging from 7.4 to 10.1 and RMI from 26.7 to 38.6. Samples of 9 or 10 lower molars from up to seven localities show a CV between 5 and 12, RMI from 17 to 37 (values rounded off). Finally, the pooling of all *M. pentelici* specimens results in generally the same values with less inter-tooth variation (N=29-43; CV=7.1-9.6; RMI=21.5-37.8). For $M_{2\text{-}3}$, it was further possible to examine values for *M. monspessulanus*, tentatively considered as a distinct species by Delson (1973). With sample sizes about 5 for teeth from Montpellier and from all other localities, CV ranged from 9.3 to 14.1, RMI from 23.2 to 35.5; the pooled samples of 10 had CV=10.3 and 12.2, RMI of 31.8 and 36.7 respectively. This indicates that with small (or perhaps just size-equal) samples, the more variable group from many localities about balanced that from the type locality, which is also the most abundant. Combining all of these specimens for $M_{2\text{-}3}$ reveals that the greater sample sizes for *M. pentelici* seem to swamp those for the smaller species, with CVs of 10.4 and 11.3, within the range for those from single sites! On the other hand, the RMI clearly stands out here, with values of 48.6 and 50.1, indicating at least a great range of size.[3]

The early hominid data given by Wolpoff indicate a comparable degree of variability for all groupings except 'all East Africa', 'all Australopithecines' and 'all Australopithecines without East African graciles'. The latter three groups have CV above 15 and RMI above 70 (often above 80), while the others have CV mostly between 11 and 15, RMI between 30 and 60. The sample labelled 'robust Australopithecines' was on the borderline between these two groups, suggesting that it is within this group that the cause of the variation

3. It must be noted that such high values of RMI may even occur in single-site samples if one individual is far beyond the mean, although the CV in such cases I observed (in *Dolichopithecus ruscinensis*) was below 13.

may lie. It appears that, while all the South African forms are dentally of similar cheek-tooth size, the difference is great in East Africa, with these 'robust' forms well beyond the average. Perhaps a sample 'total australopith except East African robust' would reveal interestingly low values.

It would also be interesting to see values for samples from single localities, such as the individual South African caves, especially Swartkrans and Sterkfontein. These results suggest that there is more variation in the australopiths than in the *Mesopithecus* samples studied by me, certainly more than accepted by Wolpoff.

By comparing the values for early hominids with those for modern pongids and hominids, Wolpoff has suggested that variability in the fossils is low. Comparison of the CV in his modern populations to *Mesopithecus*, and to values suggested by Simpson, Roe and Lewontin (1961) as acceptable for homogeneous samples, suggests that the modern hominids measured were highly variable, probably because a large number of local populations were sampled. Certainly, this is in line with what Wolpoff has argued should be the method of comparison, but it seems to lead to circularity in interpretation: if a large number of variable populations are used as a model or standard, it is likely that the fossils compared will prove less variable, and thus relatively homogeneous, fitting the single-species hypothesis. But this also can be used to suggest that more fossils should be pooled into the sample, to match the variation in the modern standard. With the use of fossil populations as a standard, the interpretation is reversed, and heterogeneity of the fossils is therefore suggested. Contrary to Wolpoff's argument, if it is clear that only one fossil species is involved, there is no greater probability of error than when using modern morphospecies such as *Pan troglodytes* as a standard.

Wolpoff goes one step further and pools the chimpanzee and gorilla measures to show that very high values of both CV and RMI result (his Table 4). Inspection of the ranges of tooth-crown area in these two species reveal almost no overlap, however, and the result is not truly comparable to the situation for the australopiths – it corresponds to pooling *Dolichopithecus* and *Mesopithecus* samples. On the other hand, the results of pooling orang measures with chimpanzee or even gorilla measures would be more comparable and might prove interesting; the analogy here would be to the pooling of the two 'species' of *Mesopithecus*. Wolpoff complains that *Pan* and *Pongo* are allopathic and thus not comparable to the australopith morphs, but in fact there are few if any cases of the latter being both present at a single site unit or horizon. I hope that the presentation of the data in Table 1 may allow for further comparisons to be made by those with additional data on early hominids and other catarrhine taxa.

Time and the single species

A complicated aspect of the single-lineage problem is the role of temporal data in these studies: comparison of temporal and geographic variation, pooling of specimens from widely disparate time levels, and the possibility of recognizing contemporary samples or individuals. Wolpoff argues (this volume) that it is not possible to show clearly that two fossils are contemporaneous. Therefore, he suggests that material from many time horizons can be pooled, again to increase sample size. His argument rests on the errors inherent in the determination of radiometric dates, such that two layers dated at 1.8 m.y., for example, could actually range from 1.6-2.0 m.y. and be nearly half a million years apart. As I will argue below, it is inadvisable to base interpretation too heavily on the age of fossils. But our knowledge of dating can be improved in several ways. First, the use of palaeomagnetic data can limit the possible range of radiometric dates – in the case mentioned, a date of 1.8 m.y. tied to a layer with normal polarity would mean sampling a time horizon within the Olduvai normal event, at most 1.6-1.9 m.y. Secondly, continued refinement of palaeontological correlation would allow other localities to be tied into a standard sequence and at least approximate ranges of time delineated. The present difficulties involved in correlating the East Rudolf and Omo successions show how complicated these problems can be, but the discussions during this conference suggest that, at least for studies of metrical characters, a time scale does exist upon which agreement is sufficiently general to allow more precise comparisons of the sort carried out by Pilbeam and Zwell (1973).

In that work, the hominid fossils thought to be older than 0.75 m.y. were separated into four time blocks, within which selected histograms of tooth size were plotted to determine whether observed variation was high compared with expectation. Their discussion of models for the study of variation is similar to mine, based on modern rather than fossil data. Unfortunately, some of their age determinations do not appear acceptable at present, and some of the following may be altered by new work. However, it does seem quite feasible to suggest replication of their study using three main 'time blocks': (1), specimens between 1.9 and 3 m.y. old, such as those from the Omo Usno Fm. and Shungura members B through F (Howell, this volume; Howell and Coppens, 1974), East Rudolf Lower Member of the Koobi Fora Fm. (Brock and Isaac, 1974; R.E.F. Leakey, this volume), the South African sites of Sterkfontein, Makapan and probably Taung (Cooke and Maglio, 1972; discussions during this meeting), the Hadar Fm. (Taieb, Johanson and Coppens, 1975); (2), specimens falling within the Olduvai normal magnetic event (1.6-1.9 m.y.), such as those from Olduvai Bed I and the Lemuta Member of Bed II (M. Leakey, this volume), Omo Shungura member G, East Rudolf lower part of the Upper Member of the Koobi

Fora Fm. and lower parts of the Ileret sequence, Peninj (Isaac, this volume), possibly Chesowanja and the South African sites of Swartkrans and perhaps Kromdraai; and (3), specimens younger than the above (i.e. 1.0-1.6 m.y.), essentially from the Omo Kalam area, East Rudolf Ileret Mb., and the major part of Bed II at Olduvai.

I would expect that findings similar to Pilbeam and Zwell's would recur with a revised attempt – namely, that variation in tooth size appears to increase upward in time. Pilbeam and Zwell interpreted the increased variability through time to reflect cladogenesis or 'branching' evolution leading to two separate hominid lineages that diverged morphologically. On the basis of data of this type, it is impossible to determine whether the change was due to evolution *in situ* or to the immigration of a more distinct form, possibly descended from a local population related to one sampled in the previous time range. Since we are dealing here with a broad sample over the entire known range, this distinction may not be more than theoretically important. However, the idea that a 'robust' lineage could persist relatively unchanged appears to disturb some workers on theoretical grounds. By way of reply, one interpretation of evolutionary speciation employing an allopatric model suggests that most species remain morphologically constant over long times through the action of homeostatic mechanisms, and that most speciation events (especially those few which 'succeed', or result in a new species surviving to become sympatric with or replace its ancestor), occur on the geographic margin of the ancestor species' range (see Eldredge and Gould, 1972, but also rebuttal by Gingerich, 1974). A long-surviving, conservative lineage of 'robust' australopiths would fit such a model well, especially alongside a more rapidly-changing lineage of progressive 'gracile' types, with a number of rather different local populations separated geographically. At successive times, some of the latter would develop new traits in isolation, then spread back through the previous range to displace the earlier populations and consolidate the new traits. In such a model, it would be possible to consider *Homo habilis*, or something like it, as a species or subspecies which had developed the trait of larger brain size while retaining australopith dentition, although this is, of course, oversimplified.

Reconstructing an ancestor in a multi-lineage model

Theory of cladistic methodology

The discussion so far has centred on several aspects of the single-lineage hypothesis. Each of these has been seen to be valid under its own assumptions, but less secure when these postulates are called into question. In my opinion, the hypothesis of a single species or lineage including all known early hominids is unsatisfactory. Although there are questions as to how certain subsamples should be grouped, the need for a multi-species model seems clear. The problem now is to determine how to present this model in clearest form, especially regarding the relationships among the several phena that have been distinguished.

By clarifying these relationships one is essentially making a model of the phylogeny of the group. It must be based mainly on morphological characters, not simply the comparison of metrical variates and their overlap or disjunction, because size may vary within or between lineages, while the development of new traits usually indicates the occurrence of speciation. The best approach seems to be offered by the major principle of the cladistic method: namely, that grouping phena on the basis of morphology must depend only on those characters which can be considered *derived* from the ancestral condition, not merely *inherited* from a common ancestor.

Hennig (1966) has been the leading architect of this approach, although some of his accessory postulates leave much to be desired. Schaeffer, Hecht and Eldredge (1972) have formulated the method as it applies to palaeontology; Eldredge and Tattersall (1975) have reviewed the arguments and offered a summary application to human palaeontology; and I have attempted to apply it more fully to the study of catarrhine evolutionary history (Delson, 1973, 1975a, 1975b, 1977; Delson and Andrews, 1975; Delson, Eldredge and Tattersall, 1977). Phrased most succinctly, the cladistic approach maintains that phena (or taxa) should be linked phyletically only if they share characters which may be termed *derived* by comparison with other members of the larger group to which they belong.

The argument runs as follows. Speciation represents a separation between an ancestral species and two (or more) daughter species. The resulting sisters will share many characters retained from their common ancestor but will also differ in a smaller number of characters. In most cases, it is likely that one of the two daughters will retain the ancestral condition (for a given character), while the other will present a derived condition. In some cases, both daughters may have different derived conditions. The several descendants of these original sister-species can be termed sister-groups, and their members will tend to retain the traits which have been called derived by comparison to the original parent species but which are ancestral for the group as a whole. In general, a new trait is always derived in the first species to present it, by comparison to that species' ancestor, but is ancestral for that species' descendants.

To apply this scheme to a real set of phena with many characters, it is necessary to devise methods to determine which characters in a group are ancestral. Those phena sharing derived characters can then be linked into a subgroup, irrespective of their relative ages. Although this concept is discussed in most works on general systematic theory (e.g. Simpson, 1961; Le Gros Clark, 1971), it is not usually followed in practice. Palaeontologists tend to accept as ancestral those characters which appear first in the geological record of a group. This may lead to circularity or error, if for example the oldest known member of a group happens to be, in fact, a highly specialized form, while some modern members are more 'generalized', retaining many ancestral characters. To avoid this problem, Schaeffer, Hecht and Eldredge (1972) have advocated that fossil and modern representatives of a group be considered together, without reference to geological age, after grouping specimens into phena by the usual methods. Thus, one is presented with the total known range of variation within the group, without prejudging which characters were ancestral. Ancestral or derived conditions are best determined by broad comparison of character states throughout the group under study and its close relatives. The most widespread characters or states, especially if also present in related groups (the 'sister(s)' of the total studied group) are likely to be retentions from an earlier ancestor. On the other hand, states which occur only once in a whole group are probably derived, but of no help in linking phena. Of greatest value are those states occurring relatively few times, enabling the phena which share them to be linked. A greater number of shared characters linking phena (if independent) indicate relatively closer phyletic relationship. Schaeffer, Hecht and Eldredge also discussed the concepts of a morphocline, or graded sequence of character states from ancestral to most derived, and of the polarity along this morphocline, which may be used to determine the set of characters to be expected in the ancestor of a group or subgroup.

This set of ancestral characters may be termed the 'morphotype' of such a group. By reconstructing a series of ancestral morphotypes within a large group, one essentially infers or deduces the attributes of some of the actual ancestor species at different points in the group's evolutionary history. On the one hand, it is possible to link modern (and fossil) phena or taxa into subgroups by comparison of their characters with the ancestral states of the morphotype. This leads to the production of a cladogram, or phylogeny without time dimension. On the other hand, it is also of great interest to compare actual fossils with the postulated ancestral morphotypes at various points along the 'evolutionary tree'. Traditionally, the concept of such a morphotype might have been altered to correspond to a known fossil, but in this method, it is argued instead that the likelihood that a given fossil is a so-called 'structural ancestor' is directly proportional to its possession of ancestral character states. With the addition of the time dimension provided only by fossils, it is possible to suggest the date at which certain derived conditions first were evolved, or the time when basic lineage divisions occurred, because of the presence of such characteristic derived conditions (see also Delson, 1975b, 1977).

Application to the Australopiths

Eldredge and Tattersall (1975) have studied some cranial and dental characters of the Hominidae with a number of interesting results. They concluded that the South African 'gracile' australopith corresponds very closely to the ancestral morphotype for Hominidae.[4] In skull shape and lightness, somewhat reduced face and incisors (compared to pongids), broad molars with low cusps and expanded occlusal surface and heavily buttressed jaws, Eldredge and Tattersall found that the known characters of 'gracile' early hominids matched those in the morphotype they postulated. On the other hand, they place the 'robust' forms as a derived lineage sharing great reduction of the anterior dentition, molarization of permanent and deciduous premolars, expanded and flattened molars with reduction or elimination of shearing wear, greater orthognathy and related cranial-vault features. Their analysis agrees well with that of Wallace (1975; this volume), who, in essence, has described a morphocline in early hominid dentition, with the ancestral features being somewhat intermediate between the two end-points. Although part of his determination of polarity rested on temporal evidence, the morphology appears to speak for itself, indicating that South African *Homo* spp. have ancestral conditions, while 'robust' forms and later 'graciles' are derived in different directions. In other words, they follow different trends in morphology, which also match well with their apparent temporal positions.

This interpretation does not correspond exactly to the views of Robinson, who, it must be noted, has at least argued that he is using a somewhat similar methodology. By comparison to Wallace's (and Eldredge and Tattersall's) interpretation, Robinson has seen the morphocline as extending from an ancestral form similar to known 'robusts', through the 'graciles' to later hominids, thus as a single line, rather than a major branching. In terms of actual phylogeny, there would be a branching which left 'robust' forms to persist without much change, but the morphocline would be linear. As Eldredge and Tattersall have said also, there must be further, more detailed analyses of the skull and teeth, as well as inclusion of evidence from

4. By comparison, *Ramapithecus* possessed only one additional ancestral feature: a 'sectorial' or C′-honing P_3. The very inclusion of *Ramapithecus* in the analysis may be thought to have biased the conclusions, but this is probably untrue. On the other hand, if this analysis had been carried out by Robinson (see below), with the inclusion of *Gigantopithecus* among the Hominidae (and without *Ramapithecus*), it is possible that more 'robust'-like gnathic characters and large size might have been determined as ancestral features of hominids. This contention is hard to prove without actually performing such an analysis, however.

Delson, Eldredge and Tattersall (1977) did undertake a partial study including both of these fossils and other hominoids which agreed with the results of the previous analysis. More recent data on dental characters of later Miocene hominoids suggest alterations in the cladogram, but substantiate the method.

the brain, post-cranium and other systems, before the question can be reconsidered in more detail. But this method seems to offer the most promise.

From the evidence and discussions during this conference, it appears that several different models of early hominid phylogeny can be consistent with present knowledge. I offer the following 'individual variant', based on the preceding arguments.

Whatever the ancestry in the 15-8 m.y. range (see Simons, this volume), the dental pattern seen in Miocene *Dryopithecus* species may have been altered by increase in relative molar size to one similar to that found in South African 'gracile' australopiths. Accompanying this change would have been some relative increase in brain size and the development of a bipedal locomotor system. There is still major disagreement among specialists (as in this volume) as to whether significant morphological or functional differences exist between 'gracile' and 'robust' early hominids in their post-cranium, especially the lower limb, or even if early hominids differ from modern ones. What is required now is a careful determination of polarity along the morphocline whose states include the characteristics of several postcranial complexes in australopiths, *Homo* and modern apes, which are partly derived in their own ways. The australopiths share some features which *may* also be derived among hominids, thus linking them in a clade separate from *Homo*. However, Robinson's (1972; this volume) arguments for a 'primitiveness' of the 'robust' locomotor system still merit full consideration as well.

On the other hand, there is no *a priori* reason to expect that, even if known 'robust' australopiths retain a more 'primitive' locomotor apparatus, their cranio-gnathic complex is also ancestral. Mosaic evolution has long been accepted as functioning for humans as well as other animal groups, and I would expect it to be especially strong in early hominids, as they adapted to new environments locally and perhaps competed with one another in certain niches. Thus, the common ancestor of the early hominids might have possessed the cranium and teeth of a 'gracile', on the body of a (small?) 'robust' form. From this ancestral stock, one or more (sub-)lineages of 'robust' form developed, following the dental trends described by Wallace, increasing absolute brain size as body size increased (and on body size our evidence is most shaky) but showing little overall 'advancement'. Tobias' interpretation (1973b) of a 'robust' superspecies with several semispecies may be a good interim taxonomic assessment.

Another lineage derived from the ancestral early hominid stock appears to have reversed the trend to increase in molar size, resulting in relatively smaller cheek teeth which retained the ancestral shearing functions. At the same time, there was increase of brain size relative to body size and improvement of the locomotor apparatus. These trends, along with some cranial shape changes, proceeded mosaically, perhaps in a set of interbreeding (sub-)lineages which we are as yet

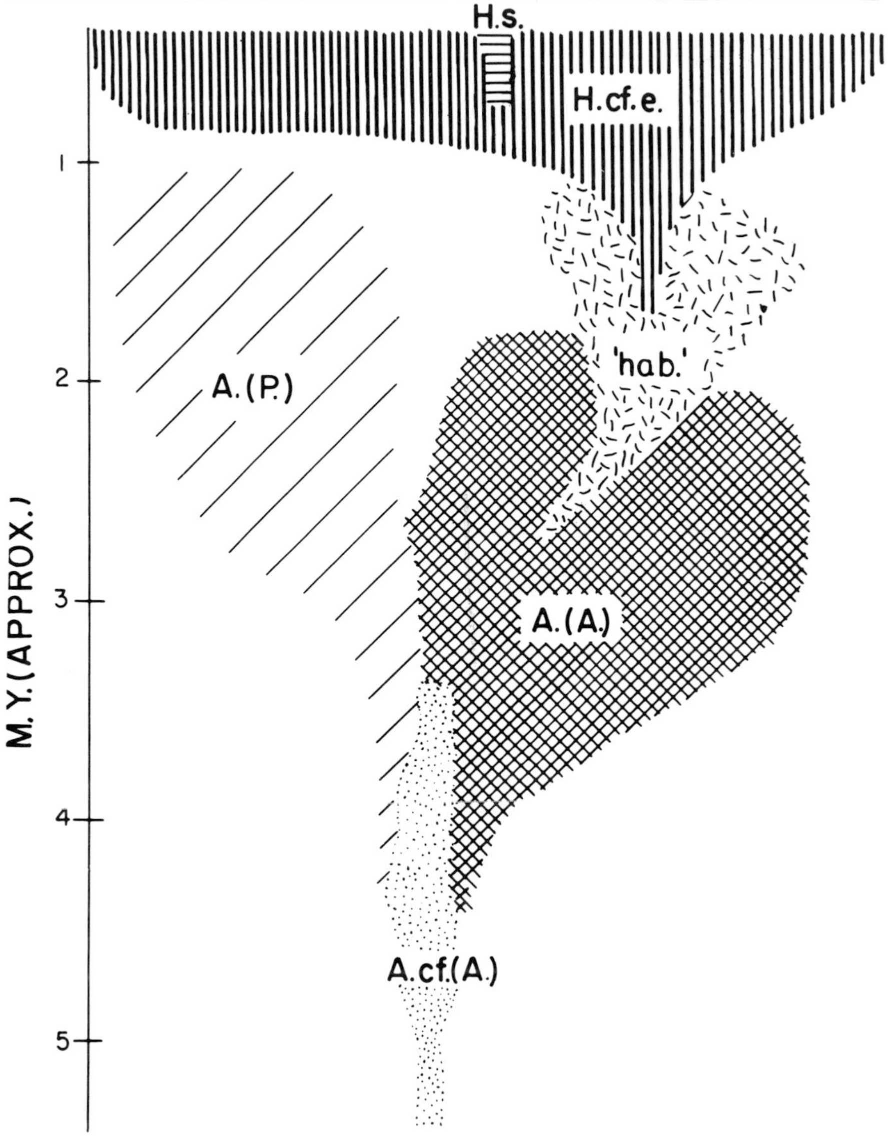

Figure 1. A model of the evolutionary history of the early hominids. The time axis is approximate, and the relative width of the funnel-shaped lineages indicates their range and diversity. Reproductive isolation between species was incomplete at first, later complete. Note that some indicated temporal range data are now incorrect: the oldest known *A.* (*Paranthropus*) is between 2.0 and 2.25 m.y. in age, while specimens assigned to *Homo habilis* may be older than 3.5 m.y. The latter are less clearly related to *A.* (*Australopithecus*) than they are to ancestral *Australopithecus*.

Abbreviations: A. = *Australopithecus*
P. = *Paranthropus*
'hab.' = *Homo habilis*
H.cf.e. = *Homo* cf. *erectus*
H.s. = *Homo sapiens* (archaic)

unable to unravel. New developments would thus originate in a peripheral population, allowing it to compete favourably and spread across the total range to replace its ancestor, only to succumb eventually in turn. The pattern is one of successive expanding (sub)species replacing one another through time. This can be illustrated (Figure 1) by a set of nested funnels, rather than by Howell's (1967) pattern of apparently contracting populations or Tobias' picture of each funnel-shaped lineage extending far back in time (1973a, 1973b). The group of 'gracile' populations might also be recognized as a superspecies, or as a set of local subspecies analogous in some ways to Campbell's evaluation (this volume). This reliance on superspecies is perhaps as much a recognition of our own uncertainties as it is a representation of evolution in progress at low taxonomic levels.

Accordingly, it seems best to recognize only two genera in the time period here considered. A strict cladist would consider the 'robust' lineage or lineages, the 'graciles', and their common ancestor as three taxa of equal rank, as Robinson has done, in part. Because what we know as *Australopithecus africanus* is morphologically so 'primitive', so retentive of common ancestral characters, it is still very similar to 'robust' forms in most complexes, as might be expected in diverse species of a single genus. Thus I hesitantly recognize only *Australopithecus* for hominids of moderate body size, with brains of 400-600(?) cc., large cheek teeth, etc. Following Howell (1967) among others, subgenera *A.* (*Australopithecus*) and *A.* (*Paranthropus*) can be distinguished; the unknown common ancestor possibly merits a third.

The morphologically 'transitional' or 'intermediate' specimens from Olduvai, Rudolf, Hadar and other regions testify to the presence of a derived 'gracile' species *Homo habilis*, which is nonetheless still difficult to diagnose or identify consistently. Present evidence suggests its origin from the as yet unknown common ancestor of *Australopithecus* species earlier than is indicated in Figure 1. Still other (later) samples can be identified as *Homo* cf. *erectus*, whose spread probably coincided causally with the demise of *A. robustus*. Swedlund (1974) found this extinction the most difficult datum to explain in a multi-lineage model under ecological constraints, but the advanced tool kits of *Homo erectus* might have permitted it indirectly to outcompete *A. robustus* in the use of resources, if not more directly. Groves and Mazak (1975) have recently suggested that specimens here allocated to *H.* cf. *erectus* be named *Homo ergaster*, although no comparison of holotypes or hypodigms was carried out in a paper which professed to apply the methods of mammalian systematics to palaeoanthropology. The description of more complete material from Koobi Fora (Leakey and Walker, 1976) once again underlines the need for the actual application of such methods to the study of fossil man where they continue to be conspicuous for their absence.

I realize that this reconstruction of early hominid evolutionary history is very speculative, but it may serve as a hypothesis to be tested, one on which I have extended myself when possible in order to be specific. The picture agrees in most respects with Jolly's (1970) well-known two-phase dietary model, especially as we both consider it more likely that the development of increased adaptations to small-object feeding would occur in later or more derived hominid populations ('robusts'), rather than being fully formed in the earliest hominids. Wallace's finding (1975) that there is no clear difference in tooth chipping (and thus grit content of food) between 'gracile' and 'robust' early hominids seems to fit in with Jolly's arguments as well as with the above. Szalay's (1975) suggestion that positively selected incorporation of the canine into the incisor row was coupled with thickened cheek-tooth enamel to facilitate meat-eating is also most valuable, although his inference of bone-crushing by this early hominid dentition requires experimental or behavioral testing.

Discussion

There may seem to be some inconsistency in this analysis with respect to the inclusion of temporal information. In dealing with metrical data, I have argued for the grouping of specimens for consideration into time blocks, so as to avoid blurring potential differences. For example, if an ancestral population had some variate with mean 2 and range $1\frac{1}{4}$ to $2\frac{3}{4}$, and two later populations had values of 1 ($\frac{1}{4}$-$1\frac{3}{4}$) and 3 ($2\frac{1}{4}$-$3\frac{3}{4}$), it would be simple to differentiate the two younger phena considered alone. But if all three were pooled to increase sample size, there would be a spurious indication of a single variable population (see also Pilbeam and Zwell, 1973). With morphological characters, however, the inclusion of temporal data at the wrong stage of the analysis could well be counter-productive. It may be necessary to pool short-period temporal evidence in the first stages of a cladistic study: incomplete specimens from a single site are included in the same phenon to produce a complete picture of the features of that phenon for comparison. What is important is not to employ relative ages in the determination of ancestral characters, so that the time dimension can be added later in order to reconstruct historical events. Time cannot be used in polarity analysis without leading to circularity.

Campbell (this volume) has chosen another route, basing his determination of taxa mainly on the contemporaneity of phena within a broad group. He has thus separated the East African 'robust' forms as one lineage, but included the South African ones as merely a subspecies of the 'graciles', mostly because it is not easy to see more than one lineage in South Africa. This is too limited an analysis, however: no positive reason is given to link the two South African morphs so closely. Clearly, any two points or clusters in morphological or geometrical space can be connected by a single line or trend, but, with biological processes, the meaning of that trend also depends on other known points or populations: in the cladistic view, the 'robust' and 'gracile' South African forms may be similar because of shared ancestral features, not having much taxonomic 'weight', while the South and East African 'robusts' share derived conditions (albeit perhaps to different degrees) and thus must be linked phyletically and taxonomically. The phyletic 'lineage' connecting South African 'gracile' and 'robust' australopiths in Campbell's interpretation in fact bypasses the major evolutionary branching point within the group. On the other hand, Tobias (1973a, 1973b) has accepted the arguments of Partridge (1973; see rebuttals by Bishop and by Butzer, this volume) and others (e.g., Butzer) that the Taung hominid is quite recent, and he has suggested, partly because it is late, that it is probably a 'robust' individual. The resulting nomenclatural problems raised by Tobias indicate a disregard for the provisions of the International Code of Zoological Nomenclature.

Summary

I have reviewed several schools of thought on models of early hominid phylogeny: single-lineage and multi-lineage with either 'gracile' or 'robust' form as common ancestor. Data on molar area in single and pooled samples of two species of the terrestrial fossil cercopithecid *Mesopithecus* are provided to serve as a standard of variability in single species of catarrhines. Consideration of this pattern with that observed in australopiths suggests that the early hominids are more variable than has been thought. Much of this variation may be due to the great size of the East African 'robust' individuals. In addition, studies supporting the single-lineage hypothesis have not considered questions of proportion along the tooth row, as emphasized by Robinson, nor of the effects of pooling specimens from different time periods. I suggest that the work of Pilbeam and Zwell (1973) along the latter lines be repeated, with more accurate delineation of time blocks.

Having determined that a multi-lineage model is required, I have suggested the application of the cladistic methodology, as exemplified by Schaeffer, Hecht and Eldredge (1972) and Eldredge and Tattersall (1975). A theory of relationships among the phena can be formulated by linking those which share derived characters, and a cladogram developed. With the addition of the time dimension, a phylogeny of the group can be drawn up, while comparisons of variation and other criteria may be used to rank the phena into formal taxa.

I have suggested an outline model of early hominid evolutionary history and systematics, developed by applying these methods superficially to published data (especially those of Eldredge and Tattersall, 1975, and Wallace, 1975 and this volume), in order to serve as the basis for further discussion and refinement after more detailed work. The common ancestor of the known early hominids is reconstructed as possessing cranio-gnathic characters found in early 'graciles', perhaps mosaically linked with a heavy body and the post-cranial features Robinson (1972) has considered distinguish 'robusts' from 'graciles' (assuming such differences do indeed exist). Taxonomically, the known 'graciles' and 'robusts' are perhaps best ranked as subgenera of *Australopithecus*, possibly with a superspecies for the 'robusts'. *Homo habilis* existed as a distinct taxon, morphologically if not phyletically intermediate between *Australopithecus* cf. *africanus* and *Homo* cf. *erectus*. The appearance of the last species probably is closely linked to the extinction of *A. Robustus*. This model or scenario is presented graphically in Figure 1.

Acknowledgments

I thank Dr Clifford Jolly for inviting me to participate in this stimulating and rewarding conference, Mrs Lita Osmundsen and the Staff of the Wenner-Gren Foundation for their hospitality and the other participants for much personal and professional interaction. Dr Jeffrey H. Schwartz and Dr Ian M. Tattersall read and commented most helpfully on an earlier draft of this manuscript, for which I am grateful.

References

Andrews, P. (1974) New species of *Dryopithecus* from Kenya. *Nature*, 249, 188-90.

Andrews, P. and Williams, D. (1973) The use of principal components analysis in physical anthropology. *Amer. J. phys. Anthrop.* 39, 291-303.

Bilsborough, A. (1972) Anagenesis in hominid evolution. *Man* (n.s.) 7, 481-3.

Bishop, W.W., this volume.

Brace, C.L. (1973) Sexual dimorphism in human evolution. *Yb. phys. Anthrop.* 16, 31-49.

Brace, C.L., Mahler, P. and Rosen, R.B. (1973) Tooth measurements and the rejection of the taxon '*Homo habilis*'. *Yb. phys. Anthrop.* 16, 51-68.

Brock, A. and Isaac, G.Ll. (1974) Palaeomagnetic stratigraphy and chronology of hominid-bearing sediments east of Lake Rudolf, Kenya. *Nature* 247, 344-8.

Butzer, K.W., this volume.

Campbell, B.G. (1972) Conceptual progress in physical anthropology: fossil man. *Ann. Rev. Anthrop.* 1, 27-54.

Campbell, B.G., this volume.

Cooke, H.B.S. and Maglio, V. (1972) Plio-Pleistocene stratigraphy in East Africa in relation to proboscidean and suid evolution. In Bishop, W.W. and Miller, J.A. (eds.), *Calibration of Hominoid Evolution*, 303-29. Toronto.

Delson, E. (1973) Fossil colobine monkeys of the circum-Mediterranean region and the evolutionary history of the Cercopithecidae (Primates, Mammalia). Thesis, Columbia University.

Delson, E. (1974) Preliminary review of Cercopithecid distribution in the circum-Mediterranean region. *Mem. Bur. Rech. geol. Min.* (France) 78, 131-5.

Delson, E. (1975a) Evolutionary history of the Cercopithecidae. *Contrib. Primat.* (Karger) 5, 167-217.

Delson, E. (1975b) Toward the origin of the Old World monkeys. *Colloques internat. Centre nat. Rech. sci.* (France) 218, 839-50.

Delson, E. (1977) Catarrhine phylogeny and classification: principles, methods and comments. *J. human Evol.* 6 (in press).

Delson, E. and Andrews, P. (1975) Evolution and interrelationships of the catarrhine primates. In Luckett, W.P. and Szalay, F.S. (eds.), *Phylogeny of the Primates: A Multidisciplinary Approach*, 405-46. New York.

Delson, E., Eldredge, N. and Tattersall, I. (1977) Reconstruction of hominid phylogeny: attestable framework based on cladistic analysis. *J. human Evol.* 6 (in press).

Eldredge, N. and Gould, S.J. (1972) Speciation and punctuated equilibria: an alternative to phyletic gradualism. In Schopf, T.J. (ed.), *Models in Paleobiology*, 82-115. San Francisco.

Eldredge, N. and Tattersall, I. (1975) Evolutionary models, phylogenetic reconstruction and another look at hominid phylogeny. *Contrib. Primat.* (Karger) 5, 218-42.

Forsten, A. (1973) New systematics and the classification of Old World *Hipparion*. *Zeits. Saugetierk.* 38, 289-94.

Gingerich, P. (1974) Stratigraphic record of Early Eocene *Hyopsodus* and the geometry of mammalian phylogeny. *Nature* 248, 107-9.

Groves, C.P. and Mazak, V. (1975) An approach to the taxonomy of the Hominidae: gracile Villafranchian hominids of East Africa. *Casopis pro Mineralogii a Geologii*, 20, 225-47.

Hennig, W. (1966) *Phylogenetic Systematics*. Chicago.

Howell, F.C. (1967) Book review of *Man-Apes or Ape-Men?* by W. Le Gros Clark. *Amer. J. phys. Anthrop.* 27, 95-102.

Howell, F.C. (1972) Recent advances in human evolutionary studies (revised). *Perspectives on Human Evolution* 2, 51-128.

Howell, F.C., this volume.

Howell, F.C. and Coppens, Y. (1976) An overview of Hominidae from the Omo succession, Ethiopia. In Coppens, Y. *et al.* (eds.), *Earliest Man and Environments in the Lake Rudolf Basin: Stratigraphy, Paleoecology and Evolution*, 522-32. Chicago.

Howells, W.W. (1973) *Evolution of the Genus Homo*. Reading, Mass.

Hull, D. (1970) Contemporary systematic philosophies. *Ann. Rev. Ecol. Syst.* 1, 19-54.

Isaac, G.Ll., this volume.

Jolly, C.J. (1970) The seed-eaters: a new model of hominid differentiation based on a baboon analogy. *Man* (n.s.) 5, 5-26.

Jolly, C.J. and Brett, F. (1973) Genetic markers and baboon biology. *J. med. Primat.* 2, 85-99.

Kowalski, C. (1972) A commentary on the use of multivariate statistical methods in anthropometric research. *Amer. J. phys. Anthrop.* 36, 119-32.

Leakey, M.D., this volume.
Leakey, R.E.F. (1973a) Further evidence of lower Pleistocene hominids from East Rudolf, North Kenya, 1972. *Nature* 242, 170-3.
Leakey, R.E.F. (1973b) Evidence for an advanced Plio-Pleistocene hominid from East Rudolf, Kenya. *Nature* 242, 447-50.
Leakey, R.E.F., this volume.
Leakey, R.E.F. and Walker, A. (1976) *Australopithecus, Homo erectus* and the single-species hypothesis. *Nature* 261, 572-4.
Le Gros Clark, W. (1971) *The Antecedents of Man* (3rd ed.). Edinburgh.
Mayr, E. (1969) *Principles of Systematic Zoology*. New York.
Oxnard, C. (1972) Some African fossil foot bones: a note on the interpolation of fossils into a matrix of extant species. *Amer. J. phys. Anthrop.* 37, 3-12.
Partridge, T.C. (1973) Geomorphological dating of cave openings at Makapansgat, Sterkfontein, Swartkrans and Taung. *Nature* 246, 75-9.
Pilbeam, D. (1972) *The Ascent of Man*. New York.
Pilbeam, D. (1973) Adaptive response of hominids to their environment as ascertained by fossil evidence. *Social Biology* 19, 115-27.
Pilbeam, D., this volume.
Pilbeam, D. and Gould, S.J. (1974) Size and scaling in human evolution. *Science* 186, 892-906.
Pilbeam, D. and Vaišnys, J.R. (1975) Hypothesis testing in paleoanthropology. In Tuttle, R.H. (ed.), *Paleoanthropology: Morphology and Paleoecology*, 3-13. The Hague.
Pilbeam, D. and Zwell, M. (1973) The single species hypothesis, sexual dimorphism, and variability in early hominids. *Yb. phys. Anthrop.* 16, 69-79.
Robinson, J.T. (1954) Prehominid dentition and hominid evolution. *Evolution* 8, 324-34.
Robinson, J.T. (1956) The dentition of the Australopithecinae. *Transvaal Mus. Mem.* No.9.
Robinson, J.T. (1961) The australopithecines and their bearing on the origin of man and of stone tool-making. *S. Afr. J. Sci.* 57, 3-13.
Robinson, J.T. (1967) Variation and the taxonomy of the early hominids. *Evol. Biol.* 1, 69-100.
Robinson, J.T. (1971) Dentition and adaptation in early hominids. *Proc. VIII Int. Cong. anth. ethnol. Sci.*, 1969 (Tokyo), 302-6.
Robinson, J.T. (1972) *Early Hominid Posture and Locomotion*. Chicago.
Robinson, J.T. and Steudel, K. (1973) Multivariate discriminant analysis of dental data bearing on early hominid affinities. *J. human Evol.* 2, 509-27.
Schaeffer, B., Hecht, M. and Eldredge, N. (1972) Phylogeny and paleontology. *Evol. Biol.* 6, 31-46.
Shaklee, A. (1973) Statistical inference from fossils. *Man* (n.s.) 8, 477-9.
Simons, E., this volume.
Simpson, G.G. (1961) *Principles of Animal Taxonomy*. New York.
Simpson, G.G. (1975) Recent advances in methods of phylogenetic inference. In Luckett, W.P. and Szalay, F.S. (eds.), *Phylogeny of the Primates: A Multidisciplinary Approach*, 3-19. New York.
Simpson, G.G. Roe, A. and Lewontin, R. (1961) *Quantitative Zoology* (rev. ed.). New York.
Swedlund, A.C. (1974) The use of ecological hypotheses in australopithecine taxonomy. *Amer. Anthrop.* 76, 515-29.

Szalay, F.S. (1975) Hunting-scavenging hominids: a model for human origins. *Man* (n.s.) 10, 420-9.

Taieb, M., Johanson, D.C. and Coppens, Y. (1975) Expédition Internationale de l'Afar, Ethiopie (3e Campagne 1974); Découverte d'hominidés Plio-Pleistocènes à Hadar. *C.R. Acad. Sci* (Paris) 2180, 1297-300.

Tobias, P. (1967) *Olduvai Gorge.* Vol. 2, *The Cranium and Maxillary Dentition of Australopithecus (Zinjanthropus) boisei.* London.

Tobias, P. (1973a) Implications of the new age estimates of the early South African hominids. *Nature* 246, 79-83.

Tobias, P. (1973b) New developments in hominid palaeontology in South and East Africa. *Ann. Rev. Anthrop.* 2, 311-34.

Walker, A. (1976) Remains attributable to *Australopithecus* in the East Rudolf succession. In Coppens, Y. *Earliest Man and Environments in the Lake Rudolf Basin: Stratigraphy, Paleoecology and Evolution.* 484-9. Chicago.

Wallace, J. (1975) Dietary adaptations of *Australopithecus* and early *Homo.* In Tuttle, R.H. (ed.), *Paleoanthropology: Morphology and Paleoecology*, 203-23. The Hague.

Wallace, J., this volume.

Wolpoff, M. (1968) 'Telanthropus' and the single species hypothesis. *Amer. Anthrop.* 70, 477-93.

Wolpoff, M. (1970) The evidence for multiple hominid taxa at Swartkrans. *Amer. Anthrop.* 72, 576-607.

Wolpoff, M. (1971a) *Metric Trends in Hominid Dental Evolution.* Case Western Reserve University Studies in Anthropology, 2.

Wolpoff, M. (1971b) Interstitial wear. *Amer. J. phys. Anthrop.* 34, 205-28.

Wolpoff, M. (1971c) Competitive exclusion among lower Pleistocene hominids: the single species hypothesis. *Man* (n.s.) 6, 601-14.

Wolpoff, M. (1973) Posterior tooth size, body size, and diet in South African gracile Australopithecines. *Amer. J. phys. Anthrop.* 39, 375-93.

Wolpoff, M. (1975) Sexual dimorphism in the Australopithecines. In Tuttle, R.H. (ed.), *Paleoanthropology: Morphology and Paleoecology*, 245-84. The Hague.

Wolpoff, M., this volume.

E.L. Simons

Diversity among the early hominids: A vertebrate palaeontologist's viewpoint

Introduction

Much of my writing has emphasized that for proper evaluation the early hominids must be considered as basically a palaeontological problem. The palaeoanthropologist merely adopts palaeontological procedures in assessing early hominids. In fact, as I will try to illustrate, lack of familiarity with these procedures has played its role in provoking unnecessary controversy in evaluating early hominid fossils.

One basic aspect of any assessment of diversity in hominids is of course the question of how many genera are to be included in Family Hominidae. It is here that vertebrate palaeontology can provide assistance in the interpretation of human ancestors; first, in evaluating long term changes – common practice in the study of fossil vertebrates – and second, in understanding the scope and definition of Taxonomic Families (among mammals, for instance). Both these questions basically ask, how different can an ancestor be? Or, alternatively, how divergent could two genera and species of mammal be and still belong in the same family? It is in this kind of assessment that some anthropologists have little background. Certainly some perplexing differences of opinion about the hominid status of certain fossils arise from this lack of experience or perspective in judging the meaning of differences between given sets of fossils. For example, throughout the history of human palaeontology there has been an often-expressed tendency to expect human ancestors to be just like modern man, a kind of 'I'm my own grandpa' problem. The reaction against the hominid claims of *Pithecanthropus* at the turn of the century and the even more well-known inability of many anthropologists to accept initially the hominid claims of *Australopithecus* both arose from widespread preconceived notions about what human ancestors *must* be like. These were notions formulated before there was any adequate evidence. It is interesting that the very first and most eloquent early support for the accuracy of Dart's initial assertion of hominid status for *Australopithecus* came in a paper by a vertebrate palaeontologist, A.S. Romer (1925).

It seems difficult for some colleagues to understand that if earliest hominids demonstrate some but not all hominid characters, this fact does not disqualify them from placement within the family. All basal members of mammalian families resemble members of earlier families from which they evolved. Basically, the earliest members of mammalian taxonomic families are singled out because they exhibit the first appearance of the 'advanced' or distinctive features which later will typify the emergent group as a whole. For instance, both *Ramapithecus* and *Australopithecus* show reduction of the size and length of canine crowns, coupled with the marked broadening and rounding out of the cheek tooth outlines, deepening of the alveolar processes of the maxillae, thickening and shallowing of the mandibular rami and increase in the relative thickness of the enamel surfaces of the molars. These features demonstrate first, that species of these two genera had acquired a new way of feeding, and second, that they are very likely to be closely related to each other. This change in the dental mechanism in *Ramapithecus* away from that of *Dryopithecus* demonstrates that adaptation to a new way of life had occurred. The structural differences are real and cannot be explained away even though differences of opinion will always exist as to detailed interpretation of actual ecology in these extinct forms. Retention of ape characteristics in *Australopithecus* and *Ramapithecus* in no way disqualifies them from placement in Hominidae. They necessarily retained primitive features if they were derived from apes and were closer to them in time or in basic adaptation than is modern man.

The earliest members of the family Pongidae show a blend of 'advanced' and 'primitive' features comparable to that seen in *Ramapithecus*, but it is always the first indications of adaptive features later to become standard that 'carry' the initial members into the younger taxonomic group. (Thus, *Hyracotherium* is universally placed with its relatives and descendants in Order Perissodactyla because it shows the first foreshadowing of the characteristics of that order. This placement in no way denies the fact that *Hyracotherium* has many characters in common with earlier members of order Condylarthra such as species of *Tetraclaenodon* and *Ectocion*, from one of which it may be descended.)

From dental-mandibular anatomy it has long been clear that *Propliopithecus* and *Aegyptopithecus* qualify at the earliest known Pongidae. Their teeth are closely similar to modern apes as are also many details of mandibular anatomy. *Aegyptopithecus* provides us with a perfect example of a basal family member which, although already exhibiting advanced or 'basic' features characterizing Pongidae, also retains striking primitive features, not seen among later catarrhines. The skull of *Aegyptopithecus* shows a dental mechanism very much like that of *Dryopithecus*, *Pan*, and *Gorilla*. The incisors are procumbent, canines large and interlocking, there is a premolar hone, and in anatomical details the cheek teeth most closely resemble those of *Gorilla*. As in the latter, molars increase in size posteriorly and are relatively large. The mandibular ascending ramus is broad, high and at right angles to the tooth row. These and other details of the dental mechanism, together with palaeoecological interpretations to be drawn from the Fayum fauna and flora, suggest that *Aegyptopithecus* was like many subsequent apes in being an arboreal herbivore; there are also resemblances to later Pongidae (specifically to the Rusinga skull of *Dryopithecus africanus* found by Mary Leakey in 1948) in the brain cavity and skull morphology. According to recent work by Radinsky (1973) significant expansion of the brain has occurred in *Aegyptopithecus*. As I have indicated elsewhere (Simons, 1970, 1972), symphyseal and frontal fusion as well as postorbital closure are all exhibited in the Fayum primates. Thus, placement of *Aegyptopithecus* in Pongidae is warranted. Nevertheless, this skull also shows large premaxillary bones with an expanded ascending branch, quite unlike later catarrhines; a bony auditory meatus does not extend out of the bulla. In both these features *Aegyptopithecus* resembles Eocene prosimians, not later pongids. Its retention of such primitive characters cannot disqualify it as a pongid.

Hominid diversity

From the above considerations it is clear that eventual agreement about the scope of diversity in family Hominidae involves acceptance of the palaeontological methods for drawing an agreed on line for its base, for as we approach the present, more and more of the various schemes come into agreement – for instance, derivation of *Homo sapiens* from *Homo erectus* is now almost universally accepted.

Diversity within the taxonomic family Hominidae may be considered in two general areas: (1) Species diversity at any one time and (2) Generic diversity. Considered in contrast with other mammalian families whose history through time has been well-documented, there is neither much pene-contemporary species diversity nor much generic diversity indicated in this family. Moreover, as is illustrated by other papers in this volume, certainty as to species distinctions often eludes scholars in this field.

Thus, how are we to measure diversity in Plio-Pleistocene hominids? A number of classificatory schemes have already been proposed and these, of themselves, affect interpretation of diversity of hominids. This happens in two ways. The systems either greatly restrict acceptance of species diversity at any one time (the single species or lineage hypothesis), or they point to different ancestral genera, which by exclusion, or inclusion alter the size of the family. Three such schemes are those of Brace, Robinson and Tobias (see Figure 1).

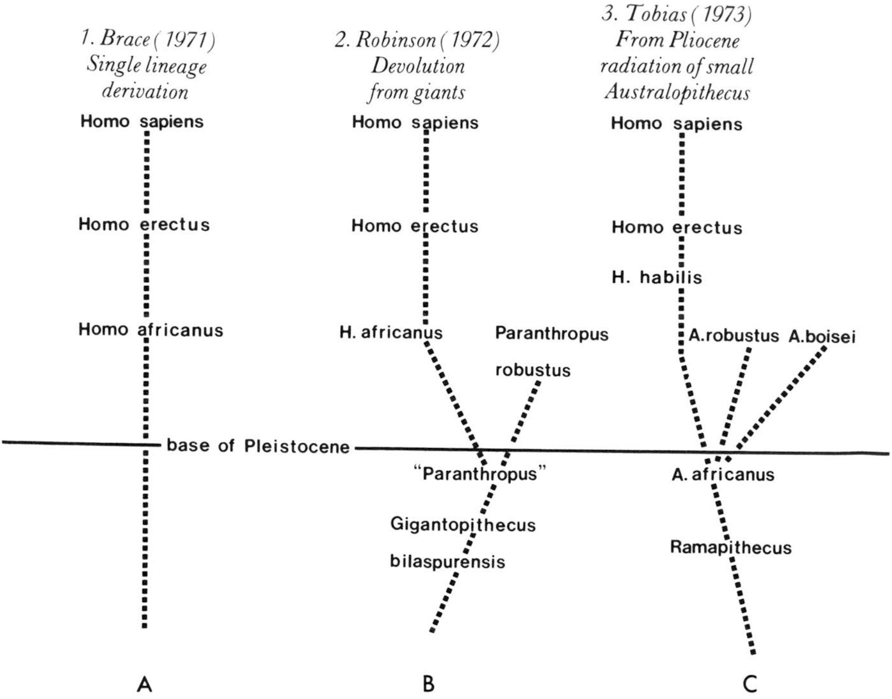

Figure 1.

Such schemes, and these three are certainly not the only ones, all share one basic and inevitable weakness. They are unclear at the base. This is because there is one remaining important period of time when hominid evolution is most poorly known. It is within the time period between three and twelve million years that the most important future discoveries about hominid evolution will be made. Most schemes about the ultimate source of hominids are either inferential or at least skip across this period and are consequently less certain than they would otherwise be.

It seems most likely that between two and three million years, we have one or more species of *Australopithecus* and *Homo* (indicated by the East Rudolf finds such as ER 1470) in Africa. Contemporaneously, in Eurasia we have *Gigantopithecus blacki* but possibly no hominids. For prior, well understood forms, one has to then jump back to the period of, say, 12 to 18 million years when specimens of *Dryopithecus* and *Ramapithecus* are abundant. Then, even for *Ramapithecus*, there are nearly twenty known specimens (Simons, Tattersall and Meyer, 1975).

Agreement as to numbers of species would be more frequent if there were greater numbers of contemporaneous specimens known from various sites, or equally if specimens were more complete than they typically are. Obviously, greater numbers of finds from the same time periods would facilitate statistical separation into groups, and the probability of their reflecting species groupings could be dealt with quantitatively.

At the generic level the family contains few taxa; either two or three genera, depending on whether *Ramapithecus* is included with *Homo* and *Australopithecus*. *Gigantopithecus* is definitely to be excluded, as I shall show.

A review of published and unpublished information about the actual or supposed fossil hominids in the three to twelve million year time period is essential to the task of delimiting the extent of diversity of early hominids. While outlining these finds I shall also endeavour to redefine the best criteria for drawing the hominid/pongid distinction. My own research of recent months brings considerable new evidence to bear on the proper criteria for distinguishing hominids and pongids. It includes reassessment of the recently described mandible of *Ramapithecus* from Greece and the excellent but long misidentified mandible of *Ramapithecus* from Hari Talyangar, now in Calcutta (Simons and Pilbeam, 1972). I have also undertaken extensive researches on *Gigantopithecus* since the discovery of *Gigantopithecus bilaspurensis* (Simons and Chopra, 1969a). Some of these problems have been touched on already (Simons and Chopra, 1969b; Simons and Pilbeam, 1972; Simons, 1972). Additional discussion about the methods for distinguishing hominids and pongids is also contained in Pilbeam (1968), Andrews (1971), and more recently, in Walker and Andrews (1973). However, there is no general, recent review of the problem.

Briefly stated a major source of confusion is that most early definitions of the distinctions between pongids and hominids were really distinctions between *Homo* and the modern great apes (see for instance, Le Gros Clark, 1964, Table 1). Some of the traditional dogmas about pongid/hominid distinctions have proven false when actual fossils have been examined. One example at this point should suffice.

Pongidae were said to have U-shaped mandibles with parallel cheek-tooth rows. My examination of all known fossil ape mandibles which include the symphysis, about two dozen specimens, has shown that none has parallel cheek tooth rows; all diverge posteriorly at an angle higher than that typical of any living ape species. All known Miocene monkey mandibles similarly diverge. Posteriorly diverging, not parallel, tooth rows are thus seen to be the primitive condition for Anthropoidea. Also, in recent years the gradually accumulating material of *Australopithecus*, and the greater dissemination of new casts and photographs of the older material, have made it clear that *Australopithecus* specimens do not have the hemi-circular dental arcade seen in many *Homo sapiens*, as is implied in Tobias (1967), and more clearly by Genet-Varcin in 1969. *Gigantopithecus* and *Ramapithecus*, like *Australopithecus*, have posteriorly diverging dental arcades which fit neither of the arcade outlines formerly supposed to distinguish hominids and pongids. Similarly, presence or absence of a simian shelf has been shown not to sort relevant fossils, but only to distinguish recent great apes from modern man. The simian shelf, a shelf-like ventral buttress whose lateral margins are confluent with the base of the horizontal mandibular rami, is not found in fossil apes of genus *Dryopithecus* but only in modern great apes. Quite similar superior and inferior transverse tori have now been demonstrated in *Ramapithecus*, *Gigantopithecus*, *Australopithecus boisei*, and *Gorilla*. Like the arrangement of the dental arcade, the structure of the symphyseal region and its cross-section do not help to distinguish hominids from pongids. Both lines of study have proved to be blind alleys.

Suggested earliest hominids

Within the crucial three to twelve million year period there are three or four principle sources of information. (1) *Ramapithecus* specimens. Material from Asia and Europe (including the new Pyrgos mandible from near Athens) is all dated faunally to between about 8 and 13 million years. African *Ramapithecus* from Fort Ternan is dated to the beginning of this period, between 12.6 and 14 million years. (2) The Ngorora molar, from the Baringo Basin of Kenya, dated at about 10 or 11 million years. (3) The type and only mandible of *Gigantopithecus bilaspurensis* from presumed Dhok Pathan beds north of Hari Talyangar, India. Recent correlation of faunas indicates that this specimen may be as little as 5 million years old. (4) The Lothagam mandible of *Australopithecus*, faunally dated to between 5 and 6 million years.

1. Ramapithecus

In considering the first group of Mio-Pliocene fossils, remains of *Ramapithecus*, as sources of information it is clear that even the best specimens give rise to differing taxonomic conclusions. This is due both to the incompleteness of the individual specimens and to the fact that there are not enough specimens to demonstrate differences in size or other consistent characters that would substantiate establishment of distinct species. However, this does not mean that we cannot clearly identify given specimens as *Ramapithecus*, rather than *Dryopithecus*, or *Gigantopithecus*. Identifications at the generic level rest on the recognition of a nexus of interrelated structural features which characterize the particular genus. Traditionally, scientists have often avoided the issue of generic placement by proposing a new genus for each new find. This practice is now declining, as growth of the scientific literature makes definition of the scope of the various genera of hominoids more and more precise. Also, with time, the necessity for erection of new genera should decline as more and more of the genera which ever existed are discerned and named. There is a fair probability, for instance, that all hominid genera that ever existed are now known. (This is not necessarily so of hominid species; differences of opinion are still rife.) The sorts of problems encountered are exemplified by *Ramapithecus*.

Previously I have stated that the type maxilla of *Kenyapithecus wickeri* cannot be separated at the specific level from maxillae of *Ramapithecus punjabicus* from India, such as Lewis' well-known specimen, YPM 13799 (Simons, 1963). More recently other students, Pilbeam (1972), Andrews (1971), Walker and Andrews (1973) have confirmed generic identity for these two, and other similar Indian finds, but consider the Fort Ternan specimen a distinct species, *Ramapithecus wickeri*. The supposed species distinctions rest on their discernment of differences in time, size, and morphology between the two. Clearly, it is the differences in morphology which must be considered the principal evidence if a dual species diversity for *Ramapithecus* is to be maintained. One part of the Fort Ternan *Ramapithecus* material upon which the judgment that there are two species is based is the anterior mandibular fragment described by Andrews (1971) and in greater detail more recently by Walker and Andrews (1973). This material was not originally considered by Leakey as belonging with the maxillary specimens. In fact, because there is no collector's association between upper and lower jaw fragments in this Fort Ternan material, and because the mandibular and maxillary fragments were not discovered and documented beside each other *in situ*, it should be remembered that we cannot be certain that they are the same individual. That is, they were not collected as one individual, although matching staining, colouration, character of weathering, seemingly identical dental age, degree of opposing tooth wear, and a tight occlusal fit between upper and lower teeth suggest that they are one. From the Fort Ternan mandibular fragment Andrews and Walker have shown that the lower incisors must have been tiny, and this in turn, demonstrates that the upper central incisor from Fort Ternan, discussed in 1967 by L.S.B. Leakey as being from this individual specimen, cannot belong with it. However, the best evidence about the relative size of the front and back teeth in *Ramapithecus* is derived not from the Fort Ternan find but from those at Hari Talyangar, India and at Pyrgos, Greece.

The recent papers of Andrews (1971) and of Walker and Andrews (1973) on Fort Ternan *Ramapithecus* deserve careful attention, not only for the new information about *Ramapithecus* which they reveal, but also because these scholars clearly do not, as some have stated, intend to imply that their discernment in *Ramapithecus* of some features transitional to apes means that either of them think that *Ramapithecus* is now challenged as a hominid. Speaking as palaeontologists both are aware that the combined features seen in *Ramapithecus* qualify it as the earliest known hominid. (This means that both of these two authors as well as all the other scientists who have ever done original research on *Ramapithecus* specimens believe that this animal is best ranked as a hominid. Such students include: Lewis, Gregory, Hrdlicka, Hellman, Simons, von Koenigswald, Leakey and Pilbeam.)

However, Andrews and Walker (1973) have now been able to deduce from the Fort Ternan specimen or specimens, several features that might not have been expected for *Ramapithecus* working from the Indian-Pakistan material; among these are shallow anterior mandible, and P_3 longer than P_4. In each case these features are not reflected in Asian material, or the Asian material is itself hard to interpret. In sum, the new mandibular evidence from Fort Ternan, for some, may not seem to be what had been expected for *Ramapithecus*, but it is largely non-comparable with the Indian type and the most certainly referred other material from India. So, is there species diversity at the outset of hominid evolution? Answer: unclear. Primary students disagree on this point.

The Pyrgos mandible

A most important newly published fossil hominid is the mandible of *Ramapithecus* from Pyrgos near Tour de la Reine in the outskirts of Athens. This was recently described by von Koenigswald (1972) as *Graecopithecus freybergi*. This specimen was found in 1944 by Professor B. von Freyberg, who published (1950) a faunal list of this site, prepared by W.O. Dietrich of Berlin. This included an identification of the mandible as *Mesopithecus pentelicus*. Later, von Koenigswald, while studying the palaeontological collections at Erlangen, identified the fossil from Tour de la Reine as a hominid. The specimen consists of a more-or-less complete mandible, with continuous apparently undistorted bone running around the symphysis ventrally and with horizontal rami complete to points a centimetre or two behind the third molars. On the right side most of P_4, and M_1 and M_2 are preserved; M_3 is broken off at the alveolar margin. On the left side all teeth are broken off but the tops of the roots from $\bar{C}$ to M_3 are indicated in cross-section. Of all known fossil hominoids from Eurasia prior to the time of *Gigantopithecus blacki* only this and the type mandible of *Gigantopithecus bilaspurensis* preserve so much information in one individual about the relative size of teeth and about mandibular conformation. The only possible runner up for this ranking is the second mandible of *Dryopithecus* from St Gaudens. But the latter find is more extensively crushed together posteriorly and ventrally, and more distorted than the Tour de la Reine mandible. Von Koenigswald (1972) played down the likelihood of this mandible being *Ramapithecus*, but there is no reason to question that it does represent that genus. Perhaps even more important than the objective of reaching full agreement soon among all scientists as to its generic identification are the facts of its place, time, and faunal associations. Other animals were recovered from the same lens of sandy reddish clay, and are now in the collection at Erlangen, Germany and a private collection in Athens, that of Professor Paraskevaides. This fauna definitely dates the site to the Pontian. But what is more remarkable is that it is a 'Steppenfauna', that is an open country or grassland fauna. As von Koenigswald stresses, the Pyrgos mandible is the only hominoid mandible ever found in Europe with such a fauna. Von Koenigswald concludes (1972, p.393) that the age of the Pyrgos mandible would be that of the Pikermian or perhaps a little younger than oldest *Pikermi*. Such faunas have been absolutely dated on the Island of Samos where volcanics are alternated with fossil sites: Van Couvering and Miller (1971) give K-Ar ages for Samos lower level, ranging around 9.3 million years. Von Koenigswald (1972) concludes that the lower level at Samos would set a maximal age for the Pyrgos mandible, but states that these authors give a date of 8.5 m.y. The presence of a single gazelle mandible at Pyrgos of a sort not found at Pikermi, but which is at Samos, suggested to von Koenigswald that the Pyrgos site might be just a little younger than other Pikermian sites in the Athens region. There is no evidence from faunal correlation with dated sites that the Greek *Ramapithecus* could be younger than the upper level, quarry 5 at Samos and this has an estimated age of 7.5 m.y. If the Pyrgos site correlates in time with the lower levels at Samos it would then be about 9 million years old. Because it is a *Hipparion* fauna and the apparent datum for *Hipparion* in Eurasia is 12.5 million years (van Couvering and Miller, 1971), the fauna containing this mandible could fall anywhere between 8 and about 12 million years or even a little earlier, depending on where the *Hipparion* and other fauna at Pyrgos fit into the sequence.

Is there then some reasonable doubt that the Pyrgos mandible is a *Ramapithecus*? Readers of his paper will find that von Koenigswald does not produce a list of defining characters of *Graecopithecus*. In fact, none can be produced for all observable details fall within the range of those known to characterize *Ramapithecus*. The body of the mandible is far too shallow and the molars much too broad to allow assignment to *Gigantopithecus* or *Dryopithecus*. Von Koenigswald discusses how the second molar on the right (the best preserved tooth) could not be matched by him in any anthropoid, 'Eine Besonderheit des Zahnes liegt darin, dass er vorne schmaler ist als hinten; ein solches Verhalten ist mir bisher noch bei keinem Anthropoidenmolar begegnet, wo gerade das umgekehrte normal ist' (1972, p.388). Both M_1 and M_2 in the Pyrgos mandible jut inwardly and outwardly beyond the planes of the inner and outer surfaces of the horizontal ramus. Thus these teeth are broader than the horizontal ramus which is also very shallow at this point, its depth under M_2 being less than the estimated combined length of M_2 and M_3. Such very large teeth are not characteristic of apes and certainly not any fossil apes.

These molars are also unlike those of *Gigantopithecus*. One of the most diagnostic features of *Gigantopithecus* is the universal presence of long lower molars, deeply indented between trigonid and talonid in a rather wasp-waisted condition, seen elsewhere only in *Oreopithecus*. Thus both the shape and the relatively large size of the molars when compared to the body of the mandible makes assignment of the Pyrgos mandible to either of the fossil apes *Gigantopithecus* or *Dryopithecus* quite implausible, as von Koenigswald tacitly recognizes. As he also emphasizes, the ecological associations are also most uncharacteristic of *Dryopithecus*. A paper currently in preparation will analyse in much greater detail the significance of this important specimen.

We may summarize its taxonomic status as follows. It can be said that this mandible possesses no unique or new generic characters, and it falls anatomically within the structural and size range of *Ramapithecus*. There are several Asian *Ramapithecus* larger than the three best specimens from Hari Talyangar (see Simons, Tattersall and Meyer, 1975). One might consider the possibility of assignment to *Australopithecus* were it not about twice as old as the Lothagam mandible, which at 5 m.y. seems to remain the oldest dated specimen of the latter genus.

Scholars might as well retain the newly coined species name, *Ramapithecus freybergi*, pending settlement of the question of whether it, *Ramapithecus punjabicus* and *R. wickeri* are distinct. Simons (1963) has posited that typical species of hominids may have been wide-ranging, and in this case the different species proposed for *Ramapithecus* may not be meaningful. Wide-ranging species may appear in faunas which otherwise contain many species which are not the same. It is worth remembering that all three proposed species come from faunas indicating the same broad period of time, equivalent to the European Land Mammal ages Vallesian, and Turolian, and with many closely related mammal species distributed between them. Moreover, in both the Nagri and Dhok Pathan age beds of India and Pakistan, at Pyrgos in Attica, and at Fort Ternan, Kenya, the faunas associated with *Ramapithecus* give evidence of much more open habitats than are those of the Middle Miocene sites where apes occur. At all these sites the habitat is clearly no longer tropical forest, but instead open woodland or woodland savannah where seasonal changes in temperature and rainfall almost surely affected plant food production through the year. Judging by the total absence of fossil apes from all the African Plio-Pleistocene sites, even the earliest, such as Lothagam and the Baringo Basin localities, the ancestors of the recent apes, like modern pongids, could not live in habitats of this type.

Perhaps the Pyrgos mandible is most important at this writing in that it is the only *Ramapithecus* jaw which goes all the way around the mid-line. Although the left ramus may have been moved slightly inwards and backwards by plastic flow, the extent of such distortion must have been minor because, seen in ventral view, the mandibular arc is without fractures or twisting. In my opinion, the shape of the mandibular arcade as determined from the ventral view of this specimen is accurate. If the lines of posterior divergence of each of the two premolar-molar series are drawn in, the angle by which they diverge is essentially the same as that estimated for the maxilla of *Ramapithecus* drawn with its mirror-image in a figure by Simons (1961). The evidence provided by each of these specimens, especially the Greek mandible, argues against the extremely narrow reconstruction recently prepared by Andrews and Walker on the basis of the Fort Ternan mandibular specimen. From this they have projected the shape of the dental arcade for this particular Fort Ternan *Ramapithecus*, but in my view in a much less certain manner than can be estimated for the Pyrgos mandible. Even so, the dental archades (in the region of cheek teeth) are diverging posteriorly in the Fort Ternan specimen at approximately the same angle, 20°, as in the Pyrgos mandible, and in Indian *Ramapithecus* (based on YPM 13799). Nevertheless there may be something wrong with their reconstruction, because the large cheek-teeth are brought very close to each other across the mid-line. To me, this seems functionally improbable and difficult to match in any living or fossil Anthropoidea. Personally I would not like to base an accurate estimate of the dental arcade alignment on so fragmentary a specimen. The slightest error at the pivot-point could have a major effect on calculating the angle of divergence of the sides of the parabola.

In spite of these reservations two important conclusions about *Ramapithecus* now seem inescapable. (1) Dental arcades diverge posteriorly and are not parallel sided as in modern apes. (2) The degree of posterior divergence is greater than in typical modern apes, more like such fossil apes as *Gigantopithecus* and *Dryopithecus*, but the divergence angle is less than that seen in *Australopithecus*.

Table 1 shows an expression of the degree of mandibular divergence in various hominoids. The distance between the labial surfaces of the canines in each specimen is expressed as percentage of the comparable distance between the second molars.

Table 1 Mean values of the index $\frac{\textbf{Intercanine breadth} \times 100}{\textbf{Inter} - \textbf{M}_2 \textbf{ breadth}}$ in some fossil and recent hominoids

African *Dryopithecus* (n = 5):	61%
Gigantopithecus (n = 4):	52.5%
Ramapithecus (Pyrgos):	60%
'Robust' *Australopithecus* (n = 3):	42%
'Early *Homo*' (n = 2):	50%
Living African apes (n = 14):	83%

Recently (Simons, 1972), I have pointed out that when the arrangements of the cheek tooth rows are actually determined in the

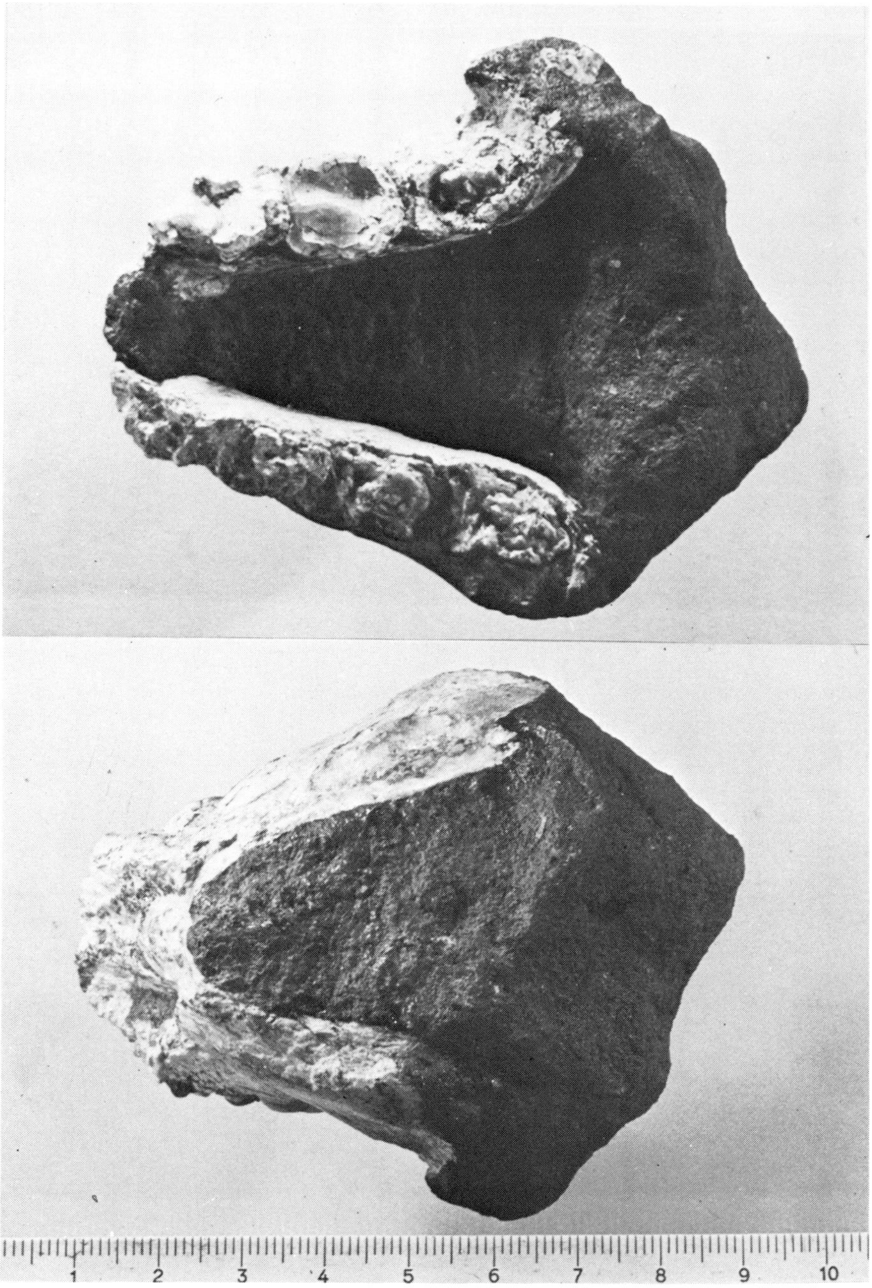

Figure 2. Crown view, above, and ventral view of the mandible, below, of *Ramapithecus freyburgi* from Pyrgos or Tour de la Reine, in the outskirts of Athens, Greece. This jaw is associated with an *Hipparion* fauna of about 8 or 9 million years in age. It exemplifies the *Ramapithecus* theory of hominid descent which puts the appearance of large broad lower molars coupled with small front teeth at a period before oldest dated *Australopithecus* in Africa.

best preserved mandibles of *Dryopithecus* from East Africa, in the three mandibles of *Gigantopithecus* from China, as well as in all other Miocene and Oliogocene Anthropoidea known from Africa and South America, these lower cheek-tooth rows in all are seen to diverge posteriorly. This posterior divergence is then plausibly judged to be the primitive condition for both apes and monkeys. The divergent condition has been largely supplanted by parallel-sided mandibular arcades in the modern Anthropoidea other than man. Classic definitions of the differences between apes and humans in dental arcade, for instance that of Le Gros Clark (1964), are inadequate because fossil forms were not included in the evaluation. Consequently, the supposed contrast between the hemi-circular arcade arrangement of hominids and the U-shaped arcade that of the pongids was initially spurious, as was its repetition by later authors (Simons and Pilbeam, 1965). One now sees that the whole history of analysis of hominid-pongid distinctions drawn from the arrangement of dental arcades was wrongly derived. Neither *Ramapithecus* nor *Australopithecus*, or even *Gigantopithecus*, resembles *Homo sapiens* in having rounded, or hemicircular dental arcades.

2. *The Ngorora molar*

This specimen was discovered in February 1968 by George R. Chapman in association with other well preserved mammalian fossils at a site within the Ngorora administrative district, some twenty miles north-west of Lake Baringo in the Northern Kenya Rift Valley. The layer containing this fossil tooth is overlain and underlain by phonolite lava flows which have yeilded potassium-argon age determinations, bracketing its age between 9 and 12 million years. In his initial assessment of this specimen, L.S.B. Leakey (in Bishop and Chapman, 1970) concluded that it was a hominid molar that showed structural resemblances to those of *Homo* and *Australopithecus* and to that of *Kenyapithecus* (meaning *Ramapithecus wickeri*) as well. Leakey stressed that the very low crown height resembled *R. wickeri*, but that anatomy of the tooth crown was also close to both *Australopithecus africanus* and to *Homo habilis*. There is no trace of a cingulum, as is often seen in both *Dryopithecus* and *Australopithecus*, and the differences from such forms as *D. sivalensis* and *D. indicus* in anatomical details of the crown is not great. Nevertheless, the low crown height weighs in favour of Leakey's assessment. If he was correct, the tooth is very important as yet another indication that the hominid-pongid split was prior to the 5 to 10 million year limits now favoured by some authorities (Washburn and Moore, 1973). It should be possible to determine the enamel thickness. If, like *Ramapithecus*, it is found to have thicker molar enamel than is typical for *Dryopithecus*, this would also indicate hominid status (Andrews and Walker, 1974).

3. The Gigantopithecus bilaspurensis *mandible*

Recently, Frayer (1973), Robinson (1972), and Robinson and Steudel (1973) have revived the idea that *Gigantopithecus* is ancestral to hominids. A short review of the see-sawing opinions as to hominid or pongid status for *Gigantopithecus* is included in Simons and Chopra (1969b). There is certainly nothing novel in such a placement, as Frayer suggests. *Gigantopithecus bilaspurensis* was recovered by an expedition operating under my direction. From the first, the possibility that this specimen bore evidence of the origin of hominids was under careful scrutiny. (If confirmed, this relationship would of course have focused much desired support and attention on our research project.) The possibility of an ancestral relation to hominids for *Gigantopithecus bilaspurensis* was then, and is now, rejected for good reasons, variously dealt with in Simons and Chopra (1969a and b), in Pilbeam (1970), and in Simons and Ettel (1970). The metrical resemblances between *Gigantopithecus* and hominids such as *Australopithecus* (specifically, robust *Australopithecus* or *Paranthropus* in the sense of Robinson (1972)) are simply due to the fact that *Gigantopithecus* is a pongid with small front teeth relative to the cheek teeth, while *Paranthropus* has relatively the smallest front teeth of any hominid. Thus in the multivariate analyses of Robinson and Steudel (1973) the extinct Asian ape is sometimes, but not always, approximated to hominids.

Close examination of tooth morphology in *Gigantopithecus* indicates that all teeth are different from those of hominids in structural detail, whereas in various significant points they resemble pongids or are *sui generis*. Canines, for example, though low-crowned, are dimorphic with large ape-like roots and show extensive crown-wear achieved at a comparatively early dental age that is wholly unlike that of early hominids. This Pilbeam (1970) regards as a case of 'molarization' of the canines. The degree of morphological difference between P_3 and P_4 (termed premolar heteromorphy) is de-emphasized in hominids, but still clearly seen in such early fossils as the type mandible of *Homo habilis*. It is about equally developed in *G. bilaspurensis* and *R. wickeri*. In this one feature both resemble conventional pongids about as much as they do hominids. Both are structurally intermediate between the two grades of organization, but only one of them can be evolutionarily intermediate. Lower molars of *Gigantopithecus* are not broad transversely and rounded in outline as in hominids but are elongate – distinctly narrower than long – showing a broad trigonid with a central constriction or 'wasp-waisted' condition between it and the other narrower talonid. All such features are unlike hominids and are in general more like features of pongid molar structure. Like the condition typical for fossil apes, mandibular horizontal rami in *Gigantopithecus* are also deep under the molars, considered relative to

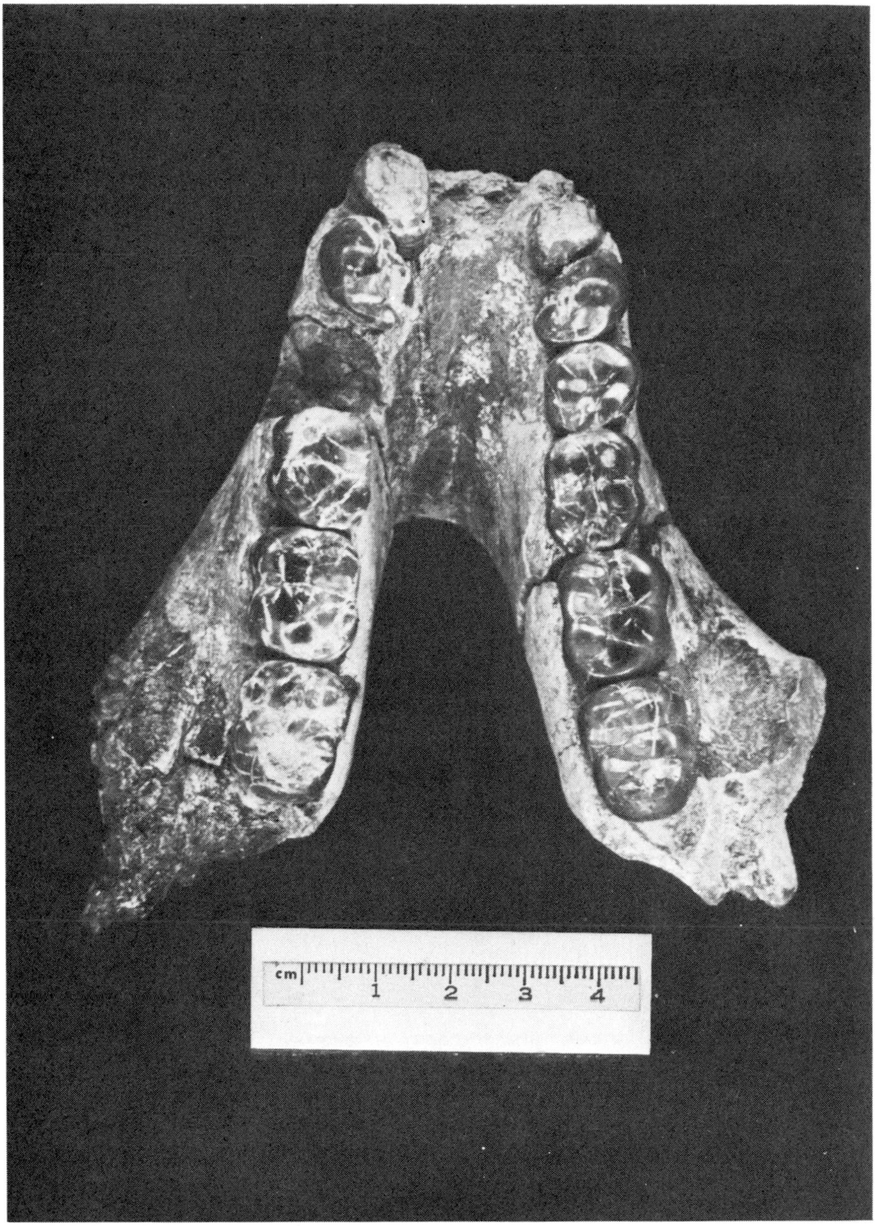

Figure 3. Mandible of *Gigantopithecus bilaspurensis* from a late Pliocene Dhok Pathan equivalent north of Hari Talyangar, India. This mandible has been made the basis of the *Gigantopithecus* theory of human descent. However, since neither this nor any other individual of *Gigantopithecus* can be shown to be older than earliest *Australopithecus* (which it does not resemble) it can hardly be supposed the ancestor of the latter genus, or of any other early hominid. *Gigantopithecus* retains a number of ape features such as long, 'wasp-waisted' lower molars and extremely deep horizontal ramus.

tooth-crown height and mandibular breadth. Moreover, this combination of pongid features seen in *Gigantopithecus* comes at a late period when in degree of advance toward the hominid condition it had already been bypassed by *Ramapithecus*. The latter, in every detail that is important in judging affinity, more closely approximates to *Australopithecus*, although in all cases it is demonstrably older than any *Gigantopithecus*. All these considerations suggest that *Gigantopithecus* and hominids were independently derived from pongids.

This conclusion seems especially likely when stratigraphic evidence is taken into account. As all agree, the Chinese fossils of *G. blacki*, whatever their exact age, are younger than about 2.5 million years and therefore most probably co-existed with both *Homo* and *Australopithecus*. Positing *Gigantopithecus* as a forbear of hominids thus rests entirely on assessment of the one and only specimen of *G. bilaspurensis* (Simons and Chopra, 1969b). This find would have to be shown to be significantly older than the oldest known African *Australopithecus* which is already distinct at 5 million years. The postulated conversion of *G. bilaspurensis* to *Australopithecus* would have to take time as they differ in virtually every dental detail which separates apes and humans. In order to draw this most implausible derivation it would be necessary, at the very least, to show that *G. bilaspurensis* is older than the 5 million year date of the Lothagam *Australopithecus* mandible. This cannot be done. Conventionally, the beds above the Nagri horizons north of Hari Talyangar have been termed Dhok Pathan. I guessed the age of the *G. bilaspurensis* find to be about 6 million years. This was based largely on a conclusion of mine that *G. bilaspurensis* was almost exactly intermediate morphologically (and hence, perhaps chrŏnologically) between *G. blacki* (at say 1 million years) and *Dryopithecus indicus* (at say 12 or 13 million years). In fact, no exact date is possible for *G. bilaspurensis* on present evidence, as there was *no* associated fauna. The region north and east of Hari Talyangar was considered by Lewis (1934) as either latest Dhok Pathan or Tatrot. Prasad (1962 and pers. comm.) considers the area a Tatrot equivalent. Recent faunal correlations such as that in Maglio (1973, Figure 12) would place the age of the *G. bilaspurensis* site as between 3 and 4 million if Tatrot, and between 4 and 5.5. million if latest Dhok Pathan. The Tatrot according to Hooijer and Colbert (1951) on faunal grounds is a Villafrancian equivalent. If so, it might be considered only 2 to 3 million years old. There is also a lengthy set of problems which arise in attempting to correlate the Pakistan type areas for the faunal zone terms used in Asia, with those faunas occurring around Hari Talyangar. Even if the beds containing the one find of *Gigantopithecus bilaspurensis* could be shown to correlate with the upper part of the Dhok Pathan in Pakistan rather than the Tatrot, the *G. bilaspurensis* site need not be more than 5 million years old. Even forgetting the morphological transformation required by the '*Gigantopithecus* as hominid ancestor' theory one must stress that a form has to be older than its descendants to be an ancestor. To date this cannot be shown to be the case for any *Gigantopithecus*.

The problems of the '*Gigantopithecus* derivation theory' do not end with the demurrals given above, for in addition to the almost insurmountable morphological and chronological problems inherent to the assumption is the zoogeographical one as well: African *Australopithecus* (or *Paranthropus* in the language of Robinson) has to have evolved late and rapidly from a source animal that otherwise appears to have been confined to East Asia.

4. *The Lothagam mandible*

This mandible has been tentatively identified as cf. *A. africanus*. The specimen consists of most of a right horizontal ramus containing roots of M_2 and M_3 and the crown of M_1. There is no doubt that this is a hominid mandible. Most consider it best placed in genus *Australopithecus*; as such, it is of gracile, not robust type. The fauna at Lothagam 1 with which it is associated has been dated at between about 5 and 5.5. million years, (Patterson, Behrensmeyer and Sill, 1970). This dating is well-founded and now seems to be widely accepted, (e.g. Howell 1972). The early dating of the specimen is its main significance.

The main theories of hominid origins

There are at least three different major hypotheses to account for hominid origins. Which one of these is accepted basically affects tabulation of the number of genera and diversity of species to be included in Hominidae. These can be listed as follows:

1. The 'chimpanzee theory': *Homo* and *Australopithecus* have an ancestor which immediately before their divergence was derived from a chimpanzee-like ape in the 5 to 10 million year period. Adherents: Washburn, Sarich.
2. The '*Gigantopithecus* theory': *Homo africanus*, by way of *Paranthropus*, is derived from *Gigantopithecus bilaspurensis*. Advocates: Robinson, Frayer.
3. The '*Ramapithecus* theory': The earliest species of *Homo* is derived from *Australopithecus* at about 3 + .75 million years and a radiation of *Australopithecus* was earlier derived from *Ramapithecus*. Exponents: Simons, Pilbeam, others.

The first of these three theories, 'chimpanzee' derivation, is based on both simplistic cultural assumptions and simplistic biochemical assumptions. Darwin originally posited the cultural assumption that huge canines in our ape-like ancestors were directly replaced in an

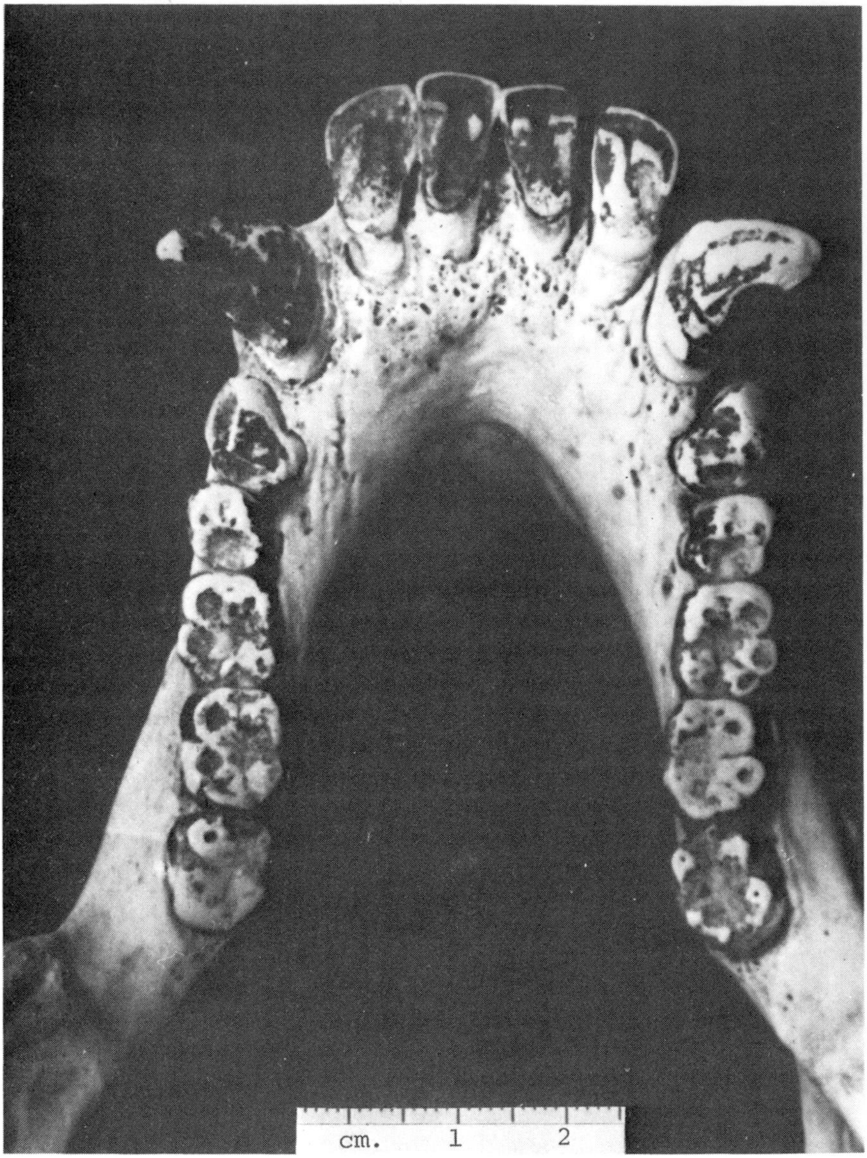

Figure 4. Mandible of the common chimpanzee *Pan troglodytes troglodytes*. Courtesy of Christian Vogel, Kiel, exemplifying the chimpanzee theory of human descent. Proponents of this theory advocate a separation between the ancestry of man and chimpanzee as late as 3 to 7 million years ago. Since hominids are the progressive group this theory requires the assumption that the common ancestor was closely similar to the modern African apes, such as this chimpanzee. Weaknesses of the theory are that *Australopithecus* is known to exist already in the 3 to 7 million year period. Its earliest known members do not approximate toward the mandibular anatomy of African apes. No African fossil apes are known in this time period nor is it clear that hominid ancestors ever had the broadened symphysis and enlarged incisors of the modern African apes.

evolutionary sense when tools were invented. There is now ample evidence for the existence of pre-tool-using or non-tool-using hominids, with small canines. It no longer seems plausible to conjecture that chimpanzee-like apes became hominids by the single stroke of luck embodied in the discovery of tool use and manufacture. In fact, the earliest dated tools at Omo and East Rudolf come from a time when there were certainly already two and perhaps three hominid species in existence. (This is at 2.6 million years ± .26, date for KBS tuff, East Rudolf, Howell, 1972.) There can no longer be any doubt that manufacture of stone tools is not the operative factor in the production of hominids, although the genus *Homo* may be defined in this way.

The implications of the 'chemical anthropology' of Sarich that the immunological distance between chimpanzee and man indicate a separation of the two from a common stock 3 to 5 million years ago are also simplistic. They require straight-line evolution, unvarying in rate throughout the primates, in order to calibrate the yardstick of chemical difference, and assume a precision of measurement that is implausible to both chemists and evolutionary biologists. The controversy has been dealt with extensively and summarized in Simons (1969) and in Uzzell and Pilbeam (1971) and will not be discussed further here except to point out that an immense disdain for the study and meaning of hominoid fossils is enextricably conjoined with acceptance or advocation of this theory. Interestingly, it is incompatible with both the other theories in terms of time. Frayer (1973) and Robinson (1972), while advocating *G. bilaspurensis* as a hominid ancestor, nevertheless agree with the suggestions of Simons (1970) and Pilbeam (1970) that the latter species is plausibly derived from *D. indicus*. Since the latter species, in turn, is dated by faunal correlation in Asia as going back as far as 12 to 13 million years ago, it also puts the branching off of the *D. indicus – G. bilaspurensis* stock back to a period that is inadmissably early in terms of the I.D. date for pongid-hominid branching advocated by Sarich and Washburn, variously given as within the range of from 3 to 10 million years ago. It might also be added that some of the new *Dryopithecus* material from the vicinity of Pasalar, Turkey recently discovered by Tobien and his co-workers is almost exactly intermediate morphologically and temporally between *D. indicus* and *D. major*. It is therefore, definitely possible to maintain that this material in turn links back the *D. indicus* lineage as a separate stock all the way to *D. major* which is a distinct taxon at Songhor, for instance, at around 20 million years. Thus, an adherent of the '*Gigantopithecus* theory' of hominid origins has to explain away a more easily demonstrable and much more ancient time of separation of the stock than is the case for any other theory.

In terms of the second and third theories listed above, if either *Gigantopithecus* or *Ramapithecus* is ancestral to hominids the split from the stock of the African apes has to be prior to the outside upper limit of 10 million years recently postulated for that event (Washburn and Moore, 1973). This is operating on the assumption that *Gigantopithecus* arose from an Asian *Dryopithecus, D. indicus.* In any event the existence of the Lothagam mandible requires that the split be prior to approximately 6 million years.

As is outlined here, *Gigantopithecus* is best interpreted as an Asian open-country, terrestrial, gorilla-like ape with a derivation from earlier *Dryopithecus indicus. Dryopithecus indicus* has been recovered by both Dehm's and von Koenigswald's expeditions in lower Dhok Pathan horizons that on faunal grounds seem to be about 6 to 9 million years old. As a probable descendant form from *D. indicus* it is unlikely that *G. bilaspurensis* is as old as this, more probably less than 6 million years and therefore, contemporary with Lothagam *Australopithecus* in Africa. This seems to rule out the '*Gigantopithecus* theory'.

The phases of hominid evolution

The third or '*Ramapithecus* theory' of hominid descent has at least one major aspect to recommend it which does not have to do with the plausibility of the argument on anatomical and geological grounds. This is that it allows ample time for hominids to shift through a series of phases or principle adaptive stages in their evolutionary progress away from ancestral arboreal apes. In consideration of the extent of the presumed behavioural and known morphological changes which typify the completed hominid condition, at least as seen in genus *Homo*, a series of minor adaptive shifts seem more plausible that a sudden one like the tool use/canine reduction dogma.

In this context Jolly (1970) is to be commended for stressing that the origin and early evolution of the Hominidae is best viewed as a succession of stages, each representing both a successful adaptation by itself and a step-wise advance in the direction of modern man as well. Unfortunately, as with earlier attempts to coin non-taxonomic names for stages in the sequence of evolving Hominidae, such as archanthropine and palaeoanthropine, his terminology of phase 1 and phase 2 hominids may be premature. Perhaps number identifications should not be used. In my view there is a phase in hominid evolution (outlined below) which comes before his phase 1.

Jolly's phase 1 hominids have been characterized in analogy with the modern Ethiopian baboon, *Theropithecus*, as presumptively tool-less, dominantly herbivorous (or granivorous) terrestrial, open country or savannah animals. The palaeoecology of *Dryopithecus* and *Ramapithecus* in the Miocene suggests a phase prior to this. The assumptions are as follows: first, that early Miocene apes [*Dryopithecus*] which were in the ancestry of Man were medium-sized herbivores that lived and fed mainly in the trees, animals in the size range of the pigmy chimpanzee and gibbons, and with analogous habits. The ecological reconstructions for sites such as Rusinga and Songhor suggest that their environment was wet, densely forested, and tropical. Under such conditions in the Congo Region and South-east Asia today, *Pan paniscus* and *Hylobates* can forage the year round on successively ripening fruits and sequentially flowering blossoms and new leaf growth. The same habits for early Miocene African apes seem probable, and such is the essential basis for the traditional or conventional arboreal-ape theory of human descent.

Nevertheless, in the middle Miocene fossil great-apes present a different picture and their environmental context is different. By this time, say 14 million years ago, apes had evidently reached their widest distribution and ranged across the whole of Eurasia from Spain in the west to China in the east. They were distributed as far north as the Rhine Valley, and although there is no fossil evidence it is plausible that they ranged far from the equator southward in Africa. This broad distribution undoubtedly subjected these apes to a maximum amount of climatic fluctuation, particularly as gradual world-wide changes toward cooler, drier weather took place. In Europe, Africa and Asia there is faunal and floral evidence for the development of broken forest, open woodland, or woodland savannah. At the northern and southern edges of their distribution, Miocene apes must have been subjected to conditions where seasonal fruiting and new leaf growth was the rule, rather than year round production of these foodstuffs as is the case in tropical forests. Similar seasonality is also indicated nearer the equator as at Fort Ternan (Andrews and Walker, 1974). In this context the first phase of hominid evolution would have been feeding on the ground but within open forest, with omnivorous foraging carried out for food stuffs available there, somewhat in the manner of the New World peccaries or in certain Eurasian suids such as *Sus* species.

This type of origin is compatible with the assumption of *Ramapithecus* as the ancestral or basal hominid, occupying the niche of a ground forager and small object feeder (perhaps roots, seeds, nuts and berries) of the open woodlands, where fruiting is seasonal and forage in the trees is inadequate at some seasons. Under this assumption, the basic hominid adaptation could have arisen anywhere throughout the whole of the earlier range of *Dryopithecus*, possibly in Africa, but not necessarily so. Gradual increases in aridity in east Asia and the prevalence of conditions favouring the spread of the typical *Hipparion* steppe faunas in east Asia could also explain the appearance at a considerably later date of a giant, terrestrially-adapted ape, *Gigantopithecus*. It is also worth considering that the reason that *Gigantopithecus* could flourish in east Asia at so late a date was perhaps because it was yet to be supplanted by the arrival of advanced hominids. It should not be forgotten that evidence of *Homo* and *Australopithecus* contemporary with *Gigantopithecus* in east Asia is not really convincing. All the foregoing lines of evidence are combined in a tentative table suggesting the degree of diversity in the family Hominidae at about the Plio-Pleistocene boundary (Table 2). In this ranking *Gigantopithecus* and its species are excluded from Hominidae and *Ramapithecus* sustained as a hominid. Viewed this way Hominidae contains three genera, each of which can be regarded, very tentatively, as having three valid species.

Table 2.

AGE IN MILLIONS B.P.	ASIA	EUROPE	AFRICA
	Homo sapiens	*Homo sapiens*	*Homo sapiens*
1	*Homo erectus*	*Homo erectus*	*Homo erectus*
2			*Homo habilis* · *Australopithecus boisei, robustus*
3			*A. africanus*
6			
9			
		Ramapithecus freybergi	
	Ramapithecus punjabicus		
12			
			Ramapithecus wickeri
15			

Acknowledgments

I should like to thank my wife Friderun Ankel Simons, David Pilbeam, and Phillip Gingerich who have read and contributed to this manuscript.

References

Andrews, P. (1971) *Ramapithecus wickeri* mandible from Fort Ternan, Kenya. *Nature*, 231, 192-194.

Andrews, P. and Walker, A. (1976) The primate and other fauna from Fort Ternan, Kenya. In Isaac, G.Ll. and McCown, E.L., *Human Origins: Louis Leakey and the East African Evidence*, 279-304. Menlo Park, Cal.

Bishop, W.W. and Chapman, G.R. (1970) Early Pliocene sediments and fossils from the northern Kenya Rift Valley. *Nature* 226, 914-18.

Brace, C.L., Nelson, H. and Korn, M. (1971) *Atlas of Fossil Man*. New York.

Clark, Wilfred Le Gros (1964) *The Fossil Evidence for Human Evolution*. 2nd ed., Chicago.

Frayer, D.W. (1973) *Gigantopithecus* and its relationship to *Australopithecus*. *Amer. J. phys. Anthrop.* 39 (3), 413-26.

Freyberg, B. von (1949) Die Pikermi-Fauna von Tour la Reine (Attika). *An. Geol. Hel.* 3, 1-10.

Freyberg, B. von (1950) Das Neogen-Gebiet nordwestlich Athen. *An Geol. Hel.* 3, 65-86.

Genet-Varcin, E. (1969) *A la recherche du primate ancêtre de l'homme*. Paris.

Hellman, M. (1918) Observations on the form of the dental arch of the Orang. *Orthodontia* 4, 3-15.

Hooijer, D.A. and Colbert, E.H. (1951) A note on the Plio-Pleistocene boundary in the Siwalik series of India and in Java. *Amer. J. Sci.* 249, 533-8.

Howell, F.C. (1972) Pliocene-Pleistocene Hominidae in eastern Africa: absolute and relative ages. In Bishop, W.W. and Miller, J.A. (eds.), *Calibration of Hominid Evolution*, Edinburgh.

Jolly, C.J. (1970) The seed-eaters: a new model of hominid differentiation based on a baboon analogy. *Man* 5, 1-26.

Johnson, G.D. (1971) Neogene molasse sedimentation in a portion of the Punjab-Himachal Pradesh Tertiary Re-entrant, Himalayan Foothill Belt, India: A vertical profile of Siwalik deposition. (Unpublished doctoral dissertation, Iowa State University, 84 pp.)

Koenigswald, G.H.R. von (1972) Ein Unterkiefer eines fossilen Hominoiden aus dem Unterpliozän Griechenlands. *Koninkl. Nederl. Akad. Wetenshap.* Ser. B, 75(5), 385-94.

Lewis, G.E. (1934) Preliminary notice of new man-like apes from India. *Amer. J. Sci.* Ser. V, 27 (159), 161-79.

Maglio, V.J. (1973) Origin and evolution of the Elephantidae. *Trans. Amer. Philos. Soc.*, N.S. 63 (3), 1-149.

Patterson, B., Behrensmeyer, A.K. and Sill, W.D. (1970) Geology and fauna of a new Pliocene locality in north-western Kenya. *Nature*, 226, 918-21.

Pilbeam, D. (1970) *Gigantopithecus* and the origins of Hominidae. *Nature* 225, 516-19.

Pilbeam, D. (1972) *The Ascent of Man: An Introduction to Human Evolution*. London.

Prasad, K.N. (1962) Fossil primates from the Siwalik beds near Hari Talyangar, Himachal Pradesh, India. *Journ. Geol. Soc. Ind.* 3, 86-96.

Radinsky, L. (1973) *Aegyptopithecus* endocasts: oldest record of a pongid brain. *Amer. J. phys. Anthrop.* 39 (2), 239-48.

Robinson, J.T. (1972) *Early Hominid Posture and Locomotion.* Chicago.
Romer, A.S. (1925) *Australopithecus* not a chimpanzee. *Science* 71(1845), 482-3.
Simons, E.L. (1963) Some fallacies in hominid phylogeny. *Science* 141(3584), 879-89.
Simons, E.L. (1969) The origin and radiation of primates. *Ann. N.Y. Acad.* 167, 3, 9-331.
Simons, E.L. (1970) The deployment and history of Old World Monkeys, Napier, J.R. and Napier, P. (eds.), *Old World Monkeys.* New York and London.
Simons, E.L. (1972) *Primate Evolution: An introduction to Man's place in nature.* New York.
Simons, E.L. and Chopra, S.R.K. (1969a) A preliminary announcement of a new *Gigantopithecus* species from India. *Proc. 2nd Int. Cong. Primatol.* 2, 135-43. Basel.
Simons, E.L. and Chopra, S.R.K. (1969b) *Gigantopithecus* (Pongidae, Hominoidea) a new species from North India. *Postilla,* Peabody Museum, Yale University, New Haven, 138, 1-18.
Simons, E.L. and Pilbeam, D. (1965) Preliminary revision of the Dryopithecinae (Pongidae, Anthropoidea). *Folia primat.* 3, 81-152.
Simons, E.L. and Ettel, P.C. (1970) *Gigantopithecus. Sci. Amer.* 222, 77-85.
Simons, E.L. and Pilbeam, D. (1972) Hominoid Palaeoprimatology. In Tuttle, R. (ed.), *The Functional and Evolutionary Biology of Primates.* Chicago.
Simons, E.L., Tattersall, I.M. and Meyer, G.E. *Ramapithecus.* In Oakley, K.P. *et al.* (eds.), *Catalogue of Fossil Hominids.* Pt. III: *Asia.* Brit. Mus. (Nat. Hist.) London, 217 pp., 1975.
Tobias, P.V. (1967) The cranium and maxillary dentition of *Australopithecus (Zinjanthropus) boisei.* Vol. 2, London, 1-264.
Tobias, P.V. (1973) Implications of the new age estimates of the early south African hominids. *Nature* 246, 79-83.
Uzzell, T. and Pilbeam, D. (1971) Phyletic divergence dates of hominoid primates. A comparison of fossil and molecular data. *Evolution* 25, 615-35.
Van Couvering, J.A. and Miller, J. (1971) Late Miocene marine and non-marine time scale in Europe. *Nature* 230, 559-63.
Walker, A. and Andrews, P. (1973) Reconstruction of the dental arcades of *Ramapithecus wickeri. Nature* 224, 313-14.
Washburn, S.L. (1973) The evolution game. *J. human Evol.* 2(6), 557-61.
Washburn, S.L. and Moore, R. (1973) *Ape Into Man: A Study of Human Evolution.* Boston.

B.G.Campbell

Some problems in hominid classification and nomenclature

This paper sets out to review some of the major problem areas in the classification of the African Plio-Pleistocene Hominidae, by means of a step-by-step discussion of the issues.

Background: variation and delineation

It cannot be said too often that variability is always underestimated. Any palaeontologist who has examined skeletal series of living biospecies, especially the chimpanzee and gorilla, is bound to be struck by their variability, especially in those parts of the skull which we learn are distinctive of gracile and robust australopitheci. Similar variations apply to other regions of the skeleton, both in terms of robusticity and shape; there is, for instance, considerable variation in the shape of the innominate bone. These considerations lead me to respect the conclusions of Lovejoy *et al.* (1973, and this volume) when they attempt to assess the differences between the ossa coxae and femora from Sterkfontein and Swartkrans. It seems to me that Robinson (1972) still greatly overestimates these differences, while Napier (1964) was obviously led badly astray by working on very poor casts. It is essential to compare such fossils with a large series of modern human bones drawn from the smaller as well as the larger races of man.

There is no doubt that anatomists still tend to overemphasize the taxonomic significance of relatively minor anatomical differences. Within single populations of any modern species, we can expect to find variation due to genetic differences between individuals and the differing environmental stresses to which they are exposed. Bones respond rapidly during both growth and maturity to changes in stress in ways which alter both their exterior form and inner structure. Among living populations differences in methods of carrying, walking and resting bring about small but recognisable differences in the detailed anatomy of the leg and foot bones. This source of variability, which can be very striking, has been almost completely overlooked. Beyond this we must expect considerable variability due to age and sex. The latter in turn varies among living primates between differences confined to primary and secondary sexual characters and much greater dimorphism effecting stature, weight and even shape.

It has to be emphasized that because of the allometric growth patterns of most organisms, two closely related individuals of the same species which are different in *size* will be different in *shape* as well (Huxley, 1942). The most obvious example of allometry in higher primates is in the relationship between jaw size and body size. One individual bigger than another has masticatory apparatus larger again than could be accounted for by a proportional size increase alone. To put it another way, a mandible which is twice as robust as another does not imply an individual twice as tall. Weidenreich may well have been rather misled in this way when he postulated giants in man's ancestry on the basis of the giant molar teeth of *Gigantopithecus*.

Sexual dimorphism involving differences in body size does therefore necessarily imply related but more emphatic differences in the size and shape of the masticatory apparatus as a whole. Other parts of the body are also altered in shape as the animal gets bigger, even beyond the differences attributable to sexual differences. At present we only know about crude weight differences due to sexual dimorphism in primates (apart from obvious primary and secondary sexual characters). We still do not know all the factors which determine the extent of the dimorphism, although some seem obvious enough. We therefore cannot accurately predict the amount that we might expect in extinct forms, though there is a fairly strong correlation of dimorphism with size.

We must also note that a single fossil population (or sample thereof) may not be representative of the biospecies, which may have been geographically wide-ranging. Geographical subspecies may have been present, showing considerable inter-populational variability, some approaching the state of incipient species. The expansion and contraction of the range of differently adapted subspecies or races may also give the appearance of very rapid change in morphology over a period of time *at a given site*, or even make it appear that more than one species is present. This is possibly the explanation of the 'second hominid' at Swartkrans (see below).

Finally, we must recognize that variation which represents evolution occurs in the dimension of time, making a chronospecies a three-dimensional taxon. According to convention (see for example Simpson, 1961), the variation in the time dimension of a chronospecies should approximately equal the variation in space of a typical biospecies. The exact morphological dimension, however, is ultimately a matter for discussion and agreement among interested taxonomists, and does not represent a biological reality (but see Campbell, 1963).

Since chronospecies are sequent, continuous and not discrete natural units, they cannot be distinguished by morphological characters alone. Somewhere, many times, an *Australopithecus* mother gave birth to a *Homo* child, and they were indistinguishable at the taxonomic level. Nothing is to be gained by following Tobias (1969) and creating intermediate taxonomic categories, for neither morphological nor behavioural boundaries exist in reality, however carefully we define them (Tobias, 1973a). Simpson (1963) discussed this problem, and it is clear that the boundaries of sequent taxa, be they genera, species or subspecies, should be conventionally agreed time-lines, rather than diagnostic morphological features such as the famed cerebral rubicon of Keith. This means that *both anatomy and dating are necessary to create the taxonomy of fossil lineages*. It follows that the development of a reliable chronology is one of the most important characteristics of the most recent period of research, and as this paper will show, new dates give us new taxonomy.

Some people feel that because taxonomy and nomenclature are so controversial, we should leave nomenclature aside as an irrelevant barrier to scientific progress. I agree absolutely that the premature naming of fossil finds should be avoided and I applaud Richard Leakey's approach which merely involves placing his discoveries into existing and rather ill-defined genera. I know he looks upon his diagnoses as provisional and would not wish to have to defend them. I will discuss his approach in the conclusions to this paper.

The reason that taxonomy is so often controversial is that its approach does imply detailed evolution hypotheses. But this is its main function. It is a way of describing the natural world, which categorizes the wealth of the exceedingly varied living material in it, and at the same time incorporates information about the relationships of the various categories (that is, populations) that we choose to label in this way. The Linnean binominal system is not ideal and is even somewhat inappropriate for the job we have to do, but there is no better system proposed at this time. The following discussion therefore works within the Linnaean system, which appeals to man, whose brain processes use words to codify and classify his environment. Therefore we face the problem of using discrete taxa to categorize variability and continuity in the fossil record.

The problems discussed

I will now tackle some of the taxonomic problems associated with an interpretation of the Pliocene and early Pleistocene Hominidae. My procedure will be to state the issue, and then follow it by the simplest hypothesis which can possibly account for the data. Scientific method (guided by Occam's razor) dictates this approach. The simplest acceptable hypothesis must form our working hypothesis, and we must use such an hypothesis to guide our thinking and research until the data no longer corroborate it, when it must be abandoned for the next simplest hypothesis.

In palaeontology the simplest hypothesis usually implies recognition of a minimum number of taxa at any given site. This is the justification for a lumper's taxonomy in general and for presenting 'single-species hypotheses' as working hypotheses. It does not imply that such simple hypotheses are necessarily true, but that if they are not falsified we should use such working hypotheses if our studies are to procede with the minimum of unnecessary controversy.

I will first discuss the South African Plio-Pleistocene Hominidae.

The South African hominids

The issue. There are 5 sites; how many taxa are represented?

There is no doubt that Robert Broom, genius though he was, did not fully admit the extent of variability in living populations. A fossil with some superficially striking differences in morphology often received a new name without reference to the variability present in the sample from which it was drawn. Broom did not really view his type specimens as part of a variable population, and quantitative taxonomy was a science of the future.

In our present position, there is no reason to remain too much influenced by his taxonomy. We may need to use some of the names he associated with the fossils, but we are by no means bound to follow his grouping of them. Three of the most important sites in South Africa lie within a mile of each other, and while the time spans they represent probably differ, they may also overlap. At the same time there is certainly morphological overlap between the sites. At Swartkrans we have the very gracile SK 847 and SK 15: at Sterkfontein we have the very robust Sts 36 and 73: at Kromdraai we have the robust TM 1517 and 1603, right alongside the gracile TM 1536 and 1601. While the means of these site samples may differ, there is certainly more overlap in robusticity than we have been led to believe in the literature.

The simplest hypothesis is to consider the samples from these three sites (and indeed from Makapan and Taung, neither of which fall outside their morphological range) as representing a single lineage. This sample may span as much as a million years, if we put Swartkrans at Bed I Olduvai times, 1.7 m.y. BP, and Sterkfontein a million years earlier, say at 2.7 m.y. BP (Cooke, 1970; Tobias, 1973b), and we can expect it to show the variability due to evolution between the earlier and later sites. Therefore the simplest hypothesis for these finds is to interpret them all as samples taken successively from an evolving lineage over a period of about a million years, showing a local increase in robusticity. Makapan is morphologically and chronologically intermediate. Obviously the correct name for this group is *Australopithecus africanus*, unless we choose to put it into the genus *Homo*, a question which is discussed later in this paper.

More complex hypotheses. Many workers feel that this solution is too simple and they recognize morphological differences between the so-called robust forms and the gracile ones which justify specific separation. Robinson has recently reviewed these (1972) and his book makes persuasive reading. However, I do feel that the differences are greatly exaggerated and given undue taxonomic weight, partly perhaps because he wishes to uphold Broom's original taxonomic differentiation. I feel that the most persuasive differences may be found in the locomotor adaptations rather than in the masticatory apparatus. If such differences fall beyond those which might be accounted for by the allometry, then we can accept that we have two biospecies with distinct locomotor adaptations. However, I look upon this hypothesis with suspicion, partly because we have such small samples (Sterkfontein: one pelvis, 2 distal femora and one proximal end very damaged without head or neck; Swartkrans: 2 proximal femora only, and two very damaged innominates; no hind limb bones from Taung and Kromdraai, but a poor ilium from the latter; and only 2 measurable ilia from Makapan). There is very little indeed here which can actually be compared *within* the total sample to establish such significant differences.

Differences in the masticatory apparatus do exist, but as I have suggested above, there is certainly an overlap in robusticity between the individual sites. While the means of many characters would certainly differ, this has little significance: the means of most measurements of most populations differ. When we consider ranges, there is no question but that in most cases extensive overlap can be demonstrated. Obviously the dental measurements are best. The means should differ in the region of about 3 × SD to attract taxonomic attention. Haldane (1949) suggested that a difference of 4 × SD between means was appropriate for chronospecies; 2 to 3 × SD differences might be used to differentiate chrono-subspecies. Has such a degree of differentiation been demonstrated for South African sites (see data in Robinson, 1967, Figure 3)?

The dental patterns differ between the Swartkrans and Sterkfontein samples, as is well known: the mandibular canine of the former is smaller in relation to the cheek teeth. Wolpoff (1971) gives the means and ranges for the relation of the lower canine to fourth premolar, and these do not overlap. It is clear that the proportions and pattern of the front and back teeth of these samples are significantly different. Though important, these differences do not invalidate the hypothesis that the two populations are two samples from the same lineage separated by one million years of evolutionary change.

The 'Telanthropus' hypothesis. With a sample size of one, it is hard to call statistics to our aid here. In point of fact, I believe that there is much other gracile material at Swartkrans which might be placed with the famous SK 847 skull for taxonomic purposes. However, as things stand, we are dealing, not so much with some simple measurements of size (the dimensions of the teeth of SK 15 are not all that small), but with morphology. The fact is that the total morphological pattern of SK 847 is strikingly different from that of SK 48, yet Wolpoff (1968) has questioned the need for specific distinction. Nevertheless, in this single skull, we have the best evidence for a second hominid taxon in South Africa. But does it have to be a separate species? Not necessarily. It could be a different and successful geographical subspecies the increasing geographical range of which has brought it to this region of the world. This very gracile form occurs most strikingly at Swartkrans and Kromdraai (TM 1535,

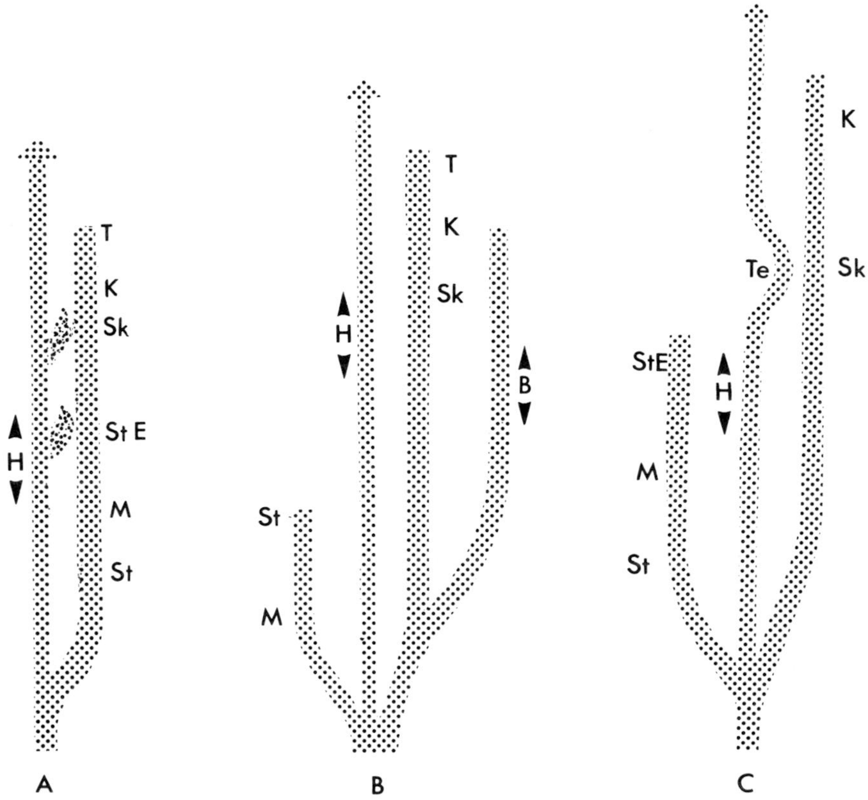

Figure 1. Simplified diagrams representing alternative hypotheses about the relationships of the South African early hominids.

A. According to Campbell. B. According to Tobias, 1973b. C. Other authorities.

Abbreviations: B: *boisei* lineage. H: *habilis* lineage. K: Kromdraai. M: Makapan. Sk: Swartkrans. St: Sterkfontein. St E: Sterkfontein Extension Site. T: Taung. Te: 'Telanthropus'.

1601) and these are the later sites. If it is specifically distinct, this implies that no genes were interchanged with the local inhabitants. In this case it requires a distinct name, and we might call it *Australopithecus capensis* (but see below).

Alternative hypotheses relating the South African hominids to each other are shown in Figure 1.

The East African hominids

First issue. How many different species do we have?

It is striking that the situation in East Africa bears such a strong resemblance to that in South Africa. But on further reflection this is perhaps not surprising. The simplest variation which isolation and selection can produce in the evolution of any related populations is that related to size. Natural selection can very readily bring about increases or decreases in the growth period which result in size differences. Living populations of *Homo sapiens* vary very strikingly in size and robusticity, and the extraordinary thing is that some very different sized populations (e.g. Watutsi and Batwa) live as neighbours. Extensive adaptation by size difference is common among geographical subspecies of a single biospecies.

The simplest hypothesis would relate the differences known among the East African hominids to most of the kinds of variation listed in the introduction to this paper. Some writers favour this approach (e.g. Buettner-Janusch 1973), and it is certainly a reasonable way of tackling the array of material we have to interpret. However, the situation in East Africa differs from that in South Africa insofar as the different sized creatures are contemporaries over a considerable period of nearly 2 million years, so we cannot use the variation introduced by evolutionary change to account for this situation as I have done in South Africa. Instead we have to lean much more heavily on sexual dimorphism. How can we test this hypothesis? The males should be bigger in all features than the females (even if there are differences in shape), and this should hold statistically even if there is an overlap in adult size range. First of all, we require samples of at least 5 to 7 individuals of each class, for a reasonably conclusive result. (This we are close to achieving, but I do not have sufficient published data.) Meanwhile the data for cranial capacity are suggestive: 'Females' range 500-810 cc; x = 648; n = 6. Our single published 'male' endocranial capacity is 530 cc. This appears to suggest that the robust individuals were indeed not the consorts of the gracile individuals, but were more probably another population which did not exchange genes with them. Two populations living in the same area over a considerable period of time which do not exchange genes are by definition two genetic and biological species. More data are needed to confirm or destroy this hypothesis. It is surprising to me that the two groups are so alike in so many other ways; this suggests that their adaptations are in fact broadly similar (and that they should share the same generic name). Evidence of *clear morphological divergence* would also be relevant to this problem, but while many minor morphological differences have been described, I do not know that a convincing and summary case has been presented. Good evidence of distinct locomotor adaptations would greatly weaken the single species hypothesis for these fossils but this has not yet appeared. The evidence presented in this volume by Day and by Wood goes some way in this direction, and is most important in our attempt to understand the different adaptations of these hominids.

More complex hypotheses. If we dismiss the single species hypothesis for East Africa we have to fall back on a two species hypothesis. This seems to be something many of us agree about although the evidence is still weak. Are there more than two species? Clark Howell hints that he has evidence of a third. This suggestion, which is not theoretically impossible, would need rather careful demonstration, and it will take a lot of good evidence with large samples to demonstrate it. When the grasslands spread through Asia, Europe and Africa in the Late Miocene, we certainly find they were populated with extensive radiations of new species, and among them were a number of terrestrial monkeys. It seems possible that, given an appropriate locomotor potential as knuckle-walkers or bipeds, the apes would also have radiated extensively into this new biome. There are, however, locomotor problems for terrestrial apes which quadrupedal monkeys do not have to face. Notwithstanding this, we do have at least two grassland 'apes': a hominid and *Gigantopithecus* (unless the first is derived from the second as a number of people now seem to think), and there could have been a third. We can be sure, however, that the species which finally won through dispatched his closest rivals as time went by, and what the palaeontologists will reveal to us will be a series (if they exist) of grassland adaptations which did not survive for long in competition with that tool-using, meat-eating creature which was to become man.

Second issue. Are the gracile hominids of East Africa related to those of South Africa?

Simplest hypothesis. Yes. The objection to this, that they are different, requires discussion. Certainly they are different. The samples are roughly contemporary and live 2000 miles apart. We can predict a degree of difference appropriate to this amount of geographical isolation, and that, in my opinion, is what we find. It is also relevant that the South African gracile specimens from Sterkfontein are certainly older than Bed I Olduvai Gorge and may be over half a million years older. Their smaller endocranial capacity would therefore also be predictable – although they themselves may not be directly ancestral to the East African sample. If this hypothesis is correct, then we can use the same species name and follow it with subspecies names to distinguish them: *Australopithecus africanus africanus* in the South and *A. africanus habilis* further north. The older East African specimens (e.g. Lothagam) could be ancestral to both samples.

Complex hypothesis. More than one species. This would require demonstration by its supporters; demonstration that the morphological divergence is appropriate to such a taxonomic distinction. I have not seen such demonstration, and those who upheld such a distinction do not now do so with much enthusiasm. It is always difficult, in any case, to demonstrate the existence of two related allopatric species. Such a thesis involves the implication that we have different contemporary tool-using hominids (at Olduvai, Swartkrans and Sterkfontein Extension), unless we postulate that 'Telanthropus' is *A. a. habilis*, from the north, arriving with his tool-making techniques. This is certainly a possibility.

Third issue. Are the East African and South African robust forms conspecific?

Simple hypothesis. Yes. This, however, is not consistent with the conclusions we have already drawn. However, this hypothesis is supported by most workers and in this matter I am in a small minority. These groups certainly have much in common, but if we are to accept the theory as commonly held (that the Sterkfontein form and *A. a. habilis* represent one lineage, and Kromdraai and Swartkrans and *A. boisei* represent another) then we have to go along with a separation of the South African hominids into two distinct lineages, a course of action which I consider quite ungrounded, as I have explained. If this simple hypothesis is correct, the ages of the different samples imply that the East African forms are probably ancestral, not vice versa. If the dates had been otherwise, we might have postulated that the South African group was, as a whole, ancestral to the two East African species, but this we cannot do. Present evidence suggests, in my opinion, that ancestral East African forms (e.g. Lothagam) gave rise to a South African race which continued to evolve in semi-isolation there. In this case, the robust fossils from each area obviously show a good deal of parallelism. The features they share, however, are products of overall size, and size increases may have evolved more than once; indeed this is the commonest of all evolutionary parallelisms. Therefore I see the South African race of *A. africanus* evolving somewhat in parallel with the *A. boisei* forms and coming to occupy a rather broad niche, which farther north is shared between two different species.

Nomenclature

The South African samples. If we accept the simplest hypothesis the trivial name is obviously *africanus*, and it remains a matter of discussion whether we accept generic separation from *Homo* (see below). If we recognize a robust and a gracile species then our interpretation of the Taung child becomes critical for establishing the correct *nomen*. If SK 15 and 847 are to be given separate specific status then it would seem best to use the name of the East African gracile form of similar age with which it has much in common – *habilis*. Its own species name (based on the jaw) is *capensis*, but this cannot be used in the genus *Homo* as it is 'occupied'.

The East African robust fossils. This sample carries the species name *boisei*. This term distinguishes this group from all other Hominidae. If we are to associate this group specifically with the Swartkrans sample, then they will be called *africanus* or *robustus* according to our interpretation of the Taung child. There seems to be general agreement that this group should be placed, with at least some of the South African samples, in the genus *Australopithecus*. If both South African samples are classified as *Homo*, then the correct generic name for *boisei* would be *Zinjanthropus*, if generic separation is required.

The East African gracile fossils. They may be distinguished from the South African finds by the name *habilis*, at either a specific or subspecific level. I prefer the latter. They can then be treated as members of the genus *Homo* or *Australopithecus*, species *erectus* or *africanus*.

Homo or Australopithecus? This is a matter of judgment which should be based on taxonomic guidelines which are established by convention. The convention is that a new genus name in a lineage or radiation should be coincident with a *new adaptive plateau*. There are three adaptive plateaus in man's evolution: (1) the forest phase, (2) the grassland phase, and (3) the unrestricted phase. There is a very real difference between forest and savannah adaptations, and I believe that there is at least an equally big break between the savannah phase and the modern phase in which man has found himself able to occupy almost every existing biome. These three phases are traditionally indicated by the generic names *Ramapithecus, Australopithecus* and *Homo*. If we sink *Australopithecus* into *Homo*, something commonly done these days, we are seriously underestimating the quite fundamental changes in adaptation represented by the coming of *Homo, senu stricto*. Huxley thought that man was entitled not only to generic distinction, but rather that he represented a whole new sub-kingdom of animals, the Psychozoa, which were of equivalent standing to the Protozoa and Metazoa; I think he had a good point. Man's coming is characterized by a whole series of new adaptations which are highly significant. They have been briefly discussed in a recent publication (Campbell, 1972) and can be seen as a whole series of related cultural developments based on language and technology, which enabled the hominids to adapt to and survive in *zones of low climatic equability*. I believe that the late, critical phases in human evolution occurred in response to stresses imposed by Eurasian temperate climates with seasonal variations in temperature which were sometimes acute. The appearance of hearths at this stage implies a whole new level of cultural and social adaptation, which enabled man to become the cosmopolitan creature that he is today. I believe this cultural and neuro-anatomical evolutionary development represents a new hominid adaptive plateau which is fittingly distinguished by the generic name *Homo*.

Discussion and conclusion

Rather than broadmindedly accept alternative classifications as equally substantiated, it now seems clear that a proper understanding of the variety and extent of variability in living species will lead us to accept what has usually been called a lumper's taxonomy. In my own opinion, only the status of the taxon *Australopithecus boisei* may fulfil the minimal conditions for recognition as a separate lineage at one period of time. Bigger samples, more complete analysis of the fossils and of sexual dimorphism in apes, should enable us to reach some clear-cut conclusions on this subject. Those of us who like to recognize and name the different varieties of *africanus* or *erectus* are justified in my opinion in working only at the rank of subspecies (see Table 1).

It seems clear that when Richard Leakey and his colleagues use generic terms to distinguish separate populations among the East Rudolf hominids, they are implying separate lineages, but attempting to avoid the use of specific names. We all feel, I think, that the use of specific names may seem to imply a greater precision in our understanding of taxonomic relationships than is justified by the material, and I would be the first to avoid any such implication. Yet the use of separate generic names in practice implies specific distinction and, while nomenclatorial problems are thereby to some extent cleverly avoided, genetic discontinuity between lineages is acknowledged. This may prove unjustified, and it is for this reason that I prefer to use *nomina* at the level of subspecies so that no genetic discontinuity is assumed. Mammalogists may maintain that it is hard enough to recognise subspecies among living species let alone fossil species, but the fact is that our precious fossil Hominidae receive incredibly detailed study of a kind rarely accorded butterflies, birds or badgers, and the very smallest differences are recognized and quantified. In fact I believe that many of the differences to which attention is drawn are of a kind associated with individual variation, or with variation between neighbouring populations, and may not even justify the use of subspecific terms. However, the advantage of using subspecific nomenclature is that it is convenient, it uses well-known names, and yet does not imply genetic discontinuities which are very hard to recognise in the fossil record. While I would use a conservative approach by not recognizing them, others believe equally

Table 1 Classification of the Hominidae

This table includes all recognized hominid taxa down to sub-species except for the lineage which is classified as *Australopithecus boisei.*

Date of taxon boundary in millions of years BP	Geographical sub-species						Species	Genus
	Europe	N. Africa	E. Africa	S. Africa	W. Asia	E. Asia		
Present								
	Living subspecies of *Homo sapiens*						*sapiens*	*Homo*
0.04								
	neanderthalensis		*rhodesiensis*		*palestinus*	*soloensis*	*sapiens*	*Homo*
0.3								
	heidelberg-ensis	*mauritanicus*				*pekinensis*	*erectus*	*Homo*
0.8								
			leakeyi			*erectus*	*erectus*	*Homo*
1.3								
			habilis			*modjokertensis*		
2.0								
			habilis	*robustus africanus*			*africanus*	*Australo-pithecus*
6.0								
					(punjabicus)		*punjabicus*	
12.0								
			(wickeri)				*wickeri*	*Rama-pithecus*

that the recognition of generic distinctions is appropriate, perhaps for the same reason. I believe that the principle of William of Occam impels us to recognize the minimum rather than the maximum of genetically discrete lineages and this is the basis of my approach to the taxonomy of fossil man, which is a symbolic representation of my working hypothesis. Though this hypothesis may prove wrong, I believe it best represents the present state of our knowledge.

Another objection which has been raised against the use of my taxonomic approach is that it is to a great extent unnecessary and even misleading insofar as it directs attention to semantic problems which are irrelevant to the real issues about man's evolution. Everyone, however, agrees that the recognition and analysis of evolutionary lineages is a question of central importance, and I am the first to agree with this. Taxonomy, in my opinion, is a method of classifying the populations which represent such lineages in a way that makes it easy to communicate our ideas about them. While the binomial/trinomial system is undoubtedly based on a pre-evolutionary folk taxonomy, we still have nothing better with which to replace it. My own classification (Table 2) is certainly intended to draw attention to lineages, but I have not given them separate generic status, which I consider inappropriate except where *Homo* is proved to be contemporary with a species of *Australopithecus*. Our subject is a branch of palaeozoology, and it seems reasonable that we should still

Table 2 Classification of the Hominidae

- *Ramapithecus* Lewis, 1934.
  - *R. wickeri* (Leakey), 1962.
  - *R. punjabicus* (Pilgrim), 1910.
- *Australopithecus* Dart, 1925.
  - *A. africanus* Dart, 1925.
    - *A. a. africanus* Dart, 1925.
    - *A. a. robustus* (Broom), 1938.
    - *A. a. habilis* (Leakey, Tobias and Napier), 1964.
  - *A. boisei* (Leakey), 1959.
- *Homo* L., 1758.
  - *H. erectus* (Dubios), 1892.
    - *H. e. erectus* (Dubois), 1892.
    - *H. e. heidelbergensis* Schoetensack, 1908.
    - *H. e. mauritanicus* (Arambourg), 1954.
    - *H. e. leakeyi* Heberer, 1963.
    - *H. e. pekinensis* (Black and Zdansky), 1927.
    - *H. e. habilis* (Leakey, Tobias & Napier), 1964.
    - *H. e. modjokertensis* (von Koenigswald), 1936.
  - *H. sapiens* L., 1758.
    - *H. s. neanderthalensis* King, 1864.
    - *H. s. palestinus* (McCowan and Keith), 1932.
    - *H. s. rhodesiensis* (Woodward), 1921.
    - *H. s. soloensis* (Oppenoorth), 1932.
    - *H. s. sapiens* L., 1758 and other living subspecies.

try and conform to the conventions of other palaeozoologists.

The *International Code of Zoological Nomenclature* lays down a whole series of rules and recommendations which if we were to follow them would reduce semantic disagreement and disharmony among palaeoanthropologists. I believe that taxonomy is a priceless tool in the analysis and understanding of human evolution and it deserves more respect than it at present receives. Without classification into taxa, and without symbols to identify them, our ability to understand the natural world is severely limited.

William of Occam rightly enjoined us to select simple hypotheses so long as they were consonant with the facts on which they were based. Our science has come a long way since the time when, not so long ago, a new *nomen* was proposed for each new fossil discovery (and a new *nomen* implies a new hypothesis). Thanks to the good sense of modern explorers, we can assess each new discovery without prejudice (which a new *nomen* creates), and only after its place in the phylogeny of man has been established need we, or should we, establish its taxonomic position. Palaeoanthropology is becoming a real science at last, where analysis can precede hypothesis, and where progress takes the form of an orderly revision of the consensual working hypothesis. This way we move step by step up the ladder of induction to a better understanding of man's place in nature.

References

Buettner-Janusch, J. (1973) *Physical Anthropology: A Perspective*. New York.

Campbell, B.G. (1963) Quantitative taxonomy and human evolution. In Washburn, S.L., *Classification and Human Evolution*, 51-3. Chicago.

Campbell, B.G. (1972) Man for all seasons. In Campbell, B.G. (ed.), *Sexual Selection and the Descent of Man, 1871-1971*, 40-58. Chicago.

Cooke, H.B.S. (1970) *Bull. Soc. Vert. Paleontol.*

Haldane, J.B.S. (1949) Suggestions as to quantitative measurement of rates of evolution. *Evolution*, 3, 51-6.

Huxley, J.S. (1942) *Essays on Growth and Form*. London.

Lovejoy, C.D., Kingsbury, G., Heiple, G. and Burstein, A.H. (1973) The Gait of *Australopithecus*. *Amer. J. phys. Anthrop.* 38, 757-80.

Napier, J.R. (1964) The evolution of bipedal walking in the hominids. *Arch. Biol.* (Liège) (suppl.) 75, 673-708.

Robinson, J.T. (1967) Variation and the taxonomy of the early hominids. In Dobzhansky, T. (ed.), *Evolutionary Biology*, Vol. I, 69-100. New York.

Robinson, J.T. (1972) *Early Hominid Posture and Locomotion*. Chicago.

Simpson, G.G. (1961) *Principles of Animal Taxonomy*. New York.

Simpson, G.G. (1963) Meaning of taxonomic statements. *Viking Fund Publ. Anthrop.* 37, 1-31.

Tobias, P.V. (1969) Bigeneric nomina: a proposal for modification of the rules of nomenclature. *Amer. J. phys. Anthrop.* 31, 103-6.

Tobias, P.V. (1973a) Darwin's prediction and the African emergence of the genus *Homo*. In *L'Origine Dell'Uomo*, Accademia Nazionale dei Lincei, Rome.

Tobias, P.V. (1973b) Implications of the New Age Estimates of the Early South African Hominids. *Nature, Lond.* 246, 79-83.

Wolpoff, M.H. (1968) 'Telanthropus' and the single species hypothesis. *Amer. Anthrop.* 70, 477-93.

Wolpoff, M.H. (1971) *Metric Trends in Hominid Dental Evolution*. Cleveland.

General Index

Index of Authors